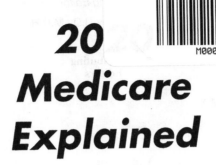

20
Medicare
Explained

Managing Editor

Kelly J. Rooney, J.D., M.P.H.

**Contributing
Editors**

Kayla R. Bryant, J.D.

Sheila Lynch-Afryl, J.D., M.A.

Anthony H. Nguyen, J.D.

Cathleen Calhoun, J.D.

Rebecca Mayo, J.D.

Patricia K. Ruiz, J.D.

Bryant Storm, J.D.

Amy Styka
Production

This publication is designed to provide accurate and authoritative information in regard to the subject matter covered. It is sold with the understanding that the publisher is not engaged in rendering legal, accounting, or other professional service. If legal advice or other expert assistance is required, the services of a competent professional person should be sought.

2700 Lake Cook Road
Riverwoods, IL 60015
866 529-6600
http://WoltersKluwerLR.com

SUSTAINABLE FORESTRY INITIATIVE — Certified Sourcing — www.sfiprogram.org — SFI-00756

Printed in the United States of America

ISBN: 978-1-5438-2118-5

Foreword

This book has been prepared for Medicare beneficiaries and others who need a relatively thorough explanation of the Medicare program with particular emphasis on services covered in institutional settings and services provided by physicians and suppliers.

Published annually, this book includes changes made by law and regulation amendments and by updates to program manuals issued by the Centers for Medicare and Medicaid Services (CMS). This edition includes changes issued during 2019 that affect Medicare beneficiaries and providers in 2020.

The 2020 highlights are as follows:

Medicare Part A (hospital insurance). For 2020, the inpatient hospital deductible is $1,408 per each beneficiary "spell of illness." Patients are responsible for a coinsurance amount for each day after the 60th and through the 90th day per spell of illness, and in 2020 daily coinsurance amount is $352 for the 61st through 90th day of hospitalization. When Medicare patients use their lifetime reserve days in 2020, their coinsurance is $704 per day. When Medicare patients are patients in skilled nursing facilities in 2020, their coinsurance is $176 for the 21st through 100th day of skilled nursing facility care (see ¶ 223, ¶ 242).

Medicare Part B (supplementary medical insurance). The Part B premium for most beneficiaries in 2020 is $144.60.

Income-adjusted premiums for 2020 are as follows: Individuals with modified adjusted gross income (MAGI) greater than $87,000 but less than or equal to $109,000 and couples with MAGI greater than $174,000 but less than or equal to $218,000 pay a monthly premium of $202.40 per beneficiary. Individuals with MAGI greater than $109,000 but less than or equal to $136,000 and couples with MAGI greater than $218,000 and less than or equal to $272,000 pay a monthly premium of $289.20 per beneficiary. Individuals with MAGI greater than $136,000 but less than or equal to $163,000 and couples with MAGI greater than $272,000 and less than or equal to $326,000 pay a monthly premium of $376 per beneficiary. Individuals with MAGI greater than $163,000 and less than $500,000 and couples with MAGI greater than $326,000 and less than $750,000 pay a monthly premium of $462.70 per beneficiary. Individuals with MAGI of at least $500,000 and couples with MAGI of at least $750,000 pay a monthly premium of $491.60 per beneficiary. The rates are modified slightly for beneficiaries who are married and lived with their spouse at any time during the taxable year but file a separate tax return from their spouse (see ¶ 320).

For 2020, the Part B deductible is $198 (see ¶ 335).

The SUPPORT for Patients and Communities Act (P.L. 115-271) added Medicare Part B coverage of opioid use disorder treatment services beginning January 1, 2020 (see ¶ 394).

Part B will provide separate coverage of home infusion therapy effective January 1, 2021. Coverage includes the following services furnished in a beneficiary's home: (1) professional services, including nursing services, furnished in accordance with the plan of care; and (2) training and education (not otherwise paid for as durable medical equipment), remote monitoring, and monitoring services for the provision of home infusion therapy and home infusion drugs furnished by a qualified home infusion therapy supplier. Home infusion therapy will be specifically excluded from the definition of home health services (see ¶ 390).

Physician reimbursement. The physician fee schedule payment amount for a service is determined by a formula that takes into consideration the relative value unit for the service, the conversion factor for the year, and the geographic adjustment factor for the service. The Medicare Access and CHIP Reauthorization Act of 2015 (MACRA) (P.L. 114-10) changed how the conversion factor is updated. Under MACRA, starting in 2019, the amounts paid to individual providers will be subject to adjustment through one of two mechanisms, depending on whether the physician chooses to participate in an Advanced Alternative Payment Model (APM) program or the Merit-Based Incentive Payment System (MIPS) program (see ¶ 855).

Home health services. Pursuant to the Bipartisan Budget Act of 2018 (P.L. 115-123), CMS changed the unit of payment for home health agencies from 60 days to 30 days, effective for 30-day periods of care that start on or after January 1, 2020.

Medicare Part C (managed care plans). Starting in 2019, there is an open enrollment period during the first three months of the year for Medicare Advantage (MA)-eligible individuals, during which an individual who is enrolled in an MA plan will be permitted to change his or her election at any time (see ¶ 401). Beginning in 2021, individuals with end-stage renal disease (ESRD) will be permitted to enroll in MA plans and organ acquisitions for kidney transplants will no longer be covered under Part C and instead will be covered by Parts A and B (see ¶ 402).

Medicare Part D (prescription drug plans). Part D sponsors are permitted to establish a drug management program for at-risk beneficiaries that limits their access to frequently abused drugs for plan years beginning on January 1, 2019. On January 1, 2022, the program will become mandatory (see ¶ 525).

For 2020, beneficiaries in standard prescription drug plans (PDPs) are subject to a $435 deductible. The coverage gap, or "donut hole," begins when a beneficiary reaches the plan's initial coverage limit ($4,020 in 2020) and ends when the beneficiary spends a total of $6,350 out of pocket in 2020. In 2020, beneficiaries will pay 25 percent of the price for generic drugs in the coverage gap. The applicable gap percentage for applicable drugs in the coverage gap is 75 percent for 2020 and later (see ¶ 507).

The 2020 base beneficiary premium is $32.74. High-income beneficiaries are subject to income-adjusted premiums for Part D, just as they are for Part B. For 2020, the income-related monthly adjustment amount for a PDP premium is $12.20 for an individual with MAGI greater that $87,000, but not more than $109,000; $31.50 for an individual with MAGI greater than $109,000, but not more than $136,000; $50.70 for an individual with MAGI greater than $136,000, but not more than $163,000; $70 for an individual with MAGI greater than $163,000 but less than $500,000; and $76.40 for an individual with MAGI equal to or more than $500,000 (see ¶ 505).

Quality of care. CMS will continue to implement a number of quality of care initiatives in 2020, many of which will affect provider and facility reimbursement.

Inpatient hospitals that do not submit required quality data on specific quality indicators to the Medicare program each year will have their applicable hospital market basket percentage increase reduced by 2 percent. Similarly, Medicare payments to hospitals can be reduced under the Hospital Readmissions Reduction Program and the Hospital-Acquired Condition Reduction Program, and hospitals can earn incentives under the Hospital Inpatient Value-Based Purchasing Program (see ¶ 810).

Outpatient hospitals that fail to report on quality measures in 2020 will have their payments reduced by 2.0 percent in calendar year 2022 (see ¶ 820).

Other Wolters Kluwer publications:

Further details on the topics covered in this book, together with the texts of pertinent laws, regulations, policy guidelines, court decisions, etc., may be found in Wolters Kluwer's MEDICARE AND MEDICAID GUIDE. The GUIDE is available as a six-volume, loose-leaf print product as well as electronically on the Internet. Other electronic databases, including the full text of the CMS program manuals and the codes and complete descriptions contained in the physician fee schedule, are offered as part of Wolters Kluwer's electronic Health Law Library. Wolters Kluwer also has an easy-to-read electronic reporter specializing in Part B issues entitled the PHYSICIANS' MEDICARE GUIDE. Wolters Kluwer also offers, in print and electronic form, a comprehensive guide to the landmark health care reform legislation passed in 2010, entitled LAW, EXPLANATION AND ANALYSIS OF THE PATIENT PROTECTION AND AFFORDABLE CARE ACT (2014 UPDATE), VOLUMES 1 AND 2.

Finally, Wolters Kluwer publishes the following related paperback books:

2020 Master Medicare Guide

2020 Social Security Benefits (Including Medicare)

2020 Social Security Explained

To find out more about these publications, call 1-888-224-7377 or visit http:// WoltersKluwerLR.com.

A note about the citations in the text:

Throughout the text, statements are documented, when possible, by citations to the law, regulations, and program manuals issued by the federal government. In the interests of simplicity and conservation of space, citations generally have been made only to the highest authority available for the statement in the text, although, when appropriate, multiple citations (i.e., citations both to a law provision and its implementing regulation) are included. In some instances, when there is no clear ranking of authorities, only the most widely available source is cited.

January 2020

Table of Contents

Detailed Table of Contents

Chapter 1—Introduction

Chapter 2—Medicare Part A—Hospital Insurance

Eligibility and Enrollment

Inpatient Hospital Services

Nursing Home Services

Chapter 7—Administrative Provisions

Chapter 8—Payment Rules

Chapter 9—Claims, Payments, and Appeals

Topical Index

Chapter 1– INTRODUCTION

[¶ 100] Introduction to Medicare

As part of the Social Security Amendments of 1965, Congress established two new programs to cover the cost of medical care for the elderly and disabled. The first of these programs, largely financed through the hospital insurance taxes, provides basic protection against the costs of inpatient hospital and other institutional provider care. Officially, this program is called "Hospital Insurance Benefits for the Aged and Disabled," although it includes much more than hospital benefits. Unofficially it is sometimes called "basic Medicare," "hospital insurance," or "Medicare Part A" (because the authorization for the program is Part A of Title XVIII of the Social Security Act).

The second of these programs is a voluntary program covering the costs of physician and other health care practitioner services and items and supplies not covered under the basic program. It is financed through monthly premiums from enrollees and contributions from the federal government. Officially, this program is called "Supplementary Medical Insurance Benefits for the Aged and Disabled," but unofficially it is called "supplementary Medicare," the "medical insurance program," or "Medicare Part B."

A third Medicare program that expands managed care options for beneficiaries who are entitled to Part A and enrolled in Part B was created under the Balanced Budget Act of 1997 (BBA) (P.L. 105-33) and expanded under the Medicare Modernization Act of 2003 (MMA) (P.L. 108-173); it is now commonly referred to as "Medicare Part C" or "Medicare Advantage." Since January 1, 1999, beneficiaries have had the option of choosing to receive their health benefits through the traditional Medicare "fee-for-service" program or through a managed care plan certified under the Medicare Advantage program. Payments Medicare makes to a Medicare Advantage plan replace the amounts Medicare otherwise would have paid under Parts A and B.

The Medicare program was also expanded by the MMA to include a prescription drug benefit, under Part D of Title XVIII of the Social Security Act. The prescription drug benefit became available to eligible individuals on January 1, 2006, and is called Medicare Part D.

Together, the four programs are known officially as "Health Insurance for the Aged and Disabled," the name of Title XVIII of the Social Security Act, which contains the basic law governing the Medicare program.

Contents of this Book

Medicare Part A, the hospital insurance program, is discussed in Chapter 2, and Medicare Part B, supplementary medical insurance, is discussed in Chapter 3. Medicare Part C, the Medicare Advantage program, is discussed in Chapter 4, and Medicare Part D, the prescription drug benefit, is discussed in Chapter 5. Certain items that are specifically excluded from coverage by Medicare are discussed in Chapter 6. Miscellaneous administrative features of the Medicare program are discussed in Chapter 7, including quality improvement organizations, electronic health data privacy, "Medigap" insurance, and initiatives used to curb health care fraud and abuse. Medicare payment to providers, physicians, and suppliers is discussed in Chapter 8. Claims filing procedures and appeals of adverse determinations are discussed in Chapter 9.

Rules concerning eligibility and applications for Medicare are discussed at the beginning of Chapter 2 in the case of Part A, and at the beginning of Chapter 3 in the case of Part B. Election and enrollment in Medicare Part C are discussed in Chapter 4 (¶ 401). Eligibility and enrollment in Medicare Part D are discussed in Chapter 5 (¶ 503).

Chapter 2– MEDICARE PART A—HOSPITAL INSURANCE

Eligibility and Enrollment

[¶ 200] Entitlement to Part A Hospital Insurance Benefits

Most individuals automatically become entitled to hospital insurance benefits under Part A of the Medicare program when they reach age 65 if they are eligible for monthly Social Security retirement or survivor benefits or railroad retirement benefits as "qualified railroad retirement beneficiaries." [Soc. Sec. Act § 226; 42 C.F.R. §§ 406.5, 406.10.]

Entitlement to Medicare for these individuals begins in the month in which they become 65 years old, regardless of whether they have elected to receive Social Security (or other) retirement benefits. [42 C.F.R. § 406.10(b)(1).] Individuals electing to receive Social Security benefits earlier than age 65 do not need not file an application for Medicare when they become 65; they will automatically receive an application. Individuals electing not to receive Social Security, however, need to file an application for Medicare (see below under "Part A Application Requirements"). [42 C.F.R. § 406.6.]

Individuals under age 65 also are entitled to benefits under Part A if they are entitled to: (1) Social Security or railroad retirement disability benefits for at least the previous 24 months (see ¶ 204); or (2) end-stage renal disease (ESRD) benefits (see ¶ 205). [Soc. Sec. Act §§ 226(a), 226A(a); 42 C.F.R. §§ 406.5(a), 406.12, 406.13.]

Individuals age 65 or over who are not entitled to Part A benefits on one of the bases outlined above can enroll voluntarily in the Part A program by paying a monthly premium (see ¶ 203). [Soc. Sec. Act § 1818(a); 42 C.F.R. §§ 406.5(b), 406.20(b).]

Individuals entitled to benefits under Part A (except people with ESRD) and enrolled in the supplementary medical insurance program (Medicare Part B—see ¶ 300–¶ 320) may choose to receive benefits under the traditional fee-for-service programs, or they may choose to enroll in a Medicare Advantage managed care plan, which offers additional benefits. [Soc. Sec. Act § 1851(a)(3).] The Medicare Advantage program, also called Medicare Part C, is discussed in detail in ¶ 400–¶ 412.

In addition, individuals entitled to benefits under Part A (except people with ESRD) and enrolled in Part B may choose to enroll in Part D, which provides coverage for prescription drugs (see ¶ 500–¶ 535). [Soc. Sec. Act § 1860D-1 *et seq.*]

Coverage Period for Part A

Medicare entitlement usually begins on the first day of the month when an individual reaches age 65. Therefore, someone whose 65th birthday is on January 6, 2020, is eligible for benefits on January 1, 2020. [Soc. Sec. Act § 226(c)(1); 42 C.F.R. § 406.10(b)(1).]

The Social Security and Medicare programs follow the rule that a person reaches a given age on the day before the anniversary of birth. A person born on April 1, 1955, for example, is considered to have reached age 65 on March 31, 2020, and Medicare hospital benefits begin March 1, 2020. [*Medicare General Information, Eligibility, and Entitlement Manual*, Pub. 100-01, Ch. 2, § 10.2.]

A Social Security applicant who applies for monthly benefits after reaching age 65 can be entitled to Part A benefits retroactively beginning with the first day of the first month in which all the requirements for benefits otherwise are met, but not more than six months (12 months for disabled widows' or widowers' benefits) before the month in which the application is filed. [42 C.F.R. § 406.6(d)(2), (4).]

Suspended Part A Benefits of Aliens

An individual whose cash Social Security benefits have been suspended under section 202(t)(1) of the Social Security Act (relating to suspension of the benefits of certain aliens who are outside the United States for more than six months) is not entitled to Part A benefits furnished in any month for which such a suspension is applicable. [Soc. Sec. Act § 202(t)(9); 42 C.F.R § 406.50.]

Conviction of Subversive Activities

If a person is convicted of espionage, sabotage, treason, sedition, subversive action, or conspiracy to establish a dictatorship, his or her income (or the income of the insured individual on whose earnings record the person became or seeks to become entitled) for the year of conviction and any previous year may not be counted in determining the insured status necessary for entitlement to hospital insurance. [Soc. Sec. Act § 202(u); 42 C.F.R § 406.52.]

Part A Application Requirements

A person age 65 or over who has filed an application and established entitlement to monthly Social Security benefits or who is a qualified railroad retirement beneficiary ordinarily does not need to file any additional application for Part A. It comes automatically with these other benefits. [42 C.F.R. § 406.6(a).]

However, an application for Medicare benefits is required for those who have not applied for Social Security benefits. An application also is required for an individual who seeks entitlement on the basis of: (1) ESRD (¶ 205); (2) "Medicare-qualified government employment" (¶ 206); (3) deemed entitlement to disabled widow's or widower's benefits under certain circumstances; or (4) voluntary Part A enrollment (¶ 203). [42 C.F.R. § 406.6(c), (e).]

Form CMS-18-F-5, "Application for Hospital Insurance Entitlement," is the form most commonly used to apply for Part A entitlement, and may also be used for enrollment in the Part B program (¶ 310). ESRD applicants use Form CMS-43, "Application for Health Insurance Benefits Under Medicare for Individuals with End-Stage Renal Disease." [42 C.F.R. § 406.7.]

Except for individuals seeking entitlement on the basis of ESRD, an application for Part A must be filed before the applicant's death—a relative or legal representative may not file for retroactive entitlement after the individual has died. [42 C.F.R. §§ 406.10(b)(2), 406.13(d)(3).]

Filing claims for Medicare benefits by Medicare beneficiaries is discussed at ¶ 900 *et seq.*

Medicare Card

As evidence of entitlement to Medicare benefits, CMS issues each beneficiary a Medicare card. This card includes the name of the beneficiary, Medicare number, and the effective date of entitlement. When receiving covered services, the cardholder should show the card to the health care provider. [Pub. 100-01, Ch. 2, § 50.]

Replacement cards. Beneficiaries may order a replacement for a lost or damaged Medicare card by visiting the Medicare Card Replacement section of the SSA's website at https://faq.ssa.gov/en-US/Topic/article/KA-01735. The new card will be mailed within 30

¶200

days to the address the SSA has on record. An individual needing immediate proof of Medicare coverage can call 1-800-772-1213 or contact a local SSA office.

Social Security numbers. Section 501(d) of the Medicare Access and CHIP Reauthorization Act of 2015 (MACRA) (P.L. 114-10) amended the Social Security Act to require the establishment of cost-effective procedures to ensure that a Social Security number is not displayed, coded, or embedded on the HI card issued to an individual entitled to Part A or Part B benefits and any other identifier displayed on the card is not identifiable as a Social Security number or derivative of a Social Security number. [Soc. Sec. Act 205(c)(2)(C)(xiii).]

For more information on CMS's initiative to replace the SSN-based Health Insurance Claim Number with a new Medicare Beneficiary Identifier, see https://www.cms.gov/Medicare/New-Medicare-Card/.

[¶ 203] Voluntary Enrollment in the Hospital Insurance Program

Hospital insurance (Part A) coverage is available on a voluntary basis, for a premium, to individuals 65 or over who are not entitled to Social Security or other Medicare-qualifying benefits (see ¶ 200). This is called premium hospital insurance.

Eligibility for Voluntary Enrollment in Part A

An individual is eligible to enroll voluntarily in Part A if he or she:

(1) has attained age 65;

(2) is enrolled in Medicare Part B;

(3) is a resident of the United States and is either:

a. a citizen of the United States; or

b. an alien lawfully admitted for permanent residence who has continuously resided in the United States for the five years immediately before the month in which application for enrollment is made; and

(4) is not otherwise entitled to Part A benefits.

[Soc. Sec. Act § 1818(a); 42 C.F.R. § § 406.5(b), 406.20.]

For purposes of determining U.S. residency, the term "United States" includes the District of Columbia, Commonwealth of Puerto Rico, the Virgin Islands, Guam, American Samoa, and the Northern Mariana Islands. [Soc. Sec. Act § § 210(i), 1861(x); Northern Mariana Islands Covenant Implementation Act (P.L. 94-241).]

Part A Voluntary Enrollment Process

An individual may accomplish voluntary enrollment in Part A only during an "enrollment period." [Soc. Sec. Act § 1818(b).] For individuals 65 years of age or older, the initial enrollment period extends for three months before and three months after the first month the individual would be eligible for Part A. Following this initial enrollment period, an individual is able to enroll for Part A benefits from January 1 to March 31 of each subsequent year. If the individual enrolls during one of the annual enrollment periods following his or her initial enrollment, the benefits are effective on July 1 of that year. [42 C.F.R. § 406.21.] Note that these enrollment periods do not apply to the majority of individuals who are automatically enrolled upon reaching the age 65 and enrolling for Social Security benefits.

In general, the provisions governing enrollment (see ¶ 310–¶ 311), coverage periods (see ¶ 313), and premiums (see ¶ 320) under Part B—excluding premium increases for late enrollment (see below)—also are applicable to voluntary enrollment in Part A. [Soc. Sec. Act § 1818(c).]

An individual meeting the conditions for voluntary enrollment and paying the appropriate premium may elect coverage under a Medicare Advantage managed care plan under Part C (see ¶ 401). [Soc. Sec. Act § 1851(a)(3).]

Payment of Premiums for Voluntary Enrollees

Voluntary enrollees must pay a monthly premium based on the total cost of Part A protection for the enrolled group. The premium is updated annually according to a formula established by law. [Soc. Sec. Act § 1818(d)(2).] For 2020, the monthly Part A premium is $458. For 2019, the monthly Part A premium was $437. [*Notice*, 84 FR 61622, Nov. 13, 2019; *Notice*, 83 FR 52455, Oct. 17, 2018.]

There is a 45 percent Part A premium reduction available to certain individuals with 30 or more quarters of Social Security coverage. One who has had at least 30 months of such coverage—or who was married to, widowed from, or divorced from such an individual for certain periods of time—is entitled to the reduction. [Soc. Sec. Act § 1818(d)(4)(A).] The reduced premium for eligible individuals in 2020 is $252. The reduced premium for eligible individuals in 2019 was $240. [*Notice*, 84 FR 61622, Nov. 13, 2019; *Notice*, 83 FR 52455, Oct. 17, 2018.]

The Part A premium is zero for certain public retirees. [Soc. Sec. Act § 1818(d)(5).] Government employees are discussed in detail at ¶ 206.

Part A Late Enrollment and Reenrollment Penalties

There is a 10 percent late enrollment penalty for individuals who enroll voluntarily in Part A 12 months or more after the expiration of the initial enrollment period. The penalty is based on the date when an individual first meets the eligibility requirements for enrollment and continues for twice the number of years (i.e., full 12-month periods) that the enrollment was delayed. [Soc. Sec. Act § 1818(c)(6); 42 C.F.R. §§ 406.32(d), 406.33.]

If an individual drops out of the program and then reenrolls, the months during which the individual was out of the program are counted in determining the re-enrollment penalty. [42 C.F.R. § 406.34.]

Example • • •

Agnes Williams was eligible to enroll during an initial enrollment period that ended May 31, 2017. She waited, and enrolled in the 2020 general enrollment period (January 1, 2020—March 31, 2020). Thirty-four months elapsed after the close of her initial enrollment period and before March 31, 2020, the close of the period in which she actually enrolled. (Delinquent enrollment is counted from the end of the initial enrollment period to the end of the enrollment period in which the individual actually enrolls—see ¶ 320.) There were, therefore, two 12-month periods during which she could have been, but was not, enrolled. She is assessed a 10 percent premium penalty, and that penalty expires after she has paid it for 48 months.

State and local government retirees who retired before January 1, 2002, can be exempt from the Part A delayed enrollment penalties. Their exemption depends on the total amount of payroll taxes they or their employers paid. [Soc. Sec. Act § 1818(d)(6).]

Group Premium Payments

A state or any other public or private organization can pay monthly premiums on a group basis for its retired or active employees age 65 and over. For group coverage, the agency or organization may make premium payments under a contract or other arrangements. The Secretary may refuse to enter into a group premium payment contract if such a method of payment is not administratively feasible. [Soc. Sec. Act § 1818(e).]

Termination of Entitlement to Voluntary Part A Benefits

An individual's entitlement to the voluntary Part A program terminates if he or she: (1) files a request for termination; (2) becomes entitled to regular Part A benefits in one of the ways described at ¶ 200; (3) is no longer entitled to Part B; (4) fails to pay voluntary Part A premiums; or (5) dies. [Soc. Sec. Act § 1818(c)(4), (5); 42 C.F.R. § 406.28.]

If the voluntary enrollee stops paying the premium, entitlement will end on the last day of the third month after the billing month. CMS will reinstate entitlement, however, if the individual can show good cause for failing to pay the premiums on time as long as all overdue premiums are paid within three calendar months after the date entitlement would have been terminated. [42 C.F.R. § 406.28(d).]

[¶ 204] Disability Beneficiaries

An individual under age 65 is entitled to hospital insurance benefits if, for 24 months, he or she has been: (1) entitled or deemed entitled to Social Security disability benefits as an insured individual, child, widow, or widower who is "under a disability;" or (2) a disabled qualified beneficiary certified under section 7(d) of the Railroad Retirement Act. [Soc. Sec. Act § 226(b); 42 C.F.R. § 406.12(a).]

"Medicare-qualified government employment" (see ¶ 206) is treated as Social Security qualifying employment for the purpose of the provision of Medicare disability benefits. [Soc. Sec. Act § 226(a)(2)(C).]

Disabled beneficiaries who are not yet 65 and continue to be disabled and no longer are entitled to benefits solely because their earnings exceed the amount permitted may purchase Part A coverage. Enrollment can occur during special enrollment periods as provided by law. Premiums are similar to the premiums required for voluntary enrollees (see ¶ 203). [Soc. Sec. Act § 1818A.]

Social Security retirees. Upon reaching the age of 65, beneficiaries who are disabled can become eligible for Medicare as Social Security retirees if they satisfy the requirements for that status (see ¶ 200).

Waiting Period

Disabled individuals may not receive Part A benefits until they have satisfied a 24-month "waiting period" during which they have continuously been disabled. An exception to this rule applies for individuals with amyotrophic lateral sclerosis (ALS), who have no waiting period. [Soc. Sec. Act § 226(b), (h).]

Months of a previous period of entitlement or deemed entitlement to disability benefits count toward the 24-month requirement if any of the following conditions is met:

(1) entitlement was as an insured individual or a disabled qualified railroad retirement beneficiary, and the previous period ended within the 60 months preceding the month in which the current disability began;

(2) entitlement was as a disabled child, widow, or widower, and the previous period ended within the 84 months preceding the month in which the current disability began; or

(3) the previous period ended on or after March 1, 1988, and the current impairment is the same as, or directly related to, the impairment on which the previous period of entitlement was based.

[Soc. Sec. Act § 226(f); 42 C.F.R. § 406.12(b).]

Termination of Coverage

Generally, entitlement to Part A ends with the earliest of the following:

- the last day of the last month in which the beneficiary was entitled or deemed entitled to disability benefits or was qualified as a disabled railroad retirement beneficiary, if he or she was notified of the termination of entitlement before that month;

- the last day of the month following the month in which he or she is mailed a notice that his or her entitlement or deemed entitlement to disability benefits, or his or her status as a qualified disabled railroad retirement beneficiary, has ended;

- the last day of the month before the month he or she attains age 65; or

- the day of death.

[Soc. Sec. Act § 226(b); 42 C.F.R. § 406.12(d)(2).]

Returning to work. If an individual's entitlement to disability benefits or status as a qualified disabled railroad retirement beneficiary ends because he or she engaged in, or demonstrated the ability to engage in, substantial gainful activity after the 36 months following the nine-month trial work period provided for by 20 C.F.R. § 404.1592, Medicare entitlement continues until the earlier of the following:

(1) the last day of the 78th month following the first month of substantial gainful activity occurring after the 15th month of the individual's reentitlement period or, if later, the end of the month following the month the individual's disability benefit entitlement ends; or

(2) the last day of the month following the month in which notice is mailed to the individual indicating that he or she is no longer entitled to hospital insurance because of an event or circumstance (for example, there has been medical improvement, or the disabled widow has remarried) that would terminate disability benefit entitlement if it had not already been terminated because of substantial gainful activity.

[Soc. Sec. Act § 226(b); 42 C.F.R. § 406.12(e).]

Employer Group Health Plan Coverage

Medicare is the secondary payer for disability beneficiaries who are covered by a large group health plan (an employer with 100 or more employees) as a current employee (or as a family member of a current employee). Thus, when an employee (or a member of the employee's family) becomes disabled, the large employer's group health plan has primary coverage responsibility and Medicare has secondary coverage responsibility. The law provides that either the federal government or the individual has a cause of action against a plan that does not meet its coverage responsibilities and that double damages may be recovered. [Soc. Sec. Act § 1862(b)(1)(B), (b)(2)(B)(iii).]

Employer group health plans are discussed in more detail at ¶ 636.

[¶ 205] End-Stage Renal Disease Beneficiaries

Medicare covers individuals who have not reached age 65 and are suffering from end-stage renal (kidney) disease (ESRD) if they are: (1) fully or currently insured for Social Security or railroad retirement benefits (see ¶ 200); (2) entitled either to monthly Social Security or railroad retirement benefits; or (3) spouses or dependent children of eligible individuals. ESRD benefits are available only after an application for Medicare benefits is filed. The application may be filed after the individual's death. [Soc. Sec. Act § 226A(a); 42 C.F.R. §§ 406.6(c), 406.13(c) and (d).]

¶205

"End-stage renal disease" is defined as "that stage of kidney impairment that appears irreversible and permanent and requires a regular course of dialysis or kidney transplantation to maintain life." [42 C.F.R. § 406.13(b).] Payment for ESRD benefits is discussed at ¶ 845.

Waiting period. Coverage for dialysis patients normally begins the third month after the month in which a course of renal dialysis is initiated. However, entitlement begins on the first day of the month in which a regular course of renal dialysis began if, before the end of the waiting period, the beneficiary participates in a self-dialysis training program offered by a participating Medicare facility. For kidney transplant candidates, coverage can begin as early as the month in which the candidate is hospitalized for transplantation provided the surgery takes place in that month or in the following two months. [Soc. Sec. Act § 226A(b), (c); 42 C.F.R. § 406.13(e).]

Termination of coverage. Coverage ends at the end of the 12th month after the month in which a course of dialysis ends, unless the individual receives a kidney transplant during that period or begins another regular course of dialysis. For a kidney transplant recipient, coverage ends with the end of the 36th month after the month in which the individual has received a kidney transplant, unless he or she receives another kidney transplant or begins a regular course of dialysis during that period. [Soc. Sec. Act § 226A(b)(2); 42 C.F.R. § 406.13(f).]

[¶ 206] Government Employees

An individual who has worked in Medicare-qualified government employment (or any related individual who would be entitled to Social Security cash benefits on the employee's record if Medicare-qualified government employment qualified for those benefits) is entitled to hospital insurance benefits if he or she: (1) would meet the requirements of 42 C.F.R. §§ 406.10 (see ¶ 200), 406.12 (see ¶ 204), or 406.13 (see ¶ 205) if Medicare-qualified government employment were Social Security covered employment; and (2) has filed an application for hospital insurance. [Soc. Sec. Act § 226(a)(2)(C); 42 C.F.R. § 406.15(e).]

"Medicare-qualified government employment" means federal, state, or local government employment that is subject only to the hospital insurance portion of the tax imposed by the Federal Insurance Contributions Act (FICA), including (1) wages paid for federal employment after December 1982; (2) wages paid to state and local government employees hired after March 31, 1986; and (3) wages paid to state and local government employees hired before April 1, 1986, but whose employment after March 31, 1986, is covered, for Medicare purposes only, under an agreement under Soc. Sec. Act § 218. [Soc. Sec. Act § 210(p); 42 C.F.R. § 406.15(a).]

Individuals entitled to Medicare by virtue of their Medicare-qualified government employment also are entitled to Medicare disability benefits (¶ 204) and end-stage renal disease benefits (¶ 205). [Soc. Sec. Act §§ 226(b)(2)(C), 226A(a)(1).]

Government Employment Not Considered "Medicare-Qualified"

Federal employees who are not considered "Medicare-qualified" include:

(1) inmates in federal penal institutions;

(2) certain interns (other than medical or dental interns or medical or dental residents in training) and student nurses employed by the federal government; and

(3) employees serving on a temporary basis in case of fire, storm, earthquake, flood, or other similar emergency.

[Soc. Sec. Act § 210(a)(6).]

State and local government employees who are not "Medicare-qualified" include:

(1) individuals employed to relieve them from unemployment;

(2) patients or inmates in a hospital, home, or other institution;

(3) employees serving on a temporary basis in case of fire, storm, snow, earthquake, flood, or other similar emergency;

(4) interns (other than medical or dental interns or medical or dental residents in training), student nurses, and other student employees of hospitals of the District of Columbia; and

(5) an election official or election worker if the remuneration paid for services performed in a calendar year is less than $1,000.

[Soc. Sec. Act § 210(p)(2).]

As noted above, state and local government employees hired before April 1, 1986, are exempt from the hospital portion of the FICA tax, so their employment is not considered to be "Medicare-qualified." A state, however, may ask the Commissioner of Social Security to enter into an agreement whereby these employees also would have their employment treated as "Medicare-qualified." In such cases, only employment occurring after March 31, 1986, is considered "Medicare-qualified." [Soc. Sec. Act § 218(n).]

Payment of Premiums for Government Employees

Government employees who have retired but are unable to qualify for Medicare benefits in the manner described above are entitled to enroll voluntarily in the Part A program and pay the appropriate premium (see ¶ 203). [42 C.F.R. § 406.11.]

Additionally, public retirees meeting certain statutory conditions do not pay the monthly premium. Specifically, the premium is zero for any individual receiving cash benefits under a qualified state or local government retirement system on the basis of the individual's employment for at least 40 calendar quarters (or a combination of such quarters and Social Security-covered quarters totalling 40). As is the case with reduced premiums, individuals who have been married to, widowed from, or divorced from such an individual for certain periods of time also are entitled to a zero premium. [Soc. Sec. Act § 1818(d)(5)(B).]

To be covered under this provision, certain conditions must be met: (1) the individual's Part A premium may not be payable in whole or part by a state (including a state Medicaid program) or a political subdivision of a state; and (2) in the preceding 84 months, the individual was enrolled in Part A and did not have had the Part A premium paid in whole or part by any governmental entity described above. [Soc. Sec. Act § 1818(d)(5)(A).]

A "qualified state or local government retirement system" is a system established or maintained by a state or political subdivision (or agency thereof) that covers positions of some or all employees of the governmental entity and does not adjust cash benefits based on eligibility for the premium relief described above. [Soc. Sec. Act § 1818(d)(5)(C).]

Inpatient Hospital Services

[¶ 210] Inpatient Hospital Services: Coverage in General

Medicare covers the following services or supplies provided while the beneficiary is an inpatient in the hospital:

(1) bed and board (see ¶ 211);

(2) nursing services (other than the services of a private-duty nurse or attendant) and other related services that ordinarily are furnished by the hospital for the care and treatment of inpatients (see ¶ 217);

¶210

(3) use of hospital facilities;

(4) medical social services (see ¶ 217);

(5) drugs, biologics, supplies, appliances, and equipment for use in the hospital that ordinarily are furnished by the hospital for the care and treatment of inpatients (see ¶ 212 and ¶ 213);

(6) certain other diagnostic and therapeutic items and services that ordinarily are furnished to inpatients (see ¶ 214);

(7) medical or surgical services provided by certain interns or residents-in-training (see ¶ 215); and

(8) transportation services, including transport by ambulance.

To be covered, these services must be provided directly by the hospital or under an arrangement made by the hospital with an outside contractor. Further, when payment can be made for an inpatient hospital stay under Part A, all Medicare-covered services furnished during that stay are paid under Part A. [Soc. Sec. Act § 1861(b); 42 C.F.R. § 409.10(a).]

Limitations and exclusions related to inpatient hospital services. Covered services do not include: (1) the services of physicians and certain other health care practitioners, which are covered under Part B (see ¶ 350); (2) services of private-duty nurses (see ¶ 217); and (3) pneumococcal, influenza, and hepatitis B vaccine and their administration, which are covered under Part B even when provided to an inpatient during a hospital stay covered under Part A. [Soc. Sec. Act § 1861(b)(4), (5); 42 C.F.R. § 409.10(b); *Medicare Benefit Policy Manual*, Pub. 100-02, Ch. 1, § § 1–60; *Medicare Claims Processing Manual*, Pub. 100-04, Ch. 18, § 10.1.]

Dental services, which are not ordinarily covered under Medicare Part A, may be covered if the individual, because of an underlying medical condition and clinical status or the severity of the dental procedure, requires hospitalization for the performance of those services. [Soc. Sec. Act § 1862(a)(12); 42 C.F.R. § 411.15(i).]

In addition, Medicare will pay for emergency services provided in a nonparticipating hospital or under arrangements if (1) those services would otherwise be covered if provided in a participating hospital; (2) the hospital has a special payment agreement with CMS; and (3) the nonparticipating hospital is the most accessible hospital available that is equipped to furnish the services needed (see discussion at ¶ 227). [42 C.F.R. § 424.103(a).]

General exclusions from Medicare coverage can be found in Chapter 6.

Benefit period. Medicare Part A covers services provided to beneficiaries who are inpatients in qualified hospitals participating in the Medicare program for up to 90 days in any one "spell of illness" (see ¶ 221). In addition, each beneficiary has a lifetime reserve of 60 days that can be used after the 90 days have been exhausted (see ¶ 222). [Soc. Sec. Act § 1812(a)(1).]

"Inpatient" Defined

An "inpatient" is a person who has been admitted to a hospital for bed occupancy to receive inpatient hospital services. Generally, a person is considered an inpatient if formally admitted as a patient with the expectation that he or she will require hospital care that is expected to span at least two midnights, even if a hospital bed is not used overnight due to discharge or transfer. [Pub. 100-02, Ch. 1, § 10.]

When a patient with a known diagnosis enters a hospital for a specific minor surgical procedure that is expected to keep him or her in the hospital for only a few hours (fewer than 24) and this expectation is realized, the individual will be considered an outpatient regardless of the hour of admission, whether a bed is used, or the hospital stay extends past midnight. [Pub. 100-02, Ch. 1, § 10.]

Special rules apply when a patient needs only extended care services but is placed in a hospital bed, including a "swing bed" (see ¶ 229).

Notice of Rights and Coverage

Hospitals must provide beneficiaries, including those enrolled in Medicare Advantage plans, the "Important Message from Medicare" (IM) notice within two days of admission. The beneficiary or a representative must sign the notice. The IM explains a Medicare beneficiary's rights as a hospital patient, including appeal rights at discharge. Hospitals must deliver a copy of the signed notice within two days prior to discharge. Beneficiaries who request an appeal must be provided a more detailed notice. [42 C.F.R. § § 405.1205, 422.620.]

Advance Beneficiary Notices

If a hospital determines items or services will no longer be covered by Medicare, it must issue an Advance Beneficiary Notice (ABN). The ABN informs a Medicare beneficiary, before he or she receives specified items or services, that Medicare certainly or probably will not provide for items or services provided on that visit. The ABN provides the beneficiary with the information necessary to decide whether to receive items or services that may require out-of-pocket payment or payment through other insurance. [42 C.F.R. § 411.408(f)(1); Pub. 100-04, Ch. 30, § 50.1.] ABNs are discussed at ¶ 900.

Hospital Discharge Planning

A hospital must have an effective discharge planning process that focuses on the patient's goals and treatment preferences and includes the patient and his or her caregivers/support persons as active partners in the discharge planning for post-discharge care. The discharge planning process and the discharge plan must be consistent with the patient's goals for care and his or her treatment preferences, ensure an effective transition of the patient from hospital to post-discharge care, and reduce the factors leading to preventable hospital readmissions. [42 C.F.R. § 482.43.]

Late Discharge from a Hospital

A stay beyond the checkout time for the comfort or convenience of the patient is not covered under the program, and the hospital's agreement to participate in the program does not preclude it from charging the patient. Medicare expects that a hospital will not impose late charges on a beneficiary unless it has given reasonable notice (for example, 24 hours) of impending discharge. When the patient's medical condition is the cause of the stay past the checkout time (for example, the patient needs further services, is bedridden and awaiting transportation to his or her home or a SNF, or dies in the hospital), the stay beyond the discharge hour is covered under the program and the hospital may not charge the patient. [Pub. 100-02, Ch. 3, § 20.1.1.]

[¶ 211] Accommodations

Part A generally will pay only for *semi-private* accommodations (rooms of two to four beds) or ward accommodations (five or more beds) in connection with inpatient hospital care or nursing care in a skilled nursing facility (SNF) (see ¶ 232). [Soc. Sec. Act § 1861(b)(1); 42 C.F.R. § 409.11(a); *Medicare Benefit Policy Manual*, Pub. 100-02, Ch. 1, § 10.1.1.]

Private Rooms

Medicare will make extra payments for a private room or other accommodations more expensive than semi-private only when such accommodations are medically necessary. Private rooms are considered medically necessary in the following circumstances:

（1) the patient's condition requires isolation for the patient's health or that of others;

（2) the hospital or critical access hospital (CAH) has no semi-private or less expensive accommodations; or

（3) semiprivate and ward accommodations are fully occupied by other patients, were so occupied at the time the patient was admitted to the hospital or CAH for treatment of a condition that required immediate inpatient hospital or inpatient CAH care, and have been so occupied during the interval.

In the situations specified in (1) and (3), Medicare pays for a private room until the patient's condition no longer requires isolation or until semi-private or ward accommodations are available. [42 C.F.R. § 409.11(b)(1), (b)(2).]

The hospital may charge the beneficiary the difference between its customary charge for the private room and its most prevalent charge for a semi-private room if (1) none of the conditions described above is met; and (2) the private room was requested by the patient or a member of the family, who, at the time of the request, was informed what the hospital's charge would be. [42 C.F.R. § 409.11(b)(3).]

Payment also will be made for intensive care facilities when medically indicated.

Example • • • _____

At the time Mary Green is admitted to the hospital, she requests a private room. It is not medically necessary that she be in a private room, and she is told by the hospital that she will be charged the difference between its "customary charge" (see below) for a private room ($2,000 per day) and the customary charge for a semi-private room at the hospital's "most prevalent rate" (see below) at the time of admission ($1,300 per day). The hospital may charge Mary $700 per day for the private room, and the rest of her bill for bed and board, less any required deductible or coinsurance amount, is covered by Part A.

_____

"Customary charges" are the current amounts that the institution uniformly charges patients for specific services and accommodations. The "most prevalent rate" for semi-private accommodations is the rate that applies to the greatest number of semi-private beds. [Pub. 100-02, Ch. 1, § 10.1.7.]

Deluxe Private Rooms

A beneficiary in need of a private room (either because isolation is needed for medical reasons or because immediate admission is needed when no other accommodations are available) may be assigned to any private room in the hospital. Part A does not pay for personal comfort items (see ¶ 616), nor does it pay for deluxe accommodations or services, such as a suite or a room that is substantially more spacious than required for treatment, specially equipped or decorated, or serviced for the comfort and convenience of persons willing to pay a differential. If a beneficiary (or the beneficiary's representative) requests deluxe accommodations, the hospital should advise the patient or representative that there will be a charge, not covered by Medicare, of a specified amount for each day the beneficiary occupies the deluxe accommodations. The maximum amount the beneficiary may be charged is the differential between the most prevalent private room rate at the time of admission and the customary charge for the room occupied. [Pub. 100-02, Ch. 1, § 10.1.4.]

The beneficiary may not be charged a differential in private room rates if that differential is based on factors other than personal comfort items. These factors might include, but are not limited to: differences between older and newer wings, proximity to a lounge, elevators or nursing stations, or a desirable view. [Pub. 100-02, Ch. 1, § 10.1.4.]

All-Private Room Hospitals

If the patient is admitted to a hospital that has only private rooms and no semi-private or ward accommodations, medical necessity will be deemed to exist for the accommodations furnished. Beneficiaries may not be subjected to an extra charge for a private room in an all-private room hospital. [Pub. 100-02, Ch. 1, § 10.1.5.]

[¶ 212] Drugs and Biologics

Drugs and biologics furnished to an inpatient are covered under Part A if they: (1) represent a cost to the institution in rendering services to the beneficiary; (2) are ordinarily furnished by the hospital for the care and treatment of inpatients; and (3) are furnished to an inpatient for use in the hospital. Medicare will, however, pay for a limited supply of drugs for use outside the hospital if it is medically necessary to facilitate the beneficiary's departure from the hospital and required until he or she can obtain a continuing supply. [Soc. Sec. Act § 1861(b)(2); 42 C.F.R. § 409.13.]

For a drug or biologic furnished by a hospital to be a covered hospital service, it must be included or approved for inclusion in the latest official edition or revision of certain drug compendia (including the *United States Pharmacopeia - National Formulary*, the *United States Pharmacopeia-Drug Information*, or the *American Dental Association Guide to Dental Therapeutics*). This does not include any drugs or biologics unfavorably evaluated in the *American Dental Association Guide to Dental Therapeutics* or expressly approved by the pharmacy and drug therapeutics committee (or equivalent committee) of the medical staff of the hospital for use in the hospital. [*Medicare Benefit Policy Manual*, Pub. 100-02, Ch. 1, § 30.]

Combination drugs are covered if the combination itself or all of the active ingredients are listed or approved for listing in any of the compendia named. Similarly, any combination drugs approved by the pharmacy and therapeutics committee for use in the hospital are covered. [Pub. 100-02, Ch. 1, § 30.3.]

Coverage is not limited to drugs and biologics routinely stocked by the hospital. A drug or biologic not stocked by the hospital that the hospital obtains from an outside source, such as a community pharmacy, also is covered if the facility rather than the patient is responsible for making payment to the supplier. [Pub. 100-02, Ch. 1, § 30.4.]

An investigational drug is not considered to meet the "reasonable and necessary" test that applies to all services (see ¶ 601) because its efficacy has not yet been established. Even if approved by an appropriate hospital committee, an investigational drug or biologic cannot be reimbursed. [Pub. 100-02, Ch. 1, § 30.2.]

Part D. The Medicare prescription drug benefit (Medicare Part D) permits eligible individuals to choose from at least two prescription drug plans (PDPs) in their region, with a standard coverage plan or an alternative coverage plan with actuarial-equivalent benefits. See Chapter 5 for a complete description of the prescription drug coverage provided under Medicare Part D. Drugs and biologics covered under Medicare Part B are discussed at ¶ 362.

¶212

[¶ 213] Supplies, Appliances, and Equipment

Medicare pays for supplies, appliances, and equipment as inpatient hospital or inpatient critical access hospital (CAH) services if they: (1) are ordinarily furnished by the hospital or CAH to inpatients; and (2) are furnished to inpatients for use in the hospital or CAH. [Soc. Sec. Act § 1861(b)(2); 42 C.F.R. § 409.14(a).]

Under certain circumstances, supplies, appliances, and equipment used during the beneficiary's stay are covered even when the items leave the hospital with the patient at the time of discharge. Medicare pays for items to be used beyond the hospital stay if: (1) the item is one that the beneficiary must continue to use after he or she leaves the hospital (for example, heart valves or a heart pacemaker); or (2) the item is medically necessary to permit or facilitate the beneficiary's departure from the hospital and is required until he or she can obtain a continuing supply (for example, tracheostomy or draining tubes). [42 C.F.R. § 409.14(b); *Medicare Benefit Policy Manual*, Pub. 100-02, Ch. 1, § 40.]

Routine Personal Hygiene Items and Services

Hospital "admission packs," containing primarily toilet articles (such as soap, tooth-brushes, toothpaste, and combs), are covered if routinely furnished by the hospital to all of its inpatients. If not routinely furnished, the packs are not covered and the hospital may charge the beneficiary. The beneficiary may not be charged, however, unless the beneficiary requests the pack with the knowledge of what is requested and what will be charged. [Pub. 100-02, Ch. 1, § 40.]

[¶ 214] Other Diagnostic and Therapeutic Items and Services

Medicare covers "other diagnostic or therapeutic items or services" that ordinarily are furnished to inpatients by the hospital. [Soc. Sec. Act § 1861(b)(3).] To be covered, the services must be of a kind ordinarily furnished to inpatients either by the hospital or critical access hospital (CAH) or under arrangements made by the hospital. They must be furnished by the hospital or others under arrangements made by the hospital, and billing for the services must be through the hospital. Included in this benefit are a number of diagnostic and therapeutic techniques, such as blood tests and x-rays. [42 C.F.R. § 409.16; *Medicare Benefit Policy Manual*, Pub. 100-02, Ch. 1, § § 50, 50.1.]

Many diagnostic and therapeutic items and services also are covered when furnished as outpatient hospital services (see ¶ 352).

Therapeutic Items

Therapeutic items are covered when ordinarily furnished by the hospital to its inpatients or when furnished to hospital inpatients by others under agreements made with the hospital. These items include, but are not limited to:

- surgical dressings, splints, casts, and other devices used for the reduction of fractures and dislocations;

- prosthetic devices (non-dental) that replace all or part of an internal body organ, including continuous tissue, or replace all or part of the function of a permanently inoperative or malfunctioning internal body organ; and

- leg, arm, back, and neck braces, trusses, and artificial legs, arms, and eyes.

Therapeutic items that leave the hospital with the patient upon discharge, such as splints or casts, are covered if they are not furnished for use only outside the hospital. Temporary or disposable items medically necessary to permit or facilitate the patient's departure from the hospital and required until the patient can obtain a continuing supply are covered. [Pub. 100-02, Ch. 1, § 50.1.]

Physical Therapy, Occupational Therapy, and Speech-Language Pathology Services

Physical therapy, occupational therapy, or speech-language pathology services must be furnished by qualified physical therapists, physical therapist assistants, occupational therapists, occupational therapy assistants, or speech-language pathologists in accordance with a care plan. The plan must be established before treatment begins by one of the following: (1) a physician; (2) a nurse practitioner, clinical nurse specialist, or physician assistant; (3) the physical therapist furnishing the physical therapy services; (4) a speech-language pathologist furnishing the speech-language pathology services; or (5) an occupational therapist furnishing the occupational therapy services. The plan must prescribe the type, amount, frequency, and duration of the physical therapy, occupational therapy, or speech-language pathology services to be furnished to the individual and indicate the diagnosis and anticipated goals. [42 C.F.R. § 409.17.]

Kidney Transplants

Medicare covers kidney transplantation surgery performed in approved renal transplantation centers. Additionally, Medicare pays for services related to the evaluation and preparation of a donor, the donation of the kidney, and postoperative recovery services related to the kidney donation when the kidney is intended for a Medicare beneficiary with end stage renal disease (ESRD) regardless of the donor's Medicare status. [42 C.F.R. § 409.18.]

Independent Clinical Laboratory Services

Part A also covers diagnostic services furnished to an inpatient by an independent clinical laboratory under arrangements with the hospital, provided the lab is certified under the Clinical Laboratory Improvement Amendments of 1988 (CLIA) (P.L. 100-578) to perform the services. An "independent laboratory" is independent of the attending or consulting physician's office and the hospital. [Pub. 100-02, Ch. 1, § 50.3.]

A "clinical laboratory" performs microbiological, serological, chemical, hematological, radiobioassay, cytological, immunohematological, or pathological examinations on materials derived from the human body to provide information for the diagnosis, prevention, or treatment of a disease or assessment of a medical condition. [Pub. 100-02, Ch. 1, § 50.3.]

Alcoholism and Drug Abuse (Chemical Dependency) Treatments

Alcohol detoxification and rehabilitation services are covered by Medicare when furnished as inpatient hospital services under Part A and as physician services under Part B. [*Medicare National Coverage Determinations Manual*, Pub. 100-03, Ch. 1, § § 130.1, 130.2.]

Inpatient hospital stays for alcohol detoxification. Inpatient hospital stays for alcohol detoxification are covered during the more acute stages of alcoholism or alcohol withdrawal when medical complications occur or are highly probable. Detoxification can usually be accomplished within two to three days with an occasional need for up to five days when the patient's condition dictates. Following detoxification, a patient may be transferred to an inpatient rehabilitation unit or discharged to a residential treatment program or outpatient treatment setting. [Pub. 100-03, Ch. 1, § § 130.1, 130.2.]

Inpatient hospital stays for alcohol rehabilitation. Part A covers inpatient hospital stays for alcohol rehabilitation for treatment of chronic alcoholism. Because alcohol rehabilitation can be provided in a variety of settings, an inpatient hospital stay for alcohol rehabilitation is only covered when it is medically necessary that care be provided in an inpatient hospital setting, not in a less costly setting or on an outpatient basis. Further, because alcoholism is classifiable as a psychiatric condition, the beneficiary must be receiving "active treatment." Generally, 16 to 19 days of rehabilitation services are considered

¶214

sufficient prior to continuing care on a basis other than an inpatient hospital setting. [Pub. 100-03, Ch. 1, § § 130.1, 130.2.]

Outpatient hospital coverage. Medicare covers both diagnostic and therapeutic services furnished to hospital outpatients for the treatment of alcoholism. The same rules that apply to outpatient hospital services in general (see ¶ 352) also apply here. All services must be reasonable and necessary for diagnosis or treatment of the patient's condition. In addition, alcoholism treatment services such as drug therapy, psychotherapy, and patient education that are provided incident to a physician's services in a freestanding clinic are covered under the same rules as clinic services (see ¶ 351). The psychiatric services limitation discussed at ¶ 387 also applies to these services. [Pub. 100-03, Ch. 1, § § 130.2, 130.5.]

Aversion therapy. Chemical aversion therapy for the treatment of alcoholism is a covered service. Electrical aversion therapy is not covered, however, because it has not been shown to be safe and effective. [Pub. 100-03, Ch. 1, § § 130.3, 130.4.]

Drug abuse. Treatment for drug abuse or other chemical dependency, when medically necessary, is covered by Medicare in all of the settings described above as long as the services provided are reasonable and necessary for the treatment of the patient's condition. [Pub. 100-03, Ch. 1, § § 130.5, 130.6, 130.7.]

[¶ 215] Services of Interns, Residents-in-Training, and Teaching Physicians

Physician services for inpatients are generally covered under Part B and excluded under Part A. Medicare Part A covers the services of interns and residents-in-training who participate in teaching programs approved by the appropriate accrediting associations. If the intern or resident is not providing services as part of an approved teaching program, those services are covered under Part B (see further ¶ 340). [Soc. Sec. Act § 1861(b)(4), (6); 42 C.F.R. § 409.15.]

The administrative and teaching services of teaching physicians are also covered under Part A. [42 C.F.R. § 415.55.] The services of teaching physicians to individual patients are covered under Part B (see ¶ 340 and ¶ 855).

[¶ 217] Nursing and Medical Social Services

Nursing and other related services are covered as inpatient hospital services if ordinarily furnished by the hospital for the care and treatment of inpatients. However, the services of a private-duty nurse or other private-duty attendant are expressly excluded. [Soc. Sec. Act § 1861(b)(2), (5); 42 C.F.R. § 409.12.]

Private-duty nurses or private-duty attendants are registered professional nurses, licensed practical nurses, or any other trained attendants whose services ordinarily are rendered to, and restricted to, a particular patient by arrangement between the patient and the private-duty nurse or attendant. Private-duty services are engaged or paid by an individual patient or by someone acting on the patient's behalf, including a hospital that initially incurs the cost and seeks reimbursement for noncovered services from the patient. When the hospital acts on behalf of a patient, the services of the private-duty nurse or other attendant are not inpatient hospital services, regardless of the control the hospital may exercise over the private services. [*Medicare Benefit Policy Manual*, Pub. 100-02, Ch. 1, § 20.]

Medical social services. Medical social services ordinarily furnished by the hospital, i.e., those social services that contribute meaningfully to the treatment of a patient's condition, are covered as inpatient hospital services under Part A. These services include, but are not limited to: (1) assessment of the social and emotional factors related to the patient's illness, the individual's need for care, the individual's response to treatment, and the individual's adjustment to care in the facility; (2) appropriate action to obtain casework services to assist in resolving problems in these areas; and (3) assessment of the relationship of the patient's medical and nursing requirements to the home situation, financial resources, and the community resources available in making the decision regarding his or her discharge. [42 C.F.R. § 409.12(a); Pub. 100-02, Ch. 1, § 20.2.]

[¶ 218] Inpatient Rehabilitation Facilities

The inpatient rehabilitation facility (IRF) benefit is designed to provide intensive rehabilitation therapy in an inpatient hospital environment for patients who, due to the complexity of their nursing, medical management, and rehabilitation needs, require and can reasonably be expected to benefit from an inpatient stay and an interdisciplinary team approach to the delivery of rehabilitation care. [*Medicare Benefit Policy Manual*, Pub. 100-02, Ch. 1, § 110.]

For an IRF claim to be considered reasonable and necessary, documentation in the medical record must demonstrate a reasonable expectation that at the time of admission to the IRF that the patient:

(1) requires the active and ongoing therapeutic intervention of multiple therapy disciplines (including physical therapy, occupational therapy, speech-language pathology, or prosthetics/orthotics therapy), one of which must be physical or occupational therapy;

(2) generally requires an intensive rehabilitation therapy program, which, under current standards, generally consists of at least three hours of therapy per day at least five days per week (in certain well-documented cases, an intensive rehabilitation therapy program might instead consist of at least 15 hours of intensive rehabilitation therapy within a seven-consecutive-day period, beginning with the date of admission to the IRF);

(3) is expected to actively participate in, and benefit significantly from, the intensive rehabilitation therapy program at the time of admission to the IRF;

(4) is sufficiently stable at the time of admission to actively participate in the intensive rehabilitation therapy program; and

(5) requires physician supervision by a rehabilitation physician, defined, effective October 1, 2019, as a licensed physician who is determined by the IRF to have specialized training and experience in inpatient rehabilitation.

The requirement for medical supervision means that the rehabilitation physician must conduct face-to-face visits with the patient at least three days per week throughout the patient's stay in the IRF to assess the patient medically and functionally and modify the course of treatment as needed to maximize the patient's capacity to benefit from the rehabilitation process. The post-admission physician evaluation described in 42 C.F.R. § 412.622(a)(4)(ii) may count as one of the face-to-face visits. [42 C.F.R. § 412.622(a)(3); *Final rule*, 84 FR 39054, Aug. 9, 2019.]

Significantly benefits. Benefit from this intensive rehabilitation therapy program is demonstrated by measurable improvement that will be of practical value to the patient in improving the patient's functional capacity or adaptation to impairments. The required therapy treatments must begin within 36 hours from midnight of the day of admission to the IRF. However, the patient need not be expected to achieve complete independence in the domain of self-care or expected to return to his or her prior level of functioning to meet this standard. [42 C.F.R. § 412.622(a)(3)(ii); Pub. 100-02, Ch. 1, § 110.2.]

Group therapy. The standard of care for IRF patients is individualized (i.e., one-on-one) therapy. Group therapies may serve as an adjunct to individual therapies. In those instances in which group therapy better meets the patient's needs on a limited basis, the situation or rationale that justifies group therapy should be specified in the patient's medical record. [Pub. 100-02, Ch. 1, § 110.2.2.]

Rehabilitation services are also discussed at ¶ 230.

IRF Documentation Requirements

The IRF must maintain documentation in the patient's medical record to demonstrate that a patient was reasonably expected to meet IRF requirements at the time of admission. The patient's medical record must include a record of the preadmission screening, the post-admission evaluation by a physician, the individualized plan of care, and all rehabilitation service orders. [42 C.F.R. § 412.622(a)(4).]

Preadmission screening. Documentation must indicate that the preadmission screening:

(1) was performed within 48 hours immediately preceding the IRF admission by a licensed or certified clinician designated by a rehabilitation physician;

(2) provides a detailed and comprehensive review of the patient's condition and medical history;

(3) served as the basis for the initial determination of whether the patient meets the requirements for an IRF admission to be reasonable and necessary;

(4) was used to inform the rehabilitation physician who reviews and, subsequently, documents his or her concurrence with the findings of the preadmission screening; and

(5) is retained in the patient's medical record.

A preadmission screening that includes all of the required elements but that is conducted more than 48 hours immediately preceding the IRF admission is acceptable as long as an update is conducted in person or by telephone to update the patient's medical and functional status within the 48 hours immediately preceding the IRF admission and is documented in the patient's medical record. [42 C.F.R. § 412.622(a)(4)(i).]

Post-admission evaluation. Documentation must include a post-admission physician evaluation that (1) is completed by a rehabilitation physician within 24 hours of the patient's admission; (2) documents the patient's status on admission to the IRF; (3) includes a comparison with the information noted in the preadmission screening documentation; and (4) serves as the basis for the development of the overall individualized plan of care. [42 C.F.R. § 412.622(a)(4)(ii), (iii).]

Individualized plan of care. Within four days of the patient's admission to the IRF, an individualized overall plan of care for the patient must be developed by a rehabilitation physician with input from the interdisciplinary team. The plan of care must be retained in the patient's medical record at the IRF. [42 C.F.R. § 412.622(a)(4)(iii).]

Rehabilitation service orders. All rehabilitation services orders must be documented in the patient's medical record in accordance with the requirements at 42 C.F.R. § 482.24. [42 C.F.R. § 482.56(b)(1).]

IRF Interdisciplinary Team

For an IRF claim to be considered reasonable and necessary, the patient must require an interdisciplinary team approach to care, as evidenced by documentation in the patient's medical record of weekly interdisciplinary team meetings that meet the following requirements:

(1) The team meetings are led by a rehabilitation physician. The team includes a registered nurse with specialized training or experience in rehabilitation; a social worker and/or case manager; and a licensed or certified therapist from each therapy discipline involved in treating the patient. All team members must have current knowledge of the patient's medical and functional status. The rehabilitation physician may lead the interdisciplinary team meeting remotely using a mode of communication such as video or telephone conferencing.

(2) The team meetings occur at least once per week throughout the duration of the patient's stay to implement appropriate treatment services; review the patient's progress toward stated rehabilitation goals; identify any problems that could impede progress towards those goals; and, when necessary, reassess previously established goals in light of impediments, revise the treatment plan in light of new goals, and monitor continued progress toward those goals.

(3) The results and findings of the team meetings, and the concurrence by the rehabilitation physician with those results and findings, are retained in the patient's medical record.

[42 C.F.R. § 412.622(a)(5).]

Rehabilitation and Physical, Occupational, and Speech Pathology Services

Rehabilitation, physical therapy, occupational therapy, audiology, and speech pathology services must be provided under the orders of a qualified and licensed practitioner who is responsible for the care of the patient, is acting within his or her scope of practice under state law, and is authorized by the hospital's medical staff to order the services in accordance with hospital policies and procedures and state laws. The organization of the service must be appropriate to the scope of the services offered and the director of the services must have the necessary knowledge, experience, and capabilities to properly supervise and administer the services. Services must be provided by qualified physical therapists, physical therapist assistants, occupational therapists, occupational therapy assistants, speech-language pathologists, or audiologists as defined in 42 C.F.R. Part 484. [42 C.F.R. § 482.56(a), (b).]

The provision of care and the personnel qualifications must be in accordance with national acceptable standards of practice and must meet the requirements of 42 C.F.R. § 409.17 (see ¶ 233). [42 C.F.R. § 482.56(b)(2).]

[¶ 221] Inpatient Benefit Period and "Spell of Illness"

The duration of inpatient hospital services and post-hospital services in a skilled nursing facility (SNF) is limited according to the beginning and ending of a "spell of illness"—commonly called a "benefit period." [42 C.F.R. § 409.60.]

A "spell of illness" is a period of consecutive days that begins with the first day (that is not included in a previous spell of illness) on which a patient is furnished inpatient hospital or SNF services by a "qualified" provider during a period in which the patient is entitled to Part A benefits. [Soc. Sec. Act § 1861(a)(1); 42 C.F.R. § 409.60(a).]

A "qualified" provider is a hospital (including a psychiatric hospital) or SNF that has been certified as satisfying the requirements of the definition of such an institution (see ¶ 229 and ¶ 249). A hospital that meets the requirements related to emergency services, which are outlined at ¶ 227, is a qualified hospital for purposes of beginning a spell of illness when it furnishes the patient covered inpatient emergency services. [*Medicare General Information, Eligibility, and Entitlement Manual*, Pub. 100-01, Ch. 3, § 10.4.1; Ch. 5, § 20.2.]

Admission to a qualified SNF will begin a spell of illness, even if payment for the services cannot be made because the prior hospitalization or transfer requirement has not been met (see ¶ 230).

Ending a Spell of Illness

The spell of illness ends with the close of a period of 60 consecutive days during which the patient was neither an inpatient of a hospital nor an inpatient of a SNF. The 60-consecutive-day period begins with the day on which the individual is discharged. [Soc. Sec. Act § 1861(a)(2); 42 C.F.R. § 409.60(b); Pub. 100-01, Ch. 3, § 10.4.2.]

A stay in a nonparticipating hospital is counted as a qualified stay for purposes of determining whether a spell of illness has ended, even if the nonparticipating hospital did not furnish covered emergency services. A stay in a SNF does not continue a spell of illness unless the stay meets Medicare skilled nursing care requirements. Thus, a beneficiary who is transferred from a hospital to a SNF, but receives only "custodial care" (see ¶ 244) at the SNF, would begin counting the 60-consecutive-day period on the day of discharge from the hospital. [42 C.F.R. § 409.60(b).]

An individual may be discharged from and readmitted to a hospital or SNF several times during a spell of illness and still be in the same spell if 60 days have not elapsed between discharge and readmission. The stay does not need to be for related physical or mental conditions. [Pub. 100-01, Ch. 3, § 10.4.3.2.]

Example • • • _____

(1) John White was entitled to Part A benefits and was hospitalized in a participating general hospital on June 1. He previously had not established a spell of illness. He remained in the hospital for 30 days and then was transferred to a SNF for 50 days, after which he was discharged to his home on August 18. John's spell of illness began on June 1 and ended on October 17, the end of the 60-day period beginning with the date of his last discharge.

(2) Assume the same set of facts as above, except that John was rehospitalized after 50 days in the SNF and remained in the hospital for another 60 days, after which he was discharged to his home on October 17. John's spell of illness still began on June 1, but it ended on December 16, the end of the 60-day period beginning with the date of his last discharge.

(3) Assume the same set of facts as in example (2), except that John was required to enter the hospital for a third time, *before* exhaustion of the 60-day period following his last hospital discharge. Assume further that he remained in the hospital until his death. No new spell of illness could begin regardless of how long John remained in the hospital during his terminal illness. The crossing from one calendar year to another does not end an ongoing spell of illness.

_____

Once a spell of illness has ended, the beneficiary's next admission to a qualified hospital or SNF will start a new spell of illness. [42 C.F.R. § 409.60(a).]

Note that when a beneficiary begins a new spell of illness as a hospital inpatient, a new inpatient hospital deductible (see ¶ 223) must be paid, even if it is within the same calendar year. [42 C.F.R. § 409.60(e).]

"Inpatient Day of Care" Defined

The number of days of care charged to a beneficiary for inpatient hospital services is always in units of full days. A day begins at midnight and ends 24 hours later. A part of a day, including the day of admission, counts as a full day, but the day of discharge or death, or a day on which a patient begins a leave of absence, is not counted as a day. If admission and discharge occur on the same day, the day is considered a day of admission and counts as one day. As noted, the day on which a patient begins a leave of absence is treated as a day of discharge and not counted (unless the patient returns to the hospital by midnight of the same day), each day during the leave is not counted as an inpatient day, and the day the patient returns to the hospital from the leave is treated as a day of admission and counted if the patient is present at midnight of that day. [Pub. 100-02, Ch. 3, § § 20.1, 20.1.2.]

[¶ 222] Inpatient Lifetime Limitation

Each beneficiary has a lifetime reserve of 60 days of inpatient hospital services to draw upon after having used 90 days of inpatient hospital services in a benefit period (see ¶ 221). The 60 days are not renewable and may be used only once during a beneficiary's lifetime. Medicare pays for such additional days of hospital care after the 90 days of benefits have been exhausted unless the individual elects to save the reserve days for a later time and not to have such payment made. [Soc. Sec. Act § 1812(a)(1), (b)(1); *Medicare Benefit Policy Manual*, Pub. 100-02, Ch. 5, § § 20, 30.1.]

For example, if a beneficiary is hospitalized for 150 days during the first covered spell of illness, all lifetime reserve days will be expended. If a beneficiary is hospitalized for only 100 days during the first spell of illness, 50 lifetime reserve days would be left for use during a subsequent spell of illness that requires hospitalization for more than 90 days. [Soc. Sec. Act § 1812(a)(1), (b)(1); Pub. 100-02, Ch. 5, § 30.1.]

A coinsurance amount equal to one-half of the inpatient hospital deductible applies to lifetime reserve days. [42 C.F.R. § 409.83(a)(3).]

There is an additional lifetime limitation of 190 days on inpatient psychiatric hospital services (see ¶ 225). [Soc. Sec. Act § 1812(b)(3).]

For coverage under Part B of inpatient "ancillary" services furnished after a beneficiary's days of entitlement under Part A are exhausted, see ¶ 361.

Election by Beneficiary Not to Use Reserve Days

Whenever a beneficiary has exhausted the 90 regular benefit days, the hospital may bill Medicare for lifetime reserve days unless the beneficiary elects not to use them or is deemed to have elected not to use them. A beneficiary will be deemed to have elected not to use lifetime reserve days if the average daily charges for such days is equal to or less than the applicable coinsurance amount, since a beneficiary would not benefit from using the days under those circumstances. [42 C.F.R. § 409.65(a)(1), (b).]

The beneficiary (or someone acting on the beneficiary's behalf) may make an election not to use lifetime reserve days at the time of admission to a hospital or any time thereafter. Ordinarily, an election *not* to use reserve days will apply prospectively. If the beneficiary files the election at the time of admission to a hospital, it may be made effective on the first day of hospitalization or on any day thereafter. If the election is filed later, it may be made effective on any day after the day it is filed. [42 C.F.R. § 409.65(c); Pub. 100-02, Ch. 5, § 30.2.]

Retroactive election. A beneficiary, within 90 days following discharge, may elect retroactively not to use reserve days, provided: (1) the beneficiary (or some other source) offers to pay the hospital for any of the services not payable under Part B; and (2) the hospital agrees to accept the retroactive election. A beneficiary may file an election not to use the lifetime reserve days later than 90 days following discharge only if benefits are available from a third-party payer and the hospital agrees to the retroactive election. [42 C.F.R. § 409.65(d); Pub. 100-02, Ch. 5, § 30.3.]

Example • • • _____

Before July 1, Henry Wong had used 90 days of inpatient hospital services in a spell of illness. Beginning July 1, he was hospitalized for 10 more days during the same spell of illness. On July 1, at the time of his admission, Henry indicated that he wanted to use his reserve days for that stay. One month after being discharged from the hospital, Henry informed the hospital that he now wished to save his reserve days for a future stay. Henry agreed to pay the hospital for the services he received during the 10 days of hospitalization and was permitted to file a retroactive election not to use his reserve days for those 10 days.

On July 1, Walter Brown was discharged from a hospital after being hospitalized for 105 days. The hospital billed Medicare for 90 regular days plus 15 lifetime reserve days. On October 20 (more than 90 days following discharge), Walter learned that a private insurer could pay for the last 15 days of the stay. Walter informed the hospital that he wished to file a retroactive election not to use lifetime reserve days for the last 15 days of the stay. The hospital agreed to the request, and Walter filed an election form. The hospital refunded the Medicare payment and billed the private carrier instead.

Period Covered by Election Not to Use Reserve Days

A beneficiary election *not* to use reserve days for a particular hospital stay may apply to the entire stay or to a single period of consecutive days in the stay, but it cannot apply to selected days in a stay. For example, a beneficiary may restrict the election to the period covered by private insurance but cannot use individual lifetime reserve days within that period. If an election (whether made prospectively or retroactively) not to use reserve days is made effective with the first day for which reserve days are available, it must remain in effect until the end of the stay unless it is revoked. [42 C.F.R. § 409.65(e).]

Exception for hospitals reimbursed under the prospective payment system. For hospitals reimbursed under the hospital inpatient prospective payment system (IPPS), the rules stated above apply with the following exceptions:

One or more regular benefit days available at time of admission. If the beneficiary has one or more regular benefit (non-lifetime reserve) days remaining in the benefit period upon entering the hospital, an election not to use lifetime reserve days will apply automatically to all days that are not outlier days (see ¶ 810 for an explanation of the term "outlier days"). There will be no advantage to a beneficiary in using any lifetime reserve days for non-outlier days if at least one day of the regular 90 days of coverage remains when the beneficiary enters the hospital. The beneficiary also may elect not to use lifetime reserve days for outlier days, but such an election must apply to all outlier days. [42 C.F.R. § 409.65(e)(2)(i); Pub. 100-02, Ch. 5, § 30.1.]

Example • • • _____

Olivia Gonzalez was admitted to a hospital on April 1 and discharged on June 29, utilizing 89 regular days of inpatient care. On August 1, Olivia entered the hospital again. For this Medicare severity diagnosis-related group (MS-DRG), outlier days would have begun August 26, but Olivia was discharged on August 23, before the commencement of outlier days. Because the first two days of the second stay were regular coverage days, Medicare will reimburse the hospital the IPPS amount for the entire stay. Because no outlier days are involved, there is no advantage to the beneficiary in using lifetime reserve days. Therefore, Olivia will be deemed to have elected *not* to use any lifetime reserve days for that stay.

Exhaustion of regular benefit days. If the beneficiary enters the hospital after completely exhausting regular benefit days, available lifetime reserve days will be used automatically for each day of the stay unless the beneficiary elects not to use lifetime reserve days or is deemed to have elected not to use lifetime reserve days. An election by a beneficiary not to use lifetime reserve days must apply to the entire hospital stay. If the beneficiary elects not to use lifetime reserve days, Medicare will not pay for any portion of the stay. A deemed election not to use lifetime reserve days must apply to the entire stay and will preclude any payment for the stay. The policy regarding the use of lifetime reserve days is the same for long-term care hospitals. [42 C.F.R. § 409.65(e)(2)(ii); Pub. 100-02, Ch. 5, § 30.4.1.]

Example • • • _____

Frances McDonald was admitted to a hospital on March 10, 2020 and discharged on June 8, utilizing 90 regular days of coverage. On August 1, Frances entered the hospital again; she was discharged on September 10. For this MS-DRG, outlier days began on August 26. At the time of the second admission, Frances still had 60 lifetime reserve days available. The hospital charges for this stay were $35,000. The sum of the coinsurance amounts for the lifetime reserve days needed to pay for this stay was $28,160 ($704 per day × 40 days). Because the charges for the stay were greater than the sum of lifetime reserve days coinsurance amounts, there was no deemed election not to use lifetime reserve days. Frances had the option: (1) of making no lifetime reserve election, in which case Medicare pays for the entire stay, including the outlier days, and she would use 40 lifetime reserve days; or (2) of electing *not* to use lifetime reserve days, in which case Medicare does not pay for any portion of the stay.

Revocation of Election Not to Use Lifetime Reserve Days

Generally, a beneficiary (or anyone authorized to execute a request for payment, if the beneficiary is incapacitated) may revoke an election not to use lifetime reserve days during hospitalization or within 90 days after discharge. The revocation must be submitted to the hospital in writing and identify the stay or stays to which it applies. [42 C.F.R. § 409.66(a), (b).]

A revocation of an election not to use lifetime reserve days may not be filed: (1) after the beneficiary dies; or (2) after the hospital has filed a claim under Part B for medical and other health services furnished to the beneficiary on the days in question. [42 C.F.R. § 409.66(c).]

[¶ 223] Inpatient Hospital Deductible and Coinsurance

The amount payable by Part A is reduced by the deductible and coinsurances described below. The inpatient deductible and coinsurance amounts are portions of the cost of covered inpatient services that Medicare does not pay. The hospital may charge these amounts to the beneficiary or someone on his or her behalf. [Soc. Sec. Act § 1813; 42 C.F.R. § 409.80.]

Inpatient Hospital Deductible

For inpatient hospital services furnished in each "spell of illness," the patient is responsible for an inpatient hospital deductible. In 2020, the deductible is $1,408 per spell of illness. [Soc. Sec. Act § 1813(b); 42 C.F.R. § 409.82; *Notice,* 84 FR 61619, Nov. 13, 2019.]

The inpatient hospital deductible for each successive year is calculated by modifying the previous year's deductible by the same percentage used to determine Medicare payments to prospective payment system (PPS) hospitals. The amount calculated is rounded to the nearest multiple of $4 (an amount midway between two multiples is rounded up). Once the

¶223

deductible is determined, the coinsurance amounts are adjusted accordingly. [Soc. Sec. Act § 1813(b)(1), (2).]

Under this formula, the inpatient hospital deductible is increased each year by about the same percentage as the increase in the average Medicare daily hospital costs. The result of the deductible increase is that the beneficiary continues to pay about the same proportion of the hospital bill. [42 C.F.R. § 409.80(b)(1).]

If the hospital stay spans two calendar years, the deductible in effect on the first day of the hospitalization is applicable. The coinsurance, however, is based on the coinsurance in effect for the year in which the cost-sharing days are incurred. [Soc. Sec. Act § 1813(b)(3).]

The applicable deductible is the one in effect during the calendar year in which the services were furnished. [42 C.F.R. 409.82(a)(4).]

The deductible is satisfied only by charges for *covered* services. Expenses for covered services count toward the deductible on an incurred, rather than a paid, basis, and expenses incurred during one spell of illness cannot be applied toward the deductible in a later spell of illness. The inpatient hospital deductible is imposed only once during a "spell of illness," even though the beneficiary may have been hospitalized more than once during that spell of illness (see the examples at ¶ 210). There can be more than one spell of illness and, thus, more than one required deductible, in a calendar year. Neither expenses incurred in meeting the blood deductible (see below) nor the monthly premiums paid by those voluntarily enrolled for hospital insurance coverage (see ¶ 203) count toward the inpatient hospital deductible. [42 C.F.R. § 409.82(a)(2); *Medicare General Information, Eligibility, and Entitlement Manual*, Pub. 100-01, Ch. 3, § 10.1.]

A reduction in benefit days resulting from the application of the psychiatric hospital carryover restriction, on and immediately preceding the date of entitlement, does not affect the amount of the deductible for which the patient is responsible. [Pub. 100-01, Ch. 3, § 10.1.] For a discussion of the psychiatric hospital carryover restriction, see ¶ 225.

The deductible and coinsurance requirements do not apply to services in connection with the donation of a kidney for transplant surgery. [42 C.F.R. § 409.89.]

Inpatient Hospital Coinsurance

When a beneficiary receives inpatient hospital services for more than 60 days during a spell of illness, he or she is responsible for a coinsurance amount for each day after the 60th and through the 90th day on which these services are furnished. There also is a coinsurance amount for each day, after the 90th and through the 150th in any spell of illness, that is chargeable against the individual's 60-day lifetime reserve (see ¶ 222). [Soc. Sec. Act § 1813(a)(1); 42 C.F.R. § 409.83(a).]

The coinsurance amount for the 61st through 90th days is equal to one-fourth of the inpatient hospital deductible, as annually adjusted ($352 in 2020). For the 91st to the 150th day (lifetime reserve days), the coinsurance amount is ½ of the inpatient deductible ($704 in 2020). When a patient's hospitalization spans two calendar years, the coinsurance amount is based on the deductible applicable for the calendar year in which the services were furnished. For example, if an individual starts a benefit period by being admitted to a hospital in 2019 and remains in the hospital long enough to use coinsurance days in 2020, the coinsurance amount charged for those days is based on the 2020 inpatient hospital deductible. [Soc. Sec. Act § 1813(a)(1), (b)(3); 42 C.F.R. § 409.83(a); *Notice*, 84 FR 61619, Nov. 13, 2019.]

In the determination of the amount of the coinsurance met, the coinsurance charge for a day of inpatient hospital services may not exceed the charges imposed for that day with respect to the individual beneficiary. Customary charges are considered actual charges if they are greater than the charges imposed. If the actual charge to the patient for the 61st through the 90th day of inpatient hospital services is less than the coinsurance amount applicable for the calendar year in which the services were furnished, the actual charge per day is the daily coinsurance amount. [Soc. Sec. Act § 1813(a)(1).] In connection with the lifetime reserve days provision, however, when the actual charge is equal to or less than the coinsurance amount, the beneficiary is deemed to have elected not to use one of the lifetime reserve days. Thus, the day is treated as a noncovered day and no coinsurance amount is chargeable to the patient (see ¶ 222). [42 C.F.R. § 409.83(c)(2).]

Deductible for Whole Blood and Packed Red Blood Cells

In addition to the inpatient hospital deductible, there is another deductible, equal to the cost of the first three pints of whole blood (or packed red blood cells) received by a beneficiary in a calendar year. The blood deductible can be satisfied under either Part A or Part B (see ¶ 335), or a combination of the two. [Soc. Sec. Act § 1813(a)(2); 42 C.F.R. § 409.87(a).]

"Whole blood" or packed red cells is the red blood cells that remain after plasma is separated from whole blood. The deductible does not apply to other blood components such as platelets, fibrinogen, plasma, gamma globulin, and serum albumin, or to the cost of processing, storing, and administering blood. [42 C.F.R. § 409.87(a).]

A beneficiary has the option of paying the hospital's charges for the blood or packed red cells or arranging for it to be replaced. However, the beneficiary is not responsible for the first three units of whole blood or packed red cells if the provider obtained it at no charge other than a processing or service charge. In that case, the blood is deemed to have been replaced. [42 C.F.R. § 409.87(b).]

Generally, a provider may charge a beneficiary its customary charge for any of the first three units of whole blood or packed red cells. A provider may not charge the beneficiary for the first three units of whole blood or packed red cells in any of the following circumstances: (1) the blood or packed red cells have been replaced; (2) the provider (or its blood supplier) receives a replacement offer from an individual or a blood bank that meets requirements; and (3) the provider obtained the blood or packed red cells at no charge other than a processing or service charge and, therefore, it is deemed to have been replaced. [Soc. Sec. Act § 1866(a)(2)(C); 42 C.F.R. § 409.87(c).]

A blood replacement offer by a beneficiary, an individual, or a blood bank on behalf of a beneficiary discharges the beneficiary's obligation to pay the blood deductible as long as the replacement blood would not endanger the health of a recipient and the donation would not endanger the donor's health. [42 C.F.R. § 409.87(d).]

[¶ 225] Psychiatric Hospital Restrictions

Payment may not be made for more than a total of 190 days of inpatient psychiatric hospital services during the patient's lifetime. Once an individual receives benefits for 190 days of care in a psychiatric hospital, no further benefits of that type are available. The period spent in a psychiatric hospital before entitlement does not count against the patient's 190-day lifetime limitation. [42 C.F.R. § 409.62; *Medicare Benefit Policy Manual*, Pub. 100-02, Ch. 4, § 50.]

Reduction of inpatient psychiatric benefit days available. In addition, if an individual was an inpatient in a psychiatric hospital on the first day of Medicare entitlement and for any of the 150 days immediately before the first day of entitlement, those days are subtracted from the 150 days (90 regular days plus 60 lifetime reserve days) that would otherwise be available in the initial benefit period for inpatient psychiatric services in a psychiatric or general hospital. Days spent in a general hospital before entitlement are not subtracted, even if the stay was for the diagnosis or treatment of mental illness. However, after entitlement, all psychiatric care days, whether in a general or a psychiatric hospital, are counted toward the number of days available in the initial benefit period. [Soc. Sec. Act § 1812(c); 42 C.F.R. § 409.63.]

[¶ 227] Emergency Services Provided in Nonparticipating Hospitals

There are emergency situations in which an individual who is eligible for Medicare goes or is taken to a hospital that does not participate in the Medicare program. For example, an accident victim might have to be taken immediately to the nearest hospital, either for outpatient diagnosis and treatment or admission as an inpatient. The law permits the payment of benefits for emergency outpatient services or inpatient care in the United States in such cases until it is no longer medically necessary to care for the patient in the nonparticipating institution. Payment will be made only when the nonparticipating facility was the most accessible hospital able to furnish necessary emergency care. [Soc. Sec. Act § 1814(d)(1).]

The following discussion applies *only* to emergency services in a hospital *not participating* in Medicare. Emergency services in a participating hospital are covered under Medicare in the same manner as nonemergency services. The special requirements applicable to participating hospitals with respect to the treatment of emergency room cases are discussed at ¶ 730.

Payment for Emergency Services in Nonparticipating Hospitals

There are two possible methods of payment to a nonparticipating hospital for emergency services. Payment can be made to the hospital if it so elects and meets the conditions described below. Otherwise, payment is made to the individual on the basis of an itemized bill. For payment to be made to the hospital:

(1) the services must be emergency services;

(2) the services must be covered inpatient hospital services under Part A or covered outpatient services;

(3) the hospital must meet the definition of "emergency services hospital" (see below);

(4) the hospital must agree to not charge the patient or any other individual for covered items or services (except to the extent that a participating hospital would be permitted to charge for these services (see ¶ 730)), and must agree to return any money incorrectly collected; and

(5) the hospital must have signed a statement of election to claim payment for all inpatient and outpatient services furnished during the year.

[Soc. Sec. Act §§ 1814(d)(1), 1835(b)(1), 1866(a); 42 C.F.R. §§ 424.104, 424.108; *Medicare General Information, Eligibility, and Entitlement Manual*, Pub. 100-01, Ch. 5, § 20.1.]

If the hospital does not elect to claim payment as discussed above, payment may be made to the beneficiary on the basis of an itemized bill, subject to applicable deductible and coinsurance amounts. [Soc. Sec. Act §§ 1814(d)(2), 1835(b)(2).]

Definition of "Emergency Services Hospital"

A facility qualifies as an "emergency services hospital" if it is licensed as a hospital under applicable state or local laws, has a full-time nursing service, is engaged primarily in furnishing medical care under the supervision of a physician, and is not engaged primarily in providing skilled nursing care and related services for inpatients who require medical or nursing care. Psychiatric hospitals that meet these requirements also can qualify as emergency services hospitals. A federal hospital need not be licensed under state or local licensing laws to meet this definition. [Soc. Sec. Act § 1861(e); 42 C.F.R. § 424.101; Pub. 100-01, Ch. 5, § 20.2.]

Definition of "Emergency Services"

"Emergency services" are inpatient or outpatient hospital services that are necessary to prevent the death or serious impairment an individual's health and that, because of the threat to the life or health, necessitate the use of the most accessible hospital available and equipped to furnish the services. [42 C.F.R. § 424.101.]

The following situations do not in themselves indicate a need for emergency services, unless there also is an immediate threat to the patient's life or health: (1) the death of the patient during hospitalization; (2) a lack of adequate care at home; or (3) a lack of transportation to a participating hospital. [42 C.F.R. § 424.102.]

Termination of Emergency Services

Payment to a nonparticipating hospital for emergency services under Part A ceases when the emergency has ended. Payment under Part B may be made, however, for certain ancillary services furnished during nonemergency inpatient stays (see ¶ 361). An emergency no longer exists when it becomes medically safe to move the patient to a participating institution or discharge the patient, whichever occurs first. The physician's supporting statement will ordinarily serve as the basis for determining that an emergency has ended. [42 C.F.R. § 424.103(b)(3).]

Emergency Services Outside the United States

Under certain circumstances, Medicare will pay for emergency inpatient hospital services furnished to a beneficiary outside the United States by a foreign hospital. See ¶ 610.

[¶ 228] Religious Nonmedical Health Care Institutions

Providers qualifying as religious nonmedical health care institutions are included as hospitals and skilled nursing facilities for Medicare purposes. [Soc. Sec. Act § 1861(e), (y), (ss).] To qualify, an institution must:

(1) be a tax-exempt organization under section 501(c)(3) of the Internal Revenue Code;

(2) be lawfully operated under all applicable federal, state, and local laws and regulations;

(3) provide only nonmedical nursing items and services exclusively to individuals who choose to rely solely upon a religious method of healing, through experienced nonmedical personnel, and on a 24-hour basis;

(4) not provide medical items or services (including screening, examination, diagnosis, or administration of drugs) to its patients or be affiliated by common ownership or otherwise with an institution that provides such services; and

(5) have in effect a specialized utilization review plan and provide the Secretary with information required to monitor quality of care and provide for coverage determinations.

[Soc. Sec. Act § 1861(ss); 42 C.F.R. § 403.720.]

Patients being treated in a religious nonmedical health care institution must make an election to receive such benefits. Additionally, Medicare reimbursement in these institutions is available only to individuals with a condition that would require them to be inpatients in a hospital or skilled nursing facility were it not for their religious beliefs. [Soc. Sec. Act § 1821(a), (b).]

Payment is on a reasonable cost basis and may be made only for items and services normally furnished in such institutions (i.e., nonmedical nursing services and related items). [Soc. Sec. Act § 1861(e), (y); 42 C.F.R. § 403.752.]

Medicare will cover specified durable medical equipment and intermittent religious nonmedical health care institution nursing visits provided in the home to beneficiaries. However, payment for nonmedical care is subject to the requirements for reasonableness and necessity. Religious nonmedical nursing personnel may not engage in any activities that are medical in nature. The remainder of the services covered under the Medicare home health benefit are medical in nature and must be provided under the order of a physician. The specified durable medical equipment items include canes, crutches, walkers, commodes, a standard wheelchair, hospital beds, bedpans, and urinals. [Soc. Sec. Act § 1862(a)(1)(A); *Medicare Benefit Policy Manual*, Pub. 100-02, Ch. 1, § 130.4.]

[¶ 229] "Hospital" Defined—Qualified Hospitals

As a general rule, Medicare will not cover a beneficiary's stay in a hospital unless the hospital is "participating" in the Medicare program (see ¶ 730). Services provided in a nonparticipating hospital, however, may be covered by Medicare in emergency situations (see ¶ 227).

To participate as a hospital in the Medicare program, an institution must be a "hospital" within the meaning of section 1861(e) of the Social Security Act and meet all of the requirements identified in the section. Nonparticipating hospitals must be primarily engaged in providing inpatients with: (1) diagnostic and therapeutic services for medical diagnosis, treatment, and care of injured, disabled, or sick persons; or (2) rehabilitation services of injured, disabled, or sick persons, The services must be provided by or under the supervision of physicians. [Soc. Sec. Act § 1861(e)(1).] In addition, hospitals must provide 24-hour nursing care, have a utilization review plan in effect, and meet certain health and safety requirements.

Psychiatric hospitals must participate in Medicare for the services they furnish to be covered. The requirements for these hospitals are similar to the requirements for other hospitals, although they differ in some respects due to their different purpose. Among the requirements psychiatric hospitals must meet, the hospital must be primarily engaged in providing, by or under the supervision of a physician, psychiatric services for the diagnosis and treatment of mentally ill persons. [Soc. Sec. Act § 1861(f).]

Medicare regulations describing the conditions of participation for hospitals are found at 42 C.F.R. Part 482.

Hospital Providers of Extended Care Services ("Swing-Bed" Facilities)

Because of the shortage of rural skilled nursing facility (SNF) beds for Medicare patients, rural hospitals with fewer than 100 beds may be paid under Part A for furnishing covered nursing home services to Medicare beneficiaries. Such a hospital, known as a swing-bed facility, can "swing" its beds between hospital and SNF levels of care on an as-needed basis if it has obtained a swing-bed approval from CMS. [Soc. Sec. Act § 1883; *Medicare General Information, Eligibility, and Entitlement Manual*, Pub. 100-01, Ch. 5, § 30.3.]

A hospital providing extended care services will be treated as a SNF for purposes of applying coverage rules. This means that those services are subject to all of the Part A coverage, physician certification, deductible, and coinsurance provisions that are applicable to SNF extended care services. For example:

(1) SNF level of care days in a swing-bed facility are counted against total SNF benefit days available to Medicare beneficiaries;

(2) Medicare beneficiaries receiving a SNF level of care in a swing-bed facility must first meet the three-day prior hospital stay requirement; and

(3) services needed and provided must be of the type and at the level to constitute extended care or SNF level services.

[Soc. Sec. Act § 1883(d); 42 C.F.R. § 409.30; *Medicare Benefit Policy Manual*, Pub. 100-02, Ch. 8, § § 10.3, 20.1, 30.]

Nursing Home Services

[¶ 230] Introduction to Covered Nursing Home Services

Extended care services furnished to inpatients of a skilled nursing facility (SNF) are covered under Part A. These services, which involve "skilled" nursing or rehabilitation services, are similar to the kinds of services provided to hospital inpatients, but at a lower level of care. [Soc. Sec. Act § § 1812(a)(2), 1814(a)(2)(B).]

Patients using this Part A coverage are entitled to have payment made on their behalf for covered extended care services furnished by the facility or a hospital with which the facility has a transfer agreement, or by others under arrangements with the facility. Generally, only the kinds of services that would be covered if furnished to a hospital inpatient are covered during a stay in a SNF. [Soc. Sec. Act § § 1814(a)(2)(B), 1861(h).]

"Extended care services" are items and services furnished to an inpatient of a SNF, including:

• nursing care provided by or under the supervision of a registered professional nurse (see ¶ 231);

• bed and board in connection with furnishing of such nursing care (see ¶ 232);

• physical or occupational therapy and/or speech-language pathology services furnished by the SNF or by others under arrangements made by the facility (see ¶ 233);

• medical social services (see ¶ 234);

• drugs, biologics, supplies, appliances, and equipment furnished for use in the SNF, as are ordinarily furnished by the facility for the care and treatment of inpatients (see ¶ 235 and ¶ 236);

• medical services provided by an intern or resident-in-training of a hospital with which the facility has in effect a transfer agreement under an approved teaching program of the hospital, and other diagnostic or therapeutic services provided by a hospital with which the facility has an agreement in effect (see ¶ 237); and

• other services necessary to the health of the patients that are generally provided by SNFs, or by others under arrangements (see ¶ 239).

[Soc. Sec. Act § 1861(h).]

Skilled Nursing and Rehabilitation Services

Medicare covers nursing home services for only a limited number of days and only if the services provided are "skilled." [Soc. Sec. Act § § 1812(a)(2), 1814(a)(2)(B).] The skilled requirement means that nursing home services must:

¶ 230

(1) be ordered by a physician;

(2) require the skills of technical or professional personnel such as registered nurses, licensed practical (vocational) nurses, physical therapists, occupational therapists, and speech-language pathologists or audiologists; and

(3) be furnished directly by, or under the supervision of, such personnel.

[42 C.F.R. § § 409.31(a), 409.32.]

Condition requirement. The beneficiary must require skilled services on a daily basis. The skilled services furnished must be for a condition:

(1) for which the beneficiary received inpatient hospital or inpatient critical access hospital (CAH) services; or

(2) that arose while the beneficiary was receiving care in a SNF or swing-bed hospital for a condition for which he or she received inpatient hospital or inpatient CAH services; or

(3) for which, in the case of a Medicare Advantage enrollee, a physician has determined that a direct admission to a SNF without an inpatient hospital or inpatient CAH stay would be medically appropriate.

[42 C.F.R. § § 409.31(b), 409.34.]

Inpatient basis. Finally, the daily skilled services must be ones that, as a practical matter, can be provided only in a SNF, on an inpatient basis. [42 C.F.R. § 409.31(b)(3).] An inpatient is a person who has been admitted to a SNF or swing bed hospital for bed occupancy for purposes of receiving inpatient services. A person is considered an inpatient if formally admitted as an inpatient with the expectation that he or she will remain at least overnight and occupy a bed. [*Medicare Benefit Policy Manual*, Pub. 100-02, Ch. 8, § 50.]

[¶ 231] Nursing Care

Nursing care provided by a skilled nursing facility (SNF) is covered under Part A if it is furnished by, or under the supervision of, a registered professional nurse. The services of a private-duty nurse or other private-duty attendant, however, are excluded. [Soc. Sec. Act § 1861(h)(1); 42 C.F.R. § § 409.20(a)(1), 409.21.]

A private-duty nurse or attendant is a registered professional nurse, licensed practical nurse, or any other trained attendant whose services are rendered and restricted to a particular patient by arrangement between the patient and the private-duty nurse or attendant. Such persons are generally engaged or paid by an individual patient or by someone acting on his or her behalf, including a SNF that initially incurs the cost and looks to the patient for reimbursement for such noncovered services. [*Medicare Benefit Policy Manual*, Pub. 100-02, Ch. 8, § 50.1.]

An individual is not considered to be a private duty nurse or attendant if he or she is an employee of the facility at the time the services are furnished. [42 C.F.R. § 409.21(b).]

[¶ 232] Accommodations

Medicare coverage of services furnished to an inpatient of a skilled nursing facility (SNF) includes bed and board in connection with the furnishing of such nursing care. Depending on the patient's care needs, Medicare Part A may cover private, semiprivate, or ward accommodations. [Soc. Sec. Act § 1861(h)(2); 42 C.F.R. § 409.22.]

Medicare covers a private room if:

(1) the patient's condition requires isolation;

(2) the SNF has no semiprivate or ward accommodations; or

(3) the SNF semiprivate and ward accommodations are fully occupied by other patients, were so occupied at the time the patient was admitted to the SNF for treatment of a condition that required immediate inpatient SNF care, and have been so occupied during the interval.

Medicare pays for a private room until the patient's condition no longer requires isolation or until semiprivate or ward accommodations are available. [42 C.F.R. § 409.22(b).]

Patients in Inappropriate Beds

When patients requiring inpatient hospital services occupy beds in a SNF or in the hospital's distinct part SNF, they are considered inpatients of the SNF. In such cases, the services furnished in the SNF may not be considered inpatient hospital services, and payment may not be made under the Medicare program for those services. Such a situation may arise where the SNF is a distinct part of an institution the remainder of which is a hospital, and either there is no bed available in the hospital, or for any other reason the institution fails to place the patient in the appropriate bed. The same rule applies where the SNF is a separate institution. [*Medicare Benefit Policy Manual*, Pub. 100-02, Ch. 8, § 50.]

In the special case of patients who require extended care services but occupy beds in a hospital, the general rule is that no payment will be made on their behalf for the hospital services furnished to them. However, when such patients occupy hospital beds because there are no SNF beds available to them, the general rule may not apply. A physician or a utilization review committee may certify to the need for continued hospitalization in these situations. [42 C.F.R. § 424.13(c).] Similarly, under Soc. Sec. Act § 1861(v)(1)(G), the HHS Secretary may require continued coverage for the extended care services at a special nursing home rate of payment. Finally, rural hospitals entering into "swing-bed" agreements, as well as other hospitals without such agreements, are eligible for special rates of reimbursement for patients inappropriately occupying hospital beds because there are no SNF beds available. [Pub. 100-02, Ch. 8, § 10.3.]

[¶ 233] Physical and Occupational Therapy and Speech-Language Pathology Services

Medicare Part A pays for physical, speech, and occupational therapy furnished by a skilled nursing facility (SNF) when those services are furnished:

(1) by (or under arrangements made by) the facility and billed by (or through) the facility;

(2) by qualified physical therapists, physical therapist assistants, occupational therapists, occupational therapy assistants, or speech-language pathologists; and

(3) in accordance with a treatment plan that meets the requirements of 42 C.F.R. § 409.17(b).

[Soc. Sec. Act § 1861(h)(3); 42 C.F.R. § 409.23.]

Therapy services must be furnished under a treatment plan that: (1) prescribes the type, amount, frequency, and duration of the physical therapy, occupational therapy, or speech-language pathology services to be furnished to the individual; and (2) indicates the diagnosis and anticipated goals for treatment. [42 C.F.R. § 409.17(c).]

Coverage for skilled therapy services turns on the beneficiary's need for skilled care, not on the presence or absence of a beneficiary's potential for improvement from therapy services. Therapy services are considered skilled when they are so inherently complex that they can be safely and effectively performed only by, or under the supervision of, a qualified therapist. These skilled services may be necessary to improve the patient's current condi-

¶233

tion, maintain the patient's current condition, or prevent or slow further deterioration of the patient's condition. [*Medicare Benefit Policy Manual*, Pub. 100-02, Ch. 8, § 30.4.]

[¶ 234] Medical Social Services

Part A covers medical social services furnished to skilled nursing facility (SNF) patients. Covered medical social services are social services that contribute meaningfully to the treatment of a patient's condition. Such services include: (1) assessment of the social and emotional factors related to the beneficiary's illness, need for care, response to treatment, and adjustment to care in the facility; (2) case work services to assist in resolving social or emotional problems that may have an adverse effect on the beneficiary's ability to respond to treatment; and (3) assessment of the relationship of the beneficiary's medical and nursing requirements to his or her home situation, financial resources, and the community resources available upon discharge from facility care. [Soc. Sec. Act § 1861(h)(4); 42 C.F.R. § 409.24; *Medicare Benefit Policy Manual*, Pub. 100-02, Ch. 8, § 50.4.]

[¶ 235] Drugs and Biologics

Medicare covers drugs and biologics as post-hospital skilled nursing facility (SNF) care if they:

> (1) represent a cost to the facility;

> (2) are ordinarily furnished by the facility for the care and treatment of inpatients; and

> (3) are furnished to an inpatient for use in the facility.

[Soc. Sec. Act § 1861(h)(5); 42 C.F.R. § 409.25(a).]

Departure from facility. Medicare generally does not cover drugs administered to inpatients for use outside the facility. However, Medicare will cover a limited supply of a drug deemed medically necessary to permit or facilitate a patient's departure from the facility. Such coverage continues until the beneficiary can obtain a continuing supply. [42 C.F.R. § 409.25(b).]

Compendia and formularies. Medicare covers only those drugs that have been approved for inclusion in the latest official edition of the United States Pharmacopoeia-National Formulary, the United States Pharmacopoeia Drug Information, or the American Dental Association Guide to Dental Therapeutics. Combination drugs are covered if the combination itself or all of the therapeutic ingredients of the combination are included, or approved for inclusion, in any of the designated drug compendia. [*Medicare Benefit Policy Manual*, Pub. 100-02, Ch. 1, § § 30, 30.1; Ch. 8, § 50.5.]

Drugs and biologics not included in the drug list or formulary maintained by the facility's pharmacy and drug therapeutics committee may be covered if the facility has a policy that permits such drugs to be furnished to a patient at the special request of a physician. [Pub. 100-02, Ch. 1, § 30.4; Ch. 8, § 50.5.]

[¶ 236] Supplies, Appliances, and Equipment

Part A covers supplies, appliances, and equipment as extended care services only if they: (1) are ordinarily furnished by the skilled nursing facility (SNF) for the care and treatment of inpatients; and (2) are furnished to an inpatient for use in the SNF. [Soc. Sec. Act § 1861(h)(5); 42 C.F.R. § 409.25(c); *Medicare Benefit Policy Manual*, Pub. 100-02, Ch. 1, § 40; Ch. 8, § 50.6.]

Supplies, appliances, and equipment furnished to a patient for use only outside the facility are generally not covered as extended care services. However, Medicare covers items to be used after the individual leaves the facility if the item: (1) is one that the beneficiary must continue to use after leaving, such as a leg brace; or (2) is necessary to permit or facilitate the beneficiary's departure from the facility and is required until he or she can obtain a continuing supply. [42 C.F.R. § 409.25(d); Pub. 100-02, Ch. 1, § 40.]

A temporary or disposable item, such as a sterile dressing, that is medically necessary to permit or facilitate a patient's departure from the facility and is required until such time as the patient can obtain a continuing supply, is covered as an extended care service. [Pub. 100-02, Ch. 1, § 40; Ch. 8, § 50.6.]

[¶ 237] Interns and Residents-in-Training

Medicare pays for medical services that are furnished by an intern or a resident-in-training under a hospital teaching program as post-hospital skilled nursing facility (SNF) care if the intern or resident is in:

> (1) a participating hospital with which the SNF has in effect a transfer agreement; or

> (2) a hospital that has swing-bed approval and is furnishing services to a SNF-level inpatient of that hospital.

[Soc. Sec. Act § 1861(h)(6); 42 C.F.R. § 409.26(a).]

An "approved teaching program" is a program approved by the Council on Medical Education of the American Medical Association or, in the case of an osteopathic hospital, approved by the Committee on Hospitals of the Bureau of Professional Education of the American Osteopathic Association. In the case of services of an intern or resident-in-training in the field of dentistry in a hospital or osteopathic hospital, the teaching program must have the approval of the Council on Dental Education of the American Dental Association. [*Medicare Benefit Policy Manual*, Pub. 100-02, Ch. 8, § 50.7.]

The medical and surgical services furnished to the facility's patients by interns and residents-in-training of a hospital with which the facility has a transfer agreement are covered under Part B if the services are not covered under Part A. [Pub. 100-02, Ch. 8, § 50.7.]

[¶ 238] Whole Blood and Packed Red Blood Cells

Medicare coverage includes the cost of unreplaced blood (after satisfaction of the three-pint blood deductible discussed at ¶ 223) and the cost of administering the blood to inpatients of participating skilled nursing facilities. [Soc. Sec. Act § 1866(a)(2)(C); *Medicare General Information, Eligibility, and Entitlement Manual*, Pub. 100-01, Ch. 3, § 20.5.]

[¶ 239] Other Diagnostic and Therapeutic Items or Services

Medicare Part A pays for other diagnostic and therapeutic services provided by skilled nursing facilities (SNFs) as posthospital SNF care if the services are generally provided by (or under arrangements made by) SNFs. Those services include:

> (1) medical and other health services described under 42 C.F.R. § 410.10;

> (2) respiratory therapy services; and

> (3) transportation by ambulance that meets the requirements of 42 C.F.R. § 410.40(e)(1).

[42 C.F.R. § 409.27.]

Excluded services. Items or services that would not be included as inpatient hospital services if furnished to an inpatient of a hospital are excluded from coverage as extended care services. For instance, the provision of personal laundry services by SNFs is not a covered service under Medicare because it would not be covered if provided to an inpatient of an acute care hospital (see *Medicare Benefit Policy Manual*, Pub. 100-02, Ch. 6, § 10, for covered inpatient hospital services). The use of an operating room and any special equipment, supplies, or services would not constitute covered extended care services except when furnished to the facility by a hospital with which the facility has a transfer agreement because operating rooms are not generally maintained by SNFs. However, supplies and nursing services connected with minor surgery performed in a SNF that does not require the use of an operating room or any special equipment or supplies associated with such a room are covered extended care services and paid as part of the SNF prospective payment system. [Pub. 100-02, Ch. 8, § 50.8.1.]

[¶ 240] SNF Services Provided by Religious Nonmedical Health Care Institutions

Medicare covers skilled nursing facility (SNF) services furnished in a Medicare-qualified religious nonmedical health care institution (RNHCI) for a beneficiary who has a condition that would render him or her eligible to receive Medicare Part A services as an inpatient in a SNF. [Soc. Sec. Act § 1821(a); 42 C.F.R. § 403.720(d).]

Medicare will pay only for nonmedical health care services furnished in RNHCIs. [Soc. Sec. Act § 1861(y); 42 C.F.R. § 403.720(a).]

Election. A Medicare beneficiary may elect to receive care in a RNHCI based on his or her own religious convictions or to revoke that election at any time if for any reason he or she decides to pursue medical care. As a condition for Part A coverage, the beneficiary must have a condition that would qualify for inpatient hospital services or extended care services furnished in a hospital or SNF that is not a RNHCI. [Soc. Sec. Act § 1821(a), (b)(3).] The beneficiary must also have a valid election in effect to receive RNHCI services. [*Medicare General Information, Eligibility, and Entitlement Manual*, Pub. 100-01, Ch. 5, § 40.]

[¶ 241] SNF "Ancillary" Services Covered Under Part B

The medical and other health services listed below are covered under Part B when furnished by a participating skilled nursing facility (SNF) either directly or under arrangements to patients who are not entitled to have payment made under Part A (e.g., benefits exhausted or three-day prior-stay requirement not met):

- diagnostic x-ray tests, diagnostic laboratory tests, and other diagnostic tests;
- x-ray, radium, and radioactive isotope therapy, including materials and services of technicians;
- surgical dressings, and splints, casts, and other devices used for reduction of fractures and dislocations;
- prosthetic devices (other than dental) that replace all or part of an internal body organ (including contiguous tissue), or all or part of the function of a permanently inoperative or malfunctioning internal body organ, including replacement or repairs of such devices;
- leg, arm, back, and neck braces; trusses; and artificial legs, arms, and eyes, including adjustments, repairs, and replacements required because of breakage, wear, loss, or a change in the patient's physical condition;
- outpatient physical and occupational and speech-language pathology services;
- screening mammography services;
- screening pap smears and pelvic exams;
- influenza, pneumococcal pneumonia, and hepatitis B vaccines;
- some colorectal screening;

- diabetes self-management;
- prostate screening;
- ambulance services;
- hemophilia clotting factors; and
- epoetin alfa (EPO) for end-stage renal disease beneficiaries when given in conjunction with dialysis.

[42 C.F.R. §§ 409.27(a), 410.60(b); *Medicare Benefit Policy Manual*, Pub. 100-02, Ch. 8, § 70.]

[¶ 242] Skilled Nursing Facility Coinsurance

The beneficiary is required to pay a coinsurance amount equal to one-eighth of the inpatient hospital deductible for each day after the 20th and before the 101st day of skilled nursing facility (SNF) services furnished during a spell of illness (see ¶ 210). [Soc. Sec. Act § 1813(a)(3).]

This coinsurance amount, like the inpatient hospital deductible on which it is dependent, is subject to annual change. Daily coinsurance for the 21st through 100th day in a SNF is $176 in 2020, up from $170.50 in 2019. [*Medicare General Information, Eligibility and Entitlement Manual*, Pub. 100-01, Ch. 3, § 10.3; *Notice*, 84 FR 61619, Nov. 13, 2019; *Notice*, 83 FR 52459, Oct. 17, 2018.]

[¶ 243] Duration of Covered SNF Services

Medicare Part A pays for post-hospital extended care services for up to 100 days during any spell of illness. [Soc. Sec. Act §§ 1812(a)(2), 1861(y); 42 C.F.R. § 409.61(b).] A spell of illness—or benefit period—is the period of consecutive days beginning with the first day during which covered skilled nursing facility (SNF) services are furnished to a patient by a qualified SNF and ending when the beneficiary has not been an inpatient of a SNF for a period of 60 consecutive days. [Soc. Sec. Act § 1861(a); 42 C.F.R. § 409.60(a), (b).] The rules defining a "spell of illness" apply to both inpatient hospital services and SNF services, and they are outlined at ¶ 210.

Beginning of the benefit period. Generally, a benefit period begins with the first day (not included in a previous benefit period) on which a patient is furnished extended care covered services by a qualified provider in a month for which the patient is entitled to hospital insurance benefits; however, noncovered services furnished by a nonparticipating provider may begin a spell of illness only if the provider is a qualified provider. A qualified provider includes a SNF that meets all requirements in the definition of such an institution even though it might not be participating. [42 C.F.R. § 409.60(a); *Medicare General Information, Eligibility, and Entitlement Manual*, Pub. 100-01, Ch. 3, § 10.4.1.]

Admission to a qualified SNF or to the SNF level of care in a swing-bed hospital begins a benefit period even though payment for the services cannot be made because the prior hospitalization or 30-day transfer requirement has not been met. In a situation where the allowable interval is 60 days or longer, the subsequent commencement of extended care services in the SNF serves to trigger the start of a new benefit period. [Pub. 100-01, Ch. 3, § 10.4.1.]

Level of care. A beneficiary is considered to be an inpatient of a SNF only when care in the SNF meets certain skilled level of care standards. This means that the beneficiary must have required and received skilled services on a daily basis that, as a practical matter, could only have been provided by a SNF on an inpatient basis. If these provisions were not met during the prior SNF stay, the beneficiary was not an inpatient of the SNF for purposes of prolonging the benefit period. Conversely, a beneficiary remains a SNF "inpatient" in this context (thus prolonging his or her current benefit period) for as long as the beneficiary continues receiving a skilled level of care in the SNF even if Medicare Part A payment has ended due to the beneficiary's exhaustion of SNF benefits. CMS uses a number of presumptions to decide whether care meets the skilled level of care standards. [42 C.F.R. § 409.60(b)(2), (c); Pub. 100-01, Ch. 3, § 10.4.4.]

Counting Days in a SNF

The number of days of care charged to a beneficiary for inpatient SNF services is always in units of full days. A day begins at midnight and ends 24 hours later. The midnight-to-midnight method is to be used in reporting days of care for beneficiaries, even if the facility uses a different definition of day for statistical or other purposes. [*Medicare Benefit Policy Manual*, Pub. 100-02, Ch. 3, § 20.1.]

A part of a day, including the day of admission, counts as a full day. The day of discharge, death, or a day on which a patient begins a leave of absence, however, is not counted as a day. Charges for ancillary services on the day of discharge or death or the day on which a patient begins a leave of absence are covered. If admission and discharge or death occur on the same day, the day is considered a day of admission and counts as one inpatient day. [Pub. 100-02, Ch. 3, § 20.1.]

Post-hospital extended care services count toward the maximum number of benefit days payable per benefit period only if: (1) payment for the services is made; (2) payment for the services would have been made if a request for payment had been properly filed and the SNF submitted all necessary evidence, including physician certification of need for services; or (3) payment could not be made because the total payment due was equal to, or less than, the applicable deductible and coinsurance amounts. [42 C.F.R. § 409.64; Pub. 100-02, Ch. 3, § 30.]

Effect of Late Discharge from a SNF

When a patient chooses to occupy accommodations in a facility beyond the normal check-out time for personal reasons, the facility may charge the patient for a continued stay. The SNF, however, must provide the beneficiary with an Advance Beneficiary Notice (ABN) before the noncovered services are provided. [Pub. 100-02, Ch. 3, § 20.1.1.]

When the patient's medical condition is the cause of the stay past the checkout time (e.g., the patient needs further services, is bedridden and awaiting transportation to his or her home or in the case of a hospital, transfer to a SNF, or dies in the SNF or hospital), the stay beyond the discharge hour is covered under the program and the hospital or SNF may not charge the patient. [Pub. 100-02, Ch. 3, § 20.1.1.]

The imposition of a late checkout charge by a hospital or SNF does not affect the counting of days for: (1) ending a benefit period; (2) the number of days of inpatient care available to the individual in a hospital or SNF; and (3) the three-day prior hospitalization requirement for coverage of post-hospital extended care services and Part A home health services. A late charge by a hospital does not affect counting of days for meeting the prior inpatient stay requirement for coverage of extended care services. [Pub. 100-02, Ch. 3, § 20.1.1.]

Leaves of Absence from a SNF

The day on which the patient begins a leave of absence is treated as a day of discharge and is not counted as an inpatient day unless the patient returns to the facility by midnight of the same day. The day the patient returns to the facility from a leave of absence is treated as a day of admission and is counted as an inpatient day if he or she is present at midnight of that day. [Pub. 100-02, Ch. 3, § 20.1.2.]

Charges to the beneficiary for admission or readmission are not allowable. However, when temporarily leaving a SNF, a resident may choose to make bed-hold payments to the SNF. Under Soc. Sec. Act § 1819(c)(1)(B)(iii) and 42 C.F.R. § 483.10(b)(6), the SNF must inform residents in advance of their option to make bed-hold payments, as well as the amount of the facility's charge. [*Medicare Claims Processing Manual*, Pub. 100-04, Ch. 1, § 30.1.1.1.]

[¶ 244] Prior Hospitalization and Transfer Requirements

To have payment made on his or her behalf for post-hospital extended care services, the individual must have been an inpatient of a hospital for at least three consecutive calendar days and have been transferred to a participating skilled nursing facility (SNF), usually within 30 days after discharge from the hospital. [Soc. Sec. Act § 1861(i); 42 C.F.R. § 409.30.]

In the determination of whether the individual's prior hospital stay meets the required minimum of three consecutive calendar days, the day of admission is counted as a hospital inpatient day, but the day of discharge is not. The hospital discharge must have occurred on or after the first day of the month in which an individual attains age 65 or becomes entitled to Medicare benefits under the disability or end-stage renal disease provisions. [42 C.F.R. § 409.30(a); *Medicare Benefit Policy Manual*, Pub. 100-02, Ch. 8, § 20.1.]

Qualifying inpatient hospital stays. An inpatient hospital stay satisfies the prior hospitalization requirement if the hospital is either a participating hospital or a hospital that meets the requirements for an emergency hospital. The hospital need not be one with which the SNF has a transfer agreement. However, time spent in observation or in the emergency room before (or in lieu of) an inpatient admission to the hospital does not count toward the three-day qualifying inpatient hospital stay. A three-day stay in a psychiatric hospital satisfies the prior hospital stay requirement but stays in religious nonmedical health care institutions (RNHCIs) do not. [Pub. 100-02, Ch. 8, § 20.1.]

A stay of three or more days in a hospital outside the United States may satisfy the prior inpatient stay requirement for post-hospital extended care services within the United States if the foreign hospital is qualified as an "emergency hospital." If a stay of three or more days in a hospital outside the U.S. is being considered to satisfy the prior inpatient stay requirement, the SNF must submit documentation to the Medicare administrative contractor. [Pub. 100-02, Ch. 8, § 20.1.1.]

Applicable conditions. To be covered, the post-hospital extended care services must have been for the treatment of a condition for which the beneficiary was receiving inpatient hospital services or a condition that arose while in the SNF for treatment of a condition for which he or she was previously hospitalized. The applicable hospital condition does not have to be the principal diagnosis that precipitated the beneficiary's admission to the hospital but may be any one of the conditions present during the qualifying hospital stay. In addition, the qualifying hospital stay must have been medically necessary. [42 C.F.R. § 409.31; Pub. 100-02, Ch. 8, § 20.1.]

Certification requirements. A physician, physician assistant, clinical nurse specialist, or nurse practitioner working in collaboration with a physician must certify the need for daily skilled nursing care or other skilled rehabilitation services, which, as a practical matter, can only be provided in an SNF on an inpatient basis. [Soc. Sec. Act § 1814(a)(2).]

30-Day Transfer Requirement

Post-hospital extended care services represent an extension of care for a condition for which the individual received inpatient hospital services. Extended care services are "post-hospital" if initiated within 30 days after the date of discharge from a hospital following a stay that included at least three consecutive days of medically necessary inpatient hospital services. [Soc. Sec. Act § 1861(i); 42 C.F.R. § 409.30.]

The day of discharge from the hospital is not counted in the 30 days. For example, a patient discharged from a hospital on August 1 and admitted to a SNF on August 31 was admitted within 30 days. The 30-day period begins to run on the day following actual discharge from the hospital and continues until the individual is admitted to a participating SNF and requires and receives a covered level of care. [42 C.F.R. § 409.30(b).]

If a beneficiary is discharged from a facility after receiving post-hospital SNF care, he or she is not entitled to additional services of this kind in the same benefit period unless he or she is: (1) readmitted to the same or another facility within 30 calendar days following the day of discharge; or (b) again hospitalized for at least three consecutive calendar days. [42 C.F.R. § 409.36; Pub. 100-02, Ch. 8, § § 20.2.1, 20.2.3.]

Exceptions to the 30-day transfer requirement. Two exceptions to the 30-day transfer requirement apply: (1) if a patient is not admitted to a SNF within 30 days after discharge from a hospital because to admit the patient within that time would not be medically appropriate, admission to the SNF will be covered if the patient is admitted within such time as would be medically appropriate to begin an active course of treatment; and (2) the beneficiary will be considered to have met the admission requirements if he or she was enrolled in a Medicare Advantage plan offering the benefits described in 42 C.F.R. § 422.101(c). [Soc. Sec. Act § 1861(i); 42 C.F.R. § 409.30(b)(2).]

[¶ 248] Rights of SNF Residents

A skilled nursing facility (SNF) must promote and protect the rights of each resident, including:

(1) to be informed of, and participate in, his or her treatment;

(2) to choose his or her attending physician;

(3) to be treated with respect and dignity;

(4) self-determination;

(5) information and communication;

(6) privacy and confidentiality;

(7) safe environment;

(8) to voice grievances; and

(9) to have contact with external entities.

[Soc. Sec. Act § 1819(c)(1)(A); 42 C.F.R. § 483.10.]

Quality of Life Rights

Each SNF resident has a right to a dignified existence, self-determination, and access to persons and services inside and outside the facility. The facility must maintain an environment that promotes maintenance or enhancement of each resident's quality of life, recognizing each resident's individuality. It is the obligation of the SNF to promote and protect these resident rights. The resident must be free to exercise the rights without interference, coercion, discrimination, or reprisal from the facility. The rights of dignity and respect include freedom from restraints, the right to retain personal possessions, the right to share a room with a willing spouse, and the right to refuse transfer under certain circumstances. [42 C.F.R. § 483.10(a), (b), (e).]

Resident Rights Related to Patient Care

A SNF resident has the right to be informed of and participate in his or her treatment. This includes participation in the development of a person-centered plan of care, including the right to revise the plan, refuse treatment, and be fully informed of the nature of services to be performed. The resident also has the right to choose his or her attending physician, assuming the physician is willing and qualified. [42 C.F.R. § 483.10(c), (d).]

Notice of Rights

The facility is required to: (1) give notice, orally and in writing at the time of admission to the facility, of the resident's legal rights during the stay at the facility; (2) make available to each resident, upon reasonable request, a written statement of such rights; and (3) inform each resident, in writing before or at the time of admission and periodically during the resident's stay, of services available in the facility and related charges for such services, including any charges for services not covered under Medicare or the facility's basic per diem charge. The written description of legal rights must include a description of the SNF's protection of personal funds (see Soc. Sec. Act § 1819(c)(6)) and a statement that a resident may file a complaint with a state survey and certification agency regarding resident abuse and neglect or misappropriation of resident property in the facility. [Soc. Sec. Act § 1819(c)(1)(B); 42 C.F.R. § 483.10(g)(4).]

Payment Issues

If a beneficiary requests a noncovered service or a service that is more expensive than the amount of Medicare payment, the provider must inform the beneficiary that there will be a specific charge for that service. [42 C.F.R. § 489.32.] However, providers, including a SNF, may not impose any of the following prepayment requirements:

(1) require an individual entitled to Part A benefits to prepay in part or in whole for inpatient services as a condition of admittance as an inpatient, except when it is clear upon admission that payment under Part A cannot be made;

(2) deny covered inpatient services to an individual entitled to have payment made for those services on the ground of inability or failure to pay a requested amount at or before admission;

(3) evict, or threaten to evict, an individual for inability to pay a deductible or a coinsurance amount required under Medicare;

(4) charge an individual for an agreement to admit or readmit him or her on some specified future date for covered inpatient services; or

(5) charge a resident for failure to remain an inpatient for any agreed-upon length of time or for failure to give advance notice of departure from the provider's facilities.

[42 C.F.R. § 489.22.]

Privacy Issues

HHS regulations protect the privacy of individually identifiable information in accordance with the Health Insurance Portability and Accountability Act (HIPAA) (P.L. 104-191). Under these regulations, a SNF must provide notice to a patient on the first service visit regarding its use of his or her medical data and the right to access that data. [45 C.F.R. § 164.520.] See ¶ 715 for a full description of HIPAA protections.

Residents of SNFs are entitled to personal privacy and confidentiality of their personal and medical records. Personal privacy includes accommodations, treatment, written and telephone communications, personal care, visits, and family and resident group meetings. However, personal privacy does not require the facility to provide a private room for each

¶248

resident. Residents are also entitled to a safe, clean, comfortable, and homelike environment. [42 C.F.R. § 483.10(h), (i).]

Discharge or Transfer from a SNF

A facility's discharge planning process must focus on residents' discharge goals and the preparation of residents for discharge. Discharge plans must identify the needs of each resident. [42 C.F.R. § 483.15.]

A SNF cannot discharge or transfer a resident from the facility unless: (1) the transfer or discharge is necessary to meet the resident's welfare; (2) the resident's health has improved to the extent that the resident no longer needs the SNF's services; (3) the safety or health of other residents is endangered; (4) the resident has failed, after reasonable and appropriate notice, to pay for a stay at the facility; or (5) the facility ceases to operate. If a transfer or discharge is warranted, the reason must be documented in the resident's clinical record. [Soc. Sec. Act § 1819(c)(2)(A); 42 C.F.R. § 483.15(c)(1), (2).]

Generally 30 days in advance of the discharge or transfer, the SNF must notify the resident (or family member or legal representative) about the transfer and discharge as well as the reasons for it. [Soc. Sec. Act § 1819(c)(2)(B)(ii); 42 C.F.R. § 483.15(c)(3), (4).]

[¶ 249] "Skilled Nursing Facility"—Conditions of Participation

As a general rule, a beneficiary's stay in a skilled nursing facility (SNF) will not be covered by Medicare unless the SNF is "participating" in the Medicare program, that is, the SNF has been approved for Medicare participation by the government and has signed a participation agreement (see ¶ 730).

A "skilled nursing facility" is an institution or a distinct part of an institution that:

(1) is primarily engaged in providing skilled nursing care and related services for residents who require medical or nursing care, or rehabilitation services for the rehabilitation of injured, disabled, or sick residents;

(2) has in effect a transfer agreement with one or more participating hospitals; and

(3) meets detailed requirements relating to services provided, residents' rights, professional standards, health and safety standards, and notification to the state of changes in ownership or control.

Facilities that primarily treat mental illness are specifically excluded from the SNF definition. [Soc. Sec. Act § 1819(a).]

The term "skilled nursing facility" includes institutions operated or listed as religious nonmedical health care institutions. A Medicare beneficiary may choose to have services in these facilities covered as post-hospital extended care services. [Soc. Sec. Act § 1861(y).] See ¶ 228 for a discussion of religious nonmedical health care institutions.

A SNF must comply with the conditions of participation (CoPs) for SNFs set out at 42 C.F.R. 483 Subpart B. The CoPs impose specific requirements regarding admission standards, care planning, resident rights, the provision of services, care quality, facilities, and administration.

A SNF of the Indian Health Service (IHS), whether operated by the IHS or a tribal organization, is eligible for Medicare payments if it meets all of the Medicare requirements for SNFs. [Soc. Sec. Act § 1880(a).]

A single set of requirements is applicable to SNFs under both Medicare and Medicaid. Thus, a SNF eligible to participate under one program is eligible to participate under the other, provided it agrees to the contract terms. The identical definition also permits a single consolidated survey to determine a facility's qualifications to participate in either program. [Soc. Sec. Act § 1919(a); 42 C.F.R. § 483.1(b).]

Skilled Nursing Beds in Hospitals

It is possible to treat part of an institution as a SNF. This may be done either by having a "distinct part" of the institution certified as a SNF or having an agreement with the HHS Secretary under which inpatient hospital beds may be used for skilled nursing care on a "swing" basis (see ¶ 229). [Soc. Sec. Act § 1819(a); 42 C.F.R. § 483.5; *Medicare Claims Processing Manual*, Pub. 100-04, Ch. 6, § 100.]

To qualify for participation in the program as a "distinct part" SNF, the "distinct part" must be physically separated from the rest of the institution, that is, it must represent an entire, physically identifiable unit consisting of all the beds within that unit, such as a separate building, floor, wing, or ward. A distinct part must include all of the beds within the designated area and cannot consist of a random collection of individual rooms or beds that are scattered throughout the physical plant. [42 C.F.R. § 483.5; *Medicare General Information, Eligibility, and Entitlement Manual*, Pub. 100-01, Ch. 5, § 30.1.]

Transfer Agreements with Participating Hospitals

To participate in Medicare, a SNF must have a written transfer agreement with one or more participating hospitals providing for the transfer of patients between the hospital and the facility and the interchange of medical and other information. If an otherwise qualified SNF has attempted in good faith, but without success, to enter into a transfer agreement, this requirement may be waived. [Soc. Sec. Act § § 1819(a)(2), 1861(l); 42 C.F.R. § 483.70(j); Pub. 100-01, Ch. 5, § 30.2.]

Home Health Services

[¶ 250] Home Health Services: Qualifying Conditions for Coverage

Home health services are covered only if furnished by a home health agency (HHA) participating in the Medicare program. The HHA must act on a physician's certification that the individual: (1) is confined to the home (see ¶ 264); (2) needs intermittent skilled nursing care or physical or occupational therapy or speech-language pathology services; and (3) is under the care of a physician who has established a plan of care (see ¶ 260, ¶ 262). [Soc. Sec. Act § 1814(a)(2)(C); 42 C.F.R. § § 409.42, 424.22.]

Coverage of skilled nursing care or therapy to perform a maintenance program is based on the patient's need for skilled care and does not require the patient to have the potential for improvement as a result of the nursing care or therapy. Skilled care may be necessary to improve or maintain a patient's current condition or to prevent or slow further deterioration of the patient's condition. [*Medicare Benefit Policy Manual*, Pub. 100-02, Ch. 7, § 20.1.2.]

Part A finances up to 100 visits during one home health spell of illness if the following criteria are met:

    (1) the beneficiary is enrolled in Part A and Part B and qualifies for home health benefits;

    (2) the beneficiary had at least a three-consecutive-day stay in a hospital or rural primary care hospital; and

    (3) the home health services are initiated and the first covered home health visit is rendered within 14 days of discharge from the three-consecutive-day stay in a hospital or rural primary care hospital or within 14 days of discharge from a skilled

¶250

nursing facility (SNF) in which the patient was provided post-hospital extended care services.

If the first home health visit is not initiated within 14 days of discharge or if the three-consecutive-day stay requirement is not met, then the services are covered under Part B. See ¶ 383 for a discussion of coverage of home health services under Part B. [Soc. Sec. Act § 1812(a)(3); Pub. 100-02, Ch. 7, § 60.1.]

If a beneficiary is enrolled only in Part A and qualifies for the Medicare home health benefit, then all of the home health services are financed under Part A. The 100-visit limit does not apply to beneficiaries who are only enrolled in Part A. If a beneficiary is enrolled only in Part B and qualifies for the Medicare home health benefit, then all of the home health services are financed under Part B. There is no 100-visit limit under Part B. [Soc. Sec. Act § 1812(a)(3); Pub. 100-02, Ch. 7, § 60.3.]

Home Health Definitions

"Post-institutional home health services" are defined as services initiated within 14 days after discharge from (1) a three-day hospital inpatient stay; or (2) a SNF stay in which post-hospital extended care services were provided. [Soc. Sec. Act § 1861(tt)(1).]

"Home health spell of illness" refers to a period of consecutive days, starting with the first day the beneficiary receives post-institutional home health services during a month in which he or she is entitled to Part A benefits. This period ends when the beneficiary has not received hospital, critical access hospital, SNF, or home health services for 60 days. [Soc. Sec. Act § 1861(tt)(2).]

The beneficiary can be covered for an unlimited number of nonoverlapping episodes or periods of care. For periods of care beginning on or after January 1, 2020, the duration of a period is 30 days. Periods of care may be shorter than 30 days. For episodes beginning before January 1, 2020, the duration of a single full-length episode is 60 days. [*Medicare Claims Processing Manual*, Pub. 100-04, Ch. 10, § 10.1.5.]

"Home health services" include the following items and services, provided on a visiting basis in a residence used as the patient's home, except as noted in item (7), below:

(1) part-time or intermittent nursing care provided by or under the supervision of a registered professional nurse;

(2) physical or occupational therapy or speech-language pathology services;

(3) medical social services under the direction of a physician;

(4) part-time or intermittent services of a home health aide who has completed an approved training program successfully;

(5) medical supplies (other than drugs and biologics), durable medical equipment, and applicable disposable devices while under the plan of care;

(6) medical services of interns and residents-in-training under an approved teaching program of a hospital with which the HHA is affiliated; and

(7) any of the items and services that: (a) are provided on an outpatient basis under arrangements made by the HHA at a hospital or SNF, or at a qualified rehabilitation center, and (b) involve the use of equipment that cannot be made readily available in the patient's residence or that are furnished at the facility while the patient is there to receive any item or service involving the use of such equipment. Transportation of the individual is not covered (see ¶ 257).

[Soc. Sec. Act § 1861(m); 42 C.F.R. § § 409.44, 409.45.]

[¶ 251] Skilled Nursing Care

If a patient qualifies for home health services, Medicare covers either part-time or intermittent skilled nursing services. For purposes of receiving home health care, "part-time or intermittent care" means skilled nursing and home health aide services furnished for up to 28 hours per week combined over any number of days per week so long as they are furnished for fewer than eight hours per day. Medicare may approve additional time of up to 35 hours per week, but for fewer than eight hours per day, on a case-by-case basis. For purposes of qualifying and payment for intermittent skilled nursing care, the term "intermittent" means skilled nursing care that is either provided or needed fewer than seven days each week, or fewer than eight hours of each day for periods up to and including 21 days, with extensions in exceptional circumstances. [Soc. Sec. Act § 1861(m); 42 C.F.R. § 409.44(b); *Medicare Benefit Policy Manual*, Pub. 100-02, Ch. 7, § 50.7.1.]

Skilled nursing care in excess of the amounts of care that meet the definitions of "part-time" or "intermittent" may be provided to a home care patient or purchased by other payers without bearing on whether the care is covered to the extent allowed by Medicare. The HHA may bill the home care patient or other payer for care that exceeds the hours of care that Medicare allows as reasonable and necessary. [Pub. 100-02, Ch. 7, § 50.7.1.]

Skilled nursing services are services that:

(1) require the skills of a registered nurse or a licensed practical nurse (or licensed vocational nurse) under the supervision of a registered nurse;

(2) are reasonable and necessary to the treatment of the patient's illness or injury; and

(3) are needed on an intermittent basis.

Coverage of skilled nursing care is based on the patient's need for skilled care, not on the potential for improvement from the nursing care. [42 C.F.R. § 409.44(b); Pub. 100-02, Ch. 7, § 40.1.] Skilled nursing services are covered when they are necessary to maintain the patient's current condition or prevent or slow further deterioration, as long as the beneficiary requires skilled care for the services to be safely and effectively provided. [Pub. 100-02, Ch. 7, § 40.1.1.]

In general, the intermittent basis requirement is met if a patient needs skilled nursing care at least once every 60 days. A one-time nursing service, such as giving a gamma globulin injection following exposure to hepatitis, for example, is not considered a need for intermittent skilled nursing care because a recurrence of the problem every 60 days is not medically predictable. If the need for a skilled nursing visit at least once every 60 days is medically predictable, but a situation arises after the first visit making additional visits unnecessary—for example, the patient is institutionalized or dies—the one visit is covered. [Pub. 100-02, Ch. 7, § 40.1.3.]

Home health records for every visit should reflect the need for the skilled medical care provided, including objective measurements of physical outcomes of treatment. [Pub. 100-02, Ch. 7, § 40.1.1.]

[¶ 252] Home Health Physical and Occupational Therapy and Speech-Language Pathology Services

Physical and occupational skilled therapy and speech-language pathology services furnished by a home health agency (HHA) or others under arrangements made by the HHA are covered when provided in accordance with a physician's orders and by, or under the supervision of, a qualified therapist. To be covered as skilled therapy, the services must require the skills of a qualified therapist and must be reasonable and necessary for the

¶251

treatment of the beneficiary's illness or injury, or the restoration or maintenance of the function affected by the illness or injury. Coverage depends on the beneficiary's need for skilled care, not on the presence or absence of the beneficiary's potential for improvement. [42 C.F.R. § 409.44(c); *Medicare Benefit Policy Manual*, Pub. 100-02, Ch. 7, § § 40.2, 40.2.1.]

For therapy services to qualify for Medicare coverage, the following requirements must be met:

(1) the patient's plan of care must describe a course of therapy treatment and therapy goals that are consistent with the evaluation of the patient's function, and both must be included in the clinical record;

(2) the therapy goals must be established by a qualified therapist in conjunction with the physician;

(3) the patient's clinical record must include documentation describing how the course of therapy treatment for the patient's illness or injury is in accordance with accepted professional standards of clinical practice;

(4) therapy treatment goals described in the plan of care must be measurable and must pertain directly to the patient's illness or injury and the patient's resultant impairments; and

(5) the patient's clinical record must demonstrate that the method used to assess his or her function includes objective measurements of function in accordance with accepted professional standards of clinical practice that will allow for a comparison of successive measurements to determine the effectiveness of therapy goals. The objective measurements that assess activities of daily living may include, but are not limited to eating, swallowing, bathing, dressing, toileting, walking, climbing stairs, or using assistive devices, and mental and cognitive factors.

[42 C.F.R. § 409.44(c)(1).]

Reasonableness and Necessity of Home Health Therapy Services

To be considered reasonable and necessary, the services must be considered under accepted standards of professional clinical practice to be a specific, safe, and effective treatment for the beneficiary's condition. In addition, the patient's function must be initially assessed and periodically reassessed by a qualified therapist of the corresponding discipline for the type of therapy being provided, using a method that includes objective measurements. If more than one discipline of therapy is being provided, a qualified therapist from each of the disciplines must perform the assessment and periodic reassessments. The measurement results and corresponding effectiveness of the therapy, or lack thereof, must be documented in the clinical record. [42 C.F.R. § 409.44(c)(2)(i)(A).]

In addition, one of the following three criteria must be met:

(1) there is an expectation that the beneficiary's condition will improve materially in a reasonable (and generally predictable) period of time based on the physician's assessment of the beneficiary's restoration potential and unique medical condition;

(2) the unique clinical condition of the patient may require the specialized skills, knowledge, and judgment of a qualified therapist or therapist assistant to design or establish a safe and effective maintenance program required in connection with the patient's specific illness or injury; or

(3) the unique clinical condition of the patient may require the specialized skills of a qualified therapist to perform a safe and effective maintenance program required in connection with the patient's specific illness or injury.

[42 C.F.R. § 409.44(c)(2)(iii); Pub. 100-02, Ch. 7, § 40.2.1.]

For each therapy discipline, a qualified therapist (not an assistant) must assess and reassess the patient's function at least once every 30 calendar days. [42 C.F.R. § 409.44(c)(2)(i); Pub. 100-02, Ch. 7, § 40.2.1.]

[¶ 253] Home Health Medical Social Services

Medical social services, such as short-term counseling, assessments of social and emotional concerns related to illness, and assistance obtaining community services, are covered as home health services if ordered by a physician and included in the plan of care. The frequency and nature of the services must be reasonable and necessary for the treatment of the beneficiary's condition. Medical social services are "dependent" services that are covered only if the beneficiary needs: (1) skilled nursing care on an intermittent basis; (2) physical therapy or speech-language pathology services; or (3) occupational therapy services on a continuing basis. [42 C.F.R. § 409.45(a), (c)(1).]

Medical social services are covered under Part A only if: (1) the services are necessary to resolve social or emotional problems that are, or are expected to become, an impediment to the effective treatment of the patient's medical condition or rate of recovery; (2) the frequency and nature of the services are reasonable and necessary for the treatment of the patient's conditions; (3) the medical social services are furnished by a qualified social worker or qualified social work assistant under the supervision of a social worker; and (4) the services needed to resolve the problems that are impeding the beneficiary's recovery require the skills of a qualified social worker or social worker assistant under the supervision of a qualified medical social worker. [42 C.F.R. § 409.45(c).]

Covered services include, but are not limited to, the following:

(1) assessment of the social and emotional factors related to the patient's illness, need for care, response to treatment, and adjustment to care;

(2) appropriate action to obtain community services to assist in resolving problems in these areas;

(3) assessment of the relationship of the patient's medical and nursing requirements to the home situation, financial resources, and availability of community resources; and

(4) counseling services required by the patient.

[*Medicare Benefit Policy Manual*, Pub. 100-02, Ch. 7, § 50.3.]

Counseling services furnished to the patient's family are covered only when the home health agency can demonstrate that a brief intervention (about two or three visits) by a medical social worker is necessary to remove a clear and direct impediment to the effective treatment of the patient's medical condition or to his or her rate of recovery. [42 C.F.R. § 409.45(c)(2)(ii); Pub. 100-02, Ch. 7, § 50.3.]

[¶ 254] Home Health Aides

Medicare covers part-time or intermittent services of a home health aide who has successfully completed a training program approved by the HHS Secretary. To be covered, these services must be ordered by a physician in the plan of care for a beneficiary who qualifies for home health services. The reason for the visits by the home health aide must be to provide hands-on personal care to the beneficiary or services that are needed to maintain the beneficiary's health or facilitate treatment of the beneficiary's illness or injury. Services provided by the home health aide must be reasonable and necessary. The physician's order should indicate the frequency of the home health aide services required. [Soc. Sec. Act §§ 1861(m)(4), 1891(a)(3); 42 C.F.R. § 409.45(b).]

To be considered reasonable and necessary, the services must: (1) meet the requirements for home health aide services; (2) be of a type that the patient cannot perform himself or herself; and (3) be of a type that no able or willing caregiver can provide, or if there is a potential caregiver, the patient must be unwilling to receive care from that caregiver. [42 C.F.R. § 409.45(b)(3).]

Covered home health aide services include the following: (1) personal care of a patient; (2) simple dressing changes that do not require the skills of a licensed nurse; (3) assistance with medications that ordinarily are self-administered and do not require the skills of a licensed nurse; (4) assistance with activities that are directly supportive of skilled therapy, such as routine exercises and the practice of functional communication skills; and (5) routine care of prosthetic and orthotic devices. [42 C.F.R. § 409.45(b)(1); *Medicare Benefit Policy Manual*, Pub. 100-02, Ch. 7, § 50.2.]

The discussion on intermittent services at ¶ 251 is applicable also to home health aides.

[¶ 255] Medical Supplies and Durable Medical Equipment

Covered medical supplies are items that, due to their therapeutic or diagnostic characteristics, are essential to enable the home health agency (HHA) to effectively carry out the plan of care that the physician ordered for the treatment or diagnosis of the patient's illness or injury. This includes such items as: catheters and catheter supplies; ostomy bags and ostomy care supplies; dressings and wound care supplies, such as sterile gloves, gauze, and applicators; and intravenous supplies. [Soc. Sec. Act §§ 1861(m)(5), 1866(a)(1)(P); 42 C.F.R. §§ 409.45(f), 489.20(k); *Medicare Benefit Policy Manual*, Pub. 100-02, Ch. 7, §§ 50.4.1.1 and 50.4.2.]

Durable medical equipment (DME) also includes applicable disposable devices, defined as: (1) disposable negative pressure wound therapy devices that are integrated systems composed of a nonmanual vacuum pump, a receptacle for collecting exudate, and dressings for the purposes of wound therapy; and (2) devices that substitute for, and are used in lieu of, negative pressure wound therapy DME items that are an integrated systems of a negative pressure vacuum pump, a separate exudate collection canister, and dressings that would otherwise be covered for individuals for such wound therapy. [Soc. Sec. Act §§ 1834(s)(2), 1861(m)(5).]

Limited amounts of medical supplies may be left in the home between visits when repeated applications are required and rendered by the patient or caregivers. These items must be part of the plan of care in which the home health staff is actively involved. For example, if the patient is independent in giving himself or herself insulin injections but the nurse visits once a day to change wound dressings, the wound dressings/irrigation solution may be left in the home between visits. Supplies that require administration by a nurse, such as needles, syringes, and catheters, should not be left in the home between visits. [Pub. 100-02, Ch. 7, § 50.4.1.3.]

HHAs must offer to furnish catheters, catheter supplies, ostomy bags, and supplies related to ostomy care to any individual who needs them as part of the provision of health services. [Soc. Sec. Act § 1866(a)(1)(P); 42 C.F.R. § 489.20(k).]

DME may be covered under the home health benefit as either a Part A or Part B service. DME furnished by an HHA as a home health service is always covered by Part A if the beneficiary is entitled to Part A. The coinsurance for DME furnished as a home health service is 20 percent of the customary charge for the services. [42 C.F.R. §§ 409.45(e), 409.50.]

Exclusion of Drugs and Biologics

Drugs and biologics are generally excluded from coverage as a home health benefit. [Soc. Sec. Act § 1861(m)(5); 42 C.F.R. § 409.49(a).] In certain cases they may be covered under Part B, such as when they are administered by a physician as a part of his or her professional services (see ¶ 351 and ¶ 362). The administration of medication also may be covered if the services of a licensed nurse are required to administer the medications safely and effectively for the reasonable and necessary treatment of the illness or injury. [Pub. 100-02, Ch. 7, § 40.1.2.4.]

Osteoporosis drugs. Injections of osteoporosis drugs are covered as non-routine medical supplies for homebound female beneficiaries in certain circumstances (the nursing visit to perform the injection may be the individual's qualifying service for home health coverage) if:

(1) the individual's physician certifies that the individual sustained a bone fracture that a physician certifies was related to post-menopausal osteoporosis and she is unable to learn the skills needed to self-administer the drug, and her family or caregivers are unable or unwilling to administer the drug, or she is otherwise physically or mentally incapable of administering the drug; and

(2) the individual is confined to the home.

[Soc. Sec. Act § 1861(kk); Pub. 100-02, Ch. 7, § 50.4.3; *Medicare Claims Processing Manual*, Pub. 100-04, Ch. 10, § 90.1.]

[¶ 256] Interns and Residents-in-Training

Home health services include the medical services of interns and residents-in-training under an approved hospital teaching program, if the services are ordered by the physician who is responsible for the plan of care and the home health agency (HHA) is affiliated with, or under common control of, a hospital providing the medical services. "Approved" means:

(1) approved by the Accreditation Council for Graduate Medical Education;

(2) in the case of an osteopathic hospital, approved by the Committee on Hospitals of the Bureau of Professional Education of the American Osteopathic Association;

(3) in the case of an intern or resident-in-training in the field of dentistry, approved by the Council on Dental Education of the American Dental Association; or

(4) in the case of an intern or resident-in-training in the field of podiatry, approved by the Council on Podiatric Education of the American Podiatric Association.

[42 C.F.R. § 409.45(g); *Medicare Benefit Policy Manual*, Pub. 100-02, Ch. 7, § 50.5.]

[¶ 257] Outpatient Services

In certain instances, the services described in ¶ 251–¶ 256, provided on an outpatient basis, can be included as home health services (see ¶ 250, item (7)). While the beneficiary ordinarily must be homebound to be eligible for home health services, such services are covered if furnished under arrangements at a hospital, skilled nursing facility (SNF), rehabilitation center, or outpatient department associated with a medical school and, if the services: (1) require the use of equipment (for example, hydrotherapy) that cannot be made available at the beneficiary's home; or (2) are furnished while the beneficiary is at the facility to receive services requiring the use of such equipment. The hospital, SNF, or outpatient

¶256

department must be a qualified provider of services. [42 C.F.R. § 409.47(b); *Medicare Benefit Policy Manual*, Pub. 100-02, Ch. 7, § 50.6.]

In some cases, special transportation arrangements may have to be made to bring the homebound patient to the institution providing these special services. The cost of transporting an individual to a facility cannot be reimbursed as a home health service. [42 C.F.R. § 409.49(b); Pub. 100-02, Ch. 7, § 50.6.]

[¶ 260] Physician Certification and Recertification of Home Health Services

The home health patient must be under the care of a physician who established the plan of care (POC). [42 C.F.R. § 424.22(a)(1)(iv).] The physician must be qualified to sign the physician certification and the POC (see ¶ 262). Doctors of medicine, osteopathy, or podiatric medicine are considered qualified, but a podiatrist may establish a POC only if consistent with the functions authorized for that specialty by state law. [42 C.F.R. § 409.42(b).]

Home Health Certification and Recertification

As a condition for payment of home health services under Medicare Part A or Medicare Part B, a physician must certify the following:

(1) the patient needs or needed intermittent skilled nursing care, or physical or occupational therapy or speech-language pathology services;

(2) home health services are or were required because the individual is or was confined to the home except when receiving outpatient services;

(3) a plan for furnishing the services has been established and is periodically reviewed by a physician who is a doctor of medicine, osteopathy, or podiatric medicine;

(4) the services were furnished while the individual was under the care of a physician who is a doctor of medicine, osteopathy, or podiatric medicine; and

(5) a face-to-face patient encounter occurred.

[Soc. Sec. Act §§ 1814(a)(2)(C), 1835(a)(2)(A); 42 C.F.R. § 424.22(a).]

The home health agency (HHA) must obtain the certification of need for home health services at the time the POC is established or as soon thereafter as possible. The physician who establishes the plan must sign and date the certification. Documentation in the certifying physician's medical records and/or the acute/post-acute care facility's medical records must used as the basis for certification of home health eligibility. In addition, for certifications and recertifications occurring on or after January 1, 2019, documentation in the medical record of the HHA may also be used. [Soc. Sec. Act §§ 1814(a) and 1835(a), as amended by Bipartisan Budget Act of 2018 (P.L. 115-123) § 51002; 42 C.F.R. § 424.22(a), (c).]

Face-to-face encounter. The physician responsible for performing the initial certification must document that a face-to-face patient encounter, related to the primary reason the patient requires home health services, has occurred no more than 90 days prior to the home health start of care date, or within 30 days of the start of the home health care. The physician must include the date of the encounter and an explanation of the clinical findings supporting the patient's homebound status and the need for either intermittent skilled nursing services or therapy services. [Soc. Sec. Act § 1814(a)(2)(C); 42 C.F.R. § 424.22(a)(1)(v).]

The face-to-face encounter may be performed by one of the following:

(1) the certifying physician;

(2) a physician with privileges who cared for the patient in an acute or post-acute care facility from which the patient was directly admitted to home health;

(3) a nurse practitioner or a clinical nurse specialist working in collaboration with either of the above physicians; or

(4) a certified nurse-midwife or a physician assistant working under the supervision of either of the above physicians.

[Soc. Sec. Act § 1814(a)(2)(C); 42 C.F.R. § 424.22(a)(1)(v)(A).]

The face-to-face patient encounter may occur through telehealth. [Soc. Sec. Act § 1814(a)(2)(C); 42 C.F.R. § 424.22(a)(1)(v)(B).]

Recertification of the Need for Home Health Services

Recertification must occur at least every 60 days, preferably at the time the plan is reviewed, when there is a need for continuous home health care after an initial 60-day episode. The physician who reviews the plan of care must sign and date the recertification. Recertification is required more often than every 60 days when there is a (1) beneficiary-elected transfer; or (2) discharge with goals met and/or no expectation of a return to home health care. [42 C.F.R. § 424.22(b)(1).]

Content of recertification. As a condition for payment of home health services under Medicare Part A or Part B, if there is a continuing need for home health services, a physician must recertify the patient's continued eligibility for the home health benefit. The need for occupational therapy may be the basis for continuing services that were initiated because the individual needed skilled nursing care or physical therapy or speech therapy. [42 C.F.R. § 424.22(b)(2).]

If a patient's underlying condition or complication requires a registered nurse to ensure that essential nonskilled care is achieving its purpose, and necessitates that a registered nurse be involved in the development, management, and evaluation of a patient's care plan, the physician must include a brief narrative describing the clinical justification of this need. If the narrative is part of the recertification form, then it must be located immediately before the physician's signature. If it exists as an addendum to the recertification form, in addition to the physician's signature on the recertification form, the physician must sign immediately following the narrative in the addendum. [42 C.F.R. § 424.22(b)(2)(ii).]

Documentation Related to Patient Eligibility for Home Health Services

Documentation in the certifying physician's medical records or the acute/post-acute care facility's medical records (if the patient was directly admitted to home health) or both must be used as the basis for certification of the patient's eligibility for home health. Documentation from the home health agency (HHA) may also be used to support the basis for certification of home health eligibility if the following requirements are met:

(1) The documentation from the HHA can be corroborated by other medical record entries in the certifying physician's medical record for the patient or the acute/post-acute care facility's medical record for the patient or both, thereby creating a clinically consistent picture that the patient is eligible for Medicare home health services.

(2) The certifying physician signs and dates the HHA documentation demonstrating that the documentation from the HHA was considered when certifying patient eligibility for Medicare home health services. HHA documentation can include, but is not limited to, the patient's plan of care required under 42 C.F.R. § 409.43 or the initial or comprehensive assessment of the patient required under 42 C.F.R. § 484.55.

[Soc. Sec. Act §§ 1814(a) and 1835(a), as amended by Bipartisan Budget Act of 2018 (P.L. 115-123) § 51002; 42 C.F.R. § 424.22(c)(1).]

¶260

The documentation must be provided upon request to review entities, CMS, or both. If the documentation used as the basis for the certification of eligibility is not sufficient to demonstrate that the patient is or was eligible to receive services under the Medicare home health benefit, CMS will not pay for the home health services provided. [Soc. Sec. Act § 1866(a)(1)(X); 42 C.F.R. § 424.22(c)(2).]

[¶ 262] Home Health Plan of Care Requirement

For home health items and services to be covered, they must be furnished under a plan of care (POC) established and periodically reviewed by a physician that specifies the services necessary to meet the patient-specific needs identified in the comprehensive assessment. The plan of care must include the identification of the responsible discipline and the frequency and duration of all visits as well as those items listed in 42 C.F.R. § 484.60(a) that establish the need for such services. All care provided must be in accordance with the plan of care. [Soc. Sec. Act § 1861(m); 42 C.F.R. §§ 409.42(d), 409.43(a); *Final rule*, 84 FR 60478, Nov. 8, 2019.]

A physician that has a financial relationship with the home health agency (HHA) providing services may not establish a POC or certify and recertify services. [42 C.F.R. § 424.22(d).] See ¶ 720 on fraud and abuse.

Content of the Home Health Plan of Care

The POC must contain the following:

(1) all pertinent diagnoses;

(2) the beneficiary's mental, psychosocial, and cognitive status;

(3) types of services, supplies, and equipment required;

(4) frequency of visits, prognosis, and rehabilitation potential;

(5) functional limitations;

(6) activities permitted;

(7) nutritional requirements;

(8) all medications and treatments;

(9) safety measures to protect against injury;

(10) a description of the patient's risk for emergency department visits and hospital readmission, and all necessary interventions to address the underlying risk factors;

(11) patient and caregiver education and training to facilitate timely discharge;

(12) patient-specific interventions and education;

(13) measurable outcomes and goals identified by the HHA and the patient;

(14) information related to any advanced directives; and

(15) any additional items the HHA or physician choose to include.

In addition, all patient care orders, including verbal orders, must be recorded in the plan of care. [42 C.F.R. § 484.60(a)(2) and (3); *Medicare Benefit Policy Manual*, Pub. 100-02, Ch. 7, § 30.2.1.]

The physician's orders in the POC must specify the medical treatments to be furnished as well as the type of home health discipline that will furnish the ordered services and at what frequency the services will be furnished. Orders that are described as "as needed" or PRN must be accompanied by a description of the patient's medical signs and symptoms that would occasion the visit. These provisions in a POC also must include a specific number of such visits to be made under the order until an additional physician order must be obtained. [42 C.F.R. § 409.43(b); Pub. 100-02, Ch. 7, § 30.2.2.]

If the physician who signed plan of care is not available at the time the HHA requests an anticipated payment of the initial percentage prospective payment in accordance with 42 C.F.R. § 484.205, the request for the anticipated payment must be based on a physician's verbal order or a referral prescribing detailed orders for the services to be rendered that is signed and dated by a physician. For the final percentage payment, the plan of care must be signed and dated: (1) by a physician as described who meets the certification and recertification requirements of 42 C.F.R. § 424.22; and (2) before the claim for each episode for services is submitted for the final percentage prospective payment. Any changes in the plan must be signed and dated by a physician. [42 C.F.R. § 409.43(c).]

If any services are provided based on a physician's oral orders, the orders must be put in writing and signed and dated with the date of receipt by the registered nurse or qualified therapist responsible for furnishing or supervising the ordered services. The physician must countersign and date the oral orders before the HHA bills for the care. [42 C.F.R. § 409.43(d); Pub. 100-02, Ch. 7, § 30.2.4A.]

Plan of Care Review

The physician who established the plan of care must review and sign it at least every 60 days. The review must occur more frequently than every 60 days if there is: (1) a beneficiary-elected transfer; (2) a significant change in condition; or (3) a discharge with goals met and/or no expectation of a return to home health care and the patient returns to home health care during the 60-day episode. Each review of a beneficiary's plan of care must contain the signature of the physician who reviewed it and the date of review. [42 C.F.R. § 409.43(e); Pub. 100-02, Ch. 7, § 30.2.6.]

[¶ 264] Patient Confined to Home

For a beneficiary to be eligible to receive covered home health services, he or she must generally be confined to home. In all cases, a physician must certify this confinement. [Soc. Sec. Act § 1814(a)(2)(C); 42 C.F.R. §§ 409.42(a), 409.47.]

A beneficiary is considered "confined to home" if the following criteria are met:

(1) The patient must either:

• need the aid of supportive devices such as crutches, canes, wheelchairs, and walkers; the use of special transportation; or the assistance of another person in order to leave his or her place of residence because of illness or injury; or

• have a condition such that leaving his or her home is medically contraindicated.

(2) The patient must also:

• have a normal inability to leave home; and

• require a considerable and taxing effort to leave home.

[*Medicare Benefit Policy Manual*, Pub. 100-02, Ch. 7, § 30.1.1.]

Beneficiaries are considered homebound even if they take an occasional absence from the home for nonmedical purposes. The absences must be infrequent, relatively short in duration, and not indicate that the patient has the ability to obtain health care outside of the home. These determinations are made by assessing the patient's condition over a period of time. [Pub. 100-02, Ch. 7, § 30.1.1.]

¶264

Attendance at a religious service is considered an absence of infrequent or short duration. Beneficiaries can be considered homebound while receiving therapeutic, psychosocial, or medical treatment in a state-licensed adult day-care program on a regular basis. [Soc. Sec. Act §§ 1814(a), 1835(a).]

Patient's Place of Residence

Home health services must be furnished on a visiting basis in a place used as the patient's residence. This may be his or her own dwelling, an apartment, a relative's home, a home for the aged, or some other type of institution. However, an institution may not be considered a patient's place of residence if it meets at least the most important requirement in the definition of "hospital" (see ¶ 229) or in the definition of "skilled nursing facility" (see ¶ 249). [42 C.F.R. § 409.47(a); Pub. 100-02, Ch. 7, § 30.1.2.]

[¶ 266] Home Health Visits

A visit occurs when a home health worker makes personal contact with the patient to provide a covered service in the patient's residence. If the HHA furnishes services in an outpatient facility under arrangements with the facility, one visit may be covered for each type of service provided. [42 C.F.R. § 409.48(c); *Medicare Benefit Policy Manual*, Pub. 100-02, Ch. 7, § 70.2.]

There is nothing to preclude an HHA from adopting telemedicine or other technologies to promote efficiency; however, those technologies will not be specifically recognized or reimbursed by Medicare under the home health benefit. [Soc. Sec. Act § 1895(e)(1)(B); Pub. 100-02, Ch. 7, § 110.]

Home Health Evaluation Visits

When HHA personnel make an initial evaluation visit, the cost of this visit is considered an administrative expense because the patient has not been accepted for care. If during the course of this initial evaluation visit the HHA determines that the patient is suitable for home health care, and provides the first skilled service as ordered under the physician's plan of treatment, the visit becomes the first billable visit. An observation and evaluation or reevaluation visit ordered by the physician for the purpose of evaluating the patient's continuing need for skilled services is covered as a skilled visit. [Pub. 100-02, Ch. 7, § 70.2C.]

A supervisory visit made by a nurse or other personnel to evaluate the patient's specific personal care needs or review whether the aide is meeting the patient's personal care needs is considered an administrative function and is not chargeable to the patient as a skilled visit. [Pub. 100-02, Ch. 7, § 70.2C.]

Home Health Patient-Specific Comprehensive Assessments

An HHA must provide a patient-specific, comprehensive assessment of each patient. An RN must conduct an initial assessment visit to determine the immediate care and support needs of the patient and determine eligibility for the Medicare home health benefit, including homebound status. The initial assessment visit must occur within 48 hours of the referral or the patient's return home, or on the physician-ordered start of care date. The RN must complete the comprehensive assessment within five days calendar after the start of care. [42 C.F.R. § 484.55(a), (b).]

The comprehensive assessment must accurately reflect the patient's status, and must include, at a minimum, the following information:

(1) the patient's current health, psychosocial, functional, and cognitive status;

(2) the patient's strengths, goals, and care preferences, including information that may be used to demonstrate the patient's progress toward achievement of the goals identified by the patient and the measurable outcomes identified by the HHA;

(3) the patient's continuing need for home care;

(4) the patient's medical, nursing, rehabilitative, social, and discharge planning needs;

(5) a review of all medications the patient is currently using in order to identify any potential adverse effects and drug reactions, including ineffective drug therapy, significant side effects, significant drug interactions, duplicate drug therapy, and non-compliance with drug therapy;

(6) the patient's primary caregiver, if any, and other available supports, including their willingness and ability to provide care and availability and schedules;

(7) the patient's representative (if any); and

(8) incorporation of the current version of the Outcome and Assessment Information Set (OASIS) items, using the language and groupings of the OASIS items, as specified by the Secretary.

[42 C.F.R. § 484.55(c).]

The comprehensive assessment must be updated and revised (including the administration of the OASIS) as frequently as the patient's condition warrants due to a major decline or improvement in the patient's health status, but not less frequently than (1) the last five days of every 60 days beginning with the start-of-care date, unless there is a beneficiary-elected transfer, significant change in condition, or discharge and return to the same HHA during the 60-day episode; (2) within 48 hours of the patient's return to the home from a hospital admission of 24 hours or more for any reason other than diagnostic tests, or on physician-ordered resumption date; and (3) at discharge. [42 C.F.R. § 484.55(d).]

Home health prospective payment system. The weighted answers to several OASIS items, including the need for therapy, provide a key element of Medicare reimbursement under the home health prospective payment system (see ¶ 830).

Advance Directives

Advance medical directives are written instructions, such as a living will or durable power of attorney for health care, recognized under state law and governing provision of care when the individual is incapacitated. HHAs must inform beneficiaries about advance directives and document their choices in medical records. HHAs must provide the information to the beneficiary before care is provided during the initial visit. [Soc. Sec. Act § 1866(f)(3); 42 C.F.R. § 489.102(a).]

Beneficiaries are not *required* to make advance directives, and the amount and type of care may not be conditioned upon the completion or noncompletion of an advance directive. HHAs must provide written information to beneficiaries about their rights under state law to make decisions concerning their medical care, including the right to accept or refuse medical care and the right to formulate medical directives before care is started. [Soc. Sec. Act § 1866(f)(1); 42 C.F.R. § 489.102(a).]

[¶ 267] Specific Exclusions from Home Health Coverage

In addition to the general exclusions applicable to both parts of the Medicare program, which are discussed in Chapter 6, the following are excluded from home health services:

(1) drugs and biologics, except for osteoporosis drugs (see ¶ 255);

¶267

(2) transportation services from place of residence to a facility to receive home health services on an outpatient basis (see ¶ 257);

(3) services that would not be covered as inpatient services (see ¶ 217);

(4) housekeeping services the sole purpose of which is to enable the patient to continue residing in his or her home (e.g., cooking, shopping, Meals on Wheels, cleaning, laundry);

(5) end-stage renal disease (ESRD) services covered under the ESRD prospective payment system;

(6) prosthetic devices covered under Part B (catheters, ostomy bags, and supplies are not considered prosthetic devices if furnished under a home health plan of care and are not subject to this exclusion);

(7) medical social services provided to members of the beneficiary's family that are not incidental to covered social services provided to the beneficiary;

(8) respiratory care furnished by a respiratory therapist in a beneficiary's home;

(9) in-home visits by dietitians or nutritionists; and

(10) beginning January 1, 2021, home infusion therapy services.

[Soc. Sec. Act § 1861(b), (m); 42 C.F.R. § 409.49; *Medicare Benefit Policy Manual*, Pub. 100-02, Ch. 7, § 80.]

[¶ 268] "Home Health Agency" Defined—Qualified Home Health Agencies

As a general rule, services furnished by a home health agency (HHA) will not be covered by Medicare unless the HHA has been approved for Medicare participation by the government and has signed a participation agreement (see ¶ 730). [42 C.F.R. § 409.41.]

To participate in Medicare as a "home health agency," an organization must:

(1) be a public agency or private organization, or a subdivision of such an agency or organization;

(2) be primarily engaged in providing skilled nursing and other therapeutic services;

(3) have policies established by a group of professional personnel (including at least one physician and one registered nurse) associated with the agency;

(4) maintain clinical records on all patients;

(5) provide for supervision of services by a physician or nurse;

(6) be licensed by the state licensing agency where required;

(7) have in effect an overall plan and budget that meets certain requirements;

(8) meet certain conditions of participation (CoPs) and health and safety and financial stability requirements;

(9) provide the Secretary with a surety bond in the form specified by the HHS Secretary (in an amount of at least $50,000), which the Secretary determines is commensurate with the volume of payments made to the HHA; and

(10) meet an any additional requirements that the Secretary finds necessary for the effective and efficient implementation of the program.

[Soc. Sec. Act § 1861(o); *Medicare General Information, Eligibility, and Entitlement Manual*, Pub. 100-01, Ch. 5, § 50.]

For Part A, but not for Part B, the definition of an HHA does not include any agency or organization that is primarily for the care and treatment of mental diseases. [Soc. Sec. Act § 1861(o).]

Arrangements may be made by an HHA with other HHAs to furnish items or services under certain circumstances. Any HHA providing items and services must agree not to charge the patient for covered services or items and must agree to return money incorrectly collected (see ¶ 830). [Pub. 100-01, Ch. 5, § 50.2.]

Home Health Conditions of Participation

The requirements for participating HHAs and the additional health and safety require-ments prescribed by the HHS Secretary are incorporated into CoPs for HHAs. These conditions are included in the regulations governing the Medicare program. [42 C.F.R. Part 484.]

HHAs that are out of compliance with CoPs may correct their performance and achieve prompt compliance through new methods, such as directed plans of correction or directed in-service training. CMS may impose sanctions on and terminate HHAs that are out of compliance with CoPs. [42 C.F.R. § § 488.810, 488.850, 488.855.]

Hospice Care

[¶ 270] Hospice Care: Coverage in General

Hospice care is an interdisciplinary approach to caring for terminally ill patients by treating pain and providing comfort, rather than seeking a cure for the terminal disease. A hospice program must be a public agency or private organization that meets Medicare conditions of participation to qualify as a Medicare provider. [Soc. Sec. Act § 1861(dd).]

A Medicare beneficiary becomes eligible for hospice care upon a physician's certifica-tion that he or she has a terminal illness, i.e., is expected to live six months or less if the illness proceeds at its normal course. The prognosis is based on the physician's clinical judgment regarding the normal course of the patient's illness. [Soc. Sec. Act § § 1814(a)(7)(A), 1861(dd)(3)(A); 42 C.F.R. § 418.20.]

When electing hospice care, the patient must be informed of the palliative, rather than curative, nature of the treatment. Palliative care is defined as patient- and family-centered care that optimizes quality of life by anticipating, preventing, and treating suffering. Palliative care addresses physical, intellectual, emotional, social, and spiritual needs and facilitates patient autonomy, access to information, and choice. [42 C.F.R. § § 418.3, 418.24(b)(2).]

A Medicare beneficiary may elect to receive hospice care for up to two periods of 90 days each, followed by an unlimited number of periods up to 60 days each. [Soc. Sec. Act § 1812(a)(4); 42 C.F.R. § 418.21(a).]

Effective for services performed on or after January 1, 2019, the Bipartisan Budget Act of 2018 (P.L. 115-123) added physician assistants (PAs), in addition to physicians and nurse practitioners (NPs), to the definition of "attending physician." This will allow them to manage and separately bill for hospice care. PAs will be able to serve as the attending physician to hospice patients and perform other functions that are otherwise consistent with their scope of practice. However, NPs and PAs may not act as attending physician for purposes of certifying that the beneficiary is terminally ill. [Soc. Sec. Act § § 1814(a)(7)(A)(i)(I) and 1861(dd)(3)(B), as amended by Bipartisan Budget Act of 2018 § 51006.]

Covered Hospice Services

"Hospice care" includes the following services and supplies:

¶270

(1) nursing care provided by or under the supervision of a registered professional nurse;

(2) physical or occupational therapy or speech-language pathology services;

(3) medical social services under the direction of a physician;

(4) homemaker services and the services of a home health aide (also known as a hospice aide) who has successfully completed an approved training program;

(5) medical supplies (including drugs and biologics) and the use of medical appliances;

(6) physicians' and nurse practitioners' services;

(7) short-term inpatient care, including both procedures necessary for pain control and symptom management and occasional respite care for periods up to five days;

(8) counseling (including dietary counseling) with respect to care of the terminally ill beneficiary and the family's and caregivers' adjustment to the beneficiary's death; and

(9) any other item or service that is specified in the plan of care and otherwise covered by Medicare.

[Soc. Sec. Act § 1861(dd)(1), (3)(B); 42 C.F.R. § 418.202.]

Nursing, home health aide, and homemaker services may be provided on a 24-hour, continuous basis during periods of crisis as necessary to allow the patient to remain at home. Respite care is short-term inpatient care provided to the patient only when necessary to relieve family members or other caregivers for no more than five consecutive days at a time. Bereavement counseling is a required hospice service, available to the family before and up to one year after the patient's death, but it is not separately reimbursable. [Soc. Sec. Act § 1861(dd)(1); 42 C.F.R. § 418.204; *Medicare Benefit Policy Manual*, Pub. 100-02, Ch. 9, § 40.2.3.]

Custodial care and personal comfort items, while generally excluded by Medicare (see ¶ 616 and ¶ 625), are covered when the beneficiary is under the care of a hospice. [Soc. Sec. Act § 1862(a)(1)(C); 42 C.F.R. § 411.15(g), (j).]

A beneficiary who is denied coverage for hospice care because services received were determined not to be reasonable or necessary may nevertheless be entitled to Medicare coverage under the waiver-of-liability rules discussed at ¶ 915.

[¶ 272] Election of Hospice Care

To receive hospice services, a beneficiary must file an election statement with a particular hospice. If the individual is physically or mentally incapacitated, his or her representative may file the election statement. [42 C.F.R. § 418.24(a)(1).]

The hospice chosen by the eligible individual must file a Notice of Election (NOE) with its Medicare administrative contractor (MAC) within five calendar days after the effective date of the election statement. If a hospice does not file the required NOE within this time period, Medicare will not cover and pay for days of hospice care from the effective date of election to the date of filing of the notice of election; these days are a provider liability, and the provider may not bill the beneficiary for them. CMS may, however, waive the consequences of failure to submit a timely filed NOE if the hospice encounters an exceptional circumstance such as fires, floods, earthquakes, or similar unusual events that inflict extensive damage to the hospice's ability to operate; a CMS or MAC systems issue that is beyond the control of the hospice; or a newly Medicare-certified hospice that is notified of that certification after the Medicare certification date, or which is awaiting its user ID from its MAC. [42 C.F.R. § 418.24(a)(2), (3).]

Change of designated hospice. An individual may change, once in each election period, the designation of the particular hospice from which he or she elects to receive hospice care. The change of the designated hospice is not considered a revocation of the election, but is a transfer. [42 C.F.R. § 418.30.]

Content of Hospice Election Statement

Election statements must:

(1) identify the hospice that will be providing care;

(2) include an acknowledgment that the individual has been given a full understanding of the palliative rather than curative nature of hospice care, as it relates to the individual's terminal illness and related conditions;

(3) include a statement that the beneficiary has been provided information on the hospice's coverage responsibility and that certain Medicare services are waived by the election; for hospice elections beginning on or after October 1, 2020, this includes providing the individual with information indicating that services unrelated to the terminal illness and related conditions are exceptional and unusual and hospice should be providing virtually all care needed by the individual who has elected hospice;

(4) include the effective date of the election;

(5) for hospice elections beginning on or after October 1, 2020, the hospice must provide information on individual cost-sharing for hospice services;

(6) for hospice elections beginning on or after October 1, 2020, the hospice must provide notification of the individual's (or representative's) right to receive an election statement addendum, if there are conditions, items, services, and drugs the hospice has determined to be unrelated to the individual's terminal illness and related conditions and would not be covered by the hospice;

(7) for hospice elections beginning on or after October 1, 2020, the hospice must provide information on the Beneficiary and Family Centered Care Quality Improvement Organization, (BFCC-QIO), including the right to immediate advocacy and BFCC-QIO contact information; and

(8) include the signature of the individual or representative.

[42 C.F.R. § 418.24(b); *Final rule*, 84 FR 38484, Aug 6, 2019.]

The election to receive hospice care continues through the initial election period and through subsequent election periods without a break in care as long as the beneficiary remains in the care of a hospice, does not revoke the election, and is not discharged from the hospice. [42 C.F.R. § 418.24(d).]

Waiver of other services. Upon electing the Medicare hospice benefit, the beneficiary waives the right to Medicare payment for any services related to the terminal illness and related conditions during a hospice election, except when provided by (1) the designated hospice; (2) another hospice under arrangements made by the designated hospice; or (3) the individual's attending physician if he or she is not employed by the designated hospice. [42 C.F.R. § 418.24(e).]

Attending physician. A beneficiary receiving hospice benefits may change the designated attending physician by filing a signed statement with the hospice. The statement must identify the new attending physician and include both the effective date of the change and the date signed. The effective date cannot be before the date the statement is signed. The

¶272

statement must also acknowledge that the change in the attending physician is the beneficiary's choice. [42 C.F.R. § 418.24(g).]

Hospice Election Statement Addendum

For hospice elections beginning on or after October 1, 2020, when a hospice determines there are conditions, items, services, or drugs that are unrelated to the individual's terminal illness and related conditions, the individual, non-hospice providers furnishing such items, services, or drugs, or Medicare contractors may request a written list as an addendum to the election statement. If the election statement addendum is requested at the time of initial hospice election, the hospice must provide this information, in writing, to the individual (or representative) within five days from the date of the election. If the addendum is requested during the course of hospice care (i.e., after the hospice election date), the hospice must provide this information, in writing, within 72 hours of the request to the requesting individual (or representative), non-hospice provider, or Medicare contractor. If there are any changes to the content on the addendum during the course of hospice care, the hospice must update the addendum and provide these updates, in writing, to the individual (or representative). [42 C.F.R. § 418.24(b); *Final rule*, 84 FR 38484, Aug. 6, 2019.]

Content of addendum. The hospice election statement addendum must include the following:

(1) titled "Patient Notification of Hospice Non-Covered Items, Services, and Drugs";

(2) hospice name;

(3) patient's name and hospice medical number identifier;

(4) patient's terminal illness and related conditions;

(5) patient's condition upon admission to hospice, or upon plan of care update, with a list of the associated items, services, and drugs not covered by the hospice, as determined by the hospice;

(6) written clinical explanation, in language the patient (or representative) can understand, as to why the identified conditions, items, services, and drugs are considered unrelated to the terminal illness and related conditions and not needed for pain or symptom management; the clinical explanation must include a general statement that the decisions were specific to the patient and that the patient should share this with other health care providers, if they seek items or services unrelated to the terminal illness;

(7) references to any relevant clinical practice, policy, or coverage guidelines;

(8) information on (a) the purpose of the addendum, which is to notify the patient that the items or services are not related to the terminal illness, and (b) the right to immediate advocacy through the BFCC-QIO, if the patient disagrees with the hospice's determination on coverage; and

(9) name and signature of the individual (or representative) and date signed, along with a statement that signing the addendum (or its updates) is only acknowledgment of receipt of the addendum (or its updates) and not necessarily the individual's agreement with the hospice's determinations.

[42 C.F.R. § 418.24(c); *Final rule*, 84 FR 38484, Aug. 6, 2019.]

Duration of Hospice Election

The duration of an election to receive hospice care will be considered to continue through the initial election period and through the subsequent election periods without a break in care as long as the individual:

(1) remains in the care of a hospice;

(2) does not revoke the election; and

(3) is not discharged from the hospice for reasons described in 42 C.F.R. § 418.26.

[42 C.F.R. § 418.24(d).]

Revoking Election of Hospice Services

An individual or representative may revoke the election of hospice care at any time in writing. To revoke the election, the individual must file a signed statement with the hospice that the individual or representative revokes the election for Medicare coverage of hospice care for the remainder of that election period, including the date that the revocation is to be effective. An individual or representative may not designate an effective date earlier than the date that the revocation is made. The individual forfeits hospice coverage for any remaining days in that election period. [42 C.F.R. § 418.28.]

Re-election of hospice benefits. If an election has been revoked, the individual (or his or her representative if the individual is mentally or physically incapacitated) may at any time file an election for any other election period that is still available to the individual. [42 C.F.R. § 418.24(f).]

[¶ 274] Certification and Care Requirements

The hospice must obtain written certification of the beneficiary's terminal illness for each election period. In addition, the hospice medical director must recommend the patient for admission to the hospice in consultation with, or with input from, the patient's attending physician, if any. The recommendation must be signed by the physician and included in the patient's medical records. [Soc. Sec. Act § 1814(a)(7)(A); 42 C.F.R. §§ 418.22, 418.25.]

Certification and Recertification of Terminal Illness

At the beginning of the initial 90-day hospice benefit period, both the patient's attending physician, if any, and the medical director or physician member of the hospice interdisciplinary group must certify in writing that the patient is terminally ill. At the beginning of each subsequent period, only the hospice physician or the physician member of the hospice interdisciplinary group must recertify the patient's terminally ill status. [Soc. Sec. Act § 1814(a)(7)(A); 42 C.F.R. § 418.22(a)(1), (c).]

The hospice must obtain an initial certification of terminal illness within two days of admission to the hospice. If the hospice cannot obtain a written certification within two days, it must obtain an oral certification, and the written certification must be obtained before submission of a claim for payment. Subsequent certifications may be made orally, but the written certification must be made before the claim is submitted for payment. Certifications must be supported by documentation. [42 C.F.R. § 418.22(a)(3).] For purposes of certifying that a beneficiary is terminally ill, neither nurse practitioners nor physician assistants are considered attending physicians. [Soc. Sec. Act § 1814(a)(7)(A)(i)(I), as amended by Bipartisan Budget Act of 2018 (P.L. 115-123) § 51006(a)(2).]

Face-to-face encounter. If a beneficiary elects to continue to receive hospice care, a hospice physician or nurse practitioner must have a face-to-face encounter with the individual to determine continued eligibility for hospice care, before the 180th-day recertification and then each subsequent recertification. [Soc. Sec. Act § 1814(a)(7)(D); 42 C.F.R. § 418.22(a)(4).]

Content of certification. Certification of terminal illness must be based on the physician's or medical director's clinical judgment regarding the normal course of the individual's illness. The certification must:

(1) specify that the prognosis is for a life expectancy of six months or less if the terminal illness runs its normal course;

(2) contain clinical information and other documentation that supports the medical prognosis;

(3) include a brief narrative explanation of the clinical findings that supports a life expectancy of six months or less;

(4) include a written attestation by the physician or nurse practitioner who performed the face-to-face encounter; and

(5) be signed and dated by the physicians, and include the benefit period dates to which the certification or recertification applies.

[42 C.F.R. § § 418.22(b), 418.25.]

Mandatory medical review. If a certain percentage of a hospice's patients receive care for over 180 days, CMS must conduct a medical review for any patient receiving care for this amount of time. The HHS Secretary establishes this percentage. [Soc. Sec. Act § 1814(a)(7)(E).]

Hospice Written Plan of Care

All hospice care must be provided according to a written plan of care (POC), established by the hospice medical director in conjunction with the hospice's interdisciplinary staff, before hospice care begins. Both the beneficiary's attending physician and the hospice medical director and interdisciplinary staff must periodically review the POC. [Soc. Sec. Act § 1814(a)(7)(B), (C); 42 C.F.R. § § 418.56, 418.200.]

The hospice must develop an individualized POC reflecting patient and family goals and interventions based on the problems identified in initial and updated comprehensive assessments. The plan must include all services necessary for the palliation and management of the terminal illness and related conditions, including: (1) interventions to manage pain and symptoms; (2) a detailed statement of the scope and frequency of services necessary to meet the specific patient and family needs; (3) measurable outcomes anticipated from implementing and coordinating the POC; (4) drugs and treatment necessary to meet the needs of the patient; (5) medical supplies and appliances necessary to meet the needs of the patient; and (6) the interdisciplinary group's documentation of the patient's or representative's level of understanding, involvement, and agreement with the POC. [42 C.F.R. § 418.56(c).]

The hospice interdisciplinary group (in collaboration with the individual's attending physician, if any) must review, revise, and document the individualized POC as frequently as the patient's condition requires, but no less frequently than every 15 calendar days. A revised POC must include information from the patient's updated comprehensive assessment and must note the patient's progress toward outcomes and goals specified in the plan. [42 C.F.R. § 418.56(d).]

Coordination of Services

The hospice must develop and maintain a system of communication and integration that: (1) ensures that the interdisciplinary group maintains responsibility for directing, coordinating, and supervising the care and services provided; (2) ensures that the care and services are provided in accordance with the POC; (3) ensures that the care and services provided are based on all assessments of the patient and family needs; (4) provides for and ensures the ongoing sharing of information between all disciplines providing care and services in all settings; and (5) provides for an ongoing sharing of information with other non-hospice health care providers furnishing services unrelated to the terminal illness and related conditions. [42 C.F.R. § 418.56(e).]

[¶ 276] Discharge from Hospice Care

A patient may be discharged from a hospice program in three situations:

(1) the hospice determines that the patient is no longer terminally ill;

(2) the patient moves out of the hospice service area or transfers to another hospice; or

(3) for cause, because the behavior of the patient (or another individual in the patient's home) is disruptive, abusive, or uncooperative to the extent that delivery of care to the patient or the ability of the hospice to operate effectively is seriously impaired.

[42 C.F.R. § 418.26(a).]

Before discharging a patient for any of these reasons, the hospice must obtain a written physician's discharge order from the hospice medical director. If a patient has an attending physician, this physician should be consulted before discharge and his or her review and decision included in the discharge note. [42 C.F.R. § 418.26(b).]

Before discharging a patient for cause, the hospice must:

(1) advise the patient that discharge is being considered;

(2) ascertain that the patient's proposed discharge is not due to the patient's use of necessary hospice services;

(3) make a serious effort to resolve the problems presented by the patient or family; and

(4) document in the patient's records both the problems and the efforts made to resolve them.

[42 C.F.R. § 418.26(a)(3).]

Discharge planning. Hospices must have a process for discharge planning and must initiate this process when the staff begins to consider discharge. The discharge planning process must include planning for any necessary family counseling, patient education, or other services before the patient is discharged because he or she is no longer terminally ill. [42 C.F.R. § 418.26(d).]

Effect of discharge. A patient who has been discharged from hospice care no longer has an election of hospice care in effect. A patient whose condition remains terminal or becomes terminal again may make a new election of hospice care. Until a new election is made, the patient is not eligible for hospice care and Medicare coverage resumes for any benefits waived during hospice election. [42 C.F.R. § 418.26(c).]

[¶ 278] Deductibles and Coinsurance

During the period of election for hospice care, no copayments or deductibles other than those for drugs, biologics, and respite care apply for hospice care services provided to the patient, regardless of the setting where care is provided. [Soc. Sec. Act § 1813(a)(4); 42 C.F.R. § 418.400.]

Drugs and biologics. The beneficiary is liable for a coinsurance payment for each palliative drug and biologic prescription provided by the hospice except when the individual is an inpatient. The amount of coinsurance for each prescription must be about 5 percent of the cost of the drug or biologic to the hospice, up to $5, in accordance with the hospice's established drug copayment schedule approved by the Medicare contractor. The cost of the drug or biologic may not exceed what a prudent buyer would pay in similar circumstances. [Soc. Sec. Act § 1813(a)(4)(A)(i); 42 C.F.R. § 418.400(a).]

Respite care. The amount of coinsurance for each respite care day is 5 percent of the Medicare payment for a respite care day. The amount of the individual's coinsurance liability for respite care during a hospice coinsurance period may not exceed the inpatient hospital deductible applicable for the year that the hospice coinsurance period began (see ¶ 223). A "hospice coinsurance period" is the period of consecutive days beginning with the first day the patient's hospice election is in effect and ending after 14 consecutive days of the election no longer being in effect. [Soc. Sec. Act § 1813(a)(4)(A)(ii); 42 C.F.R. § 418.400(b).]

[¶ 280] Hospice Program Requirements

To qualify as a Medicare provider, a hospice program must be a public agency or a private organization that is primarily engaged in providing hospice-related care and services. The services are made available as needed, on a 24-hour basis. The hospice program must provide care and services in individuals' homes, on an outpatient basis, and on a short-term inpatient basis. The total number of days of short-term inpatient care provided in any 12-month period to patients with a hospice election in effect with respect to that hospice may not exceed 20 percent of the days during that period during which hospice elections are in effect. [Soc. Sec. Act § 1861(dd)(2)(A).]

Hospices must have an interdisciplinary group of staff that includes at least a physician medical director, a registered nurse, a social worker, and a pastoral or other counselor. The group must be hospice employees except the physician, who can be under contract with the hospice, and the pastoral counselor. The functions of the group are to:

- establish and review the plan of care for each patient;
- maintain central records on each patient;
- provide or supervise the provision of hospice care and services;
- govern and set policy for the hospice;
- continue providing service even if the patient is no longer able to pay;
- use volunteers in accordance with standards set by the HHS Secretary;
- maintain records on the use of volunteers and the costs savings and expanded services achieved; and
- ensure that the hospice complies with state licensing laws and state and federal regulations.

[Soc. Sec. Act § 1861(dd)(2)(B)–(G); 42 C.F.R. §§ 418.56, 418.58.]

In addition, a hospice program is required to make reasonable efforts to arrange for volunteer clergy or other members of religious organizations to visit patients who desire such visits and to advise patients of this opportunity. Hospice programs are also required to provide counseling services. [42 C.F.R. § 418.64(d)(3).]

Generally, hospice employees and volunteer staff must provide hospice services directly. The nursing, counseling, and medical social service obligations are considered "core services," which must be provided directly by hospice employees, except that the hospice may use contracted physicians. Hospices may contract with other hospices to provide nursing or medical social services in exigent circumstances, such as an unanticipated period of high patient load, staffing shortages due to illness or other events, when a patient temporarily travels outside a hospice program's service area, and to provide highly specialized services that are not frequently required. [42 C.F.R. § 418.64.]

A hospice in a non-urban area may apply for a waiver to contract for nursing services if it: (1) was operating before January 1, 1983; and (2) demonstrates that it has made a good-faith effort to hire a sufficient number of nurses to directly provide nursing care. [Soc. Sec. Act § 1861(dd)(5).]

A hospice that contracts for services remains responsible for providing and supervising those services professionally, administratively, and financially. All authorizations and all services provided by the contractor must be documented as necessary. [42 C.F.R. § 418.310.] If a hospice makes arrangements with another hospice to provide services under exigent circumstances, the hospice that the beneficiary elected is reimbursed. [Soc. Sec. Act § 1861(dd)(5)(D); 42 C.F.R. § 418.302(d)(2).]

A provider that is certified for Medicare participation as a hospital, skilled nursing facility, or home health agency may also be certified as a hospice. If so, the provider must have separate provider agreements and must file separate cost reports. [Soc. Sec. Act § 1861(dd)(4).]

A certified hospice program is surveyed by its state or local survey agency (see ¶ 703) at least once every three years. [Soc. Sec. Act § 1861(dd)(4)(C).]

Chapter 3– MEDICARE PART B—SUPPLEMENTAL MEDICAL INSURANCE

Eligibility and Enrollment

[¶ 300] Eligibility for Medicare Part B Benefits

Unlike the inpatient hospital insurance benefits program (Part A of Title XVIII of the Social Security Act), which is largely financed by Federal Insurance Contributions Act (FICA) taxes, the Supplementary Medical Insurance (SMI) Benefits for the Aged and Disabled (Part B) program is financed by monthly premium payments by enrollees and federal contributions to the SMI Trust Fund from the federal government. Medicare Part B covers physician services, medical supplies, and other outpatient services, which are not paid by Medicare Part A. [Soc. Sec. Act § § 1833(a), 1839(a), 1844; 42 C.F.R. § § 407.2, 408.20.]

Enrollment for Part B benefits is open to all persons who are entitled to Part A benefits (see ¶ 200). An individual who is not entitled to Part A benefits may enroll in Part B if he or she is:

(1) age 65 or over;

(2) a resident of the United States; and

(3) either (a) a citizen of the United States, or (b) an alien lawfully admitted to the United States for permanent residence who has resided in the United States continuously during the five years immediately preceding he or she applies for enrollment.

[Soc. Sec. Act § 1836; 42 C.F.R. § 407.10(a).] The term "United States" includes the Commonwealth of Puerto Rico, the Virgin Islands, Guam, American Samoa, and the Northern Mariana Islands. [Soc. Sec. Act § § 210(i), 1861(x).]

For the disabled under age 65 (see ¶ 204), neither Part A nor Part B coverage can begin before the 25th month of the individual's entitlement to disability benefits, except for amyotrophic lateral sclerosis (ALS) patients (see ¶ 204) and individuals exposed to public health hazards (see below). [Soc. Sec. Act § § 226(b) and (h), 1881A.]

Exposure to Health Hazards

Certain individuals exposed to specific environmental health hazards in a geographic area subject to an emergency declaration are deemed immediately eligible for Medicare benefits, regardless of the individual's age. Deemed individuals are eligible for Medicare coverage as of the date of the deeming and are eligible to enroll in Medicare Part B beginning with the month in which such deeming occurs. [Soc. Sec. Act § 1881A(a).]

An "environmental exposure affected individual" means an individual who:

(1) is diagnosed with one or more medical conditions such as asbestosis, pleural thickening, or pleural plaques;

(2) has been present for an aggregate total of six months in a geographic area subject to an emergency declaration (a) at least 10 years before such diagnosis, and (b) before the implementation of all remedial and removal actions; and

(3) has filed an application for benefits.

[Soc. Sec. Act § 1881A(e).]

Suspended Benefits for Aliens Outside of the U.S.

Part B benefits are suspended in the same manner they are suspended under Part A in the case of certain aliens who are or were outside the United States for six consecutive months (see ¶ 200). [Soc. Sec. Act § 202(t)(1), (9).]

Conviction of Subversive Activities

An individual convicted of any of the offenses stipulated in section 202(u)(1) of the Social Security Act, relating to subversive activities, cannot enroll in the Part B plan. Such activities include spying, sabotage, treason, and conspiracy to establish a dictatorship. [Soc. Sec. Act § 202(u); 42 C.F.R. § 407.10(b).]

[¶ 310] Enrollment in Medicare Part B

An individual is automatically enrolled in Medicare Part B if he or she is entitled to Part A and resides in the United States (except in Puerto Rico). The Social Security Administration (SSA) notifies individuals who are automatically enrolled and gives them at least two months to decline enrollment. An individual can decline enrollment by submitting a signed statement to the SSA or CMS before the enrollment begins or by the deadline given in the notice of enrollment. Those who do not decline coverage before it is scheduled to begin are deemed to have automatically enrolled. If an individual declines immediate enrollment, he or she must later file a signed written enrollment request during an initial, general, or special enrollment period (see ¶ 311 for a discussion of enrollment periods). [Soc. Sec. Act § 1837(f); 42 C.F.R. § 407.17.]

Request for Enrollment in Part B

A request for enrollment is required of an individual who meets the eligibility requirements of 42 C.F.R. § 407.10 (see ¶ 300) if he or she:

(1) is not entitled to Part A;

(2) previously declined enrollment in Part B;

(3) had a previous period of Part B entitlement that terminated;

(4) resides in Puerto Rico or outside the United States; or

(5) is enrolling or reenrolling during a special enrollment period under 42 C.F.R. § 407.20.

[42 C.F.R. § 407.22(a).]

A written request for enrollment must be signed by the individual or someone acting on his or her behalf and filed during the initial enrollment period, a general enrollment period, or a special enrollment period. [Soc. Sec. Act § 1837; 42 C.F.R. § 407.22(b).]

To request enrollment, an individual may complete one of the following CMS forms (which may be obtained by mail from CMS or at any local SSA office): (1) Application for Enrollment in the Supplementary Medical Insurance Program (CMS-4040 or CMS 40-D); (2) Application for Medical Insurance (CMS-40-B or CMS 40-F); or (3) Application for Hospital Insurance Entitlement (CMS-18-F-5). Alternatively, an individual may request enrollment by either answering the Part B enrollment questions on an application for monthly Social Security benefits or signing a simple statement of request. [42 C.F.R. § 407.11.]

Medicare Card

As evidence of coverage and entitlement to Part A and/or Part B benefits, CMS issues each beneficiary a Medicare card. This card gives the beneficiary's name, Medicare number, sex, and effective date of entitlement—the beginning dates of the beneficiary's Part A and

Part B coverage. [*Medicare General Information, Eligibility, and Entitlement Manual*, Pub. 100-01, Ch. 2, § 50.] For more information on insurance cards, see ¶ 200.

Enrollment Rights Prejudiced by Governmental Fault

When an individual's enrollment rights under Part B (or voluntary enrollment rights under Part A) have been prejudiced because of the action, inaction, misrepresentation, or error on the part of the federal government or its instrumentalities, the Secretary is authorized to provide the equitable relief necessary to correct or eliminate the effects of these inequities, including: (1) designation of a special initial or general enrollment period; (2) designation of an entitlement period based on that enrollment period; (3) adjustment of premiums; and/or (4) any other remedial action that may be necessary to correct or eliminate the effects of the error, misrepresentation, or inaction. An official record or other evidence must show that the individual took reasonable appropriate and timely measures to assert his or her rights, and due to administrative fault or other action his or her rights have been or are likely to be impaired unless relief is given. [Soc. Sec. Act § 1837(h); 42 C.F.R. § 407.32; Pub. 100-01, Ch. 2, § 40.8.]

[¶ 311] Enrollment Periods for Medicare Part B

Enrollment in Medicare Part B can be accomplished only during an enrollment period. There are three kinds of enrollment periods:

(1) the "initial enrollment period," which is based on the date when an individual first meets the eligibility requirements for enrollment (see ¶ 300);

(2) the "general enrollment period," for individuals that missed their initial enrollment period or whose enrollment was terminated; and

(3) special enrollment periods for volunteers, TRICARE beneficiaries, and Medicare-eligible individuals who wish to delay enrollment because of a duplicative coverage under an employer's group health plan.

[Soc. Sec. Act § 1837; 42 C.F.R. § 407.12.]

An individual who fails to enroll during the initial enrollment period or whose enrollment has been terminated may enroll thereafter only during a general enrollment period or, if he or she meets the specified conditions, during a special enrollment period. There is no limit on how often an individual can unenroll and re-enroll. [42 C.F.R. §§ 407.12(a)(2), 407.30(b).]

Part B Initial Enrollment Period

The "initial enrollment period" begins with the first day of the third month before the month in which the individual first meets the eligibility requirements (see ¶ 300 for Part B eligibility requirements) and ends seven months later. For example, an individual first meeting the eligibility requirements in July 2020 would have a seven-month enrollment period beginning April 1, 2020, and ending October 31, 2020. An individual age 65 qualifying solely on the basis of hospital insurance entitlement is deemed to meet the eligibility requirements on the first day on which he or she becomes entitled to hospital insurance benefits. [Soc. Sec. Act § 1837(d); 42 C.F.R. § 407.14(a).]

The initial enrollment period for disability beneficiaries cannot be determined on the basis of attainment of age 65. The initial enrollment period for an individual eligible for Part B by reason of entitlement to disability benefits for a period of 24 months will begin on the first day of the third month before the 25th month of entitlement to disability benefits. Enrollment periods will recur with each continuous period of eligibility and upon attainment of age 65. [Soc. Sec. Act § 1837(g)(1).]

The Social Security Administration (SSA) or CMS will establish a deemed initial enrollment period for an individual who fails to enroll during the initial enrollment period because of a belief, based on erroneous documentary evidence, that he or she had not yet attained age 65. The period will be established as though the individual had attained age 65 on the date indicated by the incorrect information. [Soc. Sec. Act § 1837(d); 42 C.F.R. § 407.14(b).]

In most cases, individuals who do not enroll in the supplementary medical insurance program within a year of the close of their initial enrollment period are required to pay a permanently increased premium. Individuals who drop out of the program and re-enroll later also will have to pay an increased premium in most cases. [Soc. Sec. Act § 1839(b).] Increased premiums are discussed at ¶ 320.

Part B General Enrollment Period

The law also provides a "general enrollment period" for those who failed to enroll in their initial enrollment period or terminated their enrollment but want to re-enroll. The general enrollment period is from January 1 through March 31 of each year. [Soc. Sec. Act § 1837(e); 42 C.F.R. § 407.15(a).]

Medicare coverage begins on the July 1 following enrollment during a general enrollment period (see ¶ 313 for coverage periods). [*Medicare General Information, Eligibility, and Entitlement Manual*, Pub. 100-01, Ch. 2, § 40.3.2.]

Example • • • _____

Bud Green became a Social Security beneficiary when he reached age 65 in May 2019. His initial enrollment period was February 1, 2019, through August 31, 2019. Because he failed to enroll during this period, his next chance to enroll was during the next general enrollment period, January 1, 2020, through March 31, 2020. Assuming that he also fails to enroll in 2020, he may now enroll during any subsequent general enrollment period (January 1 to March 31 of each year), but he will be required to pay an increased premium due to his late enrollment (see ¶ 320).

Part B Special Enrollment Periods

In addition to the initial and general enrollment periods, select groups can accomplish enrollment during a special enrollment period. Such special enrollment periods apply to certain individuals covered under an employer group health plan, volunteers, and TRICARE beneficiaries. [Soc. Sec. Act § 1837; 42 C.F.R. §§ 407.20, 407.21.]

Employer group health plans. Elderly or disabled employees and their spouses who receive primary health coverage under an employer group health plan, as discussed at ¶ 636, are not required to enroll in the same enrollment period applicable to other individuals. They may wish to delay enrollment because Part B benefits might duplicate the employer plan's benefits. A special enrollment period applicable to these individuals is available for eight full months after they terminate participation in the employer plan (or six months in the case of disabled individuals whose group plan is involuntarily terminated). This does not apply to individuals with end-stage renal disease (ESRD). [Soc. Sec. Act § 1837(i); 42 C.F.R. § 407.20(b).]

If the individual enrolls in the first month of the special enrollment period, coverage begins on the first day of that month. If enrollment occurs in a later month, coverage will begin on the first day of the following month. [Soc. Sec. Act § 1838(e).]

¶311

Volunteers. Beneficiaries who volunteer outside of the United States for at least 12 months through a program sponsored by a tax-exempt organization also may enroll during a special enrollment period if they can demonstrate health coverage while serving in the program. This also includes individuals who terminated enrollment while in a volunteer program. The special enrollment period is the six-month period beginning on the first day of the month that includes the date that the individual no longer satisfies these requirements. The coverage period for an individual enrolling during this type of special enrollment period begins on the first day of the month following the month in which he or she enrolls. [Soc. Sec. Act §§ 1837(k), 1838(f); 42 C.F.R. § 407.21.]

TRICARE beneficiaries. TRICARE is a managed health care program for active duty and retired members of the uniformed services and their families and survivors. A special Part B enrollment period applies for military retirees, their spouses (including widows/widowers), and their dependent children, who are otherwise eligible for TRICARE and entitled to Medicare Part A based on disability or ESRD, but who have declined Part B by not enrolling during their initial enrollment period for Medicare. These individuals may elect to enroll in Medicare Part B during the 12-month period beginning on the day after the last day of the initial enrollment period of the individual or, if later, the 12-month period beginning with the month the individual is notified of deemed enrollment in Medicare Part A. This special enrollment period may be used only once during an individual's lifetime. The Medicare Part B late enrollment penalty will not apply to individuals who enroll during this special enrollment period. [Soc. Sec. Act §§ 1837(l), 1839(b).]

[¶ 313] Part B Coverage Period

The Part B coverage period of an individual enrolled in the Part B program is the period during which the individual is entitled to Part B benefits and obligated to make premium payments. The start date of the coverage period depends on the type of enrollment period used to accomplish enrollment and the date of the enrollee's Part B eligibility. [Soc. Sec. Act § 1838(a); 42 C.F.R. § 407.25.]

Enrollment during initial enrollment period. For an individual who enrolls in an initial enrollment period, coverage begins:

(1) the first month of eligibility, if the individual enrolls during the first three months of the initial enrollment period;

(2) the first month after the month of enrollment, if an individual enrolls during the fourth month of the initial enrollment period;

(3) the second month after the month of enrollment, if the individual enrolls during the fifth month of the initial enrollment period;

(4) the third month after the month of enrollment, if the individual enrolls in either of the last two months of the initial enrollment period.

[Soc. Sec. Act § 1838(a); 42 C.F.R. § 407.25(a).]

Example • • • _____

Donna first meets the eligibility requirements for enrollment in April. Therefore, the initial enrollment period runs from January through July of that year. Depending upon the month of enrollment, the coverage period will begin as follows:

Enrolls in—	Coverage period begins on—
Initial enrollment period:	
January	April 1 (month eligibility requirements first met)
February	April 1

Enrolls in—	Coverage period begins on—
March	April 1
April	May 1 (month following month of enrollment)
May	July 1 (second month after month of enrollment)
June	September 1 (third month after month of enrollment)
July	October 1 (third month after month of enrollment)

Enrollment or reenrollment during general enrollment period. If an individual enrolls or reenrolls during a general enrollment period, entitlement begins on July 1 of that calendar year. [42 C.F.R. § 407.25(b).]

Automatically enrolled individuals. An individual who becomes entitled to Social Security benefits and establishes entitlement to Medicare Part A by filing an application and meeting all other requirements during any one of the first three months of his or her initial enrollment period is deemed to have enrolled in Part B in the third month of the initial enrollment period. An individual who becomes entitled to Medicare Part A on the basis of an application filed during the last four months of his or her seven-month initial enrollment period will be deemed to have enrolled automatically in the month in which he or she files the application. [Soc. Sec. Act § 1837(g)(2)(B), (g)(3); 42 C.F.R. § 407.18(b), (c).]

An individual who defers establishing entitlement to Part A benefits until after the end of his or her initial enrollment period will be deemed to have enrolled for Part B coverage on the first day of the next general enrollment period. If an individual establishes entitlement to Part A on the basis of an application filed during a Part B general enrollment period, he or she is automatically enrolled on the first day of that period. [42 C.F.R. § 407.18(d), (e); *Medicare General Information, Eligibility, and Entitlement Manual*, Pub. 100-01, Ch. 2, § 40.2.]

[¶ 318] Termination of Medicare Part B Coverage

Medicare Part B coverage period continues until coverage is terminated. In addition to termination of coverage upon the death of a beneficiary, a beneficiary can terminate coverage by: (1) filing a written notice that he or she no longer wishes to participate in Part B; or (2) failing to pay the Part B premium. For individuals under age 65, entitlement to Medicare Part B will end when the individual's entitlement to Part A ends unless Part B coverage was terminated because the beneficiary filed a notice requesting termination or failed to pay the premium. [Soc. Sec. Act § 1838(b); 42 C.F.R. § 407.27.]

Notice of termination. If an individual gives written notice that he or she no longer wishes to participate in Part B, entitlement ends at the end of the month after the month in which the individual files the disenrollment request. A termination request filed by an individual deemed to have enrolled automatically before the month in which Part B coverage becomes effective will cancel the coverage. If an automatically enrolled individual files a notice requesting termination in or after the month in which coverage becomes effective, the termination takes effect at the close of the month following the month in which the notice is filed. [Soc. Sec. Act § 1838(b); 42 C.F.R. § 407.27(c).]

Nonpayment of premiums. A termination for nonpayment of premiums will take effect with the end of the grace period during which the overdue premiums may be paid and coverage continued. [Soc. Sec. Act § 1838(b); 42 C.F.R. § § 407.27(d), 408.8(c).]

Disability beneficiaries. In the case of an individual entitled to Medicare on the basis of 24 or more months of disability rather than on the basis of having reached age 65,

¶318

coverage and enrollment under Part B ends with the close of the last month for which the individual is entitled to Part A benefits. [Soc. Sec. Act § 1838(c).]

Reenrollment. An individual whose enrollment has terminated may reenroll only during a general enrollment period or a special enrollment period, if the requirements are met (see ¶ 311). There is no limit on how often an individual can unenroll and reenroll. [42 C.F.R. § § 407.12(a)(2), 407.30(b).]

[¶ 320] Medicare Part B Premiums

The following table shows the standard monthly premium rates in effect under the Part B program during the past several years:

Year	Premium
2020	144.60
2019	135.50
2018	134.00

[*Notice*, 84 FR 61625, Nov. 13, 2019; *Notice*, 83 FR 52462, Oct. 17, 2018.]

The standard monthly Part B premium rate for all enrollees for 2020 is $144.60, which is equal to 50 percent of the monthly actuarial rate for aged enrollees (or approximately 25 percent of the expected average total cost of Part B coverage for aged enrollees) plus $3.00. [*Notice*, 84 FR 61625, Nov. 13, 2019.]

The federal government is required by statute to supplement the remainder of Part B costs out of general revenues. [Soc. Sec. Act § 1844(a).] At times, premium rates have been set by statute rather than by the actuarial formula. [Soc. Sec. Act § 1839(b).]

Calculation. The Part B premium rate is calculated on a calendar year basis and is announced each fall for the forthcoming year, along with a public statement of actuarial assumptions or other bases for any rate change. [Soc. Sec. Act § 1839(a)(3); 42 C.F.R. § 408.20.]

Beneficiaries "held harmless." In the case of an individual who has his or her premium deducted from his or her Social Security check, if there is a Social Security cost-of-living adjustment that is less than the amount of the increased premiums, the premium increase otherwise applicable will be reduced to avoid a reduction in the individual's Social Security check. [Soc. Sec. Act § 1839(a)(5), (f); 42 C.F.R. § 408.6(a)(2)(ii).]

Income-Related Monthly Adjustment for Part B

Beneficiaries with modified adjusted gross incomes (MAGIs) above a specified threshold must pay a higher percentage of the cost of Medicare Part B medical coverage than those with MAGIs below the threshold. This beneficiary premium adjustment is called an income-related monthly adjustment amount (IRMAA). [Soc. Sec. Act § 1839(i); 20 C.F.R. § 418.1120; 42 C.F.R. § 408.28.]

CMS uses MAGI and federal income tax filing status for the tax year two years before the effective year to determine whether a beneficiary must pay an IRMAA, and if so, how much. If information is not yet available for the tax year two years before the effective year, CMS uses information from the tax year three years before the effective year until the later information becomes available. [20 C.F.R. § 418.1135.]

In 2020, if the modified adjusted gross income of an individual is—

- more than $87,000, but not more than $109,000, the monthly premium is $202.40;

- more than $109,000 but not more than $136,000, the monthly premium is $289.20;

- more than $136,000 but not more than $163,000, the monthly premium is $376.00;

  - more than $163,000 but less than $500,000, the monthly premium is $462.70;

  - at least $500,000, the monthly premium is $491.60.

For beneficiaries who file a joint tax return with income—

  - less than or equal to $174,000, there is no IRMAA and the monthly premium is $144.60 per beneficiary;

  - greater than $174,000 and less than or equal to $218,000, the monthly premium is $202.40 per beneficiary;

  - greater than $218,000 and less than or equal to $272,000, the monthly premium is $289.20 per beneficiary;

  - greater than $272,000 and less than or equal to $326,000, the monthly premium is $376.00 per beneficiary;

  - greater than $326,000, and less than $750,000, the monthly premium is $462.70 per beneficiary;

  - greater than or equal to $750,000, the monthly premium is $491.60 per beneficiary.

For beneficiaries who are married and lived with their spouse at any time during the taxable year but file a separate return with income—

  - less than or equal to $87,000, there is no IRMAA and the monthly premium is $144.60;

  - greater than $87,000 and less than $413,000, the monthly premium is $462.70;

  - greater than or equal to $413,000, the monthly premium is $491.60.

[Soc. Sec. Act § 1839(i)(3)(C), as amended by the Bipartisan Budget Act of 2018 § 53114(a), (b); 20 C.F.R. § 418.1120; *Notice*, 84 FR 61625, Nov. 13, 2019.]

Inflation adjustment. Beginning in 2008 (but excluding 2018 and 2019), each dollar amount in Soc. Sec. Act § 1839(i)(2) or (3) is increased by an amount equal to the dollar amount multiplied by the percentage by which the average of the Consumer Price Index for all urban consumers (U.S. city average) for the 12-month period ending with August of the preceding calendar year exceeds the average for the 12-month period ending with August 2006 (or, in the case of a calendar year beginning with 2020, August 2018). [Soc. Sec. Act § 1839(i)(5)(A).]

Effective February 9, 2018, the inflation adjustment does not apply to each dollar amount in Soc. Sec. Act § 1839(i)(3) of $500,000. Beginning in 2028, each dollar amount of $500,000 in the individual modified adjusted gross income chart will be increased by an amount equal to the dollar amount multiplied by the percentage by which the average of the Consumer Price Index for all urban consumers (United States city average) for the 12-month period ending with August of the preceding calendar year exceeds the average for the 12-month period ending with August 2026. [Soc. Sec. Act § 1839(i)(5)(C), as amended by Bipartisan Budget Act of 2018 § 53114(c).]

Major life-changing events. If a beneficiary provides evidence that a qualifying major life-changing event significantly reduced his or her MAGI, CMS determines the IRMAA based on data from a more recent tax year. CMS defines a significant reduction in MAGI as any change that results in a reduction or elimination of IRMAA. [20 C.F.R. §§ 418.1201, 418.1215.]

¶320

Qualifying major life-changing events include marriage, the termination of marriage, reduced hours or stoppage of work, certain reductions in income, the receipt of certain settlement payments from employers, and loss of investment property as a result of fraud, theft, or the criminal acts of a third party. [Soc. Sec. Act § 1839(i)(4)(C)(ii)(II); 20 C.F.R. §§ 418.1205, 418.1210.]

When a beneficiary asks CMS to use a more recent tax year to calculate an IRMAA based on certain changes in circumstance, he or she is required to provide documentary evidence to demonstrate that the event is a qualifying change in circumstance. [20 C.F.R. § 418.1255.]

Increased Premium for Late Enrollment

If an individual who enrolls after the "initial enrollment period" (see ¶ 311) or re-enrolls after terminating enrollment, the monthly premium otherwise applicable will be increased by 10 percent for each full 12 months (in the same "continuous period of eligibility") in which the individual could have been, but was not, enrolled. For these purposes, the length of the period of delay is computed by totalling:

(1) the months that elapsed between the close of the initial enrollment period and the close of the enrollment period in which enrollment occurred, plus

(2) in the case of an individual who re-enrolls, the months that elapsed between the date of the termination of the previous coverage period and the close of the enrollment period in which reenrollment occurred. Any premium that is not a multiple of 10 cents is rounded to the nearest multiple of 10 cents.

[Soc. Sec. Act § 1839(b), (c); 42 C.F.R. §§ 408.22, 408.27.]

The beginning of a disabled individual's "continuous period of eligibility" serves as the beginning of an initial enrollment period for purposes of determining whether the premium increase applicable to late enrollees should apply. In general, a "continuous period of eligibility" is:

(1) the period beginning with the first day a person is eligible to enroll in Part B (see ¶ 300) and ending with the person's death; or

(2) a period during all of which an individual is entitled to disability benefits that ended in or before the month preceding the month in which the individual became 65 years of age.

[Soc. Sec. Act § 1839(d).]

Examples• • • _____

(1) Paul Jones was eligible to enroll in an initial enrollment period that ended May 31, 2017. He actually enrolled in the general enrollment period January 1, 2019, through March 31, 2019. There were 22 months between the close of his initial enrollment period (May 31, 2017) and the close of the period in which he actually enrolled (March 31, 2019). Because there was only one full 12-month period during which he could have been, but was not, enrolled, his premium was (permanently) increased 10 percent.

(2) Marlene Blum became age 65 in July 2008 and first enrolled in March 2010. She paid premiums increased by 10 percent above the regular rate because there was one 12-month period (17 total months) between the end of her initial enrollment period, October 2008 (see ¶ 311), and the end of the general enrollment period, March 2010, in which she actually enrolled. A few years later, she failed to pay the premiums and her coverage was terminated (after the end of her grace period) on June 30, 2015. She enrolled for a second time in January 2016.

Added to her previous 17 months of delinquency is the period of nine months between July 2015 through March 2016 (the end of the general enrollment period in which she reenrolled), for a total of 26 months. Because this amounts to two full 12-month periods, her monthly premium is (permanently) increased 20 percent.

(3) John Foley was late in enrolling by 38 months. Accordingly, his Part B premium was permanently increased by 30 percent. Thus, in 2020, when the standard premium is $144.60 per month, he is required to pay $187.98 per month ($144.60 × 130 percent = $187.98).

Group health plans. Elderly and disabled employees and their spouses who delay enrollment in the Part B program because they elect primary health coverage under an employer group health plan have a special enrollment period applicable only to them (see ¶ 311). Therefore, the months in which they are enrolled in such a plan are not counted in determining the penalty for delinquent enrollment. [Soc. Sec. Act § 1837(i).]

International volunteers. Beneficiaries who volunteer outside of the United States for at least 12 months through a program sponsored by a tax-exempt organization also have a special enrollment period and will not incur a delayed enrollment penalty. [Soc. Sec. Act § 1839(b).]

State premium payments. Under federal-state "buy-in" agreements, state Medicaid programs enroll and pay the premiums of individuals meeting the Part B eligibility requirements. State and local governments that no longer offer health benefits packages to their employees may make periodic lump sum payments for the Part B late enrollment premium surcharges assessed to retired employees who consequently enroll or reenroll in the Medicare program. [42 C.F.R. § 408.202.]

Other special cases. There are other special rules concerning late Part B enrollment penalties applicable to the following groups: (1) aliens who first met the five-year residency requirement after attaining age 65, (2) merchant seamen, and (3) certain TRICARE and CHAMPUS beneficiaries. [Soc. Sec. Act §§ 1818, 1837(i); Tax Equity and Fiscal Responsibility Act of 1982 (P.L. 97-248) § 125.]

Liability for Part B Premiums

A monthly premium is due for each month in an individual's coverage period. A monthly premium is due for the month of death, if coverage was not previously ended, even if the individual dies on the first day of the month. Any premiums owed, including premiums for each month of the grace period, if applicable, will be collected by deduction from subsequent Social Security or Railroad Retirement benefits payable to the individual, or offset against any Part B payments due an individual as reimbursement. Premium arrears constitute an obligation enforceable against the enrollee or his or her estate. [Soc. Sec. Act § 1840(g); 42 C.F.R. §§ 408.40, 408.110.]

Refund of excess premiums. Premiums received for any month after the month in which a Part B enrollee dies are refunded. Refunds are paid to: (1) the person or persons who paid the premiums; (2) the legal representative of the estate, if the enrollee paid the premiums before death; or (3) the person or persons in the priorities specified in the law, if there is no person meeting the requirements in (1) or (2). [Soc. Sec. Act § 1870(g); 42 C.F.R. § 408.112.]

Collection and Payment of Part B Premiums

Social Security and railroad retirement beneficiaries, and civil service annuitants—except those enrolled by a state as public assistance recipients—have their premiums

¶320

deducted, when possible, from their monthly benefit, annuity, or pension checks paid in the preceding month. [Soc. Sec. Act § 1840(a)–(d); 42 C.F.R. § 408.40.]

The premiums of public assistance recipients enrolled under a state "buy-in" agreement are paid by the state that enrolled them. [Soc. Sec. Act § § 1840(h), 1843; 42 C.F.R. § 408.6(c).]

Direct payment must be made by individuals who are: (1) not entitled to a monthly cash Social Security benefit, a railroad retirement annuity or pension, or a federal civil service annuity; or (2) entitled to one of these benefits, but for some reason the benefit cannot be paid during the period in question. These individuals are sent premium notices, together with a card and envelope for use in sending payment to the proper servicing center. [42 C.F.R. § 408.60 *et seq.*]

Failure to Pay Part B Premiums

CMS terminates a beneficiary's enrollment for nonpayment of premiums. [Soc. Sec. Act § 1838(b).]

Grace period. There is a grace period extending from the date payment is due through the last day of the third month following the month in which such payment is due. For example, if an enrollee's premium payment became due on March 1, 2020, the grace period would extend to June 30, 2020. If payment is made before the end of the grace period, it is considered timely, and coverage and enrollment continue. If the beneficiary does not make payment on or before the end of the grace period, coverage and enrollment terminate. A decision to terminate enrollment is not made until 15 days after the last day of the grace period. [42 C.F.R. § § 408.8(a), (c), 408.100.]

The initial grace period may be extended for up to an additional three months if there is a finding that the enrollee had good cause for not paying the overdue premiums during the initial grace period. Good cause will be found if the enrollee establishes that the failure to pay within the initial grace period was due to conditions over which he or she had no control or reasonably could not have been expected to foresee. [Soc. Sec. Act § 1838(b); 42 C.F.R. § 408.8(d).] For example, good cause may be found if the enrollee was mentally or physically incapable of paying premiums on a timely basis or had some reasonable basis to believe that payment had been made, or if the failure to pay was due to administrative error. [*Medicare General Information, Eligibility, and Entitlement Manual*, Pub. 100-01, Ch. 2, § 40.7.4.]

Reinstatement. Coverage may be reinstated without interruption of benefits if the enrollee: (1) appeals the termination of benefits by the end of the month following the month in which the notice of termination was sent; (2) alleges, and it is found to be true, that he or she did not receive timely and adequate notice that the payments were overdue; and (3) within 30 days of a subsequent request for payment, pays all premiums due through the month in which the enrollee appealed the termination. If the evidence establishes that the enrollee acted diligently to pay the premiums and the delay in payment was not the fault of the enrollee or if the enrollee reasonably believed that the premiums were being paid by deduction from benefits or by some other means, coverage may be reinstated. Coverage may not be reinstated if it is found that the enrollee failed to make payment within the grace period due to insufficient income or the termination was appealed more than one month after the termination notice was sent. [42 C.F.R. § § 408.102, 408.104.]

Benefits

[¶ 330] Part B Benefits: In General

Medicare medical insurance benefits (Part B) supplement the coverage provided by Medicare hospital insurance benefits (Part A). Part A covers inpatient institutional services at hospitals, skilled nursing facilities, hospices, and home health services after hospitalization. Part B covers the services of physicians and other health practitioners, as well as a variety of "medical and other health services" not covered under Part A. The kinds of "medical and other health services" included in Part B are described beginning at ¶ 340.

Other services covered under Part B include: (1) ambulatory surgical center services (see ¶ 386); (2) home health services (see ¶ 383); and (3) comprehensive outpatient rehabilitation facility services (see ¶ 385).

Methods of Payment

In general, there are two methods of payment for items or services covered by the Medicare program:

(1) Medicare pays the provider or facility on the patient's behalf for services including hospital and skilled nursing care, home health services, medical and other health services, outpatient physical therapy services, and rural health clinic services, among others. [Soc. Sec. Act § 1832(a)(2); 42 C.F.R. § 410.150.] The provider or facility files the claim for payment, and the patient's obligation is fully satisfied once he or she has paid any required deductible or coinsurance amounts (see ¶ 335). The Medicare payment amount is based on prospective payment rates, reasonable costs, fee schedules, and in some cases, competitive bidding by providers (see ¶ 800 *et seq.*).

(2) In the case of all other Part B services, Medicare may pay the provider or the patient. If assignment is accepted, Medicare pays the supplier or practitioner, and the patient's obligation is fully satisfied once he or she has paid any required deductible or coinsurance amounts (see ¶ 868). If the supplier or practitioner does not accept assignment, Medicare pays the patient, and the patient is responsible for paying the supplier or practitioner.

[Soc. Sec. Act § 1832(a)(1); 42 C.F.R. § 424.53(e).]

Medicare payment and assignment rules are discussed in Chapter 8.

Limitations on Part B Coverage

Benefits provided under the Part B program have limitations. Financial limitations include an annual deductible and 20 percent coinsurance payments applicable to most services covered under Part B, as well as a deductible for the cost of outpatient blood transfusions (see ¶ 335).

Benefits are limited to named items and services listed as covered by the Medicare program. Coverage is often limited to certain kinds of services or frequencies and must be reasonable and necessary for the diagnosis or symptoms presented by the beneficiary. In addition, a number of items and services are listed as excluded from Medicare coverage. Exclusions are discussed in Chapter 6.

Payment also may not be made under Part B for services furnished to an individual if he or she is entitled to have payment made for those services under Part A. [Soc. Sec. Act § 1833(d).] In general, all services provided to an inpatient of a hospital will be paid for by Part A if they are covered Medicare services, with the exception of certain services that are only covered under Part B, such as physician services, the influenza vaccine, and screening mammography, among others. [*Medicare Benefit Policy Manual*, Pub. 100-02, Ch. 6, § 10.]

[¶ 335] Deductible and Coinsurance

In addition to the monthly premium charged to individuals enrolled in Part B (see ¶ 320), an annual deductible and a 20 percent "coinsurance" or "copayment" normally are required. The Part B deductible is $198 for 2020. It was $185 for 2019. The law requires the

¶335

deductible to be indexed to the growth in Part B expenditures. [Soc. Sec. Act § 1833(b); *Notice*, 84 FR 61625, Nov. 13, 2019; *Notice*, 83 FR 52462, Oct. 17, 2018.]

Application of the Deductible and Coinsurance

The Part B annual deductible applies only to services covered by Medicare. If the deductible is not applied because the service is not covered or because the service is included in the list under "Exceptions to Deductible and Coinsurance Requirements" below, the deductible for that year remains unsatisfied. [42 C.F.R. § 410.160.]

The deductible is satisfied by the initial expenses incurred in each calendar year. Even in cases in which an individual is not eligible for the entire calendar year (for example, when coverage begins after the first month of the year), the individual is subject to the full deductible. The date of service generally determines when expenses were incurred, but expenses are allocated to the deductible in the order in which the bills are received by the Medicare administrative contractor administering the Part B program. [*Medicare General Information, Eligibility, and Entitlement Manual*, Pub. 100-01, Ch. 3, § 20.2.]

Medicare patients normally are required to pay 20 percent of the cost of each Medicare covered service, their coinsurance amount. Medicare pays the other 80 percent. For Medicare purposes, the cost of a Medicare service is the "Medicare-approved charge" for that service. The coinsurance percentage applies to the Medicare-approved charge. [Soc. Sec. Act § 1833(a), (b).]

Examples••• _____

(1) Robert White visited his doctor in January 2020 for his annual routine checkup, which is covered as his annual "wellness visit." No deductible or copayment applies. In February, a dental checkup, which indicated that Mr. White's teeth were in good condition, cost $150. Later in the year, it was discovered that he had high blood pressure. Successive visits to the doctor during the remainder of the year in connection with the treatment for this condition resulted in a total of $600 in Medicare-approved charges for the doctor's services. The $150 for the dental checkup cannot be counted toward Mr. White's Part B deductible because it is not a covered expense. Services in connection with the care and treatment of teeth or structures directly supporting the teeth are generally not covered, with some exceptions such as treatment of an oral infection (see ¶ 634). Of the remaining $600 in covered expenses, $198 satisfies the deductible for the year and 80 percent of the remaining $402 ($321.60) is paid by Medicare. Mr. White's charges total $428 ($150 (noncovered dental checkup) + $198 deductible + $80 coinsurance).

Note the exception to deductible and copayments for prevention services described below.

(2) Sarah visits her doctor in 2020 and has various clinical diagnostic laboratory tests performed in the doctor's office lab. Because the doctor accepts assignment for these tests and is paid under the fee schedule applicable to these services, no deductible (or coinsurance) is required for the lab tests. Later, Sarah visits the doctor on another matter, incurring $250 in Medicare-approved charges for the doctor's services. She then has to pay the $198 deductible and an additional $13 as coinsurance ([$250 – $198] × 20 percent = $10).

Exceptions to Deductible and Coinsurance Requirements

Several exceptions apply to the deductible and coinsurance requirements.

Noncovered services. No deductible or coinsurance is required for items or services that are not reasonable and medically necessary. If the provider knew, or should have known, that Medicare considered such services medically unnecessary, but failed to inform the beneficiary before furnishing them, the provider is held liable for their cost. If the beneficiary made payment for such items or services, he or she can be indemnified for them. [Pub. 100-01, Ch. 3, § 20.4.1.]

Clinical diagnostic laboratory tests. Generally, neither the annual deductible nor the 20 percent coinsurance applies to: (1) clinical laboratory tests performed by a physician, laboratory, or other entity paid on an assigned basis; (2) specimen collection fees; or (3) travel allowance related to laboratory tests. [*Medicare Claims Processing Manual*, Pub. 100-04, Ch. 16, § § 30.2, 30.3.]

Home health services. No deductible or coinsurance generally is applied to home health services. When a home health agency furnishes services that are not included in the definition of "home health services," however, the deductible and coinsurance do apply. The coinsurance also applies to supplies, drugs, durable medical equipment, and prosthetics/orthotics furnished by home health agencies. [Soc. Sec. Act § 1833(a)(1), (a)(2)(A), (b)(2); Pub. 100-01, Ch. 3, § 20.4.]

Donation of kidney for transplant surgery. There are no deductible or coinsurance requirements with respect to services furnished to an individual who donates a kidney for transplant surgery. [42 C.F.R. § 410.163.]

Federally qualified health center services. No deductible is required for federally qualified health center services (see ¶ 382). [Soc. Sec. Act § 1833(b)(4).]

Blood Deductibles

Part B requires a deductible for the expenses incurred during any calendar year for the first three pints of whole blood (or equivalent quantities of packed red blood cells) furnished to outpatients. As in the case of the similar deductible for inpatients under Part A, this deductible is reduced to the extent that the blood (or equivalent quantities of packed red blood cells) has been appropriately replaced. [42 C.F.R. § 410.161.] Satisfaction of the deductible through replacement is discussed in greater detail at ¶ 223.

The blood deductible under Part B is not required to the extent it has been satisfied under Part A. [Soc. Sec. Act § § 1813(a)(2), 1833(b).]

"Welcome to Medicare" Exam and Preventive Services

No deductible applies to an initial preventive physical exam (IPPE), also called the "Welcome to Medicare" exam (see ¶ 369), including IPPE services rendered in rural health clinics. Similarly, no deductible is required for screening mammography services, screening pap smears, screening pelvic exams, ultrasound screening for abdominal aortic aneurysm, or colorectal cancer screening tests. [Soc. Sec. Act § 1833(b); 42 C.F.R. § § 410.152(l)(12), 410.160(b)(9).]

Coinsurance amounts are waived for most preventive services, including medical nutrition therapy, IPPEs, and personalized preventive plan services in connection with an annual wellness visit. [Soc. Sec. Act § 1833(a)(1)(B), (W), (X), (Y), (b)(1).]

Pneumococcal and influenza vaccines. Pneumococcal and influenza vaccines and their administration are covered without imposition of deductible or coinsurance requirements. [Soc. Sec. Act § § 1833(a)(1)(B), (b)(1), 1861(s)(10)(A).]

[¶ 340] Medical and Other Health Services

The law divides the kinds of services covered under Part B into various categories, one of which is "medical and other health services" (see ¶ 330). [Soc. Sec. Act § 1832(a).]

"Medical and other health services" includes the following items or services identified at Soc. Sec. Act § 1861(s):

(1) physicians' services (see ¶ 350);

(2) services and supplies furnished incident to a physician's professional services, of kinds that commonly are furnished in physicians' offices and that commonly either are rendered without charge or are included in the physician's bills (see ¶ 351);

(3) hospital services (including drugs and biologics that are not usually self-administered by the patient) incident to physicians' services (see ¶ 352) rendered to outpatients, and partial hospitalization services incident to such services (see ¶ 387);

(4) outpatient diagnostic services furnished by a hospital (see ¶ 352);

(5) outpatient physical and occupational therapy and speech-language pathology services (see ¶ 381);

(6) rural health clinic and federally qualified health center services (see ¶ 382);

(7) home dialysis supplies and equipment, self-care home dialysis support services, institutional dialysis services and supplies, renal dialysis services, and kidney disease education services (see ¶ 389);

(8) services of nonphysician health care practitioners, including physician assistants, nurse practitioners and clinical nurse specialists, certified registered nurse anesthetists and anesthesia assistants, certified nurse-midwives, clinical psychologists, and clinical social workers (see ¶ 351 and ¶ 366);

(9) diagnostic x-ray tests, laboratory tests, and other diagnostic tests (see ¶ 353);

(10) x-ray, radium, and radioactive isotope therapy, including materials and services of technicians (see ¶ 354);

(11) surgical dressings, splints, casts, and other devices used for reduction of fractures and dislocations (see ¶ 359);

(12) durable medical equipment (see ¶ 356);

(13) prosthetic devices (other than dental) that replace all or part of an internal body organ (including colostomy bags and supplies directly related to colostomy care), and replacement of such devices (see ¶ 357);

(14) leg, arm, back, and neck braces, and artificial legs, arms, and eyes (including required adjustments, repairs, and replacements) (see ¶ 357);

(15) certain drugs and biologics, including pneumococcal pneumonia, influenza, and hepatitis B vaccines, antigens, blood clotting factors for hemophilia patients, immunosuppressant therapy drugs furnished to an individual who receives an organ transplant, erythropoietin (EPO) for dialysis patients, oral anti-cancer drugs, anti-emetic drugs used in conjunction with chemotherapy treatments, and intravenous immune globulin administered in the home for the treatment of primary immune deficiency diseases (see ¶ 362);

(16) ambulance services, if the use of other methods of transportation is contraindicated by the individual's condition (see ¶ 355);

(17) certain preventive and screening services (if specifically exempted from the exclusion for routine checkups), including an initial preventive physical exam, personalized prevention plan services, cardiovascular screening blood tests, pap smears, pelvic exams, mammograms, bone mass measurement tests, and screening tests and services for diabetes, colorectal cancer, prostate cancer, and glaucoma (see ¶ 369);

(18) diabetes outpatient self-management training services or medical nutrition therapy services for beneficiaries who have not received diabetes self-management training (see ¶ 369);

(19) therapeutic shoes for individuals with severe diabetic conditions (see ¶ 370 and ¶ 619);

(20) ultrasound screening for abdominal aortic aneurysm (see ¶ 369);

(21) items and services furnished under a cardiac or pulmonary rehabilitation program, or an intensive cardiac rehabilitation program (see ¶ 392);

(22) beginning January 1, 2021, home infusion therapy (see ¶ 390); and

(23) beginning January 1, 2020, opioid use disorder treatment services (see ¶ 394).

[Soc. Sec. Act § 1861(s), as amended by SUPPORT for Patients and Communities Act (P.L. 115-271) § 2005(a); 42 C.F.R. § 410.10.]

All "medical and other health services" provided to an inpatient of a qualified hospital (except for the services of physicians and other practitioners and pneumococcal and hepatitis B vaccine) are paid for by Part A if Part A coverage is available. Payment may not be made under Part B for services furnished to an inpatient if the inpatient is entitled to have payment made for services under Part A. [Soc. Sec. Act § 1833(d); *Medicare Benefit Policy Manual*, Pub. 100-02, Ch. 15, § 10.]

[¶ 350] Physicians' Services

Part B covers reasonable and medically necessary physicians' services. [Soc. Sec. Act §§ 1832(a)(2)(B), 1861(s)(1).] Physicians' services are the professional services performed by physicians for a patient, including diagnosis, therapy, surgery, consultation, and care plan oversight. A service may be considered to be a physician's service when the physician either examines the patient in person or is able to visualize some aspect of the patient's condition without the interposition of a third person's judgment. [42 C.F.R. § 410.20(a), (b); *Medicare Benefit Policy Manual*, Pub. 100-02, Ch. 15, § 30.]

Services by means of a telephone call between a physician and a beneficiary or between a physician and a member of a beneficiary's family are covered under Part B; however, because the physician work resulting from telephone calls is considered to be an integral part of the prework and postwork of other physician services, the fee schedule amount for these services includes payment for the telephone calls. [Pub. 100-02, Ch. 15, § 30B.]

"Concurrent care" refers to services more extensive than consultative services and rendered by more than one physician during a period of time. The reasonable and necessary services of each physician rendering concurrent care may be covered when each physician is required to play an active role in the patient's treatment, for example, because of the existence of more than one medical condition requiring diverse specialized medical services. [Pub. 100-02, Ch. 15, § 30E.]

Part B covers patient-initiated "second opinions" related to the medical need for surgery or for major nonsurgical diagnostic and therapeutic procedures. [Pub. 100-02, Ch. 15, § 30D.]

Physicians' services furnished to a patient are ordinarily paid by Medicare according to the physician fee schedule discussed at ¶ 855.

Medical record documentation. A physician may review and verify (sign/date), rather than re-document, notes in a patient's medical record made by physicians; residents; nurses; medical, physician assistant, and advanced practice registered nurse students; or other members of the medical team including, as applicable, notes documenting the physician's presence and participation in the services. [42 C.F.R. § 410.20(e); *Final rule*, 84 FR 62998, Nov. 15, 2019.]

"Physician" Defined

The term "physician" means a licensed doctor of medicine, osteopathy (including an osteopathic practitioner), dental surgery or dental medicine, podiatric medicine, chiropractic services, or optometry. [Soc. Sec. Act § 1861(q), (r); 42 C.F.R. § 410.20(b).] However, as discussed below, only certain services of dentists, podiatrists, chiropractors, and optometrists are covered. The term "physician" does not include a Christian Science practitioner or naturopath. [*Medicare General Information, Eligibility, and Entitlement Manual*, Pub. 100-01, Ch. 5, § 70.]

For services to be covered as services of a "physician," the doctor performing them must be licensed to practice by the state. Coverage does not extend to services that the practitioner is not legally authorized to perform. For example, if state licensing law limits the scope of practice of osteopaths and osteopathic practitioners to the manipulation of bones and muscles, only these authorized osteopathic services are covered. [Pub. 100-01, Ch. 5, § 70.1.]

Part B Coverage of Dentists' Services

A dentist qualifies as a physician if he or she is a doctor of dental surgery or dental medicine who is legally authorized to practice dentistry by the state in which he or she performs such functions and who is acting within the scope of his or her license when performing such functions. Such services include any otherwise covered service that may legally and alternatively be performed by doctors of medicine, osteopathy, and dentistry, e.g., dental examinations to detect infections prior to certain surgical procedures, treatment of oral infections, and interpretations of diagnostic x-ray examinations in connection with covered services. [Soc. Sec. Act § 1861(r)(2); Pub. 100-01, Ch. 5, § 70.2.]

Because of the general exclusion of payment for dental services (see ¶ 634), payment for the services of dentists is limited to those procedures that are not primarily provided for the care, treatment, removal, or replacement of teeth or structures directly supporting teeth. The coverage or exclusion of any given dental service is not affected by the professional designation of the physician rendering the services; i.e., an excluded dental service remains excluded, and a covered dental service is covered, whether furnished by a dentist or a doctor of medicine or osteopathy. [Pub. 100-01, Ch. 5, § 70.2.]

A dentist also qualifies as a physician for purposes of (1) providing the physician's certification required for inpatient hospital services connected with a dental procedure when the patient requires hospitalization; and (2) performing outpatient ambulatory surgical procedures that can be safely performed on an ambulatory basis in the dentist's office. [42 C.F.R. § 424.13(d)(2).]

A description of inpatient hospital services connected with dental procedures is at ¶ 218.

Part B Coverage of Optometrists' Services

A doctor of optometry is considered a physician for all the covered vision care services he or she is legally authorized to perform in the state in which he or she performs them. To be covered under Medicare, the services must be medically reasonable and necessary for the diagnosis or treatment of illness or injury and meet all applicable coverage requirements. [Soc. Sec. Act § 1861(r)(4); 42 C.F.R. § 410.22; Pub. 100-01, Ch. 5, § 70.5.] Note, however, that many vision care services are excluded from Medicare coverage (see ¶ 619).

Part B Coverage of Podiatrists' Services

A doctor of podiatric medicine is included within the definition of "physician," but only with respect to functions he or she is legally authorized to perform by the state in which he or she performs them. [Soc. Sec. Act § 1861(r)(3); 42 C.F.R. § 410.25; Pub. 100-01, Ch. 5, § 70.3.] Certain types of foot treatment or foot care, however, are excluded from Medicare coverage (see ¶ 619), whether performed by a doctor of medicine or a doctor of podiatric medicine.

A doctor of podiatric medicine also is considered a "physician" with respect to satisfying the physician certification and recertification requirements, for establishing and reviewing a home health plan of treatment, and for utilization review. A podiatrist, however, is not considered a "physician" for purposes of the physician activities required to qualify an institution or organization as a skilled nursing facility. [Pub. 100-01, Ch. 5, § 70.3.]

Part B Coverage of Chiropractors' Services

A chiropractor licensed by the state—or, if the state does not license chiropractors, a chiropractor legally authorized to practice in the jurisdiction in which he or she performs services—is included in the definition of physician, but only with respect to the coverage of his or her own professional services, services and supplies "incident" to the services, and treatment by means of manual manipulation of the spine. In addition, a chiropractor's services are covered only if the treatment is to correct a subluxation demonstrated to exist by x-ray. No reimbursement may be made, however, for x-rays or other diagnostic or therapeutic services furnished or ordered by a chiropractor. [Soc. Sec. Act § 1861(r)(5); 42 C.F.R. § 410.21; Pub. 100-01, Ch. 5, § 70.6.]

Provider-Based Physician Services

The services of hospital- and other provider-based physicians (e.g., radiologists, anesthesiologists, and pathologists) include two distinct elements: the professional component and the provider component.

The *professional component* of provider-based physicians' services includes those services directly related to the medical care of the individual patient. Payment for those services is made according to the Medicare physician fee schedule (see ¶ 855) by the Part B Medicare administrative contractor. The *provider component* of provider-based physicians' services includes those services not directly related to the medical care of individual patients (e.g., teaching, administrative, and autopsy services, and other services that benefit the provider's patients as a group). Those services are reimbursed to the provider as provider services under Part A. [Pub. 100-02, Ch. 15, § 30.1.]

Physicians in federal hospitals. Physicians' services performed in hospitals operated by the federal government—military hospitals, Veterans Administration hospitals, and Public Health Service hospitals—are normally reimbursable only when that hospital provides services to the public generally as a community institution. A physician working in the scope of his or her federal employment may be considered as coming within the statutory definition of "physician" even though the physician may not have a license to practice in the state in which he or she is employed. [Pub. 100-01, Ch. 5, § 70.4.]

Interns and residents. The services of interns and residents-in-training provided in the hospital setting as part of an approved training program are normally paid under Part A as hospital services and not under Part B as physicians' services. Services not part of the training program or provided outside the hospital or in the hospital's outpatient department or emergency room are covered under Part B. [42 C.F.R. §§ 415.200–415.208; Pub. 100-01, Ch. 5, § 70.7.]

¶350

Teaching physician services. Physicians teaching or supervising in an approved teaching program are normally regarded as providing Part A provider services, reimbursable to the hospital. If the teaching or supervising physician is the patient's attending physician, however, his or her services usually will be covered under Part B as physicians' services. [Pub. 100-02, Ch. 15, § 30.2.]

Payment for the services of provider-based physicians is discussed in greater detail at ¶ 855.

Psychiatrists and Psychologists

Psychiatrists are medical doctors and their services are covered by Medicare to the same extent as other physicians' services. Note, however, that there are special limits on Medicare coverage of psychiatric services (see ¶ 225 and ¶ 387). Psychiatric services also may be covered as incident to physicians' services as an outpatient hospital benefit (see ¶ 352).

Clinical psychologists generally are not considered physicians. Their services can be covered as incident to physicians' services (see ¶ 351), and their diagnostic services can be covered additionally as "other diagnostic tests" (see ¶ 353). The services of a "qualified psychologist" are covered as a separate Part B benefit (see ¶ 366).

Care Management Services

CMS makes a separate payment for non-face-to-face chronic care management services furnished to patients with multiple chronic conditions that are expected to last at least 12 months or until the death of the patient, and that place the patient at significant risk of death, acute exacerbation/decompensation, or functional decline. [Soc. Sec. Act § 1848(b)(8); *Final rule*, 81 FR 80170, Nov. 15, 2016.]

Part B also covers transitional care management services for a patient whose medical and/or psychosocial problems require moderate or high complexity medical decision making during transitions in care from an inpatient hospital setting (including acute hospital, rehabilitation hospital, long-term acute care hospital), partial hospital, observation status in a hospital, or skilled nursing facility/nursing facility, to the patient's community setting (home, domiciliary, rest home, or assisted living). Transitional care management starts on the date of discharge and continues for the next 29 days. [*Final rule*, 81 FR 80170, Nov. 15, 2016.]

[¶ 351] Services and Supplies Furnished Incident to Physicians' Services

Medicare Part B covers services and supplies furnished incident to a physician's professional services, of kinds that are commonly furnished in physicians' offices and are commonly either furnished without charge or are included in the physicians' bills. [Soc. Sec. Act § 1861(s)(2)(A); 42 C.F.R. §§ 410.10(b), 410.26(b).]

"Incident to a physician's professional services" means that the services or supplies are furnished as an integral, although incidental, part of the physician's or nonphysician practitioner's personal professional services in the course of diagnosis or treatment of an injury or illness. To be covered incident to the services of a physician, services and supplies (including drugs and biologics not usually self-administered by the patient) must be:

(1) furnished in a noninstitutional setting to noninstitutional patients;

(2) integral, although incidental, parts of the physician's professional services;

(3) rendered without charge or included in the physician's bill;

(4) of a type that are commonly furnished in physician's offices or clinics;

(5) furnished by the physician, practitioner with an incident-to benefit, or auxiliary personnel; and

(6) furnished in accordance with applicable state law.

[Soc. Sec. Act § 1861(s)(2)(A); 42 C.F.R. § 410.26(b).]

Auxiliary personnel performing incident-to services must meet state licensing requirements. [42 C.F.R. § 410.26(a)(1).]

This provision does not apply when supplies are clearly of a type a physician would not be expected to have on hand in the office or the services are of a type not considered medically appropriate to provide in the office setting. Supplies usually furnished by the physician in the course of diagnosis and treatment, such as gauze, ointments, bandages (including ace bandages), and oxygen, are covered, but charges for the supplies must be included in the physician's bills. To be covered, supplies must represent an expense to the physician. [*Medicare Benefit Policy Manual*, Pub. 100-02, Ch. 15, § 60.1.]

See ¶ 810 for a discussion of services furnished in a prospective payment system hospital to hospital inpatients that are incident to a physician's services.

Incident-to Drugs and Biologics

To meet all the general requirements for coverage under the incident-to provision, a Food and Drug Administration-approved drug or biologic must be:

- be of a form that is not usually self-administered;

- furnished by a physician; and

- administered by the physician, or by auxiliary personnel employed by the physician and under the physician's personal supervision.

[Pub. 100-02, Ch. 15, § 50.3.]

While Medicare Part B does generally not cover drugs that can be self-administered, such as those in pill form or used for self-injection, some self-administered drugs are covered under Part B. Examples of self-administered drugs that are covered include blood-clotting factors, drugs used in immunosuppressive therapy, erythropoietin (EPO) for dialysis patients, osteoporosis drugs for certain homebound patients, and certain oral cancer drugs. [42 C.F.R. § § 410.26(c)(1), 410.29(a); Pub. 100-02, Ch. 15, § 50.]

Furthermore, the administration of a drug, regardless of the source, is a service that represents an expense to the physician. Therefore, administration of the drug is payable if the drug would have been covered if the physician purchased it. [Pub. 100-02, Ch. 15, § 60.1.]

Claims for drugs payable administered by a physician to refill an implanted item of durable medical equipment (DME) are paid under Part B to the physician as a drug incident to a physician's service and are not payable to a pharmacy/supplier as DME under Soc. Sec. Act § 1861(s)(6). [42 C.F.R. § 410.26(b)(9).]

Drugs and biologics are also subject to the limitations specified in 42 C.F.R. § 410.29. [42 C.F.R. § 410.26(c)(1).]

Direct Supervision Requirement

To be covered, incident-to services and supplies must generally be furnished under the direct supervision of the physician or other practitioner. The physician/practitioner supervising the auxiliary personnel need not be the same physician/practitioner upon whose professional service the incident-to service is based; however, only the supervising physician (or other practitioner) may bill Medicare for incident-to services. [42 C.F.R. § 410.26(b)(5).]

¶351

"Auxiliary personnel" includes any individual who is acting under the supervision of a physician (or other practitioner), regardless of whether the individual is an employee, leased employee, or independent contractor of the physician (or other practitioner) or of the same entity that employs or contracts with the physician (or other practitioner). Auxiliary personnel who have been excluded from Medicare, Medicaid, and all other federally funded health care programs or who have had their enrollment revoked for any reason are prohibited from providing incident-to services. [42 C.F.R. § 410.26(a)(1).]

"Direct supervision" in the office setting means the physician is present in the office suite and immediately available to furnish assistance and direction throughout the performance of the procedure. It does not mean that the physician must be present in the room when the procedure is performed. [42 C.F.R. §§ 410.26(a)(1) and (a)(2), 410.32(b)(3)(ii); Pub. 100-02, Ch. 15, § 60.1.]

If auxiliary personnel perform services outside the office setting, their services are covered as incident to the physician's services only if there is direct supervision by the physician. For example, if a nurse accompanies the physician on house calls and administers an injection, the nurse's services are covered; if the same nurse makes the calls alone and administers the injection, the services are not covered (even when billed by the physician) because the physician is not providing direct personal supervision. [Pub. 100-02, Ch. 15, § 60.1.]

Homebound patients. There are exceptions to the direct supervision requirement for homebound patients when home health services are not readily available. Homebound patients may receive services such as injections, venipuncture, and EKGs furnished by qualified personnel who are not under a physician's direct supervision. (See Pub. 100-02, Ch. 15, § 60.4, for the complete list of such services.)

Designated care management services. Designated care management services can be furnished under general supervision of the physician (or other practitioner) when these services or supplies are provided incident to the services of a physician or other practitioner. General supervision means the service is furnished under the physician's or other practitioner's overall direction and control, but the physician's or other practitioner's presence is not required during the performance of the service. [42 C.F.R. § 410.26(a)(3), (b)(5).]

Nonphysician Practitioners

Medicare Part B covers services and supplies incident to the services of clinical psychologists (CPs), physicians assistants (PAs), nurse practitioners (NPs), clinical nurse specialists (CNSs), and certified nurse-midwives (CNMs) if the requirements of 42 C.F.R. § 410.26 are met. [Soc. Sec. Act § 1861(gg)(1), (ii); 42 C.F.R. §§ 410.71(a)(2), 410.74(b), 410.75(d), 410.76(d), 410.77(c).] See ¶ 366 for a discussion of coverage of nonphysician practitioners' services.

Further, Part B covers the services of certain nonphysician practitioners, including CNMs, CPs, clinical social workers, PAs, NPs, and CNSs, as services incident to a physician's professional services. For services of a nonphysician practitioner to be covered as incident to the services of a physician, they must meet all of the requirements for coverage, as described in 42 C.F.R. § 410.26 and Pub. 100-02, Ch. 15, § 60. [Pub. 100-02, Ch. 15, § 60.2.]

The amount of separate Medicare payment for the services of nonphysician practitioners is discussed at ¶ 860.

Incident-to Services in Outpatient and Clinic Settings

Services furnished in a prospective payment system hospital to hospital inpatients that are "incident to" a physician's services are included within the hospital's prospective payment rate and are paid under Part A.

Except in the case of rural health clinics, to which special rules apply (see ¶ 382), the guidelines for coverage of services and supplies incident to a physician's service in a "physician-directed clinic" or group association are generally the same as the general rules described above. A "physician-directed clinic" is one in which (1) a physician (or a number of physicians) is present to perform medical (rather than administrative) services at all times the clinic is open; (2) each patient is under the care of a clinic physician; and (3) the nonphysician services are under medical supervision. [Pub. 100-02, Ch. 15, § 60.3.]

In highly organized clinics, however, "direct personal physician supervision" may be the responsibility of several physicians as opposed to an individual attending physician. The physician ordering a particular service need not be the physician who is supervising the service. Therefore, services performed by therapists and other aides are covered even though they are performed in another department of the clinic. [Pub. 100-02, Ch. 15, § 60.3.]

Supplies provided by the clinic during the course of treatment also are covered. When auxiliary personnel perform services outside the clinic premises, the services are covered as "incident to" the professional services of a physician only if performed under the direct personal supervision of a clinic physician. If the clinic refers a patient for auxiliary services performed by personnel who are not employed by the clinic, such services are not "incident to" a physician's service. [Pub. 100-02, Ch. 15, § 60.3.]

Outpatient hospital services are discussed at ¶ 352. Special rules concerning ambulatory surgical centers are discussed at ¶ 386.

[¶ 352] Outpatient Hospital Services

Hospitals and critical access hospitals (CAHs) provide two distinct types of services to outpatients: (1) *therapeutic* services that aid the physician in the treatment of the patient; and (2) *diagnostic* services such as diagnostic x-rays or diagnostic laboratory services. Both kinds of services furnished by hospitals to outpatients are covered under Part B. The following rules pertaining to the coverage of outpatient hospital services are not applicable to physical therapy, speech-language pathology, occupational therapy, or end-stage renal disease (ESRD) services furnished by hospitals to outpatients. [Soc. Sec. Act § 1861(s)(2)(C); 42 C.F.R. §§ 410.27(a), 410.28; *Medicare Benefit Policy Manual*, Pub. 100-02, Ch. 6, § 20.] See ¶ 381 for a description of coverage of therapy services.

"Hospital outpatient" defined. A "hospital outpatient" is a person who has not been admitted by the hospital as an inpatient, is registered on the hospital records as an outpatient, and receives services (rather than supplies alone) from hospital personnel. An inpatient of a participating hospital may not be considered an outpatient of that or any other hospital. An inpatient of a skilled nursing facility (SNF), however, may be considered an outpatient of a participating hospital. [42 C.F.R. § 410.2; Pub. 100-02, Ch. 6, § 20.2.]

When a tissue sample, blood sample, or specimen is taken by personnel that are neither employed nor arranged for by the hospital and is sent to the hospital for the performance of tests, the test is not an outpatient hospital service because the patient does not receive services directly from the hospital. Similarly, supplies provided by a hospital supply room for use by physicians in the treatment of private patients are not covered as an outpatient service because the patients receiving the supplies are not outpatients of the hospital. [Pub. 100-02, Ch. 6, § 20.2.]

Outpatient Hospital Therapeutic Services

Medicare Part B pays for therapeutic hospital or CAH services and supplies furnished incident to a physician's or nonphysician practitioner's service, which are defined as all services and supplies furnished to hospital outpatients that are not diagnostic services and that aid the physician or nonphysician practitioner in the treatment of the patient, including drugs and biologics that are not usually self-administered. [Soc. Sec. Act § 1861(s)(2)(B); 42 C.F.R. § 410.27(a).]

To be covered, the services must be furnished (1) by or under arrangements made by the participating hospital or CAH, except in the case of a SNF resident (see 42 C.F.R. § 411.15(p)); (2) as an integral although incidental part of a physician's or nonphysician practitioner's services; (3) in the hospital or CAH or in a department of the hospital or CAH; and (4) under the general supervision (or other level of supervision as specified by CMS for the particular service). [42 C.F.R. § 410.27(a)(1).]

Therapeutic services also include clinic services, emergency room services, and observation services. [Pub. 100-02, Ch. 6, § 20.5.2.]

Psychiatric services. Medicare Part B covers a wide range of services and programs that a hospital may provide to its outpatients who need psychiatric care. Services furnished to hospital outpatients must be: (1) provided as incident to a physician's services; and (2) reasonable and necessary for the diagnosis or treatment of the patient's condition. To be covered, the services must be prescribed by a physician and provided under an individualized written plan of treatment established by the physician and supervised and periodically evaluated by the physician. The services also must be for the purpose of diagnostic study or reasonably must be expected to improve the patient's condition. [Pub. 100-02, Ch. 6, § 70.1.]

Part B Coverage of Outpatient Observation Services

Observation care includes ongoing short-term treatment, assessment, and reassessment before a decision can be made regarding whether patients will require further treatment as hospital inpatients or if they are able to be discharged from the hospital. Observation services are covered only when ordered by a physician or another individual authorized by state law and hospital staff bylaws to admit patients to the hospital or to order outpatient tests. Only rarely will observation services span more than 48 hours. [Pub. 100-02, Ch. 6, § 20.6.]

The hospital or CAH must provide written notice to an individual who receives observation services as an outpatient for more than 24 hours, within 36 hours from the start of those services, that he or she is an outpatient receiving observation services. The notice must indicate that the patient is not an inpatient of the hospital and provide the reasons for outpatient status as well as the implications of the status, such as cost-sharing requirements and subsequent eligibility for Medicare coverage for skilled nursing facility services. In addition to the written notice, the hospital must give an oral explanation of the written notification. The individual who receives observation services as an outpatient or a person acting on the individual's behalf must sign the notice to acknowledge receipt of such notification. [Soc. Sec. Act § 1866(a)(1)(Y); 42 C.F.R. § 489.20(y).]

Outpatient Hospital Diagnostic Services

Medicare Part B covers hospital or CAH diagnostic services furnished to outpatients, including drugs and biologics required in the performance of the services (even if those drugs or biologics are self-administered), if the services: (1) are furnished by or under arrangements made by a participating hospital or participating CAH, except in the case of a SNF resident as provided in 42 C.F.R. § 411.15(p); (2) are ordinarily furnished by, or under arrangements made by, the hospital or CAH to its outpatients for the purpose of diagnostic study; and (3) would be covered as inpatient hospital services if furnished to an inpatient. The services must also be provided under the appropriate level of supervision. [Soc. Sec. Act § 1861(s)(2)(C); 42 C.F.R. § 410.28(a), (e).]

A service is "diagnostic" if it is an examination or procedure to which the patient is subjected, or that is performed on materials derived from the patient, to obtain information to aid in the assessment of a medical condition or the identification of a disease. Among these examinations and tests are diagnostic laboratory services such as hematology and chemistry, diagnostic x-rays, isotope studies, electrocardiograms (EKGs), pulmonary function studies, thyroid function tests, psychological tests, and other tests given to determine the nature and severity of an ailment or injury. [Pub. 100-02, Ch. 6, § 20.4.1.]

Covered diagnostic services to outpatients include: the services of nurses, psychologists, and technicians; drugs and biologics necessary for diagnostic study; and the use of supplies and equipment. When a hospital sends hospital personnel and hospital equipment to a patient's home to furnish a diagnostic service, the service is covered as if the patient had received the service in the hospital outpatient department. [Pub. 100-02, Ch. 6, § 20.4.4.]

Services under arrangements. When the hospital makes arrangements with another facility for diagnostic services furnished on an outpatient basis, the services may be covered whether furnished in the hospital or in the other facility. Independent laboratory services furnished to an outpatient under an arrangement with the hospital are covered under the diagnostic laboratory tests provision of Part B. Laboratory services also may be furnished to a hospital outpatient under arrangements by the laboratory of another participating hospital or by the laboratory of an emergency hospital or participating SNF that meets the hospital conditions of participation relating to laboratory services. [Pub. 100-02, Ch. 6, § 20.4.5.]

Supervision Requirement for Outpatient Hospital Services

Beginning January 1, 2020, therapeutic hospital or CAH services must be furnished under the general supervision (or other level of supervision as specified by CMS for the particular service) of a physician or a nonphysician practitioner (clinical psychologist, licensed clinical social worker, physician assistant, nurse practitioner, clinical nurse specialist, or certified nurse-midwife). General supervision means the procedure is furnished under the physician's overall direction and control, but the physician's presence is not required during the performance of the procedure. Under general supervision, the training of the nonphysician personnel who actually perform the diagnostic procedure and the maintenance of the necessary equipment and supplies are the continuing responsibility of the physician. [42 C.F.R. §§ 410.27(a)(1)(iv)(A), 410.32(b)(3)(i); *Final rule with comment period*, 84 FR 61142, Nov. 11, 2019.]

Certain therapeutic services and supplies may be assigned either direct supervision or personal supervision (i.e., a physician must be in attendance in the room during the performance of the procedure). Direct supervision means that the physician or nonphysician practitioner must be immediately available to furnish assistance and direction throughout the performance of the procedure. It does not mean that the physician or nonphysician practitioner must be present in the room when the procedure is performed. [42 C.F.R. §§ 410.27(a)(1)(iv)(B), 410.32(b)(3)(iii); *Final rule with comment period*, 84 FR 61142, Nov. 11, 2019.] However, "immediate availability" requires the immediate physical presence of the physician or nonphysician practitioner. A supervisory physician or nonphysician practitioner is not immediately available if he or she is performing another procedure or service that cannot be interrupted. Also, for services furnished on campus, the supervisory physician or nonphysician practitioner may not be so physically far away on campus from the location

¶352

where hospital outpatient services are being furnished that he or she could not intervene right away. [Pub. 100-02, Ch. 6, § 20.5.2.]

Diagnostic services. Part B covers diagnostic services only when they are furnished under the appropriate level of physician supervision specified by CMS. [42 C.F.R. § 410.28(e); Pub. 100-02, Ch. 6, § 20.4.4.]

[¶ 353] Diagnostic X-Ray, Laboratory, and Other Diagnostic Tests

Part B covers diagnostic x-ray, laboratory, and other diagnostic tests, including materials and the services of technicians. [Soc. Sec. Act § 1861(s)(3); 42 C.F.R. § 410.10(e).]

In most cases, the services must be furnished by a physician or be "incident to" a physician's services. In addition, payment for the tests usually can be made only if the physician ordering the test is also the physician treating the patient. [Soc. Sec. Act § 1861(s)(2)(A); 42 C.F.R. § 410.10(b).]

Ordering Diagnostic Tests

All diagnostic x-ray tests, diagnostic laboratory tests, and other diagnostic tests must be ordered by the physician who is treating the patient, i.e., the physician who provides a consultation or treats the patient for a specific medical problem and uses the test results in the management of the patient's specific medical problem. Nonphysician practitioners (clinical nurse specialists, clinical psychologists, clinical social workers, nurse-midwives, nurse practitioners, and physician assistants) licensed to provide physician services under state law are also subject to the physician ordering requirement. [42 C.F.R. § 410.32(a).]

An order from a physician may be delivered via the following forms of communication:

- a written document signed by the physician, which is hand-delivered, mailed, or faxed to the testing facility;

- a telephone call from the physician's office to the testing facility documented in their respective copies of the beneficiary's medical records; or

- an electronic mail from the physician's office to the testing facility.

No signature is required, however, on orders for clinical diagnostic tests paid under the clinical laboratory fee schedule or the physician fee schedule. [*Medicare Benefit Policy Manual*, Pub. 100-02, Ch. 15, § 80.6.1.]

There is an exception to the treating physician requirement: a physician who meets the qualification requirements for an interpreting physician may order a diagnostic mammogram based on the findings of a screening mammogram, even though the physician does not treat the patient. [42 C.F.R. § 410.32(a)(1).]

Physician Supervision Requirements

Generally, to be considered reasonable and necessary, all diagnostic x-ray and other diagnostic tests covered under Soc. Sec. Act § 1861(s)(3) and payable under the physician fee schedule must be furnished under the appropriate level of supervision by a physician. The degree of physician supervision (general supervision, direct supervision, or personal supervision) required at the time the test is conducted depends on the difficulty and risk of the test. General supervision means that tests may be furnished under a physician's overall direction and control, direct supervision means that a physician must be present in the office suite and immediately available during tests, and personal supervision means that a physician must be in attendance in the room where a test is performed. [42 C.F.R. § 410.32(b)(1), (3).]

Diagnostic tests that would otherwise require a personal level of supervision, when performed by a registered radiologist assistant (RRA) who is certified and registered by the American Registry of Radiologic Technologists or a radiology practitioner assistant (RPA) who is certified by the Certification Board for Radiology Practitioner Assistants, may be furnished under a direct level of physician supervision to the extent permitted by state law and state scope of practice regulations. [42 C.F.R. § 410.32(b)(4).]

There are seven exceptions to the physician supervision requirement:

(1) mammography procedures;

(2) diagnostic tests personally furnished by a qualified audiologist;

(3) diagnostic psychological testing services personally furnished by a clinical psychologist or an independently practicing psychologist or furnished under the general supervision of a physician or clinical psychologist;

(4) tests personally performed by a qualified physical therapist certified as a qualified electrophysiologic clinical specialist;

(5) diagnostic tests performed by a nurse practitioner or clinical nurse specialist under applicable state laws;

(6) pathology and laboratory procedures listed in the 80000 series of the CPT® published by the American Medical Association; and

(7) diagnostic tests performed by a certified nurse-midwife authorized to perform the tests under applicable state laws.

[42 C.F.R. § 410.32(b)(2).]

Coverage of Portable X-ray Suppliers

Part B covers diagnostic x-ray services furnished by a portable x-ray supplier when those services are furnished in a place of residence used as the patient's home or in nonparticipating institutions. Diagnostic x-ray services also are covered under Part B when provided in participating skilled nursing facilities (SNFs) and hospitals under circumstances in which they cannot be covered under Part A. These portable x-ray services must be performed under the general supervision of a physician and certain conditions relating to health and safety must be met. [Soc. Sec. Act § 1861(s)(3); 42 C.F.R. § 410.32(c); Pub. 100-02, Ch. 15, § 80.4.1.]

Covered procedures. Coverage for portable x-ray services is limited to:

(1) skeletal films involving the extremities, pelvis, vertebral column, and skull;

(2) chest and abdominal films that do not involve the use of contrast media; and

(3) diagnostic mammograms if the supplier is approved for this service.

[42 C.F.R. § 410.32(c)(4); Pub. 100-02, Ch. 15, § 80.4.3.]

The taking of an electrocardiogram tracing by an approved supplier of portable x-ray services may also be covered as an "other diagnostic test." [Pub. 100-02, Ch. 15, § 80.4.5.]

Noncovered procedures. Procedures and examinations that are not covered under the portable x-ray provision include:

(1) procedures involving fluoroscopy;

(2) procedures involving the use of contrast media;

(3) procedures requiring the administration of a substance to the patient or injection of a substance into the patient and/or special manipulation;

¶353

(4) procedures that require special medical skill or knowledge possessed by a doctor of medicine or doctor of osteopathy, or that require that medical judgment be exercised;

(5) procedures requiring special technical competency and/or special equipment or materials;

(6) routine screening procedures; and

(7) procedures that are not of a diagnostic nature.

[Pub. 100-02, Ch. 15, § 80.4.4.]

Coverage of Advanced Diagnostic Imaging Services

Part B covers the technical component (TC) of advanced imaging services only when a supplier is accredited. The HHS Secretary designated advanced diagnostic imaging accreditation organizations to accredit suppliers, including but not limited to physicians, nonphysician practitioners, and independent diagnostic testing facilities (IDTFs), that furnish the TC of advanced diagnostic imaging services. Medicare law expressly excludes from the accreditation requirement x-ray, ultrasound, and fluoroscopy procedures as well as diagnostic and screening mammography, which are subject to quality oversight by the Food and Drug Administration under the Mammography Quality Standards Act. [Soc. Sec. Act § 1834(e).]

Advanced diagnostic imaging services that are covered include:

(1) diagnostic magnetic resonance imaging;

(2) computed tomography; and

(3) nuclear medicine, including positron emission tomography.

The Secretary may designate other services, except for x-ray, ultrasound, and fluoroscopy, as diagnostic imaging services in consultation with physician specialty organizations and stakeholders. [Soc. Sec. Act § 1834(e)(1)(B).]

Appropriate use criteria. Section 218(b) of the Protecting Access to Medicare Act of 2014 (PAMA) (P.L. 113-93) required the HHS Secretary to establish a program to promote the use of appropriate use criteria for certain diagnostic imaging services to assist ordering and furnishing professionals in making the most appropriate treatment decision for a specific clinical condition for an individual. Beginning in 2020, outlier ordering professionals must begin applying for prior authorization to order imaging services. [Soc. Sec. Act § 1834(q); 42 C.F.R. § 414.94.]

Coverage of Diagnostic Laboratory Tests

Part B covers diagnostic laboratory tests when furnished by a qualified hospital, physician's office laboratory, rural health clinic, federally qualified health center, a SNF to its residents, or a laboratory that meets the applicable requirements for laboratories of 42 C.F.R. Part 493. [Soc. Sec. Act § 1861(s)(3); 42 C.F.R. § § 410.10(e), 410.32(d).]

Clinical laboratory services involve the biological, microbiological, serological, chemical, immunohematological, hematological, biophysical, cytological, pathological, or other examination of materials derived from the human body for the diagnosis, prevention, or treatment of a disease or assessment of a medical condition. These examinations also include procedures to determine, measure, or otherwise describe the presence or absence of various substances or organisms in the body. Facilities only collecting or preparing specimens (or both) or only serving as a mailing service and not performing testing are not considered laboratories. [42 C.F.R. § 493.2; Pub. 100-02, Ch. 15, § 80.1.]

The law prohibits Medicare payment to a laboratory that has a financial relationship with the referring physician. Violators are subject to civil money penalties and exclusion from the program. Laboratories are required to include information on referring physicians when submitting claims for payment (see "Stark Law" at ¶ 720). [Soc. Sec. Act § § 1833(q), 1877.]

All diagnostic laboratory tests must be ordered by the physician or nonphysician practitioner who is treating the beneficiary. Tests not ordered by the physician/practitioner who is treating the beneficiary are not reasonable and necessary. [42 C.F.R. § 410.32(a).]

Payment for clinical diagnostic laboratory tests is discussed at ¶ 875.

Coverage of Other Diagnostic Tests

"Other diagnostic tests," including materials and services connected with them, are covered under Part B only if the services are furnished by a physician or as incident to a physician's services. [Soc. Sec. Act § 1861(s)(3); 42 C.F.R. § 410.10(e).] Psychological and neuropsychological tests and hearing and balance assessment services performed by a qualified audiologist are examples of "other diagnostic tests." [Pub. 100-02, Ch. 15, § § 80.2, 80.3.]

Psychological tests. In addition to coverage of psychological tests when furnished by a physician or as an incident to a physician's services, Part B covers diagnostic testing performed by a qualified psychologist (who is not a clinical psychologist) practicing independently of an institution, agency, or physician's office, if a physician orders such testing. Examples of psychologists whose services are covered under this provision include educational psychologists and counseling psychologists. [Pub. 100-02, Ch. 15, § 80.2.]

Testing by audiologist. Diagnostic testing performed by a qualified audiologist (or a nurse practitioner or clinical nurse specialist authorized to perform the tests under applicable state laws) is covered when a physician orders such testing to evaluate the need for, or appropriate type of, treatment of a hearing deficit or related medical problem. For example, diagnostic services performed by a qualified audiologist to measure a hearing deficit or to identify the factors responsible for the deficit are covered where such services are necessary to enable the physician to determine whether otologic surgery is indicated. However, diagnostic services performed only to determine the need for, or the appropriate type of, a hearing aid are not covered. [Pub. 100-02, Ch. 15, § 80.3.]

Independent Diagnostic Testing Facilities

Diagnostic tests provided by an IDTF are covered and paid under the physician fee schedule. An IDTF may be a fixed location, a mobile entity, or an individual nonphysician practitioner. An IDTF is independent of a physician's office or hospital, but it may furnish diagnostic procedures in a physician's office. In most cases, an IDTF must have one or more supervising physicians who are responsible for direct and ongoing oversight of the quality of the testing performed, proper operation and calibration of testing equipment, and the qualification of nonphysician personnel who use the equipment. [42 C.F.R. § 410.33(a), (b).]

The physician who is treating the beneficiary must order all procedures performed by the IDTF in writing, although nonphysician practitioners may order tests in accordance with the scope of their licenses. The supervising physician for the IDTF may not order tests to be performed by the IDTF unless the IDTF's supervising physician is the beneficiary's treating physician. [42 C.F.R. § 410.33(d).]

With the exception of hospital-based and mobile IDTFs, a fixed-base IDTF may not share a practice location with another Medicare-enrolled individual or organization, lease or sublease its operations or its practice location to another Medicare-enrolled individual or organization, or share diagnostic testing equipment used in the initial diagnostic test with another Medicare-enrolled individual or organization. [42 C.F.R. § 410.33(g)(15).]

[¶ 354] X-Ray, Radium, and Radioactive Isotope Therapy

X-ray, radium, and radioactive isotope therapy, including materials and the services of technicians. are covered under the Part B program. [Soc. Sec. Act § 1861(s)(4); 42 C.F.R. §§ 410.10(f), 410.35.]

X-ray, radium, and radioactive isotope therapy furnished in a nonprovider facility require direct personal supervision of a physician. The physician need not be in the same room but must be in the area and immediately available to provide assistance and direction throughout the time the procedure is being performed. This level of physician involvement does not represent a physician's service and cannot be billed as a Part B service. Radiologists' weekly treatment management services, however, are covered. [*Medicare Benefit Policy Manual*, Pub. 100-02, Ch. 15, § 90.]

A separate charge for the services of a physicist is not recognized unless such services are covered under the "incident to" provision (see Pub. 100-02, Ch. 15, § 60.1) or the services are included as part of a technical component service billed by a freestanding radiation therapy center. The "incident to" provision also may be extended to include all necessary and appropriate services supplied by a radiation physicist assisting a radiologist when the physicist is in the physician's employ and working under his or her direct supervision. [Pub. 100-02, Ch. 15, § 90.]

[¶ 355] Ambulance Services

Medicare Part B covers ambulance services when the use of other methods of transportation is contraindicated by the individual's condition. [Soc. Sec. Act § 1861(s)(7); 42 C.F.R. § 410.10(i).] For Part B to cover ambulance services, the following conditions must be met: (1) the supplier meets the requirements of 42 C.F.R. § 410.41; (2) the services meet the medical necessity and origin and destination requirements of 42 C.F.R. § 410.40; and (3) Medicare Part A payment is not made directly or indirectly for the services. [42 C.F.R. § 410.40(b).]

Medical Necessity Requirements

Medicare covers ambulance services, including fixed wing and rotary wing ambulance services, only if they are furnished to a beneficiary whose medical condition is such that other means of transportation are contraindicated. The beneficiary's condition must require both the ambulance transportation itself and the level of service provided for the billed service to be considered medically necessary. [42 C.F.R. § 410.40(e); *Medicare Benefit Policy Manual*, Pub. 100-02, Ch. 10, § 10.2.]

Nonemergency transportation. Nonemergency transportation by ambulance is appropriate if either: (1) the beneficiary is bed-confined and it is documented that the beneficiary's condition is such that other methods of transportation are contraindicated; or (2) the beneficiary's condition, regardless of bed confinement, is such that transportation by ambulance is medically required. For a beneficiary to be considered bed-confined, the following criteria must be met:

    (1) the beneficiary is unable to get up from bed without assistance;

    (2) the beneficiary is unable to ambulate; and

    (3) the beneficiary is unable to sit in a chair or wheelchair.

[42 C.F.R. § 410.40(e)(1).]

Nonemergency, scheduled, repetitive ambulance services. Medicare covers medically necessary nonemergency, scheduled, repetitive ambulance services if the ambulance supplier or provider obtains a physician certification statement dated no earlier than 60 days before the date the service is furnished. The provider or supplier must keep appropriate documentation on file and, upon request, present it to the contractor. The presence of the signed physician certification statement does not alone demonstrate that the ambulance transport was medically necessary. [42 C.F.R. § 410.40(e)(2).] A physician certification statement is a statement signed and dated by the beneficiary's attending physician that certifies that the medical necessity provisions of 42 C.F.R. § 410.40(e)(1) are met. The statement need not be a stand-alone document and no specific format or title is required. [42 C.F.R. § 410.40(a); *Final rule*, 84 FR 62998, Nov. 15, 2019.]

Nonemergency services that are unscheduled or are scheduled on a nonrepetitive basis. Medicare covers medically necessary nonemergency ambulance services that are either unscheduled or that are scheduled on a nonrepetitive basis under one of the following circumstances:

(1) for a resident of a facility who is under the care of a physician if the ambulance provider or supplier obtains a physician certification statement within 48 hours after the transport;

(2) for a beneficiary residing at home or in a facility who is not under the direct care of a physician (physician certification is not required);

(3) if the ambulance provider or supplier is unable to obtain a signed physician certification statement from the beneficiary's attending physician, a non-physician certification statement must be obtained; or

(4) if the ambulance provider or supplier is unable to obtain the required physician or non-physician certification statement within 21 calendar days following the date of the service, it must document its attempts to obtain the requested certification and may then submit the claim. Acceptable documentation includes a signed return receipt from the U.S. Postal Service or other similar service that evidences that the supplier attempted to obtain the required signature from the beneficiary's attending physician or other individual named in 42 C.F.R. § 410.40(e)(3)(iii).

The provider or supplier must keep appropriate documentation on file and, upon request, present it to the contractor. The presence of the physician or nonphysician certification statement or signed return receipt does not alone demonstrate that the ambulance transport was medically necessary. All other program criteria must be met in order for payment to be made. [42 C.F.R. § 410.40(e); *Final rule*, 84 FR 62998, Nov. 15, 2019.]

A non-physician certification statement is a statement signed and dated by an individual, which certifies that the medical necessity provisions of 42 C.F.R. § 410.40(e)(1) are met. The statement need not be a stand-alone document and no specific format or title is required. The individual must meet the following requirements: (1) have personal knowledge of the beneficiary's condition at the time the ambulance transport is ordered or the service is furnished; (2) is employed by the beneficiary's attending physician or the hospital or facility where the beneficiary is being treated and from which the beneficiary is transported; (3) is a physician assistant, nurse practitioner, clinical nurse specialist, registered nurse, licensed practical nurse, social worker, case manager, discharge planner, with respect to whom all Medicare regulations and all applicable state licensure laws apply. [42 C.F.R. § 410.40(a).]

Effect of beneficiary death. In general, if the beneficiary dies before being transported, then Medicare does not cover the ambulance service. Medicare does, however, allow payment for an air ambulance service when the ambulance is dispatched to pick up a beneficiary but he or she is pronounced dead before being loaded onto the ambulance. The allowed amount is the appropriate base rate, but no allowance is made for mileage or for rural adjustment. If the beneficiary dies after pickup, before or upon arrival at the receiving facility, the entire ambulance service is covered. [Pub. 100-02, Ch. 10, § § 10.2.6, 10.4.9.]

Covered Levels of Ambulance Transportation

Ambulance services are divided into different levels of ground (including water) and air ambulance services based on the medically necessary treatment provided during transport. These services include several different levels of service for ground and air transport of patients.

Medicare covers the following levels of ambulance service:

- basic life support (BLS) (emergency and nonemergency);
- advanced life support, level 1 (ALS1) (emergency and nonemergency);
- advanced life support, level 2 (ALS2);
- paramedic ALS intercept (PI);
- specialty care transport (SCT);
- fixed wing air ambulance (FW); and
- rotary wing air ambulance (RW) (helicopter).

[42 C.F.R. § 410.40(b).]

Paramedic ALS intercept services are covered under specific conditions in small towns and rural areas. Intercept services are ALS services furnished by a paramedic in connection with the services of a volunteer BLS ambulance supplier. The coverage applies only if there is a state law prohibiting the volunteer ambulance supplier from billing for any services. [42 C.F.R. § 410.40(c).]

Air ambulance services. There are two categories of air ambulance services: fixed wing (airplane) and rotary wing (helicopter) aircraft. Medicare covers medically appropriate air ambulance transportation only if the beneficiary's medical condition is such that transportation by basic or advanced life support ground ambulance is not appropriate, and either (1) the point of pickup is inaccessible by ground vehicle (e.g., in Hawaii, Alaska, and remote or sparsely populated areas of the continental United States); or (2) great distances or other obstacles are involved in getting the patient to the nearest hospital with appropriate facilities. [42 C.F.R. § 410.40(b)(6), (7); Pub. 100-02, Ch. 10, § 10.4.]

A "rural air ambulance service" means fixed wing and rotary wing air ambulance service in which the point of pick up occurs in a rural area or in a rural census tract of a metropolitan statistical area. To be covered, the service must be reasonable and necessary based on the health condition of the individual being transported at or immediately before the time of transport and must comply with equipment and crew requirements established by the Secretary. [Soc. Sec. Act. § 1834(l)(14).]

Origin and Destination Requirements

Medicare covers the following ambulance transportation:

(1) from any point of origin to the nearest hospital, critical access hospital (CAH), or skilled nursing facility (SNF) that is capable of furnishing the required level and type of care for the beneficiary's illness or injury;

(2) from a hospital, CAH, or SNF to the beneficiary's home;

(3) from a SNF to the nearest supplier of medically necessary services not available at the SNF where the beneficiary is a resident, including the return trip; and

(4) for a beneficiary who is receiving renal dialysis for treatment of end-stage renal disease (ESRD), from the beneficiary's home to the nearest facility that furnishes renal dialysis, including the return trip.

[42 C.F.R. § 410.40(e).]

The reference in 42 C.F.R. § 410.40(e) to the "nearest" facility continues a long-standing policy that the Medicare beneficiary must be taken to the "nearest appropriate facility." This means that the patient must be transported to a Medicare-participating institution that is generally equipped to provide the needed hospital or skilled nursing care for the illness or injury involved. That a more distant institution is better equipped to care for the patient does not warrant a finding that a closer institution does not have "appropriate facilities." Such a finding is warranted, however, if the beneficiary's condition requires a higher level of trauma care or other specialized service available only at the more distant hospital. [Pub. 100-02, Ch. 10, § 10.3.6.]

If two or more facilities that meet the destination requirements can treat the patient appropriately and the locality of each facility encompasses the place where the ambulance transportation of the patient began, then the full mileage to any one of the facilities to which the beneficiary is taken is covered. [Pub. 100-02, Ch. 10, § 10.3.]

Requests by a home health agency. When a home health agency finds it necessary to have a beneficiary transported by ambulance to a hospital or SNF to obtain services not otherwise available, the trip is covered as a Part B service only if all the usual coverage requirements are met for ambulance transportation from wherever the patient is located. Such transportation is not covered as a home health service. [Pub. 100-02, Ch. 10, § 10.3.9.]

Ambulance Services Outside the United States

If services are furnished outside the United States, Medicare Part B covers ambulance transportation to a foreign hospital only as part of the beneficiary's admission for medically necessary inpatient services, as specified in 42 C.F.R. §§ 424.120–424.127. [42 C.F.R. § 410.40(f).] See ¶ 610.

[¶ 356] Durable Medical Equipment

Medicare Part B pays for the rental or purchase of durable medical equipment (DME), including ventilators, oxygen equipment, hospital beds, and wheelchairs, if the equipment is used in the patient's home or in an institution that is used as a home. [Soc. Sec. Act § 1861(n), (s)(6); 42 C.F.R. §§ 410.10(h), 410.38(a); *Final rule*, 84 FR 60648, Nov. 8, 2019.]

For a list of DME and the coverage status of each item, see § 280.1 in the *Medicare National Coverage Determinations Manual*, Pub. 100-03.

"Durable Medical Equipment" Defined

DME is equipment that: (1) can withstand repeated use; (2) is primarily and customarily used to serve a medical purpose; (3) generally is not useful to a person in the absence of illness or injury; and (4) is appropriate for use in the home. [*Medicare Benefit Policy Manual*, Pub. 100-02, Ch. 15, § 110.1.]

DME also includes the following:

- iron lungs, whether furnished on a rental basis or purchased;

- blood-testing strips and blood glucose monitors for individuals with diabetes regardless of whether the beneficiary has Type I or Type II diabetes or his or her use of insulin; and

  - eye tracking and gaze interaction accessories for speech generating devices furnished to individuals with a demonstrated medical need for such accessories.

With respect to a seat-lift chair, only the seat-lift mechanism (and not the chair) is considered DME. [Soc. Sec. Act § 1861(n).]

Medical supplies of an expendable nature, such as incontinence pads, catheters, bandages, and elastic stockings, are not considered durable (although they may fall into other coverage categories). There are other items that, although durable in nature, may fall into other Medicare coverage categories such as prosthetic devices, braces, or artificial arms, legs, and eyes. Implantable items for which payment may be made under Soc. Sec. Act § 1833(t), such as intraocular lenses, are not considered DME. [Soc. Sec. Act § 1834(a)(13).]

Equipment presumptively nonmedical. Equipment that is used primarily and customarily for a nonmedical purpose may not be considered "medical" equipment for which payment may be made under Medicare, even though the item has some remote medically related use. For example, devices and equipment used for environmental control or to enhance the environmental setting in which the beneficiary is placed are not considered covered DME. [Pub. 100-02, Ch. 15, § 110.1.]

Special exception items. Specified items of equipment may be covered under certain conditions even though they do not meet the definition of DME because they are not used primarily and customarily to serve a medical purpose and/or are generally useful in the absence of illness or injury. These items are covered if it is clearly established that they serve a therapeutic purpose in an individual case. Examples include heat lamps for a medical rather than a soothing or cosmetic purpose, and gel pads and pressure and water mattresses when prescribed for a patient who has bed sores or if there is medical evidence indicating the patient is highly susceptible to ulceration. [Pub. 100-02, Ch. 15, § 110.1.]

Supplies and accessories. Medicare covers supplies such as oxygen that are necessary for the effective use of DME. Such supplies include those drugs and biologics that must be put directly into the equipment to achieve the therapeutic benefit of the DME or to ensure the proper functioning of the equipment, e.g., tumor chemotherapy agents used with an infusion pump or heparin used with a home dialysis system. The coverage of such drugs or biologics, however, does not preclude the need for a determination that the drug or biologic itself is reasonable and necessary for treatment of the illness or injury or to improve the functioning of a malformed body member. [Pub. 100-02, Ch. 15, § 110.3.]

Definition of Beneficiary's Home

To be covered as DME the item must be used in the patient's home. For purposes of rental or purchase of DME, a patient's home may be his or her own dwelling, an apartment, a relative's home, a home for the aged, or some other type of institution. An institution may not be considered a beneficiary's home, however, if it is a hospital, critical access hospital, or skilled nursing facility. [Pub. 100-02, Ch. 15, § 110.1.]

Medical Necessity for DME

To be covered, the DME must be necessary and reasonable for treatment of an illness or injury, or to improve the functioning of a malformed body member. In most cases the physician's prescription for the equipment and other medical information available to the durable medical equipment Medicare administrative contractor (DME MAC) will be sufficient to establish that the equipment meets this requirement. [Pub. 100-02, Ch. 15, § 110.1.]

Reasonableness. Even though an item of DME may serve a useful medical purpose, the DME MAC also will consider to what extent, if any, it would be reasonable for the Medicare program to pay for the item prescribed. In determining reasonableness, the MAC will consider the following:

(1) Would the expense of the item to the program be clearly disproportionate to the therapeutic benefits that could ordinarily be derived from use of the equipment?

(2) Is the item substantially more costly than a medically appropriate and realistically feasible alternative pattern of care?

(3) Does the item serve essentially the same purpose as equipment already available to the beneficiary?

[Pub. 100-02, Ch. 15, § 110.1.]

Certificate of medical necessity. For items or services billed to a DME MAC, the supplier must receive a signed certificate of medical necessity (CMN) from the treating physician. A supplier must have a signed original, faxed, photocopied, or electronic CMN in its records before it can submit a claim for payment to Medicare. [*Medicare Program Integrity Manual*, Pub. 100-08, Ch. 5, § 5.3.]

Advance Beneficiary Notice. Suppliers must provide Advance Beneficiary Notices (ABNs) that advise beneficiaries, before items or services such as DME are furnished, when Medicare is likely to deny payment for them due to lack of medical necessity. [*Medicare Claims Processing Manual*, Pub. 100-04, Ch. 1, § 60.]

Written Order and Face-to-Face Encounter Requirements

Effective January 1, 2020, all DMEPOS items require a written order/prescription for Medicare payment. MACs will consider the totality of the medical records when reviewing for compliance with standardized written order/prescription elements. A written order/prescription must include the following elements: (1) beneficiary name or Medicare Beneficiary Identifier (MBI); (2) general description of the item; (3) quantity to be dispensed, if applicable; (4) order date; (5) treating practitioner name or National Provider Identifier (NPI); and (6) treating practitioner signature. For power mobility devices and other DMEPOS items selected for inclusion on the Required Face-to-Face Encounter and Written Order Prior to Delivery List, the written order/prescription must be communicated to the supplier before delivery. For all other DMEPOS, the written order/prescription must be communicated to the supplier before claim submission. [Soc. Sec. Act § 1834(a)(11)(B)(i); 42 C.F.R. § 410.38(d)(1); *Final rule*, 84 FR 60648, Nov. 8, 2019.]

Master List. The Master List includes items of DMEPOS that CMS has identified in accordance with Soc. Sec. Act § 1834(a)(11)(B) and (a)(15), the criteria for which are specified in 42 C.F.R. § 414.234. The Master List serves as a library of DMEPOS items from which items may be selected for inclusion on Required Face-to-Face Encounter and Written Order Prior to Delivery List and/or the Required Prior Authorization List. The Required Face-to-Face Encounter and Written Order Prior to Delivery List is a list of DMEPOS items selected from the Master List and subject to the requirements of a face-to-face encounter and written order prior to delivery. The list of items is published in the *Federal Register* and posted on the CMS website. The list is effective no less than 60 days following its publication. When selecting items from the Master List, CMS may consider factors such as operational limitations, item utilization, cost-benefit analysis, emerging trends, vulnerabilities identified in official agency reports, or other analysis. [42 C.F.R. § 410.38(c); *Final rule*, 84 FR 60648, Nov. 8, 2019.]

¶356

Items requiring a face-to-face encounter. For power mobility devices and other DMEPOS items selected for inclusion on the Required Face-to-Face Encounter and Written Order Prior to Delivery List, the treating practitioner must document and communicate to the supplier that he or she has had a face-to-face encounter with the beneficiary within the six months preceding the date of the written order/prescription. The encounter must be used for the purpose of gathering subjective and objective information associated with diagnosing, treating, or managing a clinical condition for which the DMEPOS is ordered. If the face-to-face encounter is a telehealth encounter, the requirements of 42 C.F.R. §§ 410.78 and 414.65 must be met. [Soc. Sec. Act § 1834(a)(11)(B)(ii); 42 C.F.R. § 410.38(d)(2); *Final rule*, 84 FR 60648, Nov. 8, 2019.]

Documentation. A supplier must maintain the written order/prescription and the supporting documentation provided by the treating practitioner and make them available to CMS and its agents upon request. On request by CMS or its agents, a supplier must submit additional documentation to CMS or its agents to support and/or substantiate the medical necessity for the DMEPOS item. The face-to-face encounter must be documented in the pertinent portion of the medical record, and the supporting documentation must include subjective and objective beneficiary specific information used for diagnosing, treating, or managing a clinical condition for which the DMEPOS is ordered. [42 C.F.R. § 410.38(d)(3); *Final rule*, 84 FR 60648, Nov. 8, 2019.]

Suspension of requirements. CMS may suspend face-to-face encounter and written order prior to delivery requirements generally or for a particular item or items at any time and without undertaking rulemaking, except those items for which inclusion on the Master List was statutorily imposed. [42 C.F.R. § 410.38(e); *Final rule*, 84 FR 60648, Nov. 8, 2019.]

Repairs, Maintenance, Replacement, and Delivery

Under certain circumstances, payment may be made for repair, maintenance, and replacement of medically required DME, including equipment that had been in use before the beneficiary enrolled in the Part B program. [Pub. 100-02, Ch. 15, § 110.2.]

Repairs. Repairs to equipment that a beneficiary owns are covered when necessary to make the equipment serviceable. If the expense for repairs exceeds the estimated expense of purchasing or renting another item of equipment for the remaining period of medical need, no payment can be made for the amount of the excess. Because renters of equipment recover from the rental charge the expenses they incur in maintaining the equipment they rent out, separately itemized charges for repair of rented equipment are not covered. [Pub. 100-02, Ch. 15, § 110.2.]

Maintenance. Routine periodic servicing, such as testing, cleaning, regulating, and checking of the beneficiary's equipment, is not covered. The owner is expected to perform such routine maintenance rather than a retailer or some other person who charges the beneficiary. More extensive maintenance, which, based on the manufacturers' recommendations, is to be performed by authorized technicians, is covered as repairs. This might include, for example, breaking down sealed components and performing tests that require specialized testing equipment not available to the beneficiary. Because renters of equipment recover from the rental charge the expenses they incur in maintaining in working order the equipment they rent out, separately itemized charges for maintenance of rented equipment are generally not covered. [Pub. 100-02, Ch. 15, § 110.2.]

Replacement. Equipment that the beneficiary owns or that is a capped rental item may be replaced in cases of loss or irreparable damage, e.g., as a result of a specific accident or a natural disaster. Replacement of equipment due to irreparable wear takes into consideration the reasonable useful lifetime of the equipment. [Pub. 100-02, Ch. 15, § 110.2.]

If equipment or a device is replaced free of charge by the warrantor, no program payment may be made because there was no charge involved. If the warrantor supplied the replaced equipment or device, but some charge or a pro rata payment was imposed, program payment may be made for the partial payment imposed for the device furnished by the warrantor. [Pub. 100-02, Ch. 16, § 40.4.]

Cases suggesting malicious damage, culpable neglect, or wrongful disposition of equipment will be investigated and denied when the MAC determines that it would be unreasonable to make program payment under the circumstances. [Pub. 100-02, Ch. 15, § 110.2.]

Delivery. Payment for delivery of DME whether rented or purchased generally is included in the fee schedule allowance for the item. [Pub. 100-02, Ch. 15, § 110.2.]

Oxygen Services in the Home

Oxygen and oxygen equipment provided in the home are covered by Medicare under the DME benefit. Oxygen is considered reasonable and necessary only for patients with significant hypoxemia if requirements for medical documentation, laboratory evidence, and health conditions are met. [*Medicare National Coverage Determinations Manual*, Pub. 100-03, Ch. 1, § 240.2.]

A patient may qualify for coverage of a portable oxygen system either by itself or to use in addition to a stationary oxygen system. Portable oxygen is not covered when it is provided only as a backup to a stationary oxygen system. A portable oxygen system is covered for a particular patient if medical documentation indicates that the patient is mobile in the home and would benefit from the use of a portable oxygen system in the home. [Pub. 100-03, Ch. 1, § 240.2.]

A new physician certification is required every 90 days for certain patients receiving home oxygen therapy. The recertification must be made if, at the time the home oxygen therapy is initiated, the patient has an initial arterial blood gas value at or above a partial pressure of 56 or an arterial oxygen saturation at or above 89 percent. The recertification must be based on a follow-up test of these indications within the final 30 days of the 90-day period. [Soc. Sec. Act § 1834(a)(5)(E).]

Payments for maintenance and servicing (for parts and labor not covered by the supplier's or manufacturer's warranty) will be made if the Secretary determines them to be reasonable and necessary. [Soc. Sec. Act § 1834(a)(5)(F)(ii)(III).]

After the 36th continuous month during which payment is made for oxygen equipment, the supplier must continue to furnish the equipment during any period of medical need for the remainder of the reasonable useful lifetime of the equipment. [Soc. Sec. Act § 1834(a)(5)(F)(ii).]

Change in the Patient's Condition

A beneficiary may sell or otherwise dispose of DME purchased under the program and for which there is no further use, for example, because of recovery from the illness or injury that gave rise to the need for the equipment. There is no authority for Medicare to repossess the equipment. If, after disposal, there is again medical need for similar equipment, payment can be made for the rental or purchase of that equipment. When, however, an arrangement is motivated solely by a desire to profit from artificial expenses to be met by the program and realize a profit thereby, such expenses are not covered. [Pub. 100-02, Ch. 15, § 110.4.]

When payments stop because the beneficiary's condition has changed and the equipment is no longer medically necessary or because the beneficiary dies, the individual or his or her estate is responsible for the remaining noncovered charges. [Pub. 100-02, Ch. 15, § 110.4.]

[¶ 357] Prosthetic Devices and Prosthetics/Orthotics

Medicare Part B covers prosthetic devices, other than dental, that replace all or part of an internal body organ, including colostomy bags and supplies directly related to colostomy care. Coverage includes replacement of prosthetic devices and one pair of conventional eyeglasses or conventional contact lenses furnished after each cataract surgery during which an intraocular lens is inserted. The conditions of payment described in 42 C.F.R. § 410.38(d) also apply to medical supplies, appliances, and devices. [Soc. Sec. Act § 1861(s)(8); 42 C.F.R. § 410.36(a)(2), (b); *Final rule*, 84 FR 60648, Nov. 8, 2019.]

Examples of prosthetic devices include parenteral and enteral nutrition (PEN), cardiac pacemakers, prosthetic lenses, breast prostheses, maxillofacial devices, and devices that replace all or part of the ear or nose as well as urinary collection and retention systems with or without a tube and a Foley catheter that replace bladder function in cases of permanent urinary incontinence. Medicare does not cover a prosthetic device dispensed before the beneficiary undergoes the procedure that makes the use of the device necessary. [*Medicare Benefit Policy Manual*, Pub. 100-02, Ch. 15, § 120; *Medicare Coverage Determinations Manual*, Pub. 100-03, Ch. 1, § 20.8.]

No payment may be made for prosthetics and certain custom-fabricated orthotics unless they are furnished by a qualified practitioner and fabricated by a qualified practitioner or a qualified supplier at an approved facility. Affected custom-fabricated orthotics are items requiring education, training, and experience to custom fabricate. [Soc. Sec. Act § 1834(h)(1)(F).]

Vacuum erection systems. Effective for claims with dates of service on or after July 1, 2015, Medicare Part B no longer covers vacuum erection system prosthetic devices and related accessories, in the same manner that erectile dysfunction drugs are excluded under Part D. [Soc. Sec. Act § 1834(a)(1)(I).]

Dentures. Dentures are excluded from coverage; however, when a denture or a portion thereof is an integral part (built-in) of a covered prosthesis (e.g., an obturator to fill an opening in the palate), it is covered as part of that prosthesis. [Pub. 100-02, Ch. 15, § 120.]

Prosthetic lenses. Prostheses replacing the lens of an eye include post-surgical lenses customarily used during convalescence from eye surgery in which the lens of the eye was removed. In addition, permanent lenses are also covered when required by an individual lacking the organic lens of the eye because of surgical removal or congenital absence. Prosthetic lenses obtained on or after the beneficiary's date of entitlement to supplementary medical insurance benefits may be covered even though the surgical removal of the crystalline lens occurred before entitlement. [42 C.F.R. § 411.15(b); Pub. 100-02, Ch. 15, § 120.]

The general exclusion applicable to refractive services regardless of the reason for them, however, means that refractive services for the purpose of prescribing or providing prosthetic lenses are not covered. [42 C.F.R. § 411.15(c).]

Repair and replacement. Replacements of prosthetic devices that are artificial limbs or the replacement of any parts of artificial limbs are covered when there is a change in the condition of the patient or a change in the condition of the device. The physician's determination in these situations is controlling, except that confirmation may be required for devices or parts that are less than three years old. [Soc. Sec. Act § 1834(h)(1)(G).] Necessary supplies, adjustments, repairs, and replacements are covered even when the device had been in use before the user enrolled in Part B of the program, so long as the device continues to be medically required. [Pub. 100-02, Ch. 15, § 120.]

Enteral and Parenteral Nutrition Therapy

For PEN to be covered under Part B, the beneficiary must have a permanently inoperative internal body organ or function thereof. Coverage of such therapy, however, does not require a medical judgment that the impairment giving rise to the therapy will persist throughout the patient's remaining years. If the medical record, including the judgment of the attending physician, indicates that the impairment will be of long and indefinite duration, the test of permanence is considered met. [Pub. 100-03, Ch. 1, § 180.2.]

The claim for PEN therapy must contain a physician's written order or prescription and sufficient medical documentation to permit an independent conclusion that the requirements of the prosthetic device benefit are met and that PEN therapy is medically necessary. If the coverage requirements for PEN therapy are met, related supplies, equipment, and nutrients are also covered. [Pub. 100-02, Ch. 15, § 120; Pub. 100-03, Ch. 1, § 180.2.]

Braces, Trusses, and Artificial Limbs

Part B covers leg, arm, back, and neck braces, trusses, and artificial legs, arms, and eyes when furnished incident to a physician's services. The conditions of payment described in 42 C.F.R. § 410.38(d) apply to these services. [Soc. Sec. Act § 1861(s)(9); 42 C.F.R. § 410.36(a)(3); *Final rule*, 84 FR 60648, Nov. 8, 2019; Pub. 100-02, Ch. 15, § 130.]

Braces include rigid and semi-rigid devices that support weak or deformed body member or restrict or eliminate motion in diseased or injured parts of the body. Back braces include, but are not limited to, special corsets, including sacroiliac, sacrolumbar and dorsolumbar corsets, and belts. Elastic stockings, garter belts, and similar devices do not come within the scope of the definition of a brace. [Pub. 100-02, Ch. 15, § 130.]

Although orthopedic shoes or other supportive devices for the feet generally are excluded from coverage, the exclusion does not apply to such a shoe if it is an integral part of a leg brace. [42 C.F.R. § 411.15(f); Pub. 100-02, Ch. 15, § 290.]

A terminal device (e.g., hand or hook) is covered under this provision regardless of whether an artificial limb is required by the patient. Stump stockings and harnesses (including replacements) also are covered when these appliances are essential to the effective use of the artificial limb. [Pub. 100-02, Ch. 15, § 130.]

Adjustments to an artificial limb or other appliance required by wear or a change in the patient's condition are covered when ordered by a physician. Adjustments, repairs, and replacements are covered even when the item had been in use before the user enrolled in Part B of the program as long as the device continues to be medically required. [Soc. Sec. Act § 1861(s)(9); 42 C.F.R. § 410.36(a)(3); Pub. 100-02, Ch. 15, § 130.]

[¶ 359] Surgical Dressings, Splints, and Casts

Medicare Part B covers surgical dressings, splints, casts, and other devices used for reduction of fractures and dislocations. [Soc. Sec. Act § 1861(s)(5); 42 C.F.R. §§ 410.10(g), 410.36(a).]

The coverage of splints and casts includes dental splints. [*Medicare Benefit Policy Manual*, Pub. 100-02, Ch. 15, § 100.]

Coverage of surgical dressings is limited to (1) primary and secondary dressings required for the treatment of a wound caused by, or treated by, a surgical procedure performed by a physician or other health care professional; and (2) surgical dressings required after debridement of a wound. Surgical dressings are covered for as long as they are medically necessary. [Pub. 100-02, Ch. 15, § 100.]

Primary dressings are therapeutic or protective coverings applied directly to wounds or lesions either on the skin or caused by an opening to the skin. Secondary dressing materials (e.g., adhesive tape, roll gauze, bandages, and disposable compression material) that serve a therapeutic or protective function and are needed to secure a primary dressing are also covered. [Pub. 100-02, Ch. 15, § 100.]

Elastic stockings, support hose, foot coverings, leotards, knee supports, surgical leggings, gauntlets, and pressure garments for the arms and hands are not covered as surgical dressings. Some items, such as transparent film, may be used as a primary or secondary dressing. [Pub. 100-02, Ch. 15, § 100.]

If a physician, certified nurse-midwife, physician assistant, nurse practitioner, or clinical nurse specialist applies surgical dressings as part of a professional service that is billed to Medicare, the surgical dressings are considered incident to the practitioner's professional services. When surgical dressings are not covered incident to the services of a health care practitioner and are obtained by a patient from a supplier pursuant to an order from a physician or other health care professional, the dressings are covered separately under Part B. [Pub. 100-02, Ch. 15, § 100.]

[¶ 361] Inpatient Ancillary Services

No payment may be made under Part B for services furnished if the beneficiary is entitled (or would be entitled, except for the deductible and coinsurances) to have payment made for these services under Part A. [Soc. Sec. Act § 1833(d).] This precludes payment under Part B and Part A for the same services. When such payment is not precluded, however—for example, when an inpatient has exhausted his or her 90 days of entitlement in a "spell of illness"— payment may be made for certain "medical and other health services" under Part B, even though they are furnished to an inpatient of a skilled nursing facility (SNF). These services are usually referred to as "Part B ancillary services."

Covered Ancillary Services Furnished to SNF Inpatients

The following medical and other health services are covered under Part B when furnished by a participating SNF either directly or under arrangements to inpatients who are not entitled to have payment made under Part A (e.g., benefits exhausted or three-day prior-stay requirement not met):

- diagnostic x-ray tests, diagnostic laboratory tests, and other diagnostic tests;

- x-ray, radium, and radioactive isotope therapy, including materials and services of technicians;

- surgical dressings and splints, casts, and other devices used for reduction of fractures and dislocations;

- prosthetic devices (other than dental) that replace all or part of an internal body organ (including contiguous tissue), or all or part of the function of a permanently inoperative or malfunctioning internal body organ, including replacement or repair of such devices;

- leg, arm, back, and neck braces; trusses; and artificial legs, arms, and eyes, including adjustments, repairs, and replacements required because of breakage, wear, loss, or a change in the patient's physical condition;

- outpatient physical and occupational therapy and speech-language pathology services;

- screening mammography services;
- screening pap smears and pelvic exams;
- influenza, pneumococcal pneumonia, and hepatitis B vaccines;
- some colorectal screening;
- prostate screening;
- ambulance services;
- hemophilia clotting factors; and
- Epoetin Alfa (EPO) for end-stage renal disease beneficiaries when given in conjunction with dialysis.

[42 C.F.R. § 410.60(b); *Medicare Benefit Policy Manual*, Pub. 100-02, Ch. 8, § 70.]

Custodial care patients. A finding that the care being furnished a patient in a hospital or SNF is custodial care and, therefore, not covered does not preclude coverage of medically necessary Part B ancillary services that are provided to the patient. [Pub. 100-02, Ch. 16, § 110.]

Reasonable and Necessary Part A Hospital Inpatient Claim Denials

If a Medicare Part A claim for inpatient hospital services is denied because the inpatient admission was not reasonable and necessary, or if a hospital determines after a beneficiary is discharged that the inpatient admission was not reasonable and necessary, and if waiver of liability payment is not made, the hospital may be paid for the following Part B inpatient services that would have been reasonable and necessary if the beneficiary had been treated as a hospital outpatient:

(1) Part B services paid under the outpatient prospective payment system (OPPS), excluding observation services and hospital outpatient visits that require an outpatient status; and

(2) the following services excluded from OPPS payment that are instead paid under the respective Part B fee schedules or prospectively determined rates for which payment is made when provided to hospital outpatients:

(a) physical therapy services, speech-language pathology services, and occupational therapy services;

(b) ambulance services;

(c) prosthetic devices, prosthetic supplies, and orthotic devices paid under the durable medical equipment, prosthetics/orthotics, and supplies (DMEPOS) fee schedule (excluding implantable prosthetic devices (other than dental) that replace all or part of an internal body organ (including colostomy bags and supplies directly related to colostomy care) and replacement of such devices);

(d) durable medical equipment (DME) supplied by the hospital for the patient to take home, except DME that is implantable;

(e) certain clinical diagnostic laboratory services;

(f) screening and diagnostic mammography services; and

(g) annual wellness visit providing personalized prevention plan services.

[42 C.F.R. § 414.5(a); Pub. 100-02, Ch. 6, § 10.1.]

Hospitals also may be paid under Part B for services included in the payment window before the point of inpatient admission for outpatient services treated as inpatient services,

¶361

including services requiring an outpatient status. [42 C.F.R. § 414.5(b); Pub. 100-02, Ch. 6, § 10.1.]

Medical and Other Services Furnished to Hospital Inpatients in Other Circumstances

Part B payment can be made to a hospital for certain medical and other services for inpatients enrolled in Part B if: (1) no Part A prospective payment is made at all for the hospital stay because of patient exhaustion of benefit days before or during the admission; or (2) the patient was not otherwise eligible for or entitled to coverage under Part A. For hospitals paid under the OPPS, certain Part B inpatient services (including diagnostic tests; x-ray, radium, and radioactive isotope therapy; certain screening tests; acute dialysis of a hospital inpatient; and immunosuppressive and oral anti-cancer drugs) are separately payable under Part B and are excluded from OPPS packaging if the primary service with which the service would otherwise be bundled is not a payable Part B inpatient service. [Pub. 100-02, Ch. 6, § 10.2.]

The following inpatient services are payable under the non-OPPS Part B fee schedules or prospectively determined rates:

(1) surgical dressings and splints, casts, and other devices used for reduction of fractures and dislocations;

(2) prosthetic devices (other than dental) that replace all or part of an internal body organ (including contiguous tissue) or all or part of the function of a permanently inoperative or malfunctioning internal body organ, including replacement of such devices;

(3) leg, arm, back, and neck braces; trusses; and artificial legs, arms, and eyes, including replacements required because of a change in the patient's physical condition;

(4) physical and occupational therapy and speech-language pathology services;

(5) screening mammography services; and

(6) ambulance services.

[Pub. 100-02, Ch. 6, § 10.2.]

The services listed below, when provided to a hospital inpatient, may be covered under Part B even if the patient has Part A coverage for the hospital stay, because these services are covered under Part B and not covered under Part A:

• physicians' services (including the services of residents and interns in unapproved teaching programs) and the services of physician assistants, certified nurse-midwives, and qualified clinical psychologists;

• influenza, pneumococcal pneumonia, and hepatitis B vaccines and their administration;

• screening mammography services, screening pap smears and pelvic exams, glaucoma screening, colorectal screening, and prostate screening;

• bone mass measurements; and

• diabetes self-management training services.

[Pub. 100-02, Ch. 6, § 10.3; Ch. 15, § 250.]

To have any Medicare coverage at all (Part A or Part B), any nonphysician service rendered to a hospital inpatient must be provided directly or arranged for by the hospital. [Pub. 100-02, Ch. 6, § 10.]

[¶ 362] Drugs and Biologics

Part B covers drugs and biologics generally if they: (1) meet the specific definition of drugs and biologics; (2) are not usually self-administered by the patient; (3) are reasonable and necessary to diagnose or treat an existing illness or condition; (4) are administered by a physician or other health professional as an "incident to" service (see ¶ 351); (5) are not excluded as noncovered immunizations; and (6) are not found by the Food and Drug Administration (FDA) to be "less than effective." [Soc. Sec. Act § 1861(s)(2); 42 C.F.R. § 410.29; *Medicare Benefit Policy Manual*, Pub. 100-02, Ch. 15, § 50.]

A drug or biologic may be covered only where it is included, or approved for inclusion, in the latest official edition of the United States Pharmacopoeia National Formulary, the United States Pharmacopoeia-Drug Information, or the American Dental Association Guide to Dental Therapeutics. Combination drugs are also included in the definition of drugs if the combination itself or all of the therapeutic ingredients of the combination are included, or approved for inclusion, in any of these drug compendia. The term "drugs" also includes any drugs or biologics used in an anticancer chemotherapeutic regimen for a medically accepted indication. [Soc. Sec. Act § 1861(t)(1); Pub. 100-02, Ch. 15, § 50.1.]

Prescription drugs are covered under Medicare Part D. A description of Medicare coverage of prescription drugs begins at ¶ 500. See ¶ 885 for a discussion of payment rules for drugs and biologics.

Determining Self-Administration

Whether a drug or biologic is a type not usually self-administered by the patient is based on the usual method of administration of the form of that drug or biologic as furnished by the physician. When, for example, a physician gives a patient pills or other oral medication, these are excluded from coverage because the form of the drug given to the patient is usually self-administered. Similarly, if a physician gives a patient an injection that is usually self-injected (e.g., insulin or calcitonin), this drug is excluded from coverage unless administered to the patient in an emergency situation. [Pub. 100-02, Ch. 15, § 50.2.]

"Usually administered" means a route of administration used more than 50 percent of the time. Therefore, if a drug is self-administered by more than 50 percent of Medicare beneficiaries, it is excluded from Medicare coverage. [Pub. 100-02, Ch. 15, § 50.2.]

In the absence of reliable statistical information on the extent of self-administration by patients, contractors are to consider the following presumptions:

- Drugs delivered intravenously or by intramuscular injection are not usually self-administered.
- Drugs delivered by subcutaneous injection are self-administered.

The *Medicare Benefit Policy Manual* discusses other factors to consider in determining a drug's self-administration status, including whether a drug is given for an acute condition, whether a patient is an inpatient or an outpatient, the frequency of administration, and what administration instructions are approved by the FDA in drug package labeling. [Pub. 100-02, Ch. 15, § 50.2.]

Whole blood is a biologic that cannot be self-administered and is covered when furnished incident to a physician's services. Part B may also pay for blood fractions if all coverage requirements are satisfied. [Pub. 100-02, Ch. 15, § 50.3.]

Drugs treated as hospital outpatient supplies. Some drugs that usually are self-administered by the patient may, nevertheless, be covered by Medicare Part B when they function as supplies, such as when they are provided as an integral component of a procedure or when they facilitate the performance of or recovery from a particular procedure. Except for the applicable copayment, hospitals may not bill beneficiaries for these types of drugs because their costs, as supplies, are packaged into the prospective payment system payment for the procedure with which they are used. When a drug is not directly related or integral to a procedure and does not facilitate the performance of or recovery from a procedure, the drug is not considered a packaged supply. [Pub. 100-02, Ch. 15, § 50.2.]

Exclusion of Immunizations

Vaccinations and inoculations are excluded as "immunizations" unless they are directly related to the treatment of an injury or direct exposure to a disease or condition, such as antirabies treatment, tetanus antitoxin or booster vaccine, botulin antitoxin, antivenin sera, or immune globulin. In the absence of injury or direct exposure, preventive immunizations (vaccinations or inoculations) against such diseases as smallpox, polio, and diphtheria are not covered. Pneumococcal pneumonia, hepatitis B, and influenza virus vaccines are exceptions to this rule and are covered (see below). [Pub. 100-02, Ch. 15, § 50.4.4.2.]

Exceptions to Coverage Rules for Drugs and Biologics

There are a number of exceptions to the rule against self-administered drugs and preventive immunizations:

Antigens. Payment may be made for a reasonable supply of antigens that have been prepared for a particular patient if: (1) the antigens are prepared by a physician who is a doctor of medicine or osteopathy; and (2) the physician who prepared the antigens has examined the patient and has determined a plan of treatment and a dosage regimen. Antigens must be administered in accordance with the plan of treatment and by a physician or by a properly instructed person (who could be the patient) under the supervision of the physician. A reasonable supply of antigens is considered to be not more than a 12-month supply of antigens that has been prepared for a particular patient at any one time. [Soc. Sec. Act § 1861(s)(2)(G); 42 C.F.R. § 410.68.]

Pneumococcal pneumonia vaccine. To protect the elderly from pneumococcal pneumonia, a disease to which they are particularly susceptible, pneumococcal pneumonia vaccine and its administration are covered without deductible or coinsurance. Typically, these are administered once in a lifetime, but coverage includes revaccination of patients at highest risk of pneumococcal infection. The vaccine may be requested by the patient; neither a physician's order nor physician supervision is required. [Soc. Sec. Act § 1861(s)(10)(A); 42 C.F.R. § 410.57; Pub. 100-02, Ch. 15, § 50.4.4.2.]

Hepatitis B vaccine. Hepatitis B vaccine and its administration are covered when furnished to an individual who is a member of a group classified as having a high or intermediate risk of contracting hepatitis B. [Soc. Sec. Act § 1861(s)(10)(B); 42 C.F.R. § 410.63(a).]

High-risk groups include: (1) end-stage renal disease (ESRD) patients; (2) hemophiliacs who receive Factor VIII or IX concentrates; (3) clients of institutions for individuals with intellectual disabilities; (4) persons who live in the same household as a hepatitis B carrier; (5) homosexual men; (6) illicit injectable drug abusers; (7) Pacific Islanders; and (8) persons diagnosed with diabetes mellitus. Intermediate risk groups include: (1) staff in institutions for individuals with intellectual disabilities and classroom employees who work with individuals with intellectual disabilities; (2) health care workers who have frequent contact with blood or blood-derived body fluids during their routine work; and (3) heterosexually active persons with multiple sexual partners (which means those Medicare beneficiaries who have had at least two documented episodes of sexually transmitted diseases within the past five years). Persons in these groups, however, are not considered at high or intermediate risk of contracting hepatitis B if they have undergone a prevaccination screening and been found to be currently positive for antibodies to hepatitis B. [42 C.F.R. § 410.63(a); Pub. 100-02, Ch. 15, § 50.4.4.2.]

Influenza virus vaccine. The Part B program covers influenza virus vaccine and its administration without deductible or coinsurance when furnished in compliance with applicable state law by a provider of services or any entity or individual with a supplier number. Typically, these vaccines are administered once a year in the fall or winter. A beneficiary may receive the vaccine upon request without a physician's order and without physician supervision. [Soc. Sec. Act § 1861(s)(10)(A); 42 C.F.R. § 410.57(b); Pub. 100-02, Ch. 15, § 50.4.4.2.]

Blood clotting factors. Medicare covers blood clotting factors for hemophilia patients competent to use such factors to control bleeding without medical or other supervision. Items related to the administration of the factors also are covered. This coverage is subject to utilization controls deemed necessary by the Medicare program for the efficient use of the factors. [Soc. Sec. Act § 1861(s)(2)(I); Pub. 100-02, Ch. 15, § 50.5.5.]

Immunosuppressive drugs. Medicare covers prescription drugs used in immunosuppressive therapy when furnished to an individual who receives a covered organ transplant. [Soc. Sec. Act § 1861(s)(2)(J); 42 C.F.R. § 410.30.]

Coverage is limited to those immunosuppressive drugs that specifically are labeled as such and approved for marketing by the FDA. Also included are prescription drugs, such as prednisone, that are used in conjunction with immunosuppressive drugs as part of a therapeutic regimen reflected in FDA-approved labeling for immunosuppressive drugs. Antibiotics, hypertensives, and other drugs not directly related to preventing organ rejection are not covered. [Pub. 100-02, Ch. 15, § 50.5.1.]

IVIG for immune deficiency diseases. Medicare covers intravenous immune globulin (IVIG), a pooled plasma derivative, for the treatment of primary immune deficiency diseases in a patient's home. The benefit does not include coverage for items or services related to the administration of the derivative. For coverage of IVIG under this benefit, it is not necessary for the derivative to be administered through a piece of durable medical equipment. [Soc. Sec. Act § 1861(s)(2)(Z), (zz); 42 C.F.R. § 410.10(y); Pub. 100-02, Ch. 15, § 50.6.]

Erythropoietin. Erythropoietin (EPO) is covered, even when self-administered, for the treatment of anemia for patients with ESRD who are on dialysis. It is covered for self-administration by a home dialysis patient if the patient (or an appropriate caregiver) is trained to inject EPO. It also may be covered for other patients; however, non-ESRD patients who are receiving EPO to treat anemia induced by other conditions such as chemotherapy or the drug zidovudine (commonly called AZT) must meet the coverage requirements in Chapter 15, Section 50 of the *Medicare Benefit Policy Manual.* [Soc. Sec. Act § 1861(s)(2)(O); Pub. 100-02, Ch. 15, § 50.5.2.]

Osteoporosis drugs. Medicare covers injectable drugs approved for the treatment of a bone fracture related to post-menopausal osteoporosis if: (1) the drugs are administered by a home health agency; (2) the patient's attending physician certifies that the patient has suffered a bone fracture related to post-menopausal osteoporosis and the patient is incapable of self-administering the drugs; and (3) the patient is confined to her home. [Soc. Sec. Act § 1861(m)(5), (kk).]

Oral anti-cancer and anti-emetic drugs. Oral anti-cancer chemotherapeutic drugs are covered, even when self-administered, if they contain the same active ingredients as intravenously administered anti-cancer drugs. [Soc. Sec. Act § 1861(s)(2)(Q), (t)(2); Pub. 100-02, Ch. 15, § 50.5.3.]

¶362

Off-label uses of FDA-approved drugs and biologics for anti-cancer chemotherapeutic regimens are covered by Medicare when they are clinically recognized for the treatment of a specific type of cancer and are listed by CMS in its benefits manual under one or more compendia or under peer-reviewed medical literature. [Pub. 100-02, Ch. 15, § 50.4.5.]

Part B also covers self-administered anti-emetic drugs when they are prescribed by a physician for use with a covered anti-cancer drug when necessary for the administration and absorption of the oral anti-cancer drug (for example, when a high likelihood of vomiting exists). The anti-emetic must be used during the period that begins immediately before and ends within 48 hours after the time of the administration of the anti-cancer drug and it must be used as a full replacement for the anti-emetic therapy that otherwise would be administered intravenously. [Soc. Sec. Act § 1861(s)(2)(T); Pub. 100-02, Ch. 15, § 50.5.4.]

[¶ 366] Other Health Care Practitioners

Medicare covers the services of nonphysician health care practitioners, including physician assistants (PAs), nurse practitioners (NPs) and clinical nurse specialists (CNSs), certified registered nurse anesthetists (CRNAs) and anesthesia assistants (AAs), certified nurse-midwives, clinical psychologists, and clinical social workers (CSWs). (See ¶ 860 for the details of payment rules for these practitioners.)

Physician Assistants, Nurse Practitioners, and Clinical Nurse Specialists

Medicare Part B covers the services of PAs, NPs, and CNSs if the services would be covered as physicians' services if furnished by a physician. Such services are covered if the PA, NP, or CNS is legally authorized to perform them in the state in which they are performed and does not perform services that are otherwise excluded from coverage because of one of the statutory exclusions. Medicare covers these services in all settings in both rural and urban areas. [Soc. Sec. Act § 1861(s)(2)(K); 42 C.F.R. §§ 410.74(a), 410.75(c), 410.76(c).]

Examples of the types of services that PAs, NPs, and CNSs may furnish include services that traditionally have been reserved to physicians, such as physical examinations, minor surgery, setting casts for simple fractures, interpreting x-rays, and other activities that involve an independent evaluation or treatment of the patient's condition. Also included are the initial preventive physical examination and the annual wellness visit. [Soc. Sec. Act § 1861(s)(2)(K); *Medicare Benefit Policy Manual*, Pub. 100-02, Ch. 15, §§ 190, 200, 210.]

Personal performance. PA, NP, and CNS professional services are covered only when they have been personally performed by the PA, NP, or CNS. Supervision of other nonphysician staff does not constitute personal performance of a professional service. [42 C.F.R. §§ 410.74(d)(1), 410.75(e)(1), 410.76(e)(1).]

Physician supervision. A PA must perform services in accordance with state law and state scope of practice rules for PAs in the state in which the professional services are furnished. In states where state laws or scope of practice rules describe the required practice relationship between physicians and physician assistants, including explicit supervisory or collaborative practice requirements, those state laws or rules define supervision for purposes of Soc. Sec. Act § 1861(s)(2)(K)(i). In states without such rules, physician supervision is a process in which a physician assistant has a working relationship with one or more physicians to supervise the delivery of their health care services. Such physician supervision is evidenced by documenting at the practice level the PA's scope of practice and the working relationships the PA has with the supervising physician when furnishing professional services. [Soc. Sec. Act § 1861(s)(2)(K)(i); 42 C.F.R. § 410.74(a)(2)(iv); *Final rule*, 84 FR 62568, Nov. 15, 2019.]

Collaboration. Both NPs and CNSs must perform services while working in collaboration with a physician. Collaboration is a process in which the practitioner works with one or more physicians to deliver health care services within the scope of the practitioner's expertise, with medical direction and appropriate supervision as provided for in jointly developed guidelines or other mechanisms as provided by the law of the state in which the services are performed. The collaborating physician does not need to be present with the NP when the services are furnished or to make an independent evaluation of each patient who is seen by the NP. [Soc. Sec. Act § 1861(s)(2)(K)(ii), (aa)(6); 42 C.F.R. §§410.75(c)(3), 410.76(c)(3).]

Documentation. PAs, NPs, and CNSs may review and verify (sign and date), rather than redocument, notes in a patient's medical record made by physicians; residents; nurses; medical, physician assistant, and advanced practice registered nurse students; or other members of the medical team, including, as applicable, notes documenting the practitioner's presence and participation in the service. [42 C.F.R. §§ 410.74(e), 410.75(f), 410.76(f); *Final rule*, 84 FR 62568, Nov. 15, 2019.]

CRNAs and Anesthesia Assistants

Medicare Part B covers anesthesia services and related care furnished by a CRNA or an AA who is legally authorized to perform the services by the state in which the services are furnished. [Soc. Sec. Act § 1861(s)(11), (bb); 42 C.F.R. § 410.69(a).]

Documentation. A CRNA may review and verify (sign and date), rather than re-document, notes in a patient's medical record made by physicians; residents; nurses; medical, physician assistant, and advanced practice registered nurse students; or other members of the medical team. For example, a CRNA may sign and date notes documenting the CRNA's presence and participation in the service. [42 C.F.R. § 410.69(b); *Final rule*, 84 FR 62568, Nov. 15, 2019.]

Nurse-Midwife Services

Medicare Part B covers certified nurse-midwife services. The term "certified nurse-midwife services" means such services furnished by a certified nurse-midwife and such services and supplies furnished as an incident to the service that the certified nurse-midwife is legally authorized to perform under state law as would otherwise be covered if furnished by a physician or as an incident to a physicians' service. [Soc. Sec. Act § 1861(s)(2)(L), (gg); 42 C.F.R. § 410.77.]

Covered services are those furnished by a certified nurse-midwife that are within the scope of practice authorized by the law of the state in which they are furnished and would otherwise be covered if furnished by a physician, including obstetrical and gynecological services. Coverage of service to the newborn continues only to the point that the newborn is or would normally be treated medically as a separate individual. [42 C.F.R. § 410.77(b)(1); Pub. 100-02, Ch. 15, § 180.]

Incident-to services. Part B covers services and supplies incident to the services of a certified nurse-midwife if the requirements of 42 C.F.R. § 410.26 are met. [42 C.F.R. § 410.77(b), (c).]

Personal performance. A nurse-midwife can be paid for professional services only when he or she personally performs the services. Supervision of other nonphysician staff by a nurse-midwife does not constitute personal performance of a professional service. [42 C.F.R. § 410.77(d); Pub. 100-02, Ch. 15, § 180.]

Place of service. There is no restriction on place of service. Nurse-midwife services are covered if provided in the nurse-midwife's office, the patient's home, or a hospital or other

¶366

facility, such as a clinic or birthing center owned or operated by a nurse-midwife. [Pub. 100-02, Ch. 15, § 180.]

Relationship with physician. Unless required by state law, nurse-midwife services are covered regardless of whether he or she is under the supervision of, or associated with, a physician or other health care provider. [42 C.F.R. § 410.77(b)(2); Pub. 100-02, Ch. 15, § 180.]

Documentation. A certified nurse-midwife may review and verify (sign and date), rather than redocument, notes in a patient's medical record made by physicians; residents; nurses; medical, physician assistant, and advanced practice registered nurse students; or other members of the medical team, including, as applicable, notes documenting the nurse-midwife's presence and participation in the service. [42 C.F.R. § 410.77(e); *Final rule*, 84 FR 62568, Nov. 15, 2019.]

Clinical Psychologists

Medicare Part B covers services furnished by a clinical psychologist that are within the scope of his or her state license, if the services would be covered if furnished by a physician or as an incident to a physician's services. [Soc. Sec. Act § 1861(s)(2)(M), (ii).]

Incident-to services and supplies. Part B also covers services and supplies furnished "incident to" a CP's services if the requirements of 42 C.F.R. § 410.26 are met. [42 C.F.R. § 410.71(a)(2).]

Requirement for consultation. A CP must agree that, upon the beneficiary's consent, the CP will attempt to consult with the beneficiary's attending or primary care physician within a reasonable time to consider any conditions contributing to the beneficiary's symptoms. If the CP's attempts to consult directly with the physician are not successful, the CP must notify the physician within a reasonable time that he or she is furnishing services to the patient. Neither the CP nor the attending or primary care physician may bill Medicare or the beneficiary for this consultation. [42 C.F.R. § 410.71(c), (e); Pub. 100-02, Ch. 15, § 160.]

Noncovered services. The services of CPs are not covered if they are otherwise excluded from Medicare coverage even though a clinical psychologist is authorized by state law to perform them. In addition, any therapeutic services that are billed by CPs under Current Procedural Terminology® (CPT®) psychotherapy codes that include medical evaluation and management services are not covered. [Pub. 100-02, Ch. 15, § 160.]

Clinical Social Workers

Part B coverage of CSW services includes the diagnosis and treatment of mental illnesses that the CSW is legally authorized to perform under state law and would otherwise be covered if performed by a physician or as incident to a physician's services. [Soc. Sec. Act § 1861(s)(2)(N), (hh)(2); 42 C.F.R. § 410.73(b)(1).]

Noncovered services. Part B does not cover services furnished to an inpatient of a hospital or skilled nursing facility that the facility is required to provide, or to a patient in a Medicare-participating dialysis facility if the services are those required by the conditions for coverage for end-stage renal disease facilities. CSW services are not covered if they are otherwise excluded from Medicare coverage even though a CSW is authorized by state law to perform them. [42 C.F.R. § 410.73(b)(2); Pub. 100-02, Ch. 15, § 170.]

Requirement for consultation. A CSW must agree that, upon the patient's consent, the CSW will attempt to consult with the patient's attending or primary care physician. Neither the CSW nor the attending or primary care physician may bill Medicare or the beneficiary for this consultation. [42 C.F.R. § 410.73(c), (d)(2).]

Registered Dietitians and Nutrition Professionals

Medicare covers medical nutrition therapy (MNT) services for certain beneficiaries who have diabetes or a renal disease when furnished by registered dietitians or nutritional professionals. [Soc. Sec. Act § 1861(s)(2)(V); 42 C.F.R. § § 410.130–410.134; *Medicare National Coverage Determinations Manual*, Pub. 100-03, Ch. 1, § 180.1.]

[¶ 369] Preventive Services

Medicare Part B covers specific preventive screening services and tests. The initial preventive physical exam (IPPE), performed within the first year of Part B enrollment, begins the process. "Preventive services" are defined as: (1) the screening and preventive services currently listed in Soc. Sec. Act § 1861(ww)(2); (2) an IPPE; and (3) personalized preventive plan services. [Soc. Sec. Act § 1861(ddd)(3).]

In addition to providing the above definition of preventive services, the Patient Protection and Affordable Care Act (ACA) (P.L. 111-148) expanded coverage of preventive services and waived coinsurance and deductibles for most preventive services. For those services, Medicare is responsible for 100 percent of the costs. [Soc. Sec. Act § 1833(a)(1)(B).] Preventive services for which no coinsurance amount will be charged to beneficiaries are those services given a grade of "A" or "B" by the United States Preventive Services Task Force (USPSTF). [Soc. Sec. Act § 1833(b)(1).]

"Welcome to Medicare" Exams

Medicare pays for one IPPE, also called the "Welcome to Medicare Physical," within the first year after the effective date of the beneficiary's first Part B coverage period, if the coverage began on or after January 1, 2009. [Soc. Sec. Act § § 1861(s)(2)(W) and (ww), 1862(a)(1)(K); 42 C.F.R. § § 410.16, 411.15(a)(1) and (k)(11).]

The IPPE means all of the following services furnished to an eligible beneficiary by a physician or other qualified nonphysician practitioner with the goal of health promotion and disease detection:

   (1) a review of the beneficiary's medical and social history with attention to modifiable risk factors for disease;

   (2) a review of the beneficiary's potential (risk factors) for depression;

   (3) a review of the beneficiary's functional ability and level of safety;

   (4) a physical examination, including measurement of height, weight, body mass index, and blood pressure;

   (5) end-of-life planning, upon the agreement of the individual;

   (6) education, counseling, and referral based on the results of the review and evaluation; and

   (7) effective January 1, 2020, a review of any current opioid prescriptions.

A review of any current opioid prescriptions includes, for an individual determined to have a current prescription for opioids: (1) a review of the potential risk factors to the individual for opioid use disorder; (2) an evaluation of the individual's severity of pain and current treatment plan; (3) the provision of information on non-opioid treatment options; and (4) a referral to a specialist, as appropriate. [Soc. Sec. Act § 1861(ww)(1), as amended by SUPPORT for Patients and Communities Act (P.L. 115-271) § 2002(a)(1)(B); Soc. Sec. Act § 1861(ww)(4), as added by SUPPORT for Patients and Communities Act § 2002(a)(3); 42 C.F.R. § 410.16.]

The statutory screening and other preventive services authorized under Part B include:

- pneumococcal, influenza, and hepatitis B vaccine and their administration;
- screening mammography;
- screening pap smear and screening pelvic exam services;
- prostate cancer screening services;
- colorectal cancer screening tests;
- diabetes outpatient self-management training services;
- bone mass measurements;
- screening for glaucoma;
- medical nutrition therapy services for individuals with diabetes or renal disease;
- cardiovascular screening tests;
- diabetes screening tests;
- ultrasound screening for abdominal aortic aneurysm;
- an electrocardiogram;
- screening for potential substance use disorders; and
- additional preventive services, as defined by Soc. Sec. Act § 1861(ddd)(1).

[Soc. Sec. Act § 1861(ww)(2), as amended by SUPPORT for Patients and Communities Act § 2002(a)(2); 42 C.F.R. § 410.16.]

The deductible and coinsurance for the IPPE are waived. [Soc. Sec. Act § 1833(b)(9); 42 C.F.R. § § 410.152(l)(12), 410.160(b)(9); *Medicare Claims Processing Manual*, Pub. 100-04, Ch. 12, § 30.6.1.1.]

Excluded coverage. Excluded routine physical checkups include: (1) examinations performed for a purpose other than the treatment or diagnosis of a specific illness, symptom, complaint, or injury (such as routine chest x-rays); and (2) examinations required by third parties such as insurance companies, business establishments, or government agencies. [42 C.F.R. § 411.15(a); *Medicare Benefit Policy Manual*, Pub. 100-02, Ch. 16, § 90.]

The routine services exclusion does not apply to services furnished in a federally qualified health center. [Soc. Sec. Act § 1862(a).]

Annual Wellness Exams

Medicare beneficiaries are eligible to receive an annual wellness visit (AWV) providing personalized prevention plan services. [Soc. Sec. Act § 1861(s)(2)(FF) and (hhh)(1); 42 C.F.R. § 410.15(c).]

"Personalized prevention plan services" means the creation of a plan for an individual that includes a health risk assessment. A plan must take into account the results of the assessment and may include elements such as:

(1) the individual's medical and family history;

(2) a list of his or her current providers or suppliers;

(3) the individual's height, weight, body mass index, blood pressure, and other measurements;

(4) detection of any cognitive impairments;

(5) establishment of a screening schedule for the next five years based on recommendations of the USPSTF and a list of risk factors and conditions for which preventive measures or treatment are recommended;

(6) personalized health advice and a referral, as necessary, to address risk factors;

(7) at the discretion of the beneficiary, advance care planning services, including discussions about future care decisions that might need to be made, how the beneficiary can let others know about care preferences, and an explanation of advance directives that may involve the completion of standard forms;

(8) effective January 1, 2020, screening for potential substance use disorders and referral for treatment as appropriate;

(9) effective January 1, 2020, a review of any current opioid prescriptions (as defined in Soc. Sec. Act § 1861(ww)(4)); and

(10) any other element identified by the HHS Secretary.

[Soc. Sec. Act § 1861(hhh), as amended by SUPPORT for Patients and Communities Act § 2002(b); 42 C.F.R. § 410.15(a).]

The health risk assessment must be performed by a health professional, which includes a physician, physician assistant, nurse practitioner, clinical nurse specialist, and other medical professionals or teams of professionals. [42 C.F.R. § 410.15(b).]

Medicare pays for an AWV for a beneficiary who is no longer within 12 months after the effective date of his or her first Medicare Part B coverage period and who has not received either an IPPE or an AWV providing personalized prevention plan services within the past 12 months. The deductible and coinsurance for personalized prevention plan services, including those performed in the outpatient department of a hospital, are waived. [Soc. Sec. Act § 1833(a)(1)(X) and (b)(10), (t)(1)(B)(iv); 42 C.F.R. § § 410.152(l)(13), 410.160(b)(12); Pub. 100-04, Ch. 12, § 30.6.1.1.]

Part B Coverage of Mammograms

Medicare Part B covers screening mammography, which includes the radiological procedure itself as well as a physician's interpretation of the results of the procedure. [Soc. Sec. Act § 1861(s)(13), (jj); 42 C.F.R. § § 410.10(r), 410.34.]

Women between the ages of 35 and 39 are covered for one screening mammogram during that five-year age period. Women age 40 and over are covered for one screening mammogram per 12-month period. [Soc. Sec. Act § 1834(c)(2)(A); 42 C.F.R. § 410.34(d).]

The usual Part B deductible is waived for screening mammograms. [Soc. Sec. Act § 1833(b)(5); 42 C.F.R. § § 410.152(l)(2), 410.160(b)(5).]

Part B Coverage of Pap Smears and Pelvic Exams

Medicare covers screening pap smears and screening pelvic examinations. Screening pap smear coverage includes routine exfoliative cytology tests and the physician's interpretation of the results of the tests. Screening pelvic exam coverage includes testing for the early detection of cervical or vaginal cancer and includes clinical breast examinations. [Soc. Sec. Act § 1861(s)(14), (nn); 42 C.F.R. § 410.56; Pub. 100-02, Ch. 15, § 280.4.]

Pap smears and pelvic exams are covered at two-year intervals. Annual exams, however, are covered for women identified as being at high risk for developing cervical or vaginal cancer and for women of childbearing age who have had an abnormality detected during any of the three preceding years. [Soc. Sec. Act § § 1861(nn), 1862(a)(1)(F); 42 C.F.R. § 410.56(b).]

The usual Part B deductible is waived for these exams. [Soc. Sec. Act § 1833(b)(6); 42 C.F.R. § § 410.152(l)(3), 410.160(b)(6); Pub. 100-04, Ch. 18, § 30.3.]

¶369

Part B Coverage of Colorectal Cancer Screening Tests

Part B covers colorectal cancer screening tests. [Soc. Sec. Act § 1861(s)(2)(R), (pp); Pub. 100-02, Ch. 15, § 280.2.2.] Covered screening procedures include: (1) one annual fecal-occult blood test every 12 months for individuals age 50 and older; (2) flexible sigmoidoscopy every four years for individuals age 50 and older; (3) colonoscopy for high-risk individuals every two years and for other individuals every 10 years, including anesthesia furnished in conjunction with the service; and (4) screening barium enemas every four years for individuals age 50 and older who are not at high risk of developing colorectal cancer or every two years for individuals who are at high risk. [Soc. Sec. Act § § 1834(d), 1861(pp); 42 C.F.R. § 410.37.]

An individual is at high risk for developing colorectal cancer if he or she has one or more of the following characteristics: (1) a close relative (sibling, parent, or child) who has had colorectal cancer or an adenomatous polyp; (2) a family history of familial adenomatous polyposis; (3) a family history of hereditary nonpolyposis colorectal cancer; (4) a personal history of colorectal cancer; (5) a personal history of adenomatous polyps; or (6) inflammatory bowel disease, including Crohn's Disease and ulcerative colitis. [42 C.F.R. § 410.37(a)(3); Pub. 100-02, Ch. 15, § 280.2.3.]

Physician assistants, nurse practitioners, and clinical nurse specialists, in addition to the beneficiary's attending physician, are allowed to order screening fecal-occult blood tests. [42 C.F.R. § 410.37(b).]

Deductibles are waived for both colorectal cancer screening tests and surgical and anesthesia services furnished in connection with, as a result of, and in the same clinical encounter (i.e., furnished on the same date) as a planned colorectal cancer screening test. [Soc. Sec. Act § 1833(b)(8); 42 C.F.R. § § 410.152(l)(5), 410.160(b)(7); Pub. 100-04, Ch. 18, § 60.1.1.]

Part B Coverage of Diabetes Screening and Self-Management Services

Medicare covers diabetes outpatient self-management educational and training services furnished by a certified provider who meets certain quality standards. This program is intended to educate beneficiaries in the successful self-management of diabetes. [Soc. Sec. Act § 1861(qq).] The program includes instructions in self-monitoring of blood glucose, education about diet and exercise, an insulin treatment plan developed specifically for the patient who is insulin-dependent, and motivation for patients to use these skills for self-management. [42 C.F.R. § 410.141(c); Pub. 100-02, Ch. 15, § 300.]

The doctor or qualified nonphysician practitioner who is managing the beneficiary's diabetic condition must certify that these services are needed. The services must be provided under a comprehensive plan of care to ensure therapy compliance or provide the patient with the necessary skills and knowledge (including the skill to self-administer injectable drugs) to participate in the management of his or her own condition. Up to 10 hours of initial training and two hours of annual additional training are authorized. [Pub. 100-02, Ch. 15, § § 300, 300.1, 300.3.]

Diabetes screening. Part B covers diabetes screening tests after a referral from a physician or qualified nonphysician practitioner to an individual at risk for diabetes for the purpose of early detection of diabetes. Medicare covers diabetes screening once every 12 months for a beneficiary who is not pre-diabetic and once every six months for a beneficiary who is pre-diabetic. [Soc. Sec. Act § 1861(s)(2)(Y), (yy); 42 C.F.R. § 410.18.]

Medicare Diabetes Prevention Program services. Beginning April 1, 2018, CMS covers Medicare Diabetes Prevention Program (MDPP) services for beneficiaries who: (1)

are enrolled in Part B; (2) attend the first core session within the most recent 12-month time period and, before attending this first core session, had not previously received the set of MDPP services in his or her lifetime; (3) have as of the date of attendance at the first core session a body mass index (BMI) of at least 25 if not self-identified as Asian and a BMI of at least 23 if self-identified as Asian; (4) have, within the 12 months before attending the first core session, a hemoglobin A1c test with a value between 5.7 and 6.4 percent, a fasting plasma glucose of 110–125 mg/dL, or a two-hour plasma glucose of 140–199 mg/dL (oral glucose tolerance test); (4) have, as of the date of attendance at the first core session, no previous diagnosis of type 1 or type 2 diabetes, other than gestational diabetes; and (5) do not have end-stage renal disease. MDPP services are structured health behavior change sessions that are furnished under the MDPP with the goal of preventing diabetes among Medicare beneficiaries with pre-diabetes and follow a CDC-approved curriculum. The sessions provide practical training in long-term dietary change, increased physical activity, and problem-solving strategies for overcoming challenges to maintaining weight loss and a healthy lifestyle. [42 C.F.R. § 410.79.]

Part B Coverage of Bone Mass Measurement Tests

Medicare covers biannual bone mass measurement tests ordered by physicians or qualified nonphysician practitioners to identify bone mass, detect bone loss, or determine bone quality for: (1) estrogen-deficient women at clinical risk for osteoporosis; (2) individuals with vertebral abnormalities; (3) individuals receiving long-term glucocorticoid steroid therapy; (4) individuals with primary hyperparathyroidism; and (5) individuals being monitored to assess the response to or efficacy of an approved osteoporosis drug therapy. A physician must interpret these test results. [Soc. Sec. Act § 1861(s)(15), (rr); 42 C.F.R. § 410.31.]

Part B Coverage of Prostate Cancer Screening Tests

Medicare covers annual prostate cancer screening tests, including digital rectal examinations and prostate-specific antigen (PSA) blood tests, for men over age 50. The tests must be performed (or in the case of the PSA blood test, ordered) by the patient's physician, physician assistant, nurse practitioner, clinical nurse specialist, or certified nurse-midwife. [Soc. Sec. Act § 1861(s)(2)(P), (oo); 42 C.F.R. § 410.39.]

The screening PSA test is not subject to the Part B deductible and coinsurance requirements. The deductible and coinsurance requirements apply to screening rectal examinations. [Pub. 100-04, Ch. 18, § 50.2.]

Part B Coverage of Screening Glaucoma Tests

Medicare covers annual screening glaucoma tests for individuals determined to be at high risk for glaucoma, including: (1) individuals with diabetes mellitus; (2) individuals with a family history of glaucoma; (3) African-Americans age 50 and over; and (4) Hispanic-Americans age 65 and over. [Soc. Sec. Act § 1861(s)(2)(U), (uu); 42 C.F.R. § 410.23; Pub. 100-02, Ch. 15, § 280.1.]

Covered screening tests include: (1) a dilated eye exam with an intraocular pressure measurement; and (2) a direct ophthalmoscopy exam or a slit-lamp biomicroscopic exam. Glaucoma screening examinations must be furnished by, or under the direct supervision of, an optometrist or opthalmologist. "Direct supervision" means the optometrist or opthalmologist must be present in the office suite and be immediately available to furnish assistance and direction throughout the performance of the procedure. [42 C.F.R. § 410.23; Pub. 100-02, Ch. 15, § 280.1.]

¶369

Part B Coverage of Abdominal Aortic Ultrasound

Medicare covers a one-time ultrasound screening for abdominal aortic aneurysm for an individual who, after a referral from a physician or a qualified nonphysician practitioner, has not been previously furnished such an ultrasound screening and is included in at least one of the following risk categories: (1) has a family history of abdominal aortic aneurysm; (2) is a man age 65 to 75 who has smoked at least 100 cigarettes in his lifetime; or (3) is a beneficiary with other factors specified in national coverage determinations. A supplier or supplier who is authorized to provide covered diagnostic services must perform the test. [Soc. Sec. Act § 1861(s)(2)(AA), (bbb); 42 C.F.R. § 410.19; Pub. 100-04, Ch. 18, § 110.2.]

Part B Coverage of Medical Nutrition Therapy Services

Medicare covers medical nutrition therapy (MNT) services for beneficiaries with diabetes or a renal disease who: (1) have not received diabetes outpatient maintenance self-management training services within a specified time period; and (2) are not receiving maintenance dialysis benefits. Services covered include nutritional diagnostic, therapy, and counseling services for the purpose of disease management. The services must be provided by a registered dietitian or nutritional professional pursuant to a referral by the beneficiary's treating physician. [Soc. Sec. Act § 1861(s)(2)(V), (vv); 42 C.F.R. §§ 410.130–410.134.]

Basic coverage of MNT for the first year a beneficiary receives MNT is three hours, and basic coverage for subsequent years is two hours. If the beneficiary's treating physician determines that both MNT and diabetes self-management training are medically necessary in the same episode of care, Medicare will cover both services without decreasing either benefit as long as MNT and diabetes self-management training are not provided on the same date of service. Additional hours are covered if the treating physician determines that there is a change in medical condition, diagnosis, or treatment regimen that requires a change in MNT and orders additional hours during that episode of care. [Pub. 100-03, Ch. 1, § 180.1.]

The Part B deductible is waived for this test. [42 C.F.R. § 410.160(b)(11).]

Part B Coverage of Cardiovascular Screening

Medicare covers cardiovascular screening tests once every five years for an asymptomatic individual. These blood tests measure cholesterol levels and other lipid or triglyceride levels. [Soc. Sec. Act § 1861(s)(2)(X), (xx); 42 C.F.R. § 410.17.]

[¶ 370] Therapeutic Shoes

Therapeutic shoes and inserts are covered for beneficiaries with severe diabetic foot disease. The beneficiary's treating physician, either a doctor of medicine or a doctor of osteopathy who is responsible for diagnosing and treating the patient's diabetic condition, must certify the need for diabetic shoes. [Soc. Sec. Act § 1861(s)(12); *Medicare Benefit Policy Manual*, Pub. 100-02, Ch. 15, § 140.]

The treating physician must:

(1) document in the medical record that the beneficiary has diabetes;

(2) certify that the beneficiary is being treated under a comprehensive plan of care for diabetes and needs diabetic shoes; and

(3) document in the patient's record that the patient has one or more of the following conditions: peripheral neuropathy with evidence of callus formation, a history of pre-ulcerative calluses, a history of previous ulceration, foot deformity, previous amputation, or poor circulation.

[Soc. Sec. Act § 1861(s)(12)(A); Pub. 100-02, Ch. 15, § 140.]

After the physician managing the beneficiary's systemic diabetic condition certifies the need for therapeutic shoes, a podiatrist or other qualified physician who is knowledgeable in the fitting of diabetic shoes and inserts may prescribe the particular type of footwear necessary. A podiatrist or other qualified individual must fit and furnish the footwear. The certifying physician may not furnish the therapeutic shoes unless he or she is the only qualified individual in the area. [Soc. Sec. Act § 1861(s)(12)(B), (C); Pub. 100-02, Ch. 15, § 140.]

Limitations. Coverage is limited to one of the following within a calendar year: (1) one pair of custom-molded shoes (including inserts provided with such shoes) and two additional pairs of inserts; or (2) one pair of depth shoes and three pairs of inserts (not including the noncustomized inserts provided with such shoes). [Pub. 100-02, Ch. 15, § 140.]

[¶ 381] Physical and Occupational Therapy and Speech-Language Pathology Services

The Part B program covers physical therapy, occupational therapy, and speech-language pathology services. [Soc. Sec. Act § 1861(s)(2)(D).]

Types of Covered Outpatient Therapy Services

Part B covers the following types of therapy services.

Occupational therapy. Occupational therapy may involve:

(1) evaluation of a patient's level of function by administering diagnostic and prognostic tests;

(2) teaching task-oriented therapeutic activities designed to restore physical function, such as woodworking activities on an inclined table to restore shoulder, elbow, and wrist range of motion lost as a result of burns;

(3) individualized therapeutic activity programs for patients with a diagnosed psychiatric illness, such as sewing activities following a pattern to reduce confusion and restore reality orientation in a schizophrenic patient;

(4) activities to increase sensory input and improve response for stroke patients with functional loss resulting in a distorted body image;

(5) teaching compensatory technique to improve the level of independence in daily activities or adapt to an evolving deterioration in health and function;

(6) designing, fabricating, and fitting of orthotics and self-help devices; and

(7) vocational and prevocational assessment and training.

[42 C.F.R. § 410.59; *Medicare Benefit Policy Manual*, Pub. 100-02, Ch. 15, § 230.2.]

Physical therapy. Covered physical therapy services are not limited to services typically provided in clinics. They may include services such as aquatic therapy in a community center pool or functional electrical stimulation to enhance walking in spinal cord injury patients. The *Medicare Benefit Policy Manual* discusses types of covered physical therapy services in Chapter 15, §§ 220 and 230. [42 C.F.R. § 410.60; Pub. 100-02, Ch. 15, § 230.1.]

Speech-language pathology. Speech-language pathology services are those services necessary for the diagnosis and treatment of speech and language disorders, which result in communication disabilities and for the diagnosis and treatment of swallowing disorders (dysphagia), regardless of the presence of a communication disability. [42 C.F.R. § 410.62; Pub. 100-02, Ch. 15, § 230.3.]

Providers of Outpatient Therapy Services

Generally, Medicare Part B pays for outpatient therapy services only if they are furnished by an individual meeting the qualifications in 42 C.F.R. part 484 for a therapist or appropriately supervised therapy assistant under the following conditions:

(1) They are furnished to a beneficiary while he or she is under the care of a physician who is a doctor of medicine, osteopathy, or podiatric medicine.

(2) They are furnished under a written plan of treatment that meets the requirements of 42 C.F.R. § 410.61.

(3) They are furnished: (a) by a provider as defined in 42 C.F.R. § 489.2, or by others under arrangements with, and under the supervision of, a provider; (b) by, or under the direct supervision of, a therapist in private practice; or (c) by, or incident to the service of, a physician, physician assistant, clinical nurse specialist, or nurse practitioner when those professionals may perform therapy services within the scope of state law.

[Soc. Sec. Act § 1861(g), (p), (ll); 42 C.F.R. §§ 410.59(a), 410.60(a), 410.62(a).]

Medicare Part B pays for outpatient therapy services furnished to an inpatient of a hospital, critical access hospital (CAH), or skilled nursing facility (SNF) who requires them but who has exhausted or is otherwise ineligible for benefit days under Medicare Part A. [42 C.F.R. § 410.59(b), 410.60(b), 410.62(c).]

Therapy services are payable under the physician fee schedule when furnished by:

(1) a provider to its outpatients in the patient's home;

(2) a provider to patients who come to the facility's outpatient department;

(3) a provider to inpatients of other institutions; or

(4) a supplier to patients in the office or in the patient's home.

[Pub. 100-02, Ch. 15, § 220.1.4.]

Comprehensive outpatient rehabilitation facilities. Comprehensive outpatient rehabilitation facilities (CORFs) may provide these outpatient therapy services in the home as long as the patient also does not receive home health benefits. The CORF plan of treatment must be reviewed every 60 days for respiratory therapy and every 90 days for physical therapy, occupational therapy, and speech-language pathology. [42 C.F.R. § 410.105(b)(3)(i), (c)(2); Pub. 100-02, Ch. 12, §§ 10, 30.]

Rehabilitation agencies. Rehabilitation agencies that are Medicare Part B providers must have a physician's signature in the clinical record of a rehabilitation plan within 30 days of an initial therapy visit and within each 90-day recertification period thereafter, or as often as the patient's condition changes. [42 C.F.R. §§ 424.24(c)(2), 485.711(b)(3).]

Private practice therapists. The Part B program covers the services of a "qualified" physical therapist, speech-language pathologist, or occupational therapist in "private practice" if the therapist or speech-language pathologist: (1) is legally authorized to engage in private practice by the state in which he or she practices and practices only within the scope of his or her license; (2) engages in private practice on a regular basis as an individual in a solo practice, partnership, or group practice, or as an employee of one of these; (3) bills Medicare only for services furnished in his or her private practice office space or in the patient's home (excluding any institution that is a hospital, a critical access hospital (CAH), or a SNF); and (4) treats individuals who are patients of the practice and for whom the practice collects fees for the services furnished. [Soc. Sec. Act § 1861(p); 42 C.F.R. §§ 410.59(c), 410.60(c), 410.62(c).]

The services must be provided either by or under the direct personal supervision of the therapist in private practice, and the supporting personnel, including other therapists, must be employees of the therapist in private practice. Services furnished by a therapist in the therapist's office under arrangements with hospitals in rural communities and public health agencies, or services provided in the beneficiary's home under arrangements with a provider of therapy services, are not covered under this provision. [Pub. 100-02, Ch. 15, § 230.4.]

Reasonableness and Necessity of Outpatient Therapy Services

To be considered reasonable and necessary to treat an illness or an injury, therapy services must meet all of the following conditions:

(1) The services must be considered under accepted standards of medical practice to be a specific and effective treatment for the patient's condition.

(2) The services must be of such a level of complexity and sophistication, or the condition of the patient must be such, that the services required can be safely and effectively performed only by a qualified therapist or under a therapist's supervision.

(3) While a beneficiary's particular medical condition is a valid factor in deciding if skilled therapy services are needed, a beneficiary's diagnosis or prognosis cannot be the sole factor in deciding that a service is or is not skilled; the key issue is whether the skills of a therapist are needed to treat the illness or injury, or whether the services can be carried out by nonskilled personnel.

(4) The amount, frequency, and duration of services must be reasonable.

Services related to activities for the general good and welfare of patients, e.g., general exercises to promote overall fitness and flexibility and activities to provide diversion or general motivation, do not constitute therapy services for Medicare purposes. [Pub. 100-02, Ch. 15, § 220.2.]

Medicare coverage does not turn on the presence or absence of a beneficiary's potential for improvement from the therapy but, rather, on the beneficiary's need for skilled care. Skilled therapy services may be necessary to improve a patient's current condition, to maintain the patient's current condition, or to prevent or slow further deterioration of the patient's condition. [Pub. 100-02, Ch. 15, § 220.2.]

Medical review. A targeted medical review process applies when the accrued annual incurred expenses reach the following medical review threshold amounts: (1) beginning with 2018 and before 2028, $3,000; and (2) for 2028 and each year thereafter, the applicable medical review threshold is determined by increasing the medical review threshold in effect for the previous year (starting with $3,000 in 2027) by the increase in the Medicare Economic Index for the current year. [42 C.F.R. §§ 410.59(e)(3), 410.60(e)(3).]

Maintenance therapy. If the specialized skill, knowledge, and judgment of a qualified therapist are required to establish or design a maintenance program to maintain the patient's current condition or to prevent or slow further deterioration, the establishment or design of a maintenance program by a qualified therapist is covered. Once a maintenance program is established, coverage of therapy services to carry out a maintenance program turns on the beneficiary's need for skilled care. [Pub. 100-02, Ch. 15, § 220.2.]

Plan of Treatment Requirements for Outpatient Rehabilitation Services

Outpatient rehabilitation services (including services furnished by a qualified physical or occupational therapist in private practice) must be furnished under a written plan of treatment. The plan must be established before the start of treatment by one of the following:

(1) a physician;

(2) a physical therapist who furnishes the physical therapy services;

(3) a speech-language pathologist who furnishes the speech-language pathology services;

(4) an occupational therapist who furnishes the occupational therapy services; or

(5) a nurse practitioner, clinical nurse specialist, or physician assistant.

[42 C.F.R. § 410.61(a), (b).]

The plan must prescribe the type, amount, frequency, and duration of the physical therapy, occupational therapy, or speech-language pathology services to be furnished to the individual and indicate the diagnosis and anticipated goals. [42 C.F.R. § 410.61(c).]

Any changes in the plan must be made in writing, incorporated in the plan immediately, and signed by one of the following: (1) the physician; (2) the physical therapist who furnished the physical therapy services; (3) the occupational therapist that furnished the occupational therapy services; (4) the speech-language pathologist who furnished the speech-language pathology services; (5) a registered professional nurse or a staff physician, in accordance with oral orders from the physician, physical therapist, occupational therapist, or speech-language pathologist who furnished the services; or (6) a nurse practitioner, clinical nurse specialist, or physician assistant. [42 C.F.R. § 410.61(d).]

Physician certification and recertification. For outpatient physical therapy and speech-language pathology services, as soon as possible after the plan of care is established, the physician, nonphysician practitioner (NPP), or therapist/pathologist that established the plan must sign the plan, certifying that: (1) the beneficiary needs therapy or speech-language pathology services; (2) the services were furnished while the beneficiary was under the care of a physician, nurse practitioner, clinical nurse specialist, or physician assistant; and (3) the services were furnished under a plan of treatment that meets the requirements of 42 C.F.R. § 410.61. If the plan of treatment was established by a physician, nurse practitioner, clinical nurse specialist, or physician assistant, the certification must be signed by that physician or nonphysician practitioner; if it was established by a physical therapist or speech-language pathologist, the certification must be signed by a physician or a nurse practitioner, clinical nurse specialist, or physician assistant who has knowledge of the case. Recertification is required at least every 90 days. [42 C.F.R. § 424.24(c).]

Outpatient Therapy Provided Under Arrangements

A provider may make arrangements with other providers to furnish covered outpatient physical, occupational, or speech therapy. [Soc. Sec. Act § 1861(p).] Services under "arrangements" are services for which receipt of payment by the provider for the arranged services must (as with services provided directly) relieve the beneficiary or any other person of further liability to pay for the services.

The provider must assume professional responsibility for the services and put into place many of the same controls applied to services furnished by salaried employees. The provider must:

(1) accept the patient for treatment in accordance with its admission policies;

(2) maintain a complete and timely clinical record on the patient that includes diagnosis, medical history, orders, and progress notes relating to all services received;

(3) maintain liaison with the attending physician or NPP with regard to the progress of the patient and to assure that the required plan of treatment is periodically reviewed by the physician;

(4) secure from the physician/NPP the required certifications and recertifications; and

(5) ensure that the medical necessity of such service is reviewed on a sample basis by the agency's staff or an outside review group.

[Pub. 100-02, Ch. 15, § 230.6.]

Providers "under an arrangement" must furnish services in accordance with the terms of a written contract specifying that the provider retains responsibility for and control and supervision of such services. The contract also must:

(1) provide that the therapy services be furnished in accordance with a plan of care;

(2) specify the geographic areas in which the services are to be furnished;

(3) provide that personnel and services meet the same requirements as if furnished directly by the provider;

(4) provide that the therapist will participate in conferences required to coordinate patient care;

(5) provide for the preparation of treatment records that will be incorporated into clinical records;

(6) specify the financial arrangements, i.e., the contracting organization or individual may not bill the patient or the health insurance program; and

(7) specify the contract's time period and manner of termination or renewal.

[Pub. 100-02, Ch. 15, § 230.6.]

Hospital billing "under arrangements." A hospital may bill Medicare for outpatient therapy (physical therapy, occupational therapy, or speech-language pathology) services that it furnishes to its outpatients, either directly or under arrangements in the hospital's outpatient department. Services provided to residents of a Medicare-certified SNF may not be billed by the hospital as services to its outpatients; these services are covered under a SNF's global prospective payment system payment for the covered Part A stay. [Pub. 100-02, Ch. 15, § 230.6.]

[¶ 382] Rural Health Clinics and Federally Qualified Health Centers

Part B covers rural health clinic (RHC) and federally qualified health center (FQHC) services in medically underserved areas. RHCs are clinics located in areas designated by the Bureau of the Census as rural and the Secretary of HHS as medically underserved or having an insufficient number of physicians. FQHCs are defined similarly but are usually located in urban areas. [Soc. Sec. Act § § 1832(a)(2)(D), 1861(aa), 1861(s)(2)(E); 42 C.F.R. § § 410.10(j), (s), 491.2.]

To be covered, RHC and FQHC services must be furnished: (1) in an RHC, FQHC, or other outpatient setting, including a patient's place of residence; or (2) during a Medicare Part A stay in a skilled nursing facility (SNF) only when provided by a physician, nurse practitioner (NP), physician assistant (PA), certified nurse-midwife (CNM), or clinical psychologist (CP) employed or under contract with the RHC or FQHC at the time the services are provided. Services are not covered in a hospital or critical access hospital. [42 C.F.R. § § 405.2411(b), 405.2446(c) and (d).]

Except for certain preventive services for which the coinsurance is statutorily waived, the beneficiary in an RHC must pay the deductible and coinsurance amount, and the beneficiary in a FQHC must pay the coinsurance amount. There is no Part B deductible in

FQHCs for FQHC-covered services. For RHCs, the coinsurance is 20 percent of the total charges. For FQHCs, the coinsurance is 20 percent of the lesser of the FQHC's charge for the specific payment code or the prospective payment system (PPS) rate. For claims with a mix of waived and nonwaived services, applicable coinsurance and deductibles are assessed only on the nonwaived services. [Soc. Sec. Act § 1833(a)(1)(Z), (b)(4); 42 C.F.R. §§ 405.2410(a)(2) and (b)(2), 405.2462(e); *Medicare Benefit Policy Manual*, Pub. 100-02, Ch. 13, § 90.]

As discussed at ¶ 607, services paid for directly or indirectly by a government entity usually are excluded from coverage under the Medicare program. The law, however, makes a specific exception to this exclusion in the case of RHC and FQHC services. [Soc. Sec. Act § 1862(a)(3).]

See ¶ 847 for a discussion of payment for RHC services and ¶ 850 for a discussion of payment for FQHC services.

Covered RHC and FQHC Services

RHC and FQHC services reimbursable under Part B include:

(1) physicians' services;

(2) services and supplies incident to a physician's services;

(3) similar services furnished by a physician assistant, nurse practitioner, certified nurse-midwife, clinical psychologist, or clinical social worker;

(4) services and supplies incident to an NP, PA, CNM, CP, or clinical social worker (CSW) service; and

(5) visiting nurse services.

[Soc. Sec. Act § 1861(aa); 42 C.F.R. §§ 405.2411(a), 405.2446.] FQHC services also include preventive primary services, medical nutrition therapy services, and diabetes outpatient self-management training services. [42 C.F.R. § 405.2446(b)(8), (9).]

Hospice services. RHCs and FQHCs can treat hospice beneficiaries for any medical conditions not related to their terminal illness; however, if a Medicare beneficiary who has elected the hospice benefit receives care from an RHC or FQHC related to his or her terminal illness, the RHC or FQHC cannot be reimbursed for the visit, even if it is a medically necessary, face-to-face visit with an RHC or FQHC practitioner, because that would result in duplicate payment for services. [Pub. 100-02, Ch. 13, § 210.]

Exceptions to this rule apply when the RHC or FQHC has a contract with the hospice provider to furnish: (1) core hospice services related to the patient's terminal illness and related conditions when extraordinary circumstances exist within the hospice; or (2) highly specialized nursing services that are provided by the hospice so infrequently that it would be impractical and prohibitively expensive for the hospice to employ a practitioner to provide these services. In these situations, all costs associated with the provision of hospice services must be carved out of the RHC or FQHC cost report, and the RHC or FQHC is reimbursed by the hospice. [Pub. 100-02, Ch. 13, § 210.]

Laboratory services. Although RHCs and FQHCs are required to furnish certain laboratory services, laboratory services are not covered under the RHC or FQHC benefit. RHCs and FQHCs must separately bill for diagnostic laboratory tests that are covered under Medicare Part B. [42 C.F.R. § 410.32(d)(1)(iv), (vi); Pub. 100-02, Ch. 13, § 60.1.]

Telehealth services. RHCs and FQHCs may serve as an originating site for telehealth services, which is the location of an eligible Medicare beneficiary at the time the service being furnished via a telecommunications system occurs, and will be paid an originating site facility fee. Although FQHC services are not subject to the Medicare deductible, the deductible must be applied when an FQHC bills for the telehealth originating site facility fee because telehealth services are not considered an FQHC service. [42 C.F.R. § 410.78(b)(3)(iii), (iv); Pub. 100-02, Ch. 13, § 200.]

RHCs and FQHCs are not authorized to serve as a distant site for telehealth consultations, which is the location of the practitioner at the time the telehealth service is furnished, and may not bill or include the cost of a visit on the cost report. This includes telehealth services that are furnished by an RHC or FQHC practitioner who is employed by or under contract with the RHC or FQHC, or a non-RHC or FQHC practitioner furnishing services through a direct or indirect contract. [Pub. 100-02, Ch. 13, § 200.]

Part B Coverage of Professional Services Provided in RHCs and FQHCs

Physicians' services are professional services furnished by a physician at the RHC or FQHC, or outside of the RHC or FQHC by a physician whose employment agreement or contract with the RHC or FQHC provides that he or she will be paid by the RHC or FQHC for such services as long as certification and cost reporting requirements are met. "Physician" includes a doctor of medicine, osteopathy, dental surgery, dental medicine, podiatry, optometry, or chiropractic who is licensed and practicing within the licensee's scope of practice and meets other requirements. Dentists, podiatrists, optometrists, and chiropractors are not considered primary care physicians and do not meet the requirements to be either a physician medical director or the physician or nonphysician practitioner that must be available at all times the clinic is open. [42 C.F.R. § 405.2412; Pub. 100-02, Ch. 13, § 110.]

Nurse practitioner and physician assistant services. Services furnished by NPs, PAs, or CNMs who are employed by or receive compensation from an RHC or FQHC are reimbursable if furnished under the medical supervision of a physician and in accordance with any medical orders prepared by a physician for the care and treatment of a patient. Such services must be of a type that the professional is legally permitted to perform by the state in which the service is rendered, and they must be services that would be covered if furnished by a physician. The NP, PA, or CNM must directly examine the patient or directly review the patient's medical information such as x-rays, EKGs and electroencephalograms, or tissue samples. [42 C.F.R. § 405.2414; Pub. 100-02, Ch. 13, § 130.]

CPs and CSWs. For CP or CSW professional services to be covered, the services must be (1) furnished by an individual who owns, is employed by, or furnishes services under contract to the FQHC; (2) of a type that the CP or CSW who furnishes the services is legally permitted to perform by the state in which the service is furnished; (3) performed by a CSW or CP who is legally authorized to perform such services under state law; and (4) covered if furnished by a physician or as incident to a physician's professional service. The services of CPs or CSWs are not covered if state law or regulations require that the services be performed under a physician's order and no such order was prepared. Services that a hospital or SNF is required to provide to an inpatient or outpatient as a requirement for participation are not included. Services may include diagnosis, treatment, and consultation. The CP or CSW must directly examine the patient or directly review the patient's medical information. [42 C.F.R. § 405.2450; Pub. 100-02, Ch. 13, § 150.]

Part B Coverage of Incident-to Services and Supplies Furnished in RHCs and FQHCs

Services and supplies incident to a physician's professional services furnished in an RHC or FQHC are reimbursable if the service or supply is:

- of a type commonly furnished in physicians' offices;

¶382

- of a type commonly rendered either without charge or included in the RHC's or FQHC's bill;

- furnished as an incidental, although integral, part of a physician's professional services;

- furnished in accordance with applicable state law; and

- furnished under the direct supervision of a physician, except that services and supplies furnished incident to transitional care management, general care management, and the Psychiatric Collaborative Care Model can be furnished under general supervision of a physician when these services or supplies are furnished by auxiliary personnel.

Direct supervision does not mean that the physician must be present in the same room; however, the physician must be in the RHC or FQHC and immediately available to provide assistance and direction throughout the time the practitioner is furnishing services. [42 C.F.R. § 405.2413(a); Pub. 100-02, Ch. 13, §§ 120, 120.1.]

Incident-to services and supplies include drugs and biologics that are not usually self-administered and Medicare-covered preventive injectable drugs (e.g., influenza, pneumococcal); venipuncture; bandages, gauze, oxygen, and other supplies; and services provided by auxiliary personnel such as a nurse, medical assistant, or other clinical personnel acting under the supervision of the physician. Supplies and drugs that must be billed to the durable medical equipment, prosthetics and orthotics, and supplies Medicare administrative contractor (DMEPOS MAC) or Medicare Part D are not included. [42 C.F.R. § 405.2413(b); Pub. 100-02, Ch. 13, § 120.]

Part B Coverage of RHC/FQHC Visiting Nurse Services

Visiting nurse services are covered if provided to a homebound patient (i.e., one who is permanently or temporarily confined to his or her place of residence because of a medical or health condition) for an RHC or FQHC located in an area that has a shortage of home health agencies (HHAs). The services must be furnished by a registered professional nurse or licensed practical nurse that is employed by or receives compensation for the services from the RHC or FQHC under a written plan of treatment. [42 C.F.R. § 405.2416(a), (d).]

HHA shortage. A shortage of HHAs exists if the Secretary determines that the RHC or FQHC: (1) is located in a county, parish, or similar geographic area in which there is no participating HHA or adequate home health services are not available to RHC or FQHC patients; (2) has (or expects to have) patients whose permanent residences are not within the area serviced by a participating HHA; or (3) has (or expects to have) patients whose permanent residences are not within a reasonable traveling distance, based on climate and terrain, of a participating HHA. [42 C.F.R. § 405.2417; Pub. 100-02, Ch. 13, § 190.3.]

Covered services. Covered services include: (1) those that must be performed by a registered professional nurse or licensed practical nurse if the safety of the patient is to be ensured and the medically desired results achieved; and (2) personal care services, to the extent covered under Medicare as home health services, including helping the patient to bathe, get in and out of bed, exercise, and take medications. However, household and other housekeeping services or other services that would constitute custodial care are not covered. [42 C.F.R. § 405.2416(b), (c).]

Treatment plan. The written treatment plan must be (1) established and reviewed every 60 days by a supervising physician of the RHC or FQHC; or (2) established by an NP, PA, or CNM and reviewed at least every 60 days by a supervising physician. The treatment plan must be signed by the supervising physician, NP, PA, or CNM of the RHC or FQHC. [42 C.F.R. § 405.2416(a)(4).]

If the patient does not receive at least one covered nursing visit in a 60-day period, the plan is considered terminated for the purpose of Medicare coverage unless (1) the supervising physician has reviewed the plan of treatment and made a recertification within the 60-day period that indicates that the lapse of visits is a part of the physician's regimen for the patient; or (2) nursing visits are required at intervals less frequent than once every 60 days, but the intervals are predictable. [Pub. 100-02, Ch. 13, § 190.5.]

Coverage of Preventive Services Provided in RHCs and FQHCs

Preventive services covered under the FQHC benefit include the following:

(1) the screening and other preventive services specified in Soc. Sec. Act § 1861(ww)(2), except for electrocardiograms;

(2) initial preventive physical examinations (see Soc. Sec. Act § 1861(ww)(1) and 42 C.F.R. § 410.16); and

(3) annual wellness visits (Soc. Sec. Act § 1861(hhh); 42 C.F.R. § 410.15).

[Soc. Sec. Act § 1861(aa)(3)(A); 42 C.F.R. § 405.2449.]

Preventive primary services. Preventive primary services are those health services that an FQHC is required to provide as preventive primary health services under section 330 of the Public Health Services Act and are furnished by or under the direct supervision of a physician, NP, PA, CNM, CP, or CSW employed by or under contract with the FQHC. Except as specifically provided in Soc. Sec. Act § 1861(s), such services include only drugs and biologics that cannot be self-administered. [Soc. Sec. Act § 1861(aa)(3)(B); 42 C.F.R. § 405.2448(a).]

42 C.F.R. § 405.2448(b) specifies the preventive primary services that may be paid for when provided by FQHCs. Preventive primary services do not include group or mass information programs, health education classes, group education activities, eyeglasses, hearing aids, or preventive dental services. Screening mammography is not considered a FQHC service but may be provided at a FQHC if it meets the applicable requirements specified in 42 C.F.R. § 410.34. [42 C.F.R. § 405.2448(b)–(e).]

Non-RHC/FQHC Services

There are items and services covered and payable under Medicare Part B that do not fall under the definition of RHC or FQHC services. If these services are authorized to be furnished by the RHC or FQHC and are covered under a separate Medicare benefit category, the services are billed separately under the payment rules that apply to the service. Items or services covered under Part B that are not RHC or FQHC services include:

- durable medical equipment (whether rented or sold), including iron lungs, oxygen tents, hospital beds, and wheelchairs used in the patient's place of residence;

- ambulance services;

- telehealth distant-site services;

- technical component of a RHC or FQHC service including diagnostic tests such as x-rays and EKGs;

- prosthetic devices (other than dental) that replace all or part of an internal body organ (including colostomy bags) and supplies directly related to colostomy care, and the replacement of such devices; and

- body braces.

[Pub. 100-02, Ch. 13, § 60.1.]

[¶ 383] Home Health Services

For Medicare beneficiaries that are enrolled in both Medicare Part A and Part B, Part A pays home health services for the first 100 visits following a "spell of illness" that required a hospital or skilled nursing home (SNF) stay, referred to as a "post institutional" stay. Part A finances up to 100 visits during one home health spell of illness if the following criteria are met:

> (1) the beneficiary is enrolled in Part A and Part B and qualifies for home health benefits;

> (2) the beneficiary meets the three-consecutive-day stay requirement; and

> (3) the home health services are initiated and the first covered home health visit is rendered within 14 days of discharge from a three-consecutive-day stay in a hospital or rural primary care hospital or within 14 days of discharge from a skilled nursing facility in which post-hospital extended care services were provided.

If the first home health visit is not initiated within 14 days of discharge or if the three-consecutive-day stay requirement is not met, then services are covered under Part B. [Soc. Sec. Act § 1812(a)(3); *Medicare Benefit Policy Manual*, Pub. 100-02, Ch. 7, § § 60.1, 60.2, 60.3.]

After a beneficiary exhausts 100 visits of Part A post-institutional home health services, Part B finances the balance of the home health spell of illness. [Pub. 100-02, Ch. 7, § 60.1.]

Post-institutional defined. Home health services are considered "post-institutional" if they were furnished to a beneficiary within 14 days of discharge from: (1) a hospital in which the individual was an inpatient for at least three consecutive days before discharge; or (2) a SNF in which the beneficiary received post-hospital extended care services. [Soc. Sec. Act § 1861(tt)(1); Pub. 100-02, Ch. 7, § 60.3.]

Spell of illness defined. For home health services, a "spell of illness" is a period of consecutive days beginning with the first day that the beneficiary receives post-institutional home health services during a month in which the patient is entitled to Part A benefits.. The home health spell of illness ends when the individual has not received inpatient hospital, SNF, or home health services for 60 consecutive days. [Soc. Sec. Act § 1861(tt)(2); Pub. 100-02, Ch. 7, § 60.1.]

Requirements for home health benefits. To qualify for home health benefits, a beneficiary must: (1) be confined to the home; (2) be under a physician's care; (3) be receiving services under a plan of care established and periodically reviewed by a physician; (4) be in need of skilled nursing care on an intermittent basis, or physical therapy or speech-language pathology services; or (5) have a continued need for occupational therapy. [Soc. Sec. Act § 1835(a)(2)(A); Pub. 100-02, Ch. 7, § 30.]

Face-to-face encounter. A physician, nurse practitioner, clinical nurse specialist, certified nurse-midwife, or physician assistant must have a face-to-face encounter with the beneficiary related to the reason for the beneficiary's admission into home health at least 90 days before or within 30 days after home health care begins. The encounter must be documented by the certifying physician. Documentation must include:

> (1) the date of the encounter;

> (2) an explanation of why the clinical findings of the encounter, which was related to the primary reason for home care, support that the patient is homebound and in need of Medicare covered home health services; and

> (3) a physician signature.

[Soc. Sec. Act § 1814(a)(2)(C); 42 C.F.R. § 424.22(a)(1)(v).]

Part A home health benefits are discussed beginning at ¶ 250. The home health prospective payment system is discussed at ¶ 830.

[¶ 385] Comprehensive Outpatient Rehabilitation Facility Services

A comprehensive outpatient rehabilitation facility (CORF) is a public or private institution that is capable of providing a broad array of rehabilitation services on an outpatient basis at a central location in a coordinated fashion. Medicare Part B covers items and services furnished by a physician or other qualified professional personnel to an individual who is an outpatient of a CORF under a plan established and periodically reviewed by a physician. Covered services include:

(1) physicians' services;

(2) physical, occupational, and respiratory therapy and speech-language pathology services;

(3) prosthetic and orthotic devices, including testing, fitting, or training in the use of such devices;

(4) social and psychological services;

(5) nursing care provided by or under the supervision of a registered professional nurse;

(6) drugs and biologics that are administered by or under the supervision of a physician or registered nurse, and are not usually self-administered by the patient;

(7) supplies and durable medical equipment (DME); and

(8) a home environment evaluation visit.

[Soc. Sec. Act §§ 1832(a)(2)(E), 1861(cc)(1); 42 C.F.R. § 410.100.]

There must be potential for restoration or improvement of lost or impaired functions for CORF services to be covered. For example, treatments involving repetitive exercises (i.e., maintenance programs, general conditioning, or ambulation) that do not require the skilled services of therapists or other professional rehabilitation practitioners are not covered because nonmedical personnel such as family members or exercise instructors could perform these services in the patient's residence. It is not reasonable and medically necessary for such activities to be performed in a CORF setting by CORF personnel. [42 C.F.R. § 410.102(b); *Medicare Benefit Policy Manual*, Pub. 100-02, Ch. 12, § 10.]

Excluded services. None of the services listed above is covered as a CORF service if it: (1) would not be covered as an inpatient hospital service if furnished to a hospital inpatient; or (2) is not reasonable and necessary for the diagnosis or treatment of illness or injury or to improve the functioning of a malformed body member. Hyperbaric oxygen services, infusion therapy services, cardiac rehabilitation services, and diagnostic sleep studies are not covered CORF services because they do not meet the definition of CORF services and/or do not relate to the rehabilitation plan of treatment. [Soc. Sec. Act § 1861(cc)(1); 42 C.F.R. § 410.102; Pub. 100-02, Ch. 12, § 10.]

Requirements for Coverage of CORF Services

To become a patient of a CORF, the beneficiary must be under the care of a physician who certifies that the beneficiary needs skilled rehabilitation services. The referring physician must certify that the individual needs skilled rehabilitation services, and make the following information available to the CORF before or at the time treatment is begun: (1) the individual's significant medical history; (2) current medical findings; (3) diagnoses and contraindications to any treatment modality; and (4) rehabilitation goals, if determined. [42 C.F.R. § 410.105(a); Pub. 100-02, Ch. 12, § 30.]

Place of service. Except for a home environment evaluation and physical, occupational, and speech-language pathology services, all CORF services must be provided on the premises of the CORF. Physical, occupational, and speech-language services may be administered at a patient's home when payment for these therapy services is not otherwise made under the Medicare home health benefit. [42 C.F.R. § 410.105(b)(2), (b)(3); Pub. 100-02, Ch. 12, § 30.]

Plan of treatment. CORF services must be furnished under a written plan of treatment that (1) is established and signed by a physician before treatment begins; and (2) prescribes the type, amount, frequency, and duration of the services to be furnished, and indicates the diagnosis and anticipated rehabilitation goals. The CORF physician or the referring physician must review the plan of treatment at least every 60 days for respiratory therapy services and every 90 days for physical therapy, occupational therapy and speech-language pathology services. The reviewing physician must certify or recertify that the plan is being followed, the patient is making progress in attaining the rehabilitation goals, and the treatment is having no harmful effects on the patient. [42 C.F.R. § 410.105(c); Pub. 100-02, Ch. 12, § 30.]

Requirements for Specific CORF Services

CORF facility physician services are administrative in nature and include consultation with and medical supervision of nonphysician staff, participation in plan of treatment reviews and patient care review conferences, and other medical and facility administration activities. Diagnostic and therapeutic services furnished to an individual CORF patient by a physician in a CORF facility are not CORF physician services. These services, if covered, are physician services under 42 C.F.R. § 410.20, and the physician is reimbursed under the physician fee schedule. [42 C.F.R. § 410.100(a); Pub. 100-02, Ch. 12, § 40.1.]

Physical therapy. Physical therapy services include: (1) testing and measurement of the function or dysfunction of the neuromuscular, musculoskeletal, cardiovascular, and respiratory systems; and (2) assessment and treatment related to dysfunction caused by illness or injury, and aimed at preventing or reducing disability or pain and restoring lost function. The establishment of a maintenance therapy program for an individual whose restoration potential has been reached is a physical therapy service, but the maintenance therapy itself is not covered as part of these services. A qualified physical therapist evaluates and reevaluates a patient's level of function; determines whether a physical therapy program could reasonably be expected to improve, restore, or compensate for lost function; develops, in consultation with the physician, the physical therapy plan of treatment; and conducts the discharge visit. [42 C.F.R. § 410.100(b); Pub. 100-02, Ch. 12, § 40.2.]

Occupational therapy. Occupational therapy services include: (1) teaching of compensatory techniques to permit an individual with a physical impairment or limitation to engage in daily activities; (2) evaluation of an individual's level of independent functioning; (3) selection and teaching of task-oriented therapeutic activities to restore sensory-integrative function; and (4) assessment of an individual's vocational potential, except when the assessment is related solely to vocational rehabilitation. Such services are covered if physical therapy services are the predominate rehabilitation services provided in the CORF. A qualified occupational therapist evaluates and reevaluates the patient's level of function and develops, in consultation with the physician, the occupational therapy plan of treatment. [42 C.F.R. § 410.100(c); Pub. 100-02, Ch. 12, § 40.3.]

Speech-language pathology services. A qualified speech-language pathologist evaluates and reevaluates a patient's level of function, determines whether a speech-language program could reasonably be expected to improve, restore, or compensate for lost function, and recommends a speech-language plan of treatment to the physician. Speech-language pathology therapy services are covered CORF services if physical therapy services are the predominant rehabilitation services provided in the CORF. [42 C.F.R. § 410.100(d); Pub. 100-02, Ch. 12, § 40.4.]

Respiratory therapy. Covered respiratory therapy services include those services that can be provided appropriately to CORF patients by a qualified respiratory therapist under a physician-established respiratory therapy plan of treatment. Respiratory therapy services are for the assessment, treatment, and monitoring of patients with deficiencies or abnormalities of cardiopulmonary function. Respiratory therapy services include: (1) application of techniques for support of oxygenation and ventilation of the patient; (2) therapeutic use and monitoring of gases, mists, and aerosols and related equipment; (3) bronchial hygiene therapy; and (4) pulmonary rehabilitation techniques to develop strength and endurance of respiratory muscles and other techniques to increase respiratory function, such as graded activity services. Respiratory therapy services include the physiological monitoring necessary to furnish these services. The facility physician must be present in the facility for a sufficient time to provide medical direction, medical care services, and consultation. [42 C.F.R. § 410.100(e); Pub. 100-02, Ch. 12, § 40.5.]

Prosthetic and orthotic devices and supplies. In general, orthotics and prosthetics are covered when furnished in conjunction with a physician's service or on a physician's order. These devices are covered CORF services if they are included as part of the rehabilitation plan of treatment. The payment for an orthosis or prosthesis includes its design, materials, measurements, fabrications, testing, fitting, adjustments and training in the use of the device. Adjustments to an artificial limb or other appliance required by a change in the patient's condition are covered when ordered by the patient's referring physician or CORF physician. [42 C.F.R. § 410.100(f), (g); Pub. 100-02, Ch. 12, § 40.6.]

Social and psychological services. Social and psychological services include the assessment and treatment of an individual's mental and emotional functioning and the response to and rate of progress as it relates to the individual's rehabilitation plan of treatment, including physical therapy services, occupational therapy services, speech-language pathology services, and respiratory therapy services. To be covered as CORF services, social and/or psychological services must contribute to the improvement of the individual's rehabilitation condition and be included as part of, or directly relate to, the rehabilitation treatment plan; the services may not relate to a mental health diagnosis. [42 C.F.R. § 410.100(h); Pub. 100-02, Ch. 12, § 40.7.]

Nursing services. Nursing care services include nursing services provided by a registered nurse that are prescribed by a physician and specified in or directly related to the rehabilitation treatment plan and necessary for the attainment of the rehabilitation goals of the physical therapy, occupational therapy, speech-language pathology, or respiratory therapy plan of treatment. Nursing services must support or further the services and goals provided in the rehabilitation plan of treatment and may not substitute for or supplant the services of physical therapists, occupational therapists, speech-language pathologists, and respiratory therapists. [42 C.F.R. § 410.100(i); Pub. 100-02, Ch. 12, § 40.8.]

Drugs and biologics. Covered drugs and biologics must: (1) be prescribed by a physician and administered by or under the supervision of a physician or by a registered professional nurse; and (2) not be excluded from Medicare Part B payment for reasons specified in 42 C.F.R. § 410.29. There are, however, no drugs and biologics currently identified as appropriate for a therapy rehabilitation plan of treatment. [42 C.F.R. § 410.100(j); Pub. 100-02, Ch. 12, § 40.9.]

¶385

Supplies and DME. Covered supplies and DME include: (1) disposable supplies; and (2) DME of the type specified in 42 C.F.R. § 410.38 (except for renal dialysis systems) for a patient's use outside the CORF, whether purchased or rented. [42 C.F.R. § 410.100(k).]

Home environment evaluation. A home environment evaluation (1) is a single home visit to evaluate the potential impact of the home situation on the patient's rehabilitation goals; and (2) requires the presence of the patient and a physical therapist, occupational therapist, or speech-language pathologist, as appropriate. The purpose of the home environment evaluation is to permit the rehabilitation plan of treatment to be tailored to take into account the patient's home environment. The home environment evaluation is covered only if there is a clear indication that the home environment might adversely affect the patient's rehabilitation. [42 C.F.R. § 410.100(l); Pub. 100-02, Ch. 12, § 40.10.]

Vaccines. Medicare pays for influenza virus vaccine and pneumococcal pneumonia vaccine and their administration as well as for hepatitis B vaccine and its administration when furnished to a beneficiary who is at high or intermediate risk of contracting hepatitis B. [Pub. 100-02, Ch. 12, § 40.11.]

[¶ 386] Ambulatory Surgical Services

There are a number of surgical procedures covered by Medicare that, though usually performed on an inpatient basis, may be performed on an outpatient basis, consistent with sound medical practice. Medicare covers surgical procedures that do not have a significant safety risk when performed in an outpatient ambulatory surgical center (ASC) and do not require an overnight stay. [42 C.F.R. § 416.166.]

ASC definition. An ASC is a distinct entity that operates exclusively for the purpose of furnishing outpatient surgical services to patients not requiring hospitalization and in which the expected duration of services would not exceed 24 hours following admission. The entity must have an agreement with CMS to participate in Medicare as an ASC and meet the conditions of participation. [42 C.F.R. § 416.2.]

Covered ASC Services

Covered surgical procedures are surgical procedures specified by the HHS Secretary and published in the *Federal Register* and/or on the CMS website that are separately paid under the hospital outpatient prospective payment system (OPPS), that would not be expected to pose a significant safety risk to a Medicare beneficiary when performed in an ASC, and for which standard medical practice dictates that the beneficiary would not typically be expected to require active medical monitoring and care at midnight following the procedure. [42 C.F.R. § 416.166(a), (b).]

Covered procedures do not include procedures that:

(1) generally result in extensive blood loss;

(2) require major or prolonged invasion of body cavities;

(3) directly involve major blood vessels;

(4) are generally emergent or life-threatening in nature;

(5) commonly require systemic thrombolytic therapy;

(6) are designated as requiring inpatient care under 42 C.F.R. § 419.22(n);

(7) can only be reported using a CPT® unlisted surgical procedure code; or

(8) are otherwise excluded under 42 C.F.R. § 411.15.

[42 C.F.R. § 416.166(c).]

Excluded services. ASC services do not include items and services outside the scope of ASC services for which payment may be made under 42 C.F.R. Part 414 in accordance with 42 C.F.R. § 410.152, including, but not limited to: (1) physicians' services (including surgical procedures and all pre-operative and post-operative services that are performed by a physician); (2) anesthetists' services; (3) radiology services (other than those integral to performance of a covered surgical procedure); (4) diagnostic procedures (other than those directly related to performance of a covered surgical procedure); (5) ambulance services; (6) leg, arm, back, and neck braces other than those that serve the function of a cast or splint; (7) artificial limbs; and (8) nonimplantable prosthetic devices and durable medical equipment (DME). [42 C.F.R. § 416.164(c).]

Services Packaged into ASC Payment for a Covered Surgical Procedure

ASC services for which payment is packaged into the ASC payment for a covered surgical procedure under 42 C.F.R. § 416.166 include, but are not limited to:

(1) nursing, technician, and related services;

(2) use of the facility where the surgical procedures are performed;

(3) laboratory testing performed under a Clinical Laboratory Improvement Amendments of 1988 (CLIA) certificate of waiver;

(4) drugs and biologics for which separate payment is not allowed under the OPPS, with the exception of non-opioid pain management drugs that function as a supply when used in a surgical procedure;

(5) medical and surgical supplies not on pass-through status;

(6) equipment;

(7) surgical dressings;

(8) implanted prosthetic devices, including intraocular lenses (IOLs), and related accessories and supplies not on pass-through status;

(9) implanted DME and related accessories and supplies not on pass-through status;

(10) splints, casts, and related devices;

(11) radiology services for which separate payment is not allowed under the OPPS and other diagnostic tests or interpretive services that are integral to a surgical procedure, except certain diagnostic tests for which separate payment is allowed under the OPPS;

(12) administrative, recordkeeping, and housekeeping items and services;

(13) materials, including supplies and equipment for the administration and monitoring of anesthesia; and

(14) supervision of the services of an anesthetist by the operating surgeon.

[42 C.F.R. § 416.164(a).]

Ancillary services. Medicare makes separate payments to ASCs for certain covered ancillary services that are provided integral to a covered ASC surgical procedure. Covered ancillary services include the following:

(1) brachytherapy sources;

(2) certain implantable items with pass-through status under the OPPS;

(3) certain items and services that CMS designates as contractor-priced, including, but not limited to, the acquisition or procurement of corneal tissue for corneal transplant procedures;

(4) certain drugs and biologics for which separate payment is allowed under the OPPS;

(5) certain radiology services for which separate payment is allowed under the OPPS; and

(6) non-opioid pain management drugs that function as a supply when used in a surgical procedure.

[42 C.F.R. § 416.164(b).]

[¶ 387] Mental Health Services

There is a wide range of services and programs that a hospital may provide to its outpatients who need psychiatric care, ranging from a few individual services to comprehensive, full-day programs and from intensive treatment programs to those that primarily provide support. In general, to be covered the services must be incident to a physician's service and reasonable and necessary for the diagnosis or treatment of the patient's condition. Services generally covered by Medicare Part B for the treatment of psychiatric patients include:

• individual and group therapy with physicians, psychologists, or other mental health professionals authorized by the state;

• occupational therapy services, if the patient requires the skills of a qualified occupational therapist and the services are performed by or under the supervision of a qualified occupational therapist or by an occupational therapy assistant;

• services of social workers, trained psychiatric nurses, and other staff trained to work with psychiatric patients;

• drugs and biologics furnished to outpatients for therapeutic purposes, but only if they are of a type that cannot be self-administered;

• activity therapies, but only those that are individualized and essential for the treatment of the patient's condition; the treatment plan must clearly justify the need for each particular therapy utilized and explain how it fits into the patient's treatment;

• family counseling services (counseling services with members of the household are covered only when the primary purpose of such counseling is the treatment of the patient's condition);

• patient education programs, but only when the educational activities are closely related to the care and treatment of the patient; and

• diagnostic services for the purpose of diagnosing those individuals for whom an extended or direct observation is necessary to determine functioning and interactions, identify problem areas, and formulate a treatment plan.

[*Medicare Benefit Policy Manual*, Pub. 100-02, Ch. 6, § 70.1.]

The following are generally not covered except as indicated: (1) meals and transportation; (2) activity therapies, group activities, or other services and programs that are primarily recreational or diversional in nature; (3) psychosocial programs; and (4) vocational training. [Pub. 100-02, Ch. 6, § 70.1.]

Length of time and frequency of services. There are no specific limits on the length of time that services may be covered. There are many factors that affect the outcome of treatment, including the nature of the illness, prior history, goals of treatment, and a patient's response. As long as a patient continues to show improvement in accordance with his or her individualized treatment plan and the frequency of services is within accepted norms of medical practice, coverage may be continued. If, however, a patient reaches a point in treatment when further improvement does not appear to be indicated, mental health treatment must be reevaluated. [Pub. 100-02, Ch. 6, § 70.1.]

Partial Hospitalization Coverage

Partial hospitalization programs (PHPs) are structured to provide intensive psychiatric care through active treatment that utilizes a combination of the clinically recognized items and services described in Soc. Sec. Act § 1861(ff). The treatment program of a PHP closely resembles that of a highly structured, short-term hospital inpatient program at a level more intense than outpatient day treatment or psychosocial rehabilitation. Programs providing primarily social, recreational, or diversionary activities are not considered partial hospitalization. [Pub. 100-02, Ch. 6, § 70.3.]

Partial hospitalization services are covered only if the individual would otherwise require inpatient psychiatric care. Under this benefit, Medicare covers:

(1) individual and group therapy with physicians or psychologists (or other authorized mental health professionals);

(2) occupational therapy;

(3) services of social workers, trained psychiatric nurses, and other staff trained to work with psychiatric patients;

(4) drugs and biologics furnished for therapeutic purposes that cannot be self-administered;

(5) individualized activity therapies that are not primarily recreational or diversionary;

(6) family counseling (for treatment of the patient's condition);

(7) patient training and education; and

(8) diagnostic services.

Meals and transportation and programs involving primarily social, recreational, or diversionary activities are specifically excluded from coverage. [Soc. Sec. Act § 1861(s)(2)(B), (ff)(2); 42 C.F.R. §§ 410.27(e), 410.43(a)(4); Pub. 100-02, Ch. 6, § 70.1.]

The services must be reasonable and necessary for the diagnosis or active treatment of the individual's condition. They also must be reasonably expected to improve or maintain the individual's condition and functional level and prevent relapse or hospitalization. [Soc. Sec. Act § 1861(ff).]

Patients must meet benefit requirements for receiving the partial hospitalization services. Patients admitted to a PHP must be:

• under the care of a physician who certifies the need for partial hospitalization; they must require a minimum of 20 hours per week of therapeutic services, as evidenced by the plan of care;

• in need of comprehensive, structured, multimodal treatment requiring medical supervision and coordination, provided under an individualized plan of care, because of an acute mental disorder that severely interferes with multiple areas of daily life, including social, vocational, and/or educational functioning; and

¶387

- able to cognitively and emotionally participate in the active treatment process and capable of tolerating the intensity of a PHP program.

[Soc. Sec. Act §§ 1835(a)(2)(F), 1861(ff); 42 C.F.R. § 410.43(c).]

Community mental health centers. Part B covers partial hospitalization services furnished by or under arrangements made by a community mental health center (CMHC) if they are provided by a CHMC that has in effect a provider agreement under 42 C.F.R. Part 489. A CMHC is defined as an entity that provides mental health services described in § 1913(c)(1) of the Public Health Service Act or provides for mental health services by contract with an approved organization, meets applicable state licensing or certification requirements, and provides at least 40 percent of its services to individuals who are not eligible for benefits under Medicare. [Soc. Sec. Act § 1861(ff)(3); 42 C.F.R. § 410.110.]

[¶ 388] Telehealth Services

Medicare covers consultations furnished by means of interactive telecommunications systems if the consultation services are provided for a Medicare patient located in certain rural areas. These services are also known as "telehealth services." [Soc. Sec. Act § 1834(m); 42 C.F.R. § 410.78.]

The teleconsultation must be referred and performed by a physician, physician assistant, nurse practitioner, clinical nurse specialist, nurse-midwife, clinical psychologist, clinical social worker, registered dietitian or nutrition professional, or certified registered nurse anesthetist. The medical examination of the patient must be under the control of the consulting practitioner. [Soc. Sec. Act § 1834(m); 42 C.F.R. § 410.78(b).]

Telecommunication system. An "interactive telecommunications system" means multimedia communications equipment that includes, at a minimum, audio and video equipment permitting two-way, real-time interactive communication between the patient and the distant site physician or practitioner. Telephones, fax machines, and e-mail systems do not meet this definition. [42 C.F.R. § 410.78(a)(3).]

For any federal telemedicine demonstration program conducted in Alaska or Hawaii, the use of store-and-forward technologies that provide for the asynchronous transmission of health care information in single or multimedia formats is permitted. [Soc. Sec. Act § 1834(m)(1); 42 C.F.R. § 410.78(a).]

Originating Site for Telehealth Services

Generally, an originating site must be:

(1) located in a rural Health Professional Shortage Area (HPSA) that is either outside of a Metropolitan Statistical Area (MSA) as of December 31 of the preceding calendar year or within rural census tracts as determined by the Office of Rural Health Policy as of December 31 of the preceding calendar year;

(2) in a county that is not included in an MSA as of December 31st of the preceding year; or

(3) participating in a federal telemedicine demonstration project that was approved by HHS as of December 31, 2000.

[Soc. Sec. Act § 1834(m)(4)(C)(i); 42 C.F.R. § 410.78(b)(4).]

Facilities that may act as an originating site include the following:

(1) the office of the physician or practitioner;

(2) critical access hospitals (CAHs);

(3) rural health clinics;

(4) federally qualified health centers;

(5) hospitals;

(6) hospital-based or CAH-based renal dialysis centers (including satellites);

(7) skilled nursing facilities;

(8) community mental health centers;

(9) a renal dialysis facility (only for purposes of the home dialysis monthly end-stage renal disease (ESRD)-related clinical assessment in Soc. Sec. Act § 1881(b)(3)(B));

(10) the home of an individual (only for purposes of the home dialysis ESRD-related clinical assessment in Soc. Sec. Act § 1881(b)(3)(B));

(11) a mobile stroke unit (only for purposes of diagnosis, evaluation, or treatment of symptoms of an acute stroke provided in accordance with Soc. Sec. Act § 1881(b)(3)(B)); and

(12) the home of an individual, only for purposes of treatment of a substance use disorder or a co-occurring mental health disorder, furnished on or after July 1, 2019, to an individual with a substance use disorder diagnosis.

[Soc. Sec. Act § 1834(m)(4)(C)(ii), as amended by SUPPORT for Patients and Communities Act (P.L. 115-271) § 2001(a)(2)(B); 42 C.F.R. § 410.78(b)(3).]

Exceptions. The geographic requirements specified in 42 C.F.R. § 410.78(b)(4) do not apply to the following telehealth services: (1) home dialysis monthly ESRD-related clinical assessment services furnished on or after January 1, 2019, at an originating site described in 42 C.F.R. § 410.78(b)(3)(vi), (ix), or (x), in accordance with Soc. Sec. Act § 1881(b)(3)(B); (2) services furnished on or after January 1, 2019, for purposes of diagnosis, evaluation, or treatment of symptoms of an acute stroke; and (3) services furnished on or after July 1, 2019 to an individual with a substance use disorder diagnosis, for purposes of treatment of a substance use disorder or a co-occurring mental health disorder. [Soc. Sec. Act § 1834(m)(5), (6), and (7), as added by SUPPORT for Patients and Communities Act § 2001(a)(3); 42 C.F.R. § 410.78(b)(4)(iv).]

Covered Telehealth Services

Changes to the list of Medicare telehealth services are made through the annual physician fee schedule rulemaking process. [Soc. Sec. Act § 1834(m)(4)(F)(ii); 42 C.F.R. § 410.78(f).] A list of covered telehealth services is available on the CMS website at http://www.cms.gov/Medicare/Medicare-General-Information/Telehealth/Telehealth-Codes.html.

The physician fee schedule final rule for calendar year (CY) 2020 added to the list of telehealth services three HCPCS codes related to office-based treatment for opioid use disorder: G2086, G2087, and G2088. The codes relate to the development of the treatment plan, care coordination, individual therapy, and group therapy. The final rule for CY 2019 added to the list HCPCS codes G0513 and G0514 for prolonged preventive services beyond the typical service time of the primary procedure, in the office or other outpatient setting, requiring direct patient contact beyond the usual service. [*Final rule*, 84 FR 62568, Nov. 15, 2019; *Final rule*, 83 FR 59836, Nov. 23, 2018; *Medicare Claims Processing Manual*, Pub. 100-04, Ch. 12, § 190.3.]

[¶ 389] End-Stage Renal Disease Services

Part B covers home dialysis supplies and equipment, self-care home dialysis support services, institutional dialysis services and supplies, and renal dialysis services. In addition, Part B covers renal dialysis services furnished by a renal dialysis facility or provider of services paid under Soc. Sec. Act § 1881(b)(14) to an individual with acute kidney injury (as defined in Soc. Sec. Act § 1834(r)(2)). [Soc. Sec. Act § 1861(s)(2)(F); 42 C.F.R. § 410.10(k).]

Dialysis treatments are covered in various settings, including hospital outpatient end-stage renal disease (ESRD) facilities, independent renal dialysis facilities, or the patient's home. Items and services furnished at ESRD facilities differ according to the types of patients being treated, the types of equipment and supplies used, the preferences of the treating physician, and the capability and makeup of the staff. [*Medicare Benefit Policy Manual*, Pub. 100-02, Ch. 11, § 20.]

Medicare covers the rental or purchase of home dialysis equipment for home use, all necessary supplies, and a wide range of home support services. This coverage includes delivery and installation service charges and maintenance expenses for the equipment. [Soc. Sec. Act § 1881(b)(8).]

The home dialysis support services covered by Medicare include periodic monitoring of the patient's home adaptation, visits by qualified provider or facility personnel in accordance with a plan prepared and periodically reviewed by a professional team (including the individual's physician), installation and maintenance of dialysis equipment, and testing and treatment of the water used during dialysis. [Soc. Sec. Act § 1881(b)(9).]

Starting in 2019, a beneficiary with ESRD receiving home dialysis may receive monthly ESRD-related clinical assessments via telehealth only if he or she receives a face-to-face clinical assessment without the use of telehealth (1) in the initial three months of home dialysis, at least monthly; and (2) after such the initial three months, at least once every three consecutive months. [Soc. Sec. Act § 1881(b)(3), as amended by Bipartisan Budget Act of 2018 (P.L. 115-123) § 50302(a).]

Education services. Medicare covers kidney disease education services that are: (1) furnished to an individual with stage IV chronic kidney disease who will require dialysis or a kidney transplant; and (2) designed to provide comprehensive information about the management of comorbidities, the prevention of uremic complications, and each option for renal replacement therapy (including hemodialysis and peritoneal dialysis at home and in-center as well as vascular access options and transplantation). Medicare Part B makes payment for up to six sessions of kidney disease education services. A session is one hour long and may be provided individually or in group settings of two to 20 individuals who need not all be Medicare beneficiaries. [Soc. Sec. Act § 1861(s)(2)(EE), (ggg); 42 C.F.R. § 410.48.]

Transplantation services. Medicare covers the cost of kidney transplantation surgery only if the surgery is performed in a renal transplantation center. [42 C.F.R. § 482.72.] Medicare also covers the costs of care for actual or potential kidney donors, including all reasonable preparatory, operation, and post-operation recovery expenses associated with the donation, without regard to the usual Medicare deductible, coinsurances, and premium payments. Payments for post-operation recovery expenses are limited, however, to the actual period of recovery. [Soc. Sec. Act § 1881(d); Pub. 100-02, Ch. 11, § 140.]

[¶ 390] Home Infusion Therapy

Pursuant to section 5012(a) of the 21st Century Cures Act (P.L. 114-255), effective January 1, 2021, Medicare Part B will separately cover home infusion therapy, which includes the following items and services furnished by a qualified home infusion therapy supplier: (1) professional services, including nursing services, furnished in accordance with the plan of care; (2) training and education (not otherwise paid for as durable medical equipment); and (3) remote monitoring and monitoring services for the provision of home infusion therapy and home infusion drugs. Home infusion therapy suppliers must provide home infusion therapy services in accordance with nationally recognized standards of practice, and in accordance with all applicable state and federal laws and regulations. [Soc. Sec. Act § 1861(s)(2)(GG), (iii); 42 C.F.R. § 486.525.]

Home infusion therapy will be specifically excluded from the definition of home health services. [Soc. Sec. Act § 1861(m), as amended by 21st Century Cures Act § 5012(c)(3).]

A home infusion drug includes a parenteral drug or biologic administered intravenously or subcutaneously for an administration period of 15 minutes or more through a pump that is an item of durable medical equipment. It does not include insulin pump systems or a self-administered drug or biologic on a self-administered drug exclusion list. [Soc. Sec. Act § 1861(iii)(3)(C); 42 C.F.R. § 486.505.]

Infusion pumps. Medicare Part B covers certain types of infusion pumps under the durable medical equipment benefit. [*National Coverage Determinations Manual*, Pub. 100-03, Ch. 1, § 280.1.]

Qualified Home Infusion Therapy Supplier

For payment to be made for home infusion therapy services, the services must be provided by or under arrangement with a qualified home infusion therapy supplier that meets applicable requirements. [42 C.F.R. § 414.1505.] A qualified home infusion therapy supplier includes a pharmacy, physician, or other provider of services or supplier licensed by the state in which it furnishes items or services and that: (1) furnishes infusion therapy to individuals with acute or chronic conditions requiring administration of home infusion drugs; (2) ensures the safe and effective provision and administration of home infusion therapy on a 7-day-a-week, 24-hour-a-day basis; (3) is accredited by an organization designated by the Secretary pursuant to Soc. Sec. Act § 1834(u)(5); and (4) meets such other requirements as the Secretary determines appropriate, taking into account the standards of care for home infusion therapy established by Medicare Advantage plans under Part C and in the private sector. [Soc. Sec. Act § 1861(iii)(3)(D); 42 C.F.R. § 486.505.]

Requirements for accreditation of home infusion therapy suppliers are discussed at 42 C.F.R. §§ 488.1000–488.1050.

Home Infusion Plan of Care Requirements

To qualify for Medicare coverage of home infusion therapy services, a beneficiary must be under the care of an applicable provider (i.e., a physician, nurse practitioner, or physician assistant) and have a plan of care established and periodically reviewed by a physician that prescribes the type, amount, and duration of the home infusion therapy services that are to be furnished. [Soc. Sec. Act § 1861(iii)(1); 42 C.F.R. §§ 414.1510, 414.1515(b), 486.520; *Final rule*, 84 FR 60478, Nov. 8, 2019.]

The physician's orders for services in the plan of care must specify at what frequency the services will be furnished, as well as the discipline that will furnish the ordered professional services. Orders for care may indicate a specific range in frequency of visits to ensure that the most appropriate level of services is furnished. The ordering physician must sign and date the plan of care before submitting a claim for payment and upon any changes to the plan of care. [42 C.F.R. § 414.1515(b), (c); *Final rule*, 84 FR 60478, Nov. 8, 2019.]

[¶ 392] Outpatient Rehabilitation Programs

Medicare Part B covers certain physician-supervised outpatient rehabilitation programs. Cardiac rehabilitation is a physician-supervised program that furnishes physician-prescribed exercise, cardiac risk factor modification, psychosocial assessment, and outcomes assessment. Pulmonary rehabilitation is a physician-supervised program for chronic obstructive

¶392

pulmonary disease (COPD) and other chronic respiratory diseases designed to optimize physical and social performance and autonomy.

Cardiac and Intensive Cardiac Rehabilitation Programs

Medicare Part B covers physician-supervised cardiac rehabilitation and intensive cardiac rehabilitation program services for beneficiaries who have experienced one or more of the following:

(1) an acute myocardial infarction within the preceding 12 months;

(2) a coronary artery bypass surgery;

(3) current stable angina pectoris;

(4) heart valve repair or replacement;

(5) percutaneous transluminal coronary angioplasty or coronary stenting;

(6) a heart or heart-lung transplant;

(7) for cardiac rehabilitation only, other cardiac conditions as specified through a national coverage determination (NCD);

(8) stable, chronic heart failure defined as patients with left ventricular ejection fraction of 35 percent or less and New York Heart Association (NYHA) class II to IV symptoms despite being on optimal heart failure therapy for at least 6 weeks, on or after February 18, 2014 for cardiac rehabilitation and on or after February 9, 2018 for intensive cardiac rehabilitation; or

(9) other cardiac conditions as specified through an NCD. The NCD process may also be used to specify noncoverage of a cardiac condition for intensive cardiac rehabilitation if clinical evidence does not support coverage.

Effective January 1, 2024, physician assistants, nurse practitioners, and clinical nurse specialists, in addition to physicians, will be permitted to supervise cardiac and intensive cardiac rehabilitation programs. [Soc. Sec. Act § 1861(eee)(1), as amended by Bipartisan Budget Act of 2018 (P.L. 115-123) §51008(a), and Soc. Sec. Act §1861(eee)(4)(B), as amended by Bipartisan Budget Act of 2018 §51004; 42 C.F.R. §410.49(b)(1); *Final rule,* 84 FR 62568, Nov. 15, 2019.]

Components of the program. Cardiac rehabilitation programs and intensive cardiac rehabilitation programs must include all of the following:

(1) physician-prescribed exercise each day cardiac rehabilitation items and services are furnished;

(2) cardiac risk factor modification, including education, counseling, and behavioral intervention, tailored to the patients' individual needs;

(3) psychosocial assessment, an evaluation of an individual's mental and emotional functioning as it relates to rehabilitation, which includes an assessment of those aspects of an individual's family and home situation that affects treatment, and psychosocial evaluation of the individual's response to and rate of progress under the treatment plan;

(4) outcomes assessment, an evaluation of progress as it relates to the individual's rehabilitation, which includes: (a) assessments from the start and conclusion of cardiac rehabilitation and intensive cardiac rehabilitation, based on patient-centered outcomes that must be measured by the physician immediately at the beginning of the program and at the end of the program, and (b) objective clinical measures of exercise performance and self-reported measures of exertion and behavior; and

¶392

(5) an individualized treatment plan detailing how components are utilized for each patient; it must be established, reviewed, and signed by a physician every 30 days.

[Soc. Sec. Act § 1861(eee)(2)(C), (3); 42 C.F.R. § 410.49(b)(2).]

Limitations on coverage of cardiac rehabilitation programs. Cardiac rehabilitation program sessions are limited to a maximum of two one-hour sessions per day for up to 36 sessions over up to 36 weeks with the option for an additional 36 sessions over an extended period of time if approved by the Medicare administrative contractor (MAC). Intensive cardiac rehabilitation program sessions are limited to 72 one-hour sessions, up to six sessions per day, over a period of up to 18 weeks. [42 C.F.R. § 410.49(f).]

Settings. Part B pays for cardiac rehabilitation and intensive cardiac rehabilitation in a physician's office or a hospital outpatient setting. All settings must have a physician (or, effective January 1, 2024, a physician assistant, nurse practitioner, or clinical nurse specialist) immediately available and accessible for medical consultations and emergencies at all times when items and services are being furnished under the program. This provision is satisfied if the physician meets the requirements for direct supervision for physician office services at 42 C.F.R. § 410.26 and for hospital outpatient services at 42 C.F.R. § 410.27. [Soc. Sec. Act § 1861(eee)(2)(A), (B), as amended by Bipartisan Budget Act of 2018 § 51008(a)(2); 42 C.F.R. § 410.49(b)(3).]

Standards for physicians. The physician responsible for a cardiac rehabilitation program or intensive cardiac rehabilitation programs and physicians acting as the supervising physician must (1) have expertise in the management of individuals with cardiac pathophysiology; (2) have cardiopulmonary training in basic life support or advanced cardiac life support; and (3) be licensed to practice medicine in the state in which the cardiac rehabilitation program is offered. [Soc. Sec. Act § 1861(eee)(5); 42 C.F.R. § 410.49(d), (e).]

Intensive cardiac rehabilitation program. Intensive cardiac rehabilitation program is a physician-supervised (and, effective January 1, 2024, physician assistants, nurse practitioners, and clinical nurse specialists) program that furnishes cardiac rehabilitation and has shown, in peer-reviewed published research, that it improves patients' cardiovascular disease through specific outcome measurements. To be approved as an intensive cardiac rehabilitation program, a program must demonstrate through peer-reviewed, published research that it has accomplished one or more of the following for its patients: (1) positively affected the progression of coronary heart disease; (2) reduced the need for coronary bypass surgery; or (3) reduced the need for percutaneous coronary interventions. In addition, it must demonstrate through peer-reviewed published research that it accomplished a statistically significant reduction in five or more of the following measures for patients from their levels before cardiac rehabilitation services to after cardiac rehabilitation services:

(1) low-density lipoprotein;

(2) triglycerides;

(3) body mass index;

(4) systolic blood pressure;

(5) diastolic blood pressure; and

(6) the need for cholesterol, blood pressure, and diabetes medications.

[Soc. Sec. Act § 1861(eee)(4), as amended by Bipartisan Budget Act of 2018 § 51008(a)(3); 42 C.F.R. § 410.49(a), (c).]

¶392

Part B Coverage of Pulmonary Rehabilitation Programs

A pulmonary rehabilitation program is a physician-supervised program that furnishes the following items and services:

(1) physician-prescribed exercise, including techniques such as exercise conditioning, breathing retraining, step, and strengthening exercises;

(2) education or training closely and clearly related to the individual's care and treatment, including information on respiratory problem management and, if appropriate, brief smoking cessation counseling;

(3) psychosocial assessment, a written evaluation of an individual's mental and emotional functioning as it relates to the individual's rehabilitation or respiratory condition that includes (a) an assessment of those aspects of an individual's family and home situation that affect the individual's rehabilitation treatment, and (b) a psychosocial evaluation of the individual's response to and rate of progress under the treatment plan;

(4) outcomes assessment, a written evaluation of the patient's progress as it relates to rehabilitation, which includes (a) beginning and end evaluations, based on patient-centered outcomes, that are conducted by the physician at the start and end of the program, and (b) objective clinical measures of effectiveness of the program for the individual patient, including exercise performance and self-reported measures of shortness of breath and behavior; and

(5) individualized treatment plan, which must be established, reviewed, and signed every 30 days by a physician who is involved in the patient's care and has knowledge related to his or her condition.

Effective January 1, 2024, physician assistants, nurse practitioners, and clinical nurse specialists, in addition to physicians, will be permitted to supervise pulmonary rehabilitation programs. [Soc. Sec. Act § 1861(fff), as amended by Bipartisan Budget Act of 2018 § 51008(b); 42 C.F.R. § 410.47(c).]

Covered beneficiaries. Medicare covers pulmonary rehabilitation for beneficiaries with moderate to very severe COPD (defined as GOLD classification II, III and IV), when referred by the physician treating the chronic respiratory disease. Additional medical indications for coverage for pulmonary rehabilitation program services may be established through an NCD. [42 C.F.R. § 410.47(b).]

Limitations. Part B pays for services provided in connection with a pulmonary rehabilitation exercise program for up to 36 sessions, no more than two sessions per day. The MAC may approve up to an additional 36 sessions based on medical necessity. [42 C.F.R. § 410.47(f).]

Settings. Part B pays for a pulmonary rehabilitation in the physicians' offices and hospital outpatient settings. All settings must have the necessary cardio-pulmonary, emergency, diagnostic, and therapeutic life-saving equipment accepted by the medical community as medically necessary (for example, oxygen, cardiopulmonary resuscitation equipment, and defibrillator) to treat chronic respiratory disease available for immediate use and accessible at all times. In addition, a physician must be immediately available and accessible for medical consultations and emergencies at all times when services are being provided under the program. This provision is satisfied if the physician meets the requirements for direct supervision for physician office services at 42 C.F.R. § 410.26 and for hospital outpatient services at 42 C.F.R. § 410.27. [42 C.F.R. § 410.47(d).]

Physician standards. For pulmonary rehabilitation services to be covered, they must be supervised by a physician who meets the following requirements:

(1) is responsible and accountable for the pulmonary rehabilitation program, including oversight of staff;

(2) is involved substantially, in consultation with staff, in directing the progress of the individual in the program including direct patient contact related to the periodic review of his or her treatment plan;

(3) has expertise in the management of individuals with respiratory pathophysiology, as well as cardiopulmonary training and/or certification; and

(4) is licensed to practice medicine in the state in which the program is offered.

[Soc. Sec. Act § 1861 (fff) (3); 42 C.F.R. § 410.47(e).]

[¶ 394] Opioid Use Disorder Treatment Services

Medicare Part B will cover opioid use disorder treatment services beginning January 1, 2020. [Soc. Sec. Act § 1861(s) (2) (HH), as added by SUPPORT for Patients and Communities Act (P.L. 115-271) § 2005(a); 42 C.F.R. § 410.67(a).]

Opioid use disorder treatment services are items and services furnished by an opioid treatment program for the treatment of opioid use disorder, including:

(1) opioid agonist and antagonist treatment medications (including oral, injected, or implanted versions) that are approved by the Food and Drug Administration under section 505 of the Federal Food, Drug, and Cosmetic Act for use in the treatment of opioid use disorder;

(2) dispensing and administration of such medications, if applicable;

(3) substance use counseling by a professional to the extent authorized under state law to furnish such services, including services furnished via two-way interactive audio-video communication technology, as clinically appropriate, and in compliance with all applicable requirements;

(4) individual and group therapy with a physician or psychologist (or other mental health professional to the extent authorized under state law), including services furnished via two-way interactive audio-video communication technology, as clinically appropriate, and in compliance with all applicable requirements;

(5) toxicology testing;

(6) intake activities, including initial medical examination services required under 42 C.F.R. § 8.12 (f) (2) and initial assessment services required under 42 C.F.R. § 8.12(f) (4); and

(7) periodic assessment services required under 42 C.F.R. § 8.12(f) (4).

[Soc. Sec. Act § 1861(jjj) (1), as added by SUPPORT for Patients and Communities Act § 2005(b); 42 C.F.R. § 410.67(b).]

"Opioid treatment program" means an entity that is an opioid treatment program (as defined in 42 C.F.R. § 8.2 or any successor regulation) that: (1) is enrolled under Soc. Sec. Act § 1866(j); (2) has in effect a certification by the Substance Abuse and Mental Health Services Administration for such a program; (3) is accredited by an accrediting body approved by the Substance Abuse and Mental Health Services Administration; and (4) has in effect a provider agreement under 42 C.F.R. part 489. [Soc. Sec. Act § 1861(jjj) (2), as added by SUPPORT for Patients and Communities Act § 2005(b); 42 C.F.R. § 410.67(b), (c); *Final rule*, 84 FR 62568, Nov. 15, 2019.]

¶394

Opioid Use Disorder Treatment Demonstration Program

SUPPORT for Patients and Communities Act § 6042 required the HHS Secretary, by January 1, 2021, to implement a four-year demonstration program to increase access of applicable beneficiaries to opioid use disorder treatment services, improve physical and mental health outcomes for such beneficiaries, and reduce expenditures under Medicare. Under the program, the Secretary will make payments to participants for furnishing opioid use disorder treatment services delivered through opioid use disorder care teams, or arranging for such services to be furnished, to applicable beneficiaries participating in the program. [Soc. Sec. Act § 1866F.]

Bundled Payment for Opioid Use Disorder Treatment Services

CMS will pay an opioid treatment program a bundled payment, which will be updated annually, for opioid use disorder treatment services that are furnished to an individual during an episode of care beginning on or after January 1, 2020. CMS will establish the following categories of bundled payments for episodes of care: (1) categories for each type of opioid agonist and antagonist treatment medication; (2) a category for medication not otherwise specified, which will be used for new FDA-approved opioid agonist or antagonist treatment medications for which CMS has not established a category; and (3) a category for episodes of care in which no medication is provided. [Soc. Sec. Act §§ 1833(a)(1)(CC) and 1834(w), as added by SUPPORT for Patients and Communities Act § 2005(c); 42 C.F.R. § 410.67(d)(1); *Final rule*, 84 FR 62568, Nov. 15, 2019.]

The bundled payment for episodes of care in which a medication is provided consists of payment for a drug component, reflecting payment for the applicable FDA-approved opioid agonist or antagonist medication in the patient's treatment plan, and a non-drug component, reflecting payment for all other opioid use disorder treatment services reflected in the patient's treatment plan (including dispensing/ administration of the medication, if applicable). The payments for the drug component and non-drug component are added together to create the bundled payment amount. The bundled payment for episodes of care in which no medication is provided consists of a single payment amount for all opioid use disorder treatment services reflected in the patient's treatment plan (excluding medication and dispensing/ administration of medication). [42 C.F.R. § 410.67(d)(2); *Final rule*, 84 FR 62568, Nov. 15, 2019.]

Drug component. The payment for the drug component for an episode of care will be determined as follows:

- For implantable and injectable medications, using the methodology set forth in Soc. Sec. Act § 1847A, except that the payment amount will be 100 percent of the average sales price (ASP), if ASP is used.

- For oral medications, if ASP data is available, the payment amount is 100 percent of ASP, which will be determined based on ASP data that has been calculated consistent with the provisions in 42 C.F.R. part 414, subpart 800 and voluntarily submitted by drug manufacturers. In cases where ASP data is not available, the payment amount for methadone will be based on the TRICARE rate and for buprenorphine will be calculated using the National Average Drug Acquisition Cost.

For the drug component of bundled payments in the medication not otherwise specified category under 42 C.F.R. § 410.67(d)(1)(iii), the payment amount is based on the applicable methodology under paragraphs 42 C.F.R. § 410.67(d)(2)(i)(A) and (B) (applying the most recent available data for such new medication), or invoice pricing until the necessary data become available. [42 C.F.R. § 410.67(d)(2)(i); *Final rule*, 84 FR 62568, Nov. 15, 2019.]

Non-drug component. The payment for calendar year (CY) 2020 for the non-drug component of the bundled payment for an episode of care is the sum of:

(1) the CY 2019 Medicare physician fee schedule non-facility rates for the following items and services: (a) psychotherapy, 30 minutes with patient; (b) group psychotherapy; (c) alcohol and/or substance (other than tobacco) abuse structured assessment and brief intervention at the non-physician practitioner rate; (d) for administration of an injectable medication, if applicable, drug administration (therapeutic, prophylactic); (e) for the insertion, removal, or insertion and removal of the implantable medication, if applicable, the applicable rate;

(2) for dispensing oral medication, if applicable, an approximation of the average dispensing fees under state Medicaid programs; and

(3) one-fourth of the sum of the CY 2019 Clinical Laboratory Fee Schedule rate for two drug tests, presumptive, capable of being read by direct optical observation only and for a drug test, definitive, 1-7 drug classes.

[42 C.F.R. § 410.67(d)(2)(ii); *Final rule*, 84 FR 62568, Nov. 15, 2019.]

Care without medication. The bundled payment amount for CY 2020 for an episode of care in which no medication is provided is based on the non-drug component rate for an episode of care in which a drug is dispensed or administered, not including any amounts reflecting the cost of dispensing or administration of a drug. [42 C.F.R. § 410.67(d)(2)(iii).]

Payment adjustments. CMS will make adjustments to the bundled payments when an opioid treatment program furnishes:

• counseling or therapy services in excess of the amount specified in the beneficiary's treatment plan and for which medical necessity is documented in the medical record; an adjustment will be made for each additional 30 minutes of counseling or individual therapy furnished during the episode of care;

• intake activities;

• periodic assessments required under 42 C.F.R. § 8.12(f)(4); and

• when oral medications are dispensed, additional take-home supply of oral drugs of up to 21 days, in increments of 7 days.

The payment amounts for the nondrug component of the bundled payment for an episode of care, and the adjustments for counseling or therapy, intake activities, and periodic assessments, will be geographically adjusted using the geographic adjustment factor described in 42 C.F.R. § 414.26 and pdated annually using the Medicare Economic Index described in 42 C.F.R. § 405.504(d). [42 C.F.R. § 410.67(d)(4); *Final rule*, 84 FR 62568, Nov. 15, 2019.]

Duplicative payments. CMS must ensure that no duplicative payments are made under Medicare Part B or Part D for items and services furnished by an opioid treatment program. Payment for medications delivered, administered, or dispensed to a beneficiary as part of the bundled payment is considered a duplicative payment if a claim for delivery, administration, or dispensing of the same medications for the same beneficiary on the same date of service was also separately paid under Medicare Part B or Part D. CMS will recoup the duplicative payment made to the opioid treatment program. [Soc. Sec. Act § 1834(w)(1); 42 C.F.R. § 410.67(d)(5); *Final rule*, 84 FR 62568, Nov. 15, 2019.]

Cost-sharing. No beneficiary copayment applies. [42 C.F.R. § 410.67(e); *Final rule*, 84 FR 62568, Nov. 15, 2019.]

¶394

Enrollment Requirements

For a program or eligible professional to receive Medicare payment for the provision of opioid use disorder treatment services, the provider must qualify as an outpatient treatment program (OTP) and enroll in the Medicare program. An OTP must meet the following requirements:

(1) Fully complete and submit the Form CMS-855B application (or its successor application) and any applicable supplement or attachment thereto to its applicable Medicare contractor.

(2) Comply with the application fee requirements in 42 C.F.R. § 424.514.

(3) Successfully complete the assigned categorical risk level screening required under, as applicable, 42 C.F.R. § 424.518(b) and (c).

(4) Have a current, valid certification by SAMHSA for an opioid treatment program consistent with the provisions and requirements of 42 C.F.R. § 8.11.

(5) Report on the Form CMS-855B and/or any applicable supplement all OTP staff who meet the definition of "managing employee" in 42 C.F.R. § 424.502.

(6) Must not employ or contract with a prescribing or ordering physician or eligible professional or with any individual legally authorized to dispense narcotics who, within the preceding 10 years, has been convicted (as that term is defined in 42 C.F.R. § 1001.2) of a federal or state felony that CMS deems detrimental to the best interests of the Medicare program and its beneficiaries based on the same categories of detrimental felonies, as well as case-by-case detrimental determinations, found at 42 C.F.R. § 424.535(a)(3).

(7) Sign (and adhere to the term of) a provider agreement in accordance with the provisions of 42 C.F.R. part 489.

(8) Comply with all other applicable requirements for enrollment specified in this section and in subpart P of 42 C.F.R. part 424.

[42 C.F.R. § 424.67(b); *Final rule*, 84 FR 62568, Nov. 15, 2019.]

Denial of enrollment. CMS may choose to deny the enrollment of an OTP because (1) the provider does not have a current, valid certification by SAMHSA as required under 42 C.F.R. § 424.67(b)(4)(i) or fails to meet any other applicable requirement; or (2) any of the denial reasons in 42 C.F.R. § 424.530 apply. [42 C.F.R. § 424.67(c); *Final rule*, 84 FR 62568, Nov. 15, 2019.]

Continued compliance. Upon and after enrollment, an OTP must: (1) remain validly certified by SAMHSA as required by 42 C.F.R. § 8.11; (2) remain subject to, and remain in full compliance with, the provisions of 42 C.F.R. § 424.67 and of 42 C.F.R. part 424 subpart P. An OTP may repeal the revocation of its enrollment. [42 C.F.R. § 424.67(d).]

[¶ 395] National and Local Coverage Determinations

The Secretary of HHS has the authority to make coverage decisions, within a broad range of categories, for specific items or services not mentioned in the law. For these items and services to be covered, the Secretary must determine them to be reasonable and necessary for the diagnosis and treatment of illnesses and injuries, or to improve the functioning of a malformed body member items and services. HHS decisions as to whether Medicare will cover new services are issued as national coverage determinations (NCDs). [Soc. Sec. Act § 1862(l).]

CMS develops NCDs to describe the circumstances for Medicare coverage nationwide for an item or service. NCDs generally outline the conditions for which an item or service is considered to be covered (or not covered) under Soc. Sec. Act § 1862(a)(1) or other applicable provisions of the Social Security Act. NCDs are usually issued as a program instruction. Once published in a CMS program instruction, an NCD is binding on all Medicare administrative contractors (MACs) and Medicare Advantage organizations. NCDs are binding on administrative law judges (ALJs) during the claim appeal process. [*Medicare Program Integrity Manual*, Pub. 100-08, Ch. 13, § 13.1.1.]

The NCD development process includes:

(1) the internal and external processes for requesting an NCD or an NCD reconsideration;

(2) a tracking system that provides public notice of acceptance of a complete, formal request and subsequent actions in a web-based format;

(3) a process to allow notice and opportunity to comment before implementation of an NCD;

(4) standardization of the information required to complete a formal request; and

(5) publication of a decision memorandum explaining the purpose and basis of the decision.

CMS considers coverage of additional services with the help of the Medicare Evidence Development & Coverage Advisory Committee, which is composed of members of the health care industry and consumer groups, or other consultants. [*Notice*, 78 FR 48164, Aug. 7, 2013.]

Local coverage determinations. MACs that process claims can issue local coverage determinations (LCDs). LCDs are made only on the reasonableness and necessity of an item or service, not addressing statutory and other exclusions. [Soc. Sec. Act § 1869(f)(2)(B); Pub. 100-08, Ch. 13, § 13.1.2.]

After an LCD is developed, the LCD information must be made available on the websites of MACs and Medicare at least 45 days before the effective date of the determination. The information made available must provide: (1) the determination in its entirety; (2) where and when the proposed LCD was first made public; (3) hyperlinks to the proposed LCD and the response to comments submitted to the MAC; (4) summary of evidence considered by the MAC during the development; and (5) an explanation of the rationale that supported the determination. [Soc. Sec. Act § 1862(l)(5)(D).]

Reconsiderations and reviews of NCDs and LCDs. For a discussion of LCD and NCD reconsiderations and reviews, see ¶ 928.

Chapter 4– MEDICARE PART C—MEDICARE ADVANTAGE

[¶ 400] Overview of Medicare Part C

The Medicare Advantage (MA) program—also known as Medicare Part C—offers beneficiaries the option of receiving all of their Medicare benefits from health plans run by private companies. According to Kaiser Family Foundation (KFF) data, in 2019, 22 million Medicare beneficiaries (34 percent) were enrolled in MA plans, which were mainly health maintenance organizations (HMOs) and preferred provider organizations (PPOs). KFF estimates that 3,148 Medicare Advantage plans will be available for individual enrollment for the 2020 plan year, an increase of 414 plans over 2019. The average beneficiary will be able to choose among 28 plans in 2020, up from 24 in 2019. KFF also estimated that the number of special needs plans (SNPs) will increase from 717 plans in 2019 to 855 plans in 2020. [Medicare Advantage 2020 Spotlight: First Look, Kaiser Family Foundation, Oct. 24, 2019.]

The MA program is administered according to federal regulations found at 42 C.F.R. Part 422. CMS also publishes updates to information regarding the administration of the MA program in the *Medicare Managed Care Manual*, CMS Pub. 100-16.

Types of Medicare Advantage Plans

MA organizations can offer three types of plans to beneficiaries: (1) a coordinated care plan (which includes special needs plans); (2) a combination of a medical savings account (MSA) plan and a contribution into a MSA; and (3) a private fee-for-service (PFFS) plan. [Soc. Sec. Act § 1851(a)(2); 42 C.F.R. § 422.4(a).] **WK Note:** "Medicare cost plans," which are available in some areas of the country and have some of the same rules as MA plans, are not MA plans and are not covered in detail in this chapter.

Coordinated care plans. Coordinated care plans include a network of providers that are under contract or arrangement with the MA organization to deliver a benefit package approved by CMS. The plans may include HMOs, provider-sponsored organizations (PSOs), regional or local PPOs, and other network plans (other than PFFS plans). [42 C.F.R. § 422.4(a)(1), (a)(1)(iii).]

SNPs, mostly HMOs, are an option for three groups of beneficiaries with significant or relatively specialized care needs. "Special needs individual" means an MA eligible individual who: (1) is dually eligible for Medicare and Medicaid; (2) requires a nursing home or institutional level of care; or (3) has severe chronic or disabling conditions. SNPs offer the same benefits as traditional Medicare, but they also must provide the Part D prescription drug benefit as well as additional services tailored to the special needs population. Section 50311 of the Bipartisan Budget Act of 2018 (P.L. 115-123) removed the temporary extension of the SNP program, set to expire on December 31, 2018, and made the SNP program permanent. [Soc. Sec. Act § 1859(f)(1), as amended by Bipartisan Budget Act of 2018 § 50311(a); 42 C.F.R. §§ 422.2, 422.4(a)(1)(iv).] See ¶ 402 for more information about SNPs.

Private fee-for-service plans. Similar to fee-for-service Medicare, PFFS plans reimburse providers at a rate determined by the plan on a fee-for-service basis, without putting the provider at risk. These plans do not vary reimbursement based on utilization, and they do not limit the selection of providers. [Soc. Sec. Act § 1859(b)(2); 42 C.F.R. § 422.4(a)(3).]

Medical savings accounts. MSA plans have two parts: (1) an MA medical savings account health insurance plan that pays for a basic set of health benefits approved by CMS and includes a uniform premium and a uniform level of cost-sharing for beneficiaries in the plan's service area; and (2) an MSA, which is a trust or custodial account into which CMS will make deposits. [Soc. Sec. Act § 1859(b)(3); 42 C.F.R. § 422.4(a)(2).]

Part D coverage. An organization that offers an MA coordinated plan in a specific area must offer qualified Part D prescription drug coverage in that plan or in another MA plan in the same area. MA organizations offering MSA plans generally are not permitted to offer prescription drug coverage. MA organizations offering PFFS plans can choose whether to offer Part D coverage. [42 C.F.R. §§ 422.4(c), 422.114.]

MA Regional Plans

CMS has established 26 regions for MA plans. [*Medicare Managed Care Manual*, Pub. 100-16, Ch. 1, § 30.2.3.] The purpose of the regions is to maximize the availability of MA regional plans to all MA-eligible individuals without regard to health status or geographic location, especially to individuals in rural areas. CMS may periodically review and revise the regions if it determines it is appropriate. By regulation, there must be no fewer than 10 regions and no more than 50 regions. [Soc. Sec. Act § 1858(a); 42 C.F.R. § 422.455.]

Minimum Medical Loss Ratio Requirements for MA Plans

MA plans must have a medical loss ratio (MLR) of at least 85 percent for contracts beginning in 2014 or later. The minimum MLR requirement is intended to create incentives for MA organizations to reduce administrative costs such as for marketing costs, profits, and other uses of the funds earned by MA organizations and to help ensure that taxpayers and enrolled beneficiaries receive value from Medicare health plans. [Soc. Sec. Act § 1857(e)(4); 42 C.F.R. § 422.2410.]

An MLR is determined based on the percentage of Medicare contract revenue spent on clinical services, prescription drugs, quality improving activities, and direct benefits to beneficiaries in the form of reduced Part B premiums. If an MA organization has an MLR of less than 85 percent, it is subject to several levels of sanctions, including remittance of funds to CMS, a prohibition on enrolling new members, and contract termination. [Soc. Sec. Act § 1857(e)(4); 42 C.F.R. § 422.2410.]

CMS releases to the public Part C MLR data, for each contract for each contract year, no earlier than 18 months after the end of the applicable contract year. [42 C.F.R. § 422.2490.]

[¶ 401] Eligibility, Election, Enrollment, and Disenrollment

An individual's eligibility for a Medicare Advantage (MA) plan is determined, in part, by his or her eligibility for Medicare Part A and Part B. [42 C.F.R. § 422.50.] CMS has issued guidance for MA eligibility and enrollment on its website at http://www.cms.hhs.gov/home/medicare.asp under the "Eligibility and Enrollment" heading.

Eligibility to Elect an MA Plan

In general, an individual is eligible to elect an MA plan if he or she is a U.S. citizen or is lawfully present in the U.S. and:

(1) is entitled to Medicare Part A and enrolled under Part B;

(2) either resides in the service area of the MA plan or resides outside this service area but is enrolled in a health plan offered by the MA organization during the month immediately preceding the month in which the individual is entitled to both Medicare Part A and Part B; and

(3) through 2020, has not been medically determined to have end-stage renal disease (ESRD).

[Soc. Sec. Act § 1851(a)(3); 42 C.F.R. § 422.50.]

¶401

Special rules for ESRD. An individual medically determined to have ESRD is not currently eligible to elect an MA plan, except that: (1) an individual who develops ESRD while enrolled in an MA plan or in a health plan offered by an MA organization may continue to be enrolled in that plan; and (2) an individual with ESRD whose enrollment in an MA plan was terminated or discontinued after December 31, 1998, because CMS or the MA organization terminated the MA organization's contract for the plan or discontinued the plan in the area in which the individual resides, is eligible to elect another MA plan; and (3) an individual with ESRD may elect an MA special needs plan (SNP) as long as that plan has chosen to enroll ESRD individuals. [Soc. Sec. Act § 1851(a)(3); 42 C.F.R. § 422.50(a)(2).]

Beginning in 2021, however, individuals with ESRD will be permitted to enroll in MA plans. [Soc. Sec. Act § 1853(a)(3), as amended by 21st Century Cures Act (P.L. 114-255) § 17006.]

SNP eligibility. The Bipartisan Budget Act of 2018 (P.L. 115-123) removed the temporary extension of the SNP program, set to expire on December 31, 2018, and made the SNP program permanent. To elect a special needs plan for a special needs individual, an individual must: (1) meet the definition of a special needs individual, i.e., an individual who is institutionalized, is entitled to assistance under a state Medicaid plan, or has a severe or disabling condition and would benefit from enrollment in a specialized MA plan; (2) meet the eligibility requirements for that specific SNP; and (3) be eligible to elect an MA plan. If a SNP determines that an enrollee no longer meets the eligibility criteria but can reasonably be expected to again meet the criteria within a six-month period, the enrollee is deemed to continue to be eligible for the MA plan for a period of not less than 30 days but not to exceed six months. [Soc. Sec. Act § 1859(f), as amended by Bipartisan Budget Act of 2018 § 50311(a); 42 C.F.R. §§ 422.2, 422.52.]

Hospice patients. MA organizations do not provide hospice care but must inform each Medicare enrollee eligible to select hospice care about the availability of hospice care under certain circumstances. [Soc. Sec. Act §§ 1852(a)(1)(B)(i), 1853(h); 42 C.F.R. §§ 422.100(c)(1), 422.320.]

Continuation of enrollment. An MA organization may offer a continuation of enrollment option to enrollees when they no longer reside in the service area of a plan and permanently move into the area designated as the MA organization's "continuation area." The beneficiary may choose whether to continue enrollment in the plan after the move or to disenroll. [Soc. Sec. Act § 1851(b)(1); 42 C.F.R. § 422.54.]

Election and Enrollment in MA Plans

Generally, each MA organization must accept without restriction individuals who are eligible to elect an MA plan that the organization offers and who elect the plan during initial coverage election periods and annual election periods. If CMS determines that a plan has a capacity limit, the MA organization may limit enrollment in the plan under certain circumstances. [42 C.F.R. §§ 422.60, 422.62.]

Beneficiaries may make elections during three different types of election periods:

- the initial coverage election period (ICEP);
- the annual election period (AEP); or
- a special election period (SEP).

[Soc. Sec. Act § 1851(e); 42 C.F.R. § 422.62.]

Initial coverage election period. The ICEP is the period during which a newly MA-eligible individual may make an initial election. The ICEP begins three months before the month an individual is first entitled to Medicare Part A and Part B and ends the last day of the individual's Part B initial enrollment period. [Soc. Sec. Act § 1851(e)(1); 42 C.F.R. § 422.62(a)(1).] An individual who fails to make an election during the initial coverage election period is deemed to have elected original fee-for-service Medicare. [Soc. Sec. Act § 1851(c)(3)(A); 42 C.F.R. § 422.66(c).]

Annual election period. The AEP for MA and Part D prescription drug plans (PDPs) runs from October 15 through December 7. During the AEP, individuals may switch to a different MA plan, or from original Medicare to an MA plan. [Soc. Sec. Act § 1851(e)(3)(B)(v); 42 C.F.R. § 422.62(a)(2).]

Open enrollment period. Beginning in 2019, an individual who is enrolled in an MA plan may make an election once during the first three months of the year to enroll in another MA plan or disenroll to obtain original Medicare. An individual who exercises this election may also make a coordinating election to enroll in or disenroll from Part D. [Soc. Sec. Act § 1851(e)(2)(G); 42 C.F.R. § 422.62(a)(3)(i).]

For 2019 and later years, a newly MA-eligible individual who is enrolled in an MA plan may change his or her election once during the period that begins the month the individual is entitled to both Part A and Part B and ends on the last day of the third month of the entitlement. An individual who exercises this election may also make a coordinating election to enroll in or disenroll from Part D. [42 C.F.R. § 422.62(a)(3)(ii).]

An individual who is eligible to elect an MA plan and who is institutionalized is not limited in the number of elections or changes he or she may make. An MA-eligible institutionalized individual may at any time elect an MA plan or change his or her election from an MA plan to original Medicare, to a different MA plan, or from original Medicare to an MA plan. [Soc. Sec. Act § 1851(e)(2)(D); 42 C.F.R. § 422.62(a)(4).]

Special election periods. SEPs constitute periods outside of the usual enrollment periods when an individual may elect a plan or change his or her current plan election. SEPs include situations when:

(1) CMS or the MA organization has terminated the organization's contract for the plan or discontinued the plan in the area in which the individual resides, or the organization has notified the individual of the impending termination of the plan or the impending discontinuation of the plan in the area in which he or she resides;

(2) an individual has made a change in residence outside of the service area or continuation area or has experienced another change in circumstances as determined by CMS (other than termination for non-payment of premiums or disruptive behavior) that causes the individual to no longer be eligible to elect the MA plan;

(3) the individual demonstrates that the MA organization offering the plan substantially violated a material provision of its contract under MA in relation to the individual, including, but not limited to, failure to provide medical services in accordance with quality standards or failure to provide medically necessary services in a timely fashion;

(4) the individual demonstrates that the MA organization materially misrepresented the plan's contract provision in marketing the plan to the individual; or

(5) the individual meets other exceptional conditions as CMS may provide.

[Soc. Sec. Act § 1851(e)(4); 42 C.F.R. § 422.62(b).]

Forms. An individual who wishes to elect an MA plan may make or change his or her election during the election periods specified above by filing the appropriate election forms with the MA organization or through other mechanisms approved by CMS. An individual

¶401

who wishes to disenroll from an MA plan may change his or her election during the election periods by either filing a new election form or by filing the appropriate disenrollment form with the MA organization or through other mechanisms determined by CMS. [42 C.F.R. § 422.66(a), (b).]

Alternate employer or union election mechanism. MA organizations that offer MA plans to employers or unions may choose to accept voluntary elections directly from that group without obtaining an MA election form from each individual. The employer or union reports to the MA organization individuals' choices of coverage. MA organizations may specify the employers or unions, if any, from which they will accept this election format and may choose to accept enrollment and/or voluntary disenrollment elections. [*Medicare Managed Care Manual*, Pub. 100-16, Ch. 2, § 20.4.1.]

Conversion of enrollment. An MA plan must accept any individual (even if the individual has ESRD) who is enrolled in a health plan offered by the MA organization during the month immediately preceding the month in which he or she is eligible for Medicare. [42 C.F.R. § 422.66(d).]

Plan closure. An MA organization has the option to voluntarily close one or more of its MA plans to open enrollment period enrollment elections. However, if an MA organization has an MA plan that is open during an open enrollment period and decides to change this process, it must notify CMS and the general public 30 calendar days in advance of the new limitations on the open enrollment process. When an MA plan is voluntarily closed for the open enrollment period, it is closed to all open enrollment period requests, but it must still accept elections made during the ICEP and SEP and be open for the AEP, unless an approved capacity limit applies and has been reached. [Pub. 100-16, Ch. 2, § 30.9.1.]

Passive enrollment. When MA plans immediately terminate or when CMS determines that continued enrollment in an MA plan poses potential harm to the members, CMS may implement passive enrollment procedures. Under passive enrollment procedures, individuals are considered to have elected a plan selected by CMS unless they: (1) decline the plan selected by CMS; or (2) request enrollment in another plan. The MA organization that receives the passive enrollment must provide notice, before the enrollment effective date, to the potential enrollee that describes the costs and benefits of the plan and the process for accessing care under the plan and clearly explains the beneficiary's ability to decline the enrollment or choose another plan. [42 C.F.R. § 422.60(g).]

Effective dates of elections.

(1) An election made during an ICEP is effective as of the first day of the month of entitlement to both Part A and Part B.

(2) Elections or changes of election made during the AEP are effective the first day of the following calendar year.

(3) Elections made during an open enrollment period are effective the first day of the first month following the month in which the election is made.

(4) The effective date of elections made during SEPs depend on the circumstances and are made by CMS in a manner consistent with protecting the continuity of health benefits coverage.

(5) The effective date for an election of coverage under original Medicare made during a SEP for an individual age 65 is the first day of the first calendar month following the month in which the election is made.

(6) The effective date for an election made from January 1 through February 14 to disenroll from an MA plan to original Medicare is effective the first day of the first month following the month in which the election is made.

[Soc. Sec. Act § 1851(f); 42 C.F.R. § 422.68.]

Disenrollment from MA Plans

An individual may disenroll from an MA plan only during one of the election periods noted above. The individual may disenroll by: (1) enrolling in another plan during a valid enrollment period; (2) giving or faxing a signed written notice to the MA organization, or through his or her employer or union where applicable; (3) submitting a request via the Internet to the MA organization, if the MA organization offers such an option; or (4) calling 1-800-MEDICARE. If an enrollee makes a verbal request, the MA organization must instruct the individual to make the request in one of the ways described above. [42 C.F.R. § 422.66(b); Pub. 100-16, Ch. 2, § 50.1.]

Disenrollment by the MA organization. Generally, an MA organization may not disenroll an individual from any MA plan it offers or request or encourage disenrollment. The organization may, however, disenroll an individual if he or she: (1) does not pay any monthly basic or supplementary premium in a timely manner; (2) engages in disruptive behavior; or (3) provides fraudulent information on an election form or permits the fraudulent use of an enrollment card. [42 C.F.R. § 422.74(a), (b)(1).]

The MA organization *must* disenroll an individual under the following circumstances:

(1) the individual no longer resides in the MA plan's service area (including when the individual is incarcerated and does not reside in the service area of the MA plan);

(2) the individual loses entitlement to Part A or Part B benefits;

(3) the individual dies;

(4) for special needs individuals enrolled in a specialized MA plan, the individual no longer meets the special needs status of that plan; or

(5) the individual is not lawfully present in the United States.

[42 C.F.R. § 422.74(b)(2), (d).]

The MA organization also *must* disenroll enrollees: if the organization has its contract with CMS terminated; if it terminates the MA plan; or if it discontinues the plan in an area where it had previously been available. However, when an MA organization discontinues offering an MA plan in a portion of its service area, it may elect to offer enrollees residing in all or portions of the affected area the option to continue enrollment in an MA plan offered by the organization, as long as there is no other MA plan offered in the affected area at the time of the organization's election. The organization may require an enrollee who chooses to continue enrollment to agree to receive the full range of basic benefits (excluding emergency and urgently needed care) exclusively through facilities designated by the organization within the plan service area. [42 C.F.R. § 422.74(b)(3).]

Notice of disenrollment. If the disenrollment is for any of the reasons other than death or loss of entitlement to Medicare Part A or Part B benefits, the MA organization must give the individual a written notice of the disenrollment with an explanation of why the MA organization is planning to disenroll the individual. The organization must provide the individual with a notice of disenrollment before submitting the disenrollment to CMS, and it must include an explanation of the individual's right to a hearing under the MA organization's grievance procedures. [42 C.F.R. § 422.74(c).]

¶401

Consequences of disenrollment. An individual who is disenrolled for nonpayment of premiums, disruptive behavior, fraud and abuse, or loss of Part A or B benefits is deemed to have elected original Medicare. If the individual is disenrolled because the plan was terminated, the area covered by the plan was reduced, or the individual no longer resides in the MA plan's service area, he or she will have a SEP to make a new choice. If the individual fails to make an election during the SEP, he or she will be enrolled in original Medicare. [42 C.F.R. § 422.74(e).] MA organizations are required to notify members of their Medigap-guaranteed issue rights when members disenroll to original Medicare during a special election period. [Pub. 100-16, Ch. 2, § 50.1.7.]

[¶ 402] Benefits and Beneficiary Protections

Medicare Advantage (MA) organizations must comply with CMS national coverage decisions (NCDs), general coverage guidelines included in original Medicare manuals and instructions (unless superseded by regulations), and written coverage decisions of local Medicare contractors. If an MA organization covers geographic areas encompassing more than one local coverage policy area, it may elect to uniformly apply to plan enrollees in all areas the coverage policy that is the most beneficial to MA enrollees. [42 C.F.R. § 422.101(b).]

Medicare as secondary payer. CMS does not pay for services to the extent that Medicare is not the primary payer (see ¶ 636). An MA organization must, for each MA plan: (1) identify payers that are primary to Medicare; (2) identify the amounts payable by those payers; and (3) coordinate its benefits to Medicare enrollees with the benefits of the primary payers. [42 C.F.R. § 422.108.]

Benefits Provided by MA Plans

Generally, an MA organization offering an MA plan must provide enrollees, at a minimum, with all basic Medicare-covered services (except that additional telehealth benefits may be, but are not required to be, offered by the MA plan) and, to the extent applicable, supplemental benefits by furnishing the benefits directly or through arrangements, or by paying for the benefits. Basic benefits are all items and services (other than hospice care or coverage for organ acquisitions for kidney transplants) for which benefits are available under Medicare Parts A and B, including additional telehealth benefits offered consistent with the requirements of 42 C.F.R. § 422.135. Supplemental benefits consist of (1) mandatory supplemental benefits, services not covered by Medicare that an MA enrollee must purchase as part of an MA plan that are paid for in full, directly by (or on behalf of) Medicare enrollees, in the form of premiums or cost-sharing; and (2) optional supplemental benefits, health services not covered by Medicare that are purchased at the option of the MA enrollee and paid for in full, directly by (or on behalf of) the Medicare enrollee, in the form of premiums or cost-sharing. These services may be grouped or offered individually. [Soc. Sec. Act § 1852(a); 42 C.F.R. § 422.100(a), (c); *Final rule*, 84 FR 15680, April 16, 2019.]

Noncontracting providers and suppliers. An MA organization must make timely and reasonable payment to or on behalf of the plan enrollee for the following services obtained from a provider or supplier that does not contract with the MA organization to provide services covered by the MA plan:

(1) ambulance services dispatched through 911 or its local equivalent;

(2) emergency and urgently needed services;

(3) maintenance and post-stabilization care services;

(4) renal dialysis services provided while the enrollee was temporarily outside the plan's service area; and

(5) services for which coverage has been denied by the MA organization and found upon appeal to be services the enrollee was entitled to have furnished, or paid for, by the MA organization.

[42 C.F.R. § 422.100(b)(1).]

An MA plan and an MA medical savings account (MSA) plan offered by an MA organization, after the annual deductible has been met, satisfy the basic requirements with respect to benefits for services furnished by a noncontracting provider if that MA plan provides payment in an amount the provider would have received under original Medicare, including balance billing permitted under Medicare Part A and Part B. [42 C.F.R. § 422.100(b)(2).]

Availability of plans. An MA organization must offer an MA plan to all Medicare beneficiaries residing in the service area of the MA plan. The organization must offer the plan at a uniform premium, with uniform benefits and level of cost-sharing throughout the plan's service area or segment of service area. [42 C.F.R. § 422.100(d).]

Review and approval of benefits and cost-sharing. CMS reviews and approves MA benefits and associated cost-sharing using written policy guidelines and requirements and other CMS instructions to ensure:

• Medicare-covered services meet CMS fee-for-service guidelines.

• MA organizations are not designing benefits to discriminate against beneficiaries, promote discrimination, discourage enrollment or encourage disenrollment, steer subsets of Medicare beneficiaries to particular MA plans, or inhibit access to services.

• Benefit design meets other MA program requirements.

• MA local plans have an out-of-pocket maximum for Medicare Parts A and B services that is no greater than the annual limit set by CMS.

• With respect to a local preferred provider organization (PPO) plan, the annual out-of-pocket limit applies only to use of network providers. Such local PPO plans must include a total catastrophic limit on beneficiary out-of-pocket expenditures for both in-network and out-of-network Parts A and B services that is: (1) consistent with the requirements applicable to MA regional plans; and (2) not greater than the annual limit set by CMS.

• Cost-sharing for Medicare Part A and B services specified by CMS does not exceed levels annually determined by CMS to be discriminatory for such services.

[42 C.F.R. § 422.100(f).]

Mammography, influenza, and pneumococcal benefits. Enrollees of MA organizations may directly access (through self-referral) mammography screening and influenza and pneumococcal vaccines. MA organizations may not impose cost-sharing for influenza vaccines and pneumococcal vaccines. [42 C.F.R. § 422.100(g).]

Coverage of durable medical equipment. An MA organization must cover and ensure enrollee access to all categories of durable medical equipment (DME) covered under Medicare Part B. However, an MA organization may, within specific categories of DME, limit coverage to certain brands, items, and supplies of preferred manufacturers, provided that:

(1) its contracts with DME suppliers ensure that enrollees have access to all DME brands, items, and supplies of preferred manufacturers;

(2) its enrollees have access to all medically necessary DME brands, items, and supplies of non-preferred manufacturers;

¶402

(3) at the request of new enrollees, it provides for a 90-day transition period during which the MA organization will ensure a supply of DME brands, items, and supplies of non-preferred manufacturers, and provide for the repair of same;

(4) it makes no negative changes to its DME brands, items, and supplies of preferred manufacturers during the plan year;

(5) it treats denials of DME brands, items, and supplies of non-preferred manufacturers as organization determinations subject to appeal;

(6) it discloses, as part of its description of benefits, DME coverage limitations and beneficiary appeal rights in the case of a denial of a DME brand, item, or supply of a non-preferred manufacturer; and

(7) it provides full coverage, without limitation on brand and manufacturer, to all DME categories or subcategories annually determined by CMS to require full coverage.

[42 C.F.R. § 422.100(l).]

Special rules for ambulance, emergency, and urgently needed services. The MA organization is financially responsible for ambulance services, including ambulance services dispatched through 911 or its local equivalent, where other means of transportation would endanger the beneficiary's health. The MA organization is also financially responsible for emergency and urgently needed services regardless of whether the services are obtained within or outside the MA organization, and regardless of whether there is prior authorization for the services. [42 C.F.R. § 422.113(a), (b).]

Special rules for maintenance and post-stabilization care services. In addition, the MA organization is financially responsible for post-stabilization care services obtained within or outside the MA organization that: (1) are pre-approved by a plan provider or other MA organization representative; (2) are not pre-approved by a plan provider or other MA organization representative, but are administered to maintain the enrollee's stabilized condition within one hour of a request to the MA organization for pre-approval of further post-stabilization care services; and (3) are not pre-approved by a plan provider or other MA organization representative, but are administered to maintain, improve, or resolve the enrollee's stabilized condition under certain conditions. [Soc. Sec. Act § 1852(d)(2); 42 C.F.R. § 422.113(c)(2).]

Additional telehealth benefits. Effective January 1, 2020, an MA plan may treat additional telehealth benefits as basic benefits covered under the original Medicare fee-for-service program for purposes of Part 422. If, however, the MA plan fails to comply with the requirements of 42 C.F.R. § 422.135, then the MA plan may not treat the benefits provided through electronic exchange as additional telehealth benefits; instead, the plan may treat them as supplemental benefits as described in 42 C.F.R. § 422.102, subject to CMS approval. "Additional telehealth benefits" is defined as services for which benefits are available under Medicare Part B but that are not payable under Soc. Sec. Act § 1834(m); and that have been identified by the MA plan for the applicable year as clinically appropriate to furnish through electronic exchange when the physician or practitioner providing the service is not in the same location as the enrollee. [Soc. Sec. Act § 1852(m); 42 C.F.R. § 422.135(a), (b); *Final rule*, 84 FR 15680, April 16, 2019.]

Supplemental benefits for chronically ill individuals. Beginning in plan year 2020, MA plans, including special needs plans (SNPs), may provide to chronically ill enrollees, in addition to any supplemental health care benefits otherwise provided, supplemental benefits that have a reasonable expectation of improving or maintaining the health or overall function of the enrollee. They may not be limited to primarily health-related benefits. The term "chronically ill enrollee" means an enrollee in an MA plan that has one or more comorbid and medically complex chronic conditions that is life threatening or significantly limits his or her overall health and function, has a high risk of hospitalization or other adverse health outcomes, and requires intensive care coordination. [Soc. Sec. Act § 1852(a)(3)(D).]

Requirements during a disaster or emergency. When a state of disaster is declared, an MA organization must ensure access to benefits by covering Part A, Part B, and supplemental Part B benefits furnished at non-contracted facilities, waive requirements for gatekeeper referrals where applicable, provide the same cost-sharing for enrollees as if the service or benefit had been furnished at a plan-contracted facility, and make changes that benefit the enrollee effective immediately without the 30-day notification requirement. [42 C.F.R. § 422.100(m).]

Return to home skilled nursing facility services. MA plans must provide coverage of post-hospital extended care services to Medicare enrollees through a home skilled nursing facility (SNF) if the enrollee elects to receive the coverage through the home SNF and the home SNF either has a contract with the MA organization or agrees to accept substantially similar payment under the same terms and conditions that apply to similar SNFs that contract with the MA organization. A home SNF is: (1) the SNF in which the enrollee resided at the time of admission to the hospital preceding the receipt of post-hospital extended care services; (2) a SNF that is providing post-hospital extended care services through a continuing care retirement community in which the MA plan enrollee was a resident at the time of admission to the hospital; or (3) the SNF in which the spouse of the enrollee is residing at the time of discharge from the hospital. [42 C.F.R. § 422.133.]

Effect of NCDs and legislative changes in benefits. If CMS determines and announces that an individual NCD or legislative change in benefits meets the criteria for "significant cost," an MA organization is not required to assume risk for the costs of that service or benefit until the contract year for which payments are appropriately adjusted to take into account the cost of the NCD service or legislative change in benefits. If CMS determines that an NCD or legislative change in benefits does not meet the "significant cost" threshold, the MA organization is required to provide coverage for the NCD or legislative change in benefits and assume risk for the costs of that service or benefit as of the effective date stated in the NCD or specified in the legislation. [Soc. Sec. Act § 1852(a)(5); 42 C.F.R. § 422.109(b).]

"Significant cost" is defined as either: (1) the average cost of furnishing a single service that exceeds a cost threshold of the preceding year's dollar threshold adjusted to reflect the national per capita growth percentage; or (2) the estimated cost of all Medicare services furnished as a result of a particular NCD or legislative change in benefits representing at least 0.1 percent of the national average per capita costs. [42 C.F.R. § 422.109(a).]

Special Rules for Self-Referral and Point-of-Service Option

If an MA plan member receives an item or service of the plan that is covered upon referral or pre-authorization from a contracted provider of that plan, the member cannot be financially liable for more than the normal in-plan cost-sharing if he or she correctly identifies himself or herself as a member of that plan to the contracted provider before receiving the covered item or service. However, if the contracted provider can show that the enrollee was notified before receiving the item or service that the item or service is covered only if further action is taken by the enrollee, then this requirement does not apply. [42 C.F.R. § 422.105(a).]

Point-of-service option. As a general rule, a point-of-service (POS) benefit is an option that an MA organization may offer in a health maintenance organization (HMO) plan to

¶402

provide enrollees with additional choice in obtaining specified health care services. The organization may offer a POS option under a coordinated care plan as an additional benefit under an HMO plan as a mandatory or optional supplemental benefit. [42 C.F.R. § 422.105(b).]

Access to Services

An MA organization offering a coordinated care plan may specify the networks of providers that enrollees can use, as long as the organization ensures that all covered services, including supplemental services contracted for the Medicare enrollee, are available and accessible under the plan. [42 C.F.R. § 422.112(a).]

To accomplish this, the MA organization must do the following:

(1) maintain and monitor a network of appropriate providers supported by written agreements that is sufficient to provide necessary access to meet the needs of enrollees (except that MA regional plans can use methods other than written agreements with CMS approval);

(2) establish a panel of primary care providers (PCPs) from which an enrollee may choose a PCP;

(3) provide or arrange for necessary specialty care and, in particular, give female enrollees the option of direct access to a women's health specialist;

(4) demonstrate, if seeking to expand the service area of an MA plan, that the number and type of providers available to the plan are sufficient to meet the needs of the population;

(5) demonstrate to CMS that its providers in a plan are credentialed;

(6) establish written standards for timely access to care, medical necessity determinations, and provider consideration of enrollee input for treatment plans;

(7) establish convenient and non-discriminatory hours of operation and make plan services available 24 hours per day, seven days per week, when medically necessary;

(8) ensure that services are provided in a culturally competent manner to all enrollees;

(9) provide coverage for ambulance services, emergency and urgently needed services, and post-stabilization care services; and

(10) ensure that coordinated care and private fee-for-service (PFFS) MA plans that meet Medicare access and availability requirements through direct contracting network providers are consistent with the prevailing community pattern of health care delivery in the areas where the network is being offered.

[Soc. Sec. Act § 1852(d)(1); 42 C.F.R. § 422.112(a).]

MA organizations also must ensure continuity of care and integration of services through arrangements with contracted providers. [42 C.F.R. § 422.112(b).]

Access to services under private fee-for-service plans. An MA organization that offers a PFFS plan must demonstrate to CMS that it has a sufficient number and range of providers willing to furnish services under the plan. An MA organization meets this requirement if it has: (1) payment rates that are not less than the rates that apply under original Medicare for the provider in question; and (2) contracts or agreements with a sufficient number and range of providers to furnish the services covered under the plan or meet the required access standards. [Soc. Sec. Act § 1852(d)(4); 42 C.F.R. § 422.114(a)(1), (2).]

Reward and Incentive Programs

MA organizations may create reward and incentive programs that focus on promoting improved health, preventing illness and injuries, and encouraging the efficient use of health care resources. These rewards or incentives must: (1) be offered in connection with an entire service or activity; (2) be offered without discrimination; (3) have a monetary cap that is determined by CMS and that is expected to affect enrollee behavior but not exceed the value of the activity or service; and (4) be compliant with all relevant fraud and abuse laws. [42 C.F.R. § 422.134.]

To be considered nondiscriminatory, a reward or incentive program must be designed so that all enrollees may earn rewards and not discriminate based on race, national origin (including limited English proficiency), gender, disability, chronic disease, whether a person resides in an institutional setting, frailty, health status, or any other prohibited basis. Moreover, reward and incentive programs within MA organizations may not offer items in the form of cash or other monetary rebates and may not be used to target potential enrollees. [42 C.F.R. § 422.134.]

Special Needs Plans

MA organizations seeking to offer a SNP serving beneficiaries eligible for both Medicare and Medicaid (dual eligibles) must have a contract with the state Medicaid agency. At a minimum, the contract must document:

(1) effective January 1, 2020, the MA organization's responsibility to (a) coordinate the delivery of Medicaid benefits for individuals who are eligible for such services, and (b) if applicable, provide coverage of Medicaid services, including long-term services and supports and behavioral health services, for individuals eligible for such services;

(2) effective January 1, 2020, the categories and criteria for eligibility for dual-eligible individuals to be enrolled under the SNP;

(3) effective January 1, 2020, the Medicaid benefits covered under a capitated contract between the state Medicaid agency and the MA organization offering the SNP, the SNP's parent organization, or another entity that is owned and controlled by the SNP's parent organization;

(4) the cost-sharing protections covered under the SNP;

(5) the identification and sharing of information on Medicaid provider participation;

(6) the verification of enrollee's eligibility for both Medicare and Medicaid;

(7) the service area covered by the SNP;

(8) the contract period for the SNP; and

(9) effective January 1, 2021, for each dual-eligible SNP that is an applicable integrated plan, a requirement for the use of the unified appeals and grievance procedures under 42 C.F.R. § § 422.629 through 422.634, 438.210, 438.400, and 438.402.

[42 C.F.R. § 422.107; *Final rule,* 84 FR 15680, April 16, 2019.]

SNPs that meet a high standard of integration and minimum performance and quality-based standards may offer additional supplemental benefits when CMS finds that such benefits could better integrate care for the dual-eligible population. To offer these additional benefits, the SNP must: (1) have operated in the MA contract year prior to the MA contract year for which it is submitting its bid; and (2) offer its enrollees such benefits without cost-sharing or additional premium charges. [42 C.F.R. § 422.102(e).]

¶402

Model of care for SNPs. MA organizations offering SNPs must implement an evidence-based model of care (MOC) with appropriate networks of providers and specialists. The organization must: (1) conduct a comprehensive initial health risk assessment of each enrollee's physical, psychosocial, and functional needs as well as an annual health risk reassessment, using a comprehensive risk assessment tool that CMS will review during oversight activities; (2) develop and implement a comprehensive individualized plan of care through an interdisciplinary care team in consultation with the beneficiary, identifying goals and objectives, including measurable outcomes as well as specific services and benefits to be provided; and (3) use an interdisciplinary team in the management of care. [42 C.F.R. § 422.101(f)(1).]

MA organizations offering SNPs must also ensure an effective management structure by developing and implementing the following MOC components: (1) target one of the three SNP populations; (2) have appropriate staff trained on the SNP plan MOC to coordinate and deliver all services and benefits; (3) coordinate the delivery of care across health care settings, providers, and services to ensure continuity of care; (4) coordinate the delivery of specialized benefits and services that meet the needs of the most vulnerable beneficiaries among the three target special needs populations, including frail or disabled beneficiaries and beneficiaries near the end of life; and (5) coordinate communication among plan personnel, providers, and beneficiaries. All MA organizations wishing to offer or continue to offer an SNP must be approved by the National Committee for Quality Assurance. [42 C.F.R. § 422.101(f)(2).]

Integration of dual-eligible SNPs. Section 50311 of the Bipartisan Budget Act of 2018 (P.L. 115-123) provides for the increased integration of dual-eligible SNPs (D-SNPs) into the MA program. A D-SNP is a plan that provides coverage to individuals that are eligible for both Medicare and Medicaid. [Soc. Sec. Act § 1859(f)(8)(A), as added by Bipartisan Budget Act of 2018 § 50311.]

Coordination of Benefits

If an MA organization contracts with an employer group health plan (EGHP) or labor union that covers enrollees in an MA plan, or with a state Medicaid agency to provide Medicaid benefits to enrollees who are eligible for both Medicare and Medicaid and who are enrolled in an MA plan, the enrollees must be provided the same benefits as all other enrollees in the MA plan, with the EGHP, labor union, or Medicaid benefits supplementing the MA plan benefits. [42 C.F.R. § 422.106(a).]

Permissible employer, labor organization, or Medicaid plan benefits include: (1) payment of a portion or all of the MA basic and supplemental premiums; (2) payment of a portion or all of other cost-sharing amounts approved for the MA plan; or (3) other employer-sponsored benefits that may require additional premium and cost-sharing, or other benefits provided by the organization under a contract with the state Medicaid agency. [42 C.F.R. § 422.106(b).]

MA organizations may request a CMS waiver or modification of those requirements that hinder the design of, the offering of, or the enrollment in MA plans under contracts between MA organizations and employers, labor organizations, or the trustees of funds established by one or more employers or labor organizations to furnish benefits to the entity's employees, former employees, or members or former members of the labor organizations. [42 C.F.R. § 422.106(c).]

Beneficiary Protections

An MA organization may not deny, limit, or condition coverage or benefits to beneficiaries on the basis of health status, including medical condition, claims experience, receipt of health care, medical history, genetic information, evidence of insurability (including conditions arising out of acts of domestic violence), or disability. [42 C.F.R. § 422.110(a).]

An MA organization may not currently enroll an individual who has been medically determined to have end-stage renal disease (ESRD). However, if an individual is diagnosed with ESRD while enrolled in an MA plan, he or she may not be disenrolled for that reason. [42 C.F.R. § 422.110(b).]

Advance directives. An MA organization must maintain written policies and procedures concerning advance directives with respect to all adults receiving medical care by or through the MA organization. [42 C.F.R. § 422.128.]

Disclosure requirements. An MA organization must disclose to each beneficiary enrolling in one of its plans a plan description, including the plan's service area, benefits, access (including out-of-area coverage), emergency coverage, supplemental benefits, prior authorization and review rules, grievance and appeals procedures, quality improvement program, disenrollment rights and responsibilities, catastrophic caps and single deductible, and claims information. This information must be provided at the time of enrollment and at least annually thereafter, 15 days before the annual coordinated election period, in a clear, accurate, and standardized form. [Soc. Sec. Act § 1852(c); 42 C.F.R. § 422.111.]

Starting with plan year 2021, MA prescription drug plans (MA-PDs) and Part D prescription drug plans (PDPs) must provide information to beneficiaries on the risks associated with prolonged opioid use and coverage of nonpharmacological therapies, devices, and nonopioid medications. Instead of providing the information to each enrollee in a MA-PD or PDP plan, the sponsor may provide the information through mail or electronic communication to a subset of enrollees, such as those who have been prescribed an opioid in the previous two years. [Soc. Sec. Act § 1860D-4(a)(1)(B)(vi) and (a)(1)(C), as added by SUPPORT for Patients and Communities Act (P.L. 115-271) § 6102.]

Confidentiality of enrollee records. For any medical records or enrollment information it maintains, an MA organization must abide by all federal and state laws regarding confidentiality and disclosure of medical records; ensure that medical information is released only in accordance with federal or state laws or under court orders or subpoenas; maintain the records in an accurate manner; and ensure timely access by enrollees to their own records. [42 C.F.R. § 422.118.]

General Rules for Medicare Advantage and Step Therapy

Step therapy is a utilization management policy for coverage of drugs that begins medication for a medical condition with the most preferred or cost effective drug therapy and progresses to other drug therapies if medically necessary. Effective January 1, 2020, if an MA plan implements a step therapy program to control the utilization of Part B-covered drugs, it must:

(1) apply step therapy only to new administrations of Part B drugs, using at least a 365-day lookback period;

(2) establish policies and procedures to educate and inform health care providers and enrollees concerning its step therapy policies; and

(3) prior to implementation of a step therapy program, ensure that the program has been reviewed and approved by the MA organization's pharmacy and therapeutics committee.

[42 C.F.R. §§ 422.2, 422.136(a); *Final rule*, 84 FR 23832, May 23, 2019.]

¶402

An MA plan may include a drug supported only by an off-label indication in step therapy protocols only if the off-label indication is supported by widely used treatment guidelines or clinical literature that CMS considers to represent best practices. A step therapy program must not include as a component of a protocol or other condition or requirement any drugs not covered by the applicable MA plan as a Part B drug or, in the case of an MA-PD, a Part D drug. [42 C.F.R. § 422.136(c), (d); *Final rule*, 84 FR 23832, May 23, 2019.]

[¶ 403] Beneficiary Grievances, Organizational Determinations, and Appeals

Medicare Advantage (MA) plans must provide meaningful procedures for hearing and resolving grievances between the plan and enrolled beneficiaries and for organization determinations and appeals. [Soc. Sec. Act § 1852(f), (g); 42 C.F.R. § 422.560.]

Grievance procedures are separate and distinct from appeal procedures, which address organization determinations. For the purposes of these procedures:

- An *"appeal"* is a procedure that deals with the review of an adverse organization determination on the health care services an enrollee believes he or she is entitled to receive. The basis of this process includes delay in providing, arranging for, or approving health care services (such that a delay would adversely affect the health of the enrollee), or disputes of any amounts the enrollee must pay for a service. These procedures include reconsiderations by the MA organization and, if necessary, an independent review entity (IRE), hearings before administrative law judges (ALJs), review by the Medicare Appeals Council, and judicial review. Disputes involving optional supplemental benefits offered by cost plans and health care prepayment plans (HCPPs) are treated as appeals.

- A *"grievance"* is any complaint or dispute, other than one involving an organization determination, expressing dissatisfaction with any aspect of an MA organization's or provider's operation, activities, or behavior, regardless of whether remedial action is requested. Grievances may include complaints regarding access to or the timeliness, appropriateness, or setting of a provided health service, procedure, or item. Grievance issues also may include complaints that a covered health service procedure or item during a course of treatment did not meet accepted standards for delivery of health care.

[42 C.F.R. §§ 422.561, 422.564(b); *Medicare Managed Care Manual*, Pub. 100-16, Ch. 13, § 10.1.]

Additional Responsibilities of Dual-Eligible SNPs

Effective January 1, 2020, an MA organization that offers a dual-eligible special needs plan (SNP) has additional responsibilities. It must offer to assist an enrollee in that SNP with obtaining Medicaid covered services and resolving grievances, including requesting authorization of Medicaid services, as applicable, and navigating Medicaid appeals and grievances in connection with the enrollee's own Medicaid coverage, regardless of whether such coverage is in Medicaid fee-for-service or a Medicaid managed care plan. If the enrollee accepts the offer of assistance, the plan must provide the assistance. The dual-eligible SNP must offer to provide this assistance whenever it becomes aware of an enrollee's need for a Medicaid-covered service; offering such assistance is not dependent on an enrollee's specific request. The plan must offer to provide and actually provide assistance using multiple methods, including coaching the enrollee on how to self-advocate. The plan must, upon request, provide CMS with documentation demonstrating its compliance with this requirement, and the obligation to provide assistance does not create an obligation for a plan to represent an enrollee in a Medicaid appeal. [42 C.F.R. § 422.562(a)(5); *Final rule*, 84 FR 15680, April 16, 2019.]

Integrated dual-eligible SNPs. CMS established requirements for unified appeals and grievance processes that applicable integrated plans must follow beginning January 1, 2021. [Soc. Sec. Act § 1859(f)(8)(B) and (C); 42 C.F.R. § 422.629(a); *Final rule*, 84 FR 23832, May 23, 2019; *Final rule*, 84 FR 15680, April 16, 2019.]

Grievance Procedures for MA Organizations

Each MA organization must provide meaningful procedures for timely hearing and resolving grievances between enrollees and the organization or any other entity or individual through which the organization provides health care services under any MA plan it offers. Upon receiving a complaint, an MA organization must promptly determine and inform the enrollee whether the complaint is subject to its grievance or appeal procedures. [Soc. Sec. Act § 1852(f); 42 C.F.R. § 422.564(a), (b).]

Grievance disposition. An MA organization must notify the enrollee of its decision as expeditiously as the case requires, based on the enrollee's health status, but no later than 30 days after the date the organization receives the oral or written grievance. The notification time frame may be extended by up to 14 days if the enrollee requests the extension or if the organization justifies a need for additional information and documents how the delay is in the interest of the enrollee. If the organization extends the deadline, it must immediately notify the enrollee in writing of the reasons for the delay. [42 C.F.R. § 422.564(e).]

The MA organization must notify the enrollee of the disposition of the grievance as follows: (1) it must respond in writing to all grievances submitted in writing; (2) it may respond either orally or in writing to grievances submitted orally, unless the enrollee requests a written response; and (3) it must respond in writing to all grievances related to quality of care, regardless of how the grievance is filed. The response must also include a description of the enrollee's right to file a written complaint with the quality improvement organization (QIO). [42 C.F.R. § 422.564(e)(3).]

Expedited grievances. An MA organization must respond to an enrollee's grievance within 24 hours if the complaint involves an MA organization's: (1) decision to invoke an extension relating to an organization determination or reconsideration; or (2) refusal to grant an enrollee's request for an expedited organization determination or reconsideration. [42 C.F.R. § 422.564(f).]

MA Organization Determinations

Each MA organization must have a procedure for making timely organization determinations regarding the benefits an enrollee is entitled to receive under an MA plan, including basic benefits and mandatory and optional supplemental benefits, and the amount, if any, that the enrollee is required to pay for a health service. The MA organization must have a standard procedure for making determinations and an expedited procedure for situations in which applying the standard procedure could seriously jeopardize the enrollee's life, health, or ability to regain maximum function. [Soc. Sec. Act § 1852(g)(1), (g)(3); 42 C.F.R. § 422.566(a).]

Organization determinations. An organization determination is any determination made by an MA organization regarding any of the following:

(1) payment for temporarily out-of-the-area renal dialysis services, emergency services, post-stabilization care, or urgently needed services;

(2) payment for any other health services furnished by a provider other than the MA organization that the enrollee believes are covered under Medicare or, if not covered under Medicare, should have been furnished, arranged for, or reimbursed by the MA organization;

¶403

(3) the MA organization's refusal to provide or pay for services, in whole or in part, including the type or level of services, that the enrollee believes should be furnished or arranged for by the MA organization;

(4) reduction or premature discontinuation of a previously authorized ongoing course of treatment; or

(5) failure of the MA organization to approve, furnish, arrange for, or provide payment for health care services in a timely manner, or to provide the enrollee with timely notice of an adverse determination, such that a delay would adversely affect the health of the enrollee.

[42 C.F.R. § 422.566(b).]

Individuals or entities who can request an organization determination include the enrollee or his or her representative; any provider that furnishes, or intends to furnish, services to the enrollee; or the legal representative of a deceased enrollee's estate. An enrollee or a physician (regardless of whether the physician is affiliated with the MA organization) can request an expedited determination. [42 C.F.R. § 422.566(c).]

Generally, an enrollee makes an oral or written request with the MA organization or, if applicable, to the entity responsible for making the determination. The enrollee must make requests for payment in writing, unless the MA organization or entity responsible for making the determination has implemented a voluntary policy of accepting verbal payment requests. [42 C.F.R. § 422.568(a).]

Notice requirements. When a party makes a request for a service or an item, the MA organization must notify the enrollee of its determination as expeditiously as the enrollee's health condition requires, but no later than 14 calendar days after receiving the request for a standard organization determination. The MA organization may extend the time frame by up to 14 calendar days if (1) the enrollee requests the extension; (2) the extension is justified and in the enrollee's interest due to the need for additional medical evidence from a noncontract provider that may change an MA organization's decision to deny an item or service; or (3) the extension is justified due to extraordinary, exigent, or other non-routine circumstances and is in the enrollee's interest. When the MA organization extends the time frame, it must notify the enrollee in writing of the reasons for the delay and inform the enrollee of the right to file an expedited grievance if he or she disagrees with the decision to grant an extension. The MA organization must notify the enrollee of its determination as expeditiously as the enrollee's health condition requires, but no later than upon expiration of the extension. [42 C.F.R. § 422.568(b)(1).]

Effective January 1, 2020, when a party has made a request for a Part B drug, the MA organization must notify the enrollee (and the prescribing physician or other prescriber involved, as appropriate) of its determination as expeditiously as the enrollee's health condition requires, but no later than 72 hours after receipt of the request. This 72-hour period may not be extended under the provisions in 42 C.F.R. § 422.568(b)(1)(i). [42 C.F.R. § 422.568(b)(2); *Final rule*, 84 FR 23832, May 23, 2019.]

Expedited Determinations

An enrollee or a physician (regardless of whether the physician is affiliated with the MA organization) may request that an MA organization expedite an organization determination involving: (1) the MA organization's refusal to provide or pay for services, in whole or in part, including the type or level of services, that the enrollee believes should be furnished or arranged for by the MA organization; or (2) discontinuation of a service if the enrollee believes that continuation of the services is medically necessary. To request an expedited determination, an enrollee or a physician must submit an oral or written request directly to the MA organization or, if applicable, to the entity responsible for making the determination. A physician may provide oral or written support for a request for an expedited determination. [Soc. Sec. Act § 1852(g)(3); 42 C.F.R. § 422.570(a), (b).]

If an MA organization denies a request for expedited determination, it must take the following actions:

> (1) automatically transfer a request to the standard time frame and make the determination within the 72-hour or 14-day time frame, as applicable, for a standard determination; the time frame begins when the MA organization receives the request for expedited determination; and

> (2) give the enrollee prompt oral notice of the denial and subsequently deliver, within three calendar days, a written letter that explains that (a) the MA organization will process the request using the 14-day time-frame for standard determinations; (b) informs the enrollee of the right to file an expedited grievance if he or she disagrees with the MA organization's decision not to expedite; (c) informs the enrollee of the right to resubmit a request for an expedited determination with any physician's support; and (d) provides instructions about the grievance process and its time frames.

[42 C.F.R. § 422.570(d); *Final rule*, 84 FR 23832, May 23, 2019.]

An MA organization that approves a request for expedited determination concerning a request for a service or item must make its determination and notify the enrollee (and the physician involved, as appropriate) of its decision, whether adverse or favorable, as expeditiously as the enrollee's health condition requires, but no later than 72 hours after receiving the request. Effective January 1, 2020, an MA organization that approves a request for expedited determination concerning a request for a Part B drug must make its determination and notify the enrollee (and the physician or prescriber involved, as appropriate) of its decision as expeditiously as the enrollee's health condition requires, but no later than 24 hours after receiving the request. This 24-hour period may not be extended. [Soc. Sec. Act § 1852(g)(3)(B)(iii); 42 C.F.R. § 422.572(a); *Final rule*, 84 FR 23832, May 23, 2019.]

Reconsiderations by MA Organizations and Outside Entities

Any party to an organization determination may, within 60 days of receipt of the request for reconsideration, request that the MA organization reconsider the determination under the procedures described in 42 C.F.R. § 422.582, which address requests for a standard reconsideration. A physician who is providing treatment to an enrollee may, upon providing notice to the enrollee, request a standard reconsideration of a pre-service request for reconsideration on the enrollee's behalf. An enrollee or physician (acting on behalf of an enrollee) may request an expedited reconsideration. [Soc. Sec. Act § 1852(g)(2); 42 C.F.R. § 422.578.]

Expedited reconsiderations. An enrollee or a physician (regardless of whether he or she is affiliated with the MA organization) may request that an MA organization expedite a reconsideration of a determination that involves issues not including requests for payment of services already furnished. To request an expedited reconsideration, an enrollee or a physician acting on behalf of an enrollee must submit an oral or written request directly to the MA organization or, if applicable, to the entity responsible for making the reconsideration. The MA organization must establish and maintain specific procedures for processing requests for expedited reconsiderations. [Soc. Sec. Act § 1852(g)(3); 42 C.F.R. § 422.584.]

Independent outside entities. When the MA organization affirms, in whole or in part, its adverse organization determination, an independent, outside entity that contracts with

¶403

CMS must review and resolve the issues that remain in dispute. The independent outside entity must conduct the review as expeditiously as the enrollee's health condition requires but must not exceed the deadlines specified in the contract. [42 C.F.R. § 422.592.]

Administrative Law Judge Hearings

If the amount remaining in controversy after reconsideration meets the threshold requirement, any party to the reconsideration (except the MA organization) who is dissatisfied with the reconsidered determination has a right to a hearing before an ALJ. A request for an ALJ hearing must be in writing and filed with the entity specified in the reconsideration notice within 60 days. The parties to a hearing are the parties to the reconsideration, the MA organization, and any other person or entity whose rights with respect to the reconsideration may be affected by the hearing. [42 C.F.R. § § 422.600, 422.602; Pub. 100-16, Ch. 13, § § 100.1, 100.2.]

Amount in controversy. In 2020, plan enrollees who are dissatisfied, either because they have not received health care to which they believe they are entitled, or because they contest the cost of a service they have received, are entitled to a hearing before an ALJ if the amount in controversy is $170 or more. [*Notice*, 84 FR 53444, Oct. 7, 2019.]

Medicare Appeals Council Review

Any party to an ALJ hearing, including the MA organization, who is dissatisfied with the ALJ hearing decision may request that the Medicare Appeals Council review the ALJ's decision or dismissal (see ¶ 924). [Soc. Sec. Act § 1852(g)(5); 42 C.F.R. § 422.608.]

Judicial Review

Any party, including the MA organization, may request judicial review of an ALJ's decision if the Medicare Appeals Council denied the party's request for review and the amount in controversy meets the threshold requirement established annually. Any party may also request judicial review of a Medicare Appeals Council decision if it is the final decision of CMS and the amount in controversy meets the threshold requirement. [Soc. Sec. Act § 1852(g)(5); 42 C.F.R. § 422.612.]

To request judicial review, a party must file a civil action in a district court of the United States. The minimum amount in controversy for judicial review of Medicare claims made on or after January 1, 2020, is $1,670, up from $1,630 in 2019. [*Notice*, 84 FR 53444, Oct. 7, 2019; *Notice*, 83 FR 47619, Sept. 20, 2018.]

Effectuating Reconsidered Determinations or Decisions

If, on reconsideration of a *request for service*, the MA organization completely reverses its determination, the organization must authorize or provide the service under dispute as expeditiously as the enrollee's health condition requires, but no later than 30 calendar days after the date the MA organization receives the request for reconsideration (or no later than upon expiration of an extension described in 42 C.F.R. § 422.590(f)). [42 C.F.R. § 422.618(a)(1).]

If, on reconsideration of a *request for payment*, the MA organization completely reverses its organization determination, the organization must pay for the service no later than 60 calendar days after the date the MA organization receives the request for reconsideration. [42 C.F.R. § 422.618(a)(2).]

If, on reconsideration of a *request for a Part B drug*, the MA organization completely reverses its determination, the MA organization must authorize or provide the Part B drug under dispute as expeditiously as the enrollee's health condition requires, but no later than seven calendar days after the date the MA organization receives the request for reconsideration. [42 C.F.R. § 422.618(a)(3); *Final rule*, 84 FR 23832, May 23, 2019.]

Reversals by the independent outside entity. If, on reconsideration of a *request for service*, the MA organization's determination is reversed in whole or in part by the independent outside entity, the MA organization must authorize the service under dispute within 72 hours from the date it receives notice reversing the determination or provide the service under dispute as expeditiously as the enrollee's health condition requires, but no later than 14 calendar days from that date. [42 C.F.R. § 422.618(b)(1).]

If, on reconsideration of a *request for payment*, the MA organization's determination is reversed in whole or in part by the independent outside entity, the MA organization must pay for the service no later than 30 calendar days from the date it receives notice reversing the organization determination. [42 C.F.R. § 422.618(b)(2).]

If, on reconsideration of a *request for a Part B drug*, the MA organization's determination is reversed in whole or in part by the independent outside entity, the MA organization must authorize or provide the Part B drug under dispute within 72 hours from the date it receives notice reversing the determination. The MA organization must inform the independent outside entity that the organization has effectuated the decision. [42 C.F.R. § 422.618(b)(3); *Final rule*, 84 FR 23832, May 23, 2019.]

Other reversals. If the independent outside entity's determination is reversed in whole or in part by the ALJ, or attorney adjudicator, or at a higher level of appeal, the MA organization must pay for, authorize, or provide the service under dispute as expeditiously as the enrollee's health condition requires, but no later than 60 calendar days from the date it receives notice reversing the determination. However, if the MA organization requests Medicare Appeals Council review, the organization may await the outcome of the review before it pays for, authorizes, or provides the service under dispute. [42 C.F.R. § 422.618(c).]

Expedited requests. If, on reconsideration of an expedited request for service, the MA organization completely reverses its determination, the MA organization must authorize or provide the service under dispute as expeditiously as the enrollee's health condition requires, but no later than 72 hours after the date the MA organization receives the request for reconsideration (or no later than upon expiration of an extension described in 42 C.F.R. § 422.590(f)). If, on reconsideration of a request for a Part B drug, the MA organization completely reverses its organization determination, the MA organization must authorize or provide the Part B drug under dispute as expeditiously as the enrollee's health condition requires, but no later than 72 hours after the date the MA organization receives the request for reconsideration. [42 C.F.R. § 422.619(a); *Final rule*, 84 FR 23832, May 23, 2019.]

If the MA organization's determination on a request for service or item is reversed in whole or in part by the independent outside entity, the MA organization must authorize or provide the service under dispute as expeditiously as the enrollee's health condition requires, but no later than 72 hours from the date it receives notice reversing the determination. If, on reconsideration of a request for a Part B drug, the MA organization's determination is reversed in whole or in part by the independent outside entity, the MA organization must authorize or provide the Part B drug under dispute as expeditiously as the enrollee's health condition requires but no later than 24 hours from the date it receives notice reversing the determination. The MA organization must inform the outside entity that the organization has effectuated the decision. [42 C.F.R. § 422.619(b); *Final rule*, 84 FR 23832, May 23, 2019.]

If the independent outside entity's expedited determination is reversed in whole or in part by the ALJ, or attorney adjudicator, or at a higher level of appeal, the MA organization

¶403

must authorize or provide the service under dispute as expeditiously as the enrollee's health condition requires, but no later than 60 days from the date it receives notice reversing the determination. The MA organization must inform the independent outside entity that the organization has effectuated the decision. [42 C.F.R. § 422.619(c)(1).]

If the independent outside entity's determination is reversed in whole or in part by an ALJ or attorney adjudicator or at a higher level of appeal, the MA organization must authorize or provide the Part B drug under dispute as expeditiously as the enrollee's health condition requires but no later than 24 hours from the date it receives notice reversing the determination. The MA organization must inform the outside entity that the organization has effectuated the decision. [42 C.F.R. § 422.619(c)(2); *Final rule*, 84 FR 23832, May 23, 2019.]

If the MA organization requests Medicare Appeals Council review consistent with 42 C.F.R. § 422.608, it may await the outcome of the review before it authorizes or provides the service under dispute. An MA organization that files an appeal with the Medicare Appeals Council must concurrently send a copy of its appeal request and any accompanying documents to the enrollee and must notify the independent outside entity that it has requested an appeal. [42 C.F.R. § 422.619(c)(3).]

Notification of Hospital Discharge Appeal Rights

Hospitals must deliver a standardized written notice of an MA enrollee's rights as a hospital inpatient, including discharge appeal rights, within two calendar days of the enrollee's admission to the hospital. The notice of rights must include: (1) the enrollee's rights as a hospital inpatient, including the right to benefits for inpatient services and for post-hospital services; (2) the enrollee's right to request an immediate review, including a description of the process and the availability of other appeals processes if the enrollee fails to meet the deadline for an immediate review; (3) the circumstances under which an enrollee will or will not be liable for charges for continued stay in the hospital; (4) the enrollee's right to receive additional information; and (5) any other information required by CMS. [42 C.F.R. § 422.620(b)(1), (2).]

For delivery of the written notice of rights to be valid, the enrollee (or the enrollee's representative) must sign and date the notice to indicate that he or she has received the notice and can understand its contents. [42 C.F.R. § 422.620(b)(3).]

Follow-up notification. The hospital must present a copy of the signed notice to the enrollee (or enrollee's representative) at least two calendar days before discharge. Before the MA organization can discharge an enrollee from the inpatient hospital level of care, the physician who is responsible for the enrollee's inpatient care must concur. [42 C.F.R. § 422.620(c), (d).]

QIO review of the decision to discharge. An enrollee who wishes to appeal a determination by an MA organization or hospital that inpatient care is no longer necessary must request immediate QIO review of the determination in writing or by telephone no later than the day of discharge. An enrollee who requests immediate QIO review may remain in the hospital with no additional financial liability for inpatient services received before noon of the day after the QIO notifies the enrollee of its review determination. [Soc. Sec. Act § 1154(a)(14); 42 C.F.R. § 422.622.]

Termination of Provider Services

Before any termination of service, the provider of the service must deliver valid written notice to the enrollee of the MA organization's decision to terminate services. "Termination of service" is defined as the discharge of an enrollee from covered provider services, or discontinuation of covered provider services, when the enrollee has been authorized by the

MA organization to receive an ongoing course of treatment from that provider (including home health agencies, skilled nursing facilities, and comprehensive outpatient rehabilitation facilities). Termination includes cessation of coverage at the end of a course of treatment pre-authorized in a discrete increment, regardless of whether the enrollee agrees that such services should end. [42 C.F.R. § 422.624(a).]

The provider must notify the enrollee of the MA organization's decision to terminate covered services no later than two days before the proposed end of the services and must use a standardized notice. The standardized termination notice must include: (1) the date that coverage of services ends; (2) the date that the enrollee's financial liability for continued services begins; (3) a description of the enrollee's right to a fast-track appeal, including information on how to contact an IRE, an enrollee's right to submit evidence showing that services should continue, and the availability of other MA appeal procedures if the enrollee fails to meet the deadline for a fast-track IRE appeal; (4) the enrollee's right to receive detailed information about the termination notice and all documents sent by the provider to the IRE; and (5) any other information required by the Secretary. [42 C.F.R. § 422.624(b).]

Enrollees have a right to a fast-track appeal of an MA organization's decision to terminate provider services. Enrollees must submit a request for appeal to an IRE under contract with CMS, in writing or by telephone, by noon of the first day after the day the termination notice was delivered. [42 C.F.R. § 422.626(a).]

[¶ 405] Contracts with Medicare Advantage Organizations

Entities seeking a contract as a Medicare organization offering a Medicare Advantage (MA) plan must fulfill certain application requirements. MA organizations offering prescription drug plans must, in addition to these requirements, follow the requirements in Chapter 5 related to the prescription drug benefit. [Soc. Sec. Act § 1857(a); 42 C.F.R. § 422.500.]

Minimum enrollment requirements. CMS will not enter into a contract with a managed care organization unless the organization enrolls: (1) at least 5,000 individuals (or 1,500 individuals if the organization is a provider-sponsored organization (PSO)) for the purpose of receiving health benefits from the organization; (2) or at least 1,500 individuals (or 500 individuals if the organization is a PSO) for the purpose of receiving health benefits from the organization and this organization primarily serves patients in rural areas. CMS may waive the minimum enrollment requirement at the time of application or during the first three years of the contract if the organization demonstrates that it is capable of administering and managing an MA contract and is able to manage the level of risk required under the contract. [Soc. Sec. Act § 1857(b); 42 C.F.R. § 422.514.]

Application Requirements for MA Organizations

An organization submitting an application for a particular contract year must first submit a completed Notice of Intent to Apply by the date established by CMS. Submitting a Notice of Intent to Apply does not bind that organization to submit an application for the applicable contract year, and failure to submit a Notice will not form the basis of any CMS action against the organization. [42 C.F.R. § 422.501(b).]

Content of application. To become an MA organization and be qualified to provide a particular type of MA plan, the applicant must fully complete all parts of a certified application, in the form and manner required by CMS, including: (1) documentation of appropriate state licensure or certification that the applicant is able to offer health insurance or health benefits coverage that meets state-specified standards applicable to MA plans, and is authorized by the state to accept prepaid capitation for providing, arranging, or paying for the comprehensive health care services to be offered under the MA contract; (2) for regional plans, documentation of application for state licensure in any state in the region that the

¶405

organization is not already licensed; (3) for specialized MA plans for special needs individuals (SNPs), documentation that the entity meets the SNP requirements of 42 C.F.R. § § 422.2, 422.4(a)(1)(iv); 422.101(f), 422.107 (if applicable), and 422.152(g); and (4) documentation that payment for all health care services or items is not begin made and will not be made to individuals and entities included in the preclusion list. [42 C.F.R. § 422.501(c).]

CMS use of information from a current or prior contract. If, during the 12 months preceding the application deadline, an MA organization fails to comply with the requirements of the MA program under any current or prior contract with CMS, or if it fails to complete a corrective action plan during the 12 months preceding the application deadline, CMS may deny an application even if the applicant currently meets all of the requirements. In the absence of 12 months of performance history, CMS may deny an application based on a lack of information available to determine an applicant's capacity to comply with the requirements of the MA program. [42 C.F.R. § 422.502(b).]

Notice of CMS determination. CMS must notify each applicant that applies for an MA contract or to be designated a SNP of its determination and the basis for the determination. If CMS finds that the applicant does not appear to meet the requirements for an MA organization and has not provided enough information to evaluate the application, it must give the applicant notice of intent to deny the application and allow the applicant 10 days to respond in writing. [42 C.F.R. § 422.502(c).]

Contract period. CMS contracts with MA plans are for a term of at least 12 months. Contracts are renewed annually only if the MA organization has not notified CMS of its intention not to renew and CMS has not provided the MA organization with a notice of its intention not to renew. Renewal of a contract is contingent on the parties reaching an agreement on the bid. [Soc. Sec. Act § 1857(c)(1); 42 C.F.R. § 422.505.]

Contract provisions. The MA organization agrees to comply with all applicable requirements and conditions, including to accept new enrollments, make enrollments effective, process voluntary disenrollments, and limit involuntary disenrollments. Other requirements include the prohibition on discrimination in beneficiary enrollment, the provision of basic and supplemental benefits, and the operation of a quality assurance and performance improvement program. [42 C.F.R. § 422.504(a).]

Contract Nonrenewal, Modification, and Termination

An MA organization may elect not to renew its contract with CMS as of the end of the term of the contract for any reason. If an MA organization does not intend to renew its contract, it must notify: (1) CMS in writing, by the first Monday in June of the year in which the contract would end; and (2) each Medicare enrollee by mail at least 90 calendar days before the date on which the nonrenewal is effective. [42 C.F.R. § 422.506(a).]

If an MA organization does not renew its contract, CMS may deny an application for a new contract or a service area expansion for two years unless there are special circumstances that warrant special consideration. During this two-year period, CMS will not contract with an organization whose covered persons also served as covered persons for the non-renewing sponsor. [42 C.F.R. § 422.506(a).]

Modification or termination by mutual consent. CMS and an MA organization may modify or terminate a contract at any time by written mutual consent. If the contract is terminated by mutual consent, the MA organization must provide notice to its Medicare enrollees and the general public within 60 days before the effective date of the termination; the MA organization is not required to provide such notice, however, if the contract is replaced the following day by a new contract. If the contract is modified by mutual consent, the MA organization must notify its Medicare enrollees of any changes that CMS determines are appropriate for notification. [42 C.F.R. § 422.508(a), (b).]

As a condition of a consent to a mutual termination, CMS will prohibit the MA organization from applying for new contracts or service area expansions for a period of two years, absent circumstances warranting special consideration. During the same two-year period, CMS will not contract with an organization whose covered persons also served as covered persons for the mutually terminating sponsor. [42 C.F.R. § 422.508(c), (d).]

Termination of contract by CMS. The HHS Secretary may cancel a contract at any time if an MA plan: (1) substantially fails to carry out the terms of its contract with CMS; (2) carries out the terms of the contract in a manner that is inconsistent with the efficient, effective administration of the MA program; or (3) no longer substantially meets applicable requirements of a contracting organization under the MA program. CMS may find that one of these three preceding events has occurred upon a finding that the MA organization did any of the following:

- based on credible evidence, has committed or participated in false, fraudulent, or abusive activities affecting the Medicare, Medicaid, or other state or federal health care programs, including submission of false or fraudulent data;

- substantially fails to comply with the requirements relating to grievances and appeals;

- fails to provide CMS with valid data;

- fails to implement an acceptable quality assessment and performance improvement program;

- substantially fails to comply with prompt payment requirements;

- substantially fails to comply with service access requirements;

- fails to comply with the requirements regarding physician incentive plans;

- fails to comply with marketing requirements;

- fails to comply with the regulatory requirements contained in Part C or Part D;

- fails to meet CMS performance requirements in carrying out the regulatory requirements contained in Part C or Part D or both;

- achieves a Part C summary plan rating of less than three stars for three consecutive contract years;

- fails to report medical loss ratio data in a timely and accurate manner;

- fails to meet preclusion list requirements;

- commits acts that support imposition of intermediate sanctions or civil money penalties; or

- does not have a sufficient number of enrollees.

[Soc. Sec. Act § 1857(c)(2); 42 C.F.R. § 422.510(a).]

Termination of contract by the MA organization. The MA organization may terminate the contract if CMS fails to substantially carry out the terms of the contract. The MA organization must give advance notice to CMS at least 90 days before the intended date of termination and to its Medicare enrollees and the general public at least 60 days before the termination effective date. The notice to beneficiaries must include a written description of alternatives available for obtaining Medicare services within the services area, including alternative MA plans, Medigap options, and original Medicare. [42 C.F.R. § 422.512(a), (b).]

¶405

CMS's liability for payment to the MA organization ends as of the first day of the month after the last month for which the contract is in effect. CMS may deny an application for a new contract or a service area expansion from an MA organization that has terminated its contract within the preceding two years unless there are circumstances that warrant special consideration. During the same two-year period, CMS will not contract with an organization whose covered persons also served as covered persons for the terminating sponsor. [42 C.F.R. § 422.512(d), (e).]

Medicare Advantage Contract Determinations

CMS can make four types of contract determinations:

(1) that an entity is not qualified to enter into a contract with CMS;

(2) to terminate a contract with an MA organization;

(3) not to authorize a renewal of a contract with an MA organization; and

(4) that an entity is not qualified to offer a specialized MA plan for special needs individuals.

[42 C.F.R. § 422.641.]

Notice of contract determination. When CMS makes a contract determination, it gives the MA organization written notice specifying the reasons for the determination and the organization's right to request a hearing. Generally, for CMS-initiated terminations, CMS mails a notice 45 calendar days before the anticipated effective date of the termination. When CMS determines that it will not authorize a contract renewal, CMS mails the notice to the MA organization by August 1 of the current contract year. [42 C.F.R. § 422.644.]

Effect of contract determination. A contract determination is final and binding unless the organization files a timely request for a hearing with a CMS office within 15 calendar days. [42 C.F.R. § § 422.646, 422.662(b).]

Right to a hearing. Parties entitled to a hearing include: (1) a contract applicant that has been determined to be unqualified to enter into a contract with CMS; (2) an MA organization whose contract has been terminated or not renewed or has had an intermediate sanction imposed; or (3) an applicant that has been determined to be unqualified to offer a specialized MA plan for special needs individuals. [42 C.F.R. § 422.660.]

Notice and effect of hearing decision. The hearing officer's decision must be based upon the evidence of record and must contain separately numbered findings of fact and conclusions of law. A copy of the hearing decision is provided to each party. The decision is final and binding unless it is reversed or modified by the Administrator following review or it is reopened and revised. [42 C.F.R. § 422.690.]

Review by Administrator. CMS or an MA organization that has received a hearing decision regarding a contract determination may request review by the Administrator within 15 calendar days of receiving the hearing decision. Both CMS and the MA organization may provide written arguments to the Administrator. The Administrator has the discretion to elect to review the hearing decision or to decline review and must notify both parties of his or her determination regarding review within 30 calendar days of receiving the request. [42 C.F.R. § 422.692.]

Reopenings. CMS may reopen and revise an initial contract determination on its own motion. The hearing officer may, on his or her own motion, reopen and revise a decision that is unfavorable to any party, but is otherwise final, within one year of the notice of the hearing decision. A decision by the Administrator that is otherwise final may be reopened and revised by the Administrator upon the Administrator's own motion within one year of the notice of the Administrator's decision. The notice of reopening and of any revisions following the reopening must be mailed to the parties and specify the reasons for revisions. [42 C.F.R. § 422.696.]

[¶ 406] Medicare Advantage Bids and Benchmarks

This section discusses the requirements for Medicare Advantage (MA) bidding payment methodology, including the submission of plan bids by MA organizations, the negotiation and approval of bids by CMS, and the calculation of benchmarks by CMS. [42 C.F.R. § 422.250.]

Submission of Bids by MA Organizations

By the first Monday in June, each MA organization must submit to CMS an aggregate monthly bid amount for each MA plan (other than a medical savings account (MSA) plan) the organization intends to offer in the upcoming year in a given service area. [42 C.F.R. § 422.254(a).] The bid amount is the organization's estimate of the revenue required for providing coverage to an MA-eligible beneficiary for: (1) the statutory nondrug bid amount (the MA plan's estimated average monthly required revenue for providing basic benefits); (2) the amount to provide basic prescription drug coverage, if any; and (3) the amount to provide supplemental health care benefits, if any. [Soc. Sec. Act § 1854(a)(6)(A)(ii); 42 C.F.R. § 422.254(b)(1).]

Each bid is for a uniform benefit package for the service area. Each bid submission must contain all estimated revenue required by the plan, including administrative costs and return on investment. Effective January 1, 2020, MA plans offering additional telehealth benefits must exclude any capital and infrastructure costs and investments directly incurred or paid by the MA plan relating to such benefits from their bid submission for the unadjusted MA statutory non-drug monthly bid amount. The bid amount is for plan payments only but must be based on plan assumptions about the amount of revenue required from enrollee cost-sharing. [42 C.F.R. § 422.254(b)(2)–(b)(4); *Final rule*, 84 FR 15680, April 16, 2019.]

Bids for coordinated care plans, including regional MA plans and specialized MA plans for special needs beneficiaries, and for MA private fee-for-service plans must include specific information, including the plan type and the actuarial basis for determining the bid amount. [42 C.F.R. § 422.254(c).]

Beneficiary rebate information. If the plan is required to provide a monthly rebate for a year, the MA organization offering the plan must inform CMS how the plan will distribute the beneficiary rebate. [42 C.F.R. § 422.254(d).]

Medical savings account plan information. MA organizations intending to offer MA MSA plans must submit: (1) the enrollment capacity (if any) for the plan; (2) the amount of the MSA monthly premium for basic benefits; (3) the amount of the plan deductible; and (4) the amount of the beneficiary supplemental premium, if any. [42 C.F.R. § 422.254(e).]

Separate bids must be submitted for Part A and Part B enrollees and Part B-only enrollees for each MA plan offered. [42 C.F.R. § 422.254(f).]

Review, Negotiation, and Approval of Bids Submitted by MA Organizations

CMS reviews the aggregate bid amounts submitted by MA organizations and conducts negotiations regarding the bids (including the supplemental benefits) and the proportions of the aggregate bid attributable to basic benefits, supplemental benefits, and prescription drug benefits. CMS may deny a bid if the plan sponsor proposes significant increases in cost-sharing or decreases in benefits offered under the plan. [42 C.F.R. § 422.256(a).]

Standards of bid review. CMS can accept bid amounts or proportions only if it determines that the bid amount and proportions are supported by actuarial bases and that the bid amount and proportions reasonably and equitably reflect the plan's estimated revenue requirements for providing the benefits under that plan. For coordinated care plans (including regional MA plans and specialized MA plans) and private fee-for-service plans, the actuarial value of plan basic cost-sharing, reduced by any supplemental benefits, may not exceed the actuarial value of deductibles, coinsurance, and copayments that would be applicable for the benefits to individuals entitled to benefits under Part A and enrolled under Part B in the plan's service area if they were not members of an MA organization for the year. [42 C.F.R. § 422.256(b).]

Negotiation process. The negotiation process may include the resubmission of information to allow MA organizations to modify their initial bid submissions to account for the outcome of CMS's regional benchmark calculations and CMS's calculation of the national average monthly bid amount. [42 C.F.R. § 422.256(c).]

Exceptions. For private fee-for-service plans, CMS will not review, negotiate, or approve the bid amount, proportions of the bid, or the amounts of the basic beneficiary premium and supplemental premium. In addition, CMS does not review, negotiate, or approve amounts submitted with regard to MA MSA plans, except to determine that the deductible does not exceed the statutory maximum. [42 C.F.R. § 422.256(d), (e).]

Release of MA bid pricing data. CMS will release to the public MA bid pricing data for MA plan bids accepted or approved by CMS for a contract year under 42 C.F.R. § 422.256. The annual release will contain MA bid pricing data from the final list of MA plan bids accepted or approved by CMS for a contract year that is at least five years before the upcoming calendar year. [42 C.F.R. § 422.272.]

Calculation of Medicare Advantage Benchmarks

CMS uses MA plan bid information to arrive at an amount to pay MA plans in each region, the monthly "benchmark" amount.

Area plans. The term "MA area-specific non-drug monthly benchmark amount" means, for a month in a year:

- for MA local plans with service areas entirely within a single MA local area, $\frac{1}{12}$ of the blended benchmark amount, adjusted as appropriate for the purpose of risk adjustment; or

- for MA local plans with service areas including more than one MA local area, an amount equal to the weighted average of the amount described above for the year for each local area (county) in the plan's service area, using as weights the projected number of enrollees in each MA local area that the plan used to calculate the bid amount, and adjusted as appropriate for the purpose of risk adjustment.

[Soc. Sec. Act § 1853(j); 42 C.F.R. § 422.258(a).]

Regional plans. For MA regional plans, the term "MA region-specific non-drug monthly benchmark amount" is the sum of two components: (1) the statutory component (based on a weighted average of local benchmarks in the region), and (2) the plan bid component (based on a weighted average of regional plan bids in the region). [42 C.F.R. § 422.258(b).] CMS calculates the monthly regional non-drug benchmark amount for each MA region using the components of described in 42 C.F.R. § 422.258(c).

"Blended benchmark" calculation. A "blended benchmark" is used to determine payments for all MA plans except for MA plans under the Program of All-inclusive Care of the Elderly (PACE). [Soc. Sec. Act § 1853(n)(1); 42 C.F.R. § 422.258(d).]

¶406

Applicable amount. The "applicable amount" is equal to the amount for the area for the previous year increased by the national per capita MA growth percentage, for that succeeding year. [Soc. Sec. Act § 1853(k); 42 C.F.R. § 422.258(d)(2).]

Specified amount. The specified amount is the product of the base payment amount for an area for a year (adjusted as required) multiplied by the applicable percentage for an area for a year. [Soc. Sec. Act § 1853(n)(2); 42 C.F.R. § 422.258(d)(3).]

Base payment amount. The "base payment amount" is calculated by taking the previous year's base payment amount and increasing it by the national per capita MA growth percentage taking into account the phase-out in indirect cost of medical education from capitation rates. [Soc. Sec. Act § 1853(n)(2)(E); 42 C.F.R. § 422.258(d)(4).]

Applicable percentage. The "applicable percentage" is as follows:

- for MA plans in the highest quartile ranking of payments for the previous year, the applicable percentage is 95 percent;

- for MA plans in the second highest quartile ranking of payments for the previous year, the applicable percentage is 100 percent;

- for MA plans in the third highest quartile ranking of payments for the previous year, the applicable percentage is 107.5 percent; and

- for MA plans in the fourth highest quartile ranking of payments for the previous year, the applicable percentage is 115 percent.

[Soc. Sec. Act § 1853(n)(2)(B); 42 C.F.R. § 422.258(d)(5).]

Increases to the applicable percentage for quality of care. Plans rated at least four stars based on a five-star system stemming from the data collected under Soc. Sec. Act § 1852(e) receive bonus payments. Plans that fail to report data receive a rating of fewer than 3.5 stars. [Soc. Sec. Act § 1853(o)(4)(B); 42 C.F.R. § 422.258(d)(7)(iii).]

MA plans that have a quality rating of four stars or higher will have their applicable percentage increased by 5.0 percent. A new plan (i.e., an organization that has not had a contract as a MA provider in the previous three years) that meets the criteria to be considered a qualifying plan will have its applicable percentage increased by 3.5 percent. [Soc. Sec. Act § 1853(o); 42 C.F.R. § 422.258(d)(7).]

Calculation of Savings for MA Plans

The average per capita monthly savings for an MA local plan is 100 percent of the difference between the plan's risk-adjusted statutory non-drug monthly bid amount and the plan's risk-adjusted area-specific non-drug monthly benchmark amount. Plans with bids equal to or greater than plan benchmarks will have zero savings. [42 C.F.R. § 422.264(b).]

The risk-adjusted MA statutory non-drug monthly bid amount is the unadjusted MA statutory non-drug monthly plan bid amount, adjusted using the factors for local and regional plans. [42 C.F.R. § 422.264(a)(1).]

The risk-adjusted MA *area-specific* non-drug monthly benchmark amount is the unadjusted benchmark amount for coverage of basic benefits by a local MA plan. The risk-adjusted MA *region-specific* non-drug monthly benchmark amount is the unadjusted benchmark amount for coverage of basic benefits by a regional MA plan. [42 C.F.R. § 422.264(a)(2), (3).]

For MA local plans, CMS has the authority to apply risk adjustment factors that are plan-specific average risk adjustment factors or statewide average risk adjustment factors or to use other factors. If CMS applies statewide average risk adjustment factors, the statewide

¶406

factor for each state is the average of the risk factors based on all enrollees in MA local plans in that state in the previous year. [42 C.F.R. § 422.264(c).]

MA regional plan computation. The average per capita monthly savings for an MA regional plan and year is 100 percent of the difference between the plan's risk-adjusted statutory non-drug monthly bid amount and the plan's risk-adjusted region-specific non-drug monthly benchmark amount, using the risk adjustment factors described below. Plans with bids equal to or greater than plan benchmarks will have zero savings. [42 C.F.R. § 422.264(d).]

Risk adjustment factors for regional plan savings. For regional plans, CMS has the authority to apply risk adjustment factors that are plan-specific average risk adjustment factors, region-wide average risk adjustment factors, or factors determined on a basis other than MA regions. In the event that CMS applies region-wide average risk adjustment factors, the region-wide factor for each MA region is the average of all risk factors, based on all enrollees in MA regional plans in that region in the previous year. [42 C.F.R. § 422.264(e).]

Medicare Advantage Beneficiary Rebates

An MA organization must provide to the enrollee a monthly rebate equal to a specified percentage of the average per capita savings for MA local plans and regional plans. This percentage is determined based on the following final rebate percentage:

- for plans with at least 4.5 stars, 70 percent of the average per capita savings;

- for plans with at least 3.5 stars and fewer than 4.5 stars, 65 percent of the average per capita savings; and

- for plans with fewer than 3.5 stars, 50 percent of the average per capita savings.

[Soc. Sec. Act § 1854(b)(1)(C); 42 C.F.R. § 422.266(a).]

New MA plans. A new MA plan is treated as having a rating of 3.5 stars for purposes of determining the beneficiary rebate amount. [Soc. Sec. Act § 1854(b)(1)(C)(vi); 42 C.F.R. § 422.266(a)(2)(iv).]

Form of rebate. MA organizations must provide the rebate by crediting the amount to the enrollee's supplemental health care benefits, payment of the premium for prescription drug coverage, or payment toward the Part B premium. [42 C.F.R. § 422.266(b).]

Disclosure of rebate. MA organizations must disclose to CMS information on the amount of the rebate provided. MA organizations must also distinguish, for each MA plan, the amount of rebate applied to enhance original Medicare benefits from the amount of rebate applied to enhance Part D benefits. [Soc. Sec. Act § 1854(b)(1)(C)(vii); 42 C.F.R. § 422.266(c).]

[¶ 407] Beneficiary Premiums and Cost-Sharing

Medicare Advantage (MA) enrollees are responsible for cost-sharing, including copayments, coinsurance, and deductibles, and premiums, which vary by plan.

Part C Beneficiary Cost-Sharing

There are three forms of beneficiary cost-sharing under the MA program: copayments, coinsurance, and deductibles. A copayment is a fixed amount that can be charged for a service; coinsurance is a fixed percentage of the total cost of a service that can be charged. [42 C.F.R. § 422.2.]

Balance billing. "Balance billing" is the amount billed by a provider that is the difference between the amount the provider charges an individual for a service, and the sum of the amount the individual's health insurer will pay, plus any cost-sharing by the individual. [42 C.F.R. § 422.2.]

An MA organization that offers a private fee-for-service plan must furnish enrolled beneficiaries with an appropriate explanation of benefits, including a clear statement of the beneficiary's liability. The organization also must require that hospitals provide notice to beneficiaries before they receive inpatient hospital or other services when the amount of balance billing could be $500 or more. This notice must include a good faith estimate of the balance billing. [42 C.F.R. § 422.216(d).]

Services of noncontracting providers. An MA organization must make timely and reasonable payment to, or on behalf of, the plan enrollee for certain services obtained from a provider or supplier that does not contract with the MA organization to provide services covered by the MA plan. These services are outlined in ¶ 402. An MA plan (and an MA medical savings account (MSA) plan, after the annual deductible has been met) offered by an MA organization satisfies the timely and reasonable payment requirements with respect to benefits for services furnished by a noncontracting provider if that MA plan provides payment in an amount the provider would have received under original Medicare, including balance billing permitted under Medicare Part A and Part B. [42 C.F.R. § 422.100(b).] An MA plan may charge a higher copayment if a beneficiary chooses to receive covered health care services from providers who do not have contracts or agreements with the MA plan. [Soc. Sec. Act § 1852(d)(4)(b).]

Cost-sharing for certain benefits. MA beneficiaries who need: (1) chemotherapy administration services; (2) renal dialysis services; (3) skilled nursing care; and (4) other services that the HHS Secretary determines appropriate generally will not be subjected to higher cost-sharing for these services than traditional fee-for-service Medicare (Medicare Parts A and B) beneficiaries pay. [Soc. Sec. Act § 1852(a)(1)(B)(iii).]

In the case of an individual who is a full-benefit dual eligible or a qualified Medicare beneficiary enrolled in an MA special needs plan (SNP), the plan may not impose cost-sharing that exceeds the amount of cost-sharing that would be permitted under Medicaid. [Soc. Sec. Act § 1852(a)(7).]

Deductibles. MA regional and local preferred provider organization (PPO) plans, to the extent they apply a deductible: (1) must have a single deductible related to all in-network and out-of-network Medicare Part A and Part B services; (2) may specify separate deductible amounts for specific in-network Medicare Part A and Part B services, to the extent these deductible amounts apply to that single deductible amount; (3) may waive other plan-covered items and services from the single deductible; and (4) must waive all Medicare-covered preventive services from the single deductible. [42 C.F.R. § 422.101(d)(1).]

Refunds. An MA organization must agree to refund all amounts incorrectly collected from its Medicare enrollees, or from others on behalf of the enrollees, and to pay any other amounts due the enrollees or others on their behalf. The MA organization must use lump-sum payments for: (1) amounts incorrectly collected that were not collected as premiums; (2) other amounts due; and (3) all amounts due if the MA organization is going out of business or terminating its MA contract for an MA plan. If the amounts incorrectly collected were in the form of premiums or included premiums as well as other charges, the MA organization may refund by adjustment of future premiums or by a combination of premium adjustment and lump-sum payments. If an enrollee has died or cannot be located after reasonable effort, the MA organization must make the refund in accordance with state law. [42 C.F.R. § 422.270(b), (c).]

¶407

If the MA organization does not make the required refund by the end of the contract period following the contract period during which an amount was determined to be due to an enrollee, CMS will reduce the premium the MA organization is allowed to charge an MA plan enrollee by the amounts incorrectly collected or otherwise due. In addition, the MA organization is subject to sanction for failure to refund amounts incorrectly collected from MA plan enrollees. [42 C.F.R. § 422.270(d).]

Beneficiary Premiums for Part C

If an MA plan has an unadjusted statutory non-drug bid amount that is less than the relevant unadjusted CMS non-drug benchmark amount (see ¶ 406), the monthly basic beneficiary premium is zero. If the plan's bid amount is equal to or greater than the relevant unadjusted non-drug benchmark amount, the basic beneficiary premium is the amount by which the bid amount exceeds the benchmark amount. The benchmark is a bidding target used by CMS and based on rates paid to MA plans before 2006. [42 C.F.R § 422.262(a).]

Consolidated monthly premium. MA organizations must charge enrollees a consolidated monthly MA premium, which is equal to the sum of the MA monthly basic beneficiary premium (if any), the MA monthly supplementary beneficiary premium (if any), and the MA monthly prescription drug beneficiary premium (if any). For MSA plans offered by an MA organization, the monthly beneficiary premium is the supplemental premium. [Soc. Sec. Act § 1854(b); 42 C.F.R § 422.262(b).]

Uniformity of premiums. Except as permitted for supplemental premiums for MA contracts with employers and labor organizations, the MA monthly bid amount, the MA monthly basic beneficiary premium, the MA monthly supplemental beneficiary premium, the MA monthly prescription drug premium, and the monthly MSA premium of an MA organization may not vary among individuals enrolled in an MA plan. In addition, the MA organization cannot vary the level of cost-sharing charged for basic benefits or supplemental benefits among individuals enrolled in an MA plan. An MA organization may apply these uniformity requirements to segments of an MA local plan service area (rather than to the entire service area) as long as such a segment is composed of one or more MA payment areas. The bid information required by 42 C.F.R. § 422.254 (see ¶ 406) is submitted separately for each segment. This rule does not apply to MA regional plans. [42 C.F.R § 422.262(c).]

Monetary inducement prohibited. An MA organization may not provide cash or other monetary rebates as an inducement for enrollment or for any other reason or purpose. [42 C.F.R § 422.262(d).]

Timing of payments. The MA organization must permit payments of MA monthly basic and supplemental beneficiary premiums and monthly prescription drug beneficiary premiums on a monthly basis. [42 C.F.R § 422.262(e).]

Method of payment. An MA organization must permit each enrollee, at his or her option, to make payment of premiums to the organization through: (1) withholding from the enrollee's Social Security benefit payments, or benefit payments by the Railroad Retirement Board or the Office of Personnel Management, in the manner that the Part B premium is withheld (a charge may not be imposed on beneficiaries for the election of this withholding option); (2) an electronic funds transfer mechanism; or (3) by other means that CMS may specify, including payment by an employer or under employment-based retiree health coverage on behalf of an employee, former employee, or by other third parties such as a state. An enrollee may opt to make a direct payment of premium to the plan. [42 C.F.R § 422.262(f).]

Retroactive premium collection. In circumstances where retroactive collection of premium amounts is necessary and the enrollee is without fault in creating the premium arrearage, the MA organization must offer the enrollee the option of payment either by lump sum, by equal monthly installment spread out over at least the same period for which the premiums were due, or through other arrangements mutually acceptable to the enrollee and the MA organization. For example, for monthly installments, if seven months of premiums are due, the member would have at least seven months to repay. [42 C.F.R § 422.262(h).]

[¶ 408] Payments to Medicare Advantage Organizations

CMS makes advance monthly payments to Medicare Advantage (MA) plans for coverage of original fee-for-service (FFS) benefits for an individual in an MA payment area for a month. [Soc. Sec. Act § 1853(a)(1); 42 C.F.R. § 422.304(a)(1).]

For MA plans that have average per capita monthly savings, i.e., bids below the benchmark (see ¶ 406), CMS pays:

- the unadjusted MA statutory non-drug monthly bid amount risk-adjusted and adjusted (if applicable) for variations in rates within the plan's service area and for the effects of risk adjustment on beneficiary premiums; and

- the amount (if any) of any rebate.

[Soc. Sec. Act § 1853(a)(1)(B)(i); 42 C.F.R. § 422.304(a).]

For MA plans that do not have average per capita monthly savings, i.e., plans with bids at or above benchmark, CMS pays the unadjusted MA area-specific non-drug monthly benchmark amount, risk-adjusted and adjusted (if applicable) for variations in rates within the plan's service area and for the effects of risk adjustment on beneficiary premiums. [Soc. Sec. Act § 1853(a)(1)(B)(ii); 42 C.F.R. § 422.304(a).]

Federal drug subsidies. MA organizations offering an MA prescription drug (MA-PD) plan also receive: (1) direct and reinsurance subsidy payments for qualified prescription drug coverage; and (2) reimbursement for premium and cost-sharing reductions for low-income individuals. [Soc. Sec. Act § 1853(a)(1)(D); 42 C.F.R. § 422.304(b).]

Enrollees with ESRD. For enrollees with end-stage renal disease (ESRD), CMS establishes special rates that are actuarially equivalent to rates in effect before the enactment of the Medicare Modernization Act of 2003 (MMA) (P.L. 108-173). CMS publishes annual changes in these capitation rates no later than the first Monday in April each year. [Soc. Sec. Act § 1853(a)(1)(H); 42 C.F.R. § 422.304(c)(1).]

Medical savings account enrollees. For medical savings account (MSA) plans, CMS pays the unadjusted MA area-specific non-drug monthly benchmark amount for the service area, subject to risk adjustment as set forth at 42 C.F.R. § 422.308(c), less $\frac{1}{12}$ of the annual lump sum amount (if any) CMS deposits to the enrollee's MA MSA. [Soc. Sec. Act § 1853(e); 42 C.F.R. § 422.304(c)(2).]

Religious fraternal benefit plan enrollees. For enrollees in religious fraternal benefit (RFB) plans, CMS adjusts the capitation payments, either on an individual or organization basis, to ensure that the payment level is appropriate for the actuarial characteristics and experience of these enrollees. [Soc. Sec. Act § 1859(e)(4); 42 C.F.R. § 422.304(c)(3).]

Annual Capitation Rates for MA Local Areas

Except for years when CMS rebases the FFS rates, the annual capitation rate for each MA local area is equal to the minimum percentage increase rate, which is the annual capitation rate for the area for the preceding year increased by the national per capita MA growth percentage for the year. [42 C.F.R. § 422.306(a); *Medicare Managed Care Manual*, Pub. 100-16, Ch. 8, § 20.2.]

¶408

In rebasing years, the annual capitation rate for each MA local area is the greater of: (1) the minimum percentage increase rate; or (2) the amount determined, no less frequently than every three years, to be the adjusted average per capita cost for the MA local area, based on 100 percent of FFS costs for individuals who are not enrolled in an MA plan for the year, adjusted: (a) as appropriate for the purpose of risk adjustment; (b) to exclude costs attributable to payments for the costs of direct graduate medical education; (c) to include CMS's estimate of the amount of additional per capita payments that would have been made in the MA local area if individuals entitled to benefits under this title had not received services from facilities of the Department of Defense or the Department of Veterans Affairs; and (d) to exclude costs attributable to Medicare FFS incentive payments for meaningful use of electronic health records. [42 C.F.R. § 422.306(b).]

Phase-out of the indirect cost of medical education as an MA capitation rate component. After CMS determines the annual capitation rate for each MA local area, it adjusts the amount to exclude the phase-in percentage for the year of the estimated costs for payments of indirect medical education costs in the area for the year. [Soc. Sec. Act § 1853(k)(4); 42 C.F.R. § 422.306(c).]

Announcement of annual capitation rate. All payment rates are annual rates, determined and promulgated by HHS. The HHS Secretary will determine and announce, not later than the first Monday in April before the calendar year concerned, the annual capitation rate, payment area, and risk adjustment factors. HHS must publish proposed changes to the payment methodology no later than 60 days before annual announcement of rates. MA organizations have at least 30 days to comment on the proposed changes. [Soc. Sec. Act § 1853(b)(2); 42 C.F.R. § 422.312.]

Special Rules for Payments to MA Organizations

Services for beneficiaries enrolled in MA plans that are subject to a plan's moral or religious exception approved by CMS (see ¶ 411) are billable as fee-for-service to Medicare contractors for coverage and payment determinations. The lists of services may vary between MA plans. Beneficiaries enrolled in such plans are responsible for applicable coinsurance for the excepted services, but the deductible will be deemed met. [42 C.F.R. § 422.206(b); *Medicare Claims Processing Manual*, Pub. 100-04, Ch. 1, § 91.]

Rules for MSA plans. A beneficiary who elects coverage under an MA MSA plan must establish an MA MSA with a trustee that meets certain requirements and, if he or she has more than one MA MSA, designate the particular account to which payments under the MA MSA plan are to be made. [42 C.F.R. § 422.314.]

Payments to the MA MSA are calculated by comparing the monthly MA MSA premium with $\frac{1}{12}$ of the annual capitation rate for the area. If the monthly MA MSA premium is less than $\frac{1}{12}$ of the annual capitation rate applied for the area, the difference is the amount to be deposited in the MA MSA for each month for which the beneficiary is enrolled in the MSA plan. CMS deposits the full amount to which a beneficiary is entitled for the calendar year, beginning with the month in which MA MSA coverage begins. If the beneficiary's coverage under the MA MSA plan ends before the end of the calendar year, CMS recovers the amount that corresponds to the remaining months of that year. [Soc. Sec. Act § 1853(e); 42 C.F.R. § 422.314.]

Special rules for payments to federally qualified health centers. If an enrollee in an MA plan receives a service from a federally qualified health center (FQHC) that has a written agreement with the MA organization offering services to the plan, CMS will pay the FQHC directly for the services at a minimum on a quarterly basis, less the amount the FQHC would receive for the MA enrollee from the MA organization and taking into account the cost-sharing amount paid by the enrollee. [Soc. Sec. Act § 1853(a)(4); 42 C.F.R. § 422.316.]

Special rules for coverage that begins or ends during an inpatient hospital stay. If coverage under an MA plan begins while the beneficiary is an inpatient, the previous MA organization or original Medicare, as appropriate, makes payment for inpatient services until the date of the beneficiary's discharge. The MA organization offering the newly elected MA plan is not responsible for the inpatient services until the date after the beneficiary's discharge. The MA organization offering the newly elected MA plan is paid the full amount otherwise payable. [Soc. Sec. Act § 1853(g); 42 C.F.R. § 422.318(b).]

If coverage under an MA plan ends while the beneficiary is an inpatient, the MA organization is responsible for the inpatient services until the date of the beneficiary's discharge. Neither original Medicare nor any succeeding MA organization offering a newly elected MA plan will make payment for those services during the remainder of the stay. The MA organization that no longer provides coverage receives no payment for the beneficiary for the period after coverage ends. [Soc. Sec. Act § 1853(g); 42 C.F.R. § 422.318(c).]

Special rules for hospice care. MA organizations do not cover hospice care. An MA organization must inform each Medicare enrollee eligible to elect hospice care about the availability of hospice care if a Medicare hospice program is located within the plan's service area or it is common practice to refer patients to hospice programs outside that area. Unless the enrollee disenrolls from the MA plan, a beneficiary electing hospice continues his or her enrollment in the MA plan and is entitled to receive, through the MA plan, any benefits other than those that are the responsibility of the Medicare hospice. No payment is made to an MA organization on behalf of a Medicare enrollee who has elected hospice care, except for the portion of the payment attributable to the beneficiary rebate for the MA plan plus the amount of the monthly prescription drug payment, if any. This no-payment rule is effective from the first day of the month following the month of election to receive hospice care until the first day of the month following the month in which the election is terminated. [Soc. Sec. Act § 1853(h); 42 C.F.R. § 422.320.]

[¶ 409] Communication Requirements

A Medicare Advantage (MA) organization may not distribute any marketing materials or election forms or make such materials or forms available to individuals eligible to elect an MA organization unless it submits the material or form to CMS for review and CMS did not disapprove the distribution. [Soc. Sec. Act § 1851(h); 42 C.F.R. § 422.2262(a).]

Definition of "Marketing Materials"

Marketing materials include: (1) brochures; posters; advertisements in media such as newspapers, magazines, television, radio, billboards, or the internet; and social media content; (2) materials used by marketing representatives such as scripts or outlines for telemarketing or other presentations; and (3) presentation materials such as slides and charts. Marketing materials exclude materials that:

(1) do not include information about the plan's benefit structure or cost sharing;

(2) do not include information about measuring or ranking standards (such as star ratings);

(3) mention benefits or cost sharing, but do not meet the definition of marketing;

(4) are required disclosure materials under 42 C.F.R. § 422.111, unless otherwise specified by CMS based on their use or purpose; or

(5) are specifically designated by CMS as not meeting the definition of the marketing definition based on their use or purpose.

¶409

[42 C.F.R. 422.2260.]

CMS Review of MA Organizations' Marketing Materials

An MA organization may not distribute any marketing materials or election forms or make such materials or forms available to individuals eligible to elect an MA organization unless, at least 45 days before the date of distribution, the organization submitted the material or form to CMS for review and CMS did not disapprove the distribution. The time period may be reduced to 10 days if the materials use CMS proposed model language and format. [Soc. Sec. Act § 1851(h)(1), (3), (5); 42 C.F.R. § 422.2262(a).]

File and use. The MA organization may distribute certain CMS-designated marketing materials five days following their submission to CMS if the organization certifies that it followed all applicable marketing guidelines and, when applicable, used CMS-specified model language without modification. When specified by CMS, organizations must use standardized formats and language in model materials. [42 C.F.R. § 422.2262(b), (c).]

Review guidelines. In reviewing marketing material or election forms, CMS determines that the materials provide, in a format, and where appropriate, print size, and using standard terminology that may be specified by CMS, adequate written description of: (1) rules (including any limitations on the providers from whom services can be obtained), procedures, basic benefits and services, and fees and other charges; and (2) any supplemental benefits and services. [42 C.F.R. § 422.2264(a).]

CMS must also make sure that the materials: (1) notify the general public of its enrollment period in an appropriate manner, through appropriate media, throughout its service area and, if applicable, continuation areas; (2) include a written notice that the MA organization is authorized by law to refuse to renew its contract with CMS, that CMS also may refuse to renew the contract, and that termination or non-renewal may result in termination of the beneficiary's enrollment in the plan; and (3) are not materially inaccurate or misleading or otherwise make material misrepresentations. [42 C.F.R. § 422.2264(b)–(d).]

Communication and Marketing Standards

In conducting communication activities, MA organizations may not:

(1) provide information that is inaccurate or misleading;

(2) engage in activities that could mislead or confuse Medicare beneficiaries, or misrepresent the MA organization;

(3) claim the MA organization is recommended or endorsed by CMS or Medicare or that CMS or Medicare recommends that the beneficiary enroll in the MA plan;

(4) use MA plan names that suggest that a plan is not available to all Medicare beneficiaries;

(5) display the names and/or logos of co-branded network providers on the organization's member identification card, unless the provider names, and/or logos are related to the member selection of specific provider organizations (such as physicians and hospitals);

(6) use a plan name that does not include the plan type; or

(7) for markets with a significant non-English speaking population, provide vital materials unless in the language of these individuals. MA organizations must translate materials into any non-English language that is the primary language of at least 5 percent of the individuals in a plan benefit package service area.

[42 C.F.R. § 422.2268(b).]

Marketing Prohibitions for MA Organizations

When conducting marketing activities, an MA plan or organization may not:

- provide cash or other monetary rebates as an inducement for enrollment or otherwise;

- offer gifts to potential enrollees, unless the gifts are of nominal value, are offered to all potential enrollees without regard to whether or not the beneficiary enrolls, and are not in the form of cash or other monetary rebates;

- market non-health care related products to prospective enrollees during any MA or Part D sales activity or presentation;

- market any health care related product during a marketing appointment beyond the scope agreed upon by the beneficiary, and documented by the plan, prior to the appointment;

- market additional health related lines of plan business not identified prior to an individual appointment without a separate scope of appointment identifying the additional lines of business to be discussed;

- distribute marketing materials for which, before expiration of the 45-day period, the MA organization receives from CMS written notice of disapproval because it is inaccurate or misleading, or misrepresents the MA organization, its marketing representatives, or CMS;

- conduct sales presentations or distribute and accept MA plan enrollment forms in provider offices or other areas where health care is delivered to individuals, except in the case where such activities are conducted in common areas in health care settings;

- conduct sales presentations or distribute and accept plan applications at educational events;

- display the names and/or logos of provider co-branding partners on marketing materials, unless the materials clearly indicate that other providers are available in the network;

- knowingly target or send unsolicited marketing materials to any MA enrollee during the Open Enrollment Period;

- engage in any other marketing activity prohibited by CMS in its marketing guidance;

- engage in any discriminatory activity such as attempting to recruit Medicare beneficiaries from higher income areas without making comparable efforts to enroll Medicare beneficiaries from lower income areas;

- solicit door-to-door for Medicare beneficiaries or through other unsolicited means of direct contact, including calling a beneficiary without the beneficiary initiating the contact;

- use providers or provider groups to distribute printed information comparing the benefits of different health plans unless the providers, provider groups, or pharmacies accept and display materials from all health plans with which the providers, provider groups, or pharmacies contract; or

- provide meals to potential enrollees, regardless of value.

[Soc. Sec. Act § 1851(h)(4) and (6), (j); 42 C.F.R. § 422.2268(b).]

¶409

Confirmation of MA Organizations' Marketing Resources

The MA organization must demonstrate to CMS that its marketing resources are allocated to marketing to the disabled Medicare population as well as to beneficiaries age 65 and over. MA organizations must also establish and maintain a system for confirming that enrolled beneficiaries have, in fact, enrolled in the MA plan and understand the rules applicable under the plan. [42 C.F.R. § 422.2272(a), (b).]

Licensing of Marketing Representatives

MA organizations must employ as marketing representatives only individuals who are licensed by the state to conduct marketing activities in that state. The organization must inform the state that it has appointed these individuals as marketing representatives as required by the appointment process provided for under state law. [Soc. Sec. Act § 1851(h)(7); 42 C.F.R. § 422.2272(c).]

The MA organization must also report the termination of any such agent or broker to the state, including the reasons for such termination if the state requires that the reasons for the termination be reported. [Soc. Sec. Act § 1851(h)(7); 42 C.F.R. § 422.2272(d).]

Broker and Agent Requirements

If an MA organization uses agents and brokers to sell its plans, it must: (1) follow compensation rules established by CMS; (2) ensure agents selling Medicare products are trained annually on Medicare rules and regulations and details specific to the plan products they intend to sell; and (3) ensure agents selling Medicare products are tested annually to ensure appropriate knowledge and understanding of Medicare rules and regulations and details specific to the plan products they intend to sell. [Soc. Sec. Act § 1851(j)(2), (h)(7); 42 C.F.R. § 422.2274(b)–(c).]

The MA organization must provide CMS with the information necessary for it to conduct oversight of marketing activities, including information about the performance of a licensed agent or broker as part of a state investigation into the individual's conduct. A plan sponsor must also report annually, as direct by CMS, whether it intends to use independent agents or brokers or both in the upcoming plan year; and if applicable, the specific amount or range of amounts independent agents or brokers or both will be paid. [42 C.F.R. § 422.2274(e)–(g).]

"Compensation" defined. Compensation includes monetary or nonmonetary remuneration of any kind relating to the sale or renewal of the policy, including commissions, bonuses, gifts, prizes, awards, and referral or finder fees. Compensation does not include: (1) the payment of fees to comply with state appointment laws, training, certification, and testing costs; (2) reimbursement for mileage to and from appointments with beneficiaries; or (3) reimbursement for actual costs associated with beneficiary sales appointments such as venue rent, snacks, and materials. [42 C.F.R. § 422.2274(a).]

Compensation amounts. If an MA organization pays compensation, it must compensate independent brokers and agents as follows. For an initial year enrollment of a Medicare beneficiary into an MA plan, the compensation must be at or below the fair market value of such services, published annually as a cut-off amount by CMS. For renewal years, compensation may be up to 50 percent of the current fair market value cut-off amounts published annually by CMS. [Soc. Sec. Act § 1851(j)(2)(D); 42 C.F.R. § 422.2274(b)(1).]

If the MA organization contracts with a third-party entity such as a field management organization or similar type entity to sell its insurance products or perform services: (1) the amount paid to the third party and its agents for enrollment of a beneficiary into a plan must be the same as paid to non-third-party agents and brokers; and (2) the amount paid to the third party for services other than selling insurance products, if any, must be fair market value and must not exceed an amount that is commensurate with the amounts paid by the MA organization to a third party for similar services during each of the previous two years. [42 C.F.R. § 422.2274(b)(1).]

Plan year compensation. Compensation may be paid only for the beneficiary's months of enrollment during a plan year. Compensation payments may be made up front for the entire current plan year or in installments throughout the year. Compensation may not be paid until January 1 of the enrollment year and must be paid in full by December 31 of the enrollment year. When a beneficiary disenrolls from an MA plan, compensation paid must be recovered for those months of the plan year for which the beneficiary is not enrolled. For disenrollments occurring within the first three months, the entire compensation must be recovered unless CMS determines that recoupment is not in the best interests of the Medicare program. [42 C.F.R. § 422.2274(b)(2).]

Finder's fees. Finder's (referral) fees paid to all agents and brokers (1) may not exceed an amount that CMS determines could reasonably be expected to provide financial incentive for an agent or broker to recommend or enroll a beneficiary into a plan that is not the most appropriate to meet his or her needs; and (2) must be included in the total compensation not to exceed the fair market value for that calendar year. [42 C.F.R. § 422.2274(h).]

Compensation structure. MA organizations must establish a compensation structure for new and replacement enrollments and renewals effective in a given plan year. Compensation structures must be in place by the beginning of the plan marketing period, October 1. [42 C.F.R. § 422.2274(b)(4).]

Employer Group Retiree Marketing

MA organizations may develop marketing materials designed for members of an employer group who are eligible for employer-sponsored benefits through the MA organization and furnish these materials only to the group members. These materials are not subject to CMS prior review and approval. [42 C.F.R. § 422.2276.]

[¶ 410] Quality Improvement Programs

Medicare Advantage (MA) organizations that offer one or more MA plans must have, for each of those plans, an ongoing quality improvement program for services provided to enrollees. An MA plan must: (1) create a quality improvement program plan that sufficiently outlines the elements of the plan's quality improvement program; (2) have a chronic care improvement program that addresses populations identified by CMS based on a review of current quality performance; and (3) encourage its providers to participate in CMS and HHS quality improvement initiatives. [Soc. Sec. Act § 1852(e); 42 C.F.R. § 422.152(a); *Medicare Managed Care Manual*, Pub. 100-16, Ch. 5, § 20.1.]

Requirements for all plan types. For all types of plans that it offers, an organization must: (1) maintain a health information system that collects, analyzes, and integrates the data necessary to implement its quality improvement program; (2) ensure that the information it receives from providers of services is reliable and complete; and (3) make all collected information available to CMS. For each plan, there must be in effect a process for formal evaluation, at least annually, of the impact and effectiveness of its quality improvement program. In addition, the organization must correct all problems that come to its attention through internal surveillance, complaints, or other mechanisms. [42 C.F.R. § 422.152(f); Pub. 100-16, Ch. 5, § § 20, 20.1.]

Requirements for MA coordinated care plans. An MA coordinated care plan (except for local and regional preferred provider organization (PPO) plans) must have a quality improvement program that: (1) in processing requests for initial or continued authorization of services, follows written policies and procedures that reflect current standards of medical practice; (2) has in effect mechanisms to detect both under-utilization and over-utilization of service; and (3) measures and reports performance. These requirements also apply to MA local PPO-type plans that are offered by an organization that is licensed or organized under state law as a health maintenance organization. [42 C.F.R. § 422.152(b).]

All coordinated care contracts (including local and regional PPOs, contracts with exclusively special needs plan (SNP) benefit packages, private fee-for-service (PFFS) contracts, and medical savings account (MSA) contracts) and all cost contracts under section 1876 of the Social Security Act with 600 or more enrollees in July of the prior year must contract with approved Medicare Consumer Assessment of Healthcare Providers and Systems (CAHPS) survey vendors to conduct the Medicare CAHPS satisfaction survey of plan enrollees and submit the survey data to CMS. [42 C.F.R. § 422.152(b)(5).]

Requirements for MA regional plans and MA local plans. MA organizations offering an MA regional plan or local PPO plan must: (1) measure performance under the plan using standard measures required by CMS and report its performance to CMS; (2) collect, analyze, and report the data; and (3) evaluate the continuity and coordination of care furnished to enrollees. If the organization uses written protocols for utilization review, the organization must: (1) base those protocols on current standards of medical practice; and (2) have mechanisms to evaluate utilization of services and to inform enrollees and providers of services of the results of the evaluation. [Soc. Sec. Act § 1852(e)(3)(A)(iii); 42 C.F.R. § 422.152(e).]

Requirements for MA PFFS plans and Medicare MSA plans. MA PFFS and MSA plans are subject to requirements that may not exceed the requirement specified for MA regional plans and MA local plans. [42 C.F.R. § 422.152(h).]

Quality Improvement for Specialized MA Plans for Special Needs Individuals

All SNPs for special needs individuals must be approved by the National Committee for Quality Assurance (NCQA) and must submit their model of care to CMS for NCQA evaluation and approval. A SNP, in addition to the requirements of 42 C.F.R. § 422.152(a) and (f), must conduct a quality improvement program that: (1) provides for the collection, analysis, and reporting of data that measures health outcomes and indices of quality pertaining to its targeted special needs population (i.e., dual eligible, institutionalized, or chronic condition) at the plan level; (2) makes available information on quality and outcomes measures that will enable beneficiaries to compare health coverage options and CMS to monitor the plan's model of care performance; and (3) measures the effectiveness of its model of care through the collection, aggregation, analysis, and reporting of data that demonstrate the following:

- access to care as evidenced by measures from the care coordination domain (e.g., service and benefit utilization rates);

- improvement in beneficiary health status as evidenced by measures from functional, psychosocial, or clinical domains (e.g., quality of life indicators, depression scales, or chronic disease outcomes);

- staff implementation of the SNP model of care as evidenced by measures of care structure and process from the continuity of care domain (e.g., NCQA accreditation measures or medication reconciliation associated with care setting transitions indicators);

- comprehensive health risk assessment as evidenced by measures from the care coordination domain (e.g., accuracy of acuity stratification, safety indicators, or timeliness of initial assessments or annual reassessments);

- implementation of an individualized plan of care as evidenced by measures from functional, psychosocial, or clinical domains;

- a provider network that has targeted clinical expertise as evidenced by measures from medication management, disease management, or behavioral health domains;

- delivery of services across the continuum of care;

- delivery of extra services and benefits that meet the specialized needs of the most vulnerable beneficiaries as evidenced by measures from the psychosocial, functional, and end-of-life domains;

- use of evidence-based practices and nationally recognized clinical protocols; and

- use of integrated systems of communication as evidenced by measures from the care coordination domain (e.g., call center utilization rates and rates of beneficiary involvement in care plan development).

[Soc. Sec. Act § 1852(e)(3)(A)(ii); 42 C.F.R. § 422.152(g).]

Compliance Deemed on the Basis of Accreditation

CMS has the authority to deem MA organizations compliant with Medicare requirements. An MA organization is deemed to meet any of the following requirements if it is fully accredited, and periodically reaccredited, for the standards by a private, national accreditation organization approved by CMS and the accreditation organization used the standards approved by CMS for the purposes of assessing the MA organization's compliance with Medicare requirements:

(1) quality improvement;

(2) antidiscrimination;

(3) access to services;

(4) confidentiality and accuracy of enrollee records;

(5) information on advance directives;

(6) provider participation rules; and

(7) certain requirements for Part D prescription drug benefit programs offered by MA programs, including access to covered drugs, drug utilization management programs, quality assurance measures and methods, medication therapy management programs, and privacy, confidentiality, and accuracy of enrollee records.

[Soc. Sec. Act § 1852(e)(4); 42 C.F.R. §§ 422.156(a) and (b), 423.165(b).]

[¶ 411] Relationships with Providers

CMS has established requirements and standards for the Medicare Advantage (MA) organization's relationships with providers, including physicians, other health care professionals, and institutional providers and suppliers, under contracts or arrangements or deemed contracts under MA private fee-for-service (PFFS) plans. [Soc. Sec. Act § 1852(j)(1); 42 C.F.R. § 422.200.]

The term "providers" means individuals who are licensed or certified by a state to deliver health care services, such as doctors, nurse practitioners, and clinical social workers. The term also refers to the entities that deliver those services, including hospitals, nursing homes, and home health agencies. [42 C.F.R. § 422.2.]

Antidiscrimination rules. In selecting practitioners, an MA organization may not discriminate, in terms of participation, reimbursement, or indemnification, against any health care professional who is acting within the scope of his or her license or certification under state law solely on the basis of the license or certification. If an organization declines to include a given provider or group of providers in its network, it must furnish written notice to the affected providers of the reason for the decision. This antidiscrimination prohibition does not preclude the MA organization from: (1) refusing to grant participation to health care professionals in excess of the number necessary to meet the needs of the plan's enrollees (except for MA PFFS plans, which may not refuse to contract on this basis); (2) using different reimbursement amounts for different specialties or for different practitioners in the same specialty; or (3) implementing measures designed to maintain quality and control costs. [Soc. Sec. Act § 1852(b)(2); 42 C.F.R. § 422.205.]

Physician incentive plans. Any physician incentive plan operated by an MA organization must meet the following basic requirements:

(1) The MA organization may not make any specific payment, directly or indirectly, to a physician or physician group as an inducement to reduce or limit medically necessary services furnished to any particular enrollee. Indirect payments may include offerings of monetary value measured in the present or future.

(2) If the physician incentive plan places a physician or physician group at substantial financial risk for services that the physician or physician group does not furnish itself, the MA organization must ensure that all physicians and physician groups at substantial financial risk have either aggregate or per-patient stop-loss protection.

[Soc. Sec. Act § 1852(j)(4); 42 C.F.R. § 422.208(c).]

An MA organization may not operate a physician incentive plan unless it provides satisfactory assurance to the HHS Secretary that these requirements are met. An MA organization must provide the following information to any Medicare beneficiary who requests it: (1) whether the organization uses a physician incentive plan that affects the use of referral services; (2) the type of incentive arrangement; and (3) whether it provides stop-loss protection. [42 C.F.R. §§ 422.208(c)(3), 422.210.]

Limits on provider indemnification. An MA organization is prohibited from having a provider or a provider group indemnify the organization against civil liability for damage arising from the organization's denial of medically necessary care. [Soc. Sec. Act § 1852(j)(5); 42 C.F.R. § 422.212.]

Special rules for noncontract providers. A provider that does not have a contract establishing the amount of payment for services furnished to a Medicare beneficiary enrolled in an MA plan must accept the amount that would have been paid under the original Medicare program as payment in full. [Soc. Sec. Act § 1852(k); 42 C.F.R. § 422.214(a)(1).]

Special rules for MA PFFS plans. For MA PFFS plans, the MA organization: (1) must establish payment rates for plan-covered items and services that apply to deemed providers; (2) may vary payment rates for providers; (3) must reimburse providers on a fee-for-service basis; and (4) must make information on its payment rates available to providers that furnish services that may be covered under the MA PFFS plan. [Soc. Sec. Act § 1852(j)(6); 42 C.F.R. § 422.216(a).]

Private contracting. An MA organization may not pay a physician or other practitioner for services (other than emergency or urgently needed services) furnished to a Medicare enrollee by a health care professional who has filed with the Medicare administrative contractor an affidavit promising to furnish Medicare-covered services to Medicare beneficiaries only through private contracts (see ¶ 872). An MA organization must pay for emergency or urgently needed services furnished by a physician or practitioner who has not signed a private contract with the beneficiary. [Soc. Sec. Act § 1852(k)(2)(B); 42 C.F.R. § 422.220.]

Provider Participation Requirements

An MA organization that operates a coordinated care plan or network medical savings account (MSA) plan must provide for the participation of individual physicians, and the management and members of groups of physicians, through reasonable procedures that include:

- written notice of rules of participation, including terms of payment, credentialing, and other rules directly related to participation decisions;

- written notice of material changes in participation rules before the changes are put in effect;

- written notice of participation decisions that are adverse to physicians; and

- a process for appealing adverse participation decisions, including the right of physicians to present information and their views on the decision.

[Soc. Sec. Act § 1852(j)(1); 42 C.F.R. § 422.202(a).]

Formal consultation with physicians. An MA organization must establish a formal mechanism to consult with the physicians who have agreed to provide services under the MA plan regarding the organization's medical policy, quality improvement programs, and medical management procedures. The organization must ensure that practice guidelines and utilization management guidelines communicated to providers and enrollees: (1) are based on reasonable medical evidence or a consensus of health care professionals in the particular field; (2) consider the needs of the enrolled population; (3) are developed in consultation with contracting health care professionals; and (4) are reviewed and updated periodically. [Soc. Sec. Act § 11852(j)(2); 42 C.F.R. § 422.202(b).]

Subcontracted groups. These provider participation procedures extend not only to direct contracting health care professionals, but also to those with subcontracted agreements. [42 C.F.R. § 422.202(c).]

Provider Selection and Credentialing

An MA organization must have written policies and procedures for the selection and evaluation of providers. The organization must follow a documented process with respect to providers and suppliers who have signed contracts or participation agreements.

- For providers (other than physicians and other health care professionals), the documented process requires determination, and redetermination at specified intervals, that each provider: (1) is licensed to operate in the state and is in compliance with any other applicable state or federal requirements; and (2) has been reviewed and approved by an accrediting body or meets the standards established by the organization itself. [42 C.F.R. § 422.204(b)(1).]

- For physicians and other health care professionals, including members of physician groups, the process must include: (1) initial credentialing that includes written application, verification of licensure or certification from primary sources, disciplinary status, eligibility for payment under Medicare, and site visits; (2) recredentialing at least every three years that updates information obtained during initial credentialing, considers performance indicators such as those collected through quality improvement programs, utilization management systems, handling of grievances and appeals, enrollee satisfaction surveys, and other plan activities, and includes an attestation of the

¶411

correctness and completeness of the new information; and (3) a process for consulting with contracting health care professionals with respect to criteria for credentialing and recredentialing. [42 C.F.R. § 422.204(b)(2).]

The documented process must also require that basic benefits be provided through, or payments be made to, providers and suppliers that meet applicable Medicare requirements. [42 C.F.R. § 422.204(b)(3).]

An MA organization may not employ or contract with a provider excluded from participation in the Medicare program. [42 C.F.R. §§ 422.204(b)(4), 422.752(a)(8).] HHS's investigatory arm, the Office of Inspector General, maintains a list of excluded providers on its website at https://exclusions.oig.hhs.gov/.

Interference with Health Care Professional Advice Prohibited

An MA organization may not prohibit or restrict a health care professional from advising, or advocating on behalf of, a patient enrolled under an MA plan regarding: (1) health status, medical care, or treatment options, including the provision of sufficient information to the patient to provide an opportunity to decide among all relevant treatment options; (2) the risks, benefits, and consequences of treatment or non-treatment; or (3) the opportunity for the patient to refuse treatment and to express preferences about future treatment. Health care professionals must provide information regarding treatment options, including the option of no treatment, in a culturally competent manner, and must ensure that individuals with disabilities have effective communications with participants throughout the health system in making decisions regarding treatment options. [Soc. Sec. Act § 1852(j)(3); 42 C.F.R. § 422.206(a).]

Conscience protection. An MA plan is not required to cover, furnish, or pay for a particular counseling or referral service if the MA organization that offers the plan objects to the provision of that service on moral or religious grounds. The organization must provide written information on its moral and religious policies: (1) to CMS, with its application for a Medicare contract, within 10 days of submitting its bid proposal or, for policy changes, in accordance with all applicable marketing requirements under 42 C.F.R. Part 422, subpart V; (2) to prospective enrollees, before or during enrollment; and (3) with respect to current enrollees, within 90 days after adopting the policy. [Soc. Sec. Act § 1852(j)(3)(B); 42 C.F.R. § 422.206(b).]

Individuals and Entities on the Preclusion List

Generally, an MA organization must not make payment for a health care item, service, or drug furnished, ordered, or prescribed by an individual or entity that is included on the preclusion list. [42 C.F.R. § 422.222(a)(1)(i); *Final rule*, 84 FR 15680, April 16, 2019.]

Preclusion list defined. Effective January 1, 2020, the preclusion list is a CMS-compiled list of individuals and entities that: (1) meets all of the following requirements: (a) the individual or entity is currently revoked from Medicare for a reason other than that stated in 42 C.F.R. § 424.535(a)(3), (b) the individual or entity is currently under a re-enrollment bar under 42 C.F.R. § 424.535(c), and (c) CMS determines that the underlying conduct that led to the revocation is detrimental to the best interests of the Medicare program; or (2) meets both of the following requirements: (a) the individual or entity has engaged in behavior, other than that described in 42 C.F.R. § 424.535(a)(3), for which CMS could have revoked the individual or entity to the extent applicable had they been enrolled in Medicare, and (b) CMS determines that the underlying conduct that would have led to the revocation is detrimental to the best interests of the Medicare program; or (3) regardless of whether they are or were enrolled in Medicare, have been convicted of a felony under federal or state law within the previous 10 years that CMS deems detrimental to the best interests of the Medicare program. [42 C.F.R. § 422.2; *Final rule*, 84 FR 15680, April 16, 2019.]

[¶ 412] Intermediate Sanctions and Civil Money Penalties

The following sanctions may be imposed on Medicare Advantage (MA) organizations for certain deficiencies: (1) suspension of enrollment of Medicare beneficiaries; (2) suspension of payment to the MA organization for Medicare beneficiaries who are enrolled in the plan after the notice of the intermediate sanction; and (3) suspension of all marketing activities to Medicare beneficiaries by the MA organization for specified MA plans. CMS may also terminate an MA organization's contract or impose civil money penalties (CMPs). [Soc. Sec. Act § 1857(g)(2), (3); 42 C.F.R. §§ 422.750, 422.752.]

Imposition of Intermediate Sanctions Against MA Organizations

CMS may impose one or more of the intermediate sanctions listed in 42 C.F.R. § 422.750(a) on an MA organization for the following violations:

(1) failing to provide a beneficiary with medically necessary services and the beneficiary is adversely affected;

(2) imposing premiums that exceed the MA monthly basic and supplemental beneficiary premiums;

(3) expelling or refusing to re-enroll a beneficiary in violation of MA requirements;

(4) engaging in any practice that would have the effect of denying or discouraging the enrollment of eligible individuals whose medical condition or history indicates a need for substantial future medical services;

(5) misrepresenting or falsifying information to CMS, an individual, or any other entity;

(6) interfering with practitioners' advice to enrollees;

(7) failing to enforce the limit on balance billing under a private fee-for service plan;

(8) employing or contracting with providers who are excluded from Medicare participation for the provision of health care, utilization review, medical social work, or administrative services;

(9) enrolling an individual in an MA plan without his or her prior consent;

(10) transferring an individual enrolled in an MA plan to another plan without his or her prior consent or solely for the purposes of making a commission;

(11) failing to comply with applicable marketing requirements or implementing guidance;

(12) employing or contracting with any individual, agent, provider, supplier, or entity that engages in any of the conduct described above; or

(13) failing to comply with provisions which prohibit making payments to excluded individuals or entities or individuals on the preclusion list.

[Soc. Sec. Act § 1857(g)(1); 42 C.F.R. § 422.752(a).]

Procedures for imposing intermediate sanctions. Before imposing intermediate sanctions, CMS must send a written notice to the MA organization stating the nature and basis of the proposed intermediate sanction and the organization's right to a hearing and send the HHS Office of Inspector General (OIG) a copy of the notice. CMS allows the MA organization 10 calendar days from receipt of the notice to provide a written rebuttal. The

MA organization may request a hearing within 15 calendar days of receipt of the intent to impose an intermediate sanction. [42 C.F.R. § 422.756(a), (b).]

Effective date and duration of sanction. The effective date of the sanction is the date specified by CMS in the notice. If, however, CMS determines that the MA organization's conduct poses a serious threat to an enrollee's health and safety, CMS may make the sanction effective on an earlier date. The sanction remains in effect until CMS is satisfied that the deficiencies that are the basis for the sanction determination have been corrected and are not likely to recur. If an immediate sanction has been imposed, CMS may require the MA organization to market and/or accept enrollments for a certain period of time in order to assess whether the deficiencies have been cured and are not like to recur. [42 C.F.R. § 422.756(c).]

Contract nonrenewal or termination. In addition to or as an alternative to the intermediate sanctions described above, CMS may decline to authorize the renewal of an organization's contract or terminate the contract. [42 C.F.R. § 422.756(d).]

Imposition of Civil Money Penalties Against MA Organizations

In addition to, or in place of, any intermediate sanctions, CMS may impose CMPs for any of the reasons for contract terminations contained in 42 C.F.R. § 422.510(a), except by reason of the existence of credible evidence that the MA organization committed or participated in false, fraudulent, or abusive activities affecting the Medicare program under 42 C.F.R. § 422.510(a)(4)(i). [42 C.F.R. § 422.752(c)(1).]

In determining the amount of the CMP, CMS will consider the following:

    (1) the nature of the conduct;

    (2) the degree of culpability;

    (3) the harm that resulted or could have resulted from the conduct;

    (4) the financial condition of the organization;

    (5) the history of prior offenses by the organization or its principals; and

    (6) such other matters as justice may require.

[42 C.F.R. § 422.760(a).]

If the deficiency on which the determination is based has directly adversely affected one or more MA enrollees, CMS may assess CMPs of up to $25,000 for each determination. For each week that a deficiency remains uncorrected after the week in which the MA organization receives notice of the determination, CMS may assess up to $10,000. If CMS makes a determination that an MA organization has failed to substantially carry out the terms of its contract, CMS may assess $250 per Medicare enrollee from the terminated MA plan or plans at the time the MA organization terminated its contract, or $100,000, whichever is greater. [42 C.F.R. § 422.760(b).]

In addition to or in place of any intermediate sanctions imposed by CMS, the OIG may impose CMPs for any of the 13 bases for intermediate sanctions listed above (see 42 C.F.R. § 422.752(a)) or determinations made based on the existence of credible evidence that the MA organization committed or participated in false, fraudulent, or abusive activities affecting the Medicare program under 42 C.F.R. § 422.510(a)(4)(i). [42 C.F.R. § 422.752(c)(2).]

Notice. If CMS makes a determination to impose a CMP, it must send the organization a written notice of the decision containing a description of the basis for the determination, the basis for the penalty, the amount of the penalty, the date the penalty is due, the MA organization's right to a hearing, and information about where to file the hearing request. [42 C.F.R. § 422.756(e).]

Collection of CMPs. When an MA organization does not request an administrative law judge (ALJ) hearing, CMS initiates collection of the CMP following the expiration of the time frame for requesting the ALJ hearing. If an MA organization requests a hearing and the ALJ upholds CMS's decision to impose a CMP, CMS may initiate collection of the CMP once the administrative decision is final. [42 C.F.R. § 422.758.]

Chapter 5– MEDICARE PART D—PRESCRIPTION DRUG BENEFIT

[¶ 500] Overview of Medicare Part D

Beneficiaries entitled to Part A and enrolled in Part B, enrollees in Medicare Advantage (MA) private fee-for-service plans, and enrollees in Part C medical savings account plans are eligible for the Part D prescription drug benefit. Under the prescription drug benefit, eligible individuals have access to at least two prescription drug plans (PDPs) in their region. In regions where eligible individuals do not have access to at least two PDPs, limited risk or fallback prescription drug plans must be offered. [Soc. Sec. Act § § 1860D-1(a), 1860D-3(a).] As a practical matter, however, fallback plans have not been necessary since the Part D program started in 2006 as at least two qualified PDPs have been offered in each region.

An individual eligible for the prescription drug benefit may enroll in a private plan during specified enrollment periods by filing the appropriate enrollment form with the PDP. Full benefit dual-eligible individuals (those eligible for both Medicare and Medicaid) who fail to enroll in a plan will be automatically enrolled by CMS (see ¶ 503).

Under the PDP program, eligible individuals have the choice of either a standard coverage plan or an alternative coverage plan with actuarially equivalent benefits. In addition to the standard coverage plan, participating plans may offer a supplemental benefit (see ¶ 510). Coinsurance and deductibles are discussed at ¶ 507, and premium and cost-sharing subsidies for low-income individuals are discussed at ¶ 508.

Establishment of Prescription Drug Service Areas

CMS established 26 MA regions and 34 PDP regions consisting of the 50 states and the District of Columbia, as well as five separate PDP regions for the territories. PDP regions were established in a manner that was consistent, to the extent practicable, with MA regions, usually on a state-by-state basis. [Soc. Sec. Act § 1860D-11(a); 42 C.F.R. § 423.112; *Final rule*, 70 FR 4194, 4246, Jan. 28, 2005.]

Covered Part D Drugs

A covered Part D drug refers to a Part D drug that is included in a Part D plan's formulary, or treated as being included in a Part D plan's formulary as a result of a coverage determination or appeal, and obtained at a network pharmacy or an out-of-network pharmacy. [42 C.F.R. § 423.100.]

To be covered, a Part D drug must be approved by the U.S. Food and Drug Administration (FDA) for use and sale in the U.S. and be prescribed and used for a medically accepted reason. Part D drugs include biological products, insulin, medical supplies associated with the injection of insulin (including syringes, needles, alcohol swabs, and gauze), vaccines and their administration, supplies directly associated with delivering insulin into the body (such as an inhalation chamber used to deliver the insulin through inhalation), and combination products approved and regulated by the FDA as a drug, vaccine, or biologic. [Soc. Sec. Act § 1860D-2(e)(1).]

Excluded drugs. Part D cannot pay for drugs when they would be covered under Medicare Part A or Part B. In addition, the following drugs cannot be included in standard coverage: (1) drugs or classes of drugs, or their medical uses, that may be excluded from coverage or otherwise restricted under Medicaid under Soc. Sec. Act § 1927(d)(2) or (d)(3), except for smoking cessation agents, benzodiazepines, and barbiturates used to treat epilepsy, cancer, or a chronic mental health disorder; (2) medical foods, defined as foods that are formulated to be consumed or administered enterally under the supervision of a physician and are intended for the specific dietary management of a disease or condition for which distinctive nutritional requirements, are established by medical evaluation, and are not regulated as drugs under section 505 of the Federal Food, Drug, and Cosmetic Act; (3) drugs for erectile dysfunction; (4) drugs for the symptomatic relief of cough and colds; (5) non-prescription drugs; (6) drugs used for cosmetic purposes or hair growth; (7) drugs used to promote fertility; (8) prescription vitamins and minerals, except prenatal vitamins and fluoride preparation products; and (9) drugs used for anorexia, weight loss, or weight gain. [Soc. Sec. Act § 1860D-2(e)(2); *Medicare Prescription Drug Manual*, Pub. 100-18, Ch. 6, § 20.1.]

Part D Medical Loss Ratio Requirements

Pursuant to the Patient Protection and Affordable Care Act (ACA) (P.L. 111-148), for contracts beginning in 2014 or later, Medicare Part D sponsors are required to report their medical loss ratio (MLR), which represents the percentage of revenue used for patient care, rather than for such other items as administrative expenses or profit.

The minimum MLR requirement is intended to (1) create incentives for Part D sponsors to reduce administrative costs such as those for marketing, profits, and other uses of the funds earned by Part D sponsors; and (2) help ensure that taxpayers and enrolled benefi-ciaries receive value from Medicare health plans. An MLR is determined based on the percentage of Medicare contract revenue spent on clinical services, prescription drugs, quality improving activities, and direct benefits to beneficiaries in the form of reduced Part B premiums. Part D sponsors must remit payment to CMS when their spending on clinical services, prescription drugs, quality improving activities, and Part B premium rebates, in relation to their total revenue, is less than the 85 percent MLR requirement. If a Part D sponsor fails to meet MLR requirements for more than three consecutive years, it will also be subject to enrollment sanctions and, after five consecutive years, to contract termination. [Soc. Sec. Act § § 1857(e)(4), 1860D-12(b)(3)(D); 42 C.F.R. § 423.2410.]

CMS will release to the public Part D MLR data, for each contract for each contract year, no earlier than 18 months after the end of the applicable contract year. [42 C.F.R. § 423.2490.]

[¶ 503] Eligibility and Enrollment

To be eligible for prescription drug benefits under Part D, an individual must (1) be entitled to Medicare benefits under Part A or enrolled in Medicare Part B; (2) live in the service area of a Part D plan; and (3) be a U.S. citizen or be lawfully present in the U.S. Except for those enrolled in a Medicare Advantage prescription drug plan (MA-PD), a Program of All-inclusive Care for the Elderly (PACE) plan, or a cost-based health mainte-nance organization (HMO) or competitive medical plan (CMP), individuals may enroll in prescription drug plans (PDPs) if they are eligible for Part D, live in the PDP service area, and are not enrolled in another Part D plan. [42 C.F.R. § 423.30(a).]

Medicare Advantage plan enrollees. A Part D eligible individual enrolled in an MA-PD plan must obtain qualified prescription drug coverage from that plan. Medicare Advan-tage enrollees may not enroll in a PDP unless they are enrolled in a MA private fee-for-services plan that does not provide qualified prescription drug coverage or they are enrolled in a medical savings account plan. [42 C.F.R. § 423.30(b).]

PACE plan enrollees. A Part D eligible individual enrolled in a PACE plan offering qualified prescription drug coverage must obtain coverage through that PACE plan. [42 C.F.R. § 423.30(c).]

Cost-based HMO or CMP enrollees. A Part D eligible individual enrolled in a cost-based HMO or CMP that provides qualified prescription drug coverage is eligible to enroll in a PDP only if he or she does not elect prescription drug coverage under the cost-based HMO or CMP and otherwise meets general PDP eligibility requirements. [42 C.F.R. § 423.30(d).]

Incarcerated individuals. Individuals incarcerated in correctional facilities are not eligible to enroll in PDPs, even when they are located within a PDP service area. [*Medicare Prescription Drug Benefit Manual*, Pub. 100-18, Ch. 3, § 20.2.]

State mental institution patients. Unlike incarcerated individuals, individuals who are residing in state mental institutions are not considered by CMS to be out of service areas. Medicare beneficiaries residing in such institutions have access to Medicare benefits under Part A and Part B and are entitled to enroll in Part D plans. However, because individuals in state mental institutions may be limited to enrolling in the pharmacy network that contracts with their institution, CMS provides a special enrollment period to enable them to join the appropriate Part D plan based upon their situation. [Pub. 100-18, Ch. 3, § § 20.2, 30.3.8.]

Enrollment in Prescription Drug Plans

An individual eligible for a Part D benefit may enroll in a private PDP during the specified regulatory enrollment periods by filing the appropriate enrollment form with the PDP or through other CMS-approved enrollment mechanisms. [42 C.F.R. § 423.32(a).]

Enrollment forms. The beneficiary must complete the enrollment form, which includes an acknowledgment of the disclosure and exchange of necessary information between CMS and the PDP sponsor. Individuals who assist in the completion of an enrollment, including authorized representatives of the beneficiary, must indicate that they provided assistance and disclose their relationship to the beneficiary. Part D eligible individuals must provide information regarding reimbursement through other insurance, group health plans, other third-party payment arrangements, or other sources, and consent to the release of such information. [42 C.F.R. § 423.32(b).]

Timely processing and prompt notice. A PDP sponsor must timely process an enrollment request in accordance with CMS enrollment guidelines and enroll a Part D eligible individual who elects to enroll or is enrolled in the plan during the specified enrollment periods. A sponsor also must provide an individual with prompt notice of acceptance or denial of an enrollment request. [42 C.F.R. § 423.32(c), (d).]

Maintenance of enrollment. An enrolled individual remains enrolled in a PDP until: (1) the individual successfully enrolls in another PDP or MA-PD; (2) the individual voluntarily disenrolls from the PDP; (3) the individual is involuntarily disenrolled from the PDP; (4) the PDP is discontinued within the individual's area of residence; or (5) the individual is enrolled after the initial enrollment. [42 C.F.R. § 423.32(e).]

Cost-based HMOs, CMPs, and PACE plans. Individuals enrolled in cost-based HMOs, CMPs, and PACE plans that offered prescription drug coverage as of December 31, 2005, were permitted to remain enrolled in those plans and receive Part D benefits offered by the plans until one of the five conditions in 42 C.F.R. § 423.32(e) is met. [42 C.F.R. § 423.32(f).]

Passive enrollment by CMS. In situations involving either immediate termination based on serious financial difficulties or other situations in which CMS determines that remaining enrolled in a plan poses potential harm to plan members, CMS may implement passive enrollment procedures. Under passive enrollment procedures, individuals are considered to have enrolled in the plan selected by CMS unless they decline the plan or request enrollment in another plan. Before the enrollment effective date (or as soon as possible after the effective date if prior notice is not practicable), the organization that receives the passive enrollment beneficiaries must provide them with notification that describes the costs and benefits of the new plan, the process for accessing care under the plan, and the beneficiary's ability to decline the enrollment or choose another plan. [42 C.F.R. § 423.32(g).]

Enrollment of Low-Income Subsidy Eligible Individuals

CMS must ensure the enrollment into Part D plans of low-income subsidy eligible individuals who fail to enroll in a Part D plan. A low-income subsidy eligible individual is an individual who meets the definition of full-subsidy eligible (see ¶ 508), including those eligible for both Medicare and Medicaid, or other subsidy-eligible individual. [42 C.F.R. § 423.34(a), (b).]

Automatic enrollment. Except for low-income subsidy eligible individuals who are qualifying covered retirees with a group health plan sponsor, CMS automatically enrolls individuals who fail to enroll in a Part D plan into a PDP offering basic prescription drug coverage in the area where they reside. The PDP must have a monthly beneficiary premium amount that does not exceed the low-income subsidy amount. If there is more than one PDP in an area with a monthly beneficiary premium at or below the low-income premium subsidy amount, individuals are enrolled on a random basis. Low-income subsidy eligible individuals enrolled in an MA private fee-for-service plan, a cost-based HMO or CMP that does not offer qualified prescription drug coverage, or a medical savings account plan, and who fail to enroll in a Part D plan, also will be enrolled automatically. [Soc. Sec. Act § 1860D-1(b)(1)(C); 42 C.F.R. § 423.34(d).]

Exception for employer group health plans. Full-benefit dual-eligible individuals who are qualifying covered retirees, and for whom CMS has approved the group health plan sponsor to receive the retiree drug subsidy (see ¶ 530), also are automatically enrolled in a Part D plan, unless they elect to decline that enrollment. Before effectuating the enrollment, however, CMS will provide notice to such individuals of their choices and advise them to discuss the potential impact of Medicare Part D coverage on their group health plan coverage. The notice informs such individuals that they will be deemed to have declined to enroll in Part D unless they affirmatively enroll in a Part D plan or contact CMS and confirm that they wish to be auto-enrolled in a PDP. Individuals who elect not to be auto-enrolled may enroll in Medicare Part D at a later time if they choose to do so. All other low-income subsidy eligible beneficiaries who are qualified covered retirees are not automatically enrolled into PDPs. [42 C.F.R. § 423.34(d)(3).]

PDP plans that voluntarily waive a de minimis premium amount. CMS may include in the automatic enrollment process PDPs that voluntarily waive a *de minimis* premium amount if CMS determines that such inclusion is warranted. [Soc. Sec. Act § 1860D-1(b)(1)(D); 42 C.F.R. § 423.34(d)(4).]

Declining enrollment or disenrollment by dual-eligible individuals. A low-income subsidy eligible individual may decline enrollment in Part D or disenroll from a Part D plan and elect to enroll in another Part D plan during the special enrollment period. [42 C.F.R. § 423.34(e).]

Full-benefit dual eligibles' effective date of enrollment. Enrollment for full-benefit dual-eligible individuals must be effective: (1) for Part D for individuals who are Medicaid eligible and subsequently become newly eligible for Part D, the first day of the month the individual is eligible for Part D; and (2) for individuals who are eligible for Part D and subsequently become newly eligible for Medicaid, the first day of the month when the individual becomes eligible for both Medicaid and Part D. [42 C.F.R. § 423.34(f).]

¶503

Effective date of enrollment for non-full-benefit dual eligibles who are low-income subsidy eligible. The effective date for non-full-benefit dual-eligible individuals who are low-income subsidy eligible is no later than the first day of the second month after CMS determines that they meet the criteria for enrollment. [42 C.F.R. § 423.34(g).]

Reassigning low-income subsidy eligible individuals. During the annual coordinated election period, CMS may reassign certain low-income subsidy eligible individuals to another PDP if CMS determines that the further enrollment is warranted. However, if a PDP offering basic prescription drug coverage in the area where the beneficiary resides has a monthly beneficiary premium amount that exceeds the low-income subsidy amount by a *de minimis* amount and the PDP volunteers to waive the *de minimis* amount, then CMS will not reassign low-income subsidy individuals who would otherwise be enrolled on the basis that the monthly beneficiary premium exceeds the low-income subsidy by a *de minimis* amount. [Soc. Sec. Act § 1860D-14(a)(5); 42 C.F.R. § 423.34(c).]

Facilitation of reassignments. Within 30 days the HHS Secretary must provide subsidy-eligible individuals enrolled in a PDP who subsequently are reassigned to a new PDP with: (1) information on formulary differences between the individual's former plan and the plan to which the individual is reassigned with respect to the individual's drug regimen; and (2) a description of the individual's right to request a coverage determination, exception, or reconsideration; bring an appeal; or resolve a grievance. [Soc. Sec. Act § 1860D-14(d).]

Part D Enrollment Periods

Under the Part D program individuals may enroll in PDPs during, as relevant, the initial enrollment period (IEP), annual coordinated election period (AEP), or special enrollment periods (SEPs).

Initial enrollment period. The IEP is the period during which an individual is first eligible to enroll in a Part D plan. [42 C.F.R. § 423.38(a).]

The IEP for an individual who is first eligible to enroll on or after March 2006 is the same as the IEP for Medicare Part B, i.e., a seven-month period beginning with the third month before the month in which an individual first meets the eligibility requirements and ending seven months later (see ¶ 311). An exception applies for individuals not eligible to enroll in Part D at any time during their IEP for Part B. Their IEP runs from three months before becoming eligible for Part D to three months following eligibility. In addition, the IEP under Part D for individuals who become entitled to Medicare Part A or enrolled in Part B for a retroactive effective date starts with the month in which notification of Medicare determination is received and ends on the last day of the third month following the month in which the notification was received. [42 C.F.R. § 423.38(a)(3).]

Annual coordinated election period. The Part D AEP for a calendar year runs from October 15 through December 7 of the preceding year. [42 C.F.R. § 423.38(b)(3).]

Special enrollment periods. SEPs allow an individual to enroll in a PDP or disenroll from a PDP and enroll in another PDP or MA-PD plan at any time under any of the following circumstances:

(1) creditable prescription drug coverage is lost or involuntarily reduced so that it is no longer creditable coverage (loss of coverage due to failure to pay premiums is not considered involuntary);

(2) the individual is not adequately informed that he or she has lost creditable prescription drug coverage, that he or she never had creditable prescription drug coverage, or that the coverage is involuntarily reduced so that the coverage is no longer creditable;

(3) the individual's enrollment or non-enrollment in a PDP is unintentional, inadvertent, or erroneous because of error, misrepresentation, or inaction of a federal employee or any person authorized to act on behalf of the federal government;

(4) the individual is a full-subsidy eligible or other subsidy eligible under 42 C.F.R. § 423.772 and is making an allowable one-time-per-calendar-quarter election between January through September;

(5) the individual elects to disenroll from an MA-PD plan and elects coverage under Medicare Part A and Part B;

(6) the PDP's contract is terminated by the PDP or CMS or the PDP plan no longer is offered in the area where the individual resides;

(7) the individual is no longer eligible for the PDP because of a change of residence;

(8) the individual demonstrates in accordance with CMS guidelines that the PDP sponsor substantially violated a material provision of its contract, including: failure to provide benefits on a timely basis, failure to provide benefits in accordance with applicable quality standards, or material misrepresentation of the plan's provisions in communications; or the individual meets other exceptional circumstances as determined by CMS, such as when an individual has a life-threatening condition or illness;

(9) the individual is making an election within three months after a gain, loss, or change to Medicaid or low-income subsidy eligibility, or notification of such a change, whichever is later; or

(10) the individual is making an election within three months after notification of a CMS or state-initiated enrollment action or that enrollment action's effective date, whichever is later.

[42 C.F.R. § 423.38(c); Pub. 100-18, Ch. 3, § 30.3.8.]

Coordination with MA enrollment. Starting in 2019, an individual who makes an MA plan election may make an election to enroll or disenroll from Part D coverage. An individual who elects original Medicare during the MA open enrollment period may elect to enroll in a PDP during this time. [42 C.F.R. § 423.38(e).]

Effective Dates of Part D Coverage and Change of Coverage

CMS must apply the effective date requirements provided under the MA program to Part D enrollments.

(1) **Initial enrollment period.** An enrollment made before the month of entitlement to Medicare Part A or enrollment in Part B is effective the first day of the month the individual is entitled to or enrolled in Part A or enrolled in Part B. Except as indicated for full-benefit dual-eligible individuals, an enrollment made during or after the month of entitlement to Part A or enrollment in Part B is effective the first day of the calendar month following the month in which the enrollment in Part D is made. However, if the individual is not eligible to enroll in Part D on the first day of the calendar month following the month in which the election to enroll is made, the enrollment is effective the first day of the month the individual is eligible for Part D. [42 C.F.R. § 423.40(a).]

(2) **Annual coordinated election period.** For an enrollment or change of enrollment in Part D made during an AEP, the coverage or change in coverage is effective as of the first day of the following calendar year. [42 C.F.R. § 423.40(b).]

(3) **Special enrollment periods.** For an enrollment or change of enrollment in Part D made during a SEP, the effective date is determined by CMS in a manner consistent with protecting the continuity of health benefits coverage. [42 C.F.R. § 423.40(c).]

Coordination with the MA open enrollment period. For 2019 and later, an enrollment made by an individual who elects original Medicare during the MA open enrollment period will be effective the first day of the month following the month in which the election is made. [42 C.F.R. § 423.40(e).]

Voluntary Disenrollment from a Prescription Drug Plan

An individual may disenroll from a PDP during the specified enrollment periods by enrolling in a different PDP, submitting a disenrollment request to a PDP, or filing an appropriate disenrollment request through other mechanisms approved by CMS. The PDP sponsor must submit a disenrollment notice to CMS within the time frames CMS specifies, provide the enrollee with a CMS notice of disenrollment, and file and retain disenrollment requests for the period specified by CMS. CMS may grant retroactive disenrollment to an individual if there never was a legally valid enrollment or if a valid request for disenrollment was properly made but not processed or acted upon. [42 C.F.R. § 423.36.]

Involuntary Disenrollment from a Prescription Drug Plan

Generally, a PDP sponsor is prohibited from involuntarily disenrolling an individual from a PDP it offers or requesting or encouraging an individual to disenroll, either through verbal or written communication or through action or inaction. The PDP sponsor is, however, required to disenroll an individual under various conditions (see below) and may disenroll an individual for failing to timely pay monthly premiums or for disruptive behavior. [42 C.F.R. § 423.44(a), (b).]

Notice requirements. If the disenrollment is for any reason other than death or loss of Part D eligibility, the PDP sponsor must give the individual timely notice of the disenrollment with an explanation of why the PDP is planning to disenroll the individual. This sponsor must provide the notice to the individual before submitting the disenrollment notice to CMS, and it must explain the individual's right to file a grievance under the PDP's grievance procedures. [42 C.F.R. § 423.44(c).]

Mandatory disenrollment. A PDP sponsor must disenroll an individual from a PDP it offers if:

(1) the individual no longer resides in the PDP's service area;

(2) the individual loses eligibility for Part D;

(3) the individual dies;

(4) the PDP's contract is terminated by CMS, by the PDP, or through mutual consent;

(5) the individual materially misrepresents information to the PDP sponsor as to whether his or her costs are expected to be reimbursed through insurance or other third-party means; or

(6) the individual is not lawfully present in the United States.

[42 C.F.R. § 423.44(b)(2).]

Optional involuntary disenrollment for unpaid premiums. A PDP sponsor may disenroll an individual from a PDP it offers for failure to pay any monthly premium if the sponsor demonstrates to CMS that it made reasonable efforts to collect the unpaid premium and the PDP gives the enrollee proper notice of disenrollment. The PDP sponsor must give the enrollee a two-month grace period to pay the past due premiums, beginning on the first day of the month the premium is unpaid or the first day of the month following the date on which the premium is requested, whichever is later. When disenrollment occurs for failure to pay monthly premiums, the PDP may refuse reenrollment of the individual until all past premiums have been paid. A PDP sponsor must not disenroll an individual who has premiums withheld from his or her Social Security, Railroad Retirement Board, or Office of Personnel Management check, or who is in "premium withhold" as defined by CMS. [42 C.F.R. § 423.44(b)(1)(i), (d)(1)(i)–(v).]

When an individual is disenrolled for failure to pay the plan premium, CMS (or a third party to which CMS has assigned this responsibility, such as a Part D sponsor) may reinstate enrollment in the PDP without interruption of coverage if he or she shows good cause for failure to pay within the initial grace period and pays all overdue premiums within three calendar months after the disenrollment date. The individual must establish by a credible statement that failure to pay premiums within the initial grace period was due to circumstances for which the individual had no control or the individual could not reasonably have been expected to foresee. However, enrollment in the PDP cannot be reinstated if the only basis for the reinstatement is a change in the individual's circumstances after the involuntary disenrollment for nonpayment of premiums. [42 C.F.R. § 423.44(d)(1)(vi), (vii).]

Optional involuntary disenrollment for disruptive behavior. A PDP may disenroll an individual whose behavior is disruptive only after: (1) the PDP sponsor makes an effort to resolve the problem; (2) the PDP sponsor documents the enrollee's behavior; and (3) CMS has reviewed and approved the proposed disenrollment. A PDP enrollee is considered disruptive if his or her behavior substantially impairs the PDP's ability to arrange or provide for services to the individual or other plan members. An individual cannot be considered disruptive if the behavior is related to the use of medical services or compliance (or noncompliance) with medical advice or treatment. The PDP sponsor must make a serious effort to resolve the problems presented by the individual, including providing reasonable accommodations for individuals with mental or cognitive conditions. [42 C.F.R. § 423.44(d)(2).]

Involuntary disenrollment for failure to pay IRMAA. CMS will disenroll individuals who fail to pay the Part D income-related monthly adjustment amount (IRMAA) (see ¶ 505). For all Part D IRMAA amounts directly billed to an enrollee, the initial grace period ends with the last day of the third month after the billing month. When an individual is disenrolled for failing to pay the IRMAA within the initial grace period, CMS (or an entity acting for CMS) may reinstate enrollment, without interruption of coverage, if he or she shows good cause and pays all IRMAA arrearages and any overdue premiums due within three calendar months after the disenrollment date. When CMS has disenrolled an individual for failure to pay the IRMAA, the PDP sponsor must provide notice of termination in a form and manner determined by CMS. The effective date of disenrollment is the first day following the last day of the initial grace period. [42 C.F.R. § 423.44(e).]

Part D Late Enrollment Penalty

A Part D eligible individual must pay a late enrollment penalty (LEP) if there is a continuous period of 63 days or longer at any time after the end of the individual's IEP during which the individual was eligible to enroll in a PDP, was not covered under any creditable prescription drug coverage, and was not enrolled in a Part D plan. [42 C.F.R. § 423.46(a).]

Part D plan sponsors are responsible for determining, at the time of enrollment, whether a member was previously enrolled in Part D or had other creditable coverage before

¶503

applying to enroll in his or her plan and whether there were any lapses in coverage of 63 days or more. [42 C.F.R. § 423.46(b).]

Reconsideration. Individuals determined to be subject to a LEP may request reconsideration, which will be conducted by CMS or an independent review entity contracted by CMS. Decisions made through this review are not subject to appeal but may be reviewed and revised at the discretion of CMS. [42 C.F.R. § 423.46(c).]

Calculation of the late enrollment penalty. The LEP is equal to 1 percent of the base beneficiary premium or another amount specified by CMS based on available analysis or other information. [42 C.F.R. § 423.286(d)(3); Pub. 100-18, Ch. 4, § 40.1.]

Determining Creditable Status of Prescription Drug Coverage

A Part D enrollee who otherwise would be subject to a late enrollment penalty may avoid the penalty if his or her previous coverage meets the standards of "creditable prescription drug coverage." Previous coverage will meet those standards only if it is determined (in a manner specified by CMS) to provide coverage of the cost of prescription drugs the actuarial value of which (as defined by CMS) to the individual equals or exceeds the actuarial value of standard prescription drug coverage. [42 C.F.R. § 423.56(a).]

The following coverage is considered creditable:

(1) coverage under a PDP or a MA-PD;

(2) Medicaid;

(3) a group health plan (including coverage provided by a federal or a nonfederal government plan and by a church plan for its employees);

(4) a State Pharmaceutical Assistance Program;

(5) veterans' coverage (including survivors and dependents) of prescription drugs;

(6) prescription drug coverage under a Medigap policy;

(7) military coverage (including TRICARE);

(8) individual health insurance coverage that includes coverage for outpatient prescription drugs and that does not meet the definition of an excepted benefit;

(9) coverage provided by the medical care program of the Indian Health Service, tribe, or tribal organization, or Urban Indian organization;

(10) coverage provided by a PACE organization;

(11) coverage provided by a cost-based HMO or CMP;

(12) coverage provided through a state high-risk pool; and

(13) other coverage as CMS may determine appropriate.

[42 C.F.R. § 423.56(b).]

Calculation of actuarial equivalence standard. The basic actuarial equivalence value test for the determination of creditable coverage or alternative coverage is determined by calculating whether the expected plan payout on average will be at least equal to the expected plan payout under defined prescription drug coverage, not taking into account the value of any discount or coverage provided during the coverage gap ("donut hole"). [Soc. Sec. Act § 1860D-22(a)(2)(A); 42 C.F.R. § 423.884(d).]

Disclosure of creditable or non-creditable coverage status. With the exception of PDPs and MA-PD plans and PACE or cost-based HMO or CMP plans that provide qualified prescription drug coverage under Part D, each entity that offers prescription drug coverage must disclose to all enrolled or eligible individuals whether the coverage offered is creditable prescription drug coverage. If the coverage is not creditable, the entity also must disclose to eligible individuals that there are limitations on the periods in a year in which the individual may enroll in Part D plans and that the individual may be subject to a late enrollment penalty. [42 C.F.R. §§ 423.56(c), (d), 423.884(e).]

Clarifying notice of creditable coverage. An individual who is not adequately informed that his or her prescription drug coverage was not creditable may apply for CMS review. If CMS determines that the individual did not receive adequate notice or received incorrect information, CMS may deem the individual to have had creditable coverage, regardless of whether it was actually creditable, so that the LEP will not be imposed. [42 C.F.R. § 423.56(g).]

[¶ 505] Payment of Part D Premiums

Generally, the monthly beneficiary premium for a prescription drug plan (PDP) must be the same for all Part D eligible individuals enrolled in a plan. The monthly beneficiary premium is the base beneficiary premium adjusted to reflect the difference between the bid and the national average monthly bid amount, any supplemental benefits, and any late enrollment penalties. [Soc. Sec. Act § 1860D-13(a); 42 C.F.R. § 423.286(a).]

2020 national average monthly bid amount. For each coverage year, CMS computes the national average monthly bid amount from the applicable Part D plan bid submissions to calculate the base beneficiary premium. The national average monthly bid amount for 2020 is $47.59, which is down from the 2019 national average monthly bid amount of $51.28. [42 C.F.R. § 423.279; *Annual Release of Part D National Average Bid Amount and Other Part C & D Bid Information*, July 30, 2019.]

Calculation of the beneficiary premium. The beneficiary premium percentage for any year is a fraction, the numerator of which is 25.5 percent. The denominator is 100 percent minus a percentage equalling (1) the total estimated reinsurance payments for the coverage year, divided by (2) the total estimated reinsurance payments plus total estimated payments to Part D plans attributable to the standardized bid amount during the coverage year. [Soc. Sec. Act § 1860D-13(a)(3); 42 C.F.R. § 423.286(b).]

Base beneficiary premium. The base beneficiary premium for a month is equal to the product of the beneficiary premium percentage and the national average monthly bid amount. If the amount of the standardized bid amount exceeds the adjusted national average monthly bid amount, the monthly base beneficiary premium is increased by the amount of the excess. If the amount of the adjusted national average monthly bid amount exceeds the standardized bid amount, the monthly base beneficiary premium is decreased by the amount of the excess. [Soc. Sec. Act § 1860D-13(a)(2); 42 C.F.R. § 423.286(c)–(e).] The Part D base beneficiary premium for 2020 is $32.74, which is down from $33.19 in 2019. [*Annual Release of Part D National Average Bid Amount and Other Part C & D Bid Information*, July 30, 2019.]

Monthly beneficiary premium. Part D beneficiary premiums are calculated as the base beneficiary premium adjusted by the following factors: (1) the difference between the plan's standardized bid amount and the national average monthly bid amount; (2) an increase for any supplemental premium; (3) an increase for any late enrollment penalty; (4) an increase for income-related monthly adjustment amount (IRMAA) (see below); and (5) elimination or decrease with the application of the low-income premium subsidy. [Soc. Sec. Act § 1860D-13(a); 42 C.F.R. § 423.286(d), (e).]

¶505

Increase in Part D Premium Based on Income

The monthly amount of the beneficiary premium for each month is increased by an IRMAA for individuals whose modified adjusted gross income (MAGI) exceeds the threshold amount applicable under Soc. Sec. Act § 1839(i) for the calendar year. This IRMAA for an individual for a month in a year is equal to the product of: (1) the quotient obtained by dividing (a) the applicable percentage described below for the individual for the calendar year reduced by 25.5 percent, by (b) 25.5 percent; and (2) the base beneficiary premium. [Soc. Sec. Act § 1860D-13(a)(7)(A), (B); 42 C.F.R. § 423.286(d)(4).]

For 2020, the MAGI amounts, percentage increases, and monthly adjustment amounts are as follows for beneficiaries who filed an individual tax return in 2019:

- if the MAGI is less than or equal to $87,000, there is no monthly adjustment amount;

- if the MAGI is more than $87,000 but not more than $109,000, the applicable percentage is 35 percent, with a monthly adjustment of $12.20;

- if the MAGI is more than $109,000 but not more than $136,000, the applicable percentage is 50 percent, with a monthly adjustment of $31.50;

- if the MAGI is more than $136,000 but not more than $163,000, the applicable percentage is 65 percent, with a monthly adjustment of $50.70;

- if the MAGI is more than $163,000 but less than $500,000, the applicable percentage is 80 percent, with a monthly adjustment of $70; and

- if the MAGI is equal to or more than $500,000, the applicable percentage is 85 percent, with a monthly adjustment of $76.40.

[Soc. Sec. Act § 1839(i)(3)(C); https://www.medicare.gov/drug-coverage-part-d/costs-for-medicare-drug-coverage/monthly-premium-for-drug-plans.]

In the case of a joint return, the MAGI dollar amount is twice the dollar amounts otherwise applicable for the calendar year and each of the joint beneficiaries will pay the same monthly adjustment amount as individual filers up to the $326,000 income level. Thereafter, joint filers with the following MAGIs will pay as follows.

- if more than $326,000 but less than $750,000, the monthly adjustment amount if $70; and

- if equal to or more than $750,000, the monthly adjustment amount is $76.40.

[Soc. Sec. Act § 1839(i)(3)(C)(ii); https://www.medicare.gov/drug-coverage-part-d/costs-for-medicare-drug-coverage/monthly-premium-for-drug-plans.]

Also, in 2020, for beneficiaries who are married but file separate tax returns from their spouses, with income: less than or equal to $87,000, there is no monthly adjustment amount; greater than $87,000 but less than $413,000, the monthly adjustment is $70; and greater than or equal to $413,000, the monthly adjustment amount is $76.40. [https://www.medicare.gov/drug-coverage-part-d/costs-for-medicare-drug-coverage/monthly-premium-for-drug-plans.]

Part D Premium Collection

Plan enrollees have the option to make premium payments to PDP sponsors using any of the methods available to enrollees in MA plans listed in 42 C.F.R. § 422.262(f), including withholding from Social Security payments, electronic funds transfers, or through employers or third parties specified by CMS. Medicare will pay a plan sponsor only the portion of a late enrollment penalty attributable to increased PDP actuarial costs not taken into account through risk adjustment. [42 C.F.R. § 423.293.]

Collection of the IRMAA. The IRMAA must be paid through withholding from the enrollee's Social Security benefit payments, or benefit payments by the Railroad Retirement Board or the Office of Personnel Management, in the same manner that the Part B premium is withheld. If an enrollee's benefit payment from one of the three sources above is insufficient to have the IRMAA withheld, or if an enrollee is not receiving any such benefits, the beneficiary must be billed directly. The beneficiary may pay the amount through an electronic funds transfer mechanism or by other means specified by CMS. CMS must terminate Part D coverage for any individual who fails to pay the IRMAA. [42 C.F.R. § 423.293(d).]

[¶ 507] Part D Deductible and Coinsurance Requirements

"Standard prescription drug coverage" consists of coverage of covered Part D drugs subject to an annual deductible, 25 percent coinsurance (or an actuarially equivalent structure) up to an initial coverage limit, and catastrophic coverage after an individual incurs out-of-pocket expenses above a certain annual threshold. [Soc. Sec. Act § 1860D-2(b); 42 C.F.R. § 423.104(d).]

Deductible. The annual deductible is increased over the previous year's amount by the annual percentage increase in average per capita aggregate expenditures for Part D drugs for the 12-month period ending in July of the previous year, rounded to the nearest multiple of $5. [Soc. Sec. Act § 1860D-2(b)(1); 42 C.F.R. § 423.104(d)(1)(ii).] For 2020, the annual deductible is $435, which is up from $415 in 2019. [*Announcement of Calendar Year 2020 Medicare Advantage Capitation Rates and Medicare Advantage and Part D Payment Policies and Final Call Letter*, April 1, 2019.]

Cost-sharing under the initial coverage limit. Coinsurance for actual costs for covered Part D drugs covered under the Part D plan above the annual deductible and up to the initial coverage limit is (1) 25 percent of the actual cost; or (2) actuarially equivalent to an average expected coinsurance of no more than 25 percent of actual cost. A Part D plan providing actuarially equivalent standard coverage may apply tiered copayments if certain requirements are met. [Soc. Sec. Act § 1860D-2(b)(2)(A) and (B); 42 C.F.R. § 423.104(d)(2).]

Drug Costs in the Coverage Gap

Before the enactment of the Patient Protection and Affordable Care Act (ACA) (P.L. 111-148), beneficiaries paid 100 percent of all costs in the coverage gap, also known as the "donut hole," which occurs between the initial coverage limit and the out-of-pocket threshold. [42 C.F.R. § 423.100.] The ACA reduced the effect of the "donut hole" through:

    (1) a 50 percent discount for brand-name drugs;

    (2) gradually increasing generic drug discounts; and

    (3) increased Medicare coverage of brand-name drugs.

[Soc. Sec. Act § 1860D-2.]

The "coverage gap" begins after a beneficiary and his or her PDP have spent a certain amount for covered drugs, known as the initial coverage limit. The initial coverage limit is increased over the previous year's amount by the annual percentage increase in average per capita aggregate expenditures for Part D drugs for the 12-month period ending in July of the previous year, rounded to the nearest multiple of $10. [Soc. Sec. Act § 1860D-2(b)(3); 42 C.F.R. § 423.104(d)(3).] For 2020, the initial coverage limit is $4,020, up from $3,820 in 2019. [*Announcement of Calendar Year 2020 Medicare Advantage Capitation Rates and Medicare Advantage and Part D Payment Policies and Final Call Letter*, April 1, 2019.]

¶507

Generic drugs in the coverage gap. In 2020 beneficiaries will pay 25 percent of the price for generic drugs in the coverage gap, down from 37 percent in 2019 and 44 percent in 2018. [Soc. Sec. Act § 1860D-2(b)(2)(C)(ii); 42 C.F.R. § 423.104(d)(4)(iii); *Announcement of Calendar Year 2020 Medicare Advantage Capitation Rates and Medicare Advantage and Part D Payment Policies and Final Call Letter,* April 1, 2019.]

Applicable name-brand drugs in the coverage gap. For drugs to be covered under Part D, a manufacturer must participate in a coverage gap discount program that provides a 50 percent discount on applicable brand-name drugs provided to applicable beneficiaries while in the coverage gap. [Soc. Sec. Act § 1860D-43(a), (b); 42 C.F.R. §§ 423.2315, 423.2325.]

Part D coverage of applicable name-brand drugs in the coverage gap also began increasing in 2013. The coinsurance for the actual cost of brand-name drugs (minus the dispensing fee and any vaccine administration fee) is equal to (1) the difference between the applicable gap percentage and the discount percentage for applicable drugs; or (2) actuarially equivalent to an average expected payment of such percentage of such costs, for covered Part D drugs that are applicable drugs. [Soc. Sec. Act § 1860D-2(b)(2)(D)(i); 42 C.F.R. § 423.104(d)(4)(ii).]

The applicable gap percentage for applicable drugs in the coverage gap is 75 percent for 2020 and later. [Soc. Sec. Act § 1860D-2(b)(2)(D)(ii); 42 C.F.R. § 423.104(d)(4)(iv).]

Annual Out-of-Pocket Threshold for Part D

Once a beneficiary's "incurred costs" reach the annual out-of-pocket threshold, the beneficiary's cost-sharing equals the greater of (1) coinsurance of 5 percent of the actual cost; or (2) copayment amounts from the previous year increased by the annual percentage increase in average per capita aggregate expenditures for Part D drugs for the 12-month period ending in July of the previous year, rounded to the nearest multiple of $.05. [Soc. Sec. Act § 1860D-2(b)(4)(A); 42 C.F.R. § 423.104(d)(5)(i), (ii).]

The annual out-of-pocket threshold for 2020 is the amount specified for 2013 increased by the annual percentage increase in average per capita aggregate expenditures for Part D drugs in the United States for Part D eligible individuals for 2014 through 2020, and rounded to the nearest $50. [Soc. Sec. Act § 1860D-2(b)(4)(B); 42 C.F.R. § 423.104(d)(5)(iii).] For 2020, the annual out-of-pocket threshold is $6,350, up from $5,100 in 2019. Once the PDP enrollee reaches the annual out-of-pocket threshold, his or her nominal cost-sharing is equal to the greater of 5 percent coinsurance or a copayment of $3.60 for a generic drug or a preferred multiple source drug and $8.95 for any other drug. [*Announcement of Calendar Year 2020 Medicare Advantage Capitation Rates and Medicare Advantage and Part D Payment Policies and Final Call Letter,* April 1, 2019.]

Incurred costs. For purposes of calculating the annual out-of-pocket threshold, costs are considered "incurred" if they are paid with respect to covered Part D drugs for the annual deductible, cost-sharing, and for amounts for which benefits were not provided due to the coverage gap (excluding costs for covered Part D drugs that are not included in the plan's formulary). Generally, costs are treated as incurred only if they are paid by the Part D eligible individual (or another person on behalf of the individual) and he or she is not reimbursed through insurance, a group health plan, or other third-party arrangement. Costs are considered incurred if they are paid (1) under Soc. Sec. Act § 1860D-14; (2) under a State Pharmaceutical Assistance Program; (3) by the Indian Health Service (IHS), an Indian tribe or tribal organization, or an urban Indian organization; or (4) by an AIDS Drug Assistance Program under Part B of Title XXVI of the Public Health Service Act. [Soc. Sec. Act § 1860D-2(b)(4)(C).]

[¶ 508] Premium and Cost-Sharing Subsidies for Low-Income Individuals

CMS subsidizes the monthly beneficiary premium and cost-sharing amounts incurred by Part D eligible individuals with low income and resources. [Soc. Sec. Act § 1860D-14.]

For purposes of low-income subsidy eligibility, "income" includes the income of the applicant and spouse who is living in the same household, if any, regardless of whether the spouse is also an applicant. Support and maintenance is exempted from income. "Resources" include the liquid resources of the applicant (and, if married, his or her spouse who is living in the same household), such as checking and savings accounts, stocks, bonds, and other resources that can be readily converted to cash within 20 days, and real estate that is not the applicant's primary residence or the land on which the primary residence is located. The value of any life insurance policy is exempted from the definition of resources. [42 C.F.R. § 423.772.]

Eligibility for Part D Low-Income Subsidies

The primary goal under the low-income subsidy program is to have nationally uniform standards and rules for determining eligibility for a subsidy. CMS has not permitted states to use the more liberal methodologies that they use to determine eligibility for Medicare savings programs under Medicaid to determine Medicare Part D low-income subsidy eligibility because CMS does not have the authority to extend more liberal methodologies to the Social Security Administration. [*Final rule*, 70 FR 4194, 4374, Jan. 28, 2005.]

Subsidy-eligible individual. A subsidy-eligible individual is a Part D eligible individual residing in a state who: (1) is enrolled in, or seeking to enroll in a Part D plan; (2) has an income below 150 percent of the federal poverty level (FPL) applicable to the individual's family size; and (3) has resources that are at or below the resource thresholds described below. [42 C.F.R. § 423.773(a).]

Full-subsidy-eligible individual. A full-subsidy-eligible individual is a subsidy-eligible individual who has: (1) income below 135 percent of the FPL applicable to the individual's family size; and (2) resources that do not exceed the amount of resources allowable for the previous year increased by the annual percentage increase in the consumer price index (all items, U.S. city average) as of September of that previous year, rounded to the nearest multiple of $10. [42 C.F.R. § 423.773(b).]

An individual must be treated as meeting the eligibility requirements for full-subsidy-eligible individuals described above if the individual is: (1) a full-benefit dual-eligible individual; (2) a recipient of Social Security Income (SSI) benefits under Title XVI of the Social Security Act; or (3) eligible for Medicaid as a qualified Medicare beneficiary (QMB), specified low-income Medicare beneficiary (SLMB), or a qualifying individual (QI) under a state's plan. [42 C.F.R. § 423.773(c)(1).]

CMS will notify all individuals treated as full-subsidy eligible that they do not need to apply for the subsidies and they are deemed eligible. For an individual deemed eligible between January 1 and June 30 of a calendar year, he or she will be deemed eligible for a full subsidy for the rest of the calendar year. If deemed eligible between July 1 and December 1 of the calendar year, the individual will be deemed eligible for the rest of the calendar year and the following calendar year. [42 C.F.R. § 423.773(c)(2).]

Other low-income subsidy individuals. Other low-income subsidy individuals are subsidy-eligible individuals who have: (1) income less than 150 percent of the FPL applicable to the individual's family size; and (2) resources that do not exceed the resource amount allowable for the previous year, increased by the annual percentage increase in the consumer price index (all items, U.S. city average) as of September of the previous year, rounded to the nearest multiple of $10. [42 C.F.R. § 423.773(d).]

Low-income Part D eligible individuals must reside in the 50 states or the District of Columbia to receive premium and cost-sharing subsidies. [42 C.F.R. §§ 423.773(a), 423.907.]

Eligibility Determinations, Redeterminations, and Applications

An individual must file an application for subsidy assistance with a state's Medicaid program office or the Social Security Administration (SSA). Part D plans are to refer individual inquiries concerning application or eligibility for the low-income subsidy to state agencies or SSA. [42 C.F.R. § 423.774(d); *Medicare Prescription Drug Benefit Manual*, Pub. 100-18, Ch. 13, § 40.1.]

Eligibility determinations. If an individual applies with the state Medicaid agency, the state makes the determination of eligibility for subsidies under its state plan under Title XIX of the Social Security Act. If an individual applies with the SSA, the Commissioner of Social Security will make the determination. [42 C.F.R. § 423.774(a).]

Effective date of initial eligibility determinations. Initial eligibility determinations are effective beginning with the first day of the month in which the individual applies and remain in effect for no more than one year. [42 C.F.R. § 423.774(b).]

Redeterminations and appeals of low-income subsidy eligibility. If the state makes an eligibility determination, it must make redeterminations and appeals of low-income subsidy eligibility determinations in the same manner and frequency as the redeterminations and appeals made under the state's Medicaid plan. Redeterminations and appeals of eligibility determinations made by the Commissioner will be made in the manner specified by the Commissioner of Social Security. [42 C.F.R. § 423.774(c).]

Application requirements. For subsidy applications to be considered complete, applicants or personal representatives applying on the applicants' behalf must: (1) complete all required elements of the application; (2) provide any statements from financial institutions, as requested, to support information in the application; and (3) certify, under penalty of perjury or similar sanction for false statements, as to the accuracy of the information provided on the application form. [42 C.F.R. § 423.774(d).]

Special eligibility rule for widows and widowers. If a spouse dies during the effective period for a favorable determination or redetermination that has been made related to an individual's eligibility for a low-income subsidy, the effective period will be extended for one year after the date on which the determination or redetermination would otherwise cease to be effective. [Soc. Sec. Act § 1860D-14(a)(3)(B)(vi); Pub. 100-18, Ch. 13, § 40.1.]

Part D Premium Subsidy Amounts

The Part D premium subsidy amounts available to subsidy-eligible individuals vary depending upon the individual's income and resources/asset levels. [Soc. Sec. Act § 1860D-14(b); 42 C.F.R. § 423.780.]

Full-subsidy-eligible individuals are entitled to a premium subsidy equal to 100 percent of the premium subsidy amount. The premium subsidy amount is the lesser of:

- under the Part D plan selected by the beneficiary, the portion of the monthly beneficiary premium attributable to basic coverage for enrollees in prescription drug plans (PDPs) or the portion of the Medicare Advantage (MA) monthly beneficiary premium attributable to basic prescription drug coverage for enrollees in MA-PD plans; or

- the greater of the low-income benchmark premium amount for a PDP region or the lowest monthly beneficiary premium for a PDP that offers basic prescription drug coverage in the PDP region.

[42 C.F.R. § 423.780(a), (b)(1).]

The low-income benchmark premium amount for a PDP region is a weighted average of the monthly beneficiary premium amounts (see below) for the Part D plans, with the weight for each PDP and MA-PD plan equal to a percentage. The numerator of the percentage is the number of Part D eligible individuals enrolled in the plan in the reference month, and the denominator is the total number of Part D eligible individuals enrolled in all PDP and MA-PD plans in a PDP region in the reference month. [42 C.F.R. § 423.780(b)(2).]

CMS publishes the regional low-income premium subsidy amounts in a file on its website: https://www.cms.gov/Medicare/Health-Plans/MedicareAdvtgSpecRateStats/ Downloads/RegionalRatesBenchmarks2020.pdf.

Premium amounts. The premium amounts used to calculate the low-income benchmark premium amount are as follows: (1) the monthly beneficiary premium for a PDP that is basic prescription drug coverage; (2) the portion of the monthly beneficiary premium attributable to basic prescription drug coverage for a PDP that is enhanced alternative coverage; or (3) the MA monthly prescription drug beneficiary premium for a MA-PD plan determined before application of the monthly rebate. [42 C.F.R. § 423.780(b)(2)(ii).]

Other low-income subsidy-eligible individuals—sliding scale premium. Other low-income subsidy-eligible individuals are entitled to a premium subsidy based on a linear sliding scale, as follows:

(1) a full premium subsidy amount (100 percent) for individuals with income at or below 135 percent of the FPL applicable to their family size;

(2) a premium subsidy equal to 75 percent of the premium subsidy amount for individuals with income greater than 135 percent but at or below 140 percent of the FPL applicable to the family size;

(3) a premium subsidy equal to 50 percent of the premium subsidy amount for individuals with income greater than 140 percent but at or below 145 percent of the FPL applicable to the family size; or

(4) a premium subsidy equal to 25 percent of the premium subsidy amount for individuals with income greater than 145 percent but below 150 percent of FPL applicable to the family size.

[42 C.F.R. § 423.780(d).]

Waiver of late enrollment penalty for subsidy-eligible individuals. Subsidy-eligible individuals are not subject to a late enrollment penalty. [42 C.F.R. § 423.780(e).]

Waiver of minimal monthly premiums. The Secretary of HHS will allow a PDP or MA-PD plan to waive the monthly beneficiary premium for a subsidy-eligible individual if the amount of the premium is minimal. If the premium is waived, the Secretary will not reassign subsidy-eligible individuals enrolled in the plan to other plans based on the fact that the monthly beneficiary premium under the plan was greater than the low-income benchmark premium amount. [Soc. Sec. Act § 1860D-14(a)(5); 42 C.F.R. § 423.780(f).]

Part D Cost-Sharing Subsidy

Full-subsidy-eligible individuals have no annual deductible, and there is no coverage gap for full-subsidy individuals. In addition, they are entitled to a reduction in cost-sharing for all covered Part D drugs covered under the PDP or MA-PD plan below the out-of-pocket limit,

¶508

including Part D drugs covered under the PDP or MA-PD plan obtained after the initial coverage limit. Finally, all cost-sharing for covered Part D drugs covered under the PDP or MA-PD plan above the out-of-pocket limit is eliminated for full-subsidy-eligible individuals. In other words, Medicare pays the full benefit once the catastrophic level is reached. [42 C.F.R. § 423.782(a).]

Elimination of cost-sharing for noninstitutionalized full-benefit dual eligibles. Full-benefit dual-eligible individuals who are institutionalized or who are receiving home and community-based services have no cost-sharing for Part D drugs covered under their PDP or MA-PD plans. [Soc. Sec. Act § 1860D-14(a)(1)(D)(i); 42 C.F.R. § 423.782(a)(2)(ii).]

2020 reductions in cost-sharing. Reductions in copayments are applied as follows:

(1) For full-benefit dual-eligible individuals who are not institutionalized and who have income above 100 percent of the FPL applicable to their family size and for individuals who have income under 135 percent of the FPL applicable to their family size who meet the resources test for costs up to the out-of-pocket threshold, copayment amounts must not exceed the copayment amounts specified for standard prescription drug coverage. For 2020, copayment amounts will not exceed $3.60 for a generic or preferred multiple source drug and $8.95 for any other drug (but see (2) below because such individuals who are receiving home and community-based services have no cost-sharing).

(2) Full-benefit dual-eligible individuals who are institutionalized or receiving home and community-based services have no cost-sharing for covered Part D drugs covered under their PDP or MA-PD plans.

(3) Full-benefit dual-eligible individuals with incomes that do not exceed 100 percent of the FPL applicable to their family size are subject to cost-sharing for covered Part D drugs equal to the lesser of: (1) the amount specified for the percentage increase in the consumer price index, rounded to the nearest multiple of 5 cents or 10 cents, respectively; or (2) the copayment amount charged to other individuals described in (1). For 2020, the costs for these individuals must be capped at $1.30 for a generic drug or preferred multiple source drug and $3.90 for any other drug (but see (2) above because such individuals who are receiving home and community-based services have no cost-sharing).

[Soc. Sec. Act § 1860D-14(a)(1)(D)(i); 42 C.F.R. § 423.782(a); *Announcement of Calendar Year 2020 Medicare Advantage Capitation Rates and Medicare Advantage and Part D Payment Policies and Final Call Letter*, April 1, 2019.]

Other low-income subsidy-eligible individuals. In addition to continuation of coverage (no coverage gap), other low-income subsidy-eligible individuals are entitled to the following:

(1) for 2020, the annual deductible for these individuals is $89;

(2) 15 percent coinsurance for all covered Part D drugs obtained after the annual deductible under the plan up to the out-of-pocket limit; and

(3) for 2020, copayments may not exceed $3.60 for a generic drug and $8.95 for any other drug.

[42 C.F.R. § 423.782(b); *Announcement of Calendar Year 2020 Medicare Advantage Capitation Rates and Medicare Advantage and Part D Payment Policies and Final Call Letter*, April 1, 2019.]

Administration of Part D Subsidy Program

CMS notifies the Part D sponsor offering the Part D plan in which a subsidy-eligible individual is enrolled of the individual's eligibility for a subsidy and the amount of the subsidy. [Soc. Sec. Act § 1860D-14(c); 42 C.F.R. § 423.800(a).]

Reduction of premium or cost-sharing by PDP sponsor or organization. The Part D sponsor offering the Part D plan in which a subsidy-eligible individual is enrolled must reduce the individual's premiums and cost-sharing as applicable and provide information to CMS on the amount of those reductions. The Part D sponsor must track the application of the subsidies to be applied to the out-of-pocket threshold. [42 C.F.R. § 423.800(b).]

Reimbursement for cost-sharing paid before notification of eligibility for low-income subsidy. The Part D sponsor must reimburse subsidy-eligible individuals and organizations that pay cost-sharing on behalf of such individuals after the effective date of the individual's eligibility for a subsidy. [42 C.F.R. § 423.800(c).]

Best available evidence. Part D sponsors must accept the best available evidence received from beneficiaries and respond to requests for assistance in securing acceptable evidence of subsidy eligibility from beneficiaries according to processes established by CMS and within the reasonable time frames as determined by CMS. [42 C.F.R. § 423.800(d).]

Retroactive adjustment time frame. Sponsors must process retroactive adjustments to cost-sharing for low-income subsidy-eligible individuals and any resulting refunds and recoveries within 45 days of the sponsor's receipt of complete information. [42 C.F.R. § 423.800(e).]

[¶ 510] Benefits and Beneficiary Protections

Requirements regarding standards for access to covered Part D drugs; Part D sponsor formularies; information dissemination by Part D sponsors; disclosure to beneficiaries of pricing information for generic versions of covered Part D drugs; and the privacy, confidentiality, and accuracy of prescription drug plan (PDP) sponsors' beneficiary records are implemented in Subpart C, Part 423 of the Part D regulations.

Requirements Related to Qualified Prescription Drug Coverage

CMS may approve as Part D sponsors only those entities proposing to offer qualified prescription drug coverage. Qualified prescription drug coverage may consist of either standard prescription drug coverage or alternative prescription drug coverage, both of which provide access to Part D drugs at negotiated prices. A sponsor offering a PDP must offer that plan to all Part D eligible beneficiaries residing in the plan's service area with the same premium, benefits, and level of cost-sharing throughout the service area. [42 C.F.R. § 423.104(b), (d).]

Alternative prescription drug coverage. Alternative prescription drug coverage provides coverage for Part D drugs and includes access to negotiated prices. Alternative prescription drug coverage also must:

(1) have an annual deductible that does not exceed the annual deductible for standard prescription drug coverage;

(2) impose cost-sharing no greater than that specified for standard prescription drug coverage once the annual out-of-pocket threshold is met;

(3) have a total or gross value that is at least equal to the total or gross value of defined standard coverage;

(4) have an unsubsidized value that is at least equal to the unsubsidized value of standard prescription drug coverage (*Note:* The unsubsidized value of coverage is the

amount by which the actuarial value of the coverage exceeds the actuarial value of the subsidy payments for the coverage); and

(5) provide coverage that is designed, based upon an actuarially representative pattern of utilization, to provide for the payment of costs that are equal to the initial coverage limit, in an amount at least equal to the product of: (a) the amount by which the initial coverage limit for the year exceeds the deductible and (b) 100 percent minus the coinsurance percentage specified for standard prescription drug coverage.

[42 C.F.R. § 423.104(e).]

Negotiated prices. A PDP sponsor is required to provide enrollees with access to negotiated prices for covered Part D drugs included in its formulary. [42 C.F.R. § 423.104(g).]

Access to Covered Part D Drugs

PDPs must secure the participation of a pharmacy network consisting of retail pharmacies sufficient to ensure that all beneficiaries residing in each state in a PDP's service area, each state in a regional Medicare Advantage (MA) organization's service area, the entire service area of a local MA organization, or the entire geographic area of a cost contract have convenient access to covered drugs. As a result, PDPs must establish pharmacy networks in which:

(1) in urban areas, at least 90 percent of Medicare beneficiaries in the PDP service area live, on average, within two miles of the retail pharmacy participating in the plan's network;

(2) in suburban areas, at least 90 percent of Medicare beneficiaries in the PDP service area live, on average, within five miles of a retail pharmacy participating in the plan's network; and

(3) in rural areas, at least 70 percent of Medicare beneficiaries in the PDP service area live, on average, within 15 miles of a retail pharmacy participating in the plan's network.

[Soc. Sec. Act § 1860D-4(b); 42 C.F.R. § 423.120(a)(1).]

Part D plans may count Indian tribes and tribal organizations, urban Indian organizations (I/T/U) pharmacies, and pharmacies operated by federally qualified health centers and rural health centers toward the required percentages for urban, suburban, and rural areas. [42 C.F.R. § 423.120(a)(2).]

A PDP's contracted pharmacy network must provide adequate access to home infusion pharmacies and convenient access and standard contracting terms and conditions to all long-term care and I/T/U pharmacies in its service area. [42 C.F.R. § 423.120(a)(4), (5), (6).]

In establishing its contracted pharmacy network, a Part D sponsor offering qualified prescription drug coverage (1) must contract with any pharmacy that meets the sponsor's standard terms and conditions; (2) may not require a pharmacy to accept insurance risk as a condition of participation in the sponsor's contracted pharmacy network; and (3) beginning January 1, 2020, may not prohibit a pharmacy from, or penalize a pharmacy for, informing a Part D plan enrollee of the availability at that pharmacy of a prescribed medication at a cash price that is below the amount that the enrollee would be charged to obtain the same medication through the enrollee's Part D plan. [Soc. Sec. Act § 1860D-4(b)(1)(A), (E); 42 C.F.R. § 423.120(a)(8); *Final rule*, 84 FR 23832, May 23, 2019.]

A PDP sponsor offering a plan that provides coverage other than defined standard coverage may reduce copayments or coinsurance for covered drugs obtained through a preferred pharmacy relative to the copayments or coinsurance applicable for such drugs when obtained through a non-preferred pharmacy. [Soc. Sec. Act § 1860D-4(b)(1)(B); 42 C.F.R. § 423.120(a)(9).]

A PDP sponsor must permit its enrollees to receive benefits, which may include an extended (90-day) supply of covered drugs, at any of its network pharmacies that are retail pharmacies. A Part D plan, however, may require an enrollee obtaining a covered drug at a retail network pharmacy to pay any higher cost-sharing applicable to that pharmacy instead of the cost-sharing applicable to the drug at the mail-order network pharmacy. [Soc. Sec. Act § 1860D-4(b)(1)(D); 42 C.F.R. § 423.120(a)(10).]

Part D Formulary Requirements

A Part D sponsor that uses a formulary under its qualified prescription drug coverage must meet the following requirements:

(1) development and revision by a pharmacy and therapeutic committee;

(2) provision of an adequate formulary;

(3) a drug transition process for enrollees prescribed Part D drugs that are not on its Part D plan's formulary;

(4) a limitation on changes in therapeutic classification;

(5) the provision of notice regarding formulary changes;

(6) a limitation on formulary changes before the beginning of a contract year; and

(7) policies and procedures to educate and inform health care providers and enrollees concerning its formulary.

[Soc. Sec. Act § 1860D-4(b)(3); 42 C.F.R. § 423.120(b).]

A Part D plan's formulary must:

(1) include within each therapeutic category and class of Part D drugs at least two Part D drugs that are not therapeutically equivalent and bioequivalent, with different strengths and dosage forms available for each of those drugs, except that only one Part D drug must be included in a particular category or class of covered Part D drugs if the category or class includes only one Part D drug;

(2) include at least one Part D drug within a particular category or class of Part D drugs to the extent the Part D plan demonstrates that (and CMS approves) only two drugs are available in that category or class of Part D drugs, and that one drug is clinically superior to the other drug in that category or class of Part D drugs;

(3) include adequate coverage of the types of drugs most commonly needed by Part D enrollees, as recognized in national treatment guidelines; and

(4) be approved by CMS consistent with 42 C.F.R. § 423.272(b)(2).

[42 C.F.R. § 423.120(b)(2).]

Until the Secretary determines, through rulemaking, criteria to identify, as appropriate, categories and classes of clinical concern, the following six classes must be included in PDP formularies:

(1) anticonvulsants;

(2) antidepressants;

(3) antineoplastics;

(4) antipsychotics;

(5) antiretrovirals; and

¶510

(6) immunosuppressants for the treatment of transplant rejection.

[Soc. Sec. Act § 1860D-4 (b) (3) (G); 42 C.F.R. § 423.120 (b) (2) (v).]

Exceptions to the requirements related to the categories and classes of clinical concern are:

(1) effective January 1, 2020, drug or biological products that are rated as either of the following: (a) therapeutically equivalent (under the FDA's most recent publication of "Approved Drug Products with Therapeutic Equivalence Evaluations"), or (b) interchangeable (under the FDA's most recent publication of the Purple Book: Lists of Licensed Biological Products with Reference Product Exclusivity and Biosimilarity or Interchangeability Evaluations);

(2) utilization management processes that limit the quantity of drugs due to safety;

(3) effective January 1, 2020, subject to CMS review and approval, for enrollees that are not on existing therapy on the protected class Part D drug, and except for antiretroviral medications, prior authorization and step therapy requirements to confirm intended use is for a protected class indication, to ensure clinically appropriate use, to promote utilization of preferred formulary alternatives, or a combination thereof; and

(4) other drugs that CMS specifies through a process that is based upon scientific evidence and medical standards of practice (and, in the case of antiretroviral medications, is consistent with HHS Guidelines for the Use of Antiretroviral Agents in HIV-1-Infected Adults and Adolescents) and that permits public notice and comment.

[42 C.F.R. § 423.120 (b) (2) (vi); *Final rule*, 84 FR 23832, May 23, 2019.]

Transition process. A Part D sponsor must provide for an appropriate transition process for enrollees prescribed Part D drugs that are not on its Part D plan's formulary (including Part D drugs that are on a sponsor's formulary but require prior authorization or step therapy under a plan's utilization management rules). The transition process must:

(1) be applicable to new enrollees into Part D plans following the annual coordinated election period, newly eligible Medicare enrollees from other coverage, individuals who switch from one plan to another after the start of the contract year, and current enrollees remaining in the plan affected by formulary changes, but not apply in cases in which a Part D sponsor substitutes a generic drug for a brand name drug;

(2) ensure access to a temporary supply of drugs within the first 90 days of coverage under a new plan for retail, home infusion, long-term care, and mail-order pharmacies;

(3) ensure the provision of a temporary fill when an enrollee requests a fill of a non-formulary drug (including Part D drugs that are on a plan's formulary but require prior authorization or step therapy under a plan's utilization management rules) within the first 90 days of coverage;

(4) ensure written notice is provided to each affected enrollee within three business days after adjudication of the temporary fill;

(5) ensure that reasonable efforts are made to notify prescribers of affected enrollees who receive a transition notice; and

(6) charge cost-sharing for a temporary supply of drugs provided under its transition process such that the following conditions are met: (a) for low-income subsidy (LIS) enrollees, a sponsor must not charge higher cost-sharing for transition supplies than the statutory maximum copayment amounts; and (b) for non-LIS enrollees, a sponsor must charge the same cost-sharing for non-formulary Part D drugs

provided during the transition that would apply for non-formulary drugs approved through a formulary exception; and the same cost-sharing for formulary drugs subject to utilization management edits provided during the transition that would apply once the utilization management criteria are met.

[42 C.F.R. § 423.120(b)(3).]

Limitation on changes in therapeutic classification. Except as CMS may permit to account for new therapeutic uses and newly approved Part D drugs, a Part D sponsor may not change the therapeutic categories and classes in a formulary other than at the beginning of each plan year. [42 C.F.R. § 423.120(b)(4).]

Provision of notice regarding formulary changes. Before removing a covered Part D drug from its Part D plan's formulary or making any change to the preferred or tiered cost-sharing status of a covered Part D drug, a Part D sponsor must provide at least 30 days' notice to CMS, State Pharmaceutical Assistance Programs, entities providing other prescription drug coverage, authorized prescribers, network pharmacies, and pharmacists. The sponsor must also either provide direct written notice to affected enrollees at least 30 days before the date the change becomes effective or, at the time an affected enrollee requests a refill of the Part D drug, provide such enrollee with an approved month's supply of the Part D drug under the same terms as previously allowed and written notice of the formulary change. [42 C.F.R. § 423.120(b)(5)(i).]

The written notice to the affected enrollee must contain:

(1) the name of the affected covered Part D drug;

(2) whether the plan is removing the covered Part D drug from the formulary or changing its preferred or tiered cost-sharing status;

(3) the reason why the plan is removing such covered Part D drug from the formulary or changing its preferred or tiered cost-sharing status;

(4) alternative drugs in the same therapeutic category or class or cost-sharing tier and expected cost-sharing for those drugs; and

(5) the means by which enrollees may obtain a coverage determination or exception.

[42 C.F.R. § 423.120(b)(5)(ii).]

Part D sponsors may immediately remove from their Part D plan formularies covered Part D drugs deemed unsafe by the Food and Drug Administration (FDA) or removed from the market by their manufacturer. Part D sponsors must provide retrospective notice of any such formulary changes to affected enrollees, CMS, and other specified entities consistent with the above requirements. [42 C.F.R. § 423.120(b)(5)(iii).]

A Part D sponsor may immediately remove a brand name drug from its formulary or change the brand name drug's preferred or tiered cost-sharing without meeting the deadlines and refill requirements described above if: (1) at the same time that it removes such brand name drug or changes its preferred or tiered cost-sharing, it adds a therapeutically equivalent generic drug to its formulary on the same or lower cost-sharing tier and with the same or less restrictive utilization management criteria; (2) the sponsor previously could not have included such therapeutically equivalent generic drug on its formulary when it submitted its initial formulary for CMS approval because the generic drug was not yet available on the market; and (3) the sponsor fulfills certain notice requirements. [42 C.F.R. § 423.120(b)(5)(iv).]

¶510

Limitation on formulary changes before the beginning of a contract year. A Part D sponsor may not remove a covered Part D drug from its Part D plan's formulary, or make any change in the preferred or tiered cost-sharing status of a covered Part D drug on its plan's formulary, between the beginning of the annual coordinated election period and 60 days after the beginning of the contract year associated with that annual coordinated election period. [42 C.F.R. § 423.120(b)(6).]

Provider and patient education. A Part D sponsor must establish policies and procedures to educate and inform health care providers and enrollees concerning its formulary. [42 C.F.R. § 423.120(b)(7).]

Use of standardized technology. A Part D sponsor must issue and reissue, as necessary, a card or other type of technology that its enrollees may use to access negotiated prices for covered Part D drugs. When processing Part D claims, a sponsor or its intermediary must comply with the electronic transaction standards established by 45 C.F.R. § 162.1102. A sponsor must require its network pharmacies to submit claims to the sponsor or its intermediary whenever the card is presented or is on file at the pharmacy unless the enrollee expressly requests that a particular claim not be submitted to the sponsor or its intermediary. [42 C.F.R. § 423.120(c)(1)–(3).]

A Part D sponsor must assign and exclusively use a unique: (1) Part D bank identification number (BIN) or RxBIN and Part D processor control number (RxPCN) combination in its Medicare line of business; and (2) Part D cardholder identification number (RxID) to clearly identify its Medicare Part D beneficiaries. [42 C.F.R. § 423.120(c)(4).]

A claim for a covered Part D drug under a Part D PDP or a Medicare Advantage prescription drug plan (MA-PD) must include a valid prescriber national provider identifier (NPI). A Part D sponsor also must reject a pharmacy claim for a Part D drug if the individual who prescribed the drug is included on the preclusion list. [Soc. Sec. Act § 1860D-4(c)(4); 42 C.F.R. § 423.120(c)(5), (6).]

Compounded drug products. For multi-ingredient compounds, a Part D sponsor must determine whether the compound is covered under Part D. A compound that contains at least one ingredient covered under Part B is considered a Part B compound, regardless of whether other ingredients in the compound are covered under Part B. Only compounds that contain at least one ingredient that independently meets the definition of a Part D drug and do not contain any Part B ingredients may be considered Part D compounds and covered under Part D. For a Part D compound to be considered on-formulary, all ingredients that independently meet the definition of a Part D drug must be considered on-formulary. For a Part D compound to be considered off-formulary, transition rules apply such that all ingredients in the Part D compound that independently meet the definition of a Part D drug must become payable in the event of a transition fill and all ingredients that independently meet the definition of a Part D drug must be covered if an exception is approved for coverage of the compound. [42 C.F.R. § 423.120(d)(1).]

Compound payment liabilities. A Part D sponsor must establish consistent rules for beneficiary payment liabilities for both ingredients of the Part D compound that independently meet the definition of a Part D drug and non-Part D ingredients. For low-income subsidy beneficiaries, the copayment amount is based on whether the most expensive ingredient that independently meets the definition of a Part D drug in the Part D compound is a generic or brand name drug. For any non-Part D ingredient of the Part D compound, the Part D sponsor's contract with the pharmacy must prohibit balance billing the beneficiary for the cost of any such ingredients. [42 C.F.R. § 423.120(d)(2).]

Out-of-Network Access to Covered Part D Drugs

PDPs are required to ensure that their enrollees have adequate access to drugs dispensed at out-of-network pharmacies when enrollees cannot reasonably be expected to obtain covered drugs at a network pharmacy and do not access covered Part D drugs at an out-of-network pharmacy on a routine basis. [42 C.F.R. § 423.124(a)(1).] Provided the enrollees do not routinely access out-of-network pharmacies, CMS expects PDPs to guarantee out-of-network access if an enrollee:

(1) is traveling outside the plan's service area, runs out of or loses covered drugs or becomes ill and needs a covered drug, and cannot access a network pharmacy;

(2) cannot obtain a covered drug in a timely manner within a service area because, for example, there is no network pharmacy within a reasonable driving distance that provides 24 hour/7 day per week service;

(3) must fill a prescription for a covered drug and that particular drug is not regularly stocked at accessible network retail or mail-order pharmacies;

(4) is provided covered drugs dispensed by an out-of-network institution-based pharmacy while a patient in an emergency department, provider-based clinic, outpatient surgery, or other outpatient setting and, as a result, cannot get the medications filled at a network pharmacy; or

(5) experiences a declared federal disaster or other declared public health emergency in which Part D enrollees are evacuated or otherwise displaced from their place of residence and cannot reasonably be expected to obtain covered Part D drugs at a network pharmacy and, in addition, in circumstances in which normal distribution channels are unavailable.

[*Medicare Prescription Drug Benefit Manual*, Pub. 100-18, Ch. 5, § 60.1.]

In addition, plans must provide coverage for vaccines and other covered Part D drugs that are appropriately dispensed and administered in a physician's office. [42 C.F.R. § 423.124(a)(2).]

Limits on out-of-network access. CMS requires PDPs to establish reasonable rules to ensure that enrollees use out-of-network pharmacies in an appropriate manner, provided that the plans also ensure adequate access to out-of-network pharmacies on a non-routine basis when enrollees cannot reasonably access network pharmacies. For example, PDPs may wish to limit the amount of covered drugs dispensed at an out-of-network pharmacy and require that a beneficiary purchase maintenance medications via mail order for extended out-of-area travel or require a plan notification or authorization process for individuals who fill their prescriptions at out-of-network pharmacies. [42 C.F.R. § 423.124(a), (c); Pub. 100-18, Ch. 5, § 60.1.]

Financial responsibility for out-of-network access. Enrollees obtaining covered Part D drugs at out-of-network pharmacies must assume financial responsibility for any differential between the out-of-network pharmacy's (or provider's) usual and customary price and the Part D sponsor's plan allowance. [42 C.F.R. § 423.124(b).]

Dissemination of Part D Plan Information

To ensure that eligible or enrolled individuals in PDPs receive the information they need to make informed choices about their coverage options, sponsors must disclose a detailed description of each qualified PDP. The description must be provided in a clear, accurate, and standardized form at the time of enrollment and annually thereafter, by the first day of the annual coordinated election period. The information required is similar to the

¶510

information MA plans must disclose to their enrollees. [Soc. Sec. Act § 1860D-4(a); 42 C.F.R. § 423.128(a).]

The description must include information regarding:

(1) service area;

(2) benefits, including applicable conditions and limitations, premiums, cost-sharing, cost-sharing for subsidy-eligible individuals, and other benefit-associated conditions;

(3) how to obtain more information on cost-sharing requirements, including tiered or other copayment levels applicable to each drug;

(4) the plan's formulary, including a list of included drugs, the manner in which the formulary functions, the process for obtaining an exception to the plan's formulary or tiered cost-sharing structure, and a description of how an eligible individual may obtain additional information on the formulary;

(5) the number, mix, and addresses of network pharmacies from which enrollees may reasonably be expected to obtain covered drugs and how the sponsor meets the access requirements;

(6) provisions for access to covered drugs at out-of-network pharmacies;

(7) all grievance, coverage determination, and appeal rights and procedures;

(8) policies and procedures for quality assurance and the medication therapy management program;

(9) disenrollment rights and responsibilities; and

(10) the fact that a sponsor may terminate or refuse to renew its contract, or reduce the service area, and the effect that this may have on plan enrollees.

[42 C.F.R. § 423.128(b).]

Starting with plan year 2021, MA-PDs and PDPs must provide information to beneficiaries on the risks associated with prolonged opioid use and coverage of nonpharmacological therapies, devices, and nonopioid medications. Instead of providing the information to each enrollee in a PDP plan, the sponsor may provide the information through mail or electronic communication to a subset of enrollees, such as those who have been prescribed an opioid in the previous two years. [Soc. Sec. Act § 1860D-4(a)(1)(B)(vi) and (a)(1)(C), as added by SUPPORT for Patients and Communities Act (P.L. 115-271) § 6102.]

Information available on request of the eligible individual. Upon request of a Part D eligible individual, a Part D sponsor must provide: general coverage information; the procedures the sponsor uses to control utilization of services and expenditures; the number of grievances, appeals, and exceptions, and their disposition in the aggregate; and the financial condition of the Part D sponsor, including the most recently audited information regarding the sponsor offering the plan. "General coverage information" includes information on: (1) how to exercise election options, (2) procedural rights, (3) benefits, (4) premiums, (5) the plan's formulary, (6) the plan's service area, and (7) quality and performance indicators for benefits under the plan. [42 C.F.R. § 423.128(c).]

Mechanisms for providing specific information to enrollees. Part D sponsors must have mechanisms in place to provide specific information requested by current and prospective enrollees. The mechanisms must include: a toll-free customer call center, an internet website, and responses in writing upon beneficiary request. [42 C.F.R. § 423.128(d).]

Explanation of benefits. Part D sponsors must furnish an explanation of benefits (EOB) to enrollees who receive covered Part D drugs. EOBs must be written in a form easily understandable to beneficiaries and be provided at least monthly for those enrollees utilizing their prescription drug benefits in a given month. EOBs for Part D plans also must:

(1) list the item or service for which payment was made and the amount of such payment for each item or service;

(2) include a notice of the individual's right to request an itemized statement;

(3) include information regarding the cumulative, year-to-date amount of benefits provided relative to the deductible, the initial coverage limit, and the annual out-of-pocket threshold for that year;

(4) include the cumulative, year-to-date total of incurred costs to the extent practicable;

(5) for each prescription drug claim, include the cumulative percentage increase (if any) in the negotiated price since the first claim of the current benefit year and therapeutic alternatives with lower cost-sharing, when available as determined by the plan, from the applicable approved plan formulary;

(6) include information regarding any applicable formulary changes; and

(7) be provided no later than the end of the month following any month when prescription drug benefits are provided, including for covered Part D spending between the initial coverage limit and the out-of-pocket threshold.

[42 C.F.R. § 423.128(e); *Final rule*, 84 FR 23832, May 23, 2019.]

Disclosure of deficiencies. CMS may require a Part D plan sponsor to disclose to its enrollees or potential enrollees the Part D plan sponsor's performance and contract compliance deficiencies in a manner specified by CMS. [42 C.F.R. § 423.128(f).]

Changes in rules. If a Part D sponsor intends to change its rules for a Part D plan, it must do all of the following: (1) submit the changes for CMS review; (2) for changes that take effect on January 1, notify all enrollees at least 15 days before the beginning of the annual coordinated election period; and (3) provide notice of all other changes in accordance with Part D notice requirements. [42 C.F.R. § 423.128(g).]

Disclosure of formulary and coverage information for auto-assigned subsidy eligibles. Subsidy-eligible individuals enrolled in a PDP who subsequently are reassigned to a new PDP by the HHS Secretary must be provided, within 30 days of the reassignment, with: (1) information on formulary differences between the individual's former plan and the plan to which the individual is reassigned with respect to the individual's drug regimen; and (2) a description of the individual's right to request a coverage determination, exception, or reconsideration, bring an appeal, or resolve a grievance. [Soc. Sec. Act § 1860D-14(d).]

Disclosure of Prices for Equivalent Drugs (Generic Differential Notice)

Part D sponsors must ensure that pharmacies inform enrollees of any differential between the price of a covered Part D drug and the price of the lowest-priced generic version available under the plan at that pharmacy. Sponsors must provide this generic price differential information at the time the plan enrollee purchases the drug or, in the case of drugs purchased by mail order, at the time of delivery. Disclosure of this information, however, is not necessary if the particular covered drug purchased by an enrollee is the lowest-priced generic version of that drug available at a particular pharmacy. [Soc. Sec. Act § 1860D-4(k); 42 C.F.R. § 423.132(a), (b).]

CMS is permitted to waive the generic differential notice requirement in the following cases:

¶510

(1) whenever a private fee-for-service MA plan offers qualified prescription drug coverage and provides plan enrollees with access to covered Part D drugs dispensed at all pharmacies, without regard to whether they are contracted network pharmacies, and does not charge additional cost-sharing for access to covered drugs dispensed at all pharmacies;

(2) at out-of-network pharmacies;

(3) at pharmacies of Indian tribes and tribal organizations, and urban Indian organizations' network pharmacies;

(4) at network pharmacies located in any of the U.S. territories (American Samoa, the Commonwealth of the Northern Mariana Islands, Guam, Puerto Rico, and the Virgin Islands);

(5) at long-term care network pharmacies; and

(6) at any other place, when CMS deems compliance is impossible or impracticable.

[Soc. Sec. Act § 1860D-4(k); 42 C.F.R. § 423.132(c).]

Privacy, Confidentiality, and Accuracy of Enrollee Records

To the extent that a PDP sponsor maintains medical records or other health information regarding Part D enrollees, the sponsor must meet the same requirements regarding confidentiality and accuracy of enrollee records as MA organizations offering MA plans. [Soc. Sec. Act § 1860D-4(i).]

PDP sponsors must:

(1) abide by all federal and state laws regarding confidentiality and disclosure of medical records or other health and enrollment information, including the Health Insurance Portability and Accountability Act of 1996 (HIPAA) and the privacy rule promulgated under HIPAA;

(2) ensure that medical information is released only in accordance with applicable federal or state law or under court orders or subpoenas;

(3) maintain the records and information in an accurate and timely manner; and

(4) ensure timely access by enrollees to records and information pertaining to them.

[42 C.F.R. § 423.136.]

PDPs are covered entities under the HIPAA privacy rule because they meet the definition of "health plan." Any violations by a PDP sponsor of its obligations under the privacy rule are subject to enforcement by the HHS Office for Civil Rights. [*Final rule*, 70 FR 4194, 4277, Jan. 28, 2005.]

[¶ 515] Grievances, Coverage Determinations, Redeterminations, and Reconsiderations

The process concerning grievances, coverage determinations, redeterminations, and reconsiderations under the Part D prescription drug benefit largely mirrors the procedures required under the Medicare Advantage (MA) program (see ¶ 403). Definitions for these terms, as used in Part D, follow.

Grievance. A grievance is any complaint or dispute expressing dissatisfaction with a Part D plan sponsor's operations, activities, or behavior. Grievances do not include coverage determinations or at-risk determinations. Grievance procedures are separate and distinct from appeal procedures, which address coverage determinations as defined in 42 C.F.R.

§ 423.566(b) and at-risk determinations made under a drug management program in accordance with 42 C.F.R. § 423.153(f). [42 C.F.R. § § 423.560, 423.564(b).]

Coverage determination. A coverage determination is a decision by a Part D sponsor regarding the benefits an enrollee is entitled to receive for drug coverage. [42 C.F.R. § 423.566.]

Reconsideration. A reconsideration is a review of an adverse coverage determination or at-risk determination by an independent review entity (IRE) and includes review of the evidence upon which the determination was based and any additional evidence the enrollee submits or the IRE obtains. [42 C.F.R. § 423.560.]

Redetermination. A redetermination is a review of an adverse coverage determination or at-risk determination by a Part D plan sponsor and includes the review of evidence upon which the determination was based and any other evidence the enrollee submits or the plan obtains. [42 C.F.R. § 423.560.]

This section sets forth the requirements related to: (1) Part D plan sponsors with respect to grievances, coverage determinations, and redeterminations; (2) Part D IREs with respect to reconsiderations; and (3) Part D enrollees' rights with respect to grievances, coverage determinations, redeterminations, and reconsiderations. The requirements regarding reopenings, administrative law judge (ALJ) hearings and ALJ and attorney adjudicator decisions, Medicare Appeals Council review, and judicial review are discussed in ¶ 516. [42 C.F.R. § 423.558.]

Responsibilities of Part D Plan Sponsors and Rights of Enrollees

For each prescription drug plan (PDP) that it offers, a Part D plan sponsor must establish and maintain:

(1) a grievance procedure addressing issues unrelated to coverage determinations;

(2) a single, uniform exceptions and appeals process that includes procedures for accepting oral and written requests for coverage determinations and redeterminations;

(3) a procedure for making timely coverage determinations, including determinations on requests for exceptions to a tiered cost-sharing formulary structure or exceptions to a formulary;

(4) appeal procedures for issues related to coverage determinations that meet the requirements of the Part D regulations; and

(5) if the Part D plan sponsor has established a drug management program under 42 C.F.R. § 423.153(f), appeal procedures for issues that involve at-risk determinations.

[Soc. Sec. Act § 1860D-4(b)(3)(H), (g), (h); 42 C.F.R. § 423.562(a)(1).]

A PDP must ensure that enrollees receive written information related to grievance and appeal procedures available to them through the plan and the complaint process available to them under the quality improvement organization process. In addition, a PDP must arrange with its network pharmacies to post or distribute notices instructing enrollees to contact their plans to obtain a coverage determination or request an exception. [42 C.F.R. § 423.562(a)(2), (3).]

Delegated responsibilities. If the Part D plan sponsor delegates any of its responsibilities to another entity or individual through which the sponsor provides covered benefits, the sponsor is ultimately responsible for ensuring that the entity or individual satisfies these requirements. [42 C.F.R. § 423.562(a)(4).]

Medical director requirement. A Part D plan sponsor must employ a medical director who is responsible for ensuring the clinical accuracy of all coverage determinations and redeterminations involving medical necessity. The medical director must be a physician with a current and unrestricted license to practice medicine in a state, territory, Puerto Rico, or the District of Columbia. [42 C.F.R. § 423.562(a)(5).]

Rights of enrollees. Enrollees have the right to: (1) have grievances between the enrollee and the Part D plan sponsor heard and resolved by the plan; (2) have the plan make a timely coverage determination, including a request for an exception to the plan's tiered cost-sharing structure or formulary; and (3) request an expedited coverage determination from the plan. [42 C.F.R. § 423.562(b).]

If an enrollee is dissatisfied with any part of a coverage determination or an at-risk determination under a drug management program, he or she has the right to:

(1) a redetermination of the adverse coverage determination or at-risk determination by the PDP sponsor;

(2) request an expedited redetermination;

(3) a reconsideration or expedited reconsideration by an IRE contracted by CMS if, as a result of a redetermination, a plan affirms, in whole or in part, its adverse coverage determination or at-risk determination;

(4) an ALJ hearing if the IRE affirms the plan's adverse coverage determination or at-risk determination, in whole or in part, and the amount-in-controversy requirement is met;

(5) request a Medicare Appeals Council review of the ALJ's or attorney adjudicator's hearing decision if the ALJ or attorney adjudicator affirms the IRE's adverse coverage determination or at-risk determination, in whole or in part; and

(6) judicial review of the Medicare Appeals Council hearing decision if it affirms the ALJ's or attorney adjudicator's adverse coverage determination or at-risk determination, in whole or in part, and the amount-in-controversy requirement is met.

[42 C.F.R. § 423.562(b)(4).]

Part D Grievance Procedure

PDPs must have meaningful procedures for timely hearing and resolution of grievances from enrollees against PDP sponsors or any other entity or individual providing covered benefits under the such plans. When the plan receives a complaint, it must promptly determine and inform the enrollee whether the complaint is subject to its grievance or appeal procedures. [42 C.F.R. § 423.564(a), (b).]

Method for filing a grievance. An enrollee must file any grievance with a plan either orally or in writing no later than 60 calendar days after the event or incident that precipitated the grievance. [42 C.F.R. § 423.564(d).]

Disposition and notification. The plan must notify the enrollee of its decision as expeditiously as the case requires based on the enrollee's health status, but no later than 30 calendar days after the date the plan receives the oral or written grievance. The 30-calendar-day time frame may be extended by up to 14 calendar days if the enrollee requests the extension or if the plan justifies a need for additional information and documents how the delay is in the interest of the enrollee. [42 C.F.R. § 423.564(e).]

Expedited grievances. A PDP is required to respond to an enrollee's grievance within 24 hours if the complaint involves a refusal by the plan to grant an enrollee's request for an expedited coverage determination or an expedited redetermination and the enrollee has not yet purchased or received the drug that is in dispute. [42 C.F.R. § 423.564(f).]

Recordkeeping. The PDP must maintain records on grievances received orally and in writing. Records minimally must include the date of receipt, final disposition of the grievance, and the date that the plan notified the enrollee of the disposition. [42 C.F.R. § 423.564(g).]

Complaint system. As part of its contract with CMS, the Part D plan sponsor must agree to address complaints received by CMS against the sponsor by (1) addressing and resolving complaints in the CMS complaint tracking system; and (2) displaying a link to the electronic complaint form on the Medicare.gov website on the Part D plan's main website. [42 C.F.R. § 423.505(b)(22).]

Coverage Determinations by Prescription Drug Plans

Each PDP must have a procedure for making timely coverage determinations regarding the prescription drug benefits an enrollee is entitled to receive under the plan, including basic coverage and supplemental benefits, and the amount, including cost-sharing, that the enrollee is required to pay. The plan must have a standard procedure and an expedited procedure when use of the standard procedure may seriously jeopardize the enrollee's life, health, or ability to regain maximum function. [Soc. Sec. Act § 1860D-4(g); 42 C.F.R. § 423.566(a).]

Only adverse coverage determinations are subject to the appeals process. Plan actions that constitute coverage decisions include:

(1) a decision not to provide or pay for a Part D drug that the enrollee believes may be covered by the plan, including a decision not to pay because: (a) the drug is not on the plan's formulary, (b) the drug is determined not to be medically necessary, (c) the drug is furnished by an out-of-network pharmacy, or (d) the PDP determines that the drug is otherwise excludable from coverage if applied to Medicare Part D;

(2) failure to provide a coverage determination in a timely manner when a delay would adversely affect the health of the enrollee;

(3) a decision concerning an exceptions request to the plan's tiered cost-sharing structure;

(4) a decision concerning an exceptions request involving a non-formulary Part D drug; or

(5) a decision on the amount of cost-sharing for a drug.

[42 C.F.R. § 423.566(b).]

The enrollee or the enrollee's appointed representative, on behalf of the enrollee, or the prescribing physician, on behalf of the enrollee, may request a standard or expedited coverage determination. [42 C.F.R. § 423.566(c).]

Medical review of coverage determinations. If a Part D plan sponsor expects to issue a partially or fully adverse medical necessity decision based on the initial review of a request, a physician or other appropriate health care professional with sufficient medical and other expertise, including knowledge of Medicare coverage criteria, must first review the coverage determination. The physician or other health care professional must have a current and unrestricted license to practice within the scope of his or her profession in a state, territory, Puerto Rico, or the District of Columbia. [42 C.F.R. § 423.566(d).]

Standard coverage determination requests. An enrollee must ask for a standard coverage determination by making a request with the Part D sponsor orally or in writing,

¶515

except that requests for payment must be in writing unless the sponsor has implemented a policy of accepting oral requests. The sponsor must establish and maintain a method of documenting all oral request and retain documentation in the case file. [42 C.F.R. § 423.568(a).]

Time frames for notification. When a party makes a request for a drug benefit, the plan sponsor must notify the enrollee and the prescribing physician involved, if appropriate, of its determination as expeditiously as the enrollee's health condition requires, but no later than 72 hours after receipt of the request or, for an exceptions request, no later than 72 hours after receipt of the physician's or other prescriber's supporting statement. [42 C.F.R. § 423.568(b).]

When a party makes a request for payment, the Part D plan sponsor must notify the enrollee of its determination and make payment (when applicable) no later than 14 calendar days after receipt of the request. [42 C.F.R. § 423.568(c).]

If the plan fails to notify the enrollee of its determination in the appropriate time frame, the failure constitutes an adverse coverage determination, and the plan must forward the enrollee's request to the IRE within 24 hours of the expiration of the adjudication time frame. [42 C.F.R. § 423.568(h).]

Written notice. If a Part D plan sponsor makes a completely favorable decision regarding a request for drug benefits, it must give the enrollee written notice of the determination. The sponsor may provide the initial notice orally as long as it sends a written follow-up notice within three calendar days. The notice must explain the conditions of the approval in a readable and understandable form. [42 C.F.R. § 423.568(d) and (e).]

If a Part D plan sponsor decides to deny a drug benefit in whole or in part, it must give the enrollee written notice of the determination. The initial notice may be oral as long as the sponsor mails a written follow-up notice within three calendar days of the oral notice. The notice of denial must:

(1) use approved notice language in a readable and understandable form;

(2) state the specific reasons for the denial;

(3) inform the enrollee of his or her right to a redetermination; and

(4) comply with any other notice requirements specified by CMS.

For drug coverage denials, the denial notice must describe both the standard and expedited redetermination processes, including the enrollee's right to obtain and conditions for obtaining an expedited redetermination, and the rest of the appeals process. For payment denials, the denial notice must describe the standard redetermination process and the rest of the appeals process. [42 C.F.R. § 423.568(f) and (g).]

Effect of a coverage determination. A coverage determination is binding on the Part D plan and the enrollee unless it is reviewed and revised by a redetermination or it is reopened and revised. [42 C.F.R. § 423.576.]

Requirements for an Expedited Coverage Determination by the PDP

An enrollee or an enrollee's prescribing physician or other prescriber may request that a PDP expedite a coverage determination. An expedited review is not available for requests for payment of Part D drugs that have been furnished. An enrollee or an enrollee's prescribing physician or other prescriber on behalf of the enrollee must submit an oral or written request directly to the plan or, if applicable, to the entity responsible for making the determination, as directed by the plan. The prescribing physician or other prescriber may provide oral or written support for an enrollee's request for an expedited determination. [Soc. Sec. Act § 1860D-4(g); 42 C.F.R. § 423.570(a), (b).]

Processing the request. When a request for an expedited review is received, the PDP must provide for an expedited determination in the following situations:

• when an enrollee makes the request, if the plan determines that applying the standard time frame for making a determination may seriously jeopardize the life or health of the enrollee or the enrollee's ability to regain maximum function; and

• when the request has been made or is supported by an enrollee's prescribing physician or other prescriber, if the physician or other prescriber indicates that applying the standard time frame for making a determination may seriously jeopardize the life or health of the enrollee or the enrollee's ability to regain maximum function.

[42 C.F.R. § 423.570(c).]

Time frame and notice for denied requests. If a plan denies a request for expedited determination, it must make the determination within the 72-hour time frame established for a standard determination. The 72-hour period begins on the day the plan receives the request for expedited determination or, for an exceptions request, the day the plan receives the physician's or other prescriber's supporting statement. [42 C.F.R. § 423.570(d)(1).]

The PDP also must give the enrollee and prescribing physician or other prescriber prompt oral notice of the denial that explains that the plan must process the request using the 72-hour time frame for standard determinations and informs the enrollee of the right to file an expedited grievance if he or she disagrees with the plan's decision not to expedite. In addition, the PDP must inform the enrollee of the right to resubmit a request for an expedited determination with the prescribing physician's or other prescriber's support and provide instructions about the plan's grievance process and its time frames. Within three calendar days of the oral notice, the plan must deliver an equivalent written notice. [42 C.F.R. § 423.570(d)(2), (3).]

Time frame and notice requirements for expedited determinations. A plan that approves a request for expedited determination must make its determination and notify the enrollee and the prescribing physician or other prescriber involved, when appropriate, of its decision whether adverse or favorable, as expeditiously as the enrollee's health condition requires, but no later than 24 hours after receiving the request or, for an exceptions request, after the physician's or other prescriber's supporting statement. If the plan fails to notify the enrollee of its determination within the 24-hour time frame, the failure constitutes an adverse coverage determination and the plan must forward the enrollee's request to the IRE within 24 hours of the expiration of the adjudication time frame. [42 C.F.R. § 423.572(a), (d).]

If the Part D plan sponsor first notifies an enrollee of an adverse or favorable expedited determination orally, it must mail written confirmation to the enrollee within three calendar days of the oral notification. If the determination is completely favorable, the notice must explain the conditions of the approval in a readable and understandable form. If the determination is not completely favorable, the notice must:

(1) use approved language in a readable and understandable form;

(2) state the specific reasons for the denial;

(3) inform the enrollee of his or her right to a redetermination; and

(4) describe the standard and expedited redetermination processes, including the enrollee's right to request an expedited redetermination; conditions for obtaining an expedited redetermination; and other aspects of the appeal process.

[42 C.F.R. § 423.572(b), (c).]

¶515

Formulary Exceptions Processes

PDP sponsors must establish exceptions processes to a plan's tiered cost-sharing structure and for receipt of an off-formulary drug. [Soc. Sec. Act § 1860D-4(g)(2); 42 C.F.R. § 423.578(a), (b).] An enrollee may not, however, use the exceptions process to request or be granted coverage for a prescription drug that does not meet the definition of a Part D drug. [42 C.F.R. § 423.578(e).]

Exception process to tiered cost-sharing structure. Under a tiered cost-sharing structure, drugs are assigned to different copayment tiers based on cost-sharing, clinical considerations, or both. An enrollee's level of cost-sharing is based on the tier into which the prescribed drug falls. Typically, drugs fall into one of three tiers—generic drugs, preferred brand-name drugs, or non-preferred brand-name drugs. All of a plan's cost-sharing tiers make up its formulary. [42 C.F.R. § 423.4.]

A plan grants an exception to its tiered cost-sharing structure whenever it determines that the non-preferred drug for treatment of the enrollee's condition is medically necessary, consistent with the physician's statement. [Soc. Sec. Act § 1860D-4(g)(2); 42 C.F.R. § 423.578(a).]

An enrollee or the enrollee's prescribing physician or other prescriber may file a request for an exception. The prescribing physician or other prescriber must provide an oral or written supporting statement that the preferred drug for the treatment of the enrollee's condition:

(1) would not be as effective for the enrollee as the requested drug; and/or

(2) would have adverse effects for the enrollee.

If the physician or other prescriber provides an oral supporting statement, the plan may require the physician or other prescriber to provide a written supporting statement to demonstrate the medical necessity of the drug or to provide additional supporting medical documentation. [42 C.F.R. § 423.578(a)(3)–(5).]

Request for exceptions involving a non-formulary Part D drug. Part D plan sponsors that offer PDPs with formularies must establish and maintain exceptions procedures subject to CMS's approval for PDP enrollees who require drugs that are not on a plan's formulary. Formulary use includes the application of cost utilization tools such as: (1) a dose restriction, including the dosage form, that causes a particular Part D drug not to be covered for the number of doses prescribed; or (2) a step therapy requirement that causes a particular Part D drug not to be covered until the requirements of the plan's coverage policy are met; or (3) a therapeutic substitution requirement. [42 C.F.R. § 423.578(b).]

The PDP must grant an exception whenever it determines that the drug is medically necessary, consistent with the physician's statement, and that the drug would be covered but for the fact that it is an off-formulary drug. The plan's formulary exceptions process must address:

(1) situations in which a formulary changes during the year and situations in which an enrollee is already using a given drug;

(2) continued coverage of a particular Part D prescription drug that the PDP is discontinuing on the formulary for reasons other than safety or because the Part D prescription drug cannot be supplied by or was withdrawn from the market by the drug's manufacturer; and

(3) an exception to a plan's coverage policy that causes a Part D prescription drug not to be covered because of cost utilization tools, such as a requirement for step therapy, dosage limitations, or therapeutic substitution.

[42 C.F.R. § 423.578(b)(1).]

An enrollee, the enrollee's appointed representative, or the prescribing physician or other prescriber on behalf of the enrollee may file a request for an exception. The prescribing physician or other prescriber must provide an oral or written supporting statement that the requested prescription drug is medically necessary to treat the enrollee's disease or medical condition. [42 C.F.R. § 423.578(b)(4), (5).]

If the plan covers a non-formulary drug, the costs incurred by the enrollee for that drug are treated as being included for purposes of calculating and meeting the annual out-of-pocket threshold. [42 C.F.R. § 423.578(b)(3).]

When a non-formulary exceptions request is approved, the plan may not require the enrollee to request approval for a refill, or a new prescription to continue using the Part D prescription drug after the refills for the initial prescription are exhausted, as long as: (1) the enrollee's prescribing physician or other prescriber continues to prescribe the drug; (2) the drug continues to be considered safe for treating the enrollee's disease or medical condition; and (3) the enrollment period has not expired. [42 C.F.R. § 423.578(c)(4).]

Coverage determination. A decision by a PDP concerning an exceptions request constitutes a coverage determination. If the plan fails to make a decision on an exceptions request and provide notice of the decision within the time frame required for a standard determination or an expedited determination, as applicable, the failure constitutes an adverse coverage determination and the plan must forward the enrollee's request to the IRE within 24 hours of the expiration of the adjudication time frame. [42 C.F.R. § 423.578(c)(1), (c)(2).]

Rules for Redeterminations

To appeal a coverage determination or an at-risk determination under a drug management program, an enrollee or an enrollee's prescribing physician or other prescriber must file a written request for redetermination with the plan that made the coverage determination or at-risk determination within 60 calendar days from the date of the notice of determination. [Soc. Sec. Act § 1860D-4(g); 42 C.F.R. §§ 423.580, 423.582.]

Who must conduct the review of an adverse coverage determination. A person who was not involved in making the coverage determination or at-risk determination must conduct the redetermination. When the issue is the denial of coverage based on a lack of medical necessity, a physician with expertise in the field of medicine that is appropriate for the services at issue must make the redetermination. The physician need not, in all cases, be of the same specialty or subspecialty as the prescribing physician. [42 C.F.R. § 423.590(f).]

Time frames for standard redetermination requests. If the Part D plan sponsor makes a redetermination that is completely favorable to the enrollee or a redetermination that affirms, in whole or in part, its adverse coverage determination or at-risk determination, the sponsor must notify the enrollee in writing of its redetermination as expeditiously as the enrollee's health condition requires, but no later than seven calendar days from the date it receives the request for a standard redetermination. If the Part D plan sponsor makes a redetermination of a request for payment that is completely favorable to the enrollee or affirms, in whole or in part, its adverse coverage determination, the sponsor must issue its redetermination and effectuate it no later than 14 calendar days from the date it receives the request for redetermination. [42 C.F.R. § 423.590(a), (b).]

If the PDP fails to provide the enrollee with a redetermination within these time frames, the failure constitutes an adverse redetermination decision and the plan must forward the enrollee's request to the IRE within 24 hours of the expiration of the adjudication time frame. [42 C.F.R. § 423.590(c).]

¶515

Notice of adverse redetermination. The notice of any adverse determination must use approved notice language in a readable and understandable form, state the specific reasons for the denial, and inform the enrollee of his or her right to a reconsideration. For adverse drug coverage redeterminations or redeterminations related to a drug management program, the notice must describe the standard and expedited reconsideration processes, including the enrollee's right to, and conditions for, obtaining an expedited reconsideration, and the remainder of the appeals process. For adverse payment redeterminations, the notice must describe the standard reconsideration process and the remainder of the appeals process. [42 C.F.R. § 423.590(g).]

Notice of completely favorable redeterminations. The notice of any completely favorable determination must explain the conditions of the approval in a readable and understandable form. [42 C.F.R. § 423.590(h).]

Expedited Redeterminations

An enrollee or an enrollee's prescribing physician or other prescriber acting on behalf of an enrollee may request that a Part D plan sponsor expedite a redetermination of a coverage determination or an at-risk determination made under a drug management program. Requests for redetermination on payment of drugs already received, however, may not be expedited because a medical emergency does not exist for an enrollee who has obtained the medication in dispute. [Soc. Sec. Act § 1860D-4(g); 42 C.F.R. § 423.584(a).]

The enrollee or prescribing physician or other prescriber must submit an oral or written request directly to the PDP or, if applicable, to the entity responsible for making the redetermination, as directed by the plan. A prescribing physician or other prescriber may provide oral or written support for an enrollee's request for an expedited redetermination. [42 C.F.R. § 423.584(b).]

Processing expedited redetermination requests. The PDP must: (1) establish an efficient and convenient means for individuals to submit oral or written expedited redetermination requests; (2) document all oral requests in writing; and (3) maintain the documentation in the case file. In addition, the PDP must decide promptly whether to expedite the redetermination or follow the time frame for standard redetermination based on the following requirements:

- for a request made by an enrollee, the plan must provide an expedited redetermination if it determines that applying the standard time frame for making a redetermination may seriously jeopardize the life or health of the enrollee or the enrollee's ability to regain maximum function; and

- for a request made or supported by a prescribing physician or other prescriber, the plan must provide an expedited redetermination if the physician indicates that applying the standard time frame for conducting a redetermination may seriously jeopardize the life or health of the enrollee or the enrollee's ability to regain maximum function.

[42 C.F.R. § 423.584(c).]

Denial of an expedited redetermination request. If a PDP denies a request for expedited redetermination, it must make the determination within the seven-calendar-day time frame that begins the day the plan receives the request for expedited redetermination. The plan must give the enrollee prompt oral notice of the denial that:

(1) explains that the plan processes the enrollee's request using the seven-calendar-day time frame for standard redetermination;

(2) informs the enrollee of the right to file an expedited grievance if he or she disagrees with the decision by the plan not to expedite;

(3) informs the enrollee of the right to resubmit a request for an expedited redetermination with the prescribing physician's or other prescriber's support; and

(4) provides instructions about the expedited grievance process and its time frames.

Within three calendar days of the oral notice to the enrollee, the PDP must deliver an equivalent written notice that contains the required information. [42 C.F.R. § 423.584(d).]

Time frame for expedited redeterminations. A Part D plan sponsor that approves a request for expedited redetermination must complete its redetermination and give the enrollee and the prescribing physician or other prescriber involved, when appropriate, notice of its decision as expeditiously as the enrollee's health condition requires, but no later than 72 hours after receiving the request. If notice of an adverse or favorable expedited redetermination is given orally, the sponsor must mail written confirmation within three calendar days of the oral notice. [42 C.F.R. § 423.590(d).]

Failure to meet time frame for expedited redetermination. If the PDP fails to provide the enrollee or the prescribing physician or other prescriber, when appropriate, with the results of its expedited redetermination within the 72-hour time frame, the failure constitutes an adverse redetermination decision and the plan must forward the enrollee's request to the IRE within 24 hours of the expiration of the adjudication time frame. [42 C.F.R. § 423.590(e).]

Reconsideration by an Independent Review Entity

An enrollee (or the prescribing physician or other prescriber, acting on behalf of the enrollee) who is dissatisfied with the redetermination of a PDP has a right to a reconsideration by an IRE that contracts with CMS. [Soc. Sec. Act § 1860D-4(h); 42 C.F.R. § 423.600(a).]

The enrollee, or the enrollee's prescribing physician or other prescriber, must file a written request for reconsideration with the IRE within 60 calendar days of the date of the redetermination by the plan. When an enrollee or an enrollee's prescribing physician or other prescriber files an appeal, the IRE is required to solicit the views of the prescribing physician or other prescriber, either orally or in writing. The IRE must maintain a written account of the prescribing physician's views, prepared by the prescribing physician, other prescriber, or IRE. [42 C.F.R. § 423.600(a), (b).]

Requirements for reconsideration for non-formulary drugs. For an enrollee to request an IRE reconsideration of a determination by a plan not to provide for a Part D drug that is not on the formulary, the prescribing physician or other prescriber must determine that all covered Part D drugs on any tier of the formulary for treatment of the same condition would not be as effective for the individual as the non-formulary drug, would have adverse effects for the individual, or both. [42 C.F.R. § 423.600(c).]

Time frame for reconsideration. The IRE must conduct the reconsideration as expeditiously as the enrollee's health condition requires but no later than seven calendar days from the date of a request for a reconsideration. When a request for an expedited reconsideration is received and granted, the IRE must conduct the reconsideration as expeditiously as the enrollee's health condition requires, but no later than 72 hours after receiving the request. [42 C.F.R. § 423.600(d).]

Medical necessity issues. When the issue is the denial of coverage based on a lack of medical necessity (or any substantively equivalent term used to describe the concept of medical necessity), a physician with expertise in the field of medicine that is appropriate for

¶515

the services at issue must make the reconsideration. The physician making the reconsideration need not, in all cases, be of the same specialty or subspecialty as the prescribing physician or other prescriber. [42 C.F.R. § 423.600(e).]

Notice of reconsideration determination. The IRE is responsible for mailing a notice of its reconsideration determination to the enrollee and the PDP and sending a copy to CMS. When the prescribing physician or other prescriber requests the reconsideration on behalf of the enrollee, the IRE is also responsible for notifying the prescribing physician or other prescriber of its decision. The notice must state the specific reasons for the IRE's decision in understandable language. If the reconsideration determination is adverse, the notice must inform the enrollee of his or her right to an ALJ hearing if the amount in controversy meets the threshold requirement and describe the procedures that the enrollee must follow to obtain an ALJ hearing. [42 C.F.R. § 423.602.]

Effect of a reconsideration determination. A reconsideration determination is final and binding on the enrollee and the plan, unless the enrollee files a request for an ALJ hearing. [42 C.F.R. § 423.604.]

Effectuation of Standard and Expedited Determinations, Reconsiderations, and Decisions

If a PDP reverses its coverage determination in a redetermination of a request for benefits, the plan must authorize or provide the benefit under dispute as expeditiously as the enrollee's health condition requires, but no later than seven calendar days from the date it receives the request for redetermination. [42 C.F.R. § 423.636(a)(1).]

If the PDP reverses its coverage determination on a redetermination of a request for payment, the Part D plan sponsor must authorize payment for the benefit within 14 calendar days from the date it receives the request for redetermination and make payment no later than 30 calendar days after the date the plan sponsor receives the request for redetermination. [42 C.F.R. § 423.636(a)(2).]

If the PDP reverses its at-risk determination on a redetermination of an at-risk determination made under a drug management program, the sponsor must implement the change to the determination as expeditiously as the enrollee's health condition requires, but no later than seven calendar days from the date it receives the request for redetermination. [42 C.F.R. § 423.636(a)(3).]

On an expedited redetermination of a request for benefits, if the plan reverses its coverage determination, the plan must authorize or provide the benefit under dispute as expeditiously as the enrollee's health condition requires, but no later than 72 hours after the date the Part D plan sponsor receives the request for redetermination. Similarly, on an expedited redetermination of an at-risk determination made under a drug management program, if the plan sponsor reverses its at-risk determination, the sponsor must implement the change to the at-risk determination as expeditiously as the enrollee's health condition requires, but no later than 72 hours after the date the sponsor receives the request for redetermination. [42 C.F.R. § 423.638(a).]

Reversals other than by the Part D plan sponsor. On appeal of a request for benefit, if the plan's determination is reversed in whole or in part by the IRE or at a higher level of appeal, the PDP must authorize or provide the benefit under dispute within 72 hours from the date it receives notice reversing the determination. On appeal of a request for payment, if the plan's determination is reversed in whole or in part by the IRE or at a higher level of appeal, the Part D plan sponsor must authorize payment for the benefit within 72 hours and make payment no later than 30 calendar days from the date it receives notice reversing the coverage determination. On appeal of an at-risk determination, if the plan's determination is reversed in whole or in part by the IRE or at a higher level of appeal, the sponsor must implement the change to the at-risk determination within 72 hours from the date it receives notice reversing the determination and inform the IRE that it effectuated the decision. [42 C.F.R. § 423.636(b).]

If the expedited determination or expedited redetermination for benefits by the plan is reversed in whole or in part by the IRE or at a higher level of appeal, the plan must authorize or provide the benefit under dispute as expeditiously as the enrollee's health condition requires, but no later than 24 hours from the date it receives notice reversing the determination. The sponsor must inform the IRE that it effectuated the decision. [42 C.F.R. § 423.638(b).]

[¶ 516] Reopenings, ALJ Hearings, Medicare Appeals Council Review, and Judicial Review

The regulations at 42 C.F.R. Part 423 Subpart U set forth the regulatory requirements for: (1) Part D sponsors, the Part D independent review entity (IRE), administrative law judges (ALJs) and attorney adjudicators, and the Medicare Appeals Council with respect to reopenings; (2) ALJs with respect to hearings and decisions or decisions of attorney adjudicators if no hearing is conducted; (3) the Medicare Appeals Council with respect to review of Part D appeals; and (4) Part D enrollees' rights with respect to reopenings, ALJ hearings and ALJ or attorney adjudicator reviews, Medicare Appeals Council reviews, and judicial review by a federal district court. [42 C.F.R. § 423.1968.] The requirements for Part D plan sponsors with respect to grievances, coverage determinations, redeterminations, and reconsiderations are covered in ¶ 515.

Reopenings

A reopening is a remedy designed to change a binding determination or decision, even though the determination or decision may have been correct at the time it was made. A reopening may be taken by:

> (1) a Part D plan sponsor to revise the coverage determination or redetermination;

> (2) an IRE to revise the reconsideration;

> (3) an ALJ or attorney adjudicator to revise his or her decision; or

> (4) the Medicare Appeals Council to revise the ALJ or attorney adjudicator decision, or its review decision.

[42 C.F.R. §§ 423.1978(a), 423.1980(a).]

When an enrollee has filed a valid request for an appeal of a coverage determination, redetermination, reconsideration, hearing, or Medicare Appeals Council review, no adjudicator has jurisdiction to reopen an issue that is under appeal until all appeal rights for that issue are exhausted. The Part D plan sponsor's, IRE's, ALJ's or attorney adjudicator's, or Medicare Appeals Council's decision on whether to reopen is binding and not subject to appeal. [42 C.F.R. §§ 423.1978(d), 423.1980(a).]

Reopening coverage determinations and redeterminations. A Part D plan sponsor may reopen its coverage determination or redetermination on its own motion: (1) within one year from the date of the coverage determination or redetermination for any reason; (2) within four years from the date of the coverage determination or redetermination for good cause; or (3) at any time if there exists reliable evidence that the coverage determination was procured by fraud or similar fault. [42 C.F.R. § 423.1980(b).]

¶516

"Good cause" for reopening may be established when: (1) there is new and material evidence that was unavailable or unknown at the time of the determination or decision and may result in a different conclusion; or (2) the evidence that was considered clearly shows on its face that an obvious error was made. Generally, a change of legal interpretation or policy by CMS in a regulation, CMS ruling, or CMS general instruction, whether made in response to judicial precedent or otherwise, is not a basis for reopening a determination or hearing decision. [42 C.F.R. § 423.1986.]

An enrollee may request that a Part D plan sponsor reopen its coverage determination or redetermination: (1) within one year from the date of the coverage determination or redetermination for any reason; or (2) within four years from the date of the coverage determination or redetermination for good cause. [42 C.F.R. § 423.1980(c).]

IRE, ALJ, and Medicare Appeals Council reopening of reconsiderations, hearings, and reviews. Reopenings of IRE reconsiderations, ALJ hearing decisions, and Medicare Appeals Council reviews may be requested by an IRE, ALJ or attorney adjudicator, or the Medicare Appeals Council on its own motion within 180 calendar days from the date of the reconsideration, decision, or review for good cause, but if the action was procured by fraud or similar fault, the reopening may be made at any time. [42 C.F.R. § 423.1980(d).]

Enrollee or sponsor request for reopening of reconsiderations, hearings, and reviews. A Part D plan sponsor or an enrollee who received an IRE reconsideration, ALJ or attorney adjudicator decision, or Medicare Appeals Council review may request a reopening within 180 calendar days from the date of its reconsideration, hearing decision, or review for good cause. [42 C.F.R. § 423.1980(e).]

Notice requirement. Regardless of whether a reopening is initiated by an adjudicator, an enrollee, or the Part D plan sponsor, when any determination or decision is reopened and revised, the Part D plan sponsor, IRE, ALJ or attorney adjudicator, or Medicare Appeals Council must mail its revised determination or decision to the enrollee at his or her last known address, and the IRE, ALJ or attorney adjudicator, or Medicare Appeals Council must mail its revised determination or decision to the Part D plan sponsor. An adverse revised determination or decision must state the rationale and basis for the reopening and revision and any right to appeal. [42 C.F.R. § 423.1982.]

Effect of revised determination or decision. A revised determination or decision is binding unless it is appealed or otherwise reopened. [42 C.F.R. § 423.1978(c).] The methods of appeal are as follows:

- **Coverage determinations.** The revision of a coverage determination is binding unless an enrollee submits a request for a redetermination that is accepted and processed.

- **Redeterminations.** The revision of a redetermination is binding unless an enrollee submits a request for an IRE reconsideration that is accepted and processed.

- **Reconsiderations.** The revision of a reconsideration is binding unless an enrollee submits a request for an ALJ hearing that is accepted and processed.

- **ALJ or attorney adjudicator decisions.** The revision of an ALJ or attorney adjudicator decision is binding unless an enrollee submits a request for a Medicare Appeals Council review that is accepted and processed.

- **Medicare Appeals Council review.** The revision of a Medicare Appeals Council determination or decision is binding unless an enrollee files a civil action in a federal district court that accepts jurisdiction and issues a decision.

[42 C.F.R. § 423.1984.]

Administrative Law Judge Hearings

An enrollee who is dissatisfied with the IRE reconsideration determination has a right to a hearing before an ALJ if he or she: (1) files a written request for an ALJ hearing within 60 calendar days after receipt of the written notice of the IRE's reconsideration (presumed to be five calendar days after the date of the written reconsideration, unless there is evidence to the contrary); and (2) meets the amount-in-controversy requirements of 42 C.F.R. § 423.2006. [42 C.F.R. § 423.2002(a), (d).]

Amount in controversy. For ALJ hearing requests, the required amount remaining in controversy must be $100, increased by a percentage increase based on the medical care component of the Consumer Price Index as measured from July 2003 to the July before the current year involved. All amount-in-controversy dollar values are rounded up to the nearest multiple of $10. [42 C.F.R. § 423.2006(a); *Final rule,* 84 FR 19855, May 7, 2019.]

If the basis for the appeal is the refusal by the Part D plan sponsor to provide drug benefits, the projected value of those benefits is used to compute the amount remaining in controversy. The projected value of a Part D drug or drugs must include any costs the enrollee could incur based on the number of refills prescribed for the drug in dispute during the plan year. If the basis for the appeal is an at-risk determination made under a drug management program under 42 C.F.R. § 423.153(f), the projected value of the drugs subject to the drug management program is used to compute the amount remaining in controversy. The projected value of the drugs subject to the drug management program must include the value of any refills prescribed for the drugs in dispute during the plan year. [42 C.F.R. § 423.2006(c); *Final rule,* 84 FR 19855, May 7, 2019.]

Under certain circumstances, two or more appeals may be aggregated by a single enrollee or multiple enrollees to meet the amount-in-controversy requirement. [42 C.F.R. § 423.2006(d); *Final rule,* 84 FR 19855, May 7, 2019.]

Filing a request for an ALJ hearing. The enrollee must file a written request for an ALJ hearing with Office of Medicare Hearings and Appeals (OMHA) office specified in the IRE's reconsideration notice within 60 calendar days of the date from the date the enrollee receives written notice of the IRE's reconsideration or dismissal being appealed. [42 C.F.R. § 423.2014.]

Expedited hearing request. An enrollee also may request that the hearing before an ALJ be expedited. An expedited hearing must involve an issue specified in 42 C.F.R. § 423.566(b), but must not include solely a request for payment of Part D drugs already furnished. The enrollee must submit a written or oral request for an expedited ALJ hearing within 60 calendar days of the date of the written notice of an IRE reconsideration determination. The request for an expedited ALJ hearing should also explain why the standard time frame may seriously jeopardize the life or health of the enrollee. [42 C.F.R. § 423.2002(b).]

Review of IRE dismissal. An enrollee has a right to have an IRE's dismissal of a request for reconsideration reviewed by an ALJ or attorney adjudicator if the enrollee files a request within 60 calendar days after receipt of the written notice of the IRE's dismissal and meets the amount-in-controversy requirements. If the ALJ or attorney adjudicator determines that the IRE's dismissal was in error, he or she must vacate the dismissal and remand the case to the IRE for reconsideration. The ALJ or attorney adjudicator may dismiss the request for review of an IRE's dismissal in accordance with 42 C.F.R. § 423.2052(b). [42 C.F.R. § 423.2004.]

Time frames for ALJ decision. When a request for an ALJ hearing is filed after an IRE has issued a written reconsideration, an ALJ or attorney adjudicator issues a decision, dismissal order, or remand, as appropriate, no later than the end of the 90-calendar-day

¶516

period beginning on the date the request for hearing is received by the entity specified in the IRE's notice of reconsideration, unless the 90-calendar-day period has been extended. The ALJ or attorney adjudicator must provide an expedited hearing decision if the appeal involves an issue specified in 42 C.F.R. § 423.566(b), but not solely a request for payment of Part D drugs already furnished, and the enrollee's prescribing physician or other prescriber indicates, or the ALJ or attorney adjudicator determines, that applying the standard time frame for making a decision may seriously jeopardize the enrollee's life, health, or ability to regain maximum function. [42 C.F.R. § 423.2016.]

Submission of evidence. An enrollee must submit any written evidence that he or she wishes to have considered at the ALJ hearing. An ALJ or attorney adjudicator will not consider any evidence submitted regarding a change in condition of an enrollee after the appealed coverage determination or at-risk determination was made. An ALJ or attorney adjudicator will remand a case to the IRE when an enrollee wishes evidence on his or her change in condition after the coverage determination or at-risk determination to be considered. A represented enrollee must submit all written evidence he or she wishes to have considered at the hearing with the request for hearing or within 10 calendar days of receiving the notice of hearing. For an expedited ALJ hearing, an enrollee must submit all written evidence with the request for hearing or within two calendar days of receiving the notice of hearing. [42 C.F.R. § 423.2018.]

Hearing notice. The ALJ must send a notice of hearing to the enrollee and other potential participants at their last known addresses or by personal service advising them of the proposed time and place of the hearing. The ALJ must mail, transmit, or serve the notice at least 20 calendar days before the hearing, except for expedited hearings, when written notice is mailed or served at least three calendar days before the hearing. [42 C.F.R. § 423.2022.]

Permissible issues. The issues before the ALJ or attorney adjudicator include all the issues brought out in the coverage determination or at-risk determination, redetermination, or reconsideration that were not decided entirely in an enrollee's favor. The ALJ or the enrollee may raise a new issue; however, the ALJ may consider a new issue relating to a determination or appealed matter specified in the request for hearing only if its resolution could have a material impact on the appealed matter and (1) there is new and material evidence that was not available or known at the time of the determination and that may result in a different conclusion; or (2) the evidence that was considered in making the determination clearly shows on its face that an obvious error was made at the time of the determination. [42 C.F.R. § 423.2032.]

Hearing process. An enrollee has the right to appear at the hearing before the ALJ to present evidence and state his or her position by video-teleconferencing or telephone or in person. An enrollee may waive his or her right to appear by sending OMHA a written statement indicating that he or she does not wish to appear at the hearing. An enrollee (or an enrollee's appointed representative) may appear before the ALJ to state the enrollee's case, present a written summary of the case, or enter written statements about the facts and law material to the case in the record. The ALJ may receive evidence at the hearing even though the evidence is not admissible in court under the rules of evidence used by the court. The ALJ, however, may not consider evidence on any change in condition of an enrollee after a coverage determination or at-risk determination. [42 C.F.R. § § 423.2000, 423.2036.]

ALJ subpoenas. An ALJ may, on his or her own initiative, issue subpoenas for the appearance and testimony of witnesses and for the enrollee or the Part D plan sponsor to make books, records, correspondence, papers, or other documents that are material to an issue at the hearing available for inspection and copying. An ALJ may not issue a subpoena to

CMS or the IRE to compel an appearance, testimony, or the production of evidence, or to the Part D plan sponsor to compel an appearance or testimony. To the extent that a subpoena compels disclosure of a matter for which an objection based on privilege, or other protection from disclosure such as case preparation, confidentiality, or undue burden, was made before an ALJ, the Medicare Appeals Council may review immediately the ruling of the ALJ on the objections to the subpoena or that portion of the subpoena, as applicable. [42 C.F.R. § 423.2036(f).]

Notice and effect of ALJ decisions. Unless the ALJ or attorney adjudicator dismisses the hearing, the ALJ or attorney adjudicator must issue a written decision that gives the findings of fact, conclusions of law, and the reasons for the decision. [42 C.F.R. § 423.2046.]

The decision of the ALJ is binding unless:

(1) an enrollee requests a review of the decision by the Medicare Appeals Council within the stated time period or the Medicare Appeals Council reviews the decision issued by an ALJ or attorney adjudicator and issues a final decision or remand order;

(2) the decision is reopened and revised by an ALJ or attorney adjudicator or the Medicare Appeals Council;

(3) the expedited access to judicial review process is used;

(4) the ALJ's or attorney adjudicator's decision is a recommended decision directed to the Medicare Appeals Council and the Medicare Appeals Council issues a decision; or

(5) in a case remanded by a federal district court, the Medicare Appeals Council assumes jurisdiction and issues a decision.

The decision of the ALJ or attorney adjudicator on a request for review of an IRE dismissal is binding on the enrollee unless the decision is reopened and revised by the ALJ or attorney adjudicator. [42 C.F.R. § 423.2048.]

Removal by the Medicare Appeals Council. If a request for hearing is pending before OMHA, the Medicare Appeals Council may assume responsibility for the hearing by requesting that OMHA forward the hearing request. If the Medicare Appeals Council holds a hearing, however, it must conduct the hearing according to the rules for ALJ hearings. [42 C.F.R. § 423.2050.]

Medicare Appeals Council Reviews

An enrollee who is dissatisfied with an ALJ's or attorney adjudicator's decision or dismissal may request that the Council review the decision or dismissal. The Council's review of an ALJ's or attorney adjudicator's decision is a new review (conducted as though no review had yet taken place). The Council issues a final decision or dismissal order or remands a case to the ALJ or attorney adjudicator no later than the end of the 90-calendar-day period beginning on the date the request for review is received (by the entity specified in the ALJ's or attorney adjudicator's written notice of decision), unless the 90-calendar-day period is extended or the enrollee requests expedited Council review. [42 C.F.R. § 423.2100.]

Filing the Medicare Appeals Council review request. An enrollee requests a Medicare Appeals Council review by submitting a written request for review within 60 calendar days after receipt of the ALJ's or attorney adjudicator's written decision or dismissal to the entity specified in the notice of the ALJ's action. An enrollee may request that Medicare Appeals Council review be expedited if the appeal involves an issue specified in 42 C.F.R. § 423.566(b) but does not include solely a request for payment of Part D drugs already furnished. If an enrollee is requesting that the Medicare Appeals Council review be expedited, the enrollee must submit an oral or written request within 60 calendar days after the receipt of the ALJ's or attorney adjudicator's written decision or dismissal. [42 C.F.R. § § 423.2102, 423.2106.]

Reviews on Medicare Appeals Council's own motion. The Medicare Appeals Council may decide on its own motion to review a decision or dismissal issued by an ALJ or attorney adjudicator. CMS or the IRE may refer a case to the Medicare Appeals Council to consider reviewing on its own motion any time within 60 calendar days of receipt of the ALJ's or attorney adjudicator's written decision or dismissal is issued if the decision or dismissal contains an error of law material to the outcome of the claim or presents a broad policy or procedural issue that may affect the public interest. CMS or the IRE also may request that the Medicare Appeals Council take own-motion review of a case if: (1) CMS or the IRE participated or requested to participate in the appeal at the OMHA level; and (2) the ALJ's or attorney adjudicator's decision or dismissal is not supported by the preponderance of evidence in the record or the ALJ or attorney adjudicator abused his or her discretion. [42 C.F.R. § 423.2110.]

Dismissing review requests. The Medicare Appeals Council must dismiss a request for review if the enrollee did not file the request within the stated period of time and the time for filing has not been extended. The Medicare Appeals Council also must dismiss the request for review if: (1) the enrollee asks to withdraw the request for review; (2) the individual or entity does not have a right to request review; or (3) the enrollee dies while the request for review is pending and the enrollee's estate or representative either has no remaining financial interest in the case or does not want to continue the appeal. [42 C.F.R. § 423.2114.]

Briefs and evidence. Upon request, the Medicare Appeals Council must give the enrollee a reasonable opportunity to file a brief or other written statement. The Medicare Appeals Council also may request, but not require, CMS, the IRE, and/or the Part D plan sponsor to file a brief if it determines that it is necessary. [42 C.F.R. § 423.2120.] When the Medicare Appeals Council reviews an ALJ's or attorney adjudicator's decision, it must consider the evidence contained in the record of the proceedings before the ALJ or attorney adjudicator and any new evidence that relates to the period before the coverage determination or at-risk determination. If the hearing decision decides a new issue that the enrollee was not afforded an opportunity to address at the OMHA level, the Medicare Appeals Council must consider any evidence related to that new issue. The Medicare Appeals Council must not consider any new evidence submitted regarding a change in condition of an enrollee after a coverage determination or at-risk determination is made. [42 C.F.R. § 423.2122(a).]

Oral argument. An enrollee may request oral argument or the Medicare Appeals Council may decide on its own that oral argument is necessary to decide the case. The Medicare Appeals Council will grant oral argument if it decides that the case raises an important question of law, policy, or fact that cannot be decided based on written submissions alone. If it decides on its own to hear oral argument, it must inform the enrollee of the time and place of the oral argument at least 10 calendar days before the scheduled date or, for an expedited review, at least two calendar days before the scheduled date. [42 C.F.R. § 423.2124.]

Medicare Appeals Council remand. The Medicare Appeals Council may remand a case when additional evidence is needed or additional action by the ALJ or attorney adjudicator is required. The Medicare Appeals Council will designate in its remand order whether the ALJ or attorney adjudicator will issue a decision or a recommended decision on remand. The case must be remanded to the appropriate Part D IRE if it determines that the enrollee wishes evidence on his or her change in condition after the coverage determination or at-risk determination to be considered in the appeal. [42 C.F.R. § 423.2126.]

Final Medicare Appeals Council action. After it has reviewed the evidence in the administrative record and any additional evidence, the Medicare Appeals Council must make a decision or remand the case to an ALJ or attorney adjudicator. The Medicare Appeals Council has the authority to adopt, modify, or reverse the ALJ hearing decision or recommended decision. A copy of the decision is mailed to the enrollee at his or her last known address, CMS, the IRE, and the Part D plan sponsor. The decision of the Medicare Appeals Council is final and binding unless a federal district court modifies it or it is revised as the result of a reopening. [42 C.F.R. § § 423.2128, 423.2130.]

Judicial Review of Medicare Appeals Council Decisions

To the extent authorized by Soc. Sec. Act § § 1876(c)(5)(B) and 1860D-4(h), an enrollee may obtain a court review of:

(1) a Council decision if it is a final decision of the Secretary and the amount in controversy meets the threshold requirements of 42 C.F.R. § 423.2006; and

(2) an ALJ's or attorney adjudicator's decision if the Council denied the enrollee's request for review and the amount in controversy meets the threshold requirements of 42 C.F.R. § 423.2006.

[Soc. Sec. Act § § 1860D-4(h), 1876(c)(5)(B); 42 C.F.R. § 423.2136(a); *Final rule*, 84 FR 19855, May 7, 2019.]

In any civil action for judicial review, the proper party defendant is the Secretary of HHS, in his or her official capacity. Upon judicial review, the findings of the Secretary as to any fact, if supported by substantial evidence, are to be considered conclusive by the federal district court. [42 C.F.R. § 423.2136(d), (e).]

Amount in controversy. To be entitled to judicial review, the enrollee must meet the amount-in-controversy requirements at the time it requests judicial review. For review requests, the required amount remaining in controversy must be $1,000 or more, annually adjusted by a percentage increase based on the medical care component of the Consumer Price Index from July 2003 to the July prior to the current year involved. [42 C.F.R. § 423.2006(b); *Final rule*, 84 FR 19855, May 7, 2019.]

If the basis for the appeal is the refusal by the Part D plan sponsor to provide drug benefits, the projected value of those benefits is used to compute the amount remaining in controversy. The projected value of a Part D drug or drugs must include any costs the enrollee could incur based on the number of refills prescribed for the drugs in dispute during the plan year. If the basis for the appeal is an at-risk determination made under a drug management program in accordance with 42 C.F.R. § 423.153(f), the projected value of the drugs subject to the drug management program is used to compute the amount remaining in controversy. The projected value of the drugs subject to the drug management program includes the value of any refills prescribed for the drugs in dispute during the plan year. [42 C.F.R. § 423.2006(c); *Final rule*, 84 FR 19855, May 7, 2019.]

Filing requirements. Any civil action for judicial review must be filed with the appropriate federal district court within 60 calendar days after the date the enrollee receives written notice of the Medicare Appeals Council's decision. The date of receipt of the notice of the Medicare Appeals Council's decision is presumed to be five calendar days after the date of the notice, unless there is a reasonable showing to the contrary. Likewise, if a case is certified for judicial review in accordance with the expedited access to judicial review process, the civil action must be filed within 60 calendar days after receipt of the review

¶516

entity's certification, unless the time for filing is extended by the ALJ or Medicare Appeals Council upon a showing of good cause. [42 C.F.R. § 423.2136(c).]

Remand of the case by the court. When a federal district court remands a case to the HHS Secretary for further consideration, the Medicare Appeals Council may (1) make a decision; or (2) remand the case to an ALJ or attorney adjudicator with instructions to take action and either issue a decision, take other action, or return the case to the Medicare Appeals Council with a recommended decision. [42 C.F.R. § 423.2138.] When a federal district court remands a case for further consideration and the Medicare Appeals Council further remands the case to an ALJ or attorney adjudicator, a decision subsequently issued by the ALJ or attorney adjudicator becomes the final decision of the Secretary unless the Medicare Appeals Council assumes jurisdiction. [42 C.F.R. § 423.2140(a).]

Written exceptions to ALJ remand decision. If an enrollee disagrees with an ALJ or attorney adjudicator decision (after remand of the case from the district court and further remand from the Medicare Appeals Council), he or she may file exceptions to the decision with the Medicare Appeals Council. The enrollee must submit a written statement setting forth the reasons for disagreeing with the ALJ or attorney adjudicator decision within 30 calendar days of receiving the decision (and the Medicare Appeals Council will grant a timely request for a 30-day extension). [42 C.F.R. § 423.2140(b).]

If the Medicare Appeals Council concludes that there is no reason to change the ALJ's or attorney adjudicator's decision, it must issue a notice addressing the exceptions and explaining why no change is necessary. When this occurs, the decision of the ALJ or attorney adjudicator is considered a final decision of the HHS Secretary. When an enrollee files written exceptions to the decision of the ALJ, the Medicare Appeals Council may decide to assume jurisdiction. If it assumes jurisdiction, it makes a new, independent decision based on its consideration of the entire record adopting, modifying, or reversing the decision of the ALJ or remanding the case to an ALJ for further proceedings, including a new decision. This new decision of the Medicare Appeals Council is the final decision of the Secretary. [42 C.F.R. § 423.2140(b).]

Medicare Appeals Council jurisdiction without written exceptions. Any time within 60 calendar days after the date of the written decision of the ALJ or attorney adjudicator, the Medicare Appeals Council may decide to assume jurisdiction of the case even though no written exceptions have been filed by the enrollee. After giving notice to the enrollee and providing the opportunity to file a brief regarding the relevant facts and law in the case (usually 30 calendar days), the Medicare Appeals Council will either issue a final decision of the HHS Secretary affirming, modifying, or reversing the decision of the ALJ or attorney adjudicator, or remand the case to an ALJ for further proceedings, including a new decision. [42 C.F.R. § 423.2140(c).]

Expedited Access to Judicial Review

To obtain expedited access to judicial review (EAJR), a "review entity" must certify that the Medicare Appeals Council does not have the authority to decide the question of law or regulation relevant to the matters in dispute and there is no material issue of fact in dispute. For purposes of EAJR, a "review entity" is defined as an entity of up to three reviewers who are ALJs or members of the Departmental Appeals Board. [42 C.F.R. § 423.1990(a).]

An enrollee may request EAJR in place of an ALJ hearing or Medicare Appeals Council review if:

> (1) an IRE has made a reconsideration determination and the enrollee has filed a request for an ALJ or attorney adjudicator hearing and a final decision, dismissal order, or remand order of the ALJ or attorney adjudicator has not been issued; or an ALJ or

attorney adjudicator has made a decision and the enrollee has filed a request for Medicare Appeals Council review and a final decision, dismissal order, or remand order of the Medicare Appeals Council has not been issued;

(2) the requestor is an enrollee;

(3) the amount remaining in controversy meets the threshold requirements;

(4) when there is more than one enrollee to the ALJ hearing or Medicare Appeals Council review, each enrollee concurs, in writing, with the request for the EAJR; and

(5) there are no material issues of fact in dispute.

[42 C.F.R. § 423.1990(b).]

Method of filing. An enrollee may include an EAJR request in his or her request for an ALJ or attorney adjudicator hearing or Medicare Appeals Council review or, if an appeal is already pending, the enrollee may file a written EAJR request with the HHS Departmental Appeals Board. The ALJ hearing office or Medicare Appeals Council must forward the EAJR request to the review entity within five calendar days of receipt. The enrollee must file a request for EAJR: (1) any time before receipt of the notice of the ALJ's or attorney adjudicator's decision, if the enrollee has requested an ALJ or attorney adjudicator hearing; or (2) any time before receipt of notice of the Medicare Appeals Council's decision, if the enrollee has requested Medicare Appeals Council review. [42 C.F.R. § 423.1990(d).]

Review entity's action on EAJR request. Within 60 calendar days after the date the review entity receives a EAJR request and the accompanying documents and materials, the review entity will issue either a certification or a denial of the request. The certification or denial by the review entity is binding and not subject to review by the HHS Secretary. If the review entity fails to certify or deny the EAJR request within the 60-calendar-day time frame, the enrollee may bring a civil action in federal district court within 60 calendar days. [42 C.F.R. § 423.1990(e).]

If the review entity certifies the EAJR request, the enrollee automatically waives any right to completion of the remaining steps in the administrative appeals process and has 60 calendar days, beginning on the date of the certification, to bring a civil action in federal district court. If a request for EAJR does not meet the conditions set forth above or if the review entity does not certify the request, the review entity must advise the enrollee in writing that the request has been denied and return the request to OMHA or the Medicare Appeals Council. The ALJ or Medicare Appeals Council will treat the rejection as a request for an ALJ hearing or for Medicare Appeals Council review. [42 C.F.R. § 423.1990(g), (h).]

[¶ 525] Cost Control and Quality Improvement Requirements

Part D sponsors must implement certain cost control and quality improvement requirements, including the establishment of a drug utilization management program, quality assurance (QA) measures and systems, and a medication therapy management program (MTMP). Part 423 Subpart D of the Medicare Part D regulations and Chapter 7 of the *Medicare Prescription Drug Benefits Manual*, Pub. 100-18, implement these administrative provisions.

Drug Utilization Management, QA, and MTMPs

Part D sponsors must establish a drug utilization management program, QA measures and systems, and an MTMP. Each of these requirements affects the quality and cost of care provided to beneficiaries. [Soc. Sec. Act § 1860D-4(c); 42 C.F.R. § 423.153(a).] The drug utilization management and MTMP requirements, however, do not apply to private fee-for-

¶525

service Medicare Advantage (MA) plans offering qualified prescription drug coverage. [Soc. Sec. Act § 1860D-21(d)(3); 42 C.F.R. § 423.153(e).]

Drug utilization management program. Sponsors have considerable flexibility in the design of their drug utilization management programs. The minimum requirements are that a plan must:

(1) maintain a program that includes incentives to reduce costs where medically appropriate;

(2) maintain policies and systems to assist in preventing over-utilization and under-utilization of prescribed medications;

(3) provide CMS with information concerning the procedures and performance of its drug utilization management program, according to guidelines specified by CMS; and

(4) establish a daily cost-sharing rate for drugs dispensed for a supply less than the approved month's supply, if the drug is in the form of a solid oral dose (except for solid oral doses of antibiotics and solid oral doses that are dispensed in their original container) and may be dispensed for less than the approved month's supply under applicable law; the co-payment is calculated by multiplying the applicable daily cost-sharing rate by the days' supply actually dispensed.

[42 C.F.R. § 423.153(b).]

Quality assurance measures and systems. A Part D sponsor must have established QA measures and systems to reduce medication errors and adverse drug interactions and improve medication use. The QA measures and systems must include:

(1) representation that network providers are required to comply with minimum standards for pharmacy practice as established by the states;

(2) concurrent drug utilization review systems, policies, and procedures designed to ensure that a review of the prescribed drug therapy is performed before each prescription is dispensed (the review must include, but not be limited to: screening for potential drug therapy problems due to therapeutic duplication; age/gender-related contraindications; over-utilization and under-utilization; drug-drug interactions; incorrect drug dosage or duration of drug therapy; drug-allergy contraindications; and clinical abuse/misuse);

(3) retrospective drug utilization review systems, policies, and procedures designed to ensure ongoing periodic examination of claims data and other records, through computerized drug claims processing and information retrieval systems, to identify patterns of inappropriate or medically unnecessary care among enrollees or patterns associated with specific drugs;

(4) internal medication error identification and reduction systems; and

(5) provision of information to CMS regarding quality assurance measures and systems.

[42 C.F.R. § 423.153(c).]

Medication therapy management programs. A Part D sponsor must establish a MTMP that is designed to:

(1) optimize therapeutic outcomes for targeted beneficiaries (described below) by improving medication use;

(2) reduce adverse drug events (including adverse drug interactions) for targeted beneficiaries;

(3) be furnished by a pharmacist or other qualified provider;

(4) distinguish between services in ambulatory and institutional settings;

(5) target beneficiaries using an opt-out method of enrollment only;

(6) target enrollees for enrollment in the MTMP at least quarterly; and

(7) offer a minimum level of MTMP services to each beneficiary.

[Soc. Sec. Act § 1860D-4(c); 42 C.F.R. § 423.153(d)(1); Pub. 100-18, Ch. 7, § 30.1.]

The minimum level of MTMP services includes:

(1) interventions for both beneficiaries and prescribers;

(2) annual comprehensive medication review with written summaries, which must include an interactive, person-to-person, or telehealth consultation performed by a pharmacist or other qualified provider (unless the beneficiary is in a long-term care setting) and may result in a recommended medication action plan;

(3) quarterly targeted medication reviews with follow-up interventions when necessary; and

(4) standardized action plans and summaries that comply with requirements for the standardized format.

[Soc. Sec. Act § 1860D-4(c)(2)(C); 42 C.F.R. § 423.153(d)(1)(vii).]

Targeted beneficiaries. Targeted beneficiaries for the MTMP are enrollees in the sponsor's Part D plan who:

(1) have multiple chronic diseases (such as diabetes, asthma, hypertension, hyperlipidemia, and congestive heart failure), with three chronic diseases being the maximum number a Part D plan sponsor may require;

(2) are taking multiple Part D drugs, with eight Part D drugs being the maximum number of drugs a plan sponsor may require; and

(3) are likely to incur annual Part D drug costs in an amount greater than or equal to $3000 increased by the annual percentage increase in average per capita aggregate expenditures for Part D drugs in the United States for Part D eligible individuals based on data for the 12-month period ending in July of the previous year.

Beginning January 1, 2021, targeted beneficiaries for the MTMP also include at-risk beneficiaries for prescription drug abuse as defined in Soc. Sec. Act § 1860D-4(c)(5)(C). [Soc. Sec. Act § 1860D-4(c)(2)(A)(ii), as amended by SUPPORT for Patients and Communities Act (P.L. 115-271) § 6064; 42 C.F.R. § 423.153(d)(2); Pub. 100-18, Ch. 7, § 30.2.]

Cooperation with pharmacists and physicians. The MTMP must be developed in cooperation with licensed and practicing pharmacists and physicians and coordinated with any care management plan established for a targeted individual under a chronic care improvement program (CCIP). A sponsor must provide drug claims data to CCIPs for those beneficiaries who are enrolled in CCIPs. [Soc. Sec. Act § 1860D-4(c)(2)(E), (F); 42 C.F.R. § 423.153(d)(3), (4); Pub. 100-18, Ch. 7, § 30.4.]

To become a Part D sponsor, an applicant must describe how it takes into account the resources used and time required to implement the MTMP it chooses to adopt in establishing fees for pharmacists or others providing MTMP services, and disclose to CMS upon request the amount of the management and dispensing fees and the portion paid for MTMP services to pharmacists. Reports of these amounts are protected. [Soc. Sec. Act § 1860D-4(c)(2)(G); 42 C.F.R. § 423.153(d)(5).]

¶525

Drug Management Program for At-Risk Beneficiaries

Part D sponsors are permitted to establish a drug management program for at-risk beneficiaries that limits their access to frequently abused drugs for plan years beginning on January 1, 2019. On January 1, 2022, the program will become mandatory. [Soc. Sec. Act § 1860D-4(c); 42 C.F.R. § 423.153(f).]

Generally, an "at-risk beneficiary for prescription drug abuse" means a Part D eligible individual (1) who is identified through the use of clinical guidelines that indicate misuse or abuse of prescription drugs; or (2) with respect to whom the PDP sponsor of a prescription drug plan, upon enrolling such individual in such plan, received notice that he or she was identified to be an at-risk beneficiary under the prescription drug plan in which the individual was most recently previously enrolled. It excludes individuals who are receiving hospice care or are residents of a long-term care (LTC) facility, intermediate care facility, or another facility for which frequently abused drugs are dispensed for residents through a contract with a single pharmacy. [Soc. Sec. Act § 1860D-4(c)(5)(C)(i), (ii).]

Utilization management tools to prevent drug abuse. A PDP sponsor must have in place a utilization management tool to prevent drug abuse. Such a tool includes any of the following: (1) a utilization tool designed to prevent the abuse of frequently abused drugs by individuals and to prevent the diversion of such drugs at pharmacies; (2) retrospective utilization review to identify (a) individuals that receive frequently abused drugs at a frequency or in amounts that are not clinically appropriate, and (b) providers or suppliers that may facilitate the abuse or diversion of frequently abused drugs by beneficiaries; or (3) consultation with the Medicare drug integrity contractor (MEDIC) to verify if an individual enrolling in a prescription drug plan offered by a PDP sponsor has been previously identified by another PDP sponsor as an individual that receives frequently abused drugs at a frequency or in amounts that are not clinically appropriate. [Soc. Sec. Act § 1860D-4(c)(1)(E), (c)(6).]

Medicare drug integrity contractors. Beginning January 1, 2019, the HHS Secretary is required to authorize MEDICs to directly accept prescription and necessary medical records from entities such as pharmacies, prescription drug plans, Medicare Advantage prescription drug plans (MA-PDs), and physicians to aid in the determination of whether such individual is an at-risk beneficiary for prescription drug abuse. MEDICs must respond to requests by prescription drug sponsors or MA-PDs within 15 days. [Soc. Sec. Act § 1893(j).]

Requirements Regarding Outlier Prescribers of Opioids

By January 1, 2021, CMS must provide a prescriber identified as an outlier prescriber of opioids an annual notification that it has been so identified, including resources on proper prescribing methods and other information. CMS will aggregate and provide persistent outlier prescriber information on the CMS website. The information will not identify any specific prescriber. [Soc. Sec. Act § 1860D-4(c)(4)(D), as added by SUPPORT for Patients and Communities Act § 6065.]

A prescriber persistently identified by CMS as an outlier prescriber of opioids may be required to enroll in an enhanced oversight program under Soc. Sec. Act § 1866(j) for a period sufficient to correct the prescribing patterns that lead to identification of the prescriber as a persistent outlier prescriber of opioids. At least annually, CMS must communicate information on persistent outlier prescribers to PDP sponsors and MA organizations offering MA-PD plans. [Soc. Sec. Act § 1860D-4(c)(4)(D)(v), as added by SUPPORT for Patients and Communities Act § 6065.]

Part D Quality Rating System

CMS calculates an overall Star Rating, Part C summary rating, and Part D summary rating for each MA-PD contract, and a Part D summary rating for each MA-only contract using the 5-star rating system. The ratings calculated and assigned for each Part D plan are used by CMS to provide: (1) comparative information on plan quality and performance to beneficiaries for their use in making knowledgeable enrollment and coverage decisions; (2) quality ratings on a 5-star rating system; and (3) a means to evaluate and oversee overall and specific compliance with certain regulatory and contract requirements by Part D plans. [42 C.F.R. §§ 423.180, 423.182.]

Requirements for Dispensing Drugs in Long-Term Care Facilities

Generally, when dispensing covered Part D drugs to enrollees who reside in long-term care facilities, a Part D sponsor must:

(1) require all pharmacies servicing LTC facilities to dispense solid oral doses of brand-name drugs in no greater than 14-day increments at a time and permit the use of uniform dispensing techniques as defined by the LTC facilities in which the enrollees reside;

(2) not penalize LTCs' choice of more efficient uniform dispensing techniques by prorating dispensing fees based on days' supply or quantity dispensed;

(3) ensure that any difference in payment methodology among LTC pharmacies incentivizes more efficient dispensing techniques; and

(4) collect and report information on the dispensing methodology used for each dispensing event described in (1).

[Soc. Sec. Act § 1860D-4(c)(3); 42 C.F.R. § 423.154(a).]

Excluded from the above LTC dispensing requirements are: (1) solid oral doses of antibiotics; and (2) solid oral doses that are dispensed in their original container as indicated in the Food and Drug Administration Prescribing Information or are customarily dispensed in their original packaging to assist patients with compliance (for example, oral contraceptives). [42 C.F.R. § 423.154(b).]

CMS waives these dispensing requirements, except for (2) and (3), for pharmacies when they service intermediate care facilities for individuals with intellectual disabilities, institutes for mental disease, and Indian Tribe and Tribal Organization, and Urban Indian Organization (I/T/U) pharmacies. [42 C.F.R. § 423.154(c).]

The terms and conditions offered by a Part D sponsor must be in accordance with federal and state law and address the disposal of drugs that have been dispensed to an enrollee in a LTC facility, but not used, and that have been returned to the pharmacy. The terms for return for credit and reuse must also be permitted under state law. [42 C.F.R. § 423.154(d).]

Customer Satisfaction Surveys for Part D Plans

Part D plans with 600 or more enrollees as of July of the prior year must contract with approved Medicare Consumer Assessment of Healthcare Providers and Systems (CAHPS) survey vendors to conduct the Medicare CAHPS satisfaction survey of Part D plan enrollees in accordance with CMS specifications and submit the survey data to CMS. [Soc. Sec. Act § 1860D-4(d); 42 C.F.R. § 423.156.]

¶525

Electronic Prescription Drug Program

Prescribers and dispensers who electronically transmit prescription and certain other information for covered drugs prescribed for Medicare Part D eligible beneficiaries are required to comply with any electronic prescription standards that are in effect. [Soc. Sec. Act § 1860D-4(e); 42 C.F.R. § § 423.159(c), 423.160(a).]

Beginning January 1, 2021, prescriptions for a schedule II, III, IV, or V controlled substance covered under a PDP or MA-PD must be transmitted in accordance with an electronic prescription drug program. CMS may waive this requirement in certain defined cases. [Soc. Sec. Act § 1860D-4(e)(7), as added by SUPPORT for Patients and Communities Act § 2003.]

In addition, to help prevent the addiction of susceptible seniors to prescription drugs, beginning with the 2021 plan year, the Part D program will require the secure electronic transmission of prior authorization requests from the prescribing health care professional for a covered Part D drug to the PDP sponsor or MA organization offering a prescription drug plan and the secure electronic transmission of a response from the PDP sponsor or MA organization to the prescriber. To be considered an electronic transmission, the transmission must comply with the technical standards adopted by CMS. [Soc. Sec. Act § 1860D-4(e)(2)(E), as added by SUPPORT for Patients and Communities Act § 6062.]

Assistance by QIOs

Quality improvement organizations (QIOs) must offer providers, practitioners, and Part D sponsors quality improvement assistance pertaining to health care services, including those related to prescription drug therapy. To accomplish this requirement, QIOs need access to data from transactions between pharmacies and Part D plans. Any such information collected by the QIOs is subject to CMS confidentiality requirements. Part D sponsors are required to provide information directly to QIOs and to CMS for distribution to QIOs. [42 C.F.R. § 423.162; Pub. 100-18, Ch. 7, § 20.8.]

Compliance Based on Accreditation

A Part D sponsor can be deemed to meet certain requirements if: (1) it is fully accredited (and periodically reaccredited) for the standards related to the applicable area by a private, national accreditation organization (AO) approved by CMS; and (2) the AO uses the standards approved by CMS for the purposes of assessing the Part D sponsor's compliance with Medicare requirements. [Soc. Sec. Act § 1860D-4(j); 42 C.F.R. § 423.165(a).]

The requirements related to the following areas are deemable:

(1) access to covered drugs (42 C.F.R. § § 423.120 and 423.124);

(2) drug utilization management programs, QA measures and systems, and MTMPs (42 C.F.R. § § 423.120 and 423.124); and

(3) privacy, confidentiality, and accuracy of enrollee records (42 C.F.R. § 423.136).

[Soc. Sec. Act § 1860D-4(j); 42 C.F.R. § 423.165(b).]

Deemed Part D sponsor obligations. A Part D sponsor that is deemed to meet Medicare requirements must submit to CMS surveys, which are intended to validate AO processes. CMS will remove part or all of a Part D sponsor's deemed status if: (1) CMS determines, on the basis of its own investigation, that the sponsor does not meet the Medicare requirements for which deemed status was granted; (2) CMS withdraws its approval of the AO that accredited the sponsor; or (3) the sponsor fails to meet the above requirements of a deemed Part D sponsor. [42 C.F.R. § 423.165(d), (e).]

Enforcement authority. CMS retains the authority to initiate enforcement action against any Part D sponsor that it determines, on the basis of a CMS survey or the results of the accreditation survey, no longer meets the Medicare requirements for which deemed status was granted. [42 C.F.R. § 423.165(f).]

[¶ 530] Payments to Sponsors of Retiree Prescription Drug Plans

The sponsors of qualified retiree prescription drug plans (PDPs) can receive an annual subsidy equal to 28 percent of specified retiree drug costs for each qualifying covered retiree. [Soc. Sec. Act § 1860D-22(a)(3); 42 C.F.R. § 423.886.]

Requirements for Qualified Retiree Prescription Drug Plans

Employment-based retiree health coverage is considered to be a qualified retiree PDP if the sponsor:

(1) submits an actuarial attestation;

(2) provides Part D eligible individuals covered under the plan with creditable coverage notices; and

(3) maintains records and makes them available for audit.

[Soc. Sec. Act § 1860D-22(a)(2); 42 C.F.R. § 423.884(a).]

Disclosure of information. The sponsor must have a written agreement with its health insurance issuer or group health plan regarding disclosure of information to CMS, and the issuer or plan must disclose to CMS, on behalf of the sponsor, the information necessary for the sponsor to comply with CMS requirements. [42 C.F.R. § 423.884(b).]

Submitting an Application for Retiree PDP Subsidy

The sponsor seeking a subsidy for a qualified retiree PDP must submit an application to CMS that includes the following information:

(1) employer tax ID number;

(2) sponsor name and address;

(3) contact name and e-mail address;

(4) actuarial attestation (see below) and any other supporting documentation required by CMS for each qualified retiree PDP for which the sponsor seeks subsidy payments;

(5) a list of all individuals the sponsor believes are qualifying covered retirees enrolled in each PDP, including spouses and dependents, if Medicare eligible, along with the listed individual's: (a) full name, (b) Health Insurance Claim (HIC) number or Social Security number, (c) date of birth, (d) gender, and (e) relationship to the retired employee (Note: a sponsor may satisfy this requirement by entering into a voluntary data sharing agreement with CMS);

(6) a signed sponsor agreement; and

(7) any other information specified by CMS.

[42 C.F.R. § 423.884(c)(1), (2).]

An authorized representative of the requesting sponsor must sign the completed application and certify that the information contained in the application is true and accurate. [42 C.F.R. § 423.884(c)(4).]

Terms and conditions for subsidy payment. To receive a subsidy payment, the sponsor must specifically accept and agree to:

(1) comply with the terms and conditions of eligibility for a subsidy payment;

(2) acknowledge that at the same time that CMS releases Part C and Part D summary payment data, it also will release Part D retiree drug subsidy payment data for the most recently reconciled year, including the name of the eligible sponsor, the total gross aggregate dollar amount of the CMS subsidy, and the number of eligible retirees;

(3) acknowledge that the information in the application is being provided to obtain federal funds; and

(4) require that all subcontractors, including plan administrators, acknowledge that information provided in connection with the subcontract is used for purposes of obtaining federal funds.

[42 C.F.R. § 423.884(c)(3).]

Application timing and required updates. A sponsor must submit an application for a given plan year before the beginning of the plan year, unless CMS approves an extension. The sponsor must provide updates of the application's information to CMS on a monthly basis or at a frequency specified by CMS. [42 C.F.R. § 423.884(c)(5), (6).]

CMS data match. Once the full application for the subsidy payment is submitted, CMS matches the names and identifying information of the individuals submitted as qualifying covered retirees with a CMS database to determine which retirees are Part D eligible individuals who are not enrolled in a Part D plan. CMS provides information concerning the results of the search (names and identifying information) to the sponsor. [42 C.F.R. § 423.884(c)(7).]

Actuarial Attestation Requirements

The sponsor of the plan must provide to CMS an attestation (in a form and manner specified by CMS) that must include the following assurances:

(1) The actuarial gross value of the retiree prescription drug coverage under the plan for the plan year is at least equal to the actuarial gross value of the defined standard prescription drug coverage under Part D for the plan year in question, not taking into account the value of any discount or coverage provided in the coverage gap.

(2) The actuarial net value of the retiree prescription drug coverage under the plan for that plan year is at least equal to the actuarial net value of the defined standard prescription drug coverage under Part D for the plan year in question, not taking into account the value of any discount or coverage provided in the coverage gap.

(3) The actuarial values is determined using the methodology described below.

[42 C.F.R. § 423.884(d)(1).]

Actuarial requirements. A qualified actuary (member of the American Academy of Actuaries) must make and sign the attestation, which must state that the attestation is true and accurate. Applicants may use qualified outside actuaries, including actuaries employed by the plan administrator or an insurer providing benefits under the plan. The attestation must contain an acknowledgment that the information being provided in the attestation is being used to obtain federal funds. [42 C.F.R. § 423.884(d)(2)–(4).]

Methodology. The attestation must be based on generally accepted actuarial principles and any actuarial guidelines established by CMS. To the extent CMS has not provided guidance on a specific aspect of the actuarial equivalence standard, an actuary providing the attestation may rely on any reasonable interpretation of the CMS regulations and Soc. Sec. Act § 1860D-22(a) consistent with generally accepted actuarial principles in determining actuarial values. [42 C.F.R. § 423.884(d)(5).]

Timing. The sponsor must provide the attestation annually at the time it submits its subsidy application. If there is a material change to the drug coverage of the sponsor's retiree prescription drug plan, the sponsor must provide its the attestation within 90 days before the implementation of the change. The term "material change" means the addition of a benefit option that does not affect the actuarial value of the retiree prescription drug coverage under the sponsor's plan. [42 C.F.R. § 423.884(d)(6).]

Notice of a failure to continue to satisfy the actuarial equivalence standard. A sponsor must notify CMS no later than 90 days before the implementation of a change to the drug coverage that affects the actuarial value of the retiree prescription drug coverage under the sponsor's plan such that it no longer meets the actuarial equivalence standards. [42 C.F.R. § 423.884(d)(7).]

Retiree Drug Subsidy Amounts

For each qualifying covered retiree enrolled with the sponsor of a qualified retiree PDP in a plan year, the sponsor receives a subsidy payment in the amount of 28 percent of the allowable retiree costs in the plan year that are attributable to gross retiree costs that exceed the cost threshold and do not exceed the cost limit (see below). The subsidy payment is calculated by first determining gross retiree costs between the cost threshold and cost limit and then determining allowable retiree costs attributable to the gross retiree costs. [Soc. Sec. Act § 1860D-22(a)(3)(A); 42 C.F.R. § 423.886(a).]

Cost threshold and cost limit. The cost threshold and cost limit for qualified retiree prescription drug plans are adjusted in the same manner as the annual Part D deductible and out-of-pocket threshold are adjusted annually. For 2020, the cost threshold is $435 and the cost limit is $8,950. [Soc. Sec. Act § 1860D-22(a)(3)(B); 42 C.F.R. § 423.886(b)(3); *Announcement of Calendar Year 2020 Medicare Advantage Capitation Rates and Medicare Advantage and Part D Payment Policies and Final Call Letter*, April 1, 2019.]

Payment Methods and Providing Necessary Information

The provisions governing payment to Part D plan sponsors for qualified prescription drug coverage, including requirements to provide information necessary to ensure accurate subsidy payments, also govern the subsidy payment to sponsors of retiree PDPs. Payment by CMS is conditioned on provision of accurate information. The sponsor must submit the information in a form and manner and at the times provided by CMS. CMS will make payment after the sponsor submits the cost data. [42 C.F.R. § 423.888(a), (b)(3).]

Timing and submission of cost data. Payment can be on a monthly, quarterly, or annual basis, as elected by the plan sponsor, unless CMS decides to restrict the options because of operational limitations. If the plan sponsor elects for payment on a monthly or quarterly basis, it must provide cost data on the same monthly or quarterly basis, or at such time as CMS specifies. If the sponsor elects an annual payment, it must submit to CMS actual rebate and other price concession data within 15 months after the end of the plan year. [42 C.F.R. § 423.888(b).]

Special rule for insured plans. Sponsors of group health plans that provide benefits through health insurance coverage and choose monthly payments, quarterly payments, or an interim annual payment may elect to determine gross covered plan-related retiree prescription drug costs for purposes of the monthly, quarterly, or interim annual payments based on a portion of the premium costs paid by the sponsor or the qualifying covered retirees. Premium costs that are determined using generally accepted actuarial principles may be attributable to the gross prescription drug costs incurred by the health insurance issuer for the sponsor's qualifying covered retirees, except that administrative costs and risk charges must be subtracted from the premium. [42 C.F.R. § 423.888(b)(5)(i).]

Maintaining records. The sponsor of the qualified retiree PDP or a designee must maintain for a period of six years and furnish to CMS or the Office of Inspector General, upon request, the following records:

(1) reports and working documents of the actuaries who wrote the attestation;

(2) all documentation of costs incurred and other relevant information utilized for calculating the amount of the subsidy payment, including the underlying claims data; and

(3) any other records specified by CMS.

[42 C.F.R. § 423.888(d).]

Appeals by Retiree Prescription Drug Plans

A sponsor is entitled to an informal written reconsideration of an adverse initial determination by CMS regarding the amount of the retiree PDP subsidy payment; the actuarial equivalence of the sponsor's retiree PDP; whether an enrollee in a retiree PDP is a qualifying covered retiree; or any other similar determination affecting eligibility for, or the amount of, a subsidy payment. An initial determination is final and binding unless reconsidered. [42 C.F.R. § 423.890(a)(1), (2).]

Informal hearing request. A sponsor dissatisfied with the CMS reconsideration decision is entitled to an informal hearing. The sponsor must make file a written hearing request with CMS within 15 days of the date the sponsor receives the CMS reconsideration decision. The CMS hearing officer is limited to the review of the record that was before CMS when CMS made both its initial and reconsideration determinations. [42 C.F.R. § 423.890(b)(1), (2), (3).]

The CMS hearing officer decides the case and sends a written decision to the sponsor, explaining the basis for the decision. The hearing officer decision is final and binding, unless the decision is reversed or modified by the Administrator. [42 C.F.R. § 423.890(b)(4), (5).]

Review by the Administrator. A sponsor that has received a hearing officer decision upholding a CMS initial or reconsidered determination may request review by the Administrator within 15 days of receipt of the decision. The Administrator's determination is final and binding. [42 C.F.R. § 423.890(c).]

Reopening of initial or reconsidered determination. CMS may reopen and revise an initial or reconsidered determination upon its own motion or upon the request of a sponsor within one year of the date of the notice of determination for any reason, within four years for good cause, and at any time when the underlying decision was obtained through fraud or similar fault. [42 C.F.R. § 423.890(d)(1).]

A decision by CMS not to reopen an initial or reconsidered determination is final and binding and cannot be appealed. [42 C.F.R. § 423.890(d)(6).]

Change of Ownership Requirements for Retiree Prescription Drug Plan Sponsors

Sponsors who apply for a retiree drug subsidy payment must comply with certain change of ownership requirements. A change of ownership includes:

- the removal, addition, or substitution of a partner, unless the partners expressly agree otherwise as permitted by applicable state law;

- transfer of all or substantially all of the assets of the sponsor to another party; or

- the merger of the sponsor's corporation into another corporation or the consolidation of the sponsor's organization with one or more other corporations, resulting in a new corporate body.

The transfer of corporate stock or the merger of another corporation into the sponsor's corporation with the sponsor surviving does not ordinarily constitute change of ownership. [42 C.F.R. § 423.892(a), (b).]

Notice requirement. A sponsor that has a retiree PDP in effect and is considering or negotiating a change in ownership must notify CMS at least 60 days before the anticipated effective date of the change. [42 C.F.R. § 423.892(c).]

Automatic assignment. When there is a change of ownership that results in a transfer of the liability for prescription drug costs, the existing sponsor agreement is automatically assigned to the new owner. The new owner to whom a sponsor agreement is assigned is subject to all applicable statutes and regulations and to the terms and conditions of the sponsor agreement. [42 C.F.R. § 423.892(d), (e).]

[¶ 535] Communication Requirements

CMS has established prohibitions and limitations on the communication, sales, and marketing activities of Medicare Advantage (MA) and prescription drug plans (PDPs).

Communication materials means all information provided to current and prospective enrollees. Marketing materials are a subset of communication materials. Marketing materials include, but are not limited to, the following:

(1) materials such as brochures; posters; advertisements in media such as newspapers, magazines, television, radio, billboards, or the internet; and social media content;

(2) materials used by marketing representatives such as scripts or outlines for telemarketing or other presentations; and

(3) presentation materials such as slides and charts.

[42 C.F.R. § 423.2260.]

Materials that do not include the following are not considered marketing materials:

(1) information about the plan's benefit structure or cost-sharing;

(2) information about measuring or ranking standards (for example, star ratings);

(3) mention benefits or cost-sharing, but do not meet the definition of marketing;

(4) unless otherwise specified by CMS based on their use or purpose, materials that are required under 42 C.F.R. § 423.128; or

(5) any materials specifically designated by CMS as not meeting the definition of the proposed marketing definition based on their use or purpose.

[42 C.F.R. § 423.2260.]

CMS Review of Part D Marketing Materials

A Part D plan may not distribute any marketing materials or make such materials or forms available to eligible individuals unless, at least 45 days before the date of distribution, the sponsor submits the material or form to CMS for review, and CMS does not disapprove of the distribution. This time period may be reduced to 10 days if the plan's marketing materials use, without modification, CMS-specified proposed model language and format, including standardized language and formatting. [Soc. Sec. Act §§ 1851(h)(1), (5), 1860D-1(b)(1)(B)(vi); 42 C.F.R. § 423.2262(a).]

The Part D sponsor may distribute certain designated marketing materials five days following their submission to CMS if the sponsor certifies that it followed all applicable marketing guidelines and, when applicable, used CMS model language without modification. [42 C.F.R. § 423.2262(b).]

CMS review guidelines. In reviewing marketing material or election forms under 42 C.F.R. § 423.2262, CMS determines that the materials:

(1) provide interested Medicare beneficiaries an adequate written description of rules, procedures, basic benefits and services, and fees and other charges in a format (and, where appropriate, print size) and using standard terminology that may be specified by CMS;

(2) notify the general public of its enrollment period in an appropriate manner, through appropriate media, throughout its service area;

(3) include in written materials notice that the Part D sponsor is authorized by law to refuse to renew its contract with CMS, CMS also may refuse to renew the contract, and termination or non-renewal may result in termination of the beneficiary's enrollment in the Part D plan; and

(4) ensure that materials are not materially inaccurate or misleading or otherwise make material misrepresentations.

[Soc. Sec. Act §§ 1851(h)(2), 1860D-1(b)(1)(B)(vi); 42 C.F.R. § 423.2264(a).]

Materials "deemed" approved. If CMS does not disapprove marketing materials within the specified review time frame, the materials are deemed approved and the Part D sponsor may use them. [Soc. Sec. Act §§ 1851(h)(3), 1860D-1(b)(1)(B)(vi); 42 C.F.R. § 423.2262(a)(2).]

Communication and Marketing Standards for Part D Plans

In conducting communication activities, a Part D plan may not:

- provide information that is inaccurate or misleading;

- engage in activities that could mislead or confuse Medicare beneficiaries or misrepresent the Part D sponsor;

- claim the sponsor is recommended or endorsed by CMS or Medicare or that CMS or Medicare recommends that the beneficiary enroll in the Part D plan;

- employ Part D plan names that suggest that a plan is not available to all Medicare beneficiaries;

- display the names and/or logos of co-branded network providers or pharmacies on the sponsor's member identification card, unless the names and/or logos are related to the member selection of specific provider organizations;

- use a plan name that does not include the plan type; and

- for markets with a significant non-English speaking population, provide vital materials, unless in the language of these individuals. Part D sponsors must translate materials into any non-English language that is the primary language of at least 5 percent of the individuals in a plan benefit package (PBP) service area.

[Soc. Sec. Act §§ 1851(h)(4), (6), (j), 1860D-4(l); 42 C.F.R. § 423.2268(a).]

In marketing, Part D sponsors may not do any of the following:

- provide cash or other monetary rebates as an inducement for enrollment or otherwise;

- offer gifts to potential enrollees, unless the gifts are of nominal value, are offered to all potential enrollees without regard to whether the beneficiary enrolls, and are not in the form of cash or other monetary rebates;

- market non-health care/nonprescription drug plan related products to prospective enrollees during any Part D sales activity or presentation;

- market any health-related product during a marketing appointment beyond the scope agreed upon by the beneficiary, and documented by the plan, prior to the appointment;

- market additional health-related lines of plan business not identified prior to an individual appointment without a separate scope of appointment identifying the additional lines of business to be discussed;

- distribute marketing materials for which, before expiration of the 45-day period, the Part D sponsor receives from CMS written notice of disapproval because it is inaccurate or misleading, or misrepresents the Part D sponsor, its marketing representatives, or CMS;

- conduct sales presentations or distribute and accept Part D plan enrollment forms in provider offices or other areas where health care is delivered to individuals, except when such activities are conducted in common areas in health care settings;

- conduct sales presentations or distribute and accept plan applications at educational events;

- display the names and/or logos of provider co-branding partners on marketing materials, unless the materials clearly indicate that other providers are available in the network;

- knowingly target or send unsolicited marketing materials to any Part D enrollee, whose prior year enrollment was in an MA plan, during the open enrollment period;

- engage in any other marketing activity prohibited by CMS in its marketing guidance;

- engage in any discriminatory activity such as attempting to recruit Medicare beneficiaries from higher income areas without making comparable efforts to enroll Medicare beneficiaries from lower income areas;

- solicit door-to-door for Medicare beneficiaries or through other unsolicited means of direct contact, including calling a beneficiary without the beneficiary initiating the contact;

- use providers or provider groups to distribute printed information comparing the benefits of different health plans unless the providers, provider groups, or pharmacies accept and display materials from all health plans with which they contract; or

- provide meals to potential enrollees, regardless of value.

[Soc. Sec. Act §§ 1851(h)(4), (6), (j), 1860D-4(l); 42 C.F.R. § 423.2268(a).]

In its marketing, the Part D organization must demonstrate to the satisfaction of CMS that marketing resources are allocated to marketing to the disabled Medicare population (under age 65) as well as beneficiaries age 65 and over. A Part D plan also must establish and maintain a system for confirming that enrolled beneficiaries have enrolled in the PDP and understand the rules applicable under the plan. [42 C.F.R. § 423.2272(a), (b).]

Licensing of Part D Marketing Representatives

A Part D organization must employ as marketing representatives only those individuals who are licensed by the state to conduct direct marketing activities in that state. The sponsor must inform the state that it has appointed these individuals as marketing representatives as required by the appointment process provided for under state law. The organization must also report the termination of any such agent or broker to the state, including the reasons for such termination if state law requires that the reasons for the termination be reported. [Soc. Sec. Act §§ 1851(h)(7), 1860D-4(l); 42 C.F.R. § 423.2272(c), (d).]

Part D Broker and Agent Requirements

A Part D sponsor must meet the following requirements if it markets Part D plan products through any broker or agent: (1) ensure agents selling Medicare products are trained and tested annually on Medicare rules and regulations and details specific to the plan products they sell; (2) upon request, provide CMS the information necessary for it to conduct oversight of marketing activities; (3) comply with state requests for information about the performance of a licensed agent or broker as part of a state investigation into the individual's conduct; and (4) report to CMS annually on whether it intends to use independent agents or brokers or both in the upcoming plan year and, if applicable, the specific amount or range of amounts independent agents or brokers or both will be paid. [42 C.F.R. § 423.2274(c)–(g).]

Compensation requirements. Part D plan sponsor may provide compensation to an independent broker or agent for the sale of a Part D plan if the following compensation rules are followed:

• The compensation amount paid to an agent or broker for enrollment of a Medicare beneficiary into a PDP is: (1) for an initial enrollment, at or below the fair market value cut-off amounts published annually by CMS; and (2) for renewals, an amount up to 50 percent of the current fair market value cut-off amounts.

• If the Part D sponsor contracts with a third-party entity such as a field marketing organization or similar type entity to sell its insurance products or perform services: (1) the amount paid to the third party, or its agents, for enrollment of a beneficiary into a plan must be the same as paid to non-third-party agents and brokers; and (2) the amount paid to the third party for services other than selling insurance products, if any, must be fair market value and must not exceed an amount that is commensurate with the amounts paid by the PDP organization to a third party for similar services during each of the previous two years.

[42 C.F.R. § 423.2274(b)(1).]

Compensation structure. A Part D sponsor must establish a compensation structure for new and replacement enrollments and renewals effective in a given plan year. They must be in place by October 1 and must be available upon CMS's request. [42 C.F.R. § 423.2274(b)(3).]

Finder's fees. Finder's (referral) fees paid to all agents and brokers may not exceed an amount that CMS determines could reasonably be expected to provide financial incentive for an agent or broker to recommend or enroll a beneficiary into a plan that is not the most appropriate to meet his or her needs. The fee must be included in the total compensation not to exceed the fair market value for that calendar year. [42 C.F.R. § 423.2274(h).]

"Compensation" defined. For the purposes of broker and agent requirements, "compensation" includes pecuniary or nonpecuniary remuneration of any kind relating to the sale or renewal of a policy including, but not limited to, commissions, bonuses, gifts, prizes, awards, and referral or finder's fees. Compensation does not include: (1) the payment of fees to comply with state appointment laws or training, certification, and testing costs; (2) reimbursement for mileage to and from appointments with beneficiaries; or (3) reimbursement for actual costs associated with beneficiary sales appointments such as venue rent, snacks, and materials. [42 C.F.R. § 423.2274(a).]

Employer Group Retirees

Part D sponsors may develop marketing materials for members of an employer group who are eligible for employer-sponsored benefits through the Part D sponsor. These materials may be furnished only to the employer group members and are exempt from prior review and approval by CMS. [42 C.F.R. § 423.2276.]

Chapter 6– EXCLUSIONS FROM COVERAGE

[¶ 600] Exclusions Under Part A and Part B

In addition to the limitations and exclusions discussed in the preceding chapters, other items or services are excluded under both Medicare Part A and Part B, as established by Soc. Sec. Act § 1862(a). In general, CMS will not cover items and services that are not reasonable or necessary for the diagnosis or treatment of illness or injury or to improve the functioning of a malformed body member. Particular services and items are also excluded from payment eligibility and are discussed in the following sections. [42 C.F.R. § 411.1 *et seq.*]

[¶ 601] Services Not Reasonable and Necessary

Items and services that are not reasonable and necessary for the diagnosis or treatment of illness or injury or to improve the functioning of a malformed body part are excluded from coverage. Many items and services are considered reasonable and necessary for some conditions but not for others. [Soc. Sec. Act § 1862(l)(1); 42 C.F.R. § 411.15(k).]

Medicare Coverage Determinations Manual, Pub. 100-03, discusses specific coverage decisions and exclusions.

Note that a beneficiary can be "held harmless" (not required to pay) in certain situations in which claims are disallowed under this exclusion. This "waiver of liability" provision is discussed at ¶ 915. [Soc. Sec. Act § 1879.]

Exclusion of Assisted Suicide

Procedures to assist a patient in committing suicide or to cause the patient's death are excluded. However, this exclusion does not prevent the withholding or withdrawal of medical treatment, nutrition, or hydration or the provision of a service for the purpose of alleviating pain or discomfort, even if the use may increase the risk of death, as long as the service is not furnished for the specific purpose of causing death. [Soc. Sec. Act § 1862(a)(16); 42 C.F.R. § 411.15(q).]

Services Related to Non-Covered Services

Services related to services that are typically excluded from coverage under Medicare Parts A and B (for instance, cosmetic surgery, non-covered organ transplants, non-covered artificial organ implants), including follow-up services and those related to complications arising out of non-covered services, are also excluded. [*Medicare Benefit Policy Manual*, Pub. 100-02, Ch. 16, § 180.] For a list of examples of services that are considered "related to" non-covered services, see Pub. 100-02, Ch. 16, § 180.

Experimental and Investigational Devices and Treatments

Medicare generally does not cover experimental and investigational devices and treatments. However, Medicare does cover the routine costs of care furnished to a beneficiary in a qualifying Category A (experimental) clinical trial. [Soc. Sec. Act § 1862(m)(1).] Medicare also covers Category B (nonexperimental/investigational) devices and routine care items and services furnished in Food and Drug Administration-approved Category B investigational device exemption studies if specified criteria are met. [42 C.F.R. §§ 405.201–405.213, 411.15(o); Pub. 100-03, Ch. 1, § 310.1.]

[¶ 604] No Legal Obligation to Pay

Medicare will not make payment for items or services for which neither the beneficiary nor any other person or organization has a legal obligation to pay or to provide. This exclusion does not apply, however, to services furnished in a federally qualified community health center (see ¶ 382). [Soc. Sec. Act § 1862(a)(2); 42 C.F.R. § 411.4(a).]

Items/services furnished free of charge. This exclusion applies when items and services are furnished free of charge regardless of the beneficiary's ability to pay and without expectation of payment from any source. An example is free x-rays or immunizations provided by health organizations. The exclusion does not apply, however, where items and services are furnished to an indigent individual without charge because of his or her inability to pay if the provider, physician, or supplier bills other patients to the extent that they are able to pay. If a provider, physician, or supplier waives his or her charges for individuals of limited means but also expects to be paid when the patient has insurance, a legal obligation to pay exists and benefits are payable for services rendered to patients with medical insurance if the provider, physician, or supplier customarily bills all insured patients, even though non-insured patients are not charged. [*Medicare Benefit Policy Manual*, Pub. 100-02, Ch. 16, § 40.]

Other health coverage. Except as discussed at ¶ 636 (involving workers' compensation, automobile and liability insurance, and certain employer group health plans), payment is not precluded under Medicare even though the patient is covered by another health insurance plan or program that is obligated to provide or pay for the same services. In these cases, the other plan pays the primary benefits and if it does not pay the entire bill, secondary Medicare benefits may be payable. [Pub. 100-02, Ch. 16, § 40.3.] The amount of secondary benefits Medicare will pay is determined by rules discussed at ¶ 636.

Items covered under a warranty. When a defective medical device such as a cardiac pacemaker is replaced under a warranty, Medicare may cover hospital and physician charges despite the warrantor's liability. If the warrantor replaces the device free of charge, Medicare will not make payment because there was no charge involved. [Pub. 100-02, Ch. 16, § 40.4.]

Members of religious orders. A legal obligation to pay exists when a religious order either pays for or furnishes services to members of the order. Medical services furnished in such a setting ordinarily would not be expressed in terms of a legal obligation; however, the religious order has an obligation to care for its members who have rendered life-long services, so the order pays for such services whether they are furnished by the religious order itself or by independent sources that customarily charge for their services. [Pub. 100-02, Ch. 16, § 40.5.]

State or local prisoners. Medicare payment may be made for services furnished to individuals who are in the custody of the police or other penal authorities only if: (1) state or local law requires the individuals to repay the cost of medical services they receive while in custody; and (2) the state or local government entity enforces the requirement to pay by billing all such individuals and by pursuing collection of the amounts they owe in the same way and with the same vigor that it pursues the collection of other debts. [42 C.F.R. § 411.4(b).]

[¶ 607] Services Paid for by Governmental Entity

Generally, Medicare does not pay for items or services that are paid for directly or indirectly by a governmental entity, including state and local governments. [Soc. Sec. Act § 1862(a)(3); 42 C.F.R. § 411.8(a).]

However, Medicare may make payment for:

(1) services furnished under a health insurance plan established for employees of the governmental entity;

¶607

(2) services furnished under a program based on a title of the Social Security Act other than Medicare, such as Medicaid;

(3) services furnished in or by a participating general or special hospital that is operated by a state or local governmental entity and serves the general community;

(4) services furnished by a hospital or elsewhere as a means of controlling infectious diseases or because of the individual's medical indigency;

(5) services furnished by participating hospitals and skilled nursing facilities of the Indian Health Service (IHS) (see below);

(6) services furnished by a public or private health facility (other than a federal provider or facility operated by a federal agency) that: (a) receives United States government funds under a federal program that provides support to facilities furnishing health care services, (b) customarily seeks reimbursement for items and services not covered under Medicare from all resources available for the health care of its patients— for example, private insurance and patients' cash resources, and (c) limits the amounts it collects or seeks to collect from a Part B beneficiary and others on the beneficiary's behalf;

(7) rural and community health clinic services (see ¶ 382);

(8) certain emergency services (see ¶ 227); and

(9) services furnished under arrangements made by a participating hospital.

[Soc. Sec. Act § 1862(a)(3); 42 C.F.R. § § 411.6, 411.8(b).]

Indian Health Service

The IHS is the primary health care provider to the American Indian/Alaska Native Medicare population. The IHS, consisting of tribal, urban, and federally operated IHS health programs, delivers clinical and preventive health services to its beneficiaries via a network of hospitals, clinics, and other entities. Although sections 1814(c) and 1835(d) of the Social Security Act generally prohibit payment to any federal agency, an exception applies to the IHS/tribally owned and operated facilities. IHS facilities may bill for Medicare Part B covered services and items, including all screening and preventive services covered by Medicare, physician services, diagnostic x-ray and other diagnostic tests, anesthesia services, practitioner services, drugs and biologics incident to physician services, physical therapy services, occupational therapy services, speech-language pathology services, ambulance services, and telehealth services. [Soc. Sec. Act § 1880(e)(1)(A); *Medicare Claims Processing Manual*, Pub. 100-04, Ch. 19, § § 10, 70.]

Social admissions. Medicare does not cover services rendered to American Indian/Alaska Native beneficiaries admitted to IHS/tribal facilities for social reasons. These social admissions are for the patients' and families' convenience and include occasions when IHS/tribal hospitals elect to admit patients before a scheduled day of surgery, or place a patient in a room after an inpatient discharge. [Pub. 100-04, Ch. 19, § 100.3.3.]

Department of Veterans Affairs

Medicare payment may not be made for any item or service that a provider, physician, or supplier provided pursuant to an authorization issued by the Department of Veterans Affairs (VA) under which the VA agrees to pay for the services. An authorization issued by the VA binds the VA to pay in full for the items and services provided. However, when the VA does not give an authorization to the party rendering the services, Medicare payment is not precluded even though the individual might have been entitled to have payment made by the VA if the individual had requested the authorization. [*Medicare Benefit Policy Manual*, Pub. 100-02, Ch. 16, § 50.1.1.]

If a physician accepts a veteran as a patient and bills the VA, the physician must accept the VA's "usual and customary" charge determination as payment in full and neither the patient nor any other party can be charged an additional amount. Therefore, Medicare cannot make payment if the physician's bill for authorized services exceeds the amount the VA paid the physician or reimbursed the beneficiary. Medicare can, however, pay secondary benefits to the beneficiary or physician to cover the VA copayment or deductible. Medicare also may pay for services not covered by the VA. [Pub. 100-02, Ch. 16, § § 50.1.1, 50.1.4.]

Under certain circumstances, Medicare reimbursement for care provided to a nonveteran Medicare beneficiary in a VA hospital is authorized if the care was provided on the mistaken (but good faith) assumption that the beneficiary was an eligible veteran. [Soc. Sec. Act § 1814(h)(1).]

TRICARE and CHAMPVA

TRICARE is a Department of Defense health care program for all branches of the armed services. Civilian Health and Medical Program of the Veterans Administration (CHAMPVA) is a health program administered by the VA under which the VA shares the cost of covered services with eligible family members of certain veterans. If a TRICARE or CHAMPVA beneficiary also has Medicare coverage, Medicare is the primary payer. TRICARE or CHAMPVA covers the Medicare deductible and coinsurance amounts and portions of the bill not covered by Medicare. [Pub. 100-02, Ch. 16, § 50.4.]

TRICARE/CHAMPVA have established policies and procedures that provide for: (1) the identification of claimants who have coverage under both TRICARE/CHAMPVA and Medicare; and (2) the detection of duplicate payments under both programs. If TRICARE or CHAMPVA inadvertently pays amounts that duplicate Medicare payments for the same items or services, TRICARE/CHAMPVA will take steps to recover the incorrect payments. [Pub. 100-02, Ch. 16, § 50.4.]

Medicare-participating hospitals are required to participate in the programs and accept patients from those programs. [Soc. Sec. Act § 1866(a)(1)(J).]

[¶ 610] Services Outside the United States

Generally, Medicare does not pay for services furnished outside the United States, which includes the 50 states, the District of Columbia, the Commonwealth of Puerto Rico, the Virgin Islands, Guam, the Northern Mariana Islands, American Samoa, and, for purposes of services rendered on a ship, the territorial waters adjoining the land areas of the United States. For Medicare purposes, services rendered aboard a ship in an American port or within six hours of the time at which the ship arrives at, or departs from, that port will be considered to have been rendered in American waters. [Soc. Sec. Act § § 210(h) and (i), 1862(a)(4); 42 C.F.R. § 411.9; *Medicare Claims Processing Manual*, Pub. 100-04, Ch. 32, § 350.1.]

Medicare will not make payment for a medical service (or a portion of it) that is subcontracted to a provider or supplier located outside the United States. For example, if a radiologist who practices in India analyzes imaging tests that were performed on a benefici-ary in the United States, Medicare will not pay the radiologist or the U.S. facility that performed the imaging test for any of the services that were performed by the radiologist in India. [*Medicare Benefit Policy Manual*, Pub. 100-02, Ch. 16, § 60.]

Qualified railroad retirement beneficiaries submit their claims for inpatient services received in Canada to the Railroad Retirement Board (RRB) for a determination of coverage.

If the RRB finds the inpatient services are covered, it forwards the claim to a Medicare administrative contractor for consideration of whether the other requirements for Part B coverage are met and for further processing. The RRB does not cover services furnished in Mexico; Medicare rules apply to services received in Mexico. [Pub. 100-04, Ch. 32, § 350.7.]

Exceptions to Geographic Limits

Medicare pays for inpatient hospital services provided to beneficiaries entitled to Part A by a hospital located outside of the United States if: (1) the beneficiary is a resident of the United States; (2) the hospital is closer to or substantially more accessible to the beneficiary's residence than the nearest hospital within the United States; (3) the hospital is adequately equipped to deal with the beneficiary's illness or injury; and (4) the hospital is available for the treatment of the illness or injury. [Soc. Sec. Act §§ 1814(f)(1), 1862(a)(4).]

Emergency inpatient hospital services are also covered when the emergency occurred while the beneficiary was in the United States or, at the time of the emergency, the beneficiary was in Canada while traveling directly between Alaska and another state without unreasonable delay and by the most direct route and the Canadian hospital was closer or more accessible with adequate facilities to care for the beneficiary's needs. An emergency occurring within the Canadian inland waterway between the states of Washington and Canada is considered to have occurred in Canada. [Soc. Sec. Act § 1814(f)(2); 42 C.F.R. § 424.122(a), (b); Pub. 100-02, Ch. 16, § 60.]

Medicare will pay 100 percent of the foreign hospital's charges. [42 C.F.R. § 413.74(b).]

Physicians' services in connection with foreign hospitalization. Physicians' services provided to a Medicare beneficiary outside a hospital on the day of admission as an inpatient are covered, as long as the services were for the same condition for which the beneficiary was hospitalized. The physician must be legally licensed to practice in the country in which he or she furnished the services. This provision includes the services of a Canadian ship's physician who furnishes emergency treatment in Canadian waters on the day the beneficiary is admitted to a Canadian hospital for a covered emergency stay. [Soc. Sec. Act § 1862(a)(4); 42 C.F.R. § 424.124(a); Pub. 100-04, Ch. 32, § 350.6.]

Ambulance services in connection with foreign hospitalizations. Payment may be made for necessary ambulance services to a hospital in conjunction with a beneficiary's admission as an inpatient; however, return trips from a foreign hospital are not covered. [Soc. Sec. Act § 1862(a)(4); 42 C.F.R. § 424.124(a), (c); Pub. 100-04, Ch. 32, § 350.6.]

Regular deductible and coinsurance requirements apply to physicians' and ambulance services rendered outside the United States. [Pub. 100-04, Ch. 32, § 350.6.]

[¶ 613] Services Resulting from War

Medicare does not cover items and services that are required as a result of war, or an act of war, occurring after the effective date of the patient's current coverage for hospital insurance benefits or supplemental medical insurance benefits. [Soc. Sec. Act § 1862(a)(5); 42 C.F.R. § 411.10.]

[¶ 616] Personal Comfort Items

Personal comfort items, meaning those items that do not contribute meaningfully to the treatment of an illness or injury or the functioning of a malformed body member, are not covered except when provided in the course of hospice care (see ¶ 270). Charges for radios, televisions, telephones, or air conditioners are examples of personal comfort items excluded from Medicare coverage. [Soc. Sec. Act § 1862(a)(6); 42 C.F.R. § 411.15(j); *Medicare Benefit Policy Manual*, Pub. 100-02, Ch. 16, § 80.]

Basic personal services, such as simple barber and beautician services (for example, shaves, haircuts, shampoos, and simple hair sets) that patients need and cannot perform for themselves, may be viewed as ordinary patient care when furnished by a long-stay institution. Such services are included in the flat rate charge covered under Part A and provided routinely without charge to the patient by a hospital or skilled nursing facility. [Pub. 100-02, Ch. 16, § 80.]

Providers may charge patients for excluded personal comfort items that the patient requests only if the patient has knowledge that he or she will be charged for those items. [Pub. 100-02, Ch. 16, § 80.]

Providers also are allowed to charge patients when they request services that are more expensive than those covered by Medicare (see ¶ 730).

[¶ 619] Eye, Ear, and Foot Care

Medicare does not cover routine eye, ear, and foot care services. [Soc. Sec. Act § 1862(a)(7), (8), (13); 42 C.F.R. § 411.15.]

Eye Care

Excluded routine eye care includes: (1) eyeglasses; (2) most contact lenses; (3) eye examinations for the purpose of prescribing, fitting, or changing eyeglasses or contact lenses for refractive error only; and (4) procedures performed in the course of any eye examination to determine the refractive state of the eyes. [Soc. Sec. Act § 1862(a)(7); 42 C.F.R. § 411.15(b), (c).]

The eye care services exclusion does not apply to: (1) physicians' services (and services incident to a physician's service) performed in conjunction with an eye disease, for example, glaucoma or cataracts; (2) post-surgical prosthetic lenses customarily used during convalescence for eye surgery in which the lens of the eye was removed (for example, cataract surgery); (3) prosthetic intraocular lenses and one pair of conventional eyeglasses or contact lenses furnished after each cataract surgery with insertion of an intraocular lens; or (4) prosthetic lenses used by beneficiaries who are lacking the natural lens of the eye and who were not furnished with an intraocular lens. [42 C.F.R. § 411.15(b)(2); *Medicare Benefit Policy Manual*, Pub. 100-02, Ch. 16, § 90.]

Note that the law specifically authorizes coverage for one pair of conventional eyeglasses or contact lenses furnished after each cataract surgery in which an intraocular lens is inserted. [Soc. Sec. Act § 1861(s)(8).]

Ear Care

Hearing aids and examinations for the purpose of prescribing, fitting, or changing hearing aids are excluded from Medicare coverage. The scope of the hearing aid exclusion encompasses all types of air conduction hearing aids that provide acoustic energy to the cochlea via stimulation of the tympanic membrane with amplified sound, and bone conduction hearing aids that provide mechanical stimulation of the cochlea via stimulation of the scalp with amplified mechanical vibration or by direct contact with the tympanic membrane or middle ear ossicles. [Soc. Sec. Act § 1862(a)(7); 42 C.F.R. § 411.15(d).]

Certain devices that produce perception of sound by replacing the function of the middle ear, cochlea, or auditory nerve are payable by Medicare as prosthetic devices. These devices are indicated only when hearing aids are medically inappropriate or cannot be utilized due to congenital malformations, chronic disease, severe sensorineural hearing loss, or surgery. The following are covered as prosthetic devices: (1) osseointegrated implants in the skull bone that provide mechanical energy to the cochlea via a mechanical transducer; or

(2) cochlear implants and auditory brainstem implants that replace the function of cochlear structures or auditory nerve and provide electrical energy to auditory nerve fibers and other neural tissue via implanted electrode arrays. [42 C.F.R. § 411.15(d)(2); Pub. 100-02, Ch. 16, § 100.]

Foot Care

Medicare does not cover the following foot-related services:

(1) routine foot care;

(2) the evaluation or treatment of subluxations (structural misalignments of the joints) of the feet; or

(3) the evaluation or treatment of flattened arches and the prescription of supportive devices.

[Soc. Sec. Act § 1862(a)(13); 42 C.F.R. § 411.15(l)(1).]

Routine foot care. Routine foot care includes the cutting or removal of corns or calluses, the trimming of nails (including mycotic nails), and other hygienic and preventive maintenance care in the realm of self-care, such as cleaning and soaking the feet, the use of skin creams to maintain skin tone of both ambulatory and bed-confined patients, and any services performed in the absence of localized illness, injury, or symptoms involving the foot. For example, foot care such as routine soaking and application of topical medication on a physician's order between required physician visits is not covered. [42 C.F.R. § 411.15(l)(1)(i); Pub. 100-02, Ch. 15, § 290.]

Exceptions to foot-care exclusion. Services may be covered: (1) for the treatment of warts; (2) for the treatment of mycotic toenails if furnished no more often than every 60 days or the billing physician documents the need for more frequent treatment; and (3) when they are incident to, at the same time as, or as a necessary integral part of a primary covered procedure performed on the foot, or initial diagnostic services (regardless of the resulting diagnosis) in connection with a specific symptom or complaint that might arise from a condition for which treatment would be covered. [42 C.F.R. § 411.15(l)(2); Pub. 100-02, Ch. 15, § 290.]

Orthopedic shoes. Expenses for orthopedic shoes or other supportive devices for the feet generally are not covered, except when the shoe is an integral part of a leg brace and its expense is included as part of the cost of the brace. [Soc. Sec. Act § 1862(a)(8); 42 C.F.R. § 411.15(f).] The exclusion also does not apply to therapeutic shoes and inserts for individuals with severe diabetic foot disease (see ¶ 370). [Soc. Sec. Act § 1861(s)(12).]

[¶ 625] Custodial Care

Custodial care, except in the case of hospice care (see ¶ 270), is excluded from Medicare coverage. [Soc. Sec. Act § 1862(a)(9); 42 C.F.R. § 411.15(g).]

Custodial care is personal care that does not require the continuing attention of trained medical or paramedical personnel and serves to assist the individual in meeting the activities of daily living. The following activities are considered custodial care: (1) help in walking and getting in or out of bed; (2) assistance in bathing, dressing, feeding, and using the toilet; (3) preparation of special diets; and (4) supervision over medication that usually can be self-administered. Institutional care that is below the level of care covered in a skilled nursing facility (SNF) is custodial care. [*Medicare Benefit Policy Manual*, Pub. 100-02, Ch. 16, § 110.] For a discussion of noncovered levels of care in a SNF, see ¶ 244.

Note that a beneficiary can be "held harmless" (i.e., not required to pay) in certain situations in which claims are disallowed under this exclusion. This provision is discussed at ¶ 915.

[¶ 628] Cosmetic Surgery

Medicare does not cover cosmetic surgery and expenses incurred in connection with such surgery. This exclusion applies to any surgical procedure directed at improving appearance, except when required for the prompt (i.e., as soon as medically feasible) repair of accidental injury or for the improvement of the functioning of a malformed body member. For example, this exclusion does not apply to surgery: (1) in connection with treatment of severe burns or repair of the face following a serious automobile accident; or (2) for therapeutic purposes that coincidentally also serve some cosmetic purpose. [Soc. Sec. Act § 1862(a)(10); 42 C.F.R. § 411.15(h); *Medicare Benefit Policy Manual*, Pub. 100-02, Ch. 16, § 120.]

[¶ 631] Charges by Immediate Relatives and Household Members

Medicare does not pay for charges imposed by physicians or other persons who are immediate relatives of the patient or members of the patient's household. The intent of this exclusion is to bar payment for items and services that would ordinarily be furnished gratuitously because of the relationship of the beneficiary to the person imposing the charge. [Soc. Sec. Act § 1862(a)(11); 42 C.F.R. § 411.12(a).]

Immediate relatives and household members. "Immediate relative" means spouse; natural or adoptive parent, child, and sibling; stepparent, stepchild, stepbrother, and stepsister; parent-in-law, child-in-law, brother-in-law, and sister-in-law; grandparent and grandchild; and spouse of grandparent and grandchild. "Members of the patient's household" means those persons sharing a common abode with the patient as part of a single family unit, including domestic employees and others who live together as part of a single family unit. A roommate or boarder is not included. [42 C.F.R. § 411.12(b).]

A brother-in-law or sister-in-law relationship does not exist between a physician (or supplier) and the spouse of his wife's (her husband's) brother or sister. A father-in-law or mother-in-law relationship does not exist between a physician and the stepfather or stepmother of the physician's spouse. A step-relationship or an in-law relationship continues to exist even if the marriage upon which the relationship is based is terminated through divorce or through the death of one of the parties. For example, if a physician provides services to a stepparent after the death of (or divorce by) the natural parent, or if the physician provides services to an in-law after the death of the spouse of the physician, the services are considered to have been furnished to an immediate relative and, therefore, excluded from coverage. [*Medicare Benefit Policy Manual*, Pub. 100-02, Ch. 16, § 130.]

Physicians' services. The exclusion applies to the charges for physicians' services furnished by an immediate relative of the beneficiary or member of the beneficiary's household, even if the bill or claim is submitted by another individual or by an entity such as a partnership or a professional corporation. It also applies to charges for services furnished incident to a physician's professional services (for example, by the physician's nurse or technician) only if the physician who ordered or supervised the services has an excluded relationship to the beneficiary. [42 C.F.R. § 411.12(c)(1).]

Services other than physicians' services. In the case of services other than physicians' services, charges are excluded if they are provided by: (1) an individually owned provider or supplier, if the owner has an excluded relationship with the patient; or (2) a partnership, if any of the partners has an excluded relationship with the patient. [42 C.F.R. § 411.12(c)(2).]

Corporations. This exclusion does not apply to charges imposed by a corporation, other than a professional corporation, regardless of the patient's relationship to any of the stockholders, officers, or directors of the corporation or to the person who furnished the service. [42 C.F.R. § 411.12(d); Pub. 100-02, Ch. 16, § 130.]

[¶ 634] Dental Services

Items and services in connection with the care, treatment, filling, removal, or replacement of teeth or structures directly supporting the teeth (i.e., the periodontium, which includes the gingivae, dentogingival junction, periodontal membrane, cementum of the teeth, and alveolar process) generally are not covered. Payment may, however, be made under Part A for inpatient hospital services in connection with the provision of such dental services if the beneficiary, because of his or her underlying medical condition and clinical status or because of the severity of the dental procedure, requires hospitalization in connection with the provision of such services. [Soc. Sec. Act § 1862(a)(12); 42 C.F.R. § 411.15(i); *Medicare Benefit Policy Manual*, Pub. 100-02, Ch. 16, § 140.]

Medicare makes payment for the wiring of teeth when this is done in connection with the reduction of a jaw fracture. The extraction of teeth to prepare the jaw for radiation treatments of neoplastic disease also is covered. [Pub. 100-02, Ch. 15, § 150; Ch. 16, § 140.]

Whether such services as the administration of anesthesia, diagnostic x-rays, and other related procedures are covered depends upon whether Medicare covers the primary procedure being performed by the dentist. An x-ray taken in connection with the reduction of a fracture of the jaw or facial bone is covered, but a single x-ray or x-ray survey taken in connection with the care or treatment of teeth or the periodontium is not covered. [Pub. 100-02, Ch. 15, § 150; Ch. 16, § 140.]

[¶ 635] Services Not Provided In-House

Any services furnished to an inpatient of a hospital or to a hospital outpatient during an encounter by an entity other than the hospital are not covered, unless the hospital has an arrangement with that entity to furnish that particular service to the hospital's patients. The Medicare program requires hospitals and skilled nursing facilities (SNFs) caring for Medicare patients to provide in-house all the services that are furnished to those patients. This requirement is satisfied if the hospital or SNF has made arrangements to have the services provided by another entity, such as an independent laboratory or physical therapy group. Services not provided in-house that are supposed to be provided in-house are excluded from coverage and will not be covered by Medicare. [Soc. Sec. Act § 1862(a)(14), (18); 42 C.F.R. § 411.15(m)(1).]

The reason for this exclusion is that under each prospective payment system (PPS), in-house services are included in the calculation of the hospital's and SNF's PPS diagnosis-related group (DRG) payment rate, and Medicare will not pay for these services twice (see ¶ 810 and ¶ 835).

This exclusion applies, but is not limited, to the following items and services: (1) clinical laboratory services; (2) pacemakers and other prostheses and prosthetic devices (other than dental) that replace all or part of an internal body organ (for example, intraocular lenses); (3) artificial limbs, knees, and hips; (4) equipment and supplies covered under the prosthetic device benefits; and (5) services furnished incident to physicians' services. [42 C.F.R. § 411.15(m)(2).]

This exclusion does *not* apply to physicians' services or to the services of the following health care practitioners: (1) physician assistants; (2) nurse practitioners and clinical nurse specialists; (3) certified nurse-midwives; (4) qualified psychologists; and (5) certified registered nurse anesthetists and anesthesiologist's assistants. [42 C.F.R. § 411.15(m)(3).]

Charges to Beneficiaries

Under the regulations governing provider agreements, hospitals are prohibited from charging beneficiaries for inpatient hospital services furnished by entities with which there is no arrangements agreement. Furthermore, because services furnished under arrangements are included in the hospital's DRG rate, if an entity other than the hospital charges the hospital inpatient for its services, that charge is treated as a charge by the hospital and is regarded as a violation of its provider agreement. [42 C.F.R. § 489.21(f).]

[¶ 636] Medicare as Secondary Payer

Medicare payment is excluded for services to the extent that payment has been made, or reasonably can be expected to be made, when the following alternate types of insurance are available:

(1) workers' compensation;

(2) automobile, no-fault, or liability insurance; and

(3) employer group health plans (GHPs).

This exclusion is referred to as the Medicare Secondary Payer (MSP) rule. [Soc. Sec. Act § 1862(b)(2)(A); 42 C.F.R. § 411.20.]

Identifying other coverage. Providers and suppliers are required to furnish information concerning potential coverage under other plans. Payment may not be made for Part B claims if the provider or supplier fails to complete MSP questions on the claim form. Entities that knowingly, willfully, and repeatedly fail to complete a claim form or fail to provide accurate MSP information are subject to fines of up to $2,000 for each incident. [Soc. Sec. Act § 1862(b)(6).]

Coordination of benefits. In instances when Medicare is secondary payer to more than one primary insurer (e.g., an individual who is covered under his or her own GHP and under the GHP of an employed spouse or under no-fault insurance), the other primary payers will customarily coordinate benefits. If a portion of the charges remains unpaid after the other insurers have paid primary benefits, a secondary Medicare payment may be made. [*Medicare Secondary Payer Manual*, Pub. 100-05, Ch. 1, § 10.9.]

Workers' Compensation

Medicare payment is excluded for any items and services to the extent that payment has been made or reasonably can be expected to be made under a workers' compensation law or plan of the United States or a state. This exclusion also applies to the workers' compensation plans of the District of Columbia, American Samoa, Guam, the Virgin Islands, Puerto Rico, and the Virgin Islands. [Soc. Sec. Act § 1862(b)(2)(A)(ii); 42 C.F.R. § 411.40; Pub. 100-05, Ch. 1, § 10.4.]

The beneficiary is responsible for taking whatever action is necessary to obtain payment under workers' compensation when payment reasonably can be expected. Failure to take proper and timely action under such circumstances will preclude Medicare payment to the extent that payment reasonably could have been expected to be made under workers' compensation had the individual exhausted benefit rights under that system. [42 C.F.R. § 411.43(a).]

If a lump-sum workers' compensation award stipulates that the amount paid is intended to compensate the individual for all future medical expenses required because of the work-related injury or disease, Medicare payments for such services are excluded until medical expenses related to the injury or disease equal the amount of the lump-sum payment. [42 C.F.R. § 411.46(a).]

Medicare will not make payment if: (1) workers' compensation pays an amount that equals or exceeds the gross amount payable by Medicare without regard to deductible and coinsurance; (2) workers' compensation pays an amount that equals or exceeds the provider's, physician's, or supplier's charges for Medicare-covered services; or (3) the provider accepts or is required under the workers' compensation law to accept such workers' compensation payment as payment in full. If workers' compensation pays less than these amounts and the provider is not obligated to accept the amount as payment in full, secondary Medicare payments can be made. [42 C.F.R. § 411.32(b).]

Liability claims. Most state laws provide that if an employee is injured at work due to the negligent act of a third party, the employee cannot receive payments from both workers' compensation and the third party for the same injury. Generally, the workers' compensation carrier pays benefits while the third-party claim is pending. However, once a settlement of the third-party claim is reached or an award has been made, the workers' compensation carrier may recover the benefits it paid from the third-party settlement and may deny any future claims for that injury up to the amount of the liability payment made to the individual. Regardless of the liabilities of any other parties to one another, Medicare is the residual payer. [Soc. Sec. Act § 1862(b)(2)(B)(ii); Pub. 100-05, Ch. 1, § 10.9.]

Automobile and Liability Insurance Coverage

Medicare payment is excluded for any items and services to the extent that payment has been made or reasonably can be expected to be made under an automobile or liability insurance policy or plan, including a self-insured plan, or under no-fault insurance. [Soc. Sec. Act § 1862(b)(2)(A)(ii); 42 C.F.R. §§ 411.20(a)(2), 411.50(c).]

In no-fault insurance cases, the beneficiary is responsible for taking whatever action is necessary to obtain any payments from the no-fault insurer that reasonably can be expected. Medicare normally will not make any payments until the beneficiary has exhausted all remedies to obtain payments from the no-fault insurer. [42 C.F.R. § 411.51.]

It is common for insurance companies to settle claims without admitting liability. Therefore, any payment by a liability insurer constitutes a liability insurance payment regardless of whether there has been a determination of liability. Medicare is entitled to seek repayment of the amount it paid, less a proportionate share of procurement costs, from any payment a claimant receives from a liability insurer or self-insured party. [42 C.F.R. § 411.37(a).]

Employer Group Health Plans

Medicare payment is excluded for employees entitled to Medicare based on old age, disability, or (during a 30-month coordination-of-benefits period) end-stage renal disease (ESRD) to the extent that health care benefit payments have been made or reasonably can be expected to be made under a GHP. [Soc. Sec. Act § 1862(b)(2)(A)(i); 42 C.F.R. § 411.20(a)(1).]

Working aged. The working aged exclusion applies to Medicare-eligible individuals age 65 or over whose employer group health coverage is based on the current employment of the individual or spouse by an employer that employs 20 or more employees. Health insurance plans for retirees or spouses of retirees are not affected because retirement does not constitute "current employment." [Soc. Sec. Act § 1862(b)(1)(A); 42 C.F.R. § 411.20(a)(1)(ii); Pub. 100-05, Ch. 2, §§ 10, 10.3.]

Under this exclusion, employers are required to offer their employees age 65 or over the same GHP coverage offered to younger workers. Similarly, employers are required to offer their workers with Medicare-eligible spouses age 65 or over the same spousal GHP benefits they offer to workers with spouses that are not Medicare-eligible. [Soc. Sec. Act § 1862(b)(1)(A)(i).] Employees and their spouses then have the option of choosing either the employer plan or Medicare as their primary health insurer. If the employee or spouse elects the employer plan, Medicare will assume back-up coverage. If the employee or spouse elects Medicare as the primary insurer, however, the employer plan may not offer back-up coverage. [42 C.F.R. § 411.172(c); Pub. 100-05, Ch. 2, § 10.]

The working aged employee provisions do not apply to disability beneficiaries or ESRD beneficiaries. [Soc. Sec. Act § 1862(b)(1)(A)–(C).]

Disabled employees. Medicare is the secondary payer for individuals under age 65 entitled to Medicare based on disability (see ¶ 204) who are covered by a "large group health plan" (LGHP) and whose coverage is based on the current employment status of the individual or of a family member. When an employee (or a member of the employee's family) becomes disabled, the LGHP has primary coverage responsibility and Medicare has secondary coverage responsibility. [Soc. Sec. Act § 1862(b)(1)(B); 42 C.F.R. § § 411.200–411.206.]

An LGHP is defined as a group health plan of either: (1) a single employer or employee organization; or (2) at least one of two or more employers or employee organizations that employed at least 100 full-time employees or part-time employees on 50 percent or more of its regular business days during the previous calendar year. [Soc. Sec. Act § 1862(b)(1)(B)(iii); Pub. 100-05, Ch. 2, § 30.2.]

As in the case of elderly employees, there is a special enrollment period for disabled employees who do not enroll in Part B because they have chosen disability coverage under the employer's plan (see ¶ 311).

ESRD beneficiaries. Medicare benefits are secondary for a limited period of time, known as the coordination-of-benefits period, for individuals who are eligible or entitled to Medicare benefits because of ESRD (see ¶ 845) and who are entitled to primary health care coverage under an employer GHP regardless of the number of employees employed by the employer and regardless of the individual's current employment status. [42 C.F.R. § 411.162(a).]

The coordination-of-benefits period begins with the first month in which the individual becomes eligible for Medicare, or the first month in which the individual would have been eligible for Medicare if he or she had filed an application for Medicare ESRD benefits. The coordination-of-benefits period ends 30 months later. During the coordination-of-benefits period, Medicare has secondary payment responsibility. After the coordination-of-benefits period ends, Medicare has primary payment responsibility, as the patient becomes entitled to Medicare. [Soc. Sec. Act § 1862(b)(1)(C); 42 C.F.R. § 411.162.]

During the coordination-of-benefits period, Medicare will pay primary benefits for Medicare covered services that: (1) are furnished to Medicare beneficiaries who have declined to enroll in the GHP; (2) are not covered by the employer plan; (3) are covered under the GHP but not available to particular enrollees because they have exhausted their benefits; or (4) are furnished to individuals whose continuation coverage under the Consolidated Omnibus Budget Reconciliation Act of 1985 (COBRA) (P.L. 99-272) (i.e., continued health insurance coverage after leaving employment) has been terminated because of the individual's Medicare entitlement. Medicare will make secondary payments to supplement the amount paid by the employer plan if that plan pays only a portion of the charge for the service. [42 C.F.R. § 411.162(a).]

¶636

Medicare benefits are primary without a coordination-of-benefits period for ESRD-eligible individuals if the following conditions are met: (1) the beneficiary was already entitled to Medicare because of age or disability; (2) either the group health insurance was not based on current employment status, or the employer had fewer than 20 employees (in the case of the aged) or fewer than 100 employees (in the case of the disabled); and (3) the plan is paying secondary to Medicare because the plan had justifiably taken into account the age-based or disability-based entitlement. The employer health plan may continue to pay benefits secondary to Medicare but may not differentiate in the services covered and the payments made between persons who have ESRD and those who do not. [42 C.F.R. § 411.163(b)(4).]

Conditional Medicare Payments

If a primary plan has not made or cannot reasonably be expected to make payment with respect to such item or service promptly, Medicare may make a conditional payment. The conditional payment will be recovered later if it is determined that Medicare's liability is secondary. Regardless of any time limit on filing a claim under an employer group health plan, the government has three years to file a claim for recovery of conditional benefits paid by Medicare, beginning on the date the item or service was furnished. [Soc. Sec. Act § 1862(b)(2)(B); 42 C.F.R. §§ 411.45, 411.52, 411.53.]

A primary payer, and an entity that receives payment from a primary payer, must reimburse CMS for any payment if it is demonstrated that the primary payer has or had a responsibility to make payment, which is demonstrated by: (1) a judgment; (2) a payment conditioned upon the recipient's compromise, waiver, or release (whether or not there is a determination or admission of liability) of payment for items and services included in a claim against the primary plan or the primary plan's insured; or (3) by other means, including a settlement, award, or contractual obligation. [Soc. Sec. Act § 1862(b)(2)(B)(ii); 42 C.F.R. § 411.22.]

Partial Payments by Alternate Insurer

If the alternate insurer pays less than the full amount of the charge for the services rendered, Medicare may make secondary payments to supplement the alternate insurer's payments. In no case, however, will the Medicare secondary payment exceed the amount that otherwise would have been payable if there were no alternate insurance. Medicare secondary payments also can be made to pay the alternate insurer's deductible and coinsurance requirements. [Soc. Sec. Act § 1862(b)(4); 42 C.F.R. §§ 411.32, 411.33.]

Some third-party payments obligate the provider, physician, or supplier to accept the payment as payment in full. No Medicare payment is payable in such a case. [42 C.F.R. § 411.32(b).]

For physicians and suppliers who are not obligated to accept the third-party payment as payment in full, the amount of the Medicare secondary benefit payable is the lowest of the following:

(1) the actual charge by the physician or supplier minus the amount paid by the third-party payer;

(2) the amount Medicare would pay if services were not covered by the third-party payer; or

(3) the higher of: (a) the Medicare fee schedule or other amount payable under Medicare (without regard to any deductible and/or coinsurance amounts), or (b) the third-party payer's allowable charge (without regard to any deductible and/or coinsur-

ance amounts imposed by the policy or plan), minus the amount actually paid by the third-party payer.

[42 C.F.R. § 411.33(a).]

For hospitals and other providers that are not obligated to accept third-party payments as payment in full, the Medicare secondary payment is the lowest of the following:

(1) the gross amount payable by Medicare minus the applicable deductible and coinsurance amount;

(2) the gross amount payable by Medicare minus the amount paid by the third-party payer for Medicare-covered services;

(3) the provider's charges (or the amount the provider is obligated to accept as payment in full) minus the amount paid by the third-party payer; or

(4) the provider's charges (or the amount the provider is obligated to accept as payment in full) minus the applicable Medicare deductible and coinsurance amount.

[42 C.F.R. § 411.33(e).]

[¶ 646] Services of Excluded Individuals and Entities

No Medicare payment may be made, except in an emergency, to an entity or individual, such as a provider, supplier, physician, or other health care practitioner, who has been excluded from the Medicare program due to program abuses (see ¶ 720). Similarly, Medicare payment will not be made for items or services furnished at the medical direction or on the prescription of a physician who is excluded from program participation if the person furnishing the items or services knew or had reason to know of the exclusion. [Soc. Sec. Act § 1862(e)(1).]

If a beneficiary submits a claim for items or services received from a physician or supplier who has been excluded from program participation, Medicare will pay for the items or services if the beneficiary did not know or did not have reason to know about the exclusion. [Soc. Sec. Act § 1862(e)(2).]

[¶ 654] Certain Services of Surgery Assistants

The following assistant-at-surgery services are excluded: (1) services of an assistant at surgery in cataract operations, including subsequent insertions of intraocular lenses, unless, before the surgery is performed, the appropriate quality improvement organization (QIO) (see ¶ 710) or a Medicare administrative contractor (MAC) has approved the use of the assistant due to the existence of a complicating medical condition; and (2) services of an assistant at surgery in a surgical procedure (or class of surgical procedures) for which assistants at surgery on average are used in fewer than 5 percent of such procedures nationally. Services subject to this exclusion include, but are not limited to, clinical laboratory services, pacemakers, artificial limbs, knees, and hips, intraocular lenses, total parenteral nutrition, and services incident to physicians' services. [Soc. Sec. Act §§ 1848(i)(2)(B), 1862(a)(15); 42 C.F.R. § 411.15(n).]

The Office of Inspector General may exclude a physician that (1) knowingly and willfully presented or caused to be presented a claim, or billed an individual enrolled under Part B of the Medicare program (or his or her representative), for services of an assistant at surgery during a cataract operation, or charges that include a charge for an assistant at surgery during a cataract operation; and (2) failed to obtain prior approval for the use of such assistant from the appropriate QIO or MAC. [42 C.F.R. § 1001.1701(a).]

Chapter 7– ADMINISTRATIVE PROVISIONS

[¶ 700] HHS and CMS Organizational Structure

The Secretary of the U.S. Department of Health and Human Services (HHS) oversees the Medicare program. Within HHS, the Medicare program is administered by the Centers for Medicare and Medicaid Services (CMS). CMS is responsible for: enrolling providers; enforcing provider standards, called "conditions of participation"; evaluating and paying claims; reviewing utilization of services; developing and reviewing policies governing coverage of services; and preventing and prosecuting fraud and abuse by providers. HHS contracts with other entities to perform many of these functions, including Medicare administrative contractors (MACs) (see ¶ 705), state and local survey and Medicaid agencies (see ¶ 703), private insurance companies, and quality improvement organizations (see ¶ 710). In addition to using such agencies or organizations under the conditions described below, the HHS Secretary is authorized to purchase or contract separately for auditing or cost analysis. [Soc. Sec. Act § 1874(b).]

CMS Programs

In addition to the Medicare program, CMS operates the state-federal Medicaid program, the Children's Health Insurance Program, and a variety of programs designed to control program costs, ensure appropriate utilization of health services by eligible beneficiaries and recipients, and eliminate provider fraud and abuse. CMS's goal is to ensure that the best possible care is delivered in the most economical manner to eligible beneficiaries and recipients. CMS also provides national policy planning for health care financing and for delivery of health services within these operating programs.

Medicare integrity. To ensure the integrity of the Medicare program, CMS has a number of fraud control and prevention initiatives, which work in collaboration with the HHS Office of Inspector General (OIG) and the Department of Justice. The HHS Secretary is also authorized to contract with private entities known as recovery audit contractors (RACs) to perform specified review and audit functions (see ¶ 711 for a full discussion of RACs). [Soc. Sec. Act § 1893(b).] The Social Security Administration is also involved in the administration of the Medicare program, primarily in the enrollment of beneficiaries in the program and the maintenance of beneficiary rolls.

Beneficiary information programs. The Secretary must issue all beneficiaries an "Explanation of Medicare Benefits" for all medical services or items furnished, including a notice of the right to request itemized statements. Within 30 days of a beneficiary's request, providers must furnish itemized statements of items or services or face a possible civil money penalty of not more than $100 for each such failure. Beneficiaries have 90 days after receiving the statement to submit written requests identifying billing irregularities to the Secretary, who must take all appropriate measures to recover any amounts unnecessarily paid. A beneficiary may elect to receive an Explanation of Medicare Benefits in an electronic format instead of by mail. [Soc. Sec. Act § 1806.]

The Secretary must provide an annual notice to beneficiaries, including a statement of the beneficiary's right to request itemized statements of items or services provided, as well as an instruction to check explanations of benefits and itemized statements carefully for accuracy. The notice also must contain a description of the Medicare fraud and abuse information collection program (see below) and a toll-free telephone number to report errors or questionable charges. [Soc. Sec. Act § 1804(c).]

Reports of fraud or abuse. Pursuant to Health Insurance Portability and Accountability Act of 1996 (HIPAA) (P.L. 104-191) § 203(b), the Secretary established a program to encourage individuals to report other individuals and entities who are engaging, or have engaged, in acts or omissions that qualify for the imposition of sanctions under the OIG's civil penalty, exclusion, or law enforcement authorities (see below). A portion of the amount collected as the result of these sanctions is paid to the reporting individual when at least $100 is collected by the Secretary or the U.S. Attorney General. [42 C.F.R. § 420.405.]

Information on program efficiency. Individuals are also encouraged to submit suggestions for improving the efficiency of the Medicare program. As with the fraud and abuse reporting program, the Secretary may make an appropriate payment to individuals whose suggestions result in program savings. [HIPAA § 203(c); 42 C.F.R. § 420.410.]

CMS Regional Offices

In addition to a central office in Baltimore, CMS maintains 10 regional offices, which are located in Atlanta, Boston, Chicago, Dallas, Denver, Kansas City (Mo.), New York, Philadelphia, San Francisco, and Seattle. CMS regional offices are often the first point of contact for beneficiaries, health care providers, state and local governments, and the general public. The regional offices provide customer service, program management, and education and outreach programs, and they develop partnerships with state and local health and social service agencies. Additional information on the CMS regional offices can be found at https://www.cms.gov/About-CMS/Agency-Information/RegionalOffices/index.html.

Medicare Beneficiary Ombudsman

The Medicare Beneficiary Ombudsman within HHS responds to beneficiaries' complaints, grievances, and inquiries. In addition, the ombudsman provides assistance: (1) collecting relevant information needed to file appeals; (2) terminating enrollment under Medicare Part C; and (3) presenting information related to income-related premium adjustments. The ombudsman cannot serve as an advocate for any increases in payments or new coverage of services but may identify issues and problems in payment or coverage policies. [Soc. Sec. Act § 1808(c).] The ombudsman's website is located at https://www.cms.gov/Center/Special-Topic/Ombudsman-Center.html.

HHS Office of Inspector General

The OIG is an independent unit within HHS that is headed by an Inspector General and a Deputy Inspector General. The OIG is charged with: (1) conducting audits and investigations relating to HHS programs and operations; (2) promoting economy and efficiency in the administration of HHS programs and operations, as well as preventing and detecting fraud and abuse; and (3) keeping the Secretary and Congress informed about problems and deficiencies relating to the administration and operation of HHS programs and the necessity of corrective action. Reports on OIG activities must be submitted annually to Congress and quarterly to the Secretary and appropriate congressional committees. The OIG must report immediately on any serious problems or abuses. [Inspector General Act of 1978 (P.L. 95-452).]

The OIG has primary responsibility for detecting abuses and applying sanctions against providers, physicians, entities, and suppliers of health care items and services that commit federal health care program abuses. The Health Care Fraud and Abuse Control Program, required by HIPAA, is administered under the joint direction of the U.S. Attorney General and the Secretary of HHS, acting through the OIG (see ¶ 720).

Health Care Reform Initiatives

The Patient Protection and Affordable Care Act (ACA) (P.L. 111-148) required the HHS Secretary to oversee various programs to enhance health care quality, some of which are

¶700

administered by CMS and some of which are administered by other HHS agencies and entities.

National Quality Strategy. Pursuant to section 3011 of the ACA, the HHS Secretary established a national strategy to improve the delivery of health care and patient outcomes and created a comprehensive strategic plan to achieve those priorities. [Public Health Service Act § 399HH(a), (a)(2)(C) and (D).] HHS's Agency for Healthcare Research and Quality submitted its first national strategy to Congress in March 2011 and updates the report annually. The national priorities for improvement of health care quality and the agency-specific strategic plans are posted on an agency website available to the public (http://www.ahrq.gov/workingforquality/).

Center for Medicare and Medicaid Innovation. Section 3021 of the ACA established the Center for Medicare and Medicaid Innovation (CMMI) within CMS. The CMMI tests systems of provider payment and delivery of services in order to cut costs while preserving or enhancing the quality of care delivered to Medicare and Medicaid beneficiaries. The HHS Secretary selects test models, giving preference to models that have the effect of improving the coordination, quality, and efficiency of health care services available to Medicare and Medicaid beneficiaries. [Soc. Sec. Act § 1115A.]

Independent Payment Advisory Board. The Independent Payment Advisory Board (IPAB), which never convened after being established by section 3403 of the ACA, was repealed by the Bipartisan Budget Act of 2018 (P.L. 115-123). IPAB was designed to make recommendations to Congress on reducing the per capita rate of growth in Medicare spending and improving access to health care. [Soc. Sec. Act § 1899A, as amended by Bipartisan Budget Act of 2018 § 52001.]

Railroad Retirement Board

CMS and the Railroad Retirement Board have agreed on a delegation of important responsibilities to the railroad agency in connection with Medicare Part B. Under this delegation, the Railroad Retirement Board has responsibility for enrolling railroad eligibles in Medicare, collecting their premiums, and selecting MACs (see ¶ 705) for railroad enrollees under Part B.

The Railroad Retirement Board applies the same policies and regulations as CMS in determining what expenses are covered and what payments are to be made. [Soc. Sec. Act § 226(a)(2)(B), (b)(2)(B).]

Private Accrediting Organizations

The HHS Secretary contracts with private national accreditation bodies to determine whether hospitals, skilled nursing facilities, home health agencies, ambulatory surgical centers, hospices, organ transplant centers, rural health clinics, laboratories, clinics, rehabilitation agencies (including comprehensive outpatient rehabilitation agencies), psychiatric hospitals, public health agencies, and suppliers of durable medical equipment, prosthetics, orthotics, and supplies meet Medicare requirements. [Soc. Sec. Act §§ 1834(a)(20)(F), 1865(a); 42 C.F.R § 488.6.]

[¶ 703] Role of the State and Local Agencies

The Social Security Act requires the HHS Secretary to enter into agreements with able and willing state agencies to determine whether a provider of services—a hospital, skilled nursing facility, home health agency, hospice, rural health clinic, critical access hospital, comprehensive outpatient rehabilitation facility, clinic, rehabilitation agency, public health agency, or ambulatory surgical center—meets the conditions of participation of federal health care programs. State agencies conduct investigations, called surveys, and certify to the Secretary that a provider meets the conditions of participation. [Soc. Sec. Act § 1864(a), (c).]

State agencies also certify compliance with respect to other health care entities, such as independent laboratories, suppliers of portable x-ray services, and public health agencies providing outpatient physical and occupational therapy or speech-language pathology services under Part B. If the state survey agency determines that a provider or facility is not in substantial compliance with the conditions of participation, it must give written notice of the deficiencies. [42 C.F.R. § 488.18.]

Providers and facilities are surveyed at the following times: on initial application to participate in Medicare; when certification or enrollment is up for renewal; when the provider or facility receives a complaint or allegation of a deficiency; and selectively, on a sample basis. [Soc. Sec. Act § 1864(a), (c).]

Public assistance recipients. State Medicaid agencies also determine eligibility of Medicare beneficiaries for the low-income subsidy, which pays for part or all of the beneficiaries' cost-sharing requirements for prescription drug plans under Medicare Part D (see ¶ 508). [Soc. Sec. Act § 1860D-14.]

If a state enters into an agreement with Medicare to pay the Part B premium on behalf of its public assistance recipients, the agreement may provide for a designated state agency to serve as a Medicare administrative contractor (MAC) on behalf of its public assistance recipients. [Soc. Sec. Act § 1843(f).]

Disclosure of Survey and Fraud Information

Within 90 days following the state agency's completion of a health facility survey, information from the survey is available to the public, including a statement of deficiencies or the survey report itself and any pertinent written statements furnished by the surveyed facility. [Soc. Sec. Act § 1864(a).]

Adverse fraud and abuse information. The National Practitioner Data Bank (NPDB) collects fraud and abuse data from state agencies and other sources and provides this data to authorized recipients. HHS's Health Resources and Services Administration administers the NPDB as a confidential clearinghouse for fraud and abuse information. The databank is located at http://www.npdb.hrsa.gov/ (see ¶ 720).

[¶ 705] Role of Medicare Administrative Contractors

Private organizations have a considerable role in the administration of Medicare. Medicare administrative contractors (MACs) process and pay both Part A and Part B claims from particular geographic areas of the country. MACs competitively bid on contracts with the federal government to perform administrative and operational tasks for the program. [Soc. Sec. Act §§ 1816, 1842(a), 1874A.]

MACs' functions include: (1) determining the amount of Medicare payments made to providers and suppliers; (2) making Medicare payments; (3) providing beneficiary education and assistance; (4) providing consultative services to institutions, agencies, and other persons to enable them to establish and maintain necessary fiscal records; (5) communicating with providers and suppliers; (6) providing education and technical assistance to providers and suppliers; (7) maintaining an improper payment outreach and education program; and (8) any additional functions as necessary. [Soc. Sec. Act § 1874A(a)(4).]

Requirements for Medicare Administrative Contractors

An entity is eligible to become a MAC only if it: (1) has demonstrated capability to carry out the MAC functions; (2) complies with conflict-of-interest standards; (3) has sufficient assets to support operation; and (4) meets other requirements as the Secretary may impose. [Soc. Sec. Act § 1874A(a)(2).]

Contract requirements. The HHS Secretary must use competitive procedures when awarding MAC contracts. If a MAC has met or exceeded performance requirements, HHS may renew the contract from term to term without the application of competitive procedures, as long as it recompetes contracts at least once every 10 years. [Soc. Sec. Act § 1847A(b)(1)(A), (B).]

The Secretary is required to develop contract performance requirements and standards for measuring the extent to which a contractor has met the requirements and make them available to the public. [Soc. Sec. Act § 1874A(b)(3).]

Beginning for contracts entered into or renewed on or after December 28, 2018, the HHS Secretary must provide incentives for MACs to reduce the improper payment error rates in their jurisdictions. [Soc. Sec. Act § 1874A(b)(1)(D).]

MAC Jurisdictions

As of October 2017, MAC jurisdictions are as follows:

- Jurisdiction 5 (Iowa, Kansas, Missouri, and Nebraska);
- Jurisdiction 6 (Illinois, Minnesota, and Wisconsin);
- Jurisdiction 8 (Indiana and Michigan);
- Jurisdiction 15 (Kentucky and Ohio);
- Jurisdiction E (California, Hawaii, Nevada, and Pacific Islands);
- Jurisdiction F (Alaska, Arizona, Idaho, Montana, North Dakota, Oregon, South Dakota, Utah, Washington, and Wyoming);
- Jurisdiction H (Arkansas, Colorado, New Mexico, Oklahoma, Texas, Louisiana, and Mississippi);
- Jurisdiction J (Alabama, Georgia, and Tennessee);
- Jurisdiction K (New York, Connecticut, Massachusetts, Rhode Island, Vermont, Maine, and New Hampshire);
- Jurisdiction L (Delaware, Maryland, Pennsylvania, New Jersey, and Washington, D.C.);
- Jurisdiction M (North Carolina, South Carolina, Virginia, and West Virginia); and
- Jurisdiction N (Florida, Puerto Rico, and U.S. Virgin Islands).

[https://www.cms.gov/Medicare/Medicare-Contracting/Medicare-Administrative-Contractors/Downloads/MACs-by-State-October-2017.pdf.]

DME MACs. Durable medical equipment (DME) MACs are responsible for processing Medicare durable medical equipment, orthotics, and prosthetics claims for a jurisdiction. CMS has established four DME MAC jurisdictions. [https://www.cms.gov/Medicare/Medicare-Contracting/Medicare-Administrative-Contractors/Downloads/DME-MAC-Jurisdiction-Map-Oct-2017.pdf.]

Home health and hospice. Four of the A/B MACs also process home health and hospice claims in addition to their typical Medicare Part A and Part B claims. [https://www.cms.gov/Medicare/Medicare-Contracting/Medicare-Administrative-Contractors/Downloads/HHH-Jurisdiction-Map-Oct-2017.pdf.]

[¶ 710] Quality Improvement Organizations

Quality improvement organizations (QIOs) review the professional activities of physicians, other health care practitioners, and providers that furnish health care services and items that may be paid for by Medicare. QIOs are private organizations staffed by professionals, mostly doctors and other health care professionals, who are trained to review medical care, help beneficiaries with complaints about quality of care, and implement quality improvements. [Soc. Sec. Act §§ 1153, 1154(a)(1); https://www.cms.gov/Medicare/Quality-Initiatives-Patient-Assessment-Instruments/QualityImprovementOrgs/index.html.]

QIO contracts last five years, with each cycle referenced as an ordinal Statement of Work (SOW). [Soc. Sec. Act § 1153(c)(3).] As a condition of participation in Medicare, all hospitals, critical access hospitals (CAHs), skilled nursing facilities, and home health agencies are required to have an agreement with a QIO. [Soc. Sec. Act § 1866(a)(1)(F).]

Scope of QIO Review

QIOs review hospitals paid by the hospital inpatient prospective payment system (IPPS), under which hospitals are paid a fixed rate per discharge according to Medicare severity diagnosis-related groups (MS-DRGs) of illnesses (see ¶ 810). QIOs review the care and services provided to a beneficiary to determine the following:

(1) whether the services were reasonable and medically necessary;

(2) whether the quality of the services meets professionally recognized standards of health care;

(3) whether inpatient services could be effectively furnished more economically on an outpatient basis or in an inpatient health care facility of a different type;

(4) the validity of diagnostic and procedural information supplied by the hospital;

(5) the completeness, adequacy, and quality of hospital care provided;

(6) the medical necessity, reasonableness, and appropriateness of hospital admissions and discharges;

(7) the medical necessity, reasonableness, and appropriateness of inpatient hospital care for which additional payment is sought; and

(8) whether a hospital has misrepresented admission or discharge information or has taken an action that results in unnecessary admissions or other inappropriate practices.

[Soc. Sec. Act § 1154(a)(1); 42 C.F.R. § 476.71(a).]

The determinations of QIOs on these matters are binding for purposes of determining whether Medicare benefits should be paid, with some exceptions. [Soc. Sec. Act § 1154(a)(2).]

If a QIO finds that an IPPS hospital has taken an action that results in unnecessary admissions, unnecessary multiple admissions of the same such individuals, or other inappropriate medical or other practices with respect to such individuals, the Secretary may: (1) deny payment, in whole or in part, for the inappropriate services; (2) require the hospital to take other corrective action necessary to prevent or correct the inappropriate practice; or (3) in the case of a pattern of inappropriate admissions and billing practices that circumvent the IPPS, terminate the provider participation agreement (see Soc. Sec. Act § 1128(c)–(g)). [Soc. Sec. Act § 1886(f)(2).]

Each QIO assumes review responsibilities in accordance with the schedule, functions, and negotiated objectives specified in its contract with CMS, including the review require-

¶710

ments detailed in the SOW, which are incorporated into the QIO contract. [42 C.F.R. § 476.74.] The SOW establishes specific tasks for QIOs in relation to hospitals, ambulatory surgical centers, clinics, rehabilitation facilities, home health agencies, and physicians. QIOs collaborate with providers to develop and institute processes to improve the quality of care and eliminate unreasonable, unnecessary, and inappropriate care provided to beneficiaries. [*Notice*, 79 FR 46830, Aug. 11, 2014; *Medicare Quality Improvement Organization Manual*, Pub. 100-10, Ch. 1, § 1005.]

The eleventh SOW, which began on August 1, 2014, was scheduled to last five years. As a part of a restructuring of the QIO program in 2014, the QIO program separated medical case review from its quality improvement activities in each state under two types of regional contracts: (1) Beneficiary and Family Centered Care QIOs (BFCC-QIOs) contractors, which perform medical case review; and (2) Quality Innovation Network QIOs (QIN-QIOs) contractors, which perform quality improvement activities and provide technical assistance to providers and practitioners. In addition, the restructured QIO program uses a non-QIO contractor to assist CMS in the monitoring and oversight of the BFCC-QIO case review activities. [*Notice*, 79 FR 46830, Aug. 11, 2014.]

QIO Mandatory Case Review

QIOs must review the following:

Beneficiary complaints. QIOs review all written beneficiary complaints regarding quality of health care and services not meeting professionally recognized standards of health care, as well as oral complaints (see below for a discussion of the alternative dispute resolution process). QIOs must receive written complaints within three years of the care giving rise to the complaint and treat all information submitted by the beneficiary or his or her representative as confidential. Providers must deliver all medical information requested in response to a Medicare beneficiary complaint within 14 calendar days of the QIO's request. The QIO peer reviewer will complete the review and notify the practitioner and/or provider of the interim initial determination within 10 calendar days of the receipt of all medical information, giving the provider an opportunity for discussion. The QIO peer reviewer then must telephone the beneficiary within three days and issue a written final initial determination to all parties within five days after completion of the review. [Soc. Sec. Act § 1154(a)(14); 42 C.F.R. § § 476.120, 476.130.]

A Medicare beneficiary, provider, or practitioner who is dissatisfied with a QIO's final initial determination may request a reconsideration by the QIO. [42 C.F.R. § 476.140.]

Noncoverage notices issued by hospitals. Hospitals issue noncoverage notices to Medicare beneficiaries informing them that Medicare will deny coverage of their continued stay if the hospital determines, and the attending physician concurs, that inpatient care no longer is required. QIOs are required to review noncoverage notices issued by a hospital on the request of the hospital, the beneficiary, or his or her representative. [Soc. Sec. Act § 1154(e); Pub. 100-10, Ch. 7, § 7000.]

Antidumping violations. QIOs review allegations of hospital emergency rooms turning away or transferring patients without screening for, or stabilizing, emergency medical conditions. [Soc. Sec. Act § 1867(d)(3); 42 C.F.R. § 489.24(h).]

Review of assistants at surgery in cataract operations. QIOs review requests for surgical assistants based on medical necessity. Medicare payment for the services of an assistant at cataract surgery is prohibited unless a QIO approves the services before the surgery based on the existence of a complicating medical condition. [Soc. Sec. Act § 1862(a)(15); Pub. 100-10, Ch. 4, § 4020.]

Requests for upward adjustment of MS-DRG. QIOs perform MS-DRG coding validation reviews of IPPS cases, including hospital requests for higher-weighted MS-DRG adjustments. DRG validation ensures that diagnostic and procedural information and the discharge status of the patient as coded and reported by the hospital on its claim match the attending physician's description and the information contained in the patient's medical record. [Soc. Sec. Act § 1866(a)(1)(F); 42 C.F.R. § 476.71(a)(4); Pub. 100-10, Ch. 4, § 4130.]

Referrals. QIOs review all cases referred by CMS, HHS, the Office of Inspector General, Medicare contractors, clinical data abstraction centers, Medicare Advantage organization contractors, or state Medicaid and survey and certification agencies. [Pub. 100-10, Ch. 4, § 4070.]

Alternative Dispute Resolution Process

QIOs offer an alternative dispute resolution option called "Immediate Advocacy" to quickly resolve an oral complaint a Medicare beneficiary or his or her representative has regarding the quality of Medicare covered health care. This process involves a QIO representative's direct contact with the provider and/or practitioner. A QIO may offer the option of resolving an oral complaint through the use of immediate advocacy if:

(1) the QIO receives the complaint within six months of the incident;

(2) after initial screening of the complaint, the QIO makes a preliminary determination that it is unrelated to the clinical quality of health care itself but relates to items or services that accompany or are incidental to the medical care; or the complaint, while related to the clinical quality of health care received by the beneficiary, does not rise to the level of being a gross and flagrant, substantial, or significant quality of care concern;

(3) the beneficiary agrees to the disclosure of his or her name to the involved provider and/or practitioner;

(4) all parties orally consent to the use of immediate advocacy; and

(5) all parties agree to confidentiality limitations on redisclosure.

The QIO or either party may discontinue participation in immediate advocacy at any time. The QIO may determine that a complaint has been abandoned, after which it will inform the parties that immediate advocacy will be discontinued. The QIO will also inform the Medicare beneficiary of his or her right to submit a written complaint. [42 C.F.R. §§ 476.1, 476.110.]

Appeals from QIO Coverage Determinations

If a QIO's determination denies coverage or a requested MS-DRG as a result of MS-DRG validation, the beneficiary, provider, or practitioner is entitled to notice and reconsideration of the determination by the QIO. An initial denial determination consists of a finding that the health care services provided were unnecessary, unreasonable, or at an inappropriate level of care. [Soc. Sec. Act §§ 1154(a)(3), 1155; 42 C.F.R. §§ 478.12, 478.15, 478.16.]

A beneficiary, provider, or attending practitioner who is dissatisfied with an initial denial determination may obtain reconsideration of the initial review by filing a written request within 60 days after the date of the initial denial determination, unless the time is extended for good cause. The date of receipt of the initial denial determination notice is presumed to be five days after the date listed on the notice unless there is a showing to the contrary. [42 C.F.R. §§ 478.12, 478.20, 478.22.]

If the QIO's reconsidered determination is adverse to the beneficiary and the amount in controversy is at least $200, the beneficiary (but not a provider or practitioner) may request a hearing by an administrative law judge (ALJ) within 60 days after the date of receipt of the notice of reconsidered determination. If the amount in controversy is $2,000 or greater, the beneficiary is entitled to judicial review of the ALJ's decision. [Soc. Sec. Act § 1155; 42 C.F.R. §§ 478.12, 478.20, 478.40, 478.46.]

Limitations on Beneficiary Liability

The law prohibits physicians, in the case of assigned claims, from billing beneficiaries for services for which payment has been denied by a QIO on the basis of substandard quality of care. [Soc. Sec. Act § 1842(b)(3)(B)(ii).] CMS also indemnifies the beneficiary for any deductible and coinsurance paid if a QIO has denied Medicare payment for services. [Soc. Sec. Act § 1879(b).]

QIO-Recommended Sanctions

If a QIO determines that a practitioner or provider has violated its obligations to furnish services that are economical, medically necessary, of proper quality, and properly documented, the QIO may recommend sanctions. Practitioners and providers are entitled to reasonable notice of a sanction determination and must be provided the opportunity for a hearing as well as judicial review. The first step is to give the provider or practitioner the opportunity to meet with three members of the QIO to discuss the potential violation and agree to a corrective action plan approved by the QIO. [Soc. Sec. Act § 1156(a), (b); 42 C.F.R. § 1004.30.]

If the practitioner or provider fails to complete its corrective action plan and the QIO determines that the provider or practitioner has violated the requirements in a substantial number of cases or has violated one or more requirements "grossly and flagrantly," the QIO must submit a report and recommendation to the Secretary on the imposition of sanctions, including exclusion from Medicare and Medicaid participation or assessment of fines. A QIO recommendation of exclusion automatically becomes effective if the Secretary fails to act within a 120-day review period. [Soc. Sec. Act § 1156(b); 42 C.F.R. §§ 1004.30, 1004.40; Pub. 100-10, Ch. 9, § 9000.]

[¶ 711] Recovery Audit Contractors

The HHS Secretary is authorized to contract with eligible private entities known as recovery audit contractors (RACs) to perform specified review and audit functions. The RAC program was designed to identify and correct Medicare improper payments through the efficient detection and collection of overpayments made on claims of health care services provided to Medicare beneficiaries and the identification of underpayments to providers. These identifications allow CMS to implement actions that will prevent future improper payments. [Soc. Sec. Act § 1893(h).]

RACs perform a variety of review and audit functions, including:

(1) review of activities of providers of services or other individuals and entities furnishing items and services for which Medicare payment may be made, including medical and utilization review and fraud review;

(2) audit of cost reports;

(3) determinations as to the appropriateness of Medicare payment, and recovery of payments that should not have been made;

(4) education of providers, beneficiaries, and other persons with respect to payment integrity and benefit quality assurance issues;

(5) developing and updating a list of items of durable medical equipment that are subject to prior authorization under Soc. Sec. Act § 1834(a)(15); and

(6) the Medicare-Medicaid Data Match Program.

[Soc. Sec. Act § 1893(b).]

RACs are paid on a contingency basis from the recovered funds. The amount of the contingency fee is a percentage of the improper payment recovered from, or reimbursed to, providers. [Soc. Sec. Act § 1893(h).]

CMS also has the authority to enter into contracts with RACs to identify and reconcile overpayments and underpayments in Medicare Parts C and D. In addition to their other responsibilities, RACs must: ensure that MA and prescription drug plans (PDPs) have antifraud plans in effect and review the effectiveness of the plans; review PDPs' estimates on enrollment of high-cost beneficiaries; and examine claims for reinsurance payments to determine whether PDPs submitting such claims incurred costs in excess of the allowable reinsurance costs permitted. [Soc. Sec. Act § 1893(h)(9).]

RAC Program Operation

The RAC program originated as a demonstration project but was later expanded to include all 50 states. Five RACs cover specific geographic areas of the nation. [https://www.cms.gov/research-statistics-data-and-systems/monitoring-programs/medicare-ffs-compliance-programs/recovery-audit-program/.]

An entity is eligible to enter into a contract under the RAC program if it meets certain requirements, one of which is to demonstrate to the Secretary that the entity's financial holdings, interests, or relationships will not interfere with its ability to perform as required. Medicare administrative contractors (MACs) (see ¶ 705) are prohibited from entering into contracts under this provision. [Soc. Sec. Act § 1893(c), (h)(6)(B).]

Appeals of RAC Determinations

Appeals of RAC determinations regarding fee-for-service claims are handled with other overpayment determinations under the regular Medicare appeals process. There are five levels of appeals for claim denials, including those resulting from RAC audits: (1) redetermination by the MAC; (2) reconsideration by a qualified independent contractor; (3) administrative law judge hearing; (4) Medicare Appeals Council review; and (5) judicial review in federal court. [Soc. Sec. Act § 1869.]

If the Part C or Part D RAC did not apply its stated payment methodology correctly, MA organizations and Part D plan sponsors may appeal the findings of the applied methodology. [42 C.F.R. § § 422.2600, 423.2600.]

See ¶ 924 for a detailed discussion of the claims appeals process.

[¶ 715] Privacy of Health Data

Pursuant to the Health Insurance Portability and Accountability Act of 1996 (HIPAA) (P.L. 104-191), HHS implemented national standards to protect individually identifiable health information. The HIPAA privacy and security standards apply to all health care plans, health care clearinghouses, and health care providers who transmit any health information in electronic form (collectively called "covered entities"). [45 C.F.R. § § 160.102, 160.103.]

Business associates. Health care providers and other covered entities are responsible for the use of protected health information (PHI) released to other organizations and must have a contract (or other written agreement) with each business associate detailing how the business associate will protect the individually identifiable information. [45 C.F.R. § 164.502(e)(2).] Business associates must provide the same protection to individually identifiable data as health care providers or other covered entities. [45 C.F.R. § 164.504(e).]

¶715

Individually Identifiable Health Information

"Individually identifiable health information" is data created or received by a health care provider, health plan, employer, or health care clearinghouse that relates to: (1) the past, present, or future physical or mental health condition of an individual; (2) the provision of health care to an individual; or (3) the past, present, or future payment for the provision of health care. It identifies the individual or could reasonably be used to identify the individual. [45 C.F.R. § 160.103.]

"Protected health information" (PHI) is individually identifiable health information that is transmitted or maintained in any medium. The regulations cover all health data, including written records and oral communications, and not just electronically maintained or transmitted data. The disclosure of health information includes the release, transfer, provision of, access to, or divulging of patient health information, in any manner, to others outside of the entity holding the information. [45 C.F.R. § 160.103.]

The term "health care" as it relates to HIPAA means care, services, or supplies related to the health of an individual, including the following services: (1) preventive, diagnostic, therapeutic, rehabilitative, counseling, service assessments, or any other procedure with respect to the physical, mental, or functional condition of a patient; and (2) the sale or dispensing of prescription drugs, equipment, or devices in accordance with a prescription. [45 C.F.R. § 160.103.]

Notice of Privacy Practices

Health care providers must issue a notice to patients during the first delivery of service describing the provider's privacy policy. Providers are required to conduct a good faith effort to obtain written acknowledgment from a patient of the receipt of the privacy notice. In an emergency situation, the provider may obtain the acknowledgment as soon as reasonably practicable. The notice also must be available at any time and publicly displayed in a clear and prominent location in the provider's office. [45 C.F.R. § 164.520(c)(2).]

The notice must describe how the patient's medical information will be used and disclosed and inform patients that they have a right to inspect, copy, amend, and receive a list of people and organizations that have requested access to their PHI. It must contain the name, title, and telephone number of a contact person in the provider's office, as well as a description of the provider's legal duties with respect to the patient's PHI. [45 C.F.R. § 164.520(a)(1), (b).]

The notice must contain the following header statement in all capital letters (or otherwise be prominently displayed):

"THIS NOTICE DESCRIBES HOW MEDICAL INFORMATION ABOUT YOU MAY BE USED AND DISCLOSED AND HOW YOU CAN GET ACCESS TO THIS INFORMATION. PLEASE REVIEW IT CAREFULLY."

[45 C.F.R. § 164.520(b)(1)(i).] In addition, providers must retain copies of the notices issued and, if applicable, any written acknowledgments of the patient's receipt of the notice, or any other documentation of the provider's good faith efforts to obtain a written acknowledgment of the patient's privacy rights. [45 C.F.R. § 164.520(e).]

Exception for inmates. Because inmates do not have a right to notice under the provisions of 45 C.F.R. § 164.520, these notice requirements do not apply to a correctional institution that is also a covered entity. [45 C.F.R. § 164.520(a)(3).]

Authorization to Release Individually Identifiable Health Information

Health care providers may not release individually identifiable health information without an authorization unless the information is released: (1) for the provider's own treatment, payment, or health care operations; (2) for treatment activities of another health care provider; (3) for payment activities of another covered entity; (4) to other providers of the patient's care; or (5) to other providers in the provider's organized health care arrangement for the purposes of treating the patient. [45 C.F.R. § 164.506.] Patients have the right to request that providers restrict the use or disclosure of their personally identifiable health data, although the provider does not have to agree to a patient's requested restriction. [45 C.F.R. § 164.522.]

Patients may grant providers authorization to disclose individually identifiable health information for the following specific purposes:

- marketing;

- sale of PHI; or

- any use or disclosure of psychotherapy notes, except: (1) to carry out treatment, payment, or health care operations, or (2) for permitted uses by the originator of the psychotherapy notes.

Disclosures must be consistent with the authorization, and providers may not condition the provision of health care based on a patient's signing of such an authorization. [45 C.F.R. § 164.508(a).]

Requirements for authorizations. Authorizations must contain: (1) a description of the information to be disclosed and how it will be used; (2) the name of the person or organization authorized to make the disclosure; (3) the name of the person or organization or a description of the class of organization to which the information will be disclosed; (4) a description of the purpose of the release ("at the request of the individual" is a sufficient description of the purpose when the patient initiates the authorization); (5) an expiration date or event; and (6) the dated signature of the patient. [45 C.F.R. § 164.508(c).]

Exemptions to Privacy Rule

Under certain circumstances, a covered entity may use or disclose PHI, as long as the individual is informed before the use or disclosure and has the opportunity to agree to or prohibit or restrict the use or disclosure. [45 C.F.R. § 164.510.]

Facility directories. Health care facilities may provide a directory of patients that includes the patient's name, location in the facility, the general condition of the patient that does not communicate specific medical information, and the individual's religious affiliation. A patient must be given the opportunity to restrict or prohibit the information placed in this directory. [45 C.F.R. § 164.510(a)(1), (2).]

Limited use and disclosure. If the patient is unable to agree or object to the use or disclosure of PHI because he or she is incapacitated, in an emergency circumstance, or not present, health care facilities may use their professional judgment to determine whether disclosure is in the best interests of the patient. If so, the facility may disclose only the PHI that is directly relevant. [45 C.F.R. § 164.510(b)(3).]

Disaster relief. Health care facilities may use or disclose PHI to a public or private entity authorized by law or by its charter to assist in disaster relief efforts, for the purpose of coordinating with such entities permitted uses or disclosures of PHI, only to the extent the facility, in the exercise of professional judgment, determines that the requirements do not

¶715

interfere with the ability to respond to the emergency circumstances. [45 C.F.R. § 164.510(b)(4).]

Deceased patient. If the patient is deceased, a health care facility may disclose the patient's relevant PHI to a family member, or other identified individuals who were involved in the patient's care or payment for health care prior to the patient's death, unless doing so is inconsistent with any prior expressed preference of the patient that is known to the facility. [45 C.F.R. § 164.510(b)(5).]

Public welfare. Health care facilities may use or disclose a patient's PHI without authorization when the use or disclosure is: (1) required by law; (2) for public health activities; (3) to protect victims of abuse, neglect, or domestic violence; (4) for health oversight activities; (5) in judicial and administrative proceedings; (6) for law enforcement purposes; (7) about decedents; (8) for cadaveric organ, eye, or tissue donation purposes; (9) for research purposes; (10) to avert a serious threat to health or safety; (11) for specialized government functions; (12) for purposes of reporting to the National Instant Criminal Background Check System the identity of an individual who is prohibited from possessing a firearm under 18 U.S.C. § 922(g)(4); or (13) related to workers' compensation. Public welfare exceptions are limited and often require informing the patient about the disclosure. [45 C.F.R. § 164.512.]

Fundraising. Health care facilities may release limited PHI data to a business associate without authorization from the patient for the purpose of raising funds for the benefit of the facility. Health care facilities must remove personally identifiable data from fundraising lists upon request of the individual. [45 C.F.R. § 164.514(f).]

Minors. Health care providers may release PHI regarding a minor to the minor's parents, or individual acting as a parent, only if allowed by state law. If a minor can consent to a medical procedure and does not require the consent of any other individual, then the PHI concerning that procedure may not be released to a parent or individual acting as a parent unless the minor agrees or has signed an authorization for the release. [45 C.F.R. § 164.502(g).]

Patients' Rights Under HIPAA

Patients may view or request a copy (including electronic copies) of their PHI. A provider may, however, deny access to a patient's records if it believes that release of that information will endanger the life or physical safety of the individual. Providers, with the consent of the patient, may provide a summary of the data instead of the actual data itself and may charge a fee for providing access or copies. [45 C.F.R. § 164.524.]

Upon request, a laboratory may provide patients and their personal representatives with access to completed test reports belonging to that patient. [42 C.F.R. § 493.1291(l).]

An individual has the right to have a covered entity amend PHI or a record about that individual, but the provider does not have to include material submitted by a patient as an amendment if it was generated by another provider, is inaccurate, or is not part of the requested records. [45 C.F.R. § 164.526.] An individual also has a right to receive an accounting of disclosures of PHI made by a covered entity in the six years before the date on which the accounting is requested. Providers do not have to provide an accounting of the release of individually identifiable health information under certain circumstances, such as pursuant to a valid authorization. [45 C.F.R. § 164.528.]

HIPAA Breach Notification

HIPAA-covered entities, such as hospitals, doctors' offices, and health insurance plans, are required to notify an individual when his or her unsecured PHI has been or is reasonably believed to have been accessed, acquired, used, or disclosed as the result of a breach. This notice must be sent without unreasonable delay and in no case later than 60 days after the discovery of a breach. [45 C.F.R. § 164.404.] The covered entity must also notify the HHS Secretary and, for breaches that involve more than 500 residents of a state or jurisdiction, the media. [45 C.F.R. §§ 164.406, 164.408.] Business associates, as defined by HIPAA, are also subject to breach notification procedures. [45 C.F.R. § 164.410.]

16 C.F.R. Part 318 requires vendors of personal health records to notify individuals in the event of a security breach.

HIPAA Complaints

Health care providers must designate a privacy official who is responsible for the development and implementation of privacy policies and procedures and a contact person who receives complaints and requests. All staff members must be trained on privacy policies and procedures. [45 C.F.R. § 164.530(a)(1), (b)(1).]

A covered entity must also provide a process for individuals to make complaints concerning the entity's HIPAA privacy policies and procedures or its compliance with such policies and procedures. [45 C.F.R. § 164.530(d).]

A HIPAA complaint must:

- be filed in writing by mail, fax, e-mail, or via the Office of Civil Rights (OCR) Complaint Portal;

- name the covered entity involved and describe the acts or omissions that violated the requirements of the Privacy, Security, or Breach Notification Rules; and

- be filed within 180 days of when the act or omission complained of occurred.

OCR may extend the 180-day deadline for complaints if "good cause" is shown. Directions for filing a complaint, including forms, are provided on the OCR website at https://www.hhs.gov/hipaa/filing-a-complaint/complaint-process/index.html.

Penalties for HIPAA Violations

CMS imposes tiered penalties against any person who violates the requirements and standards of HIPAA Administration Simplification (Soc. Sec. Act §§ 1171–1180). Penalties range from $100 to $50,000 per violation. [Soc. Sec. Act § 1176; 45 C.F.R. § 160.404.]

Preemption of State Law

Most states have laws regulating the use and release of PHI. State law that provides more stringent regulation on the use and release of PHI preempts the HIPAA regulations, so providers must follow the state's laws in these cases. In all other cases, the HIPAA privacy regulations preempt state law. [45 C.F.R. § 160.203.]

Protection of Genetic Information

Title I of the Genetic Information Nondiscrimination Act of 2008 (GINA) (P.L. 110-233) prohibits group health plans and issuers in the group market from increasing premiums for a group based on the results of an enrollee's genetic information, denying enrollment, imposing pre-existing condition exclusions, and other forms of underwriting based on genetic information. In the individual health insurance market, GINA prohibits issuers from using genetic information to deny coverage, raise premiums, or impose pre-existing condition exclusions. [45 C.F.R. §§ 146.121, 146.122.]

Further, group health plans and health insurance issuers in both the group and individual markets cannot request, require, or buy genetic information for underwriting purposes or prior to and in connection with enrollment. Plans and issuers are generally

¶715

prohibited from asking individuals or family members to undergo a genetic test. [45 C.F.R. § 146.122(a)–(c).]

[¶ 717] Electronic Health Records

The Health Information Technology for Economic and Clinical Health (HITECH) Act (enacted as part of the American Recovery and Reinvestment Act of 2009 (ARRA) (P.L. 111-5)) provided for financial incentives and penalties to encourage the use of electronic health record (EHR) technology by physicians and hospitals to better manage patient care.

Certification of Electronic Health Record Technology

The HHS Office of the National Coordinator (ONC) for Health Information Technology identified the standards and certification criteria for certified EHR technology so that eligible professionals and hospitals can be assured that the systems they adopt are capable of performing the required functions (see 42 C.F.R. § § 495.2–495.370). Regulations on certification criteria and the certification program for EHR are found at 45 C.F.R. Part 170.

Meaningful Use of EHR Technology

To improve the use of EHR technology, CMS developed a three-stage measure known as "meaningful use." Each stage includes a series of specific objectives tied to a measure to allow health care providers to demonstrate that they are "meaningful users" of EHR technology. The first stage is data capture and sharing, the second stage is advance clinical processes, and the third stage is improved outcomes. [Soc. Sec. Act § § 1848(a)(7) and (o), 1886(n).]

Penalties for EPs and Hospitals

Eligible hospitals and critical access hospitals that do not successfully demonstrate meaningful use of certified EHR technology are subject to Medicare payment adjustments beginning in 2015. [Soc. Sec. Act § 1886(b)(3)(B)(ix); 42 C.F.R. § 495.104.]

Eligible professionals such as physicians who did not make meaningful use of health information technology were subject to a payment adjustment to their Medicare physician fee schedule payment of 3 percent in 2018. [Soc. Sec. Act § 1848(a)(7), (o); 42 C.F.R. § 495.102(d).] The Medicare Access and CHIP Reauthorization Act of 2015 (MACRA) (P.L. 114-10) consolidated and replaced the EHR meaningful use program, the Physician Quality Reporting System, and the value-based payment modifier into the new Merit-Based Incentive Payment System (MIPS) program for eligible professionals. Under MACRA, starting in 2019, the amounts paid to individual providers are subject to adjustment through one of two mechanisms, depending on whether the physician chooses to participate in an Alternative Payment Model (APM) program or MIPS. [MACRA § 101(b), (c), (e)(2).] See ¶ 855 for a discussion of MACRA.

[¶ 720] Fraud and Abuse Penalties

"Fraud" is defined as obtaining something of value unlawfully through willful misrepresentation. It includes theft, embezzlement, false statements, illegal commissions, kickbacks, conspiracies, and obtaining contracts through collusive arrangements and similar devices. "Abuse" is defined as the administrative violation of agency regulations, which impair the effective and efficient execution of the program. Violations may result in federal monetary losses or in denial or reduction in lawfully authorized benefits to participants, but they do not involve fraud. [*Financial Management Manual*, Pub. 100-06, Ch. 8, § 140.1.]

The laws used to combat health care fraud and abuse under government-funded health care programs include, among others:

- the federal criminal statutes under Title 18, Criminal Penalties for Acts Involving Federal Health Care Programs;

- the False Claims Act (FCA);

- sections of the Health Insurance Portability and Accountability Act of 1996 (HIPAA) (P.L. 104-191); and

- provisions of the Social Security Act including: (1) "Criminal Penalties for Acts Involving Federal Health Care Programs," Soc. Sec. Act § 1128B(a) and (c)–(h), including the anti-kickback provisions (Soc. Sec. Act § 1128B(b)); and (2) "Limitation on Certain Physician Self-referrals," Soc. Sec. Act § 1877 (referred to as the Stark law).

Health Care Fraud and Abuse Control Program

The Health Care Fraud and Abuse Control Program is under the joint direction of the Attorney General and HHS acting through the Office of Inspector General (OIG). Under the Health Care Fraud and Abuse Control Program, the OIG and the Attorney General are required to: (1) coordinate federal, state, and local law enforcement programs to control fraud and abuse with respect to health plans; (2) conduct investigations, audits, evaluations, and inspections relating to the delivery of and payment for health care in the United States; (3) facilitate the enforcement of the provisions of the exclusion provisions, civil money penalties (CMPs) statute, and false statements and anti-kickback provisions, as well as other statutes applicable to health care fraud and abuse; and (4) provide for the establishment and modification of safe harbors and issue advisory opinions and special fraud alerts. [Soc. Sec. Act § 1128C.]

Fraud and Abuse Data Collection Program

The National Practitioner Data Bank (NPDB) (see http://www.npdb.hrsa.gov/) collects and releases data related to the professional competence of physicians, dentists, and certain other health care practitioners. The types of information included in the NPDB are medical malpractice claims payments, certain adverse licensure actions, adverse clinical privileging actions, adverse professional society membership actions, and exclusions from Medicare and Medicaid. [Soc. Sec. Act §§ 1128E, 1921.]

Anti-kickback Statute

The anti-kickback statute forbids the solicitation, receipt, offer, or payment of any kind of remuneration (including any kickback, bribe, or rebate) in return for referring an individual or for recommending or arranging the purchase, lease, or ordering of an item or service that may be wholly or partially paid for under a federal health care program. In addition to criminal prosecution and civil fines, violation of these laws subjects the violator to exclusion from Medicare, Medicaid, and other state health care programs. [Soc. Sec. Act § 1128B.]

Conviction under the anti-kickback statute may be punishable by a fine of up to $100,000, imprisonment for up to 10 years, or both. [Soc. Sec. Act § 1128B(b), as amended by Bipartisan Budget Act of 2018 (P.L. 115-123) § 50412.] Claims that include items or services resulting from a violation of the anti-kickback statute constitute false claims under the federal FCA. [Soc. Sec. Act § 1128B(g).]

Safe harbors. Congress created several exceptions to the anti-kickback prohibitions (referred to as "statutory safe harbors") to address certain permissible activities under the statute. HHS also created regulatory safe harbors that immunize various payment practices and business arrangements from criminal prosecution or civil sanctions under the anti-kickback statute. [Soc. Sec. Act § 1128B(b)(3); 42 C.F.R. § 1001.952.]

¶720

"Stark" Law: Physician Self-Referral Prohibitions

The "Limitation on Certain Physician Referrals" statute, commonly known as the "Stark" law, prohibits a physician from making referrals for certain designated health care services (DHS) to entities with which the physician (or an immediate family member) has a financial relationship. If a financial relationship exists between a referring physician and an entity providing a DHS that does not meet an exception, the Stark law is violated and no claims from the referring physician to the entity providing DHS may be submitted to Medicare. The Stark law further prohibits an entity from presenting or causing to be presented a Medicare claim or bill to any individual, third-party payer, or other entity, for clinical laboratory services furnished under a prohibited referral. [Soc. Sec. Act § 1877.]

Financial relationship. For purposes of the physician self-referral prohibition statute, a "financial relationship" includes a physician's or a physician's immediate family member's ownership or investment interest in, or compensation arrangements (i.e., contractual arrangements) with, any entity that furnishes DHS. A compensation arrangement is any arrangement involving remuneration, direct or indirect, whether cash or in kind, between a physician and an entity. [42 C.F.R. § 411.354.]

Exceptions to physician self-referral prohibitions. CMS has established categories of exceptions to the physician self-referral prohibitions. [42 C.F.R. §§ 411.355–411.357.]

Stark law penalties. The penalties for making prohibited self-referrals include: (1) denial of payment for the DHS; (2) refund of amounts collected from the government for DHS claims; (3) imposition of CMPs of up to $15,000 for each DHS for which a claim was submitted; (4) imposition of a CMP of up to $100,000 and exclusion from participation in Medicare and other federal health care programs for circumvention schemes or arrangements that the physician or entity knows or should know violates the self-referral prohibitions; and (5) imposition of CMPs up to $10,000 per day for failing to meet the reporting requirements of Soc. Sec. Act § 1877(f). [Soc. Sec. Act § 1877(g)(1)–(5); 42 C.F.R. §§ 411.361(f), 1003.300, 1003.310.]

CMS advisory opinions. Any individual or entity may request a written advisory opinion from CMS concerning whether a physician's referral relating to DHS (other than clinical laboratory services) is prohibited. In the advisory opinion, CMS determines whether a business arrangement described by the parties appears to constitute a "financial relationship" that could potentially restrict a physician's referrals and whether the arrangement or the DHS at issue appear to qualify for any of the exceptions to the referral prohibition. An advisory opinion issued by CMS is binding as to the Secretary and the party requesting the opinion. [Soc. Sec. Act § 1877(g)(6)(A); 42 C.F.R. § 411.370.]

Civil Actions Under the False Claims Act

The FCA authorizes federal prosecutors to file a civil action against any person or entity that knowingly files a false claim with a federal health care program, including Medicare or Medicaid. [31 U.S.C. § 3729 *et seq.*] The term "claim" refers to an application for payment for items and services under a "federal health care program," such as Medicare or Medicaid. [Soc. Sec. Act § 1128A(i)(2).]

A person or entity may be prosecuted under the FCA for any of the following:

- knowingly presenting, or causing to be presented, a false or fraudulent claim for payment or approval;

- knowingly making, using, or causing to be made or used a false record or statement material to a false or fraudulent claim;

- knowingly making, using, or causing to be made or used a false record or statement, or concealing, avoiding, or decreasing an obligation to pay or transmit money or property to the government; or

- conspiring to commit any of the above violations.

[31 U.S.C. §§ 3729(a)(1), 3730(a).]

Knowledge. The FCA does not require proof of specific intent to defraud a federal health care program. It is sufficient for the person to (1) have actual knowledge of the information; (2) act in deliberate ignorance of the truth or falsity of the information; or (3) act in reckless disregard of the truth or falsity of the information provided or submitted. [31 U.S.C. § 3729(b).]

Qui tam actions. The FCA authorizes private persons to bring *qui tam* actions (also known as "whistleblower" actions). The FCA's *qui tam* provisions empower private persons to sue on behalf of the government and to share in the recovery of such actions. The amount of recovery for a *qui tam* plaintiff depends on whether the government decides to intervene in the case and the extent to which the *qui tam* plaintiff contributed to the prosecution of the claim. [31 U.S.C. § 3730.]

Penalties. A party that commits any prohibited acts under the FCA is liable to the federal government for a civil penalty of not less than $5,500 and not more than $11,000, plus three times the amount of damages that the government sustains because of the act of that party (also known as treble damages). [31 U.S.C. § 3729(a).] In addition to CMPs, parties that file false claims may also be subject to criminal prosecution and exclusion from participation in federal and state health care programs.

Civil Money Penalties

Under the provisions of Social Security Act section 1128A, the HHS Secretary is authorized to impose administrative sanctions in the form of CMPs and assessments against any person, organization, agency, or public or private entity that commits any of the acts described in Soc. Sec. Act § 1128A. [Soc. Sec. Act § 1128A(a).] The law also permits an individual upon whom the Secretary imposes a CMP or assessment to be excluded from participation in the Medicare and Medicaid programs. [Soc. Sec. Act § 1128(b).]

CMPs will not be imposed in connection with certain charitable and other innocuous programs. [Soc. Sec. Act § 1128A(i)(6)(F)–(I).]

Exclusion from Program Participation

The OIG has the authority to exclude individuals and entities that have engaged in fraud or abuse from participation in Medicare, Medicaid, and other federal health care programs. The OIG imposes a mandatory exclusionary period for those individuals or entities convicted of a health care-related offense and has the discretion to exclude providers that have engaged in civil fraud, kickbacks, or other prohibited activities, including quality of care deficiencies. [Soc. Sec. Act § 1128(a), (b).]

Mandatory exclusion. Under the mandatory exclusion provisions of the Social Security Act, an individual or entity *must* be excluded from participation in any federal health care program if convicted of any of the following: (1) a criminal offense related to the delivery of an item of service under Medicare or under any state health care program; (2) a criminal offense relating to neglect or abuse of patients in connection with the delivery of a health care item or service; (3) a felony relating to fraud, theft, embezzlement, breach of fiduciary responsibility, or other financial misconduct relating to health care; or (4) a felony relating to the unlawful manufacture, distribution, prescription, or dispensing of a controlled substance. [Soc. Sec. Act § 1128(a); 42 C.F.R. § 1001.101.]

¶720

The minimum period of a mandatory exclusion is five years. If, however, the individual has (before, on, or after such date) been convicted on one previous occasion of one or more offenses for which an exclusion may be imposed under Soc. Sec. Act § 1128(a), the period of the exclusion must be at least 10 years. An exclusion will be permanent if the individual has been convicted on two or more other occasions of one or more offenses for which an exclusion may be effected under Soc. Sec. Act § 1128(a). [Soc. Sec. Act § 1128(a), (c).]

Permissive exclusion. The OIG *may* exclude individuals or entities for any of the reasons described in Soc. Sec. Act § 1128(b). The exclusion period varies based on the offense. [Soc. Sec. Act § 1128(b), (c) (3).]

Payment of claims after exclusion. If a patient submits Part B claims for services furnished by an excluded practitioner, Medicare will pay the first claim submitted and immediately notify the beneficiary of the exclusion. CMS will not pay for items or services furnished by an excluded individual or entity, or under the medical direction or on the prescription of an excluded physician or other authorized individual, more than 15 days after the date on the notice to the enrollee, or after the effective date of the exclusion, whichever is later. Additionally, payment will be made for up to 30 days after the date of the exclusion for inpatient hospital and skilled nursing facility services furnished to patients admitted before the effective date of the suspension, and for home health and hospice care furnished under a plan established before the effective date of the suspension. [42 C.F.R. § 1001.1901(c)(1)–(3).]

Criminal Medicare and Medicaid Fraud

Soc. Sec. Act § 1128B identifies the penalties corresponding to specific unlawful acts under Medicare related to: (1) false statements and representations; (2) anti-kickback violations; (3) facility qualifications; and (4) excess charges. Section 50412(b) of the Bipartisan Budget Act of 2018 (P.L. 115-123) increased the criminal fines and sentences for health care fraud, effective for acts committed after February 9, 2018. [Soc. Sec. Act § § 1107 and 1128B.]

A person need not have specific intent to commit a violation of section 1128B. [Soc. Sec. Act § 1128B(h).]

Federal health care offenses. Title 18 of the United States Code, regarding Crimes and Criminal Procedures, includes the term "federal health care offense," which involves certain offenses or criminal conspiracies to commit such offenses. [18 U.S.C. § 24.]

Section 8122 of the SUPPORT for Patients and Communities Act (P.L. 115-271) added 18 U.S.C. § 220, which prohibits, with respect to services covered by a health care benefit program, in or affecting interstate or foreign commerce, knowingly and willfully:

(1) soliciting or receiving any remuneration in return for referring a patient or patronage to a recovery home, clinical treatment facility, or laboratory; or

(2) paying or offering any remuneration (including any kickback, bribe, or rebate) to induce a referral of an individual to a recovery home, clinical treatment facility, or laboratory; or in exchange for an individual using the services of that recovery home, clinical treatment facility, or laboratory.

Those who violate section 220 will be fined up to $200,000, imprisoned up to 10 years, or both, for each occurrence. [18 U.S.C. § 220.]

Voluntary Self-Disclosure Protocols

In 2013 the OIG published a voluntary provider self-disclosure protocol (SDP), which established a process for health care providers to voluntarily identify, disclose, and resolve instances of potential fraud involving the federal health care programs. Providers should conduct an initial assessment to substantiate that there is noncompliance with program requirements before making a disclosure to the OIG. In addition, a disclosing provider should conduct an internal financial assessment and prepare a report of its findings to estimate the monetary impact of the disclosed matter. Providers that disclose under the SDP should do so with the intention of resolving their overpayment liability exposure for the conduct identified. [*OIG Letter, Recommendations for Provider Self-Disclosure*, April 17, 2013.]

In settling the matter, the OIG's general practice is to require a minimum multiplier of 1.5 times the single damages, although in each case, it determines whether a higher multiplier is appropriate. For kickback-related submissions accepted into the SDP, the OIG will require a minimum $50,000 settlement. For all other matters accepted into the SDP, the OIG will require a minimum $10,000 settlement amount to resolve the matter. [*OIG Letter, Recommendations for Provider Self-Disclosure*, April 17, 2013.]

Open Payments

Manufacturers of covered drugs, devices, biologics, or medical supplies are required to annually submit information regarding payments or other transfers of value made to physicians and teaching hospitals. Applicable manufacturers or group purchasing organizations are also required to disclose all ownership and investment interests in the applicable manufacturer or applicable group purchasing organization that were held by a physician or an immediate family member of a physician. [Soc. Sec. Act § 1128G; 42 C.F.R. § § 403.904, 403.906.] CMS has organized these reporting requirements into an Open Payments program. [http://www.cms.gov/openpayments/index.html.]

[¶ 730] Provider Participation Agreements

To qualify for payment for its services to Medicare beneficiaries, a provider must: (1) undergo a survey and be certified by the state agency or accrediting organization to be in compliance with legal and regulatory requirements; and (2) sign a participation agreement with CMS. The participation agreement includes the conditions required for the provider to maintain compliance and continue certification.

A "provider of services," for purposes of signing a participation agreement, is defined as a hospital, a critical access hospital (CAH), a skilled nursing facility (SNF), a home health agency (HHA), a hospice, a comprehensive outpatient rehabilitation facility, certain funds for payments for physicians and other practitioners provided by hospitals, a clinic, a rehabilitation agency, a public health agency, a community health center with respect to partial hospitalization services, or an opioid treatment program. [Soc. Sec. Act § 1866(e)(1), (e)(2), (u).]

The term "supplier" means a physician or other practitioner, a facility, or other entity (other than a provider of services) that furnishes items or services used in care and treatment under the Medicare statute and can bill Medicare for Part B services. [Soc. Sec. Act § 1861(d); 42 C.F.R. § 400.202; *State Operations Manual*, Pub. 100-07, Ch. 2, § 2002.] "Suppliers" include all physician specialities, dentists, optometrists, podiatrists, chiropractors, independently practicing occupational and physical therapists, suppliers of diagnostic tests, suppliers of radiology services, multi-speciality clinics, independent laboratories, mammography screening centers, independent diagnostic testing facilities, audiologists, independently billing psychologists, ambulatory surgical centers (ASCs), supplier specialties, suppliers of durable medical equipment (DME), and others. [*Medicare Claims Processing Manual*, Pub. 100-04, Ch. 1, § 30.3.12.1.]

Screening requirements. All Medicare providers are required to undergo screening before initial enrollment and revalidate their compliance with enrollment requirements every five years; suppliers of durable medical equipment, prosthetics, orthotics, and supplies must revalidate every three years. A Medicare contractor is required to screen all initial provider and supplier applications and any applications received in response to a revalidation request and assign them to a level of limited, moderate, or high. [Soc. Sec. Act § 1866(j)(2)(D)(iii); 42 C.F.R. § § 424.57(g), 424.515, 424.518.]

Essentials of Provider Agreements

To participate in the Medicare program, a provider of services must sign an agreement with the Secretary to:

(1) limit its charges to beneficiaries to the costs of noncovered services and to the deductible, coinsurance, and other charges allowed under federal law (see "Allowable Charges" below);

(2) make adequate provision for the refund of amounts incorrectly collected from beneficiaries;

(3) disclose the hiring of any individual who, at any time during the year preceding employment, was employed in a managerial, accounting, auditing, or similar capacity by the provider's Medicare administrative contractor;

(4) release, upon request, patient data to a quality improvement organization (QIO) (see ¶ 710) reviewing the provider;

(5) bill other primary payers before billing Medicare in accordance with statutory and regulatory requirements concerning alternate insurance coverage (see ¶ 636); and

(6) admit surveyors from the state health agency or accrediting organization to assess their compliance with conditions of participation.

[Soc. Sec. Act § 1866(a)(1); 42 C.F.R. § § 489.20, 489.30.]

As proof of compliance, providers, suppliers, physicians, and eligible professionals must maintain documentation, certifying compliance with Medicare regulations, for a period of seven years, and make that documentation available to CMS upon request. Such documentation must include written and electronic documents (including the National Provider Identifier (NPI) of the physician or, when permitted, other eligible professional who ordered, certified, referred, or prescribed the Part A or B service, item, or drug) relating to written orders, certifications, referrals, prescriptions, and requests for payments for Part A or B services, items, or drugs. [42 C.F.R. § 424.516(f).]

Hospitals. The conditions of participation and provisions of the provider agreement for hospitals include the following additional requirements:

(1) to either furnish directly or make arrangements for all Medicare care and services (other than physician and certain health care practitioner services) (see ¶ 635);

(2) to maintain an agreement with a QIO for the review of admissions, quality, and diagnostic information (see ¶ 710);

(3) not to charge for services rejected by a QIO on the basis of quality of care;

(4) to participate in TRICARE, CHAMPVA (Civilian Health and Medical Program of the Veterans Administration), and Veterans Administration programs (42 C.F.R. § § 489.25, 489.26);

(5) to make available to beneficiaries directories of participating physicians in the area and identify any qualified participating physicians in the area, whenever a referral is made to a nonparticipating physician;

(6) to accept as payment in full any payments made by risk-basis health maintenance organizations on behalf of their Medicare enrollees if the payments made are at the level traditional Medicare would have paid (42 C.F.R. § 422.214);

(7) to provide beneficiaries with a written notice at the time of admission to the facility explaining the beneficiary's right to Medicare benefits (see below) and right to appeal a discharge from the hospital (42 C.F.R. § 489.27);

(8) to report quality data in accordance with the HHS Secretary's requirements;

(9) to comply with the requirements of Soc. Sec. Act § 1866(f) relating to maintaining written policies and procedures respecting advance directives;

(10) if the hospital has a financial interest in an entity to which patients are discharged, it must disclose the nature of the financial interest, the number of its patients who require home health services, and the percentage of such individuals who received such services from such entity;

(11) to provide the HHS Secretary with information regarding the volume of patients, as required by Soc. Sec. Act § 1886(d)(12);

(12) to be a participating provider of medical care both (a) under the contract health services program funded by the Indian Health Service (IHS) and operated by the IHS, and Indian tribes, or tribal organizations, and (b) any program funded by the IHS and operated by an urban Indian organization with respect to the purchase of items or services for an eligible urban Indian;

(13) if not otherwise subject to the Occupational Safety and Health Act of 1970, to comply with the Bloodborne Pathogens standard under 29 C.F.R. § 1910.1030;

(14) in the case of hospitals with emergency departments, to meet the responsibilities imposed by the law with respect to treating emergency cases (see below under "Treatment of Emergency Cases—Antidumping Rules") (42 C.F.R. § 489.24); and

(15) for individuals receiving observation services as an outpatient for more than 24 hours, to explain no more than 36 hours after the start of services (or, if sooner, upon release) that he or she has the status of an outpatient receiving observation services rather than as an inpatient and why; the implications of that status on, for example, cost-sharing requirements and subsequent eligibility for coverage for SNF services; and other appropriate information.

[Soc. Sec. Act § 1866(a)(1).] Additional terms are required for CAHs, SNFs, HHAs, and hospice programs.

Treatment of Emergency Cases—Antidumping Rules

Each hospital provider agreement must include a clause requiring the provider to comply with the Emergency Medical Treatment & Labor Act (EMTALA), which is intended to ensure public access to emergency services regardless of ability to pay. [Soc. Sec. Act §§ 1866(a)(1)(I), 1867; 42 C.F.R. §§ 489.20(l), 489.24.]

Under the EMTALA "antidumping" provision, a hospital must provide for an appropriate medical screening examination (within the capability of the hospital's emergency department) for any individual who comes to the emergency department and requests a medical examination or treatment, regardless of whether that individual is a Medicare beneficiary. The screening examination must be sufficient to determine whether an emergency medical condition exists or whether the individual is in active labor. If a patient has an emergency condition or is in active labor, the hospital must provide the treatment necessary to stabilize his or her condition. For a woman in active labor, stabilization requires delivery of both the newborn and the placenta. [Soc. Sec. Act § 1867(a), (e)(3), (h).]

¶730

Transfer. The transfer of an emergency room patient whose condition has not been stabilized is not appropriate unless either: (1) the patient (or a person acting on the patient's behalf) requests a transfer in writing; or (2) a physician has certified that the medical benefits to be obtained from treatment available at the receiving hospital outweigh the risks of transfer and that the receiving facility has the space and personnel necessary to treat the patient. [Soc. Sec. Act § 1867(c); 42 C.F.R. § 489.24(e)(2)(iv), (f).]

Records. Each hospital must post a sign in its emergency department specifying patients' rights with respect to examination and treatment for emergency medical conditions and women in labor. [Soc. Sec. Act § 1866(a)(1)(I), (N)(iii).]

Policies and procedures. A hospital must have written policies and procedures in place to respond to situations in which a particular specialty is not available or the on-call physician cannot respond because of circumstances beyond the physician's control, and to provide that emergency services are available to meet the needs of individuals with emergency medical conditions. [42 C.F.R. § 489.24(j).]

Delay in treatment. Medicare-participating hospitals must not delay required screening and the stabilization of an emergency in order to: (1) obtain insurance information; (2) seek, or direct a patient to seek, authorization to provide screening or stabilizing services from the individual's health plan, managed care organization, or insurance company; or (3) prepare an Advance Beneficiary Notice and obtain a beneficiary signature. Appropriate screening and stabilization must be provided first. [42 C.F.R. § 489.24(d)(4).]

Refusal to consent. If an individual intends to leave the hospital before the screening examination, the hospital should offer further medical examination and treatment, inform the individual of the benefits of such examination and treatment, and take all reasonable steps to obtain written informed consent to refuse such examination and treatment. The hospital must document any refusal of treatment and its actions or efforts to comply with EMTALA requirements and provide treatment. [42 C.F.R. § 489.24(d)(3).]

Sanctions. If a hospital knowingly and willfully, or negligently, fails to handle emergency treatment cases, its provider agreement with Medicare may be terminated. In addition, the Secretary may impose civil money penalties against the hospital and responsible physician, and the law provides for civil actions against a hospital (but not against physicians). [Soc. Sec. Act § 1867(d).]

Except when a delay would jeopardize the health and safety of individuals, the Secretary is required to request a QIO review before making a compliance determination that would terminate a hospital's Medicare participation because of EMTALA violations. [Soc. Sec. Act § 1867(d)(3); 42 C.F.R. § 489.24(h).]

Notifying Beneficiaries of Medicare Rights

Within two days of admission, hospitals must provide each Medicare beneficiary with a written statement (using language approved by the Secretary) explaining the beneficiary's Medicare rights, i.e., the "Important Message from Medicare." The explanation of rights must include: (1) rights to inpatient hospital services and post-hospital services; (2) the circumstances under which the beneficiary will and will not be liable for charges for a continued stay at the hospital; (3) the beneficiary's right to appeal a determination that a continued inpatient hospital stay is not covered (including practical steps to initiate such an appeal); and (4) the beneficiary's liability for payment for services if the determination is upheld on appeal. The hospital must give the patient a second copy of the notice not more than two days before discharge. [Soc. Sec. Act § 1866(a)(1)(M); 42 C.F.R. § 405.1205; *Medicare Claims Processing Manual*, Pub. 100-04, Ch. 30, § 200.3.1.]

Provider Policies on Advance Directives

Hospitals and other health care facilities must maintain written policies and procedures relating to an advance directive (a written instruction, such as a living will or durable power of attorney for health care), which expresses a patient's wishes relating to the provision of care when the individual is incapacitated. Each facility must: (1) inform Medicare and Medicaid patients of their rights under state law to make an advance directive; and (2) explain the written policies of the organization respecting the implementation of such rights. [Soc. Sec. Act § 1866(a)(1)(Q), (f).]

Allowable Charges

A provider agreement requires a provider of services to limit its charges to beneficiaries to the costs of noncovered services and to the deductible and coinsurance (copayment) charges allowed under federal law and regulations. Under Medicare law and regulations, the provider may charge a beneficiary the following amounts:

(1) Providers may charge beneficiaries for the Part A inpatient hospital deductible and coinsurance, which consist of: (a) the amount of the inpatient hospital deductible or, if less, the actual charges for the services (see ¶ 223); (b) the amount of inpatient hospital coinsurance applicable for each day the individual is furnished inpatient hospital services after the 60th day during a benefit period (see ¶ 222); and (c) the post-hospital extended care services coinsurance amount (see ¶ 242). [42 C.F.R. § § 489.30–489.32.]

(2) Providers may charge beneficiaries for the Part B deductible and coinsurance, which consist of an annual deductible and a coinsurance of 20 percent of the Medicare-approved Part B payment amount in excess of that deductible (see ¶ 335 for further details and exceptions). [Soc. Sec. Act § 1833(b); 42 C.F.R. § 489.30.] For outpatient hospital services, allowable deductible charges depend on whether the hospital can determine the beneficiary's deductible status.

(3) Providers may charge beneficiaries for the blood deductible, which consists of charges for the first three pints of blood or units of packed red blood cells furnished during a calendar year (see ¶ 223). [Soc. Sec. Act § 1833(b).]

(4) Providers may not charge a deductible for certain services not subject to deductible. Many preventive services are not subject to any copayment or deductible (see ¶ 335). [Soc. Sec. Act § 1861.]

(5) For costlier services requested by a beneficiary, the difference between the provider's customary charges for services covered under Medicare and the costlier services may be charged. Whenever a provider is permitted to charge for an item or service, it may not charge the Medicare beneficiary or another person more than the amount customarily charged by the provider for such an item or service. [Soc. Sec. Act § 1866(a)(2)(B).]

Deposits and Prepayment Requests

A provider agreement contains specific requirements concerning prepayment. Under these provisions, the provider agrees not to:

(1) require an individual entitled to hospital insurance benefits to prepay in part or in whole for inpatient services as a condition of admittance, except when it is clear upon admission that payment under Part A cannot be made;

(2) deny covered inpatient services to an eligible individual on the ground of inability or failure to pay a requested amount at or before admission;

¶730

(3) evict, or threaten to evict, an individual for inability to pay a deductible or coinsurance amount required under Medicare; and

(4) charge an individual for: (a) an agreement to admit or readmit the individual on some specified future date for covered inpatient services, (b) the individual's failure to remain an inpatient for any agreed-upon length of time, or (c) the individual's failure to give advance notice of departure from the provider's facilities.

[42 C.F.R. § 489.22.]

Providers must not require advance payment of the inpatient deductible or coinsurance as a condition of admission. Additionally, providers may not require that the beneficiary prepay any Part B charges as a condition of admission, except when prepayment from non-Medicare patients is required. In such cases, only the deductible and coinsurance may be collected. [Pub. 100-04, Ch. 2, § 10.3.]

A hospice is prohibited from discontinuing care to a patient because of his or her inability to pay. [Soc. Sec. Act § 1861(dd)(2)(D).]

Termination of Provider Agreements

A provider may terminate its participation in the Medicare program voluntarily, or its participation may be terminated by the Secretary for cause. [Soc. Sec. Act § 1866(b).] A provider whose participation is terminated for cause has the right to administrative appeal and judicial review but has no right to delay of the termination pending the hearing. [Soc. Sec. Act § 1866(h); 42 C.F.R. §§ 498.5, 498.20.]

In general, no Medicare payment will be made to a provider after the effective date of the termination. However, in the case of inpatient hospital services (including inpatient psychiatric hospital services) and SNF services, payments may be made for up to 30 days for services furnished to an individual who is admitted to the institution before the effective date of the termination. Similarly, home health services and hospice care furnished under a plan established before the termination date of the participation agreement will be covered for up to 30 days after termination. [Soc. Sec. Act §§ 1128(c)(2), 1866(b)(3); 42 C.F.R. § 489.55.]

[¶ 735] Role of Medicaid

Although the Medicaid program is administered separately from Medicare, Medicaid is required to pay the Medicare premiums, deductibles, and/or coinsurance amounts for certain Medicare beneficiaries. Medicare beneficiaries eligible for Medicaid cost-sharing assistance are called "qualified Medicare beneficiaries" or "dual eligibles." [Soc. Sec. Act § 1905(p).]

Medicaid pays all Medicare cost-sharing for dual-eligible beneficiaries with incomes up to 100 percent of the federal poverty level (FPL). Medicaid pays the Part B premiums for dual eligibles with incomes between 100 and 120 percent of FPL, referred to as specified low-income beneficiaries. To the extent that funds are available, Medicaid must pay a portion of the Part B premium for Medicare beneficiaries with incomes between 120 percent and 135 percent of FPL, called "qualifying individuals." [Soc. Sec. Act §§ 1902(a)(10)(E)(iv), 1933(g).]

States also may pay Medicare Part A and Part B premiums under "buy-in" agreements with Medicare for beneficiaries who do not qualify for qualified Medicare beneficiary status. [Soc. Sec. Act §§ 1818(g), 1843.]

Prescription drug benefit. Medicaid agencies assist in the determination of eligibility for the Medicare low-income subsidies under the prescription drug benefit (see ¶ 508) by notifying CMS of each Medicaid applicant or recipient who is eligible for the low-income subsidy for Medicare Part D cost-sharing. States are required to provide this information as a condition of receiving federal Medicaid assistance. [Soc. Sec. Act § 1935.]

[¶ 740] "Medigap" Insurance

A Medicare supplemental (Medigap) policy is a health insurance policy sold by private insurance companies specifically to fill "gaps" in original Medicare coverage. A Medigap policy typically provides coverage for some or all of the deductible and coinsurance amounts applicable to Medicare-covered services and sometimes covers items and services that are not covered by Medicare. [Soc. Sec. Act § 1882(g)(1), (o)(1); 42 C.F.R. § 403.205; *Notice*, 82 FR 41684, Sept. 1, 2017.]

Overview of Medigap Insurance

A Medigap policy is a health insurance policy sold by a private insurance company to a Medicare beneficiary specifically to fill "gaps" in original Medicare coverage. Medigap policies are primarily designed, advertised, and marketed to provide coverage for some or all of the deductible and coinsurance amounts applicable to Medicare-covered services, and sometimes cover items and services that are not covered by Medicare. [Soc. Sec. Act § 1882; 42 C.F.R. § 403.205(a).]

A Medigap policy may consist of an individual policy, a group policy, a rider attached to an individual or group policy, or a stand-alone limited health benefit plan or policy that supplements Medicare benefits and is sold primarily to Medicare beneficiaries. Any rider attached to a Medigap policy is considered an integral part of the basic policy. [42 C.F.R. § 403.205(c) and (d).]

Medigap policies do not include a Medicare Advantage (MA) plan, a prescription drug plan (PDP) under Medicare Part D, or any of the other types of health insurance policies or health benefit plans that are excluded from the definition of a Medicare supplemental policy in Soc. Sec. Act § 1882(g)(1). An insurance company may not sell a Medigap policy with knowledge that the policy duplicates health benefits which the applicant is otherwise entitled to, including from Medicaid programs that cover Medicare cost-sharing (for example, the Qualified Medicare Beneficiary Program), MA plans, and individual market plans. [Soc. Sec. Act § 1882(d)(3)(A)(i); 42 C.F.R. § 403.205(e).]

The HHS Secretary is authorized to provide all Medicare beneficiaries with Medigap insurance policy information to better enable them to evaluate and choose between policies. This provision is implemented by publication of a consumer pamphlet on Medigap insurance titled, Choosing a Medigap Policy: A Guide to Health Insurance for People with Medicare, which is prepared jointly by HHS and the National Association of Insurance Commissioners (NAIC), and available free of charge to the public. [Soc. Sec. Act § 1882(e).]

Loss ratio requirements. To be certified, Medigap policies must meet loss ratio standards. A Medigap policy must return to the policyholders, in the form of aggregate benefits provided under the policy: (1) at least 75 percent of the aggregate amount of premiums in the case of group policies; and (2) at least 60 percent of the aggregate amount of premiums in the case of individual policies. For purposes of loss ratio requirements, policies issued as a result of solicitation of individuals through the mail or by mass media advertising are considered individual policies. [42 C.F.R. §§ 403.206(a)(2), 403.215.]

NAIC Model Standards and Benefit Packages

Medigap policies must meet NAIC model standards to achieve voluntary certification. These minimum model standards are found in the "Model Regulation to Implement the Individual Accident and Insurance Minimum Standards Act" (NAIC Model), initially adopted by the NAIC on June 6, 1979, and revised periodically to reflect legislative changes. [Soc.

Sec. Act § 1882(g)(2)(A); 42 C.F.R. §§ 403.206(a)(1), 403.210.] The Model Regulation adopted by NAIC on August 29, 2016, is considered to be the applicable NAIC Model Regulation for purposes of Soc. Sec. Act § 1882. [*Notice*, 82 FR 41684, Sept. 1, 2017.]

Medigap policies issued in a state are deemed to meet the federal requirements if the state's program provides for the application of standards at least as stringent as those contained in the NAIC Model Regulation, and if the state requirements are equal to or more stringent than those set forth in Soc. Sec. Act § 1882. [Soc. Sec. Act § 1882(b)(1); 42 C.F.R. § 403.222.]

Standardized NAIC benefit packages. Medigap policies generally may not be sold unless they conform to the standardized benefit packages that have been defined and designated by the NAIC. Standardized plans are designated A through D, F, G, and K through N. Plans F and J are authorized to have high deductible options that are counted as separate plans. Medigap plans E, H, I, and J are no longer available for sale. Three states (Massachusetts, Minnesota, and Wisconsin) are permitted by statute to have different standardized Medigap plans and are sometimes referred to as the "waiver" states. There are also policies issued before the OBRA '90 requirements became applicable in 1992 (pre-standardized policies) that are still in effect. [Soc. Sec. Act § 1882; *Notice*, 82 FR 41684, Sept. 1, 2017.]

Prohibition Against Prescription Drug Coverage

Effective January 1, 2006, Medigap policies can no longer be sold with a prescription drug benefit. Three of the original standardized Medigap plans, H, I and J, as well as some Medigap policies in the waiver states, may still contain coverage for outpatient prescription drugs if the policies were sold before January 1, 2006. In addition, some pre-standardized plans cover drugs. If a beneficiary holding one of these policies enrolls in Medicare Part D prescription drug coverage, the prescription drug coverage is removed from the individual's Medigap policy. [Soc. Sec. Act § 1882(v).]

Payment of Part B Deductible for Newly Eligible Beneficiaries

Some standardized Medigap plans provide first-dollar coverage for beneficiaries, which means the plan pays the Medicare deductibles, coinsurance, and copayments so that the beneficiary has no out-of-pocket costs for Medicare covered services. However, beginning on January 1, 2020, section 401 of the Medicare Access and CHIP Reauthorization Act of 2015 (MACRA) (P.L. 114-10) prohibits the sale of Medigap plans with first-dollar coverage to an individual who is a "newly eligible Medicare beneficiary," which is defined in Soc. Sec. Act § 1882(z)(2) as an individual who is neither: (1) 65 years of age before January 1, 2020; or (2) entitled to benefits under Medicare Part A as a disabled person (Soc. Sec. Act § 226(b)), a person with end-stage renal disease (Soc. Sec. Act § 226A), or as an elderly person (Soc. Sec. Act § 226(a)), before January 1, 2020. The effect of this change is that as of January 1, 2020, a "newly eligible Medicare beneficiary" will be required to pay out-of-pocket for the Medicare Part B deductible. [Soc. Sec. Act § 1882(z).]

Medicare SELECT Policies

Medicare SELECT is a type of Medigap policy available in some states. Such plans offer beneficiaries lower premiums or increased benefits if they use the Medicare SELECT plan's network of providers. Some Medicare SELECT policies may use cost savings to help pay for additional benefits. [Soc. Sec. Act § 1882(t).]

Certain Medicare supplemental policies may be approved as Medicare SELECT policies if the policy meets the NAIC model standards and otherwise complies with the statute, except that its benefits are restricted to items and services furnished by certain physicians or providers (or reduced benefits are provided when items or services are furnished by other entities), and certain other minimum federal requirements are met relating to the network of physicians and providers specified in the statute. [Soc. Sec. Act § 1882(t).]

Additional Medicare SELECT requirements. In addition to the requirements for the Medicare supplemental policies described above, Medicare SELECT issuers must ensure that—

- full benefits are provided for items and services provided outside the insurer's network of physicians and providers if the services are medically necessary and immediately required because of an unforeseen illness, injury or condition, and it is not reasonable to obtain the service through the network;

- the network provides sufficient access and there are arrangements for an ongoing quality assurance program for services provided through the network; and

- the beneficiary receives at the time of enrollment (and acknowledges receipt of) an explanation of restrictions on payment outside the network; out of area coverage; coverage of emergency and urgently needed services; and the availability and cost of Medicare supplemental policy offered by the issuer that does not include the network restrictions.

[Soc. Sec. Act § 1882(t)(1).]

Penalties for Fraud Connected with Sales of Medigap Policies

It is a criminal offense to engage in fraudulent activities connected with the sale of Medigap policies, including: making false statements and misrepresentations; falsely claiming certification by the federal government; selling policies that duplicate Medicare benefits, including selling to MA beneficiaries; and mailing into a state Medigap policies that have been disapproved by that state. Violation of these provisions is a felony. [Soc. Sec. Act § 1882(d); 42 C.F.R. § 402.105(c).]

Chapter 8– PAYMENT RULES

[¶ 800] Introduction

Medicare's method of paying for services provided to a beneficiary varies according to whether the services are furnished under Part A, Part B, Part C, or Part D. Providers of most Part A services are reimbursed by Medicare under various prospective payment systems (PPSs). Providers of most Part B services are reimbursed by Medicare under various fee schedules. Providers of managed care services are paid by Part C organizations, which are funded by Medicare, and providers of prescription drugs are paid by Part D plans, which are also funded by Medicare.

Part A Payment

Payments made to most hospitals are made under the inpatient prospective payment system (IPPS) for services covered by Medicare Part A, which covers institutional services (see ¶ 810). PPS payments are made for a hospital's inpatient operating and capital-related costs at predetermined, specific rates for each hospital discharge. Prospective payment systems also have been established for home health agencies (see ¶ 830), hospital outpatient services (combining elements of Part A and Part B; see ¶ 820), skilled nursing facilities (see ¶ 835), inpatient rehabilitation facilities (see ¶ 837), long-term care hospitals (see ¶ 815), inpatient hospital services furnished in psychiatric hospitals and units (see ¶ 840), and end-stage renal disease facilities (see ¶ 845). Other institutional providers and services not covered by a PPS are paid on the basis of "reasonable costs." Medicare payment is made directly to the provider that furnished the services.

Part B Payment

Part B services provided by physicians and other health care practitioners generally are paid on the basis of a physician fee schedule (see ¶ 855 and ¶ 860). Other suppliers of services and equipment paid under Part B are paid on the basis of different fee schedules (see, for example, the discussions about the clinical laboratory, ambulance, and durable medical equipment fee schedules at ¶ 875, ¶ 880, and ¶ 882) or on a "reasonable charge" basis (not covered in this book). Medicare payment is made to the physician or supplier who furnished the services if assignment has been accepted (see ¶ 868). Otherwise, the payment is made to the beneficiary, who then has the obligation to pay the physician or supplier.

Part C Payment

Medicare Advantage organizations are risk-bearing entities that can issue, within designated geographic areas, health plans offering a specific set of benefits at a uniform premium and uniform level of cost-sharing to each Medicare beneficiary who chooses to enroll in a such a plan under Medicare Part C, which is called the Medicare Advantage (MA) program. The payment rules for MA organizations are at ¶ 408. The MA program:

Part D Payments

Medicare covers the cost of prescription drugs under Medicare Part D. Currently, beneficiaries entitled to Part A and enrolled in Part B, and enrollees in MA private fee-for-service plans or medical savings account plans are eligible for the prescription drug benefit. Medicare Part D is covered at ¶ 500 *et seq.*

Accountable Care Organizations

Medicare services also may be delivered through accountable care organizations (ACOs), groups of service and supplier providers that work together to manage and coordinate care for Medicare fee-for-service beneficiaries. An ACO is typically a network of provider groups, often affiliated with a hospital, that work together and are jointly responsible for the cost and quality of care provided to Medicare beneficiaries. ACOs must meet certain criteria to be designated as an ACO. If an ACO meets specified quality performance standards it may receive a portion of the shared savings. ACOs are discussed at ¶ 853.

[¶ 810] Inpatient Hospital Services

The inpatient hospital prospective payment system (IPPS) applies to all short-term, acute-care hospitals unless they are specifically excluded from the IPPS. Under the IPPS, Medicare provides a single payment amount to hospitals for each hospital discharge, identified by the Medicare severity diagnosis-related group (MS-DRG) into which each discharge is classified. [42 C.F.R. § § 412.1, 412.2(a).]

DRG Classifications

Under the IPPS, all patient illnesses and injuries resulting in admission to a hospital are classified into different MS-DRGs, which are clinically coherent and relatively homogeneous with respect to resources used by a hospital. [Soc. Sec. Act § 1886(a); 42 C.F.R. § 412.1 *et seq.*]

Cases are classified into MS-DRGs based on a principal diagnosis, additional or secondary diagnoses, surgical procedures, and the age, sex, and discharge status of the patient. The amount paid under the IPPS is based upon the MS-DRG for each discharge, regardless of the number of services received or the length of the patient's stay in the hospital, and includes all inpatient operating costs. In addition, each MS-DRG (i.e., each type of illness or injury) is paid at a set rate that is weighted geographically. The MS-DRG payment covers all items and services provided by the hospital to the patient. If the hospital's costs are less than that payment, the hospital keeps the difference; if the hospital's costs are more than the set rate, the hospital absorbs the loss. Not included in the MS-DRG are services provided by the patient's physician, which are covered under Part B (see ¶ 855). [Soc. Sec. Act § 1886(a); 42 C.F.R. § 412.1 *et seq.*]

IPPS Payment Adjustments

The base payment rate to an individual hospital may be adjusted in a number of ways, usually in the form of a percentage add-on payment, including the following:

- If a hospital serves a disproportionate number of low-income patients, it will receive a disproportionate share hospital (DSH) adjustment. The adjustment to the payment is made for DSHs that: (1) serve a significantly disproportionate number of low-income patients; or (2) are located in an urban area, have 100 or more beds, and can demonstrate that more than 30 percent of their revenues are derived from state and local government payments for indigent care not covered by Medicare or Medicaid. [Soc. Sec. Act § 1886(d)(5)(F); 42 C.F.R. § 412.106(c).]

- If the hospital is an approved teaching hospital, it will receive an indirect medical education (IME) adjustment. This percentage varies depending on the ratio of residents to beds. [Soc. Sec. Act § 1886(d)(5)(B); 42 C.F.R. § 412.105.]

- If a particular case involves certain approved new medical technology, additional payments may be made. [Soc. Sec. Act § 1886(d)(5)(K); 42 C.F.R. § § 412.87, 412.88.]

- If the hospital stay is unusually long or costly, the hospital may be eligible for an additional "outlier" payment. [Soc. Sec. Act § 1886(d)(5)(A); 42 C.F.R. § § 412.80–412.86.]

See ¶ 847 for a discussion of payment issues that apply to certain rural hospitals.

Inpatient Quality Data Reporting Program

Under the Inpatient Quality Reporting (IQR) program, beginning in fiscal year (FY) 2015, IPPS hospitals that do not submit required quality data on specific quality indicators to the Medicare program each year have their applicable hospital market basket percentage increase reduced by one-fourth. [Soc. Sec. Act § 1886(b)(3)(B)(viii); 42 C.F.R. § 412.64(d)(2).]

In the FY 2020 final rule, CMS adopted the Safe Use of Opioids–Concurrent Prescribing eCQM beginning with the calendar year 2021 reporting period. It also adopted the Hybrid Hospital-Wide Readmission (HWR) Measure with Claims and Electronic Health Record Data, which will begin with two years of voluntary reporting periods running July 1, 2021 through June 30, 2022, and from July 1, 2022, through June 30, 2023. CMS removed the Claims-Based Hospital-Wide All-Cause Unplanned Readmission Measure beginning with the FY 2026 payment determination. [*Final rule*, 84 FR 42044, Aug. 16, 2019.]

In the FY 2019 final rule, CMS added a new measure removal factor. It also removed a total of 39 measures from the Hospital IQR program; 18 measures were removed entirely and 21 were retained in one of the other hospital value programs. Beginning with the calendar year 2019 reporting period/FY 2021 payment determination and subsequent years, CMS will remove three chart-abstracted measures and two claims-based measures. [*Final rule*, 83 FR 41144, Aug. 17, 2018.]

Hospital Inpatient Value-Based Purchasing Program

The Hospital Inpatient Value-Based Purchasing (VBP) program adjusts payments to hospitals for inpatient services based on their performance on an announced set of measures. [Soc. Sec. Act § 1886(o)(1); 42 C.F.R. § 412.162.]

The HHS Secretary announces performance standards, including levels of achievement and improvement, 60 days before the beginning of a performance period. The Secretary will also provide for an assessment for each hospital for each performance period. The assessment must result in an appropriate distribution of value-based incentive payments among hospitals achieving different levels of hospital performance scores, with hospitals achieving the highest hospital performance scores receiving the largest value-based incentive payments. [Soc. Sec. Act § 1886(o); 42 C.F.R. §§ 412.160–412.167.]

The Secretary selects measures for the value-based purchasing program under the criteria described at Soc. Sec. Act § 1886(o)(2)(B) that are appropriate for measuring quality of care, including acute myocardial infarction; heart failure; pneumonia; surgeries, as measured by the Surgical Care Improvement Project; and health care-associated infections, as measured by the prevention metrics and targets established in the HHS Action Plan to Prevent Healthcare-Associated Infections (or any successor plan) of HHS. [Soc. Sec. Act § 1886(o)(2)(B)(i)(I).]

Under the SUPPORT for Patients and Communities Act (P.L. 115-271), the Secretary was prohibited from including a measure that was based on the questions appearing on the Hospital Consumer Assessment of Healthcare Providers and Systems survey in 2018 or 2019 about communication by hospital staff with an individual about the individual's pain. [Soc. Sec. Act 1886(o)(2)(B)(iii), as added by the SUPPORT Act § 6104(b).]

Hospital Readmissions Reduction

The Hospital Readmissions Reduction Program (HRRP) reduces reimbursement to certain hospitals that have excess readmissions for certain conditions. For FY 2018 and later, the reduction is based on a hospital's risk-adjusted readmission rate during a three-year period for acute myocardial infarction, heart failure, pneumonia, chronic obstructive pulmonary disease, total hip arthroplasty/total knee arthroplasty, and coronary artery bypass graft. A "readmission" refers to an individual who is discharged from an applicable hospital and is admitted to the same or another applicable hospital within a time period of 30 days from the date of the discharge. [Soc. Sec. Act § 1886(q); 42 C.F.R. § § 412.152, 412.154.]

For discharges occurring during and after FY 2019, the Secretary must apply the applicable risk adjustment methodology in a manner that allows for a separate comparison of hospitals within each group. Further, the Secretary must (1) define groups based on the overall proportion of their inpatients who are entitled to, or enrolled for, benefits under Medicare Part A and are full benefit dual eligibles before applying risk adjustment methodologies; and (2) consult with the Medicare Payment Advisory Commission (MedPAC) in defining the groups; but must not impose any additional reporting requirements on the hospital. [Soc. Sec. Act § 1886(q)(3)(D).]

Hospital-Acquired Conditions

Section 3008 of the Patient Protection and Affordable Care Act (ACA) (P.L. 111-148) established the Hospital-Acquired Condition (HAC) Reduction Program to provide an incentive for hospitals to reduce HACs. The HAC Reduction Program requires the Secretary to adjust payments to applicable hospitals that rank in the worst-performing quartile of all subsection (d) hospitals with respect to risk-adjusted HAC quality measures. These hospitals have their payments reduced to 99 percent of what would otherwise have been paid for such discharges. [Soc. Sec. Act § 1886(p); 42 C.F.R. § 412.172.]

CMS will identify the top 25 percent of all applicable hospitals, relative to the national average, with the highest HAC scores as measured during the applicable period and all of the hospital's discharges for the specified FY. An applicable period, with respect to a FY, is the two-year period specified by the Secretary from which data are collected to calculate the total HAC score. CMS calculates the total HAC scores by weighing the selected measures according to the risk adjustment established methodology. [42 C.F.R. § 412.172(d), (e).]

If a selected condition that was not present on admission manifests during the hospital stay, it is considered a HAC and the case is paid as though the secondary diagnosis was not present. [Soc. Sec. Act § 1886(d)(4)(D).]

Three-Day Payment Window

Under the three-day payment window, a hospital (or an entity that is wholly owned or wholly operated by the hospital) subject to the IPPS must include on the claim for a Medicare beneficiary's inpatient stay the diagnoses, procedures, and charges for all outpatient diagnostic services and admission-related outpatient nondiagnostic services that are furnished to the beneficiary on the date of admission to the hospital and during the three calendar days immediately preceding the date of admission. [Soc. Sec. Act § 1886(a)(4); 42 C.F.R. § 412.2(c)(5); *Medicare Claims Processing Manual*, Pub. 100-04, Ch. 3, § 40.3.]

"Two Midnight" Rule

Under the "two midnight" rule, if a physician expects a beneficiary's surgical procedure, diagnostic test, or other treatment to require a stay in the hospital lasting at least two midnights and admits the beneficiary to the hospital based on that expectation, it is presumed to be appropriate that the hospital receive Medicare Part A payment. Hospital services spanning less than two midnights are provided on an outpatient basis unless there is clear documentation in the medical record that the procedure was designated by CMS as an inpatient-only service or that the physician's order clearly states an expectation of a stay spanning more than two midnights. [42 C.F.R. § § 412.3(d), 419.22(n); *Final rule*, 78 FR 50496, Aug. 19, 2013.]

¶810

Hospitals Excluded from Inpatient PPS

Certain hospitals are exempt from the IPPS, including psychiatric hospitals and units, rehabilitation hospitals and units, pediatric hospitals, long-term care hospitals, and certain cancer hospitals. Hospitals exempt from the IPPS either are reimbursed on a reasonable cost basis but are subject to a ceiling on the rate of increase in inpatient costs or have their own prospective payment system. [Soc. Sec. Act § 1886(b)(1)(C), (j); 42 C.F.R. § 412.23.]

[¶ 815] Long-Term Care Hospitals

CMS pays for both the operating and capital-related costs of hospital inpatient stays in long-term care hospitals (LTCHs) under Part A based on prospectively set rates. LTCHs are hospitals that are primarily engaged in providing inpatient services by or under the supervision of a physician to Medicare beneficiaries with medically complex conditions who require a long hospital stay. LTCH facilities must have an average inpatient length of stay greater than 25 days (or 20 days for certain hospitals focusing on cancer treatment) and further meet the requirements for hospitals set forth in Soc. Sec. Act § 1861(e). These facilities generally provide extended medical and rehabilitative care for patients who may suffer from multiple acute or chronic conditions. [Soc. Sec. Act § 1861(ccc)(1)–(3).]

Requirements for LTCHs

LTCHs are required to do the following:

(1) have a documented patient review process that includes pre-admission screening, validation within 48 hours of admission that patients meet admission criteria, and periodic evaluation of each patient's need for continued care in the LTCH and assessment of the available discharge options;

(2) have active physician involvement with patients through an organized medical staff, with physicians available on-site every day to review patients' progress and consulting physicians on call and able to be at the patient's bedside within a moderate period of time; and

(3) have interdisciplinary teams of health care professionals, including physicians, to prepare and implement an individualized treatment plan for each patient.

[Soc. Sec. Act § 1861(ccc)(4).]

Long-Term Care Hospital PPS Payment Methodology

Payment under the LTCH prospective payment system (PPS) is made on a per-discharge basis. Each patient case is classified according to the principal diagnosis, secondary diagnoses, procedures performed during the stay, and discharge status of the patient. The patient's case is classified by Medicare severity long-term care diagnosis related group (MS-LTC-DRG), based on the relative costliness of treatment for patients in the group, similar to classification under the hospital inpatient prospective payment system (IPPS). [42 C.F.R. § 412.513.]

The amount of the prospective payment is based on the standard federal rate, established under 42 C.F.R. § 412.523 and adjusted for the MS-LTC-DRG relative weights, differences in area wage levels, cost of living in Alaska and Hawaii, high-cost outliers, and other special payment provisions.

Productivity adjustment. Section 3401(c) of the Patient Protection and Affordable Care Act (ACA) (P.L. 111-148) amended the annual update to the standard federal rate under Soc. Sec. Act § 1886(m) to add a productivity adjustment for discharges in 2012 and later. The productivity adjustment is the same one applied to inpatient hospital services under Soc. Sec. Act § 1886(b)(3)(B)(xi)(II). The application of this productivity adjustment may result in the annual update being less than 0.0 for a year and may result in payment rates under the LTCH PPS for a year being less than such payment rates for the preceding year. [Soc. Sec. Act § 1886(m)(3).]

Site-neutral IPPS payment amount. Discharges in cost reporting periods beginning on or after October 1, 2019, will be paid based on a site-neutral payment rate unless the discharge meets the criteria for exclusion. The site-neutral payment rate is the lower of (1) the IPPS comparable per diem amount; or (2) 100 percent of the estimated cost of the case. For fiscal years (FYs) 2016 through 2019, payment for discharges was made using a blended payment rate, which was determined as 50 percent of the site-neutral payment rate amount for the discharge and 50 percent of the standard federal prospective payment rate amount for the discharge as determined under 42 C.F.R. § 412.523. [Soc. Sec. Act § 1886(m)(6), as amended by Bipartisan Budget Act of 2018 (P.L. 115-123) § 51005; 42 C.F.R. § 412.522.]

Patients with stays longer than three days in an intensive care unit or on a ventilator for more than 96 hours are excluded from the site-neutral payment rate and will qualify for the traditional increased rate received by LTCHs. [Soc. Sec. Act § 1886(m)(6); 42 C.F.R. § 412.522.]

One-Day Payment Window

LTCHs are subject to a one-day payment window, the "24-hour rule," for preadmission services related to the inpatient stay. In other words, outpatient diagnostic services and most nonphysician services provided during the calendar day immediately preceding the date of admission to an LTCH (excluding ambulance services and maintenance renal dialysis services) are included in the standard payment. A preadmission service is related to the inpatient stay if:

(1) it is diagnostic (including clinical diagnostic laboratory tests);

(2) it is nondiagnostic when furnished on the date of the beneficiary's inpatient admission; or

(3) it is nondiagnostic when furnished on the calendar day preceding the date of the beneficiary's inpatient admission and the hospital does not attest that such service is unrelated to the beneficiary's inpatient admission.

[42 C.F.R. § 412.540.]

LTCH Outlier Payments

The high-cost outlier is an adjustment to the applicable LTCH PPS payment rate for LTCH stays with unusually high costs that exceed the typical cost for cases with a similar case-mix. It equals 80 percent of the difference between the estimated cost of the case and the outlier threshold, and it is made in addition to the applicable LTCH PPS payment rate. [42 C.F.R. § 412.525(a).]

LTCHs are also paid adjusted rates for outlier patients who have short stays. Short-stay outliers are cases with a length of stay up to and including five-sixths of the geometric average length of stay for each MS-LTC-DRG. The short-stay outlier adjustment allows Medicare to reimburse LTCHs for costly short-stay outlier patients and yet pay less for cases that do not receive a full episode of care at the LTCH and should not be reimbursed at the full MS-LTC-DRG payment rate. [42 C.F.R. § 412.529(a)–(c).]

LTCH PPS Interrupted Stay Policy

An interruption of stay occurs when a Medicare inpatient is transferred upon discharge to an acute care hospital, an inpatient rehabilitation facility (IRF), a skilled nursing facility (SNF), or the patient's home for treatment or services that are not available in the LTCH, and returns to the same LTCH. CMS has divided interruption of stay into two categories, a "three-day or less interruption of stay" and a "greater than three-day interruption of stay." [42 C.F.R. § 412.531(a); *Medicare Claims Processing Manual*, Pub. 100-04, Ch. 3, § 150.9.1.2.]

Three or fewer days. If an interruption of stay of three or fewer days occurs during an episode of care, the entire stay is paid as a single discharge from the LTCH and CMS makes only one LTC-DRG payment for all portions of a long-term care stay. The LTCH must provide services either directly or "under arrangements" with the other provider. The LTCH is responsible for paying the other provider for the costs of services. [42 C.F.R. § 412.531(b)(1)(ii)(A).]

Greater than three-day interruption of stay. A greater than three-day interruption of stay is defined as a stay in a LTCH during which a Medicare inpatient is discharged from the LTCH to an acute care hospital, IRF, or SNF for a period of greater than three days but returns to the LTCH within the applicable fixed-day period:

- between four and nine consecutive days for a discharge to an acute care hospital;
- between four and 27 consecutive days for a discharge to an IRF; and
- between four and 45 consecutive days for a discharge to a SNF.

[42 C.F.R. § 412.531(a)(2)(i)–(iii).] In such cases, CMS will make one LTC-DRG payment for all portions of a long-term care stay and will separately pay the acute care hospital, IRF, or SNF in accordance with their respective payment systems. [42 C.F.R. § 412.531(b)(1)(ii)(B), (c).]

If, however, the applicable fixed-day time frames are exceeded, the subsequent admission to the LTCH is considered a new stay and the LTCH will receive two separate PPS payments. [42 C.F.R. § 412.531(b)(4).] For example, if an LTCH patient is discharged to an acute care hospital and is readmitted to the LTCH on any day up to and including the ninth day following the original day of discharge from the LTCH, one MS-LTC-DRG payment will be made. If the patient is readmitted to the LTCH from the acute care hospital on the tenth day after the original discharge or later, Medicare will pay for the second admission as a separate stay with a second MS-LTC-DRG assignment. [42 C.F.R. § 412.531(b)(4)(i).]

Outlier payments. Interrupted stays at an LTCH are subject to the short-stay and high-cost outlier rules. If the total number of days of a patient's stay before and following an interruption of stay is at or below five-sixths of the geometric average length of stay of the MS-LTC-DRG, CMS will make a short-stay outlier payment. An additional payment will be made if the patient's stay qualifies as a high-cost outlier. [42 C.F.R. § 412.531(b)(2), (3).]

LTCH Quality Reporting Program

LTCHs that do not report quality data are subject to a 2.0 percentage point reduction to the annual update of the standard federal rate. [Soc. Sec. Act § 1886(m)(5); 42 C.F.R. §§ 412.523(c)(4), 412.560(b)(2).] LTCHs are required to report standardized patient assessment data, data on quality measures, and data on resource use and other measures. Data measures include: (1) functional status, cognitive function, and changes in function and cognitive function; (2) skin integrity and changes in skin integrity; (3) medication reconciliation; (4) incidence of major falls; and (4) accurately communicating the individual's health information and care preferences. [Soc. Sec. Act § 1899B.]

In the FY 2020 final rule, CMS finalized the adoption of two new quality measures. The Transfer of Health Information to the Patient–Post-Acute Care and Transfer of Health Information to the Provider–Post-Acute Care measures take effect for data collection for discharges beginning October 1, 2020. [*Final rule*, 84 FR 42044, Aug. 16, 2019.]

[¶ 820] Hospital Outpatient Services

Outpatient services are covered under Medicare Part B and paid under the outpatient prospective payment system (OPPS). Under the OPPS, predetermined amounts are paid for designated services furnished to Medicare beneficiaries. [Soc. Sec. Act § 1833(t); 42 C.F.R. § 419.2.]

The OPPS is applicable to any hospital participating in the Medicare program, except for: critical access hospitals (CAHs); hospitals located in Maryland and paid under the Maryland All-Payer Model; hospitals located outside of the 50 states, the District of Columbia, and Puerto Rico; and Indian Health Service (IHS) hospitals. [42 C.F.R. § 419.20.]

Services subject to the OPPS. CMS makes payment under the OPPS for the following services:

(1) designated hospital outpatient services;

(2) certain Medicare Part B services furnished to hospital inpatients who are either not entitled to benefits under Part A or who have exhausted their Part A benefits but are entitled to benefits under Part B of the program;

(3) partial hospitalization services furnished by community mental health centers (CMHCs);

(4) antigens, splints and casts, and the hepatitis B vaccine furnished by a home health agency (HHA) to patients who are not under an HHA plan or treatment or by a hospice program furnishing services to patients outside the hospice benefit; and

(5) an initial preventive physical examination performed within first 12 months of Part B coverage.

[Soc. Sec. Act § 1833(t)(1)(B); 42 C.F.R. § 419.21.]

Services excluded from the OPPS. 42 C.F.R. § 419.22 excludes a number of services from payment under the OPPS, except when packaged as a part of a bundled payment. Section 603 of the Bipartisan Budget Act of 2015 (P.L. 114-74) provided that certain items and services furnished by certain off-campus hospital outpatient departments will no longer be paid under the OPPS beginning January 1, 2017. These services will instead be paid under the Medicare physician fee schedule. [Soc. Sec. Act § 1833(t)(1)(B)(v); 42 C.F.R. §§ 419.22(v), 419.48(a).]

Price transparency. To facilitate price transparency with respect to items and services for which payment may be made either to a hospital outpatient department or to an ambulatory surgical center (ASC), the HHS Secretary must make available to the public via a searchable Internet website: (1) the estimated payment amount for the item or service under the OPPS and the ASC PPS (see ¶ 825); and (2) the estimated amount of beneficiary liability applicable to the item or service. [Soc. Sec. Act § 1834(t).]

In addition, effective January 1, 2021, pursuant to section 2718(e) of the Public Health Service (PHS) Act, all hospitals operating in the United States (except federally owned or operated hospitals) are required to establish, update, and make public a list of their standard charges for the items and services that they provide. If a hospital is noncompliant with these requirements, CMS may provide a written warning notice to the hospital, request a corrective action plan, or impose a civil money penalty. A hospital may appeal a civil money penalty imposed by CMS. [45 C.F.R. §§ 180.10–180.110; *Final rule*, 84 FR 65524, Nov. 27, 2019.]

Determining a Payment Under OPPS

The unit of payment under the OPPS is the ambulatory payment classification (APC) system. CMS assigns individual services to APCs based on similar clinical characteristics

¶820

and similar costs. CMS assigns to each APC group an appropriate weighting factor to reflect the relative geometric mean costs for the services within the APC group compared to the geometric mean costs for the services in all APC groups. The APC weights are converted to payment rates through the application of a conversion factor. [Soc. Sec. Act § 1833(t)(3), (5); 42 C.F.R. §§ 419.31, 419.32(c).]

The items and services in an APC group are those that are recognized as contributing to the cost of the procedures or services. Items and services within a group cannot be considered comparable with respect to the use of resources if the highest median cost for an item or service within the group is more than two times greater than the lowest median cost for an item or service within the group, referred to as the "two times rule." [Soc. Sec. Act § 1833(t)(2); 42 C.F.R. § 419.31(a).]

To account for geographic differences in input prices, the labor portion of the payment rate is further adjusted by the hospital wage index for the area where payment is being made. [42 C.F.R. §§ 419.31(c), 419.43(c).]

Items and services included in the APC payment rate. Within each APC, payment for dependent, ancillary, supportive, and adjunctive items and services is packaged into payment for the primary independent service. In general, these packaged costs may include, but are not limited to, the following items and services, the payment for which is packaged or conditionally packaged into the payment for the related procedures or services:

- use of an operating suite, procedure room, or treatment room;
- use of recovery room;
- observation services;
- anesthesia; certain drugs, biologics, and other pharmaceuticals; medical and surgical supplies and equipment; surgical dressings; and devices used for external reduction of fractures and dislocations;
- supplies and equipment for administering and monitoring anesthesia or sedation;
- intraocular lenses (IOLs);
- ancillary services;
- capital-related costs;
- implantable items used in connection with diagnostic x-ray tests, diagnostic laboratory tests, and other diagnostic tests;
- durable medical equipment that is implantable;
- implantable and insertable medical items and devices, including, but not limited to, prosthetic devices (other than dental) that replace all or part of an internal body organ (including colostomy bags and supplies directly related to colostomy care), including replacement of these devices;
- costs incurred to procure donor tissue other than corneal tissue;
- image guidance, processing, supervision, and interpretation services;
- intraoperative items and services;
- drugs, biologics, and radiopharmaceuticals that function as supplies when used in a diagnostic test or procedure (including, but not limited to, diagnostic radiopharmaceuticals, contrast agents, and pharmacologic stress agents);

- drugs and biologics that function as supplies when used in a surgical procedure (including, but not limited to, skin substitutes and similar products that aid wound healing and implantable biologics);
- certain clinical diagnostic laboratory tests; and
- certain services described by add-on codes.

[Soc. Sec. Act § 1833(t)(1)(B)(iii) and (t)(2)(B); 42 C.F.R. § 419.2(b).]

Hospitals subject to the OPPS are paid for certain items and services that are outside the scope of the OPPS on a reasonable cost or other basis. The following costs are outside the scope of the OPPS:

- direct graduate medical education;
- nursing and allied health programs;
- interns and residents not in approved teaching programs;
- teaching physicians' charges for Part B services in hospitals that elect cost-based payment for teaching physicians;
- anesthesia services furnished to hospital outpatients by qualified nonphysician anesthetists such as certified registered nurse anesthetists and anesthesiologists' assistants employed by the hospital or obtained under arrangements;
- bad debts for uncollectible deductible and coinsurance amounts;
- organ acquisition costs paid under Part B; and
- corneal tissue acquisition or procurement costs for corneal transplant procedures.

[42 C.F.R. § 419.2(c).]

Adjustments and Additional Payments Under the OPPS

Hospitals may receive payments in addition to standard OPPS payments.

- **Outlier payments.** Medicare provides for additional "outlier" payments to hospitals when they provide exceptionally costly outpatient services. CMS makes an outlier payment when a hospital's charges, adjusted to cost, exceed a fixed multiple of the OPPS payment as adjusted by pass-through payments. [Soc. Sec. Act § 1833(t)(5); 42 C.F.R. § 419.43(d).]

- **Transitional pass-through payments.** The OPPS provides for additional payments, called transitional pass-through payments, for certain innovative medical devices, drugs, and biologics for a period of two to three years. The purpose of transitional pass-through payments is to allow for adequate payment of new and innovative technology until there is enough data to incorporate the costs for these items into the base APC group. [Soc. Sec. Act § 1833(t)(6); 42 C.F.R. §§ 419.64, 419.66.]

- **Certain cancer hospitals.** CMS adjusts OPPS payments to certain cancer hospitals—those exempted by law from payment under the inpatient prospective payment system for covered hospital outpatient services provided in CY 2020. [Soc. Sec. Act § 1833(t)(18); 42 C.F.R. § 419.43(i); *Final rule with comment period*, 84 FR 61142, Nov. 11, 2019.]

- **Hold-harmless status for certain cancer hospitals and children's hospitals.** If payments for outpatient department services furnished by cancer hospitals and children's hospitals are lower than those they would have received under previous policies, CMS provides additional payments to make up the difference. [Soc. Sec. Act § 1833(t)(7)(D)(ii); 42 C.F.R. § 419.70(d)(3).]

¶820

- **Small rural hospital adjustment.** For 2020, Medicare makes a 7.1 percent payment increase for rural sole community hospitals and essential access community hospitals. The adjustment is for all services and procedures paid under the OPPS, excluding separately payable drugs and biologics, devices paid under the pass-through payment policy, and items paid at charges reduced to costs. [Soc. Sec. Act § 1833(t)(13)(B); 42 C.F.R. § 419.43(g); *Final rule with comment period*, 84 FR 61142, Nov. 11, 2019.]

Prior Authorization for Certain Outpatient Services

Due to significant increases in the utilization volume of certain outpatient department services that are primarily cosmetic, pursuant to Soc. Sec. Act § 1833(t)(2)(F), CMS established prior authorization requirements for certain hospital outpatient department services as a condition of Medicare payment. [42 C.F.R. § 419.80.]

As a condition of Medicare payment for the services in the following categories of hospital outpatient department services, a provider must submit to CMS or its contractors a prior authorization request: blepharoplasty, botulinum toxin injections, panniculectomy, rhinoplasty; and vein ablation. CMS or its contractors will deny a claim for a service that requires prior authorization if the provider has not received a provisional affirmation of coverage on the claim, unless the provider is exempt under 42 C.F.R. § 419.83(c). [42 C.F.R. §§ 419.82, 419.83; *Final rule with comment period*, 84 FR 61142, Nov. 11, 2019.]

Copayment/Coinsurance Under the OPPS

Under the OPPS, coinsurance is defined as the percent of the Medicare-approved amount that beneficiaries pay for a service furnished in the hospital outpatient department (after they have met the Part B deductible—see ¶ 335). Copayment is defined as the set dollar amount that beneficiaries pay under the OPPS and is capped at the Part A deductible for that year. [42 C.F.R. §§ 419.40(c), 419.41(c)(4).]

The coinsurance percentage is calculated as the difference between the program payment percentage and 100 percent. The coinsurance percentage in any year is defined for each APC group as the greater of the ratio of the APC group unadjusted copayment amount to the annual APC group payment rate, or 20 percent. [Soc. Sec. Act § 1833(t)(3)(B), (t)(8)(C); 42 C.F.R. § 419.40.]

The Secretary must reduce the national unadjusted coinsurance amount each year so that the effective coinsurance rate for a covered service in the year does not exceed 40 percent of the APC payment rate. For a covered service furnished in a year, the national unadjusted coinsurance amount cannot be less than 20 percent of the payment rate amount. [Soc. Sec. § 1833(t)(3)(B)(ii) and (t)(8)(C); 42 C.F.R. § 419.41(c)(4)(iii).]

The coinsurance amount for the APC or APCs for a drug or biologic furnished on the same day is aggregated with the coinsurance amount for the APC that reflects the administration of the drug or biologic furnished on that day and treated as the coinsurance amount for one APC. [42 C.F.R. § 419.41(c)(4)(i)(B).]

Coinsurance for new procedures. APCs for new procedures may be adopted when the new procedures do not fit well into another APC. When an APC is added that consists of HCPCS codes for which there was no 1996 charge data to calculate the unadjusted coinsurance amount, coinsurance is based on the minimum unadjusted coinsurance, which is 20 percent of the APC payment amount. Additional payments for outlier cases and for certain medical devices, drugs, and biologics, and transitional corridor payments will not affect the coinsurance amounts. [Soc. Sec. § 1833(t)(3)(B)(iii); *Final rule*, 65 FR 18434, 18487, April 7, 2000.]

Hospital election to reduce coinsurance. A hospital may elect to reduce coinsurance for any or all APC groups on a calendar-year basis by selecting the minimum coinsurance amount; however, it may not reduce coinsurance for some, but not all, services within the same APC group. If a hospital reduces a coinsurance amount, it must notify its Medicare administrative contractor by December 1 of the preceding year by documenting the applicable APCs and the coinsurance amount that the hospital has selected. The reduced coinsurance may not be less than 20 percent of the APC payment rate. The hospital may advertise that it has reduced the level of coinsurance identifying the specific outpatient services to which the reduction is applicable. Coinsurance reductions are not allowed in physicians' offices or other ambulatory settings. [Soc. Sec. Act § 1833(t)(8)(B); 42 C.F.R. § 419.42.]

Coinsurance waiver for preventive services. Deductibles and copayments for preventive services paid under the OPPS are waived. Preventive services are defined as: screening and preventive services currently listed in Soc. Sec. Act § 1861(ww)(2); preventive "wellness" physical examinations; and personalized preventive plan services. For coinsurance to be waived, preventive services must be given a grade of "A" or "B" by the United States Preventive Services Task Force. [Soc. Sec. Act § 1833(a), (b)(1).] See ¶ 369 for a discussion of Part B coverage of preventive services.

Hospital Outpatient Quality Reporting Program

Providers of outpatient services must report quality of care data to avoid a 2.0 percent decrease in their annual market basket payment adjustments as part of the Hospital Outpatient Quality Reporting (OQR) Program. [Soc. Sec. Act § 1833(t)(17)(a)(i).]

Validation requirement. To ensure that hospitals are accurately reporting quality of care measures for chart-abstracted data, CMS may validate one or more measures by reviewing documentation of patient encounters submitted by selected participating hospitals. CMS requires hospitals to achieve a minimum 75 percent reliability score based on this validation process to receive the full OPPS update. [42 C.F.R. § 419.46(e).]

Quality measures. In the CY 2020 OPPS final rule, CMS removed OP-33: External Beam Radiotherapy for Bone Metastases (NQF # 1822) from the Hospital OQR Program beginning with the CY 2022 payment determination. [*Final rule with comment period*, 84 FR 61142, Nov. 11, 2019.]

Separately Payable Drugs, Biologics, and Radiopharmaceuticals

OPPS payment for drugs is generally divided into two categories: separately payable drugs and packaged drugs. In 2020, CMS makes a separate payment for Medicare Part B-covered drugs, biologics, and radiopharmaceuticals when estimated per day costs are greater than $130. Drugs, biologics, and radiopharmaceuticals with a per day cost less than or equal to $130 are packaged into the payment for the treatment during which the drug is administered. [Soc. Sec. Act § 1833(t)(16)(B); *Final rule with comment period*, 84 FR 61142, Nov. 11, 2019.]

In CY 2020, CMS will pay for separately payable drugs and biologics at the average sale price (ASP) plus 6 percent. [*Final rule with comment period*, 84 FR 61142, Nov. 11, 2019.]

Drugs purchased under the 340B drug pricing program. For CY 2020, separately payable Part B drugs that meet the definition of "covered outpatient drugs," except for vaccines and drugs on pass-through payment status, that are acquired through the 340B Drug Pricing Program will be paid at the ASP minus 22.5 percent (instead of ASP plus 6 percent) when billed by a hospital paid under the OPPS. Rural sole community hospitals, PPS-exempt cancer hospitals, and children's hospitals are exempt from the reduced 340B

¶820

drug payment policy for CY 2019. [*Final rule with comment period*, 84 FR 61142, Nov. 11, 2019.]

Payment for Non-Opioid Alternative Treatments

Pursuant to Soc. Sec. Act § 1833(t)(22), CMS conducted a review and evaluation of claims data and concluded that changes are not necessary at this time under the OPPS for the packaged drug policy for drugs that function as a surgical supply, nerve blocks, surgical injections, and neuromodulation products when used in a surgical procedure in the OPPS setting. Therefore, for CY 2020 CMS will continue to package payment for non-opioid pain management drugs that function as surgical supplies in the performance of surgical procedures in the hospital outpatient department setting. [*Final rule with comment period*, 84 FR 61142, Nov. 11, 2019.]

[¶ 825] Ambulatory Surgical Centers

CMS pays for surgical procedures provided in freestanding or hospital-based ambulatory surgical centers (ASCs) using a payment system based on the hospital outpatient prospective payment system (OPPS). Under the system, CMS reimburses ASCs for any covered individual "surgical procedure." ASC covered surgical procedures are those that are separately paid under the OPPS, that would not pose a significant risk to beneficiary safety, and for which standard medical practice dictates that the beneficiary would not typically be expected to require active medical monitoring and care at midnight following the procedure. [Soc. Sec. Act § 1833(i)(1), (2); 42 C.F.R. § 416.166.]

Like the OPPS, the ASC payment system sets payments for individual services using a set of relative weights, a conversion factor (or average payment amount), and adjustments for geographic differences in input prices. Medicare pays ASCs 80 percent of the lesser of: (1) the actual charge for the services; or (2) the geographically adjusted payment rate determined by CMS. The beneficiary pays the remaining 20 percent, as the Part B deductible and coinsurance amount applies to services provided at an ASC. [42 C.F.R. §§ 416.167, 416.171, 416.172.]

Medicare pays for the related physician services under the physician fee schedule (see ¶ 855). [42 C.F.R. § 416.163(b).] See ¶ 386 for a discussion of Medicare coverage of ASC services.

ASC PPS Price Transparency

To facilitate price transparency, the HHS Secretary must make public the estimated payment amount for ASC items or services payable under the ASC payment system and the estimated amount of the beneficiary liability applicable to the item or service via a searchable website such as the CMS Physician Compare website. The estimated amount of beneficiary liability for the item or service is the amount for which an individual who does not have coverage under a Medicare supplemental policy or any other supplemental insurance coverage is responsible. The Secretary must provide notification of the availability of the estimated payment amounts for the items and services as well as the amount of the beneficiary liability. [Soc. Sec. Act § 1834(t)(1)–(3).]

Reporting of ASC Quality Data

Under the ASC quality reporting (ASCQR) program, ASCs must retain and report data on several measures of the quality of care provided. ASCs that do not maintain and report this data as required will have the increase in their payments reduced by 2 percent. [Soc. Sec. Act § 1833(i)(2)(D)(iv), (i)(7)(A); 42 C.F.R. § 416.300.]

In the calendar year (CY) 2020 final rule, CMS adopted one claims-based measure beginning with the CY 2024 payment determination: ASC-19: Facility-Level 7-Day Hospital Visits after General Surgery Procedures Performed at Ambulatory Surgical Centers (NQF #3357). [*Final rule with comment period*, 84 FR 61142, Nov. 11, 2019.]

Payment for Non-opioid Alternative Treatments

Pursuant to Soc. Sec. Act § 1833(i)(8), CMS conducted a review and evaluation of payments for opioids and evidence-based non-opioid alternatives for pain management and concluded that for CY 2020 it will continue to unpackage and pay separately at average sales price plus 6 percent for the cost of non-opioid pain management drugs that function as surgical supplies when they are furnished in the ASC setting (see 42 C.F.R. § 416.164(a)(4), (b)(6)). [*Final rule with comment period*, 84 FR 61142, Nov. 11, 2019.]

[¶ 827] Hospice Reimbursement

With the exception of payment for physician services, Medicare payment for hospice care is made at one of four predetermined rates for each day that a Medicare beneficiary is under the care of the hospice. Because the rates are prospective, there are no retroactive adjustments other than the application of the statutory "caps" on overall payments made at the end of the fiscal year (FY) and on payments for inpatient care. The rate paid for any particular day varies depending on the level of care furnished to the beneficiary. The four levels of care into which each day of care is classified are:

    (1) Routine Home Care—Revenue code 0651;

    (2) Continuous Home Care—Revenue code 0652;

    (3) Inpatient Respite Care—Revenue code 0655; and

    (4) General Inpatient Care (Nonrespite)—Revenue code 0656.

For each day that a Medicare beneficiary is under the care of a hospice, the hospice is reimbursed an amount applicable to the type and intensity of the services furnished to the beneficiary for that day. [42 C.F.R. § 418.302(a), (b); *Medicare Claims Processing Manual*, Pub. 100-04, Ch. 11, § 30.1.]

The hospice payment on a continuous care day varies depending on the number of hours of continuous services provided. The continuous home care rate is divided by 24 to yield an hourly rate. The number of hours of continuous care provided during a continuous home care day is then multiplied by the hourly rate to yield the continuous home care payment for that day. A minimum of eight hours of care must be furnished on a particular day to qualify for the continuous home care rate. [42 C.F.R. § 418.302(e)(4).]

On any day on which the beneficiary is not an inpatient, the hospice is paid the routine home care rate, unless the patient receives continuous care for at least eight hours. Subject to certain limitations, on any day on which the beneficiary is an inpatient in an approved facility for inpatient care, the appropriate inpatient rate (general or respite) is paid depending on the category of care furnished. [42 C.F.R. § 418.302(e)(3) and (4), (f).]

Annual update of payment rates. The hospice payment update percentage for FY 2020 is 2.6 percent. [Soc. Sec. Act § 1814(i)(1)(C); *Final rule*, 84 FR 38484, Aug. 6, 2019.] CMS publishes general hospice payment rates annually to be used for revenue codes 0651, 0652, 0655, and 0656. These rates must then be adjusted by the Medicare administrative contractor based on the beneficiary's locality. [42 C.F.R. § 418.306; Pub. 100-04, Ch. 11, § 30.2.]

Hospice per diem payment rates for the FY 2020 period from October 1, 2019, through September 30, 2020, for hospices that submit quality data, are as follows: continuous home care $1395.63, inpatient respite care $450.10, and general inpatient care (non-respite) $1021.25. FY 2020 hospice payment rates for routine home care for hospices that submit quality data are $194.50 for days 1 through 60 and $153.72 for days 61 and later. [*Final rule*, 84 FR 38484, Aug. 6, 2019.]

Aggregate cap amount. The total amount of payments made for hospice care provided by (or under arrangements made by) a hospice program for an accounting year may not exceed the "cap amount" for the year multiplied by the number of Medicare beneficiaries in the hospice program in that year. [Soc. Sec. Act § 1814(i)(2)(A); 42 C.F.R. § 418.309.]

The hospice aggregate cap amount for the cap year ending September 30, 2020, is set at $29,964.78. The hospice must refund any payments in excess of the cap. [42 C.F.R. § 418.309; *Final rule*, 84 FR 38484, Aug. 6, 2019.]

Hospice Quality Reporting Program

CMS will reduce the hospice market basket update by 2.0 percentage points for any hospice that does not comply with quality data submission requirements. Hospices are required to complete and submit an admission Hospice Item Set (HIS) and a discharge HIS for each patient admission to hospice, regardless of payer or patient age. [Soc. Sec. Act § 1814(i)(5); 42 C.F.R. § 418.312.]

CMS is currently developing a hospice assessment tool for real-time patient assessments. The agency believes the tool, named "Hospice Outcomes and Patient Evaluation" (HOPE), will help hospice staff better understand the patient's end of life care needs, provide hospices with important information to address patient and family needs, and ensure delivery of high quality care throughout the patient stay, while minimizing the burden on providers. [*Final rule*, 84 FR 38484, Aug. 6, 2019.]

Reimbursement for Hospice Services Performed by Physicians

The following services performed by hospice physicians and nurse practitioners are included in the hospice rates described above: (1) general supervisory services of the medical director; and (2) participation in the establishment of plans of care, supervision of care and services, periodic review and updating of plans of care, and establishment of governing policies by the physician member of the interdisciplinary group. [42 C.F.R. § 418.304(a).]

For other services, the contractor pays the hospice an amount equivalent to 100 percent of the physician fee schedule (see ¶ 855) for those physician services furnished by hospice employees or under arrangements with the hospice. [42 C.F.R. § 418.304(a).]

Independent attending physician. Services of the patient's attending physician, if he or she is not an employee of the hospice or providing services under arrangements with the hospice, are not considered hospice services. These services are reimbursed under the physician fee schedule. [Soc. Sec. Act § 1861(dd)(2)(B); 42 C.F.R. § 418.304(c); Pub. 100-04, Ch. 11, § 40.1.3.]

Nurse practitioners and physician assistants. Medicare pays for attending physician services provided by nurse practitioners and, effective January 1, 2019, physician assistants to Medicare beneficiaries who have elected the hospice benefit and who have selected a nurse practitioner or physician assistant as their attending physician, even if neither is a hospice employee. Nurse practitioner and physician assistant services are paid at 85 percent of the physician fee schedule amount. [42 C.F.R. § 418.304(e)(1) and (3), (f)(1) and (3).]

Care plan oversight services. Medicare makes separate payment for physician care plan oversight services under the following conditions: (1) the services require recurrent physician supervision of therapy involving 30 or more minutes of the physician's time per month; and (2) payment is made to only one physician per patient for services furnished during a calendar month period. The physician must have furnished a service requiring a face-to-face encounter with the patient at least once during the six-month period before the month for which care plan oversight payment is first billed. [42 C.F.R. § 414.39 (b)(1), (b)(2).]

Payment for pre-election evaluation. A physician on staff of a hospice may be paid to evaluate a patient who has not yet elected hospice care to determine the patient's need for pain and symptom management and for hospice care and to help with advance care planning. [Soc. Sec. Act § 1812 (a)(5); 42 C.F.R. § 418.304 (d).]

[¶ 830] Home Health Agencies

Under the home health prospective payment system (HH PPS) a standardized payment is made for each 30-day episode of care a beneficiary receives from a home health agency (HHA). Pursuant to the Bipartisan Budget Act of 2018 (P.L. 115-123), CMS changed the unit of payment from 60 days to 30 days, effective for 30-day periods of care that start on or after January 1, 2020. [Soc. Sec. Act § 1895 (b), as amended by Bipartisan Budget Act of 2018 § 51001 (a); 42 C.F.R. § § 484.205 (a), (b), 484.215 (f); *Final rule*, 84 FR 60478, Nov. 8, 2019.] See ¶ 250–¶ 268 for a discussion of Part A coverage of home health services.

Durable medical equipment and disposable devices. Durable medical equipment (DME) provided as a home health service is paid under the durable medical equipment fee schedule. Separate payment is made for furnishing Negative Pressure Wound Therapy using a disposable device; it is not included in the national, standardized prospective payment. [Soc. Sec. Act § 1814 (k); 42 C.F.R. § 484.205 (f).]

2020 payment rates. The calendar year (CY) 2020 national, standardized 30-day episode payment rate for HHAs submitting quality data is $1,864.03. HHAs that do not submit quality data are subject to a payment reduction, resulting in a payment of $1,827.30. [Soc. Sec. Act § 1895 (b)(3)(A)(iii); *Final rule*, 84 FR 60478, Nov. 8, 2019.]

Adjustments to Standard HH PPS Payment

CMS adjusts the national, standardized payment rate by a case-mix relative weight to explain the relative resource utilization of different patients and a wage index value based on the site of service for the beneficiary. The basic pay rate is subject to adjustments based on: (1) low utilization; (2) a partial period of care; and (3) outlier visits. [Soc. Sec. Act § 1895 (b); 42 C.F.R. § § 484.205, 484.220.]

Case-mix adjustment. The case-mix index is a scale that measures the relative difference in resource intensity among different groups in the clinical model. It factors for significant variation in costs among different units of services. [Soc. Sec. Act § 1895 (b)(4); 42 C.F.R. § 484.220.]

Outlier adjustment. The outlier adjustment provides additional payment to an HHA when the cost of providing care to a beneficiary exceeds a threshold amount. The outlier payment is a proportion of the amount of estimated costs beyond a threshold defined by CMS. The total amount of outlier payments to a specific HHA for a year may not exceed 10 percent of the total payments to the specific agency under the HH PPS for the year. [Soc. Sec. Act § 1895 (b)(5); 42 C.F.R. § § 484.205 (d), 484.240.]

Partial episode payment adjustment. An HHA receives a partial period of care adjustment if a 30-day episode is interrupted by an intervening event, such as (1) a beneficiary-elected transfer to another HHA; or (2) discharge with goals met or no expectation of return to home health and the beneficiary is readmitted to home health during the

¶830

30-day episode. The original 30-day episode payment is adjusted to reflect the length of time the beneficiary remained under the care of the original HHA based on the first billable visit date through and including the last billable visit date. [42 C.F.R. § § 484.205 (d), 484.235.]

Low-utilization payment adjustment. For periods beginning on or after January 1, 2020, a low-utilization payment adjustment applies to beneficiaries who receive two or fewer visits during a 30-day period. [42 C.F.R. § § 484.205 (d), 484.230.]

Home Health Quality Reporting Program

An HHA must submit data on health care quality to CMS or its home health market basket update will be reduced by 2 percentage points. The reduction applies to reimbursement for the calendar year for which measures were not reported. [Soc. Sec. Act § 1895 (b) (3) (B) (v) (I), (II); 42 C.F.R. § § 484.225, 484.245.]

HHAs submit certain Outcome and Assessment Information Set (OASIS) assessments and Home Health Care Consumer Assessment of Healthcare Providers and Systems Survey (HHCAHPS) data to meet the quality reporting requirements. A subset of the home health quality measures is publicly reported on the Home Health Compare website, http://www.medicare.gov/homehealthcompare/. The Improving Medicare Post-Acute Care Transformation Act of 2014 (IMPACT Act) (P.L. 113-185) imposed additional data reporting requirements for certain post-acute care providers, including HHAs. HHAs must submit: (1) standardized patient assessment data; (2) data on quality measures; and (3) data on resource use and other measures. [Soc. Sec. Act § § 1895 (b) (3) (B) (v) (IV), 1899B (a) (1).]

In the CY 2020 final rule, CMS removed one measure and added two for the CY 2022 quality reporting program. [*Final rule*, 84 FR 60478, Nov. 8, 2019.]

Value-based purchasing. All Medicare-certified HHAs in selected states are required to participate in a home health value-based purchasing model, which requires these entities to compete for payment adjustments under the current PPS reimbursement schedule based on quality performance. [42 C.F.R. § § 484.300–484.330.]

Billing for Home Health Services

Generally, payment for a home health episode of care is made in two stages. The HHA may make a request for anticipated payment (RAP) at the beginning of the episode to receive a percentage of the amount expected to be payable for the episode. The balance, including any adjustments, is paid at the end of the episode of care. However, due to the reduced time frame for the unit of payment mandated by the Bipartisan Budget Act of 2018, CMS will prohibit HHAs certified for participation in Medicare effective on or after January 1, 2019, to receive RAP payments beginning in CY 2020. HHAs certified for participation in Medicare with effective dates before January 1, 2019, will continue to receive RAP payments of 20 percent upon implementation of the 30-day unit of payment for CY 2020. RAP payments will end for CY 2021 and beyond. [42 C.F.R. § § 409.43 (c), 484.205 (g); *Final rule*, 84 FR 60478, Nov. 8, 2019.]

Final payment. The remaining split percentage payment due to an HHA for an episode is made based on a claim submitted at the end of the 30-day period. Before the claim is submitted, the plan of care must be signed and dated by a physician who meets the certification and recertification requirements of 42 C.F.R. § 424.22. [42 C.F.R. § 409.43 (c) (2); *Medicare Claims Processing Manual*, Pub. 100-04, Ch. 10, § 10.1.10.4.]

Consolidated billing. All Medicare-covered home health services listed in section 1861 (m) of the Social Security Act and ordered by the physician in a plan of care must be billed to Medicare by the HHA that established a home health episode of care (see ¶ 250). [Soc. Sec. Act § 1842 (b) (6) (F); *Medicare Benefit Policy Manual*, Pub. 100-02, Ch. 7, § 40.]

Home Health Advance Beneficiary Notices and Demand Billing

An HHA may seek denials for entire claims from Medicare in cases when it knows that all services will not be covered by Medicare. To inform beneficiaries about possible noncovered charges, HHAs must use the ABN of Noncoverage, CMS-R-131, and the Home Health Change of Care Notice (HHCCN). [Pub. 100-04, Ch. 30, §§ 50.1, 60.1.]

HHAs must use the HHCCN to provide notice to a beneficiary on the first occasion that a "triggering event" occurs. Triggering events include when the HHA: (1) reduces or stops an item and/or service during a spell of illness while continuing others, including when one home health discipline ends but others continue; or (2) ends delivery of all services. [Pub. 100-04, Ch. 30, § 60.3.]

[¶ 835] Skilled Nursing Facilities

Skilled nursing facilities (SNFs) are paid under a prospective payment system (PPS) on a case-mix adjusted, per diem basis. The payment rates represent payment in full (subject to applicable coinsurance) for all routine, ancillary, and capital-related costs associated with furnishing inpatient SNF services to Medicare beneficiaries, other than costs associated with approved educational activities. The payment also covers any physical, occupational, or speech-language therapy, whether the services are furnished by, or under the supervision of, a physician or other health care professional and regardless of whether the resident who receives the services is in a covered Part A stay. [Soc. Sec. Act § 1888(e)(2)(A)(i), (B); 42 C.F.R. § 413.335.]

Exclusions. The per diem rate does not cover the following costs, for which separate Part B claims must be made:

(1) physician services furnished to individual SNF residents;

(2) certain nurse practitioner, clinical nurse specialist, and physician assistant services;

(3) services of certified nurse-midwives, qualified psychologists, and certified registered nurse anesthetists;

(4) home dialysis supplies and equipment, self-care home dialysis support services, institutional dialysis services and supplies, and renal dialysis services;

(5) erythropoietin for dialysis patients competent to use the drug without supervision;

(6) originating site telehealth services;

(7) services provided by a rural health clinic (RHC) or federally qualified health center (FQHC), if the services would have been excluded if furnished by a physician or practitioner who was not affiliated with a RHC or FQHC;

(8) certain chemotherapy items and administrative services, and radioisotope services;

(9) certain customized prosthetic devices delivered to an inpatient for use during a SNF stay and intended for use after discharge;

(10) ambulance services furnished to an individual in conjunction with renal dialysis services; and

(11) hospice care related to a beneficiary's terminal condition.

[Soc. Sec. Act § 1888(e)(2)(A)(ii)–(iv); 42 C.F.R. § 411.15(p)(2).]

SNF Resident Defined

A beneficiary who is admitted to a Medicare-participating SNF is considered to be a resident of the SNF for the duration of his or her covered Part A stay. Further, for purposes of physical, occupational, or speech-language therapy services, a beneficiary who is admitted to a Medicare-participating SNF is considered to be a resident of the SNF regardless of whether he or she is in a covered Part A stay. Whenever the beneficiary leaves the facility, the beneficiary's status as a SNF resident (along with the SNF's responsibility to furnish or make arrangements for services) ends when one of the following events occurs:

- the beneficiary is admitted as an inpatient to a Medicare-participating hospital or critical access hospital (CAH), or as a resident to another SNF;

- the beneficiary receives services from a Medicare-participating home health agency under a plan of care;

- the beneficiary receives outpatient services from a Medicare-participating hospital or CAH (but only with respect to those services that CMS designates as being beyond the general scope of SNF comprehensive care plans); or

- the beneficiary is formally discharged (or otherwise departs) from the SNF, unless he or she is readmitted (or returns) to that or another SNF before the following midnight.

[42 C.F.R. § 411.15(p)(3).]

FY 2020 SNF PPS Payments

A SNF market basket index reflects changes over time in the prices of an appropriate mix of goods and services included in covered SNF services. It consists of the most commonly used cost categories for SNF routine services, ancillary services, and capital-related expenses. The federal per diem rate is updated by using the previous fiscal year's (FY) rate increased by the SNF market basket percentage change for the current fiscal year. [Soc. Sec. Act § 1888(e)(4)(E)(ii)(IV), (e)(5); 42 C.F.R. § 413.337(d)(1).]

In 2020, for SNFs located in urban areas, the unadjusted per diem rates are:

- physical therapy (PT): $60.75;
- occupational therapy (OT): $56.55;
- speech-language pathology (SLP): $22.68;
- nursing: $105.92;
- non-therapy ancillaries (NTA): $79.91; and
- non-case-mix: $94.48.

In rural facilities, the rates are:

- PT: $69.25;
- OT: $63.60;
- SLP: $28.57;
- nursing: $101.20;
- NTA: $76.34; and
- non-case-mix: $96.59.

The market basket percentage for FY 2020 is 2.4 percent, after application of the productivity adjustment. CMS projects aggregate payments to increase by $851 million. [*Final rule*, 84 FR 38728, Aug. 7, 2019.]

Payment for residents with AIDS. SNF payment rates include a special adjustment that is intended to cover the additional services required for any SNF resident with HIV/AIDS—a 128 percent increase in the PPS per diem payment. [Soc. Sec. Act § 1888(e)(12)(A).]

SNF Quality Reporting and Value-Based Purchasing

SNFs are required to submit quality measures and standardized patient assessment data to CMS. SNFs that fail to submit the required quality data to CMS will be subject to a 2 percentage point reduction to the annual market basket percentage update factor for fiscal years beginning with FY 2018. [Soc. Sec. Act §§ 1888(e)(6), 1899B.]

Any payment reductions that are taken will begin approximately one year after the end of the data submission period for that FY and approximately two years after CMS first adopts the measure for the SNF quality reporting program (QRP). CMS adopted two new quality measures beginning with FY 2022: (1) Transfer of Health Information to the Provider—Post-Acute Care (PAC); and (2) Transfer of Health Information to the Patient—PAC. These measures assess whether a current reconciled medication list has been provided to the appropriate provider and to the patient or patient's caregivers following discharge from the SNF. CMS also updated the measure Discharge to Community—PAC to exclude baseline nursing facility residents from the measure. [*Final rule*, 84 FR 38728, Aug. 7, 2019.]

Value-based purchasing program. The HHS Secretary established a SNF value-based purchasing (VBP) program beginning with FY 2019 under which value-based incentive payments are made to SNFs based on performance. The SNF VBP will use the Skilled Nursing Facility 30-Day All-Cause Readmission Measure to measure and rank SNF performance; high-measuring SNFs will receive an incentive payment. Beginning in 2019, the achievement threshold for quality under the VBP program will be set as the 25th percentile of achievement on VBP program measures. CMS adopted FY 2020 (October 1, 2019 through September 30, 2020) as the performance period for the FY 2022 SNF VBP program year. [Soc. Sec. Act § 1888(h); 42 C.F.R. § 413.338; *Final rule*, 84 FR 38728, Aug. 7, 2019.]

Patient-Driven Payment Model and Minimum Data Set

Resource Utilization Groups (RUGs) was the system used to classify SNF residents into mutually exclusive groups based on clinical, functional, and resource-based criteria. Effective October 1, 2019, the RUG IV model was replaced with a revised case-mix methodology called the Patient-Driven Payment Model (PDPM). Under the PDPM, reimbursement is based upon each aspects of a patient's care, including Non-Therapy Ancillaries (NTAs)—items and services not related to the provision of therapy, such as drugs and medical supplies. Additionally, under the PDPM, reimbursement will adjust per diem rates to reflect changes in patient needs throughout a stay. SNFs will also receive incentives to ensure consistent care. [*Final rule*, 84 FR 38728, Aug. 7, 2019.]

Minimum Data Set. The Minimum Data Set (MDS) is a resident assessment instrument used by SNFs to assess patient needs and create a plan of treatment to classify patients into RUG groups. The MDS contains a core set of screening, clinical, and functional status elements, including common definitions and coding categories, that form the basis of a comprehensive assessment. The amount reimbursed to the nursing home for care of a particular patient is adjusted for the clinical condition of the patient. [*Final rule*, 74 FR 40288, Aug. 11, 2009.]

SNFs must report assessment data according to an assessment schedule. This schedule must include performance of patient assessments no later than the eighth day of posthospital SNF care and such other assessments that are necessary to account for changes in patient care needs. SNFs that fail to perform assessments timely are paid a federal default payment

¶835

for the days of a resident's care for which they are not in compliance with this schedule. [42 C.F.R. § 413.343.]

Swing-Bed Facilities

Certain small rural hospitals may enter into a Medicare swing-bed agreement under which the hospital can use its beds to provide either acute or SNF care, as needed. [Soc. Sec. Act § 1883(a)(1).] For CAHs, Part A pays on a reasonable cost basis for SNF services furnished under a swing-bed agreement. SNF services furnished under a swing-bed agreement by non-CAH rural hospitals are paid under the SNF PPS. [Soc. Sec. Act § 1888(e)(7); 42 C.F.R. § 413.114(a)(2).]

[¶ 837] Inpatient Rehabilitation Facilities

An inpatient rehabilitation facility (IRF) is a hospital or hospital unit that has been excluded from the inpatient hospital prospective payment system (IPPS) and serves an inpatient population requiring intensive rehabilitation services for treatment. Patients must require physical and/or occupational therapy, along with other active and ongoing therapeutic intervention of multiple-therapy disciplines such as speech-language pathology or prosthetics/orthotics therapy. [Soc. Sec. Act § 1886(j); 42 C.F.R. § § 412.23(b), 412.622(a)(3).]

IRF Compliance Threshold

To be excluded from the IPPS and instead be paid under the IRF PPS, a facility must meet the requirements for classification as an IRF. One criterion that Medicare uses to classify a hospital or unit of a hospital as an IRF is that at least 60 percent of the facility's total inpatient population must require intensive rehabilitative services for the treatment of at least one of 13 medical conditions:

(1) stroke;

(2) spinal cord injury;

(3) congenital deformity;

(4) amputation;

(5) major multiple trauma;

(6) hip fracture;

(7) brain injury;

(8) neurological disorders, including multiple sclerosis, motor neuron diseases, polyneuropathy, muscular dystrophy, and Parkinson's disease;

(9) burns;

(10) active, polyarticular rheumatoid arthritis, psoriatic arthritis, and seronegative arthropathies resulting in significant functional impairment of ambulation and other activities of daily living;

(11) systemic vasculidities with joint inflammation, resulting in significant functional impairment of ambulation and other activities of daily living;

(12) severe or advanced osteoarthritis (osteoarthrosis or degenerative joint disease) involving two or more major weight-bearing joints (elbow, shoulders, hips, or knees, but not counting a joint with a prosthesis) with joint deformity and substantial loss of range of motion, atrophy of muscles surrounding the joint, and significant functional impairment of ambulation and other activities of daily living; or

(13) knee or hip joint replacement, or both, during an acute hospitalization immediately preceding the inpatient rehabilitation stay and also meeting one or more of the following specific criteria: (a) the patient underwent bilateral knee or bilateral hip joint

replacement surgery during the acute hospital admission immediately preceding the IRF admission; (b) the patient is extremely obese with a Body Mass Index of at least 50 at the time of admission to the IRF; or (c) the patient is age 85 or older at the time of admission to the IRF.

[42 C.F.R. §§ 412.23(b), 412.29(b).]

IRF Patient Assessment Instrument

IRFs must use the IRF patient assessment instrument (IRF-PAI) to assess each Medicare Part A fee-for-service and Medicare Advantage IRF patient upon admission and discharge. [42 C.F.R. §§ 412.604(c), 412.606.] The admission assessment is used to place a patient in a case-mix group (CMG). Each CMG is a functional-related group, determined by distinguishing classes of IRF patient discharges on the basis of impairment, age, comorbidities, functional capability of the patient, and other factors that may improve the ability of the functional-related groups to estimate variations in resource use. The CMG determines the base payment rate that the IRF receives for the Medicare-covered Part A services furnished by the IRF during the beneficiary's episode of care. [Soc. Sec. Act § 1886(j)(2); 42 C.F.R. § 412.620.]

IRFs must electronically report patient assessment data for all admission and discharge assessment data, including any interruption in stay data, to CMS. [42 C.F.R. §§ 412.614(b)–(c), 412.618(b).]

IRF PPS Payment Rate

Under the IRF PPS, IRFs receive a predetermined amount per discharge for inpatient services furnished to Medicare Part A beneficiaries. PPS rates encompass the inpatient operating costs and capital costs, including routine and ancillary costs, of furnishing covered rehabilitation services. In addition to payments based on prospective payment rates, IRFs receive payments for the bad debts of Medicare beneficiaries and a payment amount per unit for blood clotting factor provided to Medicare inpatients who have hemophilia. Payment rates are calculated using relative weights to account for variations in resource needs in CMGs. [Soc. Sec. Act § 1886(j)(3)(A); 42 C.F.R. § 412.622.]

Payment adjustments. Facility-level adjustments include area wage adjustments and adjustments for facilities located in rural areas, for treating low-income patients, and for teaching facilities. CMS makes additional payments for outlier cases that incur extraordinarily high costs and also makes case-level adjustments for interrupted stays, transfers, and short stays. [Soc. Sec. Act § 1886(j)(3)(A), (4); 42 C.F.R. § 412.624; *Medicare Claims Processing Manual*, Pub. 100-04, Ch. 3, §§ 140.2.4, 140.2.5.]

FY 2020 update. The market basket increase for fiscal year (FY) 2020, after the application of the productivity adjustment mandated by the Patient Protection and Affordable Care Act (ACA) (P.L. 111-148), is 2.5 percent. The high-cost outlier threshold in FY 2020 was decreased to $9,300 from $9,402 in FY 2019, which will maintain estimated outlier payments at 3 percent of all cases. [*Final rule*, 84 FR 39054, Aug. 8, 2019.]

IRF Quality Reporting Program

IRFs are required to submit data on specified quality measures under the IRF quality reporting program (QRP). IRFs that fail to successfully participate in the IRF QRP receive a 2.0 percent payment reduction in their IRF market basket update, which could result in payment decreases for non-complying IRFs if the IRF payment update is less than 2.0 percent in any given year. [Soc. Sec. Act § 1886(j)(7); 42 C.F.R. §§ 412.624(c)(4), 412.634(b)(1); Pub. 100-04, Ch. 3, § 140.2.11.]

¶837

Further, IRFs must report standardized patient assessment data, data on quality measures, and data on resource use and other measures. Data measures include: (1) functional status, cognitive function, and changes in function and cognitive function; (2) skin integrity and changes in skin integrity; (3) medication reconciliation; (4) incidence of major falls; and (4) accurately communicating the individual's health information and care preferences. [Soc. Sec. Act §§ 1886(j)(7)(F), 1899B.]

In the FY 2020 final rule, CMS adopted, effective for discharges beginning October 1, 2020: (1) the Transfer of Health Information to the Provider—Post Acute Care measure; and (2) Transfer of Health Information to the Patient—Post Acute Care measure. CMS also adopted a number of standardized patient assessment data elements, which key domain areas, including functional status, cognitive function and mental status, special services, treatments and interventions, medical conditions and comorbidities, impairments, and social determinants of health. [*Final rule*, 84 FR 39054, Aug. 8, 2019.]

Measures currently included in the IRF QRP can be found on CMS's website at https://www.cms.gov/Medicare/Quality-Initiatives-Patient-Assessment-Instruments/IRF-Quality-Reporting/IRF-Quality-Reporting-Program-Measures-Information-.html.

One-Day Payment Window

Under the IRF PPS, IRFs are subject to a one-day payment window, or the "24-hour rule," for pre-admission services. The "24-hour rule" requires outpatient diagnostic services and most non-physician services provided during the calendar day immediately preceding the date of admission to an IRF to be included in the IRF case-mix group payment. [Soc. Sec. Act § 1886(a)(4); 42 C.F.R. § 413.40(c)(2); *Medicare Claims Processing Manual*, Pub. 100-04, Ch. 3, § 40.3.]

IRFs and hospitals reimbursed under IRF PPS are not subject to the three-day payment window for pre-admission services. The three-day payment window applies only to acute inpatient hospitals paid under the IPPS (see ¶ 810). [Pub. 100-04, Ch. 3, § 140.2.]

IRF Accreditation Requirements

IRFs must meet accreditation requirements to ensure the quality of suppliers of durable medical equipment, prosthetics, and supplies (DMEPOS). This rule requires that suppliers be accredited by independent accrediting organizations to meet quality standards to bill the Medicare program for items such as walkers, wheelchairs, and hospital beds furnished to Medicare beneficiaries. [42 C.F.R. § 424.57(c).]

[¶ 840] Psychiatric Hospitals and Units

Under the inpatient psychiatric facility (IPF) prospective payment system (PPS), CMS reimburses on a per diem basis for covered inpatient hospital services furnished to Medicare Part A beneficiaries by psychiatric hospitals and distinct-part units in acute care hospitals and critical access hospitals (CAHs). [Soc. Sec. Act § 1886(s); 42 C.F.R. § 412.400.]

A payment under the IPF PPS represents payment in full, subject to applicable deductibles and coinsurance, for labor, inpatient operating, and capital-related costs associated with furnishing Medicare covered services in an IPF, but not the cost of an approved medical education program (see 42 C.F.R. §§ 413.75–413.85). In addition to the federal per diem amounts, IPFs receive payment for bad debts of Medicare beneficiaries (see 42 C.F.R. § 413.89). [42 C.F.R. § 412.422(b).]

For a discussion of Part B coverage of outpatient mental health services, see ¶ 387. For information on lifetime and "spell of illness" restrictions on inpatient psychiatric hospital coverage, see ¶ 225.

Requirements for IPFs

An IPF is certified under Medicare as an inpatient psychiatric hospital, which means an institution that: (1) is primarily engaged in providing, by or under the supervision of a physician, psychiatric services for the diagnosis and treatment of mentally ill patients; (2) maintains clinical records necessary to determine the degree and intensity of the treatment provided to the mentally ill patient; and (3) meets staffing requirements sufficient to carry out active programs of treatment for individuals who are furnished care in the institution. A distinct-part psychiatric unit may also be certified if it meets the clinical record and staffing requirements in 42 C.F.R. § 412.27 for a "psychiatric hospital." [42 C.F.R. § § 412.23(a), 412.27; *Medicare Benefit Policy Manual*, Pub. 100-02, Ch. 2, § 10.3.]

For all IPFs, a provisional or admitting diagnosis must be made on every patient at the time of admission, and it must include the diagnosis of comorbid diseases as well as the psychiatric diagnosis. In addition, distinct-part psychiatric units of acute care hospitals are required to admit only those patients whose admission to the unit is required for active treatment, of an intensity that can be provided appropriately only in an inpatient hospital setting, of a psychiatric principal diagnosis that is listed in the International Classification of Diseases, Tenth Revision, Clinical Modification. [42 C.F.R. § 412.27(a), (c)(1)(ii).]

Services Covered Under the IPF PPS

The IPF must furnish all necessary covered services to an inpatient Medicare beneficiary, either directly or under arrangements. Psychiatric hospital inpatient services payable under the IPF PPS do not include the services of physicians, physician assistants, nurse practitioners, clinical nurse specialists, certified nurse-midwives, qualified psychologists, or certified registered nurse anesthetists. These services are paid by Medicare under applicable provider fee schedule provisions. [42 C.F.R. § 412.404(d).]

Pre-admission services otherwise payable under Medicare Part B and furnished to a beneficiary either on the day of admission or the day preceding admission are paid under the IPF PPS as long as the services are: (1) furnished by the IPF or by an entity wholly owned or wholly operated by the IPF; (2) diagnostic, including clinical diagnostic laboratory tests; or (3) nondiagnostic when furnished on the date of the beneficiary's inpatient admission, nondiagnostic when furnished on the calendar day preceding the date of the beneficiary's inpatient admission and the hospital does not demonstrate that such services are unrelated to the beneficiary's inpatient admission, and are not ambulance services or maintenance renal dialysis services. [42 C.F.R. § 412.405.]

IPF PPS Payment Methodology

Under the IPF PPS, IPFs receive a predetermined federal per diem base rate for inpatient hospital services furnished to Medicare Part A fee-for-service beneficiaries. The federal per diem payment amount is based on the federal per diem base rate plus applicable adjustments. [42 C.F.R. § 412.422.]

Patient- and facility-level adjustments. The federal per diem payment under the IPF PPS is composed of the federal per diem base rate and certain patient- and facility-level payment adjustments that are associated with statistically significant per diem cost differences. Patient-level adjustments include age, diagnosis-related group (DRG) assignment, comorbidities, and variable per diem adjustments to reflect higher per diem costs in the early days of an IPF stay. Facility-level adjustments include adjustments for the IPF's wage index, rural location, teaching status, a cost-of-living adjustment for IPFs located in Alaska and Hawaii, and the presence of a qualifying emergency department. [42 C.F.R. § 412.424(d).]

¶840

The IPF PPS provides additional payment policies for outlier cases, interrupted stays, and a per-treatment adjustment for patients who undergo electroconvulsive therapy (ECT). [42 C.F.R. § 412.424(d)(3).]

Productivity adjustments. The Patient Protection and Affordable Care Act (ACA) (P.L. 111-148) § 10319(e) amended the annual update to add a productivity adjustment beginning in fiscal year (FY) 2012. The productivity adjustment is the same one applied to inpatient hospital services under Soc. Sec. Act § 1886(b)(3)(B)(xi)(II). [Soc. Sec. Act § 1886(s)(2)(A)(i).]

FY 2020 per diem rates. The standard per diem base rate for FY 2020 is $798.55 for providers that report quality data, up from the per diem base rate of $782.78 in FY 2019. The ECT payment for FY 2020 will increase from $337 per treatment to $343.79. [*Final rule*, 84 FR 38424, Aug. 6, 2019.]

The IPF PPS provides for gradually reduced per diem rates for consecutive days of an IPF stay. The first day of any psychiatric stay provides IPFs with the highest reimbursement due to costly admitting services; the rate is even higher for IPFs with emergency departments. The payments are adjusted downward from day 2 through day 21 of an IPF stay. For day 22 and thereafter, the variable per diem adjustment remains the same each day for the remainder of the stay. [*Final rule*, 84 FR 38424, Aug. 6, 2019.]

IPF Quality Reporting Program

IPFs are required to submit data on specified quality measures that are selected from those endorsed by qualified consensus-based entities or established by a different process. IPFs that do not participate in the program are subject to a 2.0 percent reduction in their annual market basket update. IPFs are required to submit data on specified quality measures to receive a full market basket adjustment. [Soc. Sec. Act § 1886(s)(4); 42 C.F.R. § 412.424(d)(1)(vi).]

Quality measures. In the FY 2020 IPF PPS final rule, CMS added the Medication Continuation Following Inpatient Psychiatric Discharge (NQF #3205) measure for the FY 2021 payment determination and later. [*Final rule*, 84 FR 38424, Aug. 6, 2019.]

Lifetime Limitation on Inpatient Psychiatric Services

Payment may not be made for more than a total of 190 days of inpatient psychiatric hospital services during the patient's lifetime. [42 C.F.R. § 409.62.] This limitation applies only to services furnished in a free-standing psychiatric hospital and does not apply to inpatient psychiatric services furnished in a distinct-part psychiatric unit of an acute care hospital or CAH. [Pub. 100-02, Ch. 2, § 80.]

[¶ 845] End-Stage Renal Disease

End-stage renal disease (ESRD) is permanent kidney failure that is severe enough to require a regular course of dialysis or a kidney transplant to maintain life. The ESRD prospective payment system (PPS) provides a case-mix adjusted single payment to ESRD facilities for renal dialysis services provided in an ESRD facility or in a beneficiary's home. The ESRD PPS covers renal dialysis services and home dialysis services, support, and equipment. [Soc. Sec. Act § 1881(b)(14); 42 C.F.R. §§ 413.172, 413.217.]

For renal dialysis services furnished to Medicare Part B fee-for-service beneficiaries, ESRD facilities receive a predetermined per-treatment payment amount that is the sum of: (1) the per-treatment base rate adjusted for wages, and adjusted for facility-level and patient-level characteristics; (2) any outlier payment; (3) any training adjustment add-on; (4) any transitional drug add-on payment adjustment; and (5) any transitional add-on payment adjustment for new and innovative equipment and supplies. In addition to the per-treatment payment amount, the ESRD facility may receive payment for bad debts of Medicare beneficiaries. [42 C.F.R. § 413.230.]

If the beneficiary has incurred the full Part B deductible before the dialysis treatment, Medicare pays a dialysis facility 80 percent of the prospective rate; if the beneficiary did not incur the full deductible before treatment, CMS subtracts the amount applicable to the deductible from the ESRD facility's prospective rate and pays the facility 80 percent of the remainder, if any. [42 C.F.R. § 413.176.]

See ¶ 205 for a discussion of the coverage period for ESRD beneficiaries. Part B coverage of ESRD services is discussed at ¶ 389.

Payment for acute kidney injury dialysis. CMS established a payment system for renal dialysis services furnished to beneficiaries with an acute kidney injury (AKI) in or under the supervision of an ESRD facility. An individual with acute kidney injury means a person who has acute loss of renal function and does not receive renal dialysis services for which payment is made under Soc. Sec. Act § 1881(b)(14). [Soc. Sec. Act § 1834(r); 42 C.F.R. §§ 413.370, 413.371.]

The payment amount for AKI dialysis services is the ESRD PPS base rate, as adjusted by the wage index. CMS may apply other adjustments provided under Soc. Sec. Act § 1881(b)(14). The AKI dialysis payment rate applies to renal dialysis services furnished under Medicare Part B by a renal dialysis facility or provider of services paid under Soc. Sec. Act § 1881(b)(14). Other items and services furnished to beneficiaries with AKI that are not considered to be renal dialysis services, but that are related to their dialysis treatment as a result of their AKI, are separately payable. [Soc. Sec. Act § 1834(r); 42 C.F.R. §§ 413.372, 413.373, 413.374.]

Quality Incentive Program for ESRD Services

Under the quality incentive program (QIP), an ESRD facility is required to report to CMS on quality measures. If the provider of services or a renal dialysis facility does not meet those requirements, payments will be reduced by up to 2 percent. Each year, a provider's performance score is based on reported compliance with quality measures, based on data from two years prior to the reimbursement year (for example, 2020 data affects 2022 reimbursement). [Soc. Sec. Act § 1881(h); 42 C.F.R. § 413.177.]

The measures for a payment year include, but are not limited to: (1) measures on anemia management that reflect the labeling approved by the Food and Drug Administration for such management; (2) measures on dialysis adequacy; (3) to the extent feasible, measures of patient satisfaction; (4) to the extent feasible, measures on iron management, bone mineral metabolism, and vascular access (including for maximizing the placement of arterial venous fistula); and (5) measures specific to the conditions treated with oral-only drugs and that are, to the extent feasible, outcomes based. [Soc. Sec. Act § 1881(h)(2); 42 C.F.R. § 413.178(c).]

Current measures. Beginning in payment year 2022, updates to the scoring methodology for the National Healthcare Safety Network (NHSN) Dialysis Event reporting measure will allow new facilities (and facilities that are eligible to report data on the measure for less than 12 months) to receive a score on that measure, and the Standardized Transfusion Ratio (STrR) clinical measure (NQF #2979) is converted to a reporting measure while CMS examines concerns raised by stakeholders regarding the measure's validity. [*Final rule*, 84 FR 60648, Nov. 8, 2019.]

¶845

CMS lists measures for the ESRD QIP on its website at https://www.cms.gov/Medicare/Quality-Initiatives-Patient-Assessment-Instruments/ESRDQIP/06_MeasuringQuality.html.

Reimbursement for ESRD Drugs

Medicare Part B pays for drugs medically necessary in the treatment of patients for ESRD if they are furnished in approved ESRD facilities. [42 C.F.R. § 410.50.] The drugs and biologics include but are not limited to:

(1) drugs and biologics included under the composite rate as of December 31, 2010;

(2) former separately billable Part B injectable drugs;

(3) oral or other forms of injectable drugs used for the treatment of ESRD formerly billed under Part D; and

(4) oral or other forms of drugs and biologics without an injectable form.

Note, however, that payment under the ESRD PPS for ESRD-related oral-only drugs has been postponed until January 1, 2025. [Achieving a Better Life Experience Act of 2014 (ABLE Act) (P.L. 113-295) § 204; 42 C.F.R. § 413.174(f)(5), (6).]

New renal dialysis drugs or biological products are included in the ESRD PPS bundled payment using a drug designation process. For dates of service occurring on or after January 1, 2020, CMS also allows a transitional add-on payment adjustment for furnishing new and innovative renal dialysis equipment and supplies. [42 C.F.R. § § 413.234(b), 413.236(a); *Final rule*, 84 FR 60648, Nov. 8, 2019.]

Physician Reimbursement for ESRD Services

Physicians and practitioners managing patients on dialysis are paid a "monthly capitation payment" (MCP) for most outpatient dialysis-related physician services furnished to a Medicare ESRD beneficiary regardless of the volume of the services provided. Under the MCP method, the Medicare administrative contractor (MAC) pays an MCP amount for each patient to cover all professional services furnished by the physician, except those listed as exclusions from MCP. The payment amount varies based on the number of visits provided within each month and the age of the ESRD beneficiary. [42 C.F.R. § 414.314.]

Exclusions from MCP. The MCP does not apply to the following physician services, which are paid according to the physician fee schedule:

(1) administration of hepatitis B vaccine;

(2) covered physician services furnished by another physician when the patient is not available to receive the outpatient services as usual, for example, when the patient is traveling out of town;

(3) covered physician services furnished to hospital inpatients, including services related to inpatient dialysis, by a physician who elects not to continue to receive the MCP during the period of inpatient stay;

(4) surgical services;

(5) interpretation of tests that have a professional component;

(6) complete evaluation for renal transplantation;

(7) evaluation of potential living transplant donors;

(8) the training of patients to perform home hemodialysis, self-hemodialysis, and the various forms of self-peritoneal dialysis;

    (9) non-renal related physician's services; and

    (10) all physician services that pre-date the initiation of outpatient dialysis.

[42 C.F.R. § 414.314(b)(1); *Medicare Claims Processing Manual*, Pub. 100-04, Ch. 8, § 140.]

"Initial method" of payment. Physicians may elect a different method of reimbursement under a modified version of the former "initial method." Under this method, physicians may be paid for their services to patients in the form of an "add-on" payment. To be eligible for payment under this method, all physicians in a facility must elect this method of payment for all the ESRD facility patients they serve. [42 C.F.R. §§ 414.310(e), 414.313.]

Self-dialysis training services. Physicians are paid for providing self-dialysis training services as a flat fee (subject to deductible and coinsurance requirements) for each patient a physician supervises during the training course. If the training is not completed, the payment amount is proportionate to the time spent in training. [42 C.F.R. § 414.316; Pub. 100-04, Ch. 8, § 140.2.]

Transplants. Surgeons performing renal transplants are paid on a comprehensive payment basis, subject to the deductible and coinsurance, that covers all surgical services in connection with a renal transplant, including pre-operative and post-operative surgical care and for immunosuppressant therapy supervised by the attending transplant surgeon for 60 days. Medically necessary services rendered after that period are reimbursed under the physician fee schedule. [42 C.F.R. § 414.320.]

[¶ 847] Rural Health Facilities

The Medicare program reimburses rural health facilities for providing health care services to Medicare beneficiaries. Health care entities in low-population rural areas include critical access hospitals (CAHs), sole community hospitals (SCHs), rural referral centers (RRCs), and rural health clinics (RHCs). Medicare also makes payment adjustments to qualifying low-volume rural hospitals and certain small rural hospitals for which Medicare patients make up a significant percentage of inpatient days or discharges.

Critical Access Hospitals

To qualify as a CAH, a hospital must be located in a county in a rural area or treated as being located in a rural area and (1) located more than a 35-mile drive (or, in the case of mountainous terrain or in areas with only secondary roads available, a 15-mile drive) from a hospital or CAH; or (2) certified before January 1, 2006, by the state as being a necessary provider of health care services to residents in the area. [Soc. Sec. Act § 1820(c)(2).]

Unlike traditional hospitals, which are paid under the inpatient prospective payment system (IPPS), Medicare pays CAHs based on each hospital's reported costs. Each CAH receives 101 percent of its costs for outpatient, inpatient, laboratory services, and certain ambulance services. [42 C.F.R. § 413.70.]

CAHs, which are limited to 25 beds, must provide 24-hour emergency services. Generally, they may not provide acute inpatient care for a period longer than, as determined on an annual average basis, 96 hours per patient. In addition to 25 acute beds, CAHs are allowed to have distinct-part 10-bed psychiatric units and 10-bed rehabilitation units; however, these distinct departments of the CAH are paid through Medicare's various prospective payment systems and are not eligible for cost-based reimbursement. [Soc. Sec. Act § 1820(c)(2); 42 C.F.R. § 485.610, 485.620; *Medicare Claims Processing Manual*, Pub. 100-04, Ch. 3, § 30.1.]

Sole Community Hospitals

Special reimbursement rules apply to SCHs, which are hospitals located in rural areas and the sole source of care available to residents of the area. A hospital qualifies for sole community status under the IPPS if it is located more than 35 miles from other like hospitals, or it is located in a rural area and meets one of the following conditions:

(1) the hospital is rural and located between 25 and 35 miles from other like hospitals and meets one of the following criteria:

(a) no more than 25 percent of residents who become hospital inpatients or no more than 25 percent of the Medicare beneficiaries who become hospital inpatients in the hospital's service area are admitted to other like hospitals located within a 35-mile radius of the hospital or, if larger, within its service area;

(b) the hospital has fewer than 50 beds and the Medicare administrative contractor (MAC) certifies that the hospital would have met the criteria in paragraph (1)(a) above were it not for the fact that some beneficiaries or residents were forced to seek care outside the service area due to the unavailability of necessary specialty services at the community hospital; or

(c) because of local topography or periods of prolonged severe weather conditions, the other like hospitals are inaccessible for at least 30 days in each of two out of three years;

(2) the hospital is rural and located between 15 and 25 miles from other like hospitals but because of local topography or periods of prolonged severe weather conditions, the other like hospitals are inaccessible for at least 30 days in each of two out of three years; or

(3) the hospital is rural and because of distance, posted speed limits, and predictable weather conditions, the travel time between the hospital and the nearest like hospital is at least 45 minutes.

[42 C.F.R. § 412.92(a).]

SCHs are paid at whichever of the following rates yield the greatest aggregate payment for the cost reporting period: (1) the federal national rate applicable to the hospital pursuant to 42 C.F.R. § 412.64; or (2) the hospital-specific rate, commonly referred to as the hospital's "target amount," as determined under 42 C.F.R. § 412.78. [Soc. Sec. Act § 1886(d)(5)(D)(i); 42 C.F.R. § 412.92(d)(1).]

Rural Referral Centers

To qualify for RRC status, rural hospitals must have operating costs that are more similar to urban hospitals than smaller community hospitals because of bed size, a large number of complicated cases, a high number of discharges, or a large number of referrals from other hospitals or physicians outside the hospital's service areas. [Soc. Sec. Act § 1886(d)(5)(C)(i).]

A hospital qualifies for RRC status if it meets either of the following criteria:

(1) the hospital is located in a rural area and has 275 or more beds during its most recently completed cost reporting period, unless the hospital submits written documentation with its application that its bed count has changed since the close of its most recently completed cost reporting period for one or more of the following reasons: (a) merger of two or more hospitals; (b) reopening of acute care beds previously closed for renovation; (c) transfer to the IPPS of acute care beds previously classified as part of an excluded unit; or (d) expansion of acute care beds available for use and permanently maintained for lodging inpatients, excluding beds in corridors and other temporary beds; or

(2) the hospital shows that at least 50 percent of its Medicare patients are referred from other hospitals or from physicians not on the staff of the hospital, and at least 60

percent of the hospital's Medicare patients live more than 25 miles from the hospital and at least 60 percent of all the services that the hospital furnishes to Medicare beneficiaries are furnished to beneficiaries who live more than 25 miles from the hospital.

[42 C.F.R. § 412.96(b).]

In the alternative, a hospital that does not meet the criteria of above is classified as an RRC if it is located in a rural area and meets the case-mix or discharge criteria. To determine whether the hospital meets the case-mix index criteria, CMS uses the case-mix index from the hospital's own billing records for Medicare discharges as processed by the MAC. [42 C.F.R. § 412.96(c)(1).] To determine whether the hospital meets the discharge criteria, the number of discharges (not including discharges from units excluded from the IPPS or from newborn units) for the designated cost reporting period must be at least equal to 5,000 discharges or, if less, the median number of discharges for urban hospitals located in each region. [42 C.F.R. § 412.96(c)(2).]

Rural Health Clinics

RHCs are facilities located in rural areas in which there are insufficient numbers of needed health care practitioners (as determined by HHS). RHCs can be either independent or provider-based. Within the previous three-year period, RHCs must have been designated and certified as being in an area with a shortage of personal health services. [Soc. Sec. Act. § 1861(aa)(2); 42 C.F.R. §§ 405.2401, 405.2462(a), (b).] See ¶ 382 for a discussion of Part B coverage of RHC services.

A provider-based RHC that is authorized to bill under the reasonable cost system is paid in accordance with 42 C.F.R. Parts 405 and 413 if it is an integral and subordinate part of a hospital, skilled nursing facility, or home health agency participating in Medicare and operated with other departments of the provider under common licensure, governance, and professional supervision. Independent RHCs that are authorized to bill under the reasonable cost system are paid on the basis of an all-inclusive rate for each beneficiary visit for covered services, as determined by the MAC. [42 C.F.R. § 405.2462(a), (b); Pub. 100-04, Ch. 9, § 20.1.]

Low-Volume Hospitals

Medicare provides an additional payment to qualifying rural hospitals for the higher incremental costs associated with a low volume of discharges. For fiscal years (FYs) 2011 through 2022, the term "low-volume hospital" means an acute hospital that is located more than 15 road miles from another acute care hospital. Beginning in FY 2023, a low-volume hospital is an acute hospital that is located more than 25 road miles from another acute care hospital. [Soc. Sec. Act § 1886(d)(12), as amended by Bipartisan Budget Act of 2018 (P.L. 115-123) § 50204(a)(1) and (a)(2)(A); 42 C.F.R. § 412.101(b)(1), (b)(2)(i), (c)(1).]

In addition, to be considered a low-volume hospital, the hospital must have:

(1) for FYs 2011 through 2018, fewer than 1,600 discharges of individuals entitled to, or enrolled for, benefits under Part A during the fiscal year or portion of fiscal year;

(2) for FYs 2019 through 2022, fewer than 3,800 discharges during the fiscal year; and

(3) for FY 2023 and later, fewer than 800 discharges during the fiscal year.

[Soc. Sec. Act § 1886(d)(12)(C)(i), as amended by Bipartisan Budget Act of 2018 § 50204(a)(2)(A); 42 C.F.R. § 412.101(b).]

¶847

Medicare-Dependent Hospital Program

The Medicare-Dependent Hospital program, which provides increased Medicare reimbursement to certain small rural hospitals for which Medicare patients make up a significant percentage of inpatient days or discharges, has been extended a number of times, most recently through October 1, 2022. [Soc. Sec. Act § 1886(d)(5)(G)(i), as amended by Bipartisan Budget Act of 2018 § 50205(a)(3), (a)(4); 42 C.F.R. § 412.108.]

A hospital is classified as a Medicare-dependent, small rural hospital if it meets the following conditions:

(1) the hospital is located in a rural area, or if in a state with no rural area, it satisfies any of the criteria in Soc. Sec. Act § 1886(d)(8)(E)(ii) subclause (I), (II), or (III) or under 42 C.F.R. § 412.103(a)(1)–(a)(3);

(2) the hospital has 100 or fewer beds during the cost reporting period;

(3) the hospital is not classified as a SCH; and

(4) at least 60 percent of the hospital's inpatient days or discharges were attributable to individuals entitled to Medicare Part A benefits during at least two of the last three most recent audited cost reporting periods for which the Secretary has a settled cost report. If the cost reporting period is for less than 12 months, the hospital's most recent 12-month or longer cost reporting period before the short period is used.

[Soc. Sec. Act § 1886(d)(5)(G)(iv), as amended by Bipartisan Budget Act of 2018 § 50205(a)(3); 42 C.F.R. § 412.108(a)(1).]

[¶ 850] Federally Qualified Health Centers

Soc. Sec. Act § 1834(o) established a system of payment for the costs of federally qualified health center (FQHC) services under Medicare Part B based on prospectively set rates. The FQHC prospective payment system (PPS) is based on an average of reasonable costs of FQHCs and pays FQHCs the lesser of their actual charges for services or a single encounter-based rate for professional services furnished per beneficiary per day. [Soc. Sec. Act § 1834(o); 42 C.F.R. § 405.2467(a).] Part B coverage of FQHC services is described at ¶ 382.

Deductible and coinsurance. Except for preventive services, for which Medicare pays 100 percent, beneficiaries pay a coinsurance amount of 20 percent of the lesser of the FQHC's actual charge or the PPS encounter rate. No deductible is applicable to FQHC services. [Soc. Sec. Act § 1833(a)(1)(Z), (b)(4); 42 C.F.R. §§ 405.2410(a)(2) and (b)(2), 405.2462(e).]

FQHC PPS Payment Rates

FQHCs billing under the PPS receive a single, per diem rate based on the prospectively set rate for each beneficiary visit for covered services. CMS calculates the per diem rate by dividing total FQHC costs by total FQHC daily encounters to establish an average per diem cost. The per diem rate is adjusted for the following:

(1) geographic differences in cost based on the geographic practice cost indices (GPCIs) in accordance with the physician fee schedule (see ¶ 855) during the same period, limited to only the work and practice expense GPCIs;

(2) furnishing care to a beneficiary that is a new patient; and

(3) furnishing care to a beneficiary receiving a comprehensive initial Medicare visit (an initial preventive physical examination or an initial annual wellness visit) or a subsequent annual wellness visit.

[Soc. Sec. Act § 1834(o); 42 C.F.R. §§ 405.2462(c), 405.2464(b).]

Rates are increased by the percentage increase in a market basket of FQHC goods and services as established through regulations or, if not available, the Medicare Economic Index (MEI). [Soc. Sec. Act § 1834(o)(2)(B)(ii); 42 C.F.R. § 405.2467(c).]

Supplemental payments. FQHCs under contract with Medicare Advantage (MA) organizations are eligible for supplemental payments for covered services furnished to enrollees in MA plans to cover any difference, if any, between their payments from the MA plan and what they would receive under: (1) the FQHC PPS; or (2) the Medicare outpatient per visit rate as set annually by the Indian Health Service for grandfathered tribal FQHCs. If the contracted rate is less than the Medicare PPS rate, Medicare will pay the FQHC the difference, less any cost-sharing amounts owed by the beneficiary. [Soc. Sec. Act § 1833(a)(3)(B); 42 C.F.R. § 405.2469.]

Additional Payment for FQHCs with Physicians Receiving DATA 2000 Waivers

Beginning January 1, 2019, an FQHC will receive an additional payment if a physician or practitioner who is employed by the FQHC and first receives a waiver under section 303(g) of the Controlled Substances Act (i.e., DATA 2000 waivers) on or after January 1, 2019, provides FQHC services for the treatment of opioid use disorder. The payment will be an amount determined by the Secretary, based on an estimate of the average costs of training for purposes of receiving such a waiver, and may be made only one time with respect to each such physician or practitioner. [Soc. Sec. Act § 1834(o)(3), as added by SUPPORT for Patients and Communities Act (P.L. 115-271) § 6083(a).]

Beneficiary Appeals Concerning Reimbursement for FQHC Services

A beneficiary may request a hearing by a Medicare administrative contractor (MAC) if he or she: (1) is dissatisfied with a MAC's determination denying a request for payment made on his or her behalf by an FQHC; (2) is dissatisfied with the amount of payment; or (3) believes the request for payment is not being acted upon with reasonable promptness. [42 C.F.R. § 405.2472.]

[¶ 853] Accountable Care Organizations

Accountable care organizations (ACOs) are groups of service and supplier providers that work together to manage and coordinate care for Medicare fee-for-service (FFS) beneficiaries. The program is an alternative payment system that rewards provider groups for promoting accountability for patients, coordinating items and services under Medicare Part A and Part B, and encouraging investment in infrastructure and redesigned care processes to ensure high quality and efficient delivery. ACOs are generally networks of provider groups, often affiliated with a hospital, that work together and are jointly responsible for the cost and quality of care provided to Medicare beneficiaries. ACOs must meet certain criteria and specified quality performance standards to receive a portion of the shared savings they create. [Soc. Sec. Act § 1899(a)–(b); 42 C.F.R. §§ 425.10, 425.100.]

Eligibility to participate. The following types of providers of services and suppliers are eligible to participate in the program: (1) ACO professionals in group practice arrangements; (2) networks of individual practices of ACO professionals; (3) partnerships or joint venture arrangements between hospitals and ACO professionals; (4) hospitals employing ACO professionals; (5) critical access hospitals (CAHs) that bill under Method II; (6) rural health clinics (RHCs); (7) federally qualified health centers (FQHCs); and (8) teaching hospitals that have elected to receive payment on a reasonable cost basis for the direct medical and surgical services of their physicians. [Soc. Sec. Act § 1899(b)(1); 42 C.F.R. § 425.102.]

Participation requirements. There are a number of requirements that ACOs must satisfy to participate. ACOs must:

(1) agree to be accountable for the quality, cost, and overall care of Medicare fee-for-service beneficiaries;

(2) agree to participate for at least a three-year period;

(3) have a formal legal structure allowing them to receive and distribute payments;

(4) include enough primary-care ACO professionals to accommodate no fewer than 5,000 beneficiaries;

(5) provide the HHS Secretary with information regarding ACO professionals as deemed appropriate;

(6) have leadership and management in place to support clinical and administrative systems;

(7) define processes to promote evidence-based medicine and patient engagement, report on quality and cost measures, and coordinate care through the use of methods such as telehealth, remote patient monitoring, and other enabling technologies; and

(8) demonstrate to the Secretary that they meet patient-centeredness criteria, such as patient and caregiver assessments and individualized care plans.

[Soc. Sec. Act § 1899(b)(2); 42 C.F.R. §§ 425.104–425.112.]

Providers that participate in models under Soc. Sec. Act § 1115A or any other program or demonstration project that involves shared savings or the independence at home medical practice pilot program under Soc. Sec. Act § 1866E are ineligible to participate as ACOs. [Soc. Sec. Act § 1899(b)(4); 42 C.F.R. § 425.114.] The Secretary assigns beneficiaries to an ACO based on the utilization of primary care services. [Soc. Sec. Act § 1899(c); 42 C.F.R. §§ 425.400–425.404.]

An ACO may be sanctioned if it attempts to keep costs down by avoiding high-risk patients. Furthermore, the Secretary may terminate an agreement with an ACO if the organization does not meet the Secretary's quality-performance standards. [Soc. Sec. Act § 1899(d)(3), (4).]

ACO Shared Savings and Losses

ACO participants continue to receive payment under the traditional Medicare FFS program under Parts A and B. Only if an ACO meets certain quality and savings requirements and has per capita costs for beneficiaries that are below specified benchmarks and above a minimum savings rate will the ACO qualify for shared savings, which will be based on the quality score it receives. [Soc. Sec. Act § 1899(d)(1); 42 C.F.R. §§ 425.500–425.506.]

There are several different models in which the ACOs may elect to participate. For agreement periods beginning July 1, 2019, or later, CMS retired the Track 1 and Track 2 models. CMS renamed Track 3 as the ENHANCED track and created a new BASIC track, which will allow ACOs to gain experience with more modest levels of performance-based risk on their way to accepting greater levels of performance-based risk over time. [42 C.F.R. § 425.600(a)(1); *Final rule*, 83 FR 67816, Dec. 31, 2018.]

ENHANCED track. An ACO in the ENHANCED track operates under a two-sided model, sharing both savings and losses with the Medicare program for the agreement period. The ENHANCED track includes Track 3. [42 C.F.R. §§ 425.600(a)(3), 425.610.]

BASIC track. For agreement periods beginning on July 1, 2019, and in later years, an ACO in the BASIC track operates under either a one-sided model or a two-sided model, either sharing savings only or sharing both savings and losses with the Medicare program. Under the BASIC track's "glide path," the level of risk and potential reward phases are phased in over the course of the agreement period from one-sided in Levels A and B (42 C.F.R. §425.605(d)(1)(i), (ii)) to two-sided in Levels C through E (42 C.F.R. §425.605(d)(1)(iii)–(v)). Except for an ACO that previously participated in Track 1 or a new ACO identified as a re-entering ACO because more than 50 percent of its ACO participants have recent prior experience in a Track 1 ACO, an ACO eligible to enter the BASIC track's glide path may elect to enter its agreement period at any of the levels of risk and potential reward available under 42 C.F.R. §425.600(a)(4)(i)(A)(1) through (5). [42 C.F.R. §§425.600(a)(4), 425.605.]

[¶ 855] Physician Fee Schedule

Physicians are paid by Medicare on the basis of a national physician fee schedule. The physician fee schedule applies to all "physicians' services" (see ¶ 350 for the meaning of "physician") and certain services performed by other health care professionals. Specifically, the fee schedule applies to the following:

(1) professional services of doctors of medicine and osteopathy (including osteopathic practitioners), doctors of optometry, doctors of podiatry, doctors of dental surgery and dental medicine, and chiropractors (see ¶ 350);

(2) services and supplies furnished as an incident to a physician's professional service (see ¶ 351), excluding drugs, which are separately payable;

(3) outpatient physical and occupational therapy services and outpatient speech-language pathology services furnished by a therapist (not a provider such as a hospital, other facility, or agency) (see ¶ 381);

(4) diagnostic x-ray tests and other diagnostic tests (see ¶ 353), except diagnostic laboratory tests paid under a separate fee schedule (see ¶ 875);

(5) x-ray, radium, and radioactive isotope therapy, including materials and services of technicians (see ¶ 354);

(6) antigens (see ¶ 362); and

(7) preventive services (see ¶ 369).

[Soc. Sec. Act § 1848(j)(3); 42 C.F.R. § 414.2.]

How the Physician Fee Schedule Works

Under the physician fee schedule, Medicare generally pays 80 percent of the lower of: (1) the fee schedule amount; or (2) the actual charge billed by the physician or other health care practitioner (the other 20 percent is paid by the patient as coinsurance—see ¶ 335). The fee schedule payment amount for a service is determined by a formula that takes into consideration the relative value unit (RVU) for the service, the conversion factor (CF) for the year, and the geographic adjustment factor (GAF) for the service. The net effect of the physician fee schedule is that, in any particular geographical area, only one fee may be paid for each allowable service. [Soc. Sec. Act §§ 1833(a), 1848(a)(1), (b)(1); 42 C.F.R. §§ 414.20, 414.21.]

Relative value unit. The Social Security Act requires CMS to establish payments under the physician fee schedule based on national uniform RVUs that account for the relative resources used in furnishing a service. CMS establishes RVUs for three categories of resources:

¶855

(1) work required, which reflects the relative time and intensity associated with furnishing a service;

(2) practice expense (PE), which reflects the costs of maintaining a practice (such as renting office space, buying supplies and equipment, and staff costs); and

(3) malpractice insurance expense.

[Soc. Sec. Act § 1848(c)(1)(S); 42 C.F.R. § 414.22.]

Geographic adjustment factor. The GAF compares the relative value of physicians' work effort in each of the different fee schedule areas to the national average of that work effort. CMS uses a geographic practice cost index (GPCI) to establish the GAF for every Medicare payment locality for each of the three components (work, PE, and malpractice). The GPCIs are applied in the calculation of a fee schedule payment amount by multiplying the RVU for each component times the GPCI for that component. [Soc. Sec. Act § 1848(e); 42 C.F.R. § 414.26.]

Soc. Sec. Act § 1848(e)(1)(E) provides for a 1.0 floor for the work GPCIs. Most recently, the Further Consolidated Appropriations Act, 2020 (P.L. 116-94) extended it through May 22, 2020. [Soc. Sec. Act § 1848(e)(1)(E), as amended by Further Consolidated Appropriations Act, 2020 division N title I § 101.]

Conversion factor. The sum of the geographically adjusted RVUs is multiplied by a dollar CF. For 2020 through 2025, the CF will be 0.0 percent. [Soc. Sec. Act § 1848(d); 42 C.F.R. § 414.30.]

Payment for Facility-Based Physicians' Services

There are two parts to Medicare payment for the services of physicians who are hospital-based (e.g., radiologists, anesthesiologists, pathologists, teaching physicians, and interns and residents) or otherwise facility-based. The portion of the physician's activities representing services that are not directly related to an identifiable part of the medical care of the individual patient is the "provider component." Payment for provider component services can be made only to a provider and is included in the provider's prospective payment system rate. The "professional component" services, which relate to the portion of the physician's activities that is directly related to the medical care of the individual patient, are generally paid under the physician fee schedule. [*Medicare Claims Processing Manual*, Pub. 100-04, Ch. 6, § 80; Ch. 12, § 60; Ch. 13, § 20.1.]

Another distinction is made between the technical and professional components. The technical component is for nonphysician work, including the taking of a test. The professional component includes the physician's professional services, such as the interpretation of a test. [42 C.F.R. § 414.40(b)(2).]

Medicare pays for physician services furnished to beneficiaries in providers on a fee schedule basis if the following requirements are met: (1) the services are personally furnished for an individual beneficiary by a physician; (2) the services contribute directly to the diagnosis or treatment of an individual beneficiary; (3) the services ordinarily require performance by a physician; and (4) in the case of radiology or laboratory services, the additional requirements in 42 C.F.R. §§ 415.120 or 415.130 are met. [42 C.F.R. § 415.102(a); Pub. 100-04, Ch. 12, § 80.]

Anesthesiologists. For anesthesia services performed, medically directed, or medically supervised by a physician, Medicare pays the lesser of the actual charge or the anesthesia fee schedule amount. [42 C.F.R. § 414.46; Pub. 100-04, Ch. 12, § 50.]

Radiologists. A radiologist's services are paid under the physician fee schedule if the services are "patient services" and they are identifiable, direct, and discrete diagnostic or therapeutic services furnished to an individual patient, such as interpretation of x-ray plates, angiograms, myelograms, pyelograms, or ultrasound procedures. [42 C.F.R. § 415.120(a); Pub. 100-04, Ch. 13, § 20.1.]

Pathologists. A pathologist's services are paid under the physician fee schedule if the services meet the conditions for payment in 42 C.F.R. § 415.102 and are one of the following services: (1) surgical pathology services; (2) specific cytopathology, hematology, and blood banking services that have been identified as requiring performance by a physician and are listed in program operating instructions; (3) clinical consultation services; or (4) clinical laboratory interpretive services meeting some of the same requirements for clinical consultative services. [42 C.F.R. § 415.130(b).]

Physicians in teaching hospitals. A physician in a teaching hospital personally furnishing Part B physician services is paid under the physician fee schedule on the same basis as physicians providing those services in other settings. Payment is made only if a physician in a teaching hospital supervising residents is present during the "key portion" of the service or procedure. [42 C.F.R. § 415.172.]

The services of a resident in an approved teaching program provided as part of that program are covered as inpatient hospital services and not as physician services, even if the resident is licensed as a physician under state law. [42 C.F.R. § 415.200.]

Assistants at surgery. The law permits payment under Part B for a physician assistant at surgery in a teaching hospital only under certain conditions. When payment is authorized for the services of assistants at surgery, Medicare will pay no more than 16 percent of the fee schedule amount otherwise payable to the primary physician for the global surgical service involved. In a teaching hospital setting, Medicare does not pay for assistant-at-surgery services when a resident physician at the hospital could have assisted but did not. [Soc. Sec. Act §§ 1842(b)(7)(D)(i), 1848(i)(2); 42 C.F.R. § 415.190(c); Pub. 100-04, Ch. 12, § 20.4.3.]

Payment for "Incident to" Services and Drugs

Services provided by the physician's staff that are incident to the physician's services are paid under the physician fee schedule as if the physician had personally furnished the services. [42 C.F.R. § 414.34(b).]

Office medical supplies are considered to be part of a physician's practice expense, and payment for them is included in the practice expense portion of the payment to the physician for the medical or surgical service to which they are incidental. [42 C.F.R. § 414.34(a)(1).]

Services of certain health care practitioners (e.g., nurse practitioners, physician assistants, etc.) can be billed and paid separately (see ¶ 366). When this occurs, no payment is made to the physician.

Drugs supplied by physician offices are separably payable (see ¶ 885). [42 C.F.R. §§ 405.517, 414.36.]

Global Payments for Surgery

The global surgical package includes all necessary services normally furnished by a surgeon before, during, and after a procedure. The global period for major surgeries includes the day immediately before the day of surgery, the day of surgery, and 90 days following the day of surgery. The period for minor surgeries includes the day of surgery and a post-operative period that varies from 0 to 10 days. [Soc. Sec. Act § 1848(c)(1)(A)(ii); Pub. 100-04, Ch. 12, § 40.1.]

¶855

Services not included in the global surgical package. Procedure code modifiers are used to identify the most common services not included in the global fee, such as (1) evaluation and management services on the day before major surgery or the day of major surgery that result in the initial decision to operate; or (2) return trips to the operating room during the post-operative period. [Pub. 100-04, Ch. 12, § 40.2.]

Payment for Telehealth Services

Medicare pays a physician or practitioner located at a distant site who furnishes a telehealth service the same amount that would have been paid for the service under the physician fee schedule had it been furnished without the use of a telecommunications system. Only the consulting practitioner may bill for the consultation, and payments made to the practitioner at the distant site may not be shared with the referring practitioner or telepresenter. [Soc. Sec. Act § 1834(m)(2)(A); 42 C.F.R. § 414.65(a).]

The facility fee for the originating site is updated by the Medicare Economic Index. Only the originating site may bill for the originating site facility fee and only on an assignment-related basis. [Soc. Sec. Act § 1834(m)(2)(B); 42 C.F.R. § 414.65(b); Pub. 100-04, Ch. 12, § 190.6.] No facility fee will be paid if the originating site is the home for a mobile stroke unit; or the home for (1) home dialysis therapy or (2) beneficiaries with a substance use disorder diagnosis for the purposes of treatment of that disorder or a co-occurring mental health disorder. [Soc. Sec. Act § 1834(m)(2)(B)(ii), as amended by SUPPORT for Patients and Communities Act (P.L. 115-271) § 2001(a)(1)(B); 42 C.F.R. § 414.65(b)(3).]

The payment for the professional service and originating site facility fee is subject to coinsurance and deductible requirements. [42 C.F.R. § 414.65(c).]

Quality Payment Program

Under the Medicare Access and CHIP Reauthorization Act of 2015 (MACRA) (P.L. 114-10), the amounts paid to practitioners will be subject to adjustment through one of two mechanisms, depending on whether the physician chooses to participate in an Advanced Alternative Payment Model (Advanced APM) or the Merit-Based Incentive Payment System (MIPS). [MACRA § 101(c)(1), (e)(2); 42 C.F.R. § 414.1310(a).] The Bipartisan Budget Act of 2018 extended the MIPS transition period through 2021, with full implementation in 2022. [Soc. Sec. Act § 1848(q), as amended by Bipartisan Budget Act of 2018 § 51003(a)(1).]

MACRA consolidated and replaced the electronic health record (EHR) meaningful use program, Physician Quality Reporting System (PQRS), and the value-based payment modifier into the MIPS program. MACRA sunsetted the three programs at the end of 2018. [MACRA § 101(b), (c).]

MIPS. Providers who opt to participate in MIPS will receive payments that are subject to positive or negative performance adjustments. The performance adjustment for an individual provider will depend on that provider's performance compared to a threshold. [Soc. Sec. Act § 1848(q); 42 C.F.R. § 414.1405.]

APMs. An APM requires participation in an entity that assumes a meaningful financial risk, reporting of quality measures, and use of certified EHR technology. From 2019 through 2024, eligible professionals receiving a substantial portion of their revenue from APMs will receive a lump-sum payment after each year equal to 5 percent of their Medicare payments in that year. [Soc. Sec. Act § 1833(z).]

[¶ 860] Nonphysician Practitioners

As discussed at ¶ 351, separate Medicare coverage is provided for several kinds of nonphysician practitioners. Health care practitioners such as nurse practitioners (NPs) are authorized to bill Medicare separately when they perform specialized services or stand in the place of a physician. The Medicare payment amount for nonphysician practitioners is normally a certain percentage of the physician fee schedule for the same services (or less if their actual charges are less).

Assignment. Medicare claims for payment for services of nonphysician practitioners such as physician assistants (PAs), NPs, clinical nurse specialists (CNSs), certified nurse-midwives (CNMs), and certified registered nurse anesthetists (CRNAs) may be submitted on an assignment basis only (see ¶ 868). [42 C.F.R. §§ 410.74(d)(2), 410.75(e)(2), 410.76(e)(2), 410.77(d)(2), 414.60(c).]

Physician Assistants, Nurse Practitioners, and Nurse-Midwives

The Medicare payment amount for the services of NPs, CNSs, and PAs (other than assistant-at-surgery services) is based on 85 percent of the fee schedule payment for physicians furnishing the same service. [Soc. Sec. Act §§ 1833(a)(1)(O), 1842(b)(18); 42 C.F.R. §§ 414.52(d), 414.56(c).]

Physician assistants. PAs must have their own "nonphysician practitioner" national provider identifier (NPI). The NPI is used for identification purposes only when billing for PA services because only an appropriate PA employer or a provider/supplier for whom the PA furnishes services as an independent contractor can bill for PA services. [Soc. Sec. Act § 1842(b)(6)(C); 42 C.F.R. § 410.74(a)(2)(v); *Medicare Claims Processing Manual*, Pub. 100-04, Ch. 12, § 110.4.]

Nurse practitioners and clinical nurse specialists. Payment may be made directly to a NP or CNS for their professional services when furnished in collaboration with a physician. NPs and CNSs must have their own "nonphysician practitioner" NPI number for billing purposes. [Pub. 100-04, Ch. 12, § 120.3.]

Certified nurse-midwives. CNMs services are paid at 80 percent of the lesser of: (1) the actual charge for the services, or (2) 100 percent of the physician fee schedule amount. [Soc. Sec. § 1833(a)(1)(K); 42 C.F.R. § 414.54(b).]

Payment for CNM services is made directly to CNMs for their professional services and services furnished incident to their professional services. [Pub. 100-04, Ch. 12, § 130.1.]

Global surgical payments. When a PA, NP, or CNS furnishes services to a patient during a global surgical period, Medicare administrative contractors must determine the level of PA, NP, or CNS involvement in furnishing part of the surgeon's global surgical package. PA, NP, or CNS services furnished during a global surgical period are paid at 80 percent of the lesser of the actual charge or 85 percent of what a physician is paid under the physician fee schedule. [Pub. 100-04, Ch. 12, §§ 110.1, 120.]

When a CNM is providing most of the care to a Medicare beneficiary that is part of a global service and a physician also provides a portion of the care for this same global service, the fee paid to the CNM is based on the portion of the global fee that would have been paid to the physician for the service provided by the CNM. [Pub. 100-04, Ch. 12, § 130.2.]

Certified Registered Nurse Anesthetists

Anesthesia services furnished by a qualified nonphysician anesthetist (including both CRNAs and anesthesia assistants (AAs)) are paid at the lesser of the actual charge, the physician fee schedule, or the anesthesia fee schedule. [Soc. Sec. Act § 1833(a)(1)(H), (I); 42 C.F.R. § 414.60.]

Payment may be made to the qualified nonphysician anesthetist who furnished the anesthesia services or to a hospital, physician, group practice, or ambulatory surgical center with which the anesthetist has an employment or contractual relationship. [Soc. Sec. Act § 1842(b)(18); 42 C.F.R. § 414.60; Pub. 100-04, Ch. 12, § 140.2.]

Medicare does not pay for CRNA services when an anesthesiologist is personally involved in the case unless it is determined to be medically necessary for both to be involved. [42 C.F.R. § 414.46(c)(1)(iv).]

Teaching CRNAs. A teaching CRNA is reimbursed 100 percent of the physician fee schedule amount if the teaching CRNA, who is not under medical direction of a physician, is present with the student nurse anesthetist for the pre- and post-anesthesia services included in the anesthesia base units payment and is continuously present during anesthesia time in a single case with a student nurse anesthetist. If the teaching CRNA is involved with two concurrent anesthesia cases, he or she can be involved only with those two concurrent cases and may not perform services for other patients. [Medicare Improvements for Patients and Providers Act of 2008 (MIPPA) (P.L. 110-275) § 139(b); 42 C.F.R. § 414.61.]

Clinical Psychologists and Social Workers

Clinical psychologists are paid 80 percent of the lesser of: (1) the actual charge for the services; or (2) 100 percent of the amount determined for corresponding services under the physician fee schedule. [Soc. Sec. Act § 1833(a)(1)(L); 42 C.F.R. § 414.62.] Direct payment may be made to clinical psychologists under Part B for professional services, and they are required to accept assignment for all Medicare claims for their services. [Pub. 100-04, Ch. 1, § 30.3.1; Ch. 12, § § 170, 170.1.]

Clinical social workers. For therapeutic and other diagnostic services, clinical social workers are paid 80 percent of the lesser of: (1) the actual charge for the services; or (2) 75 percent of the amount determined for payment of a clinical psychologist. [Soc. Sec. Act § 1833(a)(1)(F).]

Physical Therapists, Occupational Therapists, and Speech-Language Pathologists

The Medicare physician fee schedule is the method of payment for outpatient physical therapy, occupational therapy, speech-language pathology services. [Soc. Sec. Act § 1834(k); Pub. 100-04, Ch. 5, § 10.] Outpatient therapists may bill Medicare directly for their services. [Soc. Sec. Act § § 1832(a)(2)(C), 1833(a)(8).]

Outpatient services furnished by a therapy assistant. Payment for outpatient physical therapy services or outpatient occupational therapy services furnished on or after January 1, 2022, by a therapy assistant (in whole or in part) will be 85 percent of the amount of payment otherwise applicable for the service. [Soc. Sec. Act § 1834(v), added by Bipartisan Budget Act of 2018 (P.L. 115-123) § 53107.]

Therapy caps. The Bipartisan Budget Act of 2018 repealed outpatient therapy payment caps effective January 1, 2018. [Soc. Sec. Act § 1833(g)(1)(A), (g)(3)(A), as amended by Bipartisan Budget Act of 2018 § 50202(1)(B) and 50202(2)(B).]

Targeted medical review. Claims for therapy services above certain threshold levels of incurred expenses will be subject to targeted medical review under Soc. Sec. Act § 1833(g)(5)(E). The Bipartisan Budget Act lowered the threshold for targeted medical review from $3,7000 to $3,000 through 2027; thereafter, the threshold is the preceding year's threshold increased by the percentage increase in the Medicare Economic Index (MEI) and rounded to the nearest multiple of $10. The threshold is applied separately to (1) physical therapy services and speech-language pathology services; and (2) occupational therapy services. [Soc. Sec. Act § 1833(g)(7)(B)(i)–(iii), as added by Bipartisan Budget Act of 2018 § 50202(4).]

KX modifier threshold. In addition, claims for therapy services above a certain amount of incurred expenses, which is the same amount as the previous therapy caps, must include the KX modifier indicating that such services are medically necessary as justified by appropriate medical record documentation. [Soc. Sec. Act § 1833(g)(1)(B), (g)(3)(B), as added by Bipartisan Budget Act of 2018 § 50202(1)(C) and (2)(C), and Soc. Sec. Act § 1833(g)(7)(A), as added by Bipartisan Budget Act of 2018 § 50202(4).]

[¶ 865] Actual Charge Restrictions

To protect beneficiaries from excessive charges by Medicare physicians and suppliers, the Medicare program has several rules that limit how much beneficiaries can be charged (actual charge restrictions). These rules apply only to physicians and suppliers who do not accept assignment, including "nonparticipating" physicians and suppliers (see ¶ 870 for an explanation of the Participation Program). Payments to physicians and suppliers who accept assignment are governed by separate rules (see ¶ 868). If these actual charge restrictions did not exist, a physician or supplier who does not accept assignment would be free to set any amount as the actual charge and could require the beneficiary to pay that amount. Medicare would, as usual, pay 80 percent of the amount it determines to be allowable, and the beneficiary would have to pay the difference between the Medicare payment amount and the physician's or supplier's actual charge.

The Limiting Charge

As discussed at ¶ 868, when assignment is accepted, a physician agrees to the Medicare-approved charge as the full charge and bills the patient only the 20 percent coinsurance amount not paid by Medicare. Physicians, suppliers, or other practitioners who do not accept assignment are subject to a "limiting charge" that places restrictions on how much they are allowed to charge a Medicare patient. [Soc. Sec. Act § 1848(g).]

The limiting charge is 115 percent of the fee schedule amount for "nonparticipating" physicians and suppliers, which is 95 percent of the physician fee schedule amount for each service. [Soc. Sec. Act §§ 1834(b)(5)(B), 1848(a)(3) and (g)(2)(C); 42 C.F.R. § 414.48.] A nonparticipating physician/supplier that does not take assignment must reduce charges to the beneficiary to reflect the Medicare limiting charge. A physician who charges a patient more than the limiting charge must refund the difference. [Soc. Sec. Act § 1848(g)(1)(A)(iv).]

In cases when a payment basis other than the physician fee schedule is used, the 115 percent limiting charge is applied to the recognized payment amount for nonparticipating providers, which is defined by the statute as 95 percent of the applicable payment basis. [Soc. Sec. Act § 1848(g)(2)(D); 42 C.F.R. § 414.48(b).]

The limiting charge applies to all of the following services and supplies, regardless of who provides or bills for them, if they are covered by the Medicare program:

- physicians' services;

- services and supplies furnished incident to a physician's services that are commonly furnished in a physician's office;

- outpatient physical or occupational therapy services furnished by an independently practicing therapist;

- diagnostic tests; and

- radiation therapy services (including x-ray, radium, and radioactive isotope therapy, and materials and services of technicians).

[*Medicare Claims Processing Manual*, Pub. 100-04, Ch. 1, § 30.3.12.3.]

Example • • • _____

Carla visits Dr. Kent for a series of medical tests and services for which Dr. Kent would charge private-pay patients $800. The physician fee schedule amount for those services is $510. Carla has paid the Part B deductible for the year.

(1) If Dr. Kent is a participating physician, Medicare will pay Dr. Kent $408 and Carla will pay the $102 coinsurance (that is, 20 percent of $510).

(2) If Dr. Kent is a nonparticipating physician, the Medicare-approved amount is 5 percent less than the fee schedule ($485), and the Medicare payment amount is $388 (80 percent of the reduced approved amount).

(a) If Dr. Kent accepts assignment and, thus, agrees to accept the reduced Medicare-approved amount as his full charge, Medicare will pay Dr. Kent $388 and Carla will pay the other $97.

(b) If Dr. Kent does not accept assignment and wants to charge Carla more than the reduced Medicare-approved amount, Dr. Kent may not charge Carla more than 15 percent over the reduced Medicare-approved amount (i.e., 15 percent over $485, or $557.75). The Medicare-approved payment amount ($388) is sent to Carla, and Carla is responsible for paying the other $169.75.

_____

Medicare secondary payments. The rules for calculating Medicare secondary benefits apply regardless of whether the limiting charge applies. However, when the limiting charge is less than the actual charge, the limiting charge will be considered to be the actual charge as well as the plan's allowable charge. [*Medicare Secondary Payer Manual*, Pub. 100-05, Ch. 5, § 40.7.4.]

Sanctions. If a physician knowingly and willfully bills above the limiting charge, the Secretary may apply sanctions, including: (1) barring the physician from participating in the Medicare program for up to five years; and (2) imposing a civil money penalty or assessment. [Soc. Sec. Act § 1842(j)(1)(A), (j)(2).] The Secretary may use any penalties so collected to reimburse the beneficiary for the overcharge. [Soc. Sec. Act § 1842(j)(4).]

Other Actual Charge Restrictions

While a number of limitations on actual charges became obsolete with the adoption of the physician fee schedule and the limiting charge, other actual charge restrictions affect how much health care providers may charge or bill Medicare beneficiaries.

Services not reasonable or necessary. When a physician furnishes otherwise-covered services on an unassigned basis to a Medicare beneficiary and Medicare determines that those services were not covered because they were not reasonable or necessary, the physician is required to refund to the beneficiary any payments collected for those services (including deductible and coinsurance amounts). A program payment, however, may be made to the physician if neither the physician nor the patient knew, or could reasonably have been expected to know, that Medicare would not pay for the items and services provided. [Soc. Sec. Act §§ 1834(a)(18)(A), 1842(l)(1)(A); 42 C.F.R. § 411.408(a).]

Elective surgery on an unassigned basis. When a physician performs an elective surgical procedure on an unassigned basis for a Medicare beneficiary and the charge for that procedure is at least $500, the physician must refund to the patient any payment collected above the Medicare allowed charge for the procedure unless the physician discloses to the beneficiary in advance (1) the physician's estimated charge; (2) the estimated Medicare payment; (3) the excess of the physician's actual charge over the estimated Medicare payment; and (4) the coinsurance amount applicable to the procedure. A physician who knowingly and willfully fails to make a required refund for an elective surgery procedure may be subject to civil money penalties or be suspended from program participation. The Secretary is required to monitor elective surgery claims to assure that required refunds are being made. [Soc. Sec. Act § 1842(m).]

[¶ 868] Assignment

An assignment is an agreement between a physician or supplier and a Medicare beneficiary. Under the terms of the assignment, the beneficiary transfers to the physician or supplier his right to Medicare benefits for the services received and the physician or supplier accepts the Medicare-approved charge as the full charge for the items or services provided. The physician or supplier submits a claim for payment for the services rendered to the Medicare administrative contractor (MAC). If the MAC approves the charges, Medicare pays the physician or supplier the Medicare-approved "fee schedule" amount (see ¶ 855) and the beneficiary is responsible for paying the coinsurance and any remaining deductible (see ¶ 335). [Soc. Sec. Act § 1842(b)(3)(B)(ii); 42 C.F.R. § 424.55; *Medicare Claims Processing Manual*, Pub. 100-04, Ch. 1, §§ 30.2 and 30.3.]

Some physicians and suppliers do not accept assignment and some beneficiaries may want Medicare to sent payment directly to them. In these situations, a Medicare payment is sent directly to the beneficiary after an itemized bill is submitted to the MAC on the appropriate form (Form CMS-1500). The beneficiary is responsible for paying the physician or supplier (see also ¶ 900). [42 C.F.R. §§ 424.50–424.56; Pub. 100-04, Ch. 1, § 30.3.]

Signature of patient. The signature of the patient on the billing form, or that of a person qualified to sign on his or her behalf, is necessary to assign payment of benefits to the physician or supplier. The signature should be obtained on the billing form, on the provider's records, or, in the case of a prolonged illness, on a special statement having the effect of a general consent to assignment. [Pub. 100-04, Ch. 1, § 50.1.3.]

Mandatory Assignment

Certain practitioners who provide services under the Medicare program are required to accept assignment for all Medicare claims for their services. This means that they must accept the Medicare allowed amount as payment in full for their practitioner services. The beneficiary's liability is limited to any applicable deductible plus the 20 percent coinsurance. Assignment is mandated for the following claims:

- clinical diagnostic laboratory services and physician lab services (see Soc. Sec. Act § 1833(h)(5)(C));

- physician services to individuals dually entitled to Medicare and Medicaid;

- services of physician assistants, nurse practitioners, clinical nurse specialists, nurse-midwives, certified registered nurse anesthetists, clinical psychologists, clinical social workers, registered dietitians/nutritionists, and anesthesiologist assistants (see 42 C.F.R. §§ 410.74(d)(2), 410.75(e)(2), 410.76(e)(2), 414.60(c); Pub. 100-04, Ch. 12, §§ 110–170);

- mass immunization roster billers (billing only for influenza and pneumococcal vaccinations and administrations, services not subject to the deductible or the 20 percent coinsurance);

- ambulatory surgical center services (no deductible and 25 percent coinsurance applies for colorectal cancer screening colonoscopies);

- home dialysis supplies and equipment paid under Method II for dates of service before January 1, 2011 (see Pub. 100-04, Ch. 1, § 30.3.8);

- drugs and biologics (see 42 C.F.R. § 414.707(b); Pub. 100-04, Ch. 17, § 50);

- ambulance services (see 42 C.F.R. § 414.610(b); Pub. 100-04, Ch. 15, § 10.4);

- competitive bidding items of durable medical equipment, prosthetics, orthotics, and supplies (42 C.F.R. § 414.408) and upgrades from a competitive bid item to a non-bid item; and

- telehealth services (see 42 C.F.R. § 414.65(d)).

[Pub. 100-04, Ch. 1, § 30.3.1; Ch. 36, § § 40, 40.11, 40.12.]

Accepting assignment is not mandatory for the services of physicians, independently practicing physical and occupational therapists, or for suppliers of radiology services or diagnostic tests. [Pub. 100-04, Ch. 1, § 30.3.1.]

Limitation on Physician/Supplier Charges to Beneficiaries

By submitting the claims form with the beneficiary's assignment authorization, the physician or supplier agrees to accept the Medicare-approved charge as the full charge for the items or services provided. A physician or supplier agrees not to charge the beneficiary for services for which Medicare pays 100 percent of the approved amount. In addition, the physician or supplier agrees to collect only: (1) the difference between the Medicare-approved amount and the Medicare Part B payment; (2) any applicable deductible; and (3) any applicable coinsurance amount for which Medicare does not pay 100 percent of the approved amount. [42 C.F.R. § 424.55(b); Pub. 100-04, Ch. 1, § 30.3.2.] If the physician or supplier is dissatisfied with the amount of the Medicare-approved charge, the remedy is to request a review and hearing with the MAC. The physician may not ask the beneficiary for more money. [Soc. Sec. Act § 1842(b)(3)(B)(ii).]

If a beneficiary has private insurance in addition to Medicare (e.g., a Medigap policy— see ¶ 740), the physician or supplier who has accepted assignment is in violation of the assignment agreement if that physician or supplier bills or collects from the beneficiary or the private insurer an amount that, when added to the Medicare benefit received, exceeds the approved charge. [Pub. 100-04, Ch. 1, § 30.3.2.]

Physicians and suppliers who do not accept assignment also are limited on the amount they may charge beneficiaries. This "limiting charge" is 115 percent of the Medicare-approved charge for nonparticipating physicians and suppliers (see ¶ 865).

A physician or supplier who accepts assignment for some services (that is, on a case-by-case basis) is not ordinarily precluded from billing the patient for other services; however, a physician or supplier may not accept assignment for some services and claim payment from the beneficiary for other services he or she performed for that same beneficiary at the same place on the same occasion. [Pub. 100-04, Ch. 1, § 30.3.2.]

Exception. When a physician is required to accept assignment for certain services as a condition for any payment or for Medicare payment to be made (for example, for clinical diagnostic laboratory services (see ¶ 875) and the services of physician assistants (see ¶ 860)), the physician may accept assignment for those services while billing on an unas-signed basis for other services the physician furnishes at the same place and on the same occasion. [Pub. 100-04, Ch. 1, § 30.3.2.]

Prohibition Against Reassignment

While a beneficiary may assign his or her right to Medicare payment for Medicare services received, providers, physicians, and suppliers generally may not reassign the right to receive payments assigned to them. [Soc. Sec. Act § § 1815(c), 1842(b)(6); 42 C.F.R. § § 424.73(a), 424.80(a); Pub. 100-04, Ch. 1, § 30.2.2.]

Any person who accepts an assignment of benefits under Medicare and "knowingly, willfully, and repeatedly" violates the assignment agreement is guilty of a misdemeanor and subject to a fine of not more than $4,000, imprisonment of up to six months, or both. Further, if the physician or supplier violates the prohibition against assignment or reassignment, CMS may terminate a provider agreement or revoke the party's right to receive assigned benefits. [Soc. Sec. Act § 1128A, as amended by Bipartisan Budget Act of 2018 (P.L. 115-123) § 50412; 42 C.F.R. §§ 424.74, 424.82; Pub. 100-04, Ch. 1, § 30.2.15.]

A power of attorney may not be used to circumvent the prohibition against reassignment. [Soc. Sec. Act § 1842(b)(6); 42 C.F.R. § 424.73(a).]

Exceptions. There are several exceptions to the reassignment prohibition. Medicare payment may be made to the employer of a physician or other practitioner providing services if the physician or practitioner is required as a condition of his or her employment to turn over the fee to his or her employer and, if the services are provided in a hospital, clinic, or other facility, payment may be made to the facility if there is a contractual arrangement between the physician or other person and the facility under which the facility submits the bill for the services. [Soc. Sec. Act § 1842(b)(6); 42 C.F.R. § 424.80(b)(1); Pub. 100-04, Ch. 1, § 30.2.7.]

In addition, payment may be made to an entity that provides coverage of the services under a complementary health benefits plan—a plan that provides coverage complementary to Medicare benefits and covers only the amount by which the Part B payment falls short of the approved charge for the service—under the circumstances described at 42 C.F.R. § 424.66. [Pub. 100-04, Ch. 1, § 30.2.8.3.]

Medicare payment may be made to a substituting physician when the patient's first physician arranges for substitution services by a second physician because the first physician is unavailable to provide the services and the services are not provided by the second physician over a continuous period longer than 60 days. [Soc. Sec. Act § 1842(b)(6)(D); Pub. 100-04, Ch. 1, § 30.2.11.]

For other exceptions to the prohibition against assignment and reassignment, see regulations beginning at 42 C.F.R. § 424.70 and Pub. 100-04, Ch. 1, § 30.2.1.

[¶ 870] Participation Program for Physicians and Suppliers

Under Medicare's "Participating Physicians and Suppliers Program," physicians and suppliers are encouraged to sign a participation agreement with the HHS Secretary binding them to accept assignment (see ¶ 868) for services provided to all Medicare patients for the following calendar year. [Soc. Sec. Act § 1842(h)(1).]

Participation agreements run on a calendar-year basis and are normally effective for one year. They are automatically renewed unless cancelled. Once the year has begun, physicians and suppliers will not be permitted to enter or drop out of the program until the end of the year. However, a newly licensed physician, a physician who begins a practice in a new area, or a new supplier who begins a new business may enter into a participation agreement for the remainder of the year. [Soc. Sec. Act § 1842(h)(1); *Medicare Claims Processing Manual*, Pub. 100-04, Ch. 1, § 30.3.12.]

Note: The "participation" program relates only to how physicians or suppliers are paid; it does not affect whether the services provided are covered. Thus, for coverage purposes, it makes no difference whether the physician or supplier providing the items or services is "participating" or "nonparticipating."

¶870

Incentives to Participate in Medicare

The "participation program" provides incentives to encourage physicians and suppliers to participate in Medicare. These include the following:

(1) the establishment and free distribution of participating physician and supplier directories (see discussion below) (Soc. Sec. Act § 1842(h)(4));

(2) toll-free telephone numbers through which beneficiaries may obtain the names, addresses, specialties, and telephone numbers of participating physicians and suppliers (Soc. Sec. Act § 1842(h)(2));

(3) electronic transmission of claims to Medicare contractors (Soc. Sec. Act § 1842(h)(3));

(4) higher payment rates (nonparticipating physicians are paid 95 percent of the payment rates applied to participating physicians) (Pub. 100-04, Ch. 1, § 30.3); and

(5) limitations on the actual charges that can be billed by nonparticipating physicians, including important refund and disclosure rules (Pub. 100-04, Ch. 1, § 30.3.12.3).

[Pub. 100-04, Ch. 1, § 30.3.12.1(I).]

Directory of Participating Physicians and Suppliers

At the beginning of each year CMS publishes local directories containing the names, addresses, specialties, and telephone numbers of all local "participating" physicians and suppliers. These directories, called "Medicare Participating Physicians/Suppliers Directories" (abbreviated MEDPARD), are made available at all Social Security and Medicare administrative contractor (MAC) offices and at some senior citizen organization centers. MACs are required to mail directories to beneficiaries at no charge upon request. [Soc. Sec. Act § 1842(h)(2), (4), (5)(A).]

Each time a Medicare Summary Notice is sent to beneficiaries with respect to claims made on an unassigned basis, the Secretary is required to remind them about the existence of the participation program, the charge limits applicable to nonparticipants, the local MAC's toll-free telephone number, and an offer to help the beneficiary locate a participating physician or supplier. [Soc. Sec. Act § 1842(h)(7).]

Hospitals and critical access hospitals are required to make available to patients the directory of participating physicians for the area. [Soc. Sec. Act § 1866(a)(1)(N).]

[¶ 872] Private Non-Medicare Contracts with Health Care Practitioners

CMS allows Medicare beneficiaries and their physicians (and certain nonphysician practitioners) to enter into private contracts for health care services outside the Medicare system. A physician or practitioner may opt out of Medicare for a two-year period by entering into a private contract with a Medicare beneficiary and submitting an affidavit. Services furnished under such private contracts are not covered services under Medicare, and no Medicare payment will be made for such services either directly or indirectly, except in limited cases. [Soc. Sec. Act §§ 1802(b)(1), 1862(a)(19); 42 C.F.R. §§ 405.405, 405.410.]

Physicians who may opt out of Medicare include dentists, podiatrists, and optometrists. Practitioners who may opt out include: (1) physician assistants, nurse practitioners, and clinical nurse specialists; (2) certified registered nurse anesthetists; (3) certified nurse-midwives; (4) clinical social workers; (5) clinical psychologists; and (6) registered dietitians or nutrition professionals. [Soc. Sec. Act § 1802(b)(6).]

Medicare's limiting charge (see ¶ 865) does not apply to private contract arrangements. [Soc. Sec. Act § 1802(b)(4).] Also, a physician or practitioner who opts out is not required to submit claims on behalf of beneficiaries. [*Medicare Benefit Policy Manual*, Pub. 100-02, Ch. 15, § 40.]

The HHS Secretary posts information concerning opt-out physicians and practitioners on the HHS website at https://data.cms.gov/Medicare-Enrollment/Opt-Out-Affidavits/7yuw-754z. [Soc. Sec. Act § 1802(b)(5).]

Requirements for Private Physician Contracts

For an opt out to be effective, the contract between the beneficiary and physician/practitioner must be in writing and signed by the beneficiary before any item or service is provided, and not at a time when the beneficiary is facing an emergency or urgent health care situation. It also must clearly state whether the physician or practitioner is excluded from Medicare under Soc. Sec. Act §§ 1128, 1156, or 1892. [Soc. Sec. Act § 1802(b)(2); 42 C.F.R. § 405.415.]

By signing the contract, the beneficiary:

(1) agrees not to submit a claim (or to request that the physician or practitioner submit a claim) for the items or services, even if they are otherwise covered by Medicare;

(2) agrees to be responsible, through insurance or otherwise, for payment and understands that no reimbursement will be provided;

(3) acknowledges that no limits under Title XVIII (including the limiting charge) apply to amounts that may be charged for such items or services;

(4) acknowledges that Medigap plans under Soc. Sec. Act § 1882 do not, and other supplemental insurance plans may elect not to, make payments for the items and services because payment is not made by Medicare; and

(5) acknowledges that the beneficiary has the right to have the items or services provided by other physicians or practitioners for whom payment would be made by Medicare.

[Soc. Sec. Act § 1802(b)(2)(B); 42 C.F.R. § 405.415.]

Opt-out period. Opt outs last two years and are automatically extended for additional two-year periods unless the physician or practitioner provides notice to the Secretary 30 days before the end of the previous two-year period that he or she does not want to extend the contract. [Soc. Sec. Act § 1802(b)(3); 42 C.F.R. §§ 405.400, 405.405(b), 405.410(c).]

Physician affidavit. For the private contract to be effective, the physician or practitioner must sign and file with the HHS Secretary an affidavit stating that for the opt-out period he or she will not submit any claims to Medicare nor receive any payment from Medicare for items or services provided to any Medicare beneficiary. [Soc. Sec. Act § 1802(b)(3); 42 C.F.R. § 405.420.]

Enforcement. A physician or practitioner who knowingly and willfully submits a claim to Medicare or receives any payment from Medicare during the affidavit's opt-out period will lose the rights provided under the private contract provision for the remainder of the period and will not be eligible to receive Medicare payments for the remainder of the period. [Soc. Sec. Act § 1802(b)(3)(C); 42 C.F.R. § 405.435(a).]

Medicare payment may be made for the claims submitted by a beneficiary for the services of an opt-out physician or practitioner when the physician or practitioner did not privately contract with the beneficiary for services that were not emergency care services or urgent care services and were furnished no later than 15 days after the date of a notice by the

Medicare administrative contractor that the physician or practitioner has opted out of Medicare. [42 C.F.R. § 405.435(c).]

Emergency or urgent care. A physician or practitioner who has opted out of Medicare does not need to enter into a private contract to furnish emergency care services or urgent care services to a Medicare beneficiary. Accordingly, a physician or practitioner will not have failed to maintain opt out if he or she furnishes emergency care services or urgent care services to a Medicare beneficiary with whom the physician or practitioner has not previously entered into a private contract. In such circumstances, the physician or practitioner must submit a claim and may collect no more than the Medicare limiting charge, in the case of a physician, or the deductible and coinsurance, in the case of a practitioner. [42 C.F.R. § 405.440; Pub. 100-02, Ch. 15, § 40.28.]

Terminating opt outs and appeals. A physician or practitioner may terminate an opt out by satisfying certain notification and refund requirements. Further, a physician or practitioner who is dissatisfied with a determination by CMS that a physician or practitioner has failed to properly opt out, failed to maintain opt out, failed to timely renew opt out, failed to privately contract, or failed to properly terminate opt out may utilize the enrollment appeals process currently available for providers and suppliers addressed in 42 C.F.R. Part 498. [42 C.F.R. §§ 405.445, 405.450(a).]

[¶ 875] Clinical Diagnostic Laboratory Tests

Under section 216 of the Protecting Access to Medicare Act of 2014 (PAMA) (P.L. 113-93), outpatient clinical diagnostic laboratory tests (CDLTs) furnished on and after January 1, 2018, are paid on a private payer rate-based fee schedule. [Soc. Sec. Act § 1834A.]

Other methods of payment. Certain outpatient laboratory services can be paid in other ways, including:

- under the physician fee schedule (see *Medicare Claims Processing Manual*, Pub. 100-04, Ch. 16, §§ 100, 100.2);

- at 101 percent of reasonable cost for critical access hospitals only;

- under the outpatient prospective payment system (OPPS) when packaged into the payment for related procedures (see 42 C.F.R. § 419.2(b)); or

- the reasonable charge payment method.

[Pub. 100-04, Ch. 16, § 10.2.]

Mandatory assignment. Payment for clinical diagnostic tests performed by clinical laboratories, excluding tests performed by rural health clinics (RHCs), may be made only on an assignment-related basis. If a person repeatedly bills beneficiaries for clinical diagnostic laboratory tests on other than an assignment-related basis, he or she will be subject to exclusion from the program and civil money penalties. [Soc. Sec. Act § 1833(h)(5)(C), (D).]

Deductibles. The usual Part B deductible does not apply to clinical diagnostic laboratory tests paid (1) under Soc. Sec. Act § 1833(a)(1)(D)(i) or (a)(2)(D)(i) on an assignment-related basis, or to a provider having an agreement under Soc. Sec. Act § 1866; or (2) for tests furnished before January 1, 2018, on the basis of a negotiated rate. [Soc. Sec. Act § 1833(b)(3).]

Independent laboratories. An independent laboratory may not bill the Medicare administrative contractor (MAC) for the technical component (TC) of physician pathology services furnished to a hospital inpatient or outpatient. [42 C.F.R. § 415.130(d).]

Payment for Laboratory Services

The payment amount under Soc. Sec. Act § 1834A is equal to the weighted median for the test for the period, as determined by the Secretary based on the information reported under Soc. Sec. Act § 1834A(a). Reductions from the implementation of the private payer rate will be phased in from 2018 through 2023. [Soc. Sec. Act § 1834A(b); 42 C.F.R. § 414.507.]

Advanced diagnostic laboratory tests. An "advanced diagnostic laboratory test" (ADLT) is defined as a clinical diagnostic laboratory test covered under Medicare Part B that is offered and furnished only by a single laboratory and not sold for use by a laboratory other than the single laboratory that designed the test or a successor owner of that laboratory, and meets one of the following criteria:

(1) The test (a) is an analysis of multiple biomarkers of deoxyribonucleic acid (DNA), ribonucleic acid (RNA), or proteins; (b) when combined with an empirically derived algorithm, yields a result that predicts the probability a specific individual patient will develop certain conditions or respond to particular therapies; (c) provides new clinical diagnostic information that cannot be obtained from any other test or combination of tests; and (d) may include other assays.

(2) The test is cleared or approved by the FDA.

[42 C.F.R. § 414.502.] For advanced diagnostic laboratory tests, the payment rate is based upon the test's actual list charge, up to 130 percent of the weighted medial private payer rate. [42 C.F.R. § 414.522.]

Reporting of payment rates. Beginning January 1, 2016, and every three years thereafter, each "applicable laboratory" is required to report to CMS, with respect to a laboratory test for the previous 12-month period, the following: (1) the payment rate that was paid by each private payer (health insurance issuers, group health plans, Medicare Advantage plans, and Medicaid managed care organizations) for the test during the period; and (2) the volume of such tests for each such payer for that period. To be defined as an "applicable laboratory," the labortatory must:

(1) be a laboratory, as defined in 42 C.F.R. § 493.2;

(2) bill Medicare Part B under its own National Provider Identifier (NPI) (for hospital outreach laboratories, bills Medicare Part B on the CMS-1450 under bill type 14x);

(3) in a data collection period, receive more than 50 percent of its Medicare revenues, which includes fee-for-service payments under Medicare Parts A and B, prescription drug payments under Medicare Part D, and any associated Medicare beneficiary deductible or coinsurance for services furnished during the data collection period from one or a combination of 42 C.F.R. part 414 subparts B or G; and

(4) receive at least $12,500 of its Medicare revenues from 42 C.F.R. part 414 subpart G; however, for a single laboratory that offers and furnishes an ADLT, this $12,500 threshold does not apply with respect to the ADLTs it offers and furnishes, and applies with respect to all the other clinical diagnostic laboratory tests (CDLTs) it furnishes.

[Soc. Sec. Act § 1834A(a); 42 C.F.R. §§ 414.502, 414.504.]

The applicable laboratory must then report this data to CMS between January 1 and March 31 of the following year, to be used in calculating the clinical laboratory fee schedule for three years beginning the subsequent year. [42 C.F.R. § 414.504.]

¶875

Who May Bill for Laboratory Tests

In most cases, only the person or entity that performed or supervised performance of a clinical diagnostic laboratory test can receive payment. Thus, a physician will not be paid for a test unless the physician (or another physician with whom the physician shares his or her practice) personally performed or supervised the performance of the test. Similarly, in most cases a laboratory that refers tests to another laboratory will cannot receive payment. There is an exception for hospitals when the tests are performed under arrangements made by the hospital and the referring laboratory meets certain conditions and does not have a financial relationship with the referring physician. [Soc. Sec. Act §§ 1833(h)(5)(A), 1887.]

Payment for clinical diagnostic laboratory tests normally can be made only if the physician ordering the tests is also the physician treating the patient. [42 C.F.R. § 410.32(a).]

When a laboratory bills for a test on the basis of a physician referral, the laboratory is required to include the name and national provider identifier of the referring physician and indicate whether the referring physician is an investor in the laboratory. [Soc. Sec. Act § 1833(q).]

Prohibition on referrals to related labs. Physicians (and their immediate relatives) are generally prohibited from referring laboratory tests to labs with which the physician has a financial relationship (see ¶ 720). [Soc. Sec. Act § 1877(a)–(g).]

Prohibition on Mark-Up of Clinical Laboratory Services

If a physician bills for a laboratory test performed by an outside laboratory and identifies both the laboratory and the amount the laboratory charged, payment for the test will be based on the lower of the following amounts:

(1) the outside laboratory's reasonable charge for the service; or

(2) the amount that the laboratory charged the physician for the service.

[42 C.F.R. § 405.515(b).]

If the bill or request for payment does not indicate that the test was personally performed or supervised either by the physician who submitted the bill or another physician with whom that physician shares his or her practice and if the outside laboratory and the amount the laboratory charged are not identified, payment will be based on the lowest charge at which the MAC estimates the test could have been secured from a laboratory serving the physician's locality. [42 C.F.R. § 405.515(c).]

[¶ 880] Ambulance Fee Schedule

Ambulance services, except for services furnished by certain critical access hospitals (CAHs), are reimbursed under a fee schedule payment system. Under the fee schedule, Medicare-covered ambulance services are paid based on the lower of the actual billed amount or the ambulance fee schedule amount. [Soc. Sec. Act § 1834(l); 42 C.F.R. §§ 414.601, 414.610(a).]

The fee schedule payment for ambulance services equals a base rate for the level of service plus a separate payment for mileage to the nearest appropriate facility and applicable adjustment factors. Oxygen and other items and services provided as part of the transport are included in the base payment rate and are not separately payable. [Soc. Sec. Act § 1834(l); 42 C.F.R. § 414.610(a); *Medicare Claims Processing Manual*, Pub. 100-04, Ch. 15, § 20.1.1.]

Ground ambulance service. To compute the fee schedule amount for ground ambulance services, the conversion factor (CF), an amount that serves as a nationally uniform base rate, is multiplied by the applicable relative value units (RVUs) for each level of service to produce a service-level base rate. The service-level base rate is then adjusted by the geographic adjustment factor (GAF) (equal to the practice expense (PE) portion of the geographic practice cost index (GPCI) for the physician fee schedule for each ambulance fee schedule locality area). The lesser of the actual charge or the GAF adjusted base rate amount is added to the lesser of the actual mileage charges or the payment rate per mile, multiplied by the number of miles that the beneficiary was transported. [42 C.F.R. § 414.610(c)(1), (c)(4).]

Air ambulance service. The base payment rate for the applicable type of air ambulance service is adjusted by the GAF and, when applicable, by the appropriate rural adjustment factor, to determine the amount of payment. Air ambulance services have no CF or RVUs. This amount is compared to the actual charge. The lesser of the charge or the adjusted GAF rate amount is added to the payment rate per mile, multiplied by the number of miles that the beneficiary was transported. [42 C.F.R. § 414.610(c)(2).]

Adjustments to Ambulance Fee Schedule Amounts

Soc. Sec. Act § 1834(l)(12)(A) provides for a "super rural bonus," a percent increase in the base rate of the fee schedule for transportation originating in a qualified rural area. The payment amount for the ground ambulance base rate is increased by 22.6 percent where the point of pickup is in a rural area determined to be in the lowest 25 percent of rural population arrayed by population density. Most recently, the Bipartisan Budget Act of 2018 (P.L. 115-123) extended the bonus through December 31, 2022. [Soc. Sec. Act § 1834(l)(12)(A), as amended by Bipartisan Budget Act of 2018 § 50203(a)(2); 42 C.F.R. § 414.610(c)(5)(ii).]

Soc. Sec. Act § 1834(l)(13)(A) also provides for temporary increases to ground ambulance services. For covered ground ambulance transports that originate in a rural area or in a rural census tract of a metropolitan statistical area (MSA), the fee schedule amount is increased by 3 percent, and for covered ground ambulance transports that originate in an urban area, the fee schedule amounts are increased by 2 percent. Most recently, the Bipartisan Budget Act of 2018 extended the bonus through December 31, 2022. [Soc. Sec. Act § 1834(l)(13)(A), as amended by Bipartisan Budget Act of 2018 § 50203(a)(1); 42 C.F.R. § 414.610(c)(1)(ii).]

Productivity adjustment. Section 3401(j) of the Patient Protection and Affordable Care Act (ACA) (P.L. 111-148) amended the annual update under Soc. Sec. Act § 1834(l)(3)(B) to add a productivity adjustment for ambulance services, effective for services in 2011 and later. The productivity adjustment is the same one applied to inpatient hospital services under Soc. Sec. Act § 1886(b)(3)(B)(xi)(II). The application of this productivity adjustment may result in the annual percentage increase being less than 0.0 for a year and may result in payment rates under the ambulance fee schedule for a year being less than such payment rates for the preceding year. [Soc. Sec. Act § 1834(l)(3)(C).]

ESRD beneficiaries. For services furnished on or after October 1, 2018, the ambulance fee schedule amount normally paid for non-emergency basic life support services to transport a beneficiary with end-stage renal disease (ESRD) for dialysis services is reduced by 23 percent if furnished by a provider or renal dialysis facility. [Soc. Sec. Act § 1834(l)(15), as amended by the Bipartisan Budget Agreement of 2018 § 53108; 42 C.F.R. § 414.610(c)(8).]

Transporting multiple patients. The allowable amount per beneficiary for a single ambulance transport when more than one patient is transported simultaneously is based on the total number of patients (both Medicare and non-Medicare) on board:

    (1) If two patients are transported at the same time in one ambulance to the same destination, the adjusted payment allowance for each Medicare beneficiary is 75

¶880

percent of the single-patient allowed amount applicable to the level of service furnished a beneficiary, plus 50 percent of the total mileage payment allowance for the entire trip.

(2) If three or more patients are transported at the same time in one ambulance to the same destination, the adjusted payment for each Medicare beneficiary is 60 percent of the single-patient allowed amount applicable to the level of service furnished that beneficiary. A single payment allowance for mileage, however, will be prorated by the number of patients on board.

[42 C.F.R. § 414.610(c)(6); *Medicare Benefit Policy Manual*, Pub. 100-02, Ch. 10, § 10.3.10.]

"Patient Transportation" Covered Under Part A

Ambulance services are separately reimbursable only under Part B. Once a beneficiary is admitted to a hospital, CAH, or skilled nursing facility (SNF), it may be necessary to transport the beneficiary to another hospital or other site temporarily for specialized care while the beneficiary maintains inpatient status with the original provider. This movement of the patient is considered "patient transportation" and is covered as an inpatient hospital or CAH service under Part A and as a SNF service when the SNF is furnishing it as a covered SNF service and Part A payment is made for that service. Because the service is covered and payable as a beneficiary transportation service under Part A, the service cannot be classified and paid for as an ambulance service under Part B. This includes intra-campus transfers between different departments of the same hospital, even when the departments are located in separate buildings. Such intra-campus transfers are not separately payable under the Part B ambulance benefit. [Pub. 100-04, Ch. 15, § 10.4.]

Reporting of Cost and Other Information

Pursuant to Bipartisan Budget Act of 2018 section 50203(b), CMS developed a data collection system to collect cost, revenue, utilization, and other information determined appropriate from providers of services and suppliers of ground ambulance services. In calendar years (CYs) 2020 through 2024, a representative sample will submit information under the system. [Soc. Sec. Act § 1834(l)(17)(A), (B); 42 C.F.R. §§ 414.601, 414.626; *Final rule*, 84 FR 62568, Nov. 15, 2019.]

Data submission. A ground ambulance service provider selected for data collection must do the following:

(1) within 30 days of the date that CMS notifies the provider, select a data collection period that corresponds with its annual accounting period and provide the start date of that data collection period to the ground ambulance organization's Medicare administrative contractor;

(2) collect during its selected data collection period the data necessary to complete the Medicare Ground Ambulance Data Collection Instrument; and

(3) submit to CMS a completed Medicare Ground Ambulance Data Collection Instrument during the data reporting period that corresponds to the ground ambulance organization's selected data collection period.

[Soc. Sec. Act § 1834(l)(17)(C); 42 C.F.R. § 414.626(b)(1); *Final rule*, 84 FR 62568, Nov. 15, 2019.]

Reductions for failure to report. If a ground ambulance organization selected by CMS for a year does not sufficiently submit data under and is not granted a hardship exemption, the payments made to the organization are reduced by 10 percent for the applicable period. The applicable period is the calendar year that begins following the date that CMS provided written notification to the ground ambulance organization under 42 C.F.R. § 414.626(e)(1) that it did not sufficiently submit the required data. [Soc. Sec. Act § 1834(l)(17)(D); 42 C.F.R. § 414.610(c)(9).]

[¶ 882] Durable Medical Equipment, Prosthetics, Orthotics, and Other Supplies

Medicare pays for durable medical equipment, prosthetics, orthotics, and other supplies (DMEPOS) based on regional fee schedules. Payment for those items equals 80 percent of the lower of the actual charge for the DME or the fee schedule amount. [Soc. Sec. Act § 1834(a)(1), (h)(1).]

Fee schedule classes. DMEPOS are categorized into the following classes, with a separate fee schedule for each class:

- inexpensive or routinely purchased items;
- items requiring frequent and substantial servicing;
- certain customized items;
- oxygen and oxygen equipment;
- prosthetic and orthotic devices;
- capped rental items; and
- transcutaneous electrical nerve stimulants (TENS) units.

[Soc. Sec. Act § 1834(a); 42 C.F.R. § 414.210(b).]

Blood-testing strips and glucose monitors. The payment amounts for diabetic testing supplies, including test strips, that are not mail-order items are the same as the single payment amounts established under the national mail order competition for diabetic supplies under Soc. Sec. Act § 1847, when such single payment amounts are implemented. [Soc. Sec. Act § 1834(a)(1)(H).]

Productivity adjustment. Pursuant to § 3401(m) of the Patient Protection and Affordable Care Act (ACA) (P.L. 111-148), the annual payment update for DME is reduced by the productivity adjustment applicable to hospital inpatient services. The application of this productivity adjustment may result in the annual percentage increase being less than 0.0 for a year and may result in payment rates for DME for a year being less than such payment rates for the preceding year. [Soc. Sec. Act § 1834(a)(14)(L) and (h)(4).]

Maintenance, Servicing, and Replacement of DME

Generally, Medicare pays the reasonable and necessary charges for maintenance and servicing of beneficiary-owned equipment. Reasonable and necessary charges are those made for parts and labor not otherwise covered under a manufacturer's or supplier's warranty. The contractor establishes a reasonable fee for labor associated with repairing, maintaining, and servicing the item. Payment is made for replacement parts in a lump sum based on the contractor's consideration of the item. [42 C.F.R. § 414.210(e)(1).]

Exceptions. No payments are made for maintenance and servicing of the following: (1) items requiring frequent and substantial servicing; (2) capped rental items that are not beneficiary owned; and (3) oxygen equipment. [42 C.F.R. § 414.210(e)(3).]

Replacement. If an item of DME or a prosthetic or orthotic device paid for under the DMEPOS fee schedule has been in continuous use by the patient for the equipment's reasonable useful lifetime (of at least five years) or if the contractor determines that the item is lost, stolen, or irreparably damaged, the beneficiary may elect to obtain a new piece of equipment. If the beneficiary elects to obtain replacement oxygen equipment, payment is made in accordance with 42 C.F.R. § 414.226(a). If the beneficiary elects to obtain a replacement capped rental item, payment is made in accordance with 42 C.F.R.

§ 414.229(a)(2) or (a)(3). For all other beneficiary-owned items, if the beneficiary elects to obtain replacement equipment, payment is made on a purchase basis. [42 C.F.R. § 414.210(f).]

Prior Authorization Process for Certain DME

Pursuant to section 1834(a)(15) of the Social Security Act, the Secretary developed a list of DMEPOS that are frequently subject to unnecessary utilization, as well as a prior authorization process for these items. [42 C.F.R. § 414.234.]

Inclusion criteria for the Master List of Items Potentially Subject to Face-To-Face Encounter and Written Order Prior to Delivery and/or Prior Authorization Requirements are as follows:

(1) any DMEPOS items included in the DMEPOS fee schedule:

(a) with an average purchase fee of $500 (or greater) adjusted annually for inflation using consumer price index for all urban consumers (CPI-U)) and reduced by the 10-year moving average of changes in annual economy-wide private nonfarm business multifactor productivity (MFP);

(b) with an average monthly rental fee schedule of $50 (or greater) adjusted annually for inflation using consumer price index for all urban consumers, and reduced by the 10-year moving average of changes in annual economy-wide private nonfarm business MFP; or

(c) identified as accounting for at least 1.5 percent of Medicare expenditures for all DMEPOS items over a 12-month period and that are identified as having a high rate of fraud or unnecessary utilization in an Office of Inspector General (OIG) or Government Accounability Office (GAO) report that is national in scope and published in 2015 or later; or listed in the 2018 or later Comprehensive Error Rate Testing (CERT) Medicare Fee-for-Service (FFS) Supplemental Improper Payment Data report as having a high improper payment rate;

(2) the annual Master List updates must include any items with at least 1,000 claims and $1 million in payments during a recent 12-month period that are determined to have aberrant billing patterns and lack explanatory contributing factors (e.g., new technology or coverage policies). Items with aberrant billing patterns would be identified as those items with payments during a 12-month time frame that exceed payments made during the preceding 12-months by the greater of:

(a) double the percent change of all DMEPOS claim payments for items that meet the above claim and payment criteria, from the preceding 12-month period; or

(b) exceeding a 30 percent increase in payment; or

(3) any item statutorily requiring a face-to-face encounter, a written order prior to delivery, or prior authorization.

The Master List is self-updating annually, and items remain on it for 10 years. [42 C.F.R. § 414.234(b)(1), (2); *Final rule,* 84 FR 60648, Nov. 8, 2019.]

In addition, DMEPOS items identified as having a high rate of fraud or unnecessary utilization in any of the following reports that are national in scope and meeting the payment threshold criteria set forth in 42 C.F.R. § 414.234(b)(1) are added to the Master List: (1) OIG reports published after 2020; (2) GAO reports published after 2020; or (3) listed in the CERT Medicare FFS Supplemental Improper Payment Data report published after 2020 as having a high improper payment rate. [42 C.F.R. § 414.234(b)(3); *Final rule,* 84 FR 60648, Nov. 8, 2019.]

CMS denies a claim for an item that requires prior authorization if the claim has not received a provisional affirmation. Claims receiving a provisional affirmation may be denied based on either of the following: (1) technical requirements that can only be evaluated after the claim has been submitted for formal processing; or (2) information not available at the time of a prior authorization request. [42 C.F.R. § 414.234(c)(2).]

DME Competitive Acquisition Program

The Secretary implemented a competitive bidding program that replaces the current DMEPOS fee schedule methodology for determining payment rates for certain DMEPOS items in competitive bidding areas. This fee schedule methodology continues to be used for payment of Medicare covered DMEPOS non-competitively bid items or services. [Soc. Sec. Act § 1847(a)(1)(A); *Medicare Claims Processing Manual*, Pub. 100-04, Ch. 36, § 10.]

The payment rates for DMEPOS competitively bid items are determined by using bids submitted by DMEPOS suppliers. The intent is to improve the methodology for setting DMEPOS payment amounts. These payments will reduce beneficiary out-of-pocket expenses and save the Medicare program money while ensuring beneficiary access to quality DME-POS items and services from qualified suppliers. [Soc. Sec. Act § 1847(a)(1)(A); Pub. 100-04, Ch. 36, § 10.]

For items and services furnished on or after January 1, 2019, the HHS Secretary must solicit and take into account stakeholder input in making certain adjustments and also take into account the highest amount bid by a winning supplier in a competitive acquisition area and a comparison of each of the following with respect to non-competitive acquisition areas and competitive acquisition areas: (1) the average travel distance and cost associated with furnishing items and services in the area; (2) the average volume of items and services furnished by suppliers in the area; and (3) the number of suppliers in the area. [Soc. Sec. Act § 1834(a)(1)(G), as amended by 21st Century Cures Act (P.L. 114-255) § 16008.]

Items Requiring Frequent and Substantial Servicing

Items requiring frequent and substantial servicing to avoid risk to the patient's health include the following:

- ventilators (except those that are either continuous airway pressure devices or respiratory assist devices with bi-level pressure capability with or without a backup rate);
- continuous and intermittent positive pressure breathing machines;
- continuous passive motion machines;
- other items specified in CMS program instructions; and
- other items identified by the Medicare administrative contractor (MAC).

[Soc. Sec. Act § 1834(a)(3)(A); 42 C.F.R. § 414.222(a); *Medicare Claims Processing Manual*, Pub. 100-04, Ch. 20, § 130.3.]

For this type of equipment, contractors pay the fee schedule amounts on a monthly rental basis until medical necessity ends. Medicare does not pay for purchase of this type of equipment. [Soc. Sec. Act § 1834(a)(3)(A); 42 C.F.R. § 414.22(c); Pub. 100-04, Ch. 20, § 30.2.]

The payment amount is based on the national limited payment amount (the cost of purchasing the equipment in a national market), as updated by changes in the Consumer Price Index. [Soc. Sec. Act § 1834(a)(3)(B), (C); 42 C.F.R. § 414.222(d).]

Multi-function ventilators. Effective January 1, 2019, the monthly rental fee schedule amount for a multi-function ventilator is equal to the monthly rental fee schedule amount for

¶882

the ventilator established in 42 C.F.R. § 414.22(c) and (d) plus the average of the lowest monthly cost for one additional function and the monthly cost of all additional functions, increased by the annual covered item updates of Soc. Sec. Act § 1834(a)(14). A multi-function ventilator is a ventilator as defined in 42 C.F.R. § 414.222(a)(1) that also performs medically necessary functions for the patient at the same time that would otherwise be performed by one or more different items classified under 42 C.F.R. §§ 414.220 (inexpensive or routinely purchased items), 414.226 (oxygen and oxygen equipment), or 414.229 (capped rental items). [42 C.F.R. § 414.222(f)(1), (2).]

Inexpensive or Routinely Purchased Items

Payment for inexpensive or routinely purchased items is made on a rental basis or in a lump-sum purchase amount that is based on the national limited payment amount (the cost of purchasing the DME in a national market), as updated by changes in the Consumer Price Index. If rental rather than lump-sum purchase is chosen, the total amount of rental payments may not exceed the allowed lump-sum purchase amount. [Soc. Sec. Act § 1834(a)(2)(B)(iv), (C); 42 C.F.R. § 414.220(b); Pub. 100-04, Ch. 20, § 30.1.]

DME is "inexpensive" if the average purchase price of it did not exceed $150 from July 1986 through June 1987. DME is routinely purchased if it was acquired by purchase on a national basis at least 75 percent of the time from July 1986 through June 1987. Included in the definition of inexpensive or routinely purchased equipment are accessories used in conjunction with a nebulizer, aspirator, or ventilator that is either a continuous airway pressure device or a respiratory assist device with bi-level pressure capability. [Soc. Sec. Act § 1834(a)(2)(A); 42 C.F.R. § 414.220(a); Pub. 100-04, Ch. 20, § 130.2.]

Payment for TENS units is made on a purchase basis with the purchase price determined using the methodology for purchase of inexpensive or routinely purchased items. However, the payment amount for TENS computed under 42 C.F.R. § 414.220(c)(2) is reduced. [Soc. Sec. Act § 1834(a)(1)(D); 42 C.F.R. § 414.232(a).]

Customized Items

Payment is made on a lump sum basis for the purchase of a customized item based on the DME MAC's individual consideration and judgment of a reasonable payment amount for each customized item, which takes into account written documentation on the costs of the item including at least the cost of labor and materials used in customizing an item. [Soc. Sec. Act § 1834(a)(4); 42 C.F.R. § 414.224(b).]

To be considered a customized item for payment purposes, a covered item (including a wheelchair) must be uniquely constructed or substantially modified for a specific beneficiary according to the description and orders of a physician and be so different from another item used for the same purpose that the two items cannot be grouped together for pricing purposes. [Soc. Sec. Act § 1834(a)(4); 42 C.F.R. § 414.224(a).] According to the *Medicare Claims Processing Manual*, customized items are rarely necessary and rarely furnished. [Pub. 100-04, Ch. 20, § 130.4.]

Oxygen and Oxygen Equipment

Payment for rental of oxygen equipment is made based on a monthly fee schedule amount during the period of medical need, but for no longer than a period of continuous use of 36 months. A period of continuous use is determined under the provisions in 42 C.F.R. § 414.230. Payment for purchase of oxygen contents is made based on a monthly fee schedule amount until medical necessity ends. [42 C.F.R. § 414.226(a).]

National limited monthly payment rates are calculated and paid as the monthly fee schedule amounts for the following classes of items:

(1) stationary oxygen equipment (including stationary concentrators) and oxygen contents (stationary and portable);

(2) portable gaseous equipment only;

(3) portable liquid equipment only;

(4) oxygen-generating portable equipment only;

(5) stationary oxygen contents only;

(6) portable oxygen contents only, except for portable liquid oxygen contents for prescribed flow rates greater than four liters per minute; and

(7) portable liquid oxygen contents only for prescribed flow rates of more than four liters per minute.

Effective January 1, 2019, CMS split the portable oxygen equipment only (gaseous and liquid tanks) class into two classes and added a separate payment class for portable liquid oxygen contents for prescribed flow rates of more than four liters per minute. [Soc. Sec. Act § 1834(a)(5); 42 C.F.R. § 414.226(e)(1).]

Payment for oxygen equipment after rental cap. A supplier that furnishes oxygen equipment after the 36-month rental cap must (1) continue to furnish the equipment during any period of medical need for the remainder of the reasonable useful lifetime of the equipment in accordance with 42 C.F.R. § 414.226(h)(1); or (2) arrange for furnishing the oxygen equipment with another supplier if the beneficiary relocates to an area outside the supplier's normal service area. [Soc. Sec. Act § 1834(a)(5)(F)(ii); 42 C.F.R. § 414.226(h)(1).]

A supplier that furnishes liquid or gaseous oxygen equipment (stationary or portable) for the 36th continuous month must (1) continue to furnish the oxygen contents necessary for the effective use of the liquid or gaseous equipment during any period of medical need for the remainder of the reasonable useful lifetime established for the equipment in accordance with 42 C.F.R. § 414.226(h)(1); or (2) arrange for furnishing the oxygen contents with another supplier if the beneficiary relocates to an area outside the supplier's normal service area. [Soc. Sec. Act § 1834(a)(5)(F)(ii); 42 C.F.R. § 414.226(h)(2).]

Capped Rental Items

For rented DME not subject to the payment provisions of 42 C.F.R. §§ 414.220 through 414.228, during the first three months of use, payment is limited to 10 percent of the "recognized purchase price"; thereafter, payment is limited to 7.5 percent of the recognized purchase price. [Soc. Sec. Act § 1834(a)(7)(A)(i)(II); 42 C.F.R. § 414.229(b)(2); Pub. 100-04, Ch. 20, § 30.5.1.]

For power-driven wheelchairs, payment equals 15 percent of the recognized purchase price for the first three months and 6 percent of the recognized purchase price for the remaining months. [Soc. Sec. Act § 1834(a)(7)(A)(i)(III); 42 C.F.R. § 414.229(b)(3).]

The purchase price is based on the national limited payment amount (the cost of purchasing the DME in a national market), as updated by changes in the Consumer Price Index. [Soc. Sec. Act § 1834(a)(8); 42 C.F.R. § 414.229(c)(3).]

Replacement. If the reasonable lifetime (five years) of an item has been reached during a continuous period of medical need, or the MAC determines that the item is lost or irreparably damaged, payment for replacement may be made on either a rental or a purchase basis. [Soc. Sec. Act § 1834(a)(7)(C); Pub. 100-04, Ch. 20, § 50.1.]

Complex rehabilitative power-driven wheelchairs. Suppliers must offer beneficiaries the option to purchase complex rehabilitative power-driven wheelchairs at the time the equipment is initially furnished. Medicare pays on a lump-sum purchase basis if the beneficiary chooses this option. [Soc. Sec. Act § 1834(a)(7)(A)(iii); 42 C.F.R. § 414.229(d)(1), (h).]

Ownership after rental. Medicare pays for most capped rental items during the period of medical need, but no longer than a period of continuous use of 13 months. On the first day after the 13th continuous month, the supplier must transfer title of the item to the beneficiary. [Soc. Sec. Act § 1834(a)(7)(A)(i)(I), (ii); 42 C.F.R. § 414.229(f).]

Prosthetic Devices and Prosthetics/Orthotics

Medicare pays for prosthetic devices (excluding parenteral and enteral nutrition, nutrients, supplies, and equipment) and prosthetics and orthotics (excluding intraocular lenses and medical supplies furnished by a home health agency) on a lump sum basis. [Soc. Sec. Act § 1834(h)(1)(A), (4); 42 C.F.R. § 414.228(a); Pub. 100-04, Ch. 20, § 30.4.] Ostomy supplies, tracheostomy supplies, and urologicals are reimbursed as inexpensive or other routinely purchased DME under Soc. Sec. Act § 1834(a)(2). [Soc. Sec. Act § 1834(h)(1)(E).]

The payment rules of Soc. Sec. Act § 1834(h) apply to reimbursement for therapeutic shoes for diabetics. [Soc. Sec. Act § 1833(o)(2); 42 C.F.R. § 414.228(c).]

Parenteral and Enteral Nutrition, Splints, Casts, and Certain Intraocular Lenses

For parenteral and enteral nutrition (PEN) items and services, splints and casts, and intraocular lenses (IOLs) inserted in a physician's office, Medicare pays for the items and services on the basis of 80 percent of the lesser of: (1) the actual charge for the item or service; or (2) the fee schedule amount for the item or service, as determined in accordance with 42 C.F.R. §§ 414.104 through 414.108. [Soc. Sec. Act § 1842(s)(2); 42 C.F.R. § 414.102(a).]

CMS or the MAC determines fee schedules for these items, and CMS designates the specific items and services in each category through program instructions. The fee schedule amounts of the preceding year are updated by the percentage increase in the CPI-U for the 12-month period ending with June of the preceding year. [Soc. Sec. Act § 1842(s)(1)(B)(ii); 42 C.F.R. § 414.102(b), (c).]

PEN. Payment is made in a lump sum for PEN nutrients and supplies that are purchased and on a monthly basis for equipment that is rented. The fee schedule amounts may be adjusted based on information on the payment determined as part of the DME competitive acquisition program using the methodologies described in 42 C.F.R. § 414.210(g). [Soc. Sec. Act § 1842(s)(3); 42 C.F.R. §§ 414.104(a), 414.105; Pub. 100-04, Ch. 20, § 30.7.]

Splints and casts. Medicare pays for splints and casts in a lump sum. The fee schedule amount for payment for an item or service furnished in 2014 was the reasonable charge amount for 2013, updated by the percentage increase in the CPI-U for the 12-month period ending with June of 2013. [42 C.F.R. § 414.106; Pub. 100-04, Ch. 20, § 170.]

Certain IOLs. Medicare pays for IOLs inserted in a physician's office in a lump sum. The fee schedule amount for payment for an IOL furnished in 2014 was the national average allowed charge for the IOL furnished in calendar year 2012, updated by the percentage increase in the CPI-U for the 24-month period ending with June of 2013. [42 C.F.R. § 414.108.]

[¶ 885] Payment for Drugs and Biologics

Payment for drugs (other than prescription drugs) furnished by physicians usually is based on the lower of the actual charge or the manufacturer's average sales price (ASP). This payment policy is applicable to drugs furnished to Medicare beneficiaries that are not "paid for on a cost or prospective payment basis." [Soc. Sec. Act § § 1842(o), 1847A; 42 C.F.R. § § 414.900, 414.904; *Medicare Claims Processing Manual*, Pub. 100-04, Ch. 17, § 20.1.]

Drugs furnished incident to a physician's services fall within this category. [42 C.F.R. § § 405.517(a)(3), 414.36.] Incident-to services and supplies are defined as services and supplies (including drugs and biologics that are not usually self-administered by the patient) furnished as an incident to a physician's professional service that commonly are furnished in physicians' offices and either rendered without charge or included in the physicians' bills. [Soc. Sec. Act § 1861(s)(2)(A).] See ¶ 855 for an explanation of Part B payment for incident-to items and services.

Assignment. All billing for drugs and biologics covered under Part B must be on an assignment-related basis. Sanctions may be imposed against violators. [Soc. Sec. Act § 1842(o)(3).]

Use of Average Sales Price Methodology

The payment allowance limit for Medicare Part B drugs and biologics that are not paid on a cost or prospective payment basis is 106 percent of the ASP. [42 C.F.R. § 414.904(a)(2).]

The payment allowance limits for end-stage renal disease (ESRD) drugs when separately billed by freestanding and hospital-based ESRD facilities, specified covered outpatient drugs, and drugs and biologics with pass-through status under the outpatient prospective payment system (OPPS) are paid based on 106 percent of the ASP. [42 C.F.R. § 414.904(d)(2); Pub. 100-04, Ch. 17, § 20.1.2.]

Except for infusion drugs, payment limits are updated quarterly. The payment amount is subject to coinsurance and deductibles. [Soc. Sec. Act § 1847A(b)(5); 42 C.F.R. § 414.904(f), (h).]

Price substitution. When the Inspector General finds that the ASP exceeds the widely available market price (WAMP) or the average manufacturer price (AMP) by an applicable threshold percentage, CMS must substitute the payment amount for the drug or biologic. [42 C.F.R. § 414.904(d)(3).]

Payment at 103 percent of the AMP for a billing code will occur when the following conditions are met:

(1) the ASP for the billing code has exceeded the AMP for the billing code by 5 percent or more in two consecutive quarters, or three of the previous four quarters immediately preceding the quarter to which the price substitution would be applied;

(2) the AMP for the billing code is calculated using the same set of National Drug Codes used for the ASP for the billing code;

(3) 103 percent of the AMP is less than the 106 percent of the ASP for the quarter in which the price substitution would be applied; and

(4) the drug and dosage form represented by the Healthcare Common Procedure Coding System (HCPCS) code are not reported by the Food and Drug Administration (FDA) on its Current Drug Shortage List to be in short supply at the time the ASP payment limits are finalized.

[42 C.F.R. § 414.904(d)(3).]

The applicable percentage threshold for AMP price comparisons is 5 percent. [42 C.F.R. § 414.904(d)(3)(iv).]

Exceptions to the ASP. The following exceptions to the ASP apply:

¶885

- The payment limits for hepatitis B vaccine furnished to individuals at high or intermediate risk of contracting hepatitis B, pneumococcal vaccine, and influenza vaccine are calculated using 95 percent of the average wholesale price (AWP).

- The payment limits for infusion drugs furnished before January 1, 2017, through a covered item of durable medical equipment (DME) were calculated using 95 percent of the AWP in effect on October 1, 2003.

- For blood and blood products (other than clotting factors), the payment limits are determined in the same manner as they were determined October 1, 2003.

- For an initial period in which data on the sale prices for drugs is not sufficiently available to compute the ASP, the payment limit for drugs and biologicals furnished before January 1, 2019, is based on the wholesale acquisition cost (WAC) or the Part B drug methodology in effect on November 1, 2003; for drugs and biologicals furnished on or after January 1, 2019, payment is at an amount not to exceed 103 percent of the WAC or based on the methodologies in effect on November 1, 2003.

Effective January 1, 2019, WAC-based payments for Part B drugs determined under Soc. Sec. Act § 1847A, during the first quarter of sales when ASP is unavailable, will be subject to a 3 percent add-on in place of the 6 percent add-on. [Soc. Sec. Act § 1847A(b)(4), (c)(4), as amended by Sustaining Excellence in Medicaid Act of 2019 (P.L. 116-39) § 6; 42 C.F.R. § 414.904(e); Pub. 100-04, Ch. 17, § 20.1.3.]

[¶ 890] Home Infusion Therapy

Pursuant to the 21st Century Cures Act (P.L. 114-255), CMS implemented a payment system under which a single payment is made to a qualified home infusion therapy supplier for items and services furnished by a qualified home infusion therapy supplier in coordination with the furnishing of home infusion drugs. [Soc. Sec. Act § 1834(u), as added by 21st Century Cures Act § 5012(b).] For home infusion therapy services furnished beginning January 1, 2021, payment is made on the basis of 80 percent of the lesser of the actual charge for the item or service or the fee schedule amount for the item or service. A single unit of payment is made for items and services furnished by a qualified supplier per payment category for each infusion administration calendar day. [Soc. Sec. Act § 1833(a)(1)(BB); 42 C.F.R. § 414.1550(a), (b); *Final rule*, 84 FR 60478, Nov. 8, 2019.]

Medical review. All payments for home infusion therapy services may be subject to a medical review adjustment reflecting beneficiary eligibility, plan of care requirements, and medical necessity determinations. [42 C.F.R. § 414.1550(e); *Final rule*, 84 FR 60478, Nov. 8, 2019.]

Initial Establishment of Home Infusion Payment Amounts

CMS determined the initial single payment amounts for calendar year 2021 using the equivalent to five hours of infusion services in a physician's office as determined by codes and units of such codes under the physician fee schedule. [42 C.F.R. § 414.1550(c); *Final rule*, 84 FR 60478, Nov. 8, 2019.]

Category 1. Category 1 includes certain intravenous infusion drugs for therapy, prophylaxis, or diagnosis, including antifungals and antivirals; inotropic and pulmonary hypertension drugs; pain management drugs; chelation drugs; and other intravenous drugs as added to the durable medicare equipment local coverage determination for external infusion pumps. Payment equals one unit of 96365 plus 4 units of 96366. [42 C.F.R. § 414.1550(c)(1); *Final rule*, 84 FR 60478, Nov. 8, 2019.]

Category 2. Category 2 includes certain subcutaneous infusion drugs for therapy or prophylaxis, including certain subcutaneous immunotherapy infusions. Payment equals one unit of 96369 plus four units of 96370. [42 C.F.R. § 414.1550(c)(2); *Final rule*, 84 FR 60478, Nov. 8, 2019.]

Category 3. Category 3 includes intravenous chemotherapy infusions, including certain chemotherapy drugs and biologicals. Payment equals one unit of 96413 plus four units of 96415. [42 C.F.R. § 414.1550(c)(3); *Final rule*, 84 FR 60478, Nov. 8, 2019.]

Initial visit. For each of these three categories, the payment amounts are set higher for the first visit by the supplier to initiate the furnishing of home infusion therapy services in the patient's home, and lower for subsequent visits in the patient's home. The difference in payment amounts is a percentage based on the relative payment for a new patient rate over an existing patient rate using the annual physician fee schedule evaluation and management payment amounts for a given year and calculated in a budget-neutral manner. The first visit payment amount is subject to the following requirements if a patient has previously received home infusion therapy services:

(1) The previous home infusion therapy services claim must include a patient status code to indicate a discharge.

(2) If a patient has a previous claim for home infusion therapy services, the first visit home infusion therapy services claim subsequent to the previous claim must show a gap of more than 60 days between the last home infusion therapy services claim and must indicate a discharge in the previous period before a supplier may submit a home infusion therapy services claim for the first visit payment amount.

[42 C.F.R. § 414.1550(c)(4); *Final rule*, 84 FR 60478, Nov. 8, 2019.]

Adjustments to Single Payment Amount

The single payment amount represents payment in full for all costs associated with the furnishing of home infusion therapy services and is subject to the following adjustments:

(1) an adjustment for a geographic wage index and other costs that may vary by region, using an appropriate wage index based on the site of service of the beneficiary;

(2) beginning in 2022, an annual increase in the single payment amounts from the prior year by the percentage increase in the Consumer Price Index (CPI) for all urban consumers (United States city average) for the 12-month period ending with June of the preceding year; and

(3) an annual reduction in the percentage increase by the productivity adjustment described in Soc. Sec. Act § 1886(b)(3)(B)(xi)(II), which may result in a percentage being less than zero for a year or payment being less than the payment rates for the preceding year.

[42 C.F.R. § 414.1550(d); *Final rule*, 84 FR 60478, Nov. 8, 2019.]

Temporary Transitional Payment

CMS implemented a temporary transitional payment system under which an eligible home infusion therapy supplier will be paid under the physician fee schedule in connection with the furnishing of transitional home infusion drugs provided in 2019 and 2020. CMS established three payment categories, assigned drugs and Healthcare Common Procedure Coding System (HCPCS) codes to each category, and established a single payment amount for each payment category for each infusion drug administration calendar day in the individual's home for drugs. Payment category 1 includes antifungals and antivirals, uninterrupted long-term infusions, and pain management, inotropic, and chelation drugs. Payment category 2 includes subcutaneous immunotherapy infusions. Payment category 3 includes certain chemotherapy drugs. Medicare administrative contractors will determine the pay-

¶890

ment category for subsequent transitional home infusion drug additions to the local coverage determinations (LCDs) and compounded infusion drugs not otherwise classified, as identified by HCPCS codes J7799 and J7999. [Soc. Sec. Act § 1834(u)(7)(B), (C), as added by Bipartisan Budget Act of 2018 (P.L. 115-123) § 50401(a).]

A reference to payment for an "infusion drug administration calendar day" means payment only for the date on which professional services were furnished to administer drugs to the individual beneficiary, and includes all infusion drugs administered to that individual on that day. The skilled services provided on that day must be so inherently complex that they can only be safely and effectively performed by, or under the supervision of, professional or technical personnel. An "eligible home infusion therapy supplier" is a supplier enrolled in Medicare as a pharmacy that provides external infusion pumps and external infusion pump supplies, and maintains all pharmacy licensure requirements in the state in which the applicable infusion drugs are administered. [Soc. Sec. Act § 1834(u)(7)(E), as added by Bipartisan Budget Act of 2018 § 50401(a); 42 C.F.R. § 486.505.]

[¶ 893] Opioid Use Disorder Treatment Services

CMS will pay an opioid treatment program a bundled payment, which will be updated annually, for opioid use disorder treatment services that are furnished to an individual during an episode of care beginning on or after January 1, 2020. CMS will establish the following categories of bundled payments for episodes of care: (1) categories for each type of opioid agonist and antagonist treatment medication; (2) a category for medication not otherwise specified, which will be used for new FDA-approved opioid agonist or antagonist treatment medications for which CMS has not established a category; and (3) a category for episodes of care in which no medication is provided. [Soc. Sec. Act § § 1833(a)(1)(CC) and 1834(w), as added by SUPPORT for Patients and Communities Act § 2005(c); 42 C.F.R. § 410.67(d)(1); *Final rule*, 84 FR 62568, Nov. 15, 2019.]

The bundled payment for episodes of care in which a medication is provided consists of payment for a drug component, reflecting payment for the applicable FDA-approved opioid agonist or antagonist medication in the patient's treatment plan, and a non-drug component, reflecting payment for all other opioid use disorder treatment services reflected in the patient's treatment plan (including dispensing/administration of the medication, if applicable). The payments for the drug component and non-drug component are added together to create the bundled payment amount. The bundled payment for episodes of care in which no medication is provided consists of a single payment amount for all opioid use disorder treatment services reflected in the patient's treatment plan (excluding medication and dispensing/administration of medication). [42 C.F.R. § 410.67(d)(2); *Final rule*, 84 FR 62568, Nov. 15, 2019.]

Payment adjustments. CMS will make adjustments to the bundled payments when an opioid treatment program furnishes:

- counseling or therapy services in excess of the amount specified in the beneficiary's treatment plan and for which medical necessity is documented in the medical record; an adjustment will be made for each additional 30 minutes of counseling or individual therapy furnished during the episode of care;

- intake activities;

- periodic assessments required under 42 C.F.R. § 8.12(f)(4); and

- when oral medications are dispensed, additional take-home supply of oral drugs of up to 21 days, in increments of 7 days.

The payment amounts for the nondrug component of the bundled payment for an episode of care, and the adjustments for counseling or therapy, intake activities and periodic assessments will be geographically adjusted using the geographic adjustment factor described in 42 C.F.R. § 414.26 and updated annually using the Medicare Economic Index described in 42 C.F.R. § 405.504(d). [42 C.F.R. § 410.67(d)(4); *Final rule*, 84 FR 62568, Nov. 15, 2019.]

Duplicative payments. CMS must ensure that no duplicative payments are made under Medicare Part B or Part D for items and services furnished by an opioid treatment program. Payment for medications delivered, administered, or dispensed to a beneficiary as part of the bundled payment is considered a duplicative payment if a claim for delivery, administration, or dispensing of the same medications for the same beneficiary on the same date of service was also separately paid under Medicare Part B or Part D. CMS will recoup the duplicative payment made to the opioid treatment program. [Soc. Sec. Act § 1834(w)(1); 42 C.F.R. § 410.67(d)(5); *Final rule*, 84 FR 62568, Nov. 15, 2019.]

Cost-sharing. No beneficiary copayment applies. [42 C.F.R. § 410.67(e); *Final rule*, 84 FR 62568, Nov. 15, 2019.]

Chapter 9– CLAIMS, PAYMENTS, AND APPEALS

[¶ 900] Claims and Payments

Medicare defines a claim as a filing from a provider, supplier, or beneficiary that includes or refers to a beneficiary's request for Medicare payment and furnishes the Medicare administrative contractor (MAC) with sufficient information to determine whether payment of Medicare benefits is due and the payment amount. [42 C.F.R. §§ 424.5(a)(5), (6).] A claim must contain sufficient identifying information about the beneficiary to allow any missing information to be obtained through routine methods, such as a file check, microfilm reference, mail, or telephone contact based on an address or telephone number in the file. [*Medicare Claims Processing Manual*, Pub. 100-04, Ch. 1, § 50.1.7.]

Payments under Part C Medicare Advantage (MA) plans and Part D prescription drug plans are not subject to the same requirements for submitting claims for payment and appeals that apply to services provided under Parts A and B. For a detailed discussion of payment and appeals under Part C and Part D, see Chapter 4 and Chapter 5, respectively.

Beneficiary Notices

Providers, physicians, and suppliers are required to notify beneficiaries when they believe that Medicare will not cover charges or when services may be terminated. An Advance Beneficiary Notice (ABN) is evidence of beneficiary knowledge about the likelihood of Medicare denial for the purpose of determining financial liability for expenses incurred for services furnished to a beneficiary. An ABN must: (1) be in writing, using approved notice language; (2) cite the particular service or services for which payment is likely to be denied; and (3) cite the notifier's reasons for believing Medicare payment will be denied. [42 C.F.R. § 411.408(f)(1).]

Beneficiaries may select one of several billing options they prefer when notified by the provider that it anticipates Medicare will not cover a service. If the beneficiary signs a request for payment using the ABN, the provider is required to submit a claim. The beneficiary becomes fully responsible for payments after being notified that Medicare may not pay the claim. [Pub. 100-04, Ch. 1, § 60.4.1; Ch. 30, § 50.]

Medicare summary notice. After the MAC processes and either approves or denies the claim, it sends the results to the beneficiary in the form of a Medicare summary notice (MSN). The MSN explains which charges were allowed, any deductible or coinsurance amount, and what Medicare paid on the claim and why. It also explains various features of the Medicare program of interest to the beneficiary. If the claim is denied in whole or in part, the MSN provides the procedures for an appeal (see ¶ 924). The beneficiary is responsible for any applicable deductible or coinsurance (for Part A, see ¶ 223). [Soc. Sec. Act § 1806(a); Pub. 100-04, Ch. 21, §§ 10, 10.1.]

Beneficiaries can elect to receive MSNs electronically. [Soc. Sec. Act § 1806(c).]

Submission of Claims

All initial claims for Medicare reimbursement, except claims from small providers, must be submitted electronically (with limited exceptions). Initial Medicare claims are those claims submitted to the appropriate MAC for payment under Part A or Part B for initial processing, including claims sent to Medicare for the first time for secondary payment purposes, resubmitted previously rejected claims, claims with paper attachments, demand bills, claims in situations in which Medicare is secondary and there is only one primary payer, and nonpayment claims. Initial claims do not include adjustments submitted to MACs on previously submitted claims or appeal requests. [Soc. Sec. Act § 1862(a)(22), (h); 42 C.F.R. § 424.32(d)(1)–(3); Pub. 100-04, Ch. 24, § 30.1.]

The Secretary may waive the electronic claims submission requirement in unusual cases as the Secretary finds appropriate. Unusual cases are deemed to exist in the following situations: (1) the submission of dental claims; (2) there is a service interruption in the mode of submitting the electronic claim that is outside the control of the entity submitting the claim, for the period of the interruption; (3) the entity submitting the claim submits fewer than 10 claims to Medicare per month, on average; (4) the entity submitting the claim furnishes services outside of the U.S. territory only; or (5) other extraordinary circumstances precluding submission of electronic claims. [42 C.F.R. § 424.32(d)(4); Pub. 100-04, Ch. 24, § 90.]

Every entity that submits electronic claims to the Medicare program is required to complete an Electronic Data Interchange (EDI) Enrollment Form. New electronic billers must sign and submit the enrollment form before their first billing will be accepted. A provider must obtain a National Provider Identifier (NPI) and furnish that NPI to its MAC before completion of an initial EDI Enrollment Agreement and issuance of an initial EDI number and password by the MAC. [Pub. 100-04, Ch. 24, § 30.1.]

Part A benefits. Hospitals, skilled nursing facilities (SNFs), home health agencies, hospices, and other providers submit claims for payment for items and services rendered under Part A to the MAC. As discussed at ¶ 730, providers charge beneficiaries for applicable deductible and coinsurance amounts as well as for any noncovered or extra services requested by the beneficiary. When a provider knows or believes that no Medicare payment will be made because of the lack of medical necessity or the service or item is excluded from coverage, the provider must notify the beneficiary in writing in the form of an ABN.

Part B benefits. Physicians, practitioners, durable medical equipment suppliers, and outpatient facilities (physician or supplier) that furnish items or services to beneficiaries covered under Part B are required to complete and submit a claim for payment to a MAC. Beneficiaries may not be charged for this service. [Soc. Sec. Act § 1848(g)(4)(A).] Payment will be made to the physician or supplier if the physician or supplier has accepted assignment (see ¶ 868), or to the beneficiary directly if the physician or supplier does not accept assignment. If payment is made to a physician or supplier that is entitled to receive payment on the beneficiary's behalf, the beneficiary is responsible for any applicable deductible or coinsurance requirements (see ¶ 330 and ¶ 335).

Claims forms. Form CMS-1490S, "Patient's Request for Medicare Payment Form," is used only by beneficiaries (or their representatives) who complete and file their own claims. It contains the first six comparable items of data that are on Form CMS-1500 (provider form). When Form CMS-1490S is used, an itemized bill must be submitted with the claim. Beneficiaries use Form CMS-1490S to submit Part B claims only if the service provider refuses to do so. [42 C.F.R. § 424.32(b); Pub. 100-04, Ch. 1, § 70.8.4.]

Under Part B, a claim can be any writing submitted by or on behalf of the beneficiary; however, when the writing constituting a Part B claim is not submitted on a claim form, there must be enough information about the nature of the medical or other health service to enable the MAC to determine that the service was furnished by a physician or supplier. [42 C.F.R. § 424.32(a); Pub. 100-04, Ch. 1, § 50.1.7.]

Physicians and suppliers (except ambulance suppliers) normally submit requests for payment on Form CMS-1500, the "Health Insurance Claim Form," whether or not the claim is assigned. The form is identical to forms used by other health insurance plans in addition to

¶900

Medicare. Form CMS-1500 contains a patient's signature line or reference to the patient signature incorporating the patient's request for payment of benefits, authorization to release information, and assignment of benefits. When the billing form is used as the request for payment, there must be a signature, except in limited circumstances. [42 C.F.R. § 424.32(b); Pub. 100-04, Ch. 1, § § 50.1.1, 70.8.4; Ch. 26, § 10.]

Request for Payment Signature Requirements

For an eligible provider of services to receive payment from Medicare for services furnished to a beneficiary under either Part A or Part B, a written request for payment must be signed by the individual who receives the services. [Soc. Sec. Act § § 1814(a)(1), 1835(a)(1); 42 C.F.R. § § 424.32(a)(3), 424.36.]

Signature of beneficiary's representative. If the beneficiary is physically or mentally unable to sign the claim, the following individuals may sign it: (1) the beneficiary's legal guardian; (2) a relative or other individual that receives Social Security or other governmental benefits on behalf of the beneficiary; (3) a relative or other person that arranges for the beneficiary's treatment or takes responsibility for the beneficiary's affairs; (4) a representative of an agency or institution that did not furnish the care in question but that did furnish other care for the beneficiary; (5) a representative of the provider or of the nonparticipating hospital providing the services in question if the provider is unable to have the claim signed in another way outlined above after making reasonable efforts; or (6) an ambulance provider or supplier that provided emergency or non-emergency transport services if certain conditions are met. [42 C.F.R. § 424.36(b).]

Beneficiary not present for the service. If a provider, nonparticipating hospital, or supplier files a claim for services that involved no personal contact between the provider, hospital, or supplier and the beneficiary (for example, a physician sent a blood sample to the provider for diagnostic tests), a representative of the provider, hospital, or supplier may sign the claim on the beneficiary's behalf. [42 C.F.R. § 424.36(c); Pub. 100-04, Ch. 1, § 50.1.3.]

Refusal to sign. A patient on admission to a hospital or SNF may refuse to request Medicare payment and agree to pay for the services out of his or her own funds or from other insurance. If the patient refuses to request Medicare payment, the provider should obtain a signed statement of refusal whenever possible. If the patient is unwilling to sign the statement of refusal, the provider should record that the patient refused to file a request for payment and was unwilling to sign the statement of refusal. [Pub. 100-04, Ch. 1, § 50.1.5.]

Death of beneficiary. If the patient dies before the request for payment is signed, it may be signed by the legal representative of the estate or by any of the persons or institutions (including an authorized official of the provider) who could have signed it had the patient been alive and incompetent. [Pub. 100-04, Ch. 1, § 50.1.3.]

Time Limits for Submitting Claims

Claims must be submitted no later than one calendar year after the date of service. [Soc. Sec. Act § § 1814(a)(1), 1835(a)(1); 42 C.F.R. § 424.44(a)(1).]

Exceptions to the one-year time limit. The following exceptions apply to the one calendar year time limit for filing fee-for-service claims: (1) administrative error; (2) retroactive Medicare entitlement; (3) retroactive Medicare entitlement involving state Medicaid agencies; and (4) retroactive disenrollment from an MA plan or Program of All-inclusive Care for the Elderly (PACE) provider organization. [42 C.F.R. § 424.44(b).]

When a provider or supplier makes the initial request for an exception to the timely filing limit, the MAC must determine whether a late claim may be honored based on all pertinent documentation submitted by the provider or supplier. [Pub. 100-04, Ch. 1, § 70.7.]

Prompt Payment of Claims

MACs are required to pay at least 95 percent of all "clean claims" within 30 days after the clean claims are received. A clean claim is a claim for which payment is not made on a periodic interim payment basis, and one that has no defect, impropriety, or particular circumstance requiring special treatment that prevents timely payment from being made. [Soc. Sec. Act § § 1816(c)(2)(A) and (B), 1842(c)(2)(A) and (B); Pub. 100-04, Ch. 1, § 80.2.]

If a clean claim payment is not issued, mailed, or otherwise transmitted within the specified time period, the government will be required to pay interest on the amount of payment it should have made, beginning with the day after the required payment date and ending on the date on which the payment is made. [Soc. Sec. Act § § 1816(c)(2)(C), 1842(c)(2)(C); Pub. 100-04, Ch. 1, § 80.2.2.]

MACs are prohibited from paying electronic claims within 13 days after their receipt. As an incentive to encourage health care providers to submit claims electronically, this prohibition on payment is expanded to 28 days for all other claims. [Soc. Sec. Act § § 1816(c)(3)(A) and (B), 1842(c)(3)(A) and (B).]

[¶ 902] Certification and Recertification of Medical Necessity

Medicare requires, as a condition of coverage, that the physician who ordered the services certify on the claim form that the services were medically necessary and, in some instances, recertify that the services continue to be required. [42 C.F.R. § § 424.10(a), 424.13.]

When a certification or recertification is required, it is the responsibility of the provider to obtain the physician's certifying statement. [42 C.F.R. § 424.5(a)(4).] In the case of services furnished by an institutional provider, the provider must maintain on file a written description that specifies the time schedule for certifications and recertifications and indicates whether utilization review of long-stay cases fulfills the requirement for second and subsequent recertifications. [42 C.F.R. § § 424.13(h), 424.14(e), 424.20(g).]

In certain situations, nonphysician practitioners such as nurse practitioners, clinical nurse specialists, or physician assistants may certify as to medical necessity. The content requirements and time factors related to certifications and recertifications vary according to the items or services furnished and the facility or institution furnishing them. [Soc. Sec. Act § 1814(a)(2).]

[¶ 904] Guarantee of Payment to Hospitals

Under the guarantee of payment provisions, if a hospital or critical access hospital (CAH) acted reasonably and in good faith and did not have knowledge that an individual was not entitled to Medicare benefits but instead assumed that entitlement existed, the hospital or CAH may be paid for: (1) inpatient hospital services furnished to a beneficiary whose eligibility for inpatient hospital benefit days has been exhausted; or (2) inpatient psychiatric hospital services after the 190-day psychiatric lifetime benefit has been exhausted. [Soc. Sec. Act § 1814(e); *Medicare Benefit Policy Manual*, Pub. 100-02, Ch. 5, § 10.1.]

The guarantee provisions are not applicable until the individual has exhausted his or her 60-day lifetime reserve days for inpatient hospital services, except in situations in which the beneficiary is deemed to have elected not to use lifetime reserve days. In these cases, the guarantee of payment generally applies because the reserve days cannot be used. [Soc. Sec. Act § 1814(e); Pub. 100-02, Ch. 5, § 10.1.]

Conditions for Guarantee of Payment

Payment may be made for inpatient hospital or inpatient CAH services furnished to a beneficiary after he or she has exhausted the available benefit days if the following conditions are met:

(1) The services were furnished before CMS or the Medicare contractor notified the hospital or CAH that the beneficiary had exhausted the available benefit days and was not entitled to have payment made for those services.

(2) At the time the hospital or CAH furnished the services, it was unaware that the beneficiary had exhausted the available benefit days and could reasonably have assumed that he or she was entitled to have payment made for these services.

(3) Payment would be precluded solely because the beneficiary has no benefit days available for the particular hospital or CAH stay.

(4) The hospital or CAH claims reimbursement for the services and refunds any payments made for those services by the beneficiary or by another person on his or her behalf.

[42 C.F.R. § 409.68.]

Limitation on Guarantee of Payment

Payment cannot be made if the hospital has received prior notification that all days of entitlement have been used and, in any event, payment cannot be made beyond the sixth day after the day of admission to the hospital (excluding Saturdays, Sundays, and legal holidays). [Soc. Sec. Act § 1814(e); 42 C.F.R. § 409.68(b).] Benefits paid to a hospital under the guarantee provision are subject to recovery from the beneficiary or third-party payers in the same way as other overpayments are subject to recovery. [Soc. Sec. Act § 1870; 42 C.F.R. § 409.68(c).]

The guarantee of payment provisions apply to inpatient services furnished to individuals who have exhausted their eligibility for inpatient hospital services, but they do not extend to individuals who have no coverage for other reasons. For example, hospitals are not guaranteed payment by Medicare when an individual is not entitled under hospital insurance or when entitlement has been terminated. [Pub. 100-02, Ch. 5, § 10.1.]

[¶ 905] Payments on Behalf of a Deceased Beneficiary

When a beneficiary dies after receiving covered Part B services, whom Medicare pays depends upon on whether the bill has been paid and, if the bill has been paid, who made the payment. [42 C.F.R. §§ 424.62, 424.64.]

Beneficiary dies and bill has been paid. If a beneficiary has received covered services for which he or she could receive direct payment under 42 C.F.R. § 424.53 but dies without receiving Medicare payment and the bill has been paid, Medicare pays the following people in the specified circumstances:

• The person or persons who, without a legal obligation to do so, paid for the services with their own funds, before or after the beneficiary's death.

• The legal representative of the beneficiary's estate if the services were paid for by the beneficiary before he or she died, or with funds from the estate.

• If the deceased beneficiary or his or her estate paid for the services and no legal representative of the estate has been appointed, the survivors, in order of priority.

• If none of the specified relatives survive, no payment is made.

- If the services were paid for by a person other than the deceased beneficiary, and that person died before payment was completed, Medicare does not pay that person's estate. Medicare pays a surviving relative of the deceased beneficiary in accordance with the priorities referenced above. If none of those relatives survive, Medicare pays the legal representative of the deceased beneficiary's estate. If there is no legal representative of the estate, no payment is made.

[Soc. Sec. Act § 1870(e); 42 C.F.R. § 424.62(b), (c).]

For a payment to be made to the person other than the beneficiary, the person who claims payment must: (1) submit a claim on a CMS-prescribed form and include an itemized bill; (2) provide evidence that the services were furnished if the Medicare contractor requests it; and (3) provide evidence of payment of the bill and the identity of the person who paid it. Evidence of payment includes: a receipted bill or a properly completed "Report of Services" section of a claim form showing who paid the bill; a cancelled check; a written statement from the provider or supplier or an authorized staff member; or other probative evidence. [42 C.F.R. § 424.62(e), (f).]

Request for payment signed on behalf of a deceased beneficiary. If a patient dies before he or she can sign the request for payment for Part A or Part B services, the request may be signed on his or her behalf by the legal representative of his or her estate or by a representative payee (a person designated by the Social Security Administration or other governmental agency to receive an incompetent beneficiary's monthly cash benefits), relative, friend, representative of an institution providing him or her care or support, or by a governmental agency providing assistance. Claims for Part B services may be filed by physicians and suppliers without a request for payment signed by the beneficiary when the beneficiary is deceased, the bill is unpaid, and the physician or supplier agrees to accept the Medicare-approved amount as the full charge. [42 C.F.R. § 424.62; *Medicare Claims Processing Manual*, Pub. 100-04, Ch. 1, §§ 50.1.3, 50.1.6.]

Beneficiary dies and bill has not been paid. If a beneficiary has received covered services from a Medicare physician or supplier, the beneficiary dies without making an assignment to the physician or supplier, and the bill has not been paid, Medicare pays the physician or supplier if it:

(1) files a claim on a CMS-prescribed form;

(2) upon request from the contractor, provides evidence that the services for which it claims payment were furnished; and

(3) agrees in writing to accept the reasonable charge as the full charge for the services.

[42 C.F.R. § 424.64(c)(1).]

If the physician or other supplier does not agree to accept the reasonable charge as full charge for the service, Medicare will pay any other person who submits all of the following to the Medicare contractor:

(1) a statement indicating that he or she has assumed legal obligation to pay for the services;

(2) a claim on a CMS-prescribed form;

(3) an itemized bill that identifies the claimant as the person to whom the physician or other supplier holds responsible for payment; and

(4) if the contractor requests it, evidence that the services were actually furnished.

¶905

[42 C.F.R. § 424.64(c)(2).]

[¶ 906] Overpayments and Underpayments

Overpayments are Medicare payments a provider or beneficiary has received in excess of amounts due and payable under the statute and regulations. Overpayments are defined as "any funds that a person receives or retains under Medicare or Medicaid to which the person, after applicable reconciliation, is not entitled under such title." [Soc. Sec. Act § 1128J(d)(4)(B).]

Once a determination of an overpayment has been made, the amount is a debt owed by the debtor to the United States government. Providers, suppliers, Medicare Advantage organizations, prescription drug sponsors, and Medicaid managed care organizations that receive an overpayment from Medicare or Medicaid must, by the later of 60 days after the date the overpayment was identified or the date any corresponding cost report is due: (1) report and return the overpayment to the Secretary of HHS, CMS, the state, or the Medicare administrative contractor (MAC), as appropriate; and (2) provide written notification of the reason for the overpayment. [Soc. Sec. Act § 1128J(d); *Medicare Financial Management Manual*, Pub. 100-06, Ch. 3, § 10.]

The requirement to report and return overpayments is enforced under the False Claims Act (FCA), which means that the retention of an overpayment beyond the 60-day period exposes a provider to civil money penalties plus treble damages and penalties, even if the provider voluntarily discloses and repays the overpayment after the 60-day period has elapsed. Exposure to the penalties under the FCA exists only if the provider "knew" of the overpayment for more than 60 days. Under the FCA, "knowingly" is defined to include reckless disregard and deliberate ignorance. [Soc. Sec. Act § 1128J(d)(3); 31 U.S.C. § 3729; 28 C.F.R. § 85.3.] In addition, the Office of Inspector General (OIG) may exclude individuals or entities that know of an overpayment and do not report and return it. [Soc. Sec. Act § 1128A(a)(10).]

Examples of individual overpayment cases include: (1) payment for provider, supplier, or physician services after benefits have been exhausted, or when the individual was not entitled to benefits; (2) incorrect application of the deductible or coinsurance; (3) payment for noncovered items and services, including medically unnecessary services or custodial care furnished to an individual; (4) payment based on a charge that exceeds the reasonable charge; (5) duplicate processing of charges or claims; (6) payment to a physician on a nonassigned claim or to a beneficiary on an assigned claim (payment made to wrong payee); (7) primary payment for items or services for which another entity is the primary payer; and (8) payment for items or services rendered during a period of nonentitlement. [Pub. 100-06, Ch. 3, § 10.2.]

Beneficiary Liability for Overpayments

The law provides that any Medicare payment made for a beneficiary's benefit will be considered a payment to the beneficiary, even if the payment is received by someone other than the beneficiary. Accordingly, if the MAC determines that the overpayment cannot be recouped from the provider, physician, or supplier or that the provider, physician, or supplier was without fault with respect to the overpayment, the beneficiary then becomes liable. A provider is deemed to be without fault if, in the absence of evidence to the contrary, the overpayment was made after the fifth year following the year in which notice of the payment was sent to the individual. [Soc. Sec. Act § 1870(a), (b); 42 C.F.R. § 405.350.]

If payment is made directly to the beneficiary, liability always lies with the beneficiary unless recovery is waived under the limitation of liability provision. [Pub. 100-06, Ch. 3, § 70.]

Recovery from beneficiary. In a recovery action, the Secretary will make the proper adjustment by: (1) decreasing any Social Security (or Railroad Retirement) benefits to which the individual is entitled; (2) requiring the individual or his or her estate to refund the amount in excess of the correct amount; (3) decreasing any Social Security payments to the estate of the individual or to any other person on the basis of the wages and self-employment income (or compensation) that were the basis of the payments to the individual; or (4) applying any combination of these adjustments. [Soc. Sec. Act § 1870(b); 42 C.F.R. § 405.352; Pub. 100-06, Ch. 3, § 110.]

If an individual who is overpaid dies before the overpayment has been recovered, the Secretary may initiate a recovery action, as necessary, against any other individual who is receiving cash Social Security benefits on the same earnings record as the deceased overpaid beneficiary. [Soc. Sec. Act § 1870(b).]

Waiver of beneficiary liability. The Secretary may not pursue recovery of the overpayment if: (1) the overpaid beneficiary is without fault (or the survivor of the deceased overpaid beneficiary who is liable for repayment of a Medicare overpayment is without fault); and (2) the recovery would be against equity and good conscience or defeat the purposes of titles II or XVIII the Social Security Act. Adjustment or recovery of an incorrect payment against an individual who is without fault is deemed to be against equity and good conscience if the Secretary determines that the payment was incorrect after the fifth year following the year in which notice of the payment was sent to such individual; the Secretary may, however, reduce such five-year period to not less than one year. [Soc. Sec. Act § 1870(c); 42 C.F.R. § § 405.355, 405.358; Pub. 100-06, Ch. 3, § § 70.3, 110.10.]

When collection of a beneficiary overpayment is from a provider (or physicians or other persons who have accepted assignments), after three years, the provider (or the physician or other person) is prohibited from charging the beneficiary for services found by the Secretary to be medically unnecessary or custodial in nature, in the absence of fault on the part of the individual who received the services. The Secretary is authorized to make the presumption before the three years have expired (but not before one year) if to do so would be consistent with the objectives of the Medicare program. [Soc. Sec. Act § § 1842(b)(3)(B)(ii), 1866(a)(1)(B).]

Interest Charges on Overpayments and Underpayments

When a final determination is made that a provider of services under Part A or a physician or supplier that accepted assignment under Part B has received an overpayment or underpayment from Medicare, and payment of the excess or deficit is not made within 30 days of the determination, interest charges will be applied to the balance due. The interest rate on overpayments is determined in accordance with regulations promulgated by the Secretary of the Treasury and is the higher of the private consumer rate or the current value of fund rates prevailing on the date of final determination. No interest is assessed for a period of less than 30 days; interest is calculated in full 30-day periods. Interest is assessed on the principal amount only and is calculated on a simple rather than a compound basis. [Soc. Sec. Act § § 1815(d), 1833(j); 42 C.F.R. § 405.378.]

Suspension, Offset, and Recoupment of Overpayments

Under the Federal Claims Collection Act of 1966, each agency of the federal government must attempt collection of claims for the federal government for money arising out of the activities of the agency in a timely and aggressive manner. The MAC will not be liable for overpayments it makes to debtors in the absence of fraud or gross negligence on its part; however, once the MAC determines an overpayment has been made, it must attempt recovery of overpayments in accordance with CMS regulations. [31 U.S.C. § § 3701–3720A;

¶906

Pub. 100-06, Ch. 3, § 10.] CMS may, under certain circumstances, suspend, offset, and recoup Medicare payments to providers and suppliers of services to recover overpayments. [42 C.F.R. § 405.371(a).]

Suspension of payments. CMS or a MAC may suspend, in whole or in part, Medicare payments to providers and suppliers: (1) if CMS or the MAC possesses reliable information that an overpayment exists or that the payments to be made may not be correct, although additional information may be needed for a determination; or (2) in cases of suspected fraud, if CMS or the MAC has consulted with the OIG and, as appropriate, the Department of Justice, and determined that a credible allegation of fraud exists against a provider or supplier, unless there is good cause not to suspend payments. [42 C.F.R. § 405.371(a)(1), (2).]

Once the determination has been made that a suspension of payments should be put into effect, notice ordinarily will be given to the provider or supplier along with a written statement of the reasons for the suspension. Notice to the provider or supplier is not necessary if: (1) the intended suspension involves fraud or misrepresentation; (2) CMS or the MAC determines that the Medicare Trust Fund would be harmed by giving prior notice; or (3) the intended suspension is the result of the provider's or supplier's failure to submit requested information necessary to determine amounts due the provider or supplier. [42 C.F.R. § 405.372(a).]

If prior notice is required, the MAC must give the provider or supplier 15 days to submit a statement of rebuttal. If, by the end of the period specified in the notice, the MAC has not received a rebuttal, the suspension will go into effect automatically. With certain exceptions, the period of suspension is limited to 180 days. [42 C.F.R. § § 405.372(b), (d), 405.374.]

Offset or recoupment. CMS or a MAC may offset or recoup Medicare payments, in whole or in part, if it determines that the provider or supplier to whom payments are to be made has been overpaid. An offset is the recovery by Medicare of a non-Medicare debt by reducing present or future Medicare payments and applying the amount withheld to the indebtedness. A recoupment, on the other hand, refers to the recovery by Medicare of outstanding Medicare debt by reducing present or future Medicare payments and applying the amount withheld to the indebtedness. [42 C.F.R. § § 405.370(a), 405.371(a)(3).]

When CMS or the MAC determines that an offset or recoupment should be put in place, the provider or supplier must receive notice and an opportunity for rebuttal. If no rebuttal statement is received within the time period specified in the notice, the recoupment or offset will go into effect immediately. A recoupment or offset remains in effect until the earliest of the following: (1) the overpayment and any assessed interest are liquidated; (2) the MAC obtains a satisfactory agreement from the provider or supplier for liquidation of the overpayment; or (3) the MAC, on the basis of subsequently acquired evidence or otherwise, determines that there is no overpayment. [42 C.F.R. § 405.373.]

Rebuttals. The rebuttal process occurs before the appeals process and permits the provider a vehicle to indicate why the recoupment or offset should not take place. If the provider or supplier submits a statement as to why a suspension, offset, or recoupment should not be put into effect, CMS or the MAC must, within 15 days from the date the statement is received, consider the statement and determine whether the facts justify the suspension, offset, or recoupment. CMS or the MAC must send written notice of the determination to the provider or supplier, including an explanatory statement of the determination and: (1) in the case of offset or recoupment, the rationale for the determination; or (2) in the case of suspension of payment, specific findings on the conditions upon which the suspension is initiated, continued, or removed. Suspension, offset, or recoupment is not delayed beyond the date stated in the notice to review the statement. Such a determination is not an initial determination and, therefore, is not appealable. [42 C.F.R. § 405.375.]

Requests for reconsideration and redetermination. When a provider or supplier seeks a redetermination by a MAC or reconsideration by a qualified independent contractor (QIC) on an overpayment determination, CMS may not recoup or demand a Medicare overpayment until the decision on the redetermination or reconsideration is rendered. When a valid request for a redetermination or reconsideration has been received from a provider, the MAC will cease recoupment or not begin recoupment at the normally scheduled time (41 days from the date of the initial overpayment demand for the redetermination and 76 days for the reconsideration). Interest paid to a provider or supplier whose overpayment is reversed at subsequent levels of appeal will accrue from the date of the original determination. [Soc. Sec. Act § 1893(f)(2); 42 C.F.R. § 405.379(a), (d); Pub. 100-06, Ch. 3, § § 200, 200.3.]

Once both the redetermination and reconsideration are completed and CMS prevails, collection activities, including demand letters and internal recoupment, may resume. [Pub. 100-06, Ch. 3, § 200.]

Extended repayment schedule. If the repayment of an overpayment within 30 days would constitute a hardship, a provider or supplier can enter into a plan with the Secretary to repay the overpayment over a period of six to 36 months (or, in the case of extreme hardship, no longer than five years). [Soc. Sec. Act § 1893(f)(1); 42 C.F.R. § § 401.607(c)(2), 405.379(h).]

[¶ 915] Limitation of Liability

Medicare law provides financial relief to beneficiaries, providers, practitioners, physicians, and suppliers by permitting Medicare payment to be made, or requiring refunds to be made, for certain services and items for which Medicare payment would otherwise be denied. This is referred to as "the limitation on liability provision." The purpose of this provision is to protect beneficiaries and other claimants from liability in denial cases under certain conditions when services they received are found to be excluded from coverage for one of the reasons specified below. [Soc. Sec. Act § 1879; *Medicare Claims Processing Manual*, Pub. 100-04, Ch. 30, § 20.]

Services for Which the Limitation on Liability Provisions Apply

The limitation on liability (LOL) of claims payment and beneficiary indemnification provisions are applicable only to claims for beneficiary items or services submitted by providers or suppliers, including physicians or other practitioners, or entities other than providers, that furnish health care services under Medicare and that have taken assignment. The LOL provisions are triggered by two factors: (1) the provider, practitioner, physician, supplier, or beneficiary must not have known or could not reasonably have been expected to know that items or services were not covered; and (2) the denied claims were for one of the following items or services:

> (1) services and items or additional preventive services that are found not to be reasonable and necessary for the diagnosis or treatment of illness or injury or to improve the functioning of a malformed body member under section 1861(a)(1)(A) of the Social Security Act;

> (2) pneumococcal vaccine and its administration, influenza vaccine and its administration, and hepatitis B vaccine and its administration, furnished to an individual who is at high or intermediate risk of contracting hepatitis B, which are not reasonable and necessary for the prevention of illness;

(3) in the case of hospice care, services and items that are not reasonable and necessary for the palliation or management of terminal illness;

(4) clinical care items and services provided with the concurrence of the Secretary and, with respect to research and experimentation conducted by, or under contract with, the Medicare Payment Advisory Commission or the Secretary, that are not reasonable and necessary;

(5) services and items that, in the case of research conducted pursuant to Soc. Sec. Act § 1142, are not reasonable and necessary to carry out the purposes of the governing law;

(6) screening mammography that is performed more frequently than is covered under Soc. Sec. Act § 1834(c)(2) or that is not conducted by a facility described in Soc. Sec. Act § 1834(c)(1)(B), and screening pap smears and screening pelvic exams performed more frequently than is provided for under Soc. Sec. Act § 1861(nn);

(7) screening for glaucoma that is performed more frequently than is provided for under Soc. Sec. Act § 1861(uu);

(8) prostate cancer screening tests that are performed more frequently than is covered under Soc. Sec. Act § 1861(oo);

(9) colorectal cancer screening tests that are performed more frequently than is covered under Soc. Sec. Act § 1834(d);

(10) the frequency and duration of home health services (see ¶ 250) that are in excess of normative guidelines established by the Secretary;

(11) a drug or biological specified in Soc. Sec. Act § 1847A(c)(6)(C) for which payment is made under Part B that is furnished in a competitive area that is not furnished by an entity under a contract under Soc. Sec. Act § 1847B;

(12) an initial preventive physical examination that is performed more than one year after the date the individual's first coverage period begins under Part B;

(13) cardiovascular screening blood tests that are performed more frequently than is covered under Soc. Sec. Act § 1861(xx)(1);

(14) a diabetes screening test that is performed more frequently than is covered under Soc. Sec. Act § 1861(yy)(1);

(15) ultrasound screening for abdominal aortic aneurysm that is performed more frequently than is provided for under Soc. Sec. Act § 1861(s)(2)(AA);

(16) kidney disease education services that are furnished in excess of the number of sessions covered under Soc. Sec. Act § 1861(ggg);

(17) personalized prevention plan services that are performed more frequently than is covered under Soc. Sec. Act § 1861(hhh)(1);

(18) custodial care as described in Soc. Sec. Act § 1862(a)(9) (see ¶ 625);

(19) inpatient hospital services or extended care services if payment is denied solely because of an unintentional, inadvertent, or erroneous action that resulted in the beneficiary's transfer from a certified bed in a skilled nursing facility (SNF) or hospital (Soc. Sec. Act § 1879(e));

(20) home health services determined to be noncovered because the beneficiary was not homebound or did not require intermittent skilled nursing care; and

(21) hospice care (see ¶ 270) determined to be noncovered because the beneficiary was not "terminally ill" (as required by Soc. Sec. Act § 1861(dd)(3)(A), as referenced by Soc. Sec. Act § 1879(g)(2)).

[Soc. Sec. Act §§ 1862(a)(1) and (a)(9), 1879; 42 C.F.R. § 411.400(a); Pub. 100-04, Ch. 30, § 20.]

Services not subject to the LOL provisions. Medicare payment under the LOL provision cannot be made when Medicare coverage is denied on any basis other than one of the provisions of the law specified above. There are certain claims that may appear to involve a question of medical necessity, as described in section 1862(a)(1) of the Social Security Act, but Medicare payment denial is based on a different statutory provision. Under these circumstances, Medicare payment under the LOL provision cannot be made because the denial is not based on one of the statutory provisions specified above. [Pub. 100-04, Ch. 30, § 20.2.]

Third-party payers. The waiver of liability provision applies to third-party payers. Accordingly, a provider, practitioner, or supplier that is determined liable may not seek payment from a third-party payer without being subject to recovery action that could occur if it sought payment from the beneficiary. [Pub. 100-04, Ch. 30, § 30.2.2.]

Determination of Liability

The Medicare administrative contractor (MAC) determines whether the provider, physician, or beneficiary is liable for the overpayment and whether to waive liability. [*Medicare Financial Management Manual*, Pub. 100-06, Ch. 3, § 70.] In addition, quality improvement organization (QIO) determinations (see ¶ 710) are conclusive for payment purposes as to whether the provider and the beneficiary knew or could reasonably be expected to have known that services were excluded because of the reasonableness, medical necessity, and appropriateness of placement at an acute level of patient care. [42 C.F.R. § 476.86(a)(4).]

There are three possible outcomes of a determination of liability.

(1) If the beneficiary had knowledge (or could have been expected to know) of the noncoverage of services for the reasons specified above, the ultimate liability will rest with the beneficiary.

(2) When neither the beneficiary nor the provider, practitioner, or supplier knew or reasonably could have been expected to know that services were not covered, the government will accept liability.

(3) When the beneficiary did not have such knowledge, but the provider, practitioner, or supplier knew or could have been expected to know of the exclusion of the items or services, the liability for the charges for the denied items or services rests with the provider, practitioner, or supplier.

[Pub. 100-04, Ch. 30, § 20.]

If the Medicare program accepts liability and makes payment, CMS will put the provider and beneficiary on notice that the service was noncovered and, in any subsequent cases involving similar situations and further stays or treatments (or similar types of cases in the instance of the provider), will consider that the provider and beneficiary had knowledge that payment would not be made. [Soc. Sec. Act § 1879(a).]

If the provider did not exercise due care, but there was good faith on the part of the beneficiary, liability will shift to the provider. The provider can appeal the MAC's decision as to coverage of the services and whether it exercised due care. If the provider received reimbursement from the beneficiary, the program will indemnify the beneficiary (although deductibles and coinsurance apply). Medicare treats the indemnification as an overpayment against the provider and recoups the amount of the payment through an offset against any amounts otherwise payable to the provider. [Soc. Sec. Act § 1879(b), (d); Pub. 100-04, Ch. 30, §§ 20, 30.1.1.]

¶915

Waiver of Beneficiary Liability

The waiver of liability provision provides that the beneficiary will not have to pay for noncovered services if the beneficiary did not know, and did not have reason to know, that the services were not covered. The MAC presumes that the beneficiary did not know that services are not covered unless the evidence indicates that written notice was given to the beneficiary by the QIO, the MAC, the utilization review committee responsible for the provider that furnished the services, or the provider, practitioner, or supplier that furnished the service. [Soc. Sec. Act § 1879(a); 42 C.F.R. §§ 411.404, 411.408(f); Pub. 100-04, Ch. 30, §§ 30.1, 30.1.1.]

If the MAC waives the beneficiary's liability for the services, liability shifts either to the government or to the provider—depending upon whether the provider utilized due care in applying Medicare policy in its dealings with the beneficiary and the government. [Soc. Sec. Act § 1879(a), (b), and (c); 42 C.F.R. § 411.402; Pub. 100-04, Ch. 30, § 30.2.1; Pub. 100-06, Ch. 3, §§ 70, 70.1.]

Waiver of Provider Liability

The issue of whether a practitioner or other supplier is liable for payment for services not covered by Medicare arises only when the beneficiary has been found not liable. A physician's or supplier's liability will not be waived for noncovered services unless the physician or supplier accepted assignment for the services (see ¶ 868). [42 C.F.R. § 411.400(a); Pub. 100-06, Ch. 3, §§ 70.3, 90.]

For the initial determination, the practitioner or other supplier is presumed to have had the requisite knowledge of likely Medicare denial of payment for denied services or items and will be liable unless the practitioner or supplier gave the beneficiary a proper Advance Beneficiary Notice (ABN) that Medicare will likely deny payment for the service or item to be furnished. A provider, practitioner, or supplier will not be held liable when the provider, practitioner, or supplier indicates on the claim that the beneficiary has been given an ABN before the items or services were furnished. In that case, the MAC will hold the beneficiary liable for the denied services or items at the initial determination because the notice constitutes proof that the beneficiary and the practitioner or supplier had prior knowledge that Medicare payment would be denied for the service or item in question. When the beneficiary and the practitioner or other supplier are found to have had the requisite knowledge of likely Medicare denial, the beneficiary is held liable. [42 C.F.R. § 411.406; Pub. 100-04, Ch. 30, § 30.2.1.]

A provider, practitioner, or supplier that furnished services that constitute custodial care or are not reasonable and necessary is considered to have known that the services were not covered if:

- the MAC had informed the provider, practitioner, or supplier that the services furnished were not covered, or that similar or reasonably comparable services were not covered;

- the utilization review committee for the provider or the beneficiary's attending physician had informed the provider that these services were not covered;

- before the services were furnished, the provider, practitioner, or supplier informed the beneficiary that the services were not covered or the beneficiary no longer needed covered services; or

- the provider, practitioner, or supplier could have been expected to have known that the services were excluded from coverage based on the receipt of CMS notices, including manual issuances, bulletins, or other written guides or directives from

Medicare contractors, including: (1) QIO screening criteria and preadmission review; (2) *Federal Register* publications containing notice of national coverage decisions or of other specifications regarding noncoverage of an item or service; and (3) knowledge of acceptable standards of practice by the local medical community.

[42 C.F.R. § 411.406.] A provider, practitioner, or supplier that is determined liable for all or a portion of the charges for noncovered items and services furnished to a beneficiary may appeal such a decision by the contractor. [Pub. 100-04, Ch. 30, § 30.2.2.]

[¶ 920] Medicare Entitlement and Enrollment Appeals

The Social Security Administration (SSA) makes an initial determination on an application for Medicare benefits and entitlement of an individual to receive Medicare benefits. Entitlement is about whether an individual has a right to Medicare benefits, not whether a particular item or service is covered or how much Medicare pays for it. Any individual dissatisfied with the SSA's initial determination as to whether he or she is *entitled to* or *enrolled in* Medicare may request reconsideration of the determination in the same manner provided for Social Security (or Railroad Retirement) benefit claims if the requirements for obtaining a reconsideration are met. [20 C.F.R. § 404.909; 42 C.F.R. 405.904(a).]

The SSA mails written notice of the government's determination that an individual is not eligible for Medicare to the individual at his or her last known address. An initial determination becomes final and binding on the parties unless reconsideration is requested or the determination is reopened and revised within the specified time limits. [20 C.F.R. § § 404.904, 404.905.]

The claimant (or his or her representative) may request a reconsideration of this determination by letter or on a special form available at any district Social Security office. The request for a reconsideration should be in writing and filed at a district office within 60 days from the date of receipt of the original adverse determination. [20 C.F.R. § 404.909.]

The SSA reviews the evidence considered in making the initial determination and any other evidence received and makes its determination on the preponderance of the evidence. The reconsideration is binding unless a request for a hearing is made within the stated time period and a decision is made, the expedited appeals process is used, or the determination is revised. The SSA mails a written notice of the reconsidered determination stating the specific reasons for the determination and the right to a hearing before an administrative law judge (ALJ). [20 C.F.R. § § 404.900(b), 404.913(a), 404.920, 404.921, 404.922.]

Following the reconsideration, the individual may request a hearing before an ALJ under the Medicare appeal rules. If the individual is dissatisfied with the ALJ decision, he or she may request that the Medicare Appeals Council review the case. If dissatisfied with the Medicare Appeals Council decision, the individual is entitled to file a suit in federal district court. [42 C.F.R. § 405.904(a).]

[¶ 924] Medicare Part A and B Claims Appeals

There are four levels of administrative appeals to challenge a coverage or payment decision under Part A or Part B. The first level of appeal is a redetermination made by the Medicare administrative contractor (MAC). The second administrative appeal is a "reconsideration," conducted by a qualified independent contractor (QIC). The third level of appeal is to an administrative law judge (ALJ), and the final administrative review is conducted by the Medicare Appeals Council. [Soc. Sec. Act § § 1869(b)–(d).]

For beneficiaries that have enrolled in Medicare Advantage plans, specific requirements have been established with respect to administrative determinations, reconsiderations, appeals, and judicial review. These requirements are outlined at ¶ 403. For beneficiaries enrolled in Part D, the voluntary prescription drug benefit, administrative determinations, appeals, grievances, and judicial review are discussed at ¶ 515–¶ 516.

Initial Determinations

When a medical service provider, supplier, or beneficiary submits a bill containing a request for payment for benefits, the MAC will make an initial determination approving, denying, or partially denying the claim. The MAC will notify the beneficiary of its initial determination with a Medicare summary notice (MSN) and the provider or supplier with an electronic or paper remittance advice (RA) describing the action taken. The MSN states in detail the basis for the determination, informs beneficiaries of the right to appeal the determination if they are dissatisfied, and provides instructions on how to obtain information on the specific provision of the policy, manual, or regulation used in making the determination or redetermination. [Soc. Sec. Act § 1869(a)(4); 42 C.F.R. § § 405.920, 405.921.]

An initial determination on claims made by or on behalf of a beneficiary includes, but is not limited to, determinations with respect to:

(1) coverage of furnished items and services;

(2) if the beneficiary, physician, or supplier who accepts assignment knew or could reasonably be expected to know that the items or services were not covered;

(3) whether the deductible is met;

(4) computation of the coinsurance amount;

(5) the number of inpatient hospital days used for inpatient hospital, psychiatric hospital, or post-hospital extended care;

(6) periods of hospice care used;

(7) requirements for certification and plan of treatment for physician services, durable medical equipment, therapies, inpatient hospitalization, skilled nursing care, home health, hospice, and partial hospitalization services;

(8) the beginning and ending of a spell of illness;

(9) the medical necessity of the services, or the reasonableness or appropriateness of placement of an individual at an acute level of patient care made by the quality improvement organization (QIO) on behalf of the MAC;

(10) any other issues affecting the amount of benefits payable, including underpayments;

(11) a determination with respect to the waiver of liability provision;

(12) if a particular claim is not payable to Medicare based on the application of Medicare Secondary Payer (MSP) provisions;

(13) under MSP provisions, that Medicare has a recovery claim against a provider, supplier, or beneficiary for services or items that were already paid by the Medicare program, except when the recovery claim is based on failure to file a proper claim;

(14) if a claim is not payable to a beneficiary for the services of a physician who has opted out; and

(15) under the MSP provisions, that Medicare has a recovery claim if Medicare is pursuing recovery directly from an applicable plan (defined as liability insurance, no-fault insurance, or a workers' compensation law or plan).

[42 C.F.R. § 405.924(b).]

An initial determination also includes a determination made by a QIO that: (1) a provider can terminate services provided to an individual when a physician certified that failure to continue the provision of those services is likely to place the individual's health at significant risk; or (2) a provider can discharge an individual from that provider. [42 C.F.R. § 405.924(c).] See ¶ 926 for a discussion of expedited appeals of provider service terminations to QIOs. See also ¶ 710 for a discussion of beneficiary complaints and appeals to QIOs regarding quality of care issues.

Parties to initial determinations. The parties to the initial determination are: (1) the beneficiary who files a claim for payment under Medicare Part A or Part B or has had a claim for payment filed on his or her behalf, or in the case of a deceased beneficiary, when there is no estate, any person obligated to make or entitled to receive payment, except that payment by a third-party payer does not entitle that entity to party status; (2) a supplier who has accepted assignment for items or services furnished to a beneficiary that are at issue in the claim; (3) a provider of services who files a claim for items or services furnished to a beneficiary; and (4) an applicable plan for an initial determination under 42 C.F.R. § 405.924(b)(16) where Medicare is pursuing recovery directly from the applicable plan. [42 C.F.R. § 405.906(a).]

Deadlines for making initial determinations. Initial determinations must be concluded no later than the 45-day period beginning on the day the claim is received. [Soc. Sec. Act § 1869(a)(2)(A).]

Parties to Redeterminations, Reconsiderations, ALJ Hearings, and Medicare Appeals Council Reviews

Parties to a redetermination, reconsideration, hearing, and Medicare Appeals Council review are: (1) the parties to the initial determination, except when a beneficiary has assigned appeal rights pursuant to 42 C.F.R. § 405.912; (2) a Medicaid state agency (see 42 C.F.R. § 405.908); (3) a provider or supplier that has accepted an assignment of appeal rights from the beneficiary pursuant to 42 C.F.R. § 405.912; (4) a nonparticipating physician not billing on an assigned basis who may be liable to refund monies collected for services furnished to the beneficiary because those services were denied due to their exclusion from coverage; and (5) a nonparticipating supplier not billing on an assigned basis who may be liable to refund monies collected for items furnished to the beneficiary. [42 C.F.R § 405.906(b).]

Except for an initial determination with respect to an applicable plan under 42 C.F.R § 405.924(b)(16), if a provider or supplier is not a party to an initial determination, it may appeal an initial determination related to services it rendered to a beneficiary who subsequently dies if there is no other party available to appeal the determination. [42 C.F.R § 405.906(c).]

Redeterminations

A person or entity that may be a party to a redetermination in accordance with 42 C.F.R. § 405.906(b) that is dissatisfied with an initial determination may request a redetermination by a MAC. [Soc. Sec. Act § 1869(a)(3); 42 C.F.R. § 405.940.]

A request for redetermination must be filed with the MAC indicated on the notice of the initial determination. The request for redetermination must be in writing and should be made on a standard CMS form. A written request that is not made on a standard form is accepted if it contains the required elements, i.e., the beneficiary's name, health insurance claim number, the specific services or items for which the redetermination is being requested and the dates the services or items were furnished, and the name and signature of the party or the party's representative. [42 C.F.R. § 405.944(a), (b).]

¶924

The request for redetermination must be filed within 120 calendar days after receipt of an initial determination (presumed to be five days after the date of the notice), unless the MAC grants the appellant an extension to the filing deadline. [Soc. Sec. Act § 1869(a)(3)(C)(i); 42 C.F.R. § 405.942(a), (b).]

The request for redetermination must include an explanation of why the party disagrees with the MAC's determination and should include any evidence that the MAC should consider in making the redetermination. If parties cannot submit relevant documentation along with their redetermination requests, then they can provide later submissions. When a party submits additional evidence after filing the request for redetermination, however, the MAC's 60 calendar-day decision-making time frame is automatically extended 14 calendar days for each submission. [42 C.F.R. § 405.946.]

MACs are required to process all redeterminations within 60 calendar days. The time frame may be extended when a MAC grants an extension of the 120-day deadline for filing a request for redetermination, multiple parties request a redetermination, or a party submits evidence after the request for redetermination is filed. [Soc. Sec. Act § 1869(a)(3)(C)(ii); 42 C.F.R. § 405.950.]

Written notice of the redetermination affirming, in whole or in part, the initial determination must be mailed to the parties. For decisions that are affirmations, in whole or in part, of the initial determination, the redetermination must be written in a manner calculated to be understood by a beneficiary and contain, among other explanations and information, a summary of the rationale of the redetermination, rules for submitting evidence and missing documentation, and the right to a reconsideration and the procedures to request a reconsideration. For decisions that are full reversals of the initial determination, the redetermination must be in writing, contain a clear statement indicating that the redetermination is wholly favorable, and include any other requirements specified by CMS. [Soc. Sec. Act § 1869(a)(5); 42 C.F.R. §§ 405.954, 405.956.]

The redetermination is binding on all parties unless a timely appeal is filed, the redetermination is revised, or the expedited appeals process is used. [42 C.F.R. § 405.958.]

When a contractor dismisses a request, it must send a written notice to the parties that states that the party has a right to request that the contractor vacate the dismissal. The contractor may vacate the dismissal within 180 calendar days of the date of the notice of dismissal upon a showing of good and sufficient cause. [42 C.F.R. § 405.952(c), (d); *Final rule*, 84 FR 19855, May 7, 2019.]

Reconsiderations

A person or entity that is a party to a redetermination made by a MAC and is dissatisfied with that determination may request a reconsideration, regardless of the amount in controversy. A reconsideration is an independent, on-the-record review of an initial determination, including the redetermination and all the issues related to payment of the claim, performed by a QIC. A QIC may reconsider an initial determination only after the MAC has performed a redetermination of the initial determination. [Soc. Sec. Act § 1869(c)(3)(B); 42 C.F.R. §§ 405.960, 405.968(a).]

A reconsideration is final and binding on all parties unless a timely appeal is filed and a higher appeal overturns the reconsideration decision or the reconsideration is reopened and revised by the QIC. [42 C.F.R. §§ 405.974(b)(3), 405.978.]

If the initial determination involves a finding as to whether an item or service is reasonable and necessary, the QIC's reconsideration must involve consideration by a panel of physicians or other appropriate health care professionals and be based on clinical

similar or related services. The amount-in-controversy threshold amount is $170 for ALJ hearing requests filed on or after January 1, 2020. [Soc. Sec. Act § 1869(b)(1)(E); 42 C.F.R. § 405.1006(b); *Notice*, 84 FR 50308, Oct. 7, 2019.]

Request for an ALJ hearing. If an appellant disagrees with how a statistical sample and/or extrapolation was conducted, in the hearing request the appellant must: (1) include the above information for each sample claim that the appellant wants to appeal; (2) file the request for hearing for all sampled claims that the appellant wishes to appeal within 60 calendar days of the date the party receives the last reconsideration for the sample claims; and (3) assert the reasons the appellant disagrees with how the statistical sample and/or extrapolation was conducted. [42 C.F.R. § 405.1014(a); *Final rule*, 84 FR 19855, May 7, 2019.]

If a request is not complete, the appellant will be provided with an opportunity to complete the request, and if an adjudication time frame applies, it does not begin until the request is complete. If the appellant fails to provide the information necessary to complete the request within the time frame provided, the appellant's request for hearing or review will be dismissed. If supporting materials submitted with a request clearly provide information required for a complete request, the materials will be considered in determining whether the request is complete. [42 C.F.R. § 405.1014(b).]

Evidence. Generally, parties must submit all written evidence they wish to have considered at the hearing with the request for hearing (or within 10 calendar days of receiving the notice of hearing). Any evidence submitted by a provider, supplier, or beneficiary represented by a provider or supplier that is not submitted before the issuance of the QIC's reconsideration determination must be accompanied by a statement explaining why the evidence was not previously submitted to the QIC or to a prior decision maker. However, these requirements do not apply to oral testimony given at a hearing or evidence submitted by an unrepresented beneficiary. [42 C.F.R. § 405.1018.]

The hearing. The ALJ hearing results in a new decision by an independent reviewer and a decision based on the hearing. The ALJ conducts the hearing in person, by video-teleconference, or by telephone. The ALJ will conduct a *de novo* review (i.e., an in-depth review conducted as if for the first time) and issue a decision based on the hearing record. If the beneficiary or his or her representative waives the right to appear at the hearing, the ALJ will make a decision based on the evidence that is in the file and any new evidence that may have been submitted for consideration. [42 C.F.R. § 405.1000(b), (d), (e).]

The issues before the ALJ include all the issues brought out in the initial determination, redetermination, or reconsideration that were not decided entirely in a party's favor. In addition, the ALJ may consider a new issue at the hearing if he or she notifies all of the parties about the new issue any time before the start of the hearing. The new issues may result from the participation of CMS at the ALJ level of adjudication and from any evidence and position papers submitted by CMS for the first time to the ALJ. The ALJ may consider a new issue only if its resolution could have a material impact on the claim or claims that are the subject of the request for hearing and is permissible under the rules governing reopening of determinations and decisions. [42 C.F.R. § 405.1032(a), (b).]

ALJs are bound by all NCDs whether based on Soc. Sec. Act § 1862(a)(1) or on other grounds, as well as the Medicare Act, applicable regulations, and CMS rulings. ALJs also must give substantial deference to nonbinding CMS and MAC policies such as local coverage determinations, manual instructions, and program memoranda, and if the ALJ declines to follow a policy in a particular case, his or her decision must explain the reasons. [42 C.F.R. §§ 405.1060(a)(4), (b), 405.1062.]

Time frame for ALJ's decision. The ALJ must issue a decision, dismissal order, or remand to the QIC within 90 calendar days of when the request for hearing is received by the entity specified in the QIC's notice of reconsideration. When an appellant escalates an appeal from the QIC level to the ALJ level, the proceedings before the ALJ are not subject to the 90-calendar-day limit. In these cases, ALJs must complete their action within 180 calendar days of receipt of the escalation request, unless the 180-calendar-day period has been extended. When CMS is a party to the hearing and a party requests discovery against another party, these adjudication periods are tolled. [42 C.F.R. § 405.1016.]

Dismissal. At any time before notice of the decision, dismissal, or remand is mailed, if only one party requested the hearing or review of the QIC dismissal and that party asks to withdraw the request, an ALJ or attorney adjudicator may dismiss the request for hearing or for review of a QIC dismissal. [42 C.F.R. § 405.1052(c).] There is a right to request that the ALJ or attorney adjudicator vacate the dismissal action. If good and sufficient cause is established, the ALJ or attorney adjudicator may vacate his or her dismissal of a request for hearing or review within 180 calendar days of the date of the notice of dismissal. The dismissal of a request for a hearing is binding, unless it is vacated by the ALJ or attorney adjudicator or the Medicare Appeals Council. The dismissal of a request for review of a QIC dismissal of a request for reconsideration is binding and not subject to further review unless it is vacated by the ALJ or attorney adjudicator. [42 C.F.R. §§ 405.1052(d), (e), 405.1054; *Final rule*, 84 FR 19855, May 7, 2019.]

Notice of ALJ's decision. The notice of the ALJ's decision must be in writing, in a manner that is understood by the beneficiary, and must include: (1) the specific reasons for the determination, including, to the extent appropriate, a summary of the clinical or scientific evidence used in making the determination; (2) the procedures for obtaining additional information concerning the decision; and (3) notification of the right to appeal the decision and instructions on how to initiate the appeal. [42 C.F.R. § 405.1046(b).]

Escalation. If the ALJ does not issue a decision within the deadline, the parties may escalate the case to the next level of appeal. A party may request Medicare Appeals Council review if: (1) the party files a written request with the ALJ to escalate the appeal to the Medicare Appeals Council after the adjudication period has expired; and (2) the ALJ does not issue a decision, dismissal order, or remand order within the later of five calendar days of receiving the request for escalation or five calendar days from the end of the applicable adjudication period. [42 C.F.R. § 405.1104.]

If the ALJ is not able to issue a decision, dismissal order, or remand order within the time period, he or she sends notice to the appellant acknowledging receipt of the request for escalation and confirming that the ALJ is not able to issue a decision, dismissal order, or remand order within the statutory time frame. If the ALJ does not act on a request for escalation within the time period or does not send the required notice to the appellant, the QIC decision becomes the decision that is subject to Medicare Appeals Council review. [42 C.F.R. §§ 405.1104, 405.1106(b).]

Escalation affects the next level's deadlines for making a decision. For example, although the decision-making deadline for the Medicare Appeals Council is generally 90 days, if a case is escalated from the ALJ to the Medicare Appeals Council, the Medicare Appeals Council has 180 calendar days from receipt of a request for escalation to complete its action. [42 C.F.R. § 405.1100(d).]

Medicare Appeals Council Review

A party to the ALJ hearing may request a Medicare Appeals Council review by filing a written request for review with the Medicare Appeals Council or appropriate ALJ office within 60 calendar days after receiving the ALJ's decision. The request should be made on a standard form but will be accepted if it contains the required elements. [42 C.F.R. §§ 405.1102(a), 405.1106(a), 405.1112(a).] Effective July 8, 2019, CMS removed the requirement that appellants sign appeal requests. [42 C.F.R. § 405.1112; *Final rule*, 84 FR 19855, May 7, 2019.]

In addition, any time within 60 calendar days after the date of an ALJ decision or dismissal, the Medicare Appeals Council may decide on its own motion to review the ALJ's action. CMS or any of its MACs also may refer a case to the Medicare Appeals Council for it to consider reviewing under this authority any time within 60 calendar days of an ALJ's decision or dismissal. [42 C.F.R. § 405.1110(a).] The date of receipt of the ALJ's or attorney adjudicator's decision or dismissal is presumed to be five calendar days after the date of the notice of the decision or dismissal, unless there is evidence to the contrary. [42 C.F.R. § 405.1110(e); *Final rule*, 84 FR 19855, May 7, 2019.]

The review. The Medicare Appeals Council conducts a *de novo* review of an ALJ decision and limits its review to the evidence contained in the record of the proceedings before the ALJ. If the hearing decision identifies a new issue that the parties were not afforded an opportunity to present at the ALJ level, the Medicare Appeals Council considers any evidence related to that issue that is submitted with the request for review. If the Medicare Appeals Council determines that additional evidence is necessary to resolve the issues in the case and the hearing record indicates that the previous decision makers have not attempted to obtain the evidence, it may remand the case to an ALJ to obtain the evidence and issue a new decision. [42 C.F.R. §§ 405.1108(a), 405.1122(a), 405.1126(a).] A party also may request to appear before the Medicare Appeals Council to present oral argument. [42 C.F.R. § 405.1124.]

If the Medicare Appeals Council is reviewing a case that was escalated from the ALJ level, it will decide the case based on the record constructed by the QIC and any additional evidence that was entered into the record by the ALJ before the case was escalated. The Medicare Appeals Council may remand the case to an ALJ to consider or obtain evidence and issue a new decision if it: (1) receives additional evidence with the request for escalation that is material to the question to be decided; or (2) determines that additional evidence is needed to resolve the issues in the case. [42 C.F.R. §§ 405.1122(b), 405.1126(a).]

Final action. Subject to the limitations on Medicare Appeals Council consideration of additional evidence, it issues a final action or remands a case to the ALJ for further proceedings within 90 calendar days of receipt of the appellant's request for review, unless the 90-day period is extended. [42 C.F.R. § 405.1100(c).] The Medicare Appeals Council may adopt, modify, or reverse the ALJ hearing decision or recommended decision. It mails a copy of its decision to all the parties. [42 C.F.R. § 405.1128.]

The Medicare Appeals Council's decision is final and binding on all parties unless a federal district court issues a decision modifying the decision or it is revised as the result of a reopening. [42 C.F.R. § 405.1130.]

Escalation. If the Medicare Appeals Council does not issue a decision or dismissal or remand the case to an ALJ within the applicable time frame, the appellant may request that the appeal, other than an appeal of an ALJ dismissal, be escalated to the federal district court. If the Medicare Appeals Council is unable to issue a decision or dismissal or remand within five calendar days of the receipt of the request or five calendar days of the end of the applicable adjudication period, it will send a notice to the appellant acknowledging receipt and confirming that it is not able to issue a decision, dismissal, or remand within the statutory time frame. A party may file an action in a federal district court within 60 calendar days after it receives the Medicare Appeals Council's notice. [42 C.F.R. § 405.1132.]

Judicial Review

A party dissatisfied with the Medicare Appeals Council review may request court review of the decision if the amount in controversy meets the threshold and all of the above administrative remedies have been exhausted. For 2019 the threshold amount is $1,630. [Soc. Sec. Act §§ 1155(b)(4), 1869(b)(1)(E); *Notice*, 83 FR 47619, Sept. 20, 2018.]

The party must file the complaint in the U.S. district court for the judicial district in which the party resides or where the individual, institution, or agency has its principal place of business, within 60 calendar days after the date it receives notice of the Medicare Appeals Council's decision or notice that the Council is not able to issue a final decision, dismissal order, or remand order. If the party does not reside within any judicial district, or if the individual, institution, or agency does not have its principal place of business within any such judicial district, the civil action must be filed in the District Court of the United States for the District of Columbia. [42 C.F.R. §§ 405.1130, 405.1132, 405.1134, 405.1136.]

Standard of review. In general, federal courts will liberally construe the Medicare Act to include rather than exclude coverage and any doubts are resolved in favor of coverage. The courts, however, are required to give deference to CMS's actions. The federal court may hold unlawful or set aside agency action, findings, and conclusions that are found to be: (1) arbitrary or capricious; (2) an abuse of discretion; (3) not in accordance with the law; or (4) not supported by substantial evidence. [Administrative Procedure Act, 5 U.S.C. § 706.] Judicial review of administrative determinations of Medicare cases is limited by the substantial evidence rule. The finding of the Secretary as to any fact, if supported by substantial evidence, is considered conclusive. [Soc. Sec. Act § 205(g); 42 C.F.R. § 405.1136(f).]

Assignment of Appeal Rights

Only a provider or supplier that is not a party to the initial determination and that furnished an item or service to the beneficiary may seek assignment of appeal rights from the beneficiary for that item or service. An individual or entity that is not a provider or supplier may not be an assignee. [42 C.F.R. § 405.912(a), (b).]

The assignee must waive the right to collect payment for the item or service for which the assignment of appeal rights is made. If the assignment is revoked, the waiver of the right to collect payment remains valid. In addition, a waiver of the right to collect payment remains in effect regardless of the outcome of the appeal decision. The assignee, however, is not prohibited from recovering payment associated with coinsurance or deductibles or when an Advance Beneficiary Notice (ABN) is properly executed. [42 C.F.R. § 405.912(d).]

When a valid assignment of appeal rights is executed, the assignor transfers all appeal rights involving the particular item or service to the assignee. These rights include, but are not limited to, obtaining information about the claim to the same extent as the assignor; submitting evidence; making statements about facts or law; and making any request, or giving or receiving any notice about, appeal proceedings. When an assignment of appeal rights is revoked, the rights to appeal revert to the assignor. [42 C.F.R. § 405.912(f)–(g).]

Appointment of Representatives

An appointed representative may act on behalf of an individual or entity in exercising his or her right to an initial determination or appeal. Appointed representatives do not have party status and may take action only on behalf of the individual or entity that they represent. [42 C.F.R. § 405.910(a).]

If the requestor is the beneficiary's legal guardian, no appointment is necessary, and the requestor is defined as the authorized representative. [*Medicare Claims Processing Manual*, Pub. 100-04, Ch. 29, § 270.1.1.]

¶924

A representative may be appointed at any point in the appeals process. To file an appeal, the representative must file a copy of the Appointment of Representative (AOR) form or other written instrument with the appeal request. [42 C.F.R. § 405.910(c); Pub. 100-04, Ch. 29, § 270.1.2.]

Duration of appointment. Unless revoked, an appointment is considered valid for one year from the date that the AOR form or other conforming written instrument contains the signatures of both the party and the appointed representative. If the initial determination involves an MSP recovery, an appointment signed in connection with the party's efforts to make a claim for third-party payment is valid for the duration of any later appeal. [42 C.F.R. § 405.910(e); Pub. 100-04, Ch. 29, § 270.1.5.]

Authority and responsibilities of appointed representative. An appointed representative has an affirmative duty to inform the party of the scope and responsibilities of the representation and of the status of the appeal and the results of actions taken, including notification of appeal determinations, decisions, and further appeal rights. The representative must also disclose to the beneficiary any financial risk and liability of a non-assigned claim that the beneficiary may have. An appointed representative may, on behalf of the party, obtain appeals information about the claim to the same extent as the party, submit evidence, make statements about facts and law, and make any request, or give or receive, any notice about the appeal proceedings. [42 C.F.R. § 405.910(g), (h).]

Fees. An appointed representative may charge a fee, if approved by the Secretary, for an appeal before the Secretary; however, no fees may be charged against the Medicare trust funds, and services rendered below the ALJ level are not considered proceedings before the Secretary. [42 C.F.R. § 405.910(f)(1)–(2).]

Representation by provider or supplier. A provider, physician, or supplier cannot represent a beneficiary if there is a conflict of interest under the waiver of liability provision (i.e., if there is a question as to who knew or had reason to know that the services would not be covered) (see ¶ 915). A provider, physician, or supplier cannot impose any financial liability on the beneficiary in connection with such a representation. [Soc. Sec. Act § 1869(b)(1)(B); 42 C.F.R. § 405.910(f)(3).]

An appeal request filed by a provider or supplier must include a signed statement that no financial liability is imposed on the beneficiary in connection with the representation. If applicable, the appeal request also must include a signed statement that the provider or supplier waives the right to payment from the beneficiary for services or items regarding issues related to items and services considered under the limitation on liability provisions. [42 C.F.R. § 405.910(g)(2).]

[¶ 926] Expedited Appeals of Provider Service Terminations

Expedited determination and reconsideration procedures are available to beneficiaries when a home health agency, skilled nursing facility, hospice, or comprehensive outpatient rehabilitation facility informs the beneficiary of a decision that Medicare coverage of their services is about to end. [42 C.F.R. § 405.1200(a)(1).]

Termination of Medicare-covered service is considered a discharge of a beneficiary from a residential provider of services or a complete cessation of coverage at the end of a course of treatment, regardless of whether the beneficiary agrees that the services should end. A termination does not include a reduction in services, nor does it include the termination of one type of service by the provider if the beneficiary continues to receive other Medicare-covered services from the provider. [42 C.F.R. § 405.1200(a)(2).]

The provider of the service must deliver valid written notice to the beneficiary of the decision to terminate covered services no later than two days before the proposed end of the services. The provider must use a standardized notice as specified by CMS and include the date the services are to terminate and the date financial liability is to begin, as well as a description of the beneficiary's right to an expedited determination. Quality improvement organizations (QIOs) conduct the expedited determination, and qualified independent contractors (QICs) conduct the expedited reconsideration. [42 C.F.R. §§ 405.1200(b), 405.1202, 405.1204.]

QIO's Expedited Redetermination

A beneficiary has a right to an expedited determination by a QIO for services furnished by a nonresidential provider if he or she disagrees with the provider that services should be terminated and a physician certifies that failure to continue the provision of the services may place the beneficiary's health at significant risk. For services furnished by a residential provider or a hospice, a beneficiary has a right to an expedited determination if he or she disagrees with the provider's decision to discharge him or her. Coverage of provider services continues until the date and time designated on the termination notice, unless the QIO reverses the provider's service termination decision. [42 C.F.R. § 405.1202(a), (c).]

A beneficiary must submit a request for an expedited determination to the QIO in the state in which he or she is receiving the services, in writing or by telephone no later than noon of the calendar day following receipt of the notice of termination. The beneficiary, or his or her representative, must be available to answer questions or supply information that the QIO may request to conduct its review. The beneficiary may, but is not required to, submit evidence to be considered by a QIO in making its decision. [42 C.F.R. § 405.1202(b).]

When a beneficiary requests an expedited determination by a QIO, the burden of proof rests with the provider to demonstrate that termination of coverage is the correct decision, based either on medical necessity or other Medicare coverage policies. [42 C.F.R. § 405.1202(d).]

Within 72 hours of receiving the request for an expedited determination, the QIO must notify the beneficiary, the beneficiary's physician, and the provider of services of its determination of whether termination of Medicare coverage is the correct decision. [42 C.F.R. § 405.1202(e)(6).]

QIC Expedited Reconsiderations

A beneficiary who is dissatisfied with a QIO's expedited determination may request an expedited reconsideration by a QIC. The request for reconsideration must be submitted to the appropriate QIC in writing or by telephone no later than noon of the calendar day following initial notification of receipt of the QIO's determination. When a beneficiary requests an expedited reconsideration in accordance with the required deadline, the provider may not bill the beneficiary for any disputed services until the QIC makes its determination. [42 C.F.R. § 405.1204(a), (b), (f).]

On the day the QIC receives the request for reconsideration, it must notify the QIO that made the expedited determination and the provider of services of the request. When a QIC notifies a QIO that a beneficiary has requested an expedited reconsideration, the QIO must supply all information that the QIC needs to make its expedited reconsideration as soon as possible, but no later than by close of business of the day that the QIC notifies the QIO of the request for an expedited reconsideration. At a beneficiary's request, the QIO must furnish the beneficiary with a copy of, or access to, any documentation that it sends to the QIC. A provider may, but is not required to, submit evidence to be considered by a QIC in making its decision. If a provider fails to comply with a QIC's request for additional information beyond that furnished to the QIO for purposes of the expedited determination, the QIC makes its reconsideration decision based on the information available. [42 C.F.R. § 405.1204(c)–(e).]

QICs must provide their reconsideration decisions no later than 72 hours after receiving the appeal request and related medical records. The decisions must be provided by telephone and in writing to the provider of services, the beneficiary requesting the appeal, and the attending physician of the beneficiary. [42 C.F.R. § 405.1204(c).]

See ¶ 710 for a discussion of QIO coverage determinations and reconsideration determinations related to: (1) reasonableness, medical necessity, and appropriateness of the services furnished or proposed to be furnished; (2) appropriateness of the setting in which the services were, or are proposed to be, furnished; (3) financial liability for the services; and (4) diagnosis-related group (DRG) validation reviews.

Hospital Inpatient Expedited Determinations

A beneficiary has a right to request an expedited determination by the QIO when a hospital, acting directly or through its utilization review committee, with physician concurrence, determines that inpatient care is no longer necessary. [42 C.F.R. § 405.1206(a).] If the hospital acting directly or through its utilization review committee believes that the beneficiary does not require further inpatient hospital care but is unable to obtain the agreement of the physician, it may request an expedited determination by the QIO. [42 C.F.R. § 405.1208(a).]

A beneficiary who wishes to exercise his or her right to an expedited determination must submit a request no later than the day of discharge. The request must be made in writing or by telephone to the QIO that has an agreement with the hospital. Upon request by the QIO, the beneficiary, or his or her representative, must be available to discuss the case and may, but is not required to, submit written evidence to be considered by a QIO in making its decision. [42 C.F.R. § § 405.1206(b)(1)–(3).]

When the QIO issues an expedited determination, it must notify the beneficiary, physician, and hospital of its decision by telephone, followed by a written notice that includes: (1) the basis and rationale for the determination; (2) an explanation of the Medicare payment consequences of the determination, including the date the beneficiary becomes fully liable for the services; and (3) information about the beneficiary's right to a reconsideration of the QIO's determination, including how to request a reconsideration and the time period for doing so. [42 C.F.R. § § 405.1206(d)(8), 405.1208(d).] When the hospital requests a determination, the QIO must make a determination and notify the beneficiary, hospital, and physician within two working days of the hospital's request and receipt of any pertinent information submitted by the hospital. [42 C.F.R. § 405.1208(c)(4).]

The QIO determination is binding upon the beneficiary, physician, and hospital, except: (1) if the beneficiary is still an inpatient in the hospital and is dissatisfied with the determination, he or she may request a QIC reconsideration (see discussion above); or (2) if the beneficiary is no longer an inpatient in the hospital and is dissatisfied with this determination, the determination is subject to the general claims appeal process (see ¶ 924). [42 C.F.R. § § 405.1206(g), 405.1208(e).]

[¶ 928] NCD and LCD Appeals

The term "national coverage determination" (NCD) means a determination by the HHS Secretary with respect to whether a particular item or service is covered under the Medicare program. However, an NCD does not include a determination of what code, if any, is assigned to a particular item or service covered or a determination with respect to the amount of payment made for a particular item or service so covered. The term "local coverage determination" (LCD) means a determination by a contractor under Part A or Part B concerning whether a particular item or service is covered on a Medicare administrative contractor-wide basis in accordance with Social Security Act section 1862(a)(1)(A), which sets the reasonable and necessary standard for covered services. [Soc. Sec. Act § 1869(f)(1)(B), (f)(2)(B).]

Avenues of appeals. The right to challenge NCDs and LCDs is distinct from the rights that beneficiaries have for appealing Medicare claims (see ¶ 924). [42 C.F.R. § 426.310(a).]

There are two avenues of appeals for LCDs and NCDs: reconsideration and review. The main differences between an LCD/NCD review and a reconsideration are the avenue an individual chooses to take to initiate a change to a coverage policy and who may initiate the review. The reconsideration process allows any individual, not just an aggrieved party, to submit new evidence for reconsideration of an LCD or NCD. The review process permits only an "aggrieved party" to file a complaint to initiate the review of an LCD or NCD. The Secretary established specific procedures for filing a written complaint for a review of an LCD and separate procedures for filing a written complaint for a review of an NCD (see 42 C.F.R. §§ 426.400 *et seq.*; 426.500 *et seq.*).

Mediation for disputes related to LCDs. CMS established a mediation process to mediate disputes between groups representing providers of services, suppliers, and the medical director for a Medicare administrative contractor whenever the regional administrator involved determines that there is a systematic pattern and a large volume of complaints from such groups regarding decisions of the director or there is a complaint from the co-chair of the advisory committee of that contractor to the regional administrator regarding the dispute. [Soc. Sec. Act § 1869(i).]

LCD/NCD Reviews

Under CMS's appeals process for NCDs and LCDs, beneficiaries who qualify as aggrieved parties can challenge NCDs and LCDs by filing a complaint. An aggrieved party is defined as a Medicare beneficiary who is entitled to benefits under Part A, enrolled under Part B, or both (including an individual enrolled in fee-for-service Medicare, a Medicare Advantage plan, or another Medicare managed care plan), and is in need of coverage for a service that is the subject of an applicable LCD (in the relevant jurisdiction) or NCD, as documented by the beneficiary's treating physician. The HHS Departmental Appeals Board (DAB) conducts NCD reviews and administrative law judges (ALJs) review LCDs. [Soc. Sec. Act § 1869(f)(1), (2), (5); 42 C.F.R. §§ 426.110, 426.300, 426.320.]

Only LCDs or NCDs (including deemed NCDs) that are currently effective may be challenged. The following items are not reviewable:

(1) pre-decisional materials, including draft LCDs, template LCDs or suggested LCDs, and draft NCDs, including NCD memoranda;

(2) retired LCDs or withdrawn NCDs;

(3) LCD or NCD provisions that are no longer in effect due to revisions or reconsiderations;

(4) interpretive policies that are not an LCD or NCD;

(5) contractor decisions that are not based on Soc. Sec. Act § 1862(a)(1)(A);

(6) contractor claims processing edits;

(7) payment amounts or methodologies;

(8) procedure coding issues, including determinations, methodologies, definitions, or provisions;

(9) contractor bulletin articles, educational materials, or website frequently asked questions;

(10) any Medicare Advantage organization or managed care plan policy, rule, or procedure;

(11) an individual claim determination; or

(12) any other policy that is not an LCD or an NCD as set forth in 42 C.F.R. § 400.202.

[42 C.F.R. § 426.325.]

LCD review. An aggrieved party may initiate a review of an LCD by filing a timely written complaint that meets the requirements and includes all the necessary elements with the office designated by CMS on the Medicare website. [42 C.F.R. § 426.400.]

After a complete review of a coverage challenge, the applicable adjudicator is required to issue a description of the appeal rights or provide notice that the decision is pending. An ALJ's decision must include one of the following findings: (1) the provision of the LCD is valid under the reasonableness standard; (2) the provision of the LCD is not valid under the reasonableness standard; (3) the complaint regarding the LCD is dismissed, with a rationale for the dismissal; or (4) the LCD record is complete and adequate to support the validity of the LCD provisions under the reasonableness standard. [42 C.F.R. §§ 426.447, 426.450, 426.462, 426.482.]

An aggrieved party, CMS, or a CMS contractor may appeal the ALJ's decision if it states that a provision of the LCD is valid under the reasonableness standard or the complaint is dismissed. If the DAB determines the appeal is acceptable, it will permit the party that did not file the appeal an opportunity to respond, hear oral arguments, review the LCD record and the parties' arguments, and issue a written decision either upholding, modifying, or reversing the ALJ decision or remanding the ALJ decision for further proceedings. [42 C.F.R. §§ 426.465, 426.476(a).]

NCD review. An aggrieved party may initiate a review of an NCD by filing with the DAB a timely written complaint that meets applicable requirements. [42 C.F.R. § 426.500.] The DAB's decision must include one of the following: (1) a determination that the provision of the NCD is valid under the reasonableness standard; (2) a determination that the provision of the NCD is not valid under the reasonableness standard; (3) a statement dismissing the complaint regarding the NCD and a rationale for the dismissal; or (4) a determination that the NCD record is complete and adequate to support the validity of the NCD provisions under the reasonableness standard. [42 C.F.R. § 426.550.]

After the DAB makes a decision regarding an NCD complaint, it sends a written notice of the decision to each party stating the outcome of the review and informing each party to the determination of his or her rights to seek further review if he or she is dissatisfied with the determination, and the time limit under which an appeal must be requested. CMS may not appeal a DAB decision. [42 C.F.R. §§ 426.562, 426.566.]

A decision by the DAB constitutes a final agency action and is subject to judicial review. A party may bypass DAB review in favor of judicial review if he or she alleges an absence of material issues of the facts in dispute and the only issue concerns the constitutionality of the law or the validity of the regulation. [Soc. Sec. Act § 1869(f)(3); 42 C.F.R. § 426.560(a).]

NCD Reconsiderations

When an NCD currently exists, any individual or entity may request that CMS reconsider any provision of that NCD by filing a complete formal request for reconsideration. CMS will consider accepting a request for reconsideration if the requestor submits evidence of one of the following:

- additional scientific evidence that was not considered in the most recent review; or

- plausible arguments that the conclusion reached in the last review along with a sound premise that new evidence may change the conclusion.

[*Notice*, 78 FR 48167, Aug. 7, 2013.]

CMS considers a request complete and formal only if the following conditions are met:

(1) the requester provides a final letter of request and clearly identifies the request as a "Formal Request for NCD Reconsideration";

(2) the requester identifies the scientific evidence that he or she believes supports the request for reconsideration; and

(3) the written request includes and supports any additional Medicare Part A or Part B benefit categories in which the requester believes the item or service falls.

The request for reconsideration must be submitted electronically. CMS will usually make a decision within 60 days. [*Notice*, 78 FR 48167, Aug. 7, 2013.]

[¶ 930] Recovery Audit Contractor, Cost Report, Status, Exclusion, and Suspension Appeals

Provider and supplier appeals include appeals of recovery audit contractor (RAC) determinations, provider status determinations, and suspension and exclusion from participation in Medicare and other federal health care programs. Cost report reviews pertain only to certain providers, such as hospitals, critical access hospitals, and skilled nursing facilities, because those providers are required to submit annual cost reports.

Recovery Audit Contractor Appeals

Although RACs do not make initial determinations, as Medicare contractors, they are able to reopen claims based on their audits of providers' claims to detect improper payments. [Soc. Sec. Act § 1893(h); *Final rule*, 74 FR 65296, Dec. 9, 2009.] Appeals of RAC determinations regarding fee-for-service claims are handled with other overpayment determinations under the fee-for-service Medicare appeals process (see ¶ 924). [*Medicare Financial Management Manual*, Pub. 100-06, Ch. 4, §§ 100.6, 100.7.] For a discussion of RAC responsibilities, see ¶ 711.

Administrative Review of Disputed Cost Reports

Hospitals and certain other providers that participate in the Medicare program are required to submit an annual accounting of the costs they incur to operate their facilities, including direct patient costs for Medicare and non-Medicare patients and operating costs such as depreciation, capital-related costs, and other expenses. The cost report is the vehicle for reporting costs and income to CMS.

Appeals of cost report determinations must follow specific administrative procedures found at 42 C.F.R. § 405.1801 *et seq.* If the amount in dispute is less than $10,000, review is available through the Medicare administrative contractor (MAC), which will appoint a hearing officer or a panel of hearing officers. [42 C.F.R. § 405.1809.] A provider that is

¶930

dissatisfied with the outcome of this review may request review by a CMS official. [42 C.F.R. § 405.1834.]

PRRB review. Any provider of services that has filed a timely cost report may appeal an adverse final decision of the MAC to the Provider Reimbursement Review Board (PRRB) if the amount at issue is $10,000 or more. Groups of providers may appeal adverse final decisions of the MAC to the PRRB when the matters at issue share a common question of fact or law and the total amount in controversy, in the aggregate, is $50,000 or more. Providers also may appeal to the PRRB on a late cost report decision by the MAC if the amount involved is $10,000 or more. The appeal must be filed within 180 days after the provider receives notice of the MAC's or Secretary's final determination. [Soc. Sec. Act § 1878(a), (b); 42 C.F.R. § 405.1835(a)(2), (a)(3).]

CMS review. A party to a PRRB appeal or CMS may request a CMS Administrator review, or the CMS Administrator, at his or her discretion, may immediately review any decision of the PRRB related to: (1) a hearing decision; (2) a dismissal of a request for hearing; (3) a decision for an expedited judicial review, but only to the question of whether there is PRRB jurisdiction over a specific matter at issue in the decision (the Administrator may not review the PRRB's determination in a decision of its authority to decide a legal question relevant to the matter at issue); or (4) any other final decision of the PRRB. [42 C.F.R. § 405.1875(a), (c).]

Judicial review. A provider has a right to obtain judicial review of a final decision of the PRRB, or of a timely reversal, affirmation, or modification by the Administrator, by filing a civil action within 60 days of receipt of the decision. When judicial review is sought, the amount in controversy is subject to annual interest beginning on the first day of the first month that begins after the 180-day period following the notice of the Medicare contractor's final determination. [Soc. Sec. Act § 1878(f)(1), (2); 42 C.F.R. § 405.1877.]

Providers also have the right to obtain judicial review of any action of the MAC involving a question of law or regulations relevant to the matters in controversy, whenever the PRRB determines (on its own motion or at the request of the provider) that it is without authority to decide the question. [Soc. Sec. Act § 1878(f)(1).]

Appeals of Provider Status Determinations

CMS makes the initial determination as to whether a provider or supplier meets the conditions for participation or coverage in the Medicare program. Providers and suppliers may appeal adverse decisions to an administrative law judge (ALJ) and the Departmental Appeals Board (DAB). [Soc. Sec. Act § 1866(h); 42 C.F.R. § 498.5.] The determinations and appeals procedures are outlined in 42 C.F.R. Part 498 and are applicable to these and other status determinations.

Appeals Concerning Suspensions and Fines

The Secretary has the authority (see ¶ 720), delegated to the HHS Inspector General, to exclude from participation in the Medicare program, or impose sanctions upon, entities or individuals if they are determined to have committed certain program abuses. An excluded entity or individual is entitled to reasonable notice of an opportunity for hearing by the Secretary. Any practitioner, provider, or supplier that has been suspended, whose services have been excluded from coverage, or that has been sanctioned is entitled to a hearing before an ALJ. Any suspended or excluded practitioner, provider, or supplier dissatisfied with a hearing decision may request a DAB review and has a right to seek judicial review of the DAB's decision by filing an action in federal district court. [Soc. Sec. Act § 1128(f); 42 C.F.R. § 498.5(i).]

Any person adversely affected by a determination of the Secretary with respect to the imposition of a civil money penalty may obtain review of the determination by a U.S. Court of Appeals in the area the person resides (see ¶ 720). [Soc. Sec. Act § 1128A(e).]

¶930

Topical Index

→ *References are to paragraph numbers*

experience, the patient's medical records, and medical, technical, and scientific evidence of record, to the extent applicable. When the claim pertains to the furnishing of treatment by a physician, or the provision of items and services by a physician, the reviewing professional must be a physician. National coverage determinations (NCDs), CMS rulings, and applicable laws and regulations are binding on the QIC. [42 C.F.R. § 405.968.]

Request for reconsideration. A request for reconsideration must be in writing and filed with the QIC indicated on the notice of redetermination within 180 calendar days after receipt of the notice of redetermination (presumed to be five days after the date of the notice). The written request should be on a standard CMS form. A written request that is not made on a standard CMS form is accepted if it contains the beneficiary's name, Medicare health insurance claim number, specific services and items for which the reconsideration is being requested, name and signature of the party or the representative of the party, and the name of the MAC that made the redetermination. [42 C.F.R. § § 405.962(a), 405.964; *Medicare Claims Processing Manual*, Pub. 100-04, Ch. 29, § 320.1.]

Time frame for reconsideration. QICs must complete their reconsiderations within 60 calendar days of receiving a timely filed request. [42 C.F.R. § 405.970(a).] However, when a party submits additional evidence after filing the request for redetermination, the QIC's 60 calendar-day decision-making time frame is automatically extended by up to 14 calendar days for each submission. [Soc. Sec. Act § 1869(c)(3)(C); 42 C.F.R. § § 405.966(b), 405.970(b)(3).]

Escalation. If the QIC does not issue its decision within the 60-calendar-day deadline, the parties may submit a written request directing the QIC to escalate the appeal to an ALJ. When a QIC receives an escalation request, it has five days to complete its reconsideration and notify the parties of its decision or acknowledge the escalation request and forward the case file to the ALJ. [42 C.F.R. § 405.970(d), (e).]

Expedited access to judicial review. A beneficiary, provider, or supplier may obtain expedited access to judicial review (EAJR) after the QIC completes a reconsideration if the review entity determines that the Medicare Appeals Council does not have the authority to decide the question of law or regulation relevant to the matters in controversy and there is no material issue of fact to dispute. The requester has 60 calendar days from the date of certification to bring a civil action in federal court. [42 C.F.R. § 405.990(a), (c), (h).]

Administrative Law Judge Review

The third level of the claims appeal process, which follows a QIC reconsideration, is a review by an ALJ. [42 C.F.R. § 405.1000.]

Parties to an ALJ hearing. Any party to the QIC's reconsideration may request a hearing before an ALJ. The party who filed the request for hearing and all other parties to the reconsideration are parties to the ALJ hearing. [42 C.F.R. § 405.1008.]

CMS or its MAC may enter an appeal at the ALJ level as a party unless an unrepresented beneficiary brings the appeal. CMS will have all the rights of a party, including the right to call witnesses, submit additional evidence within the time frame specified by the ALJ, and seek review of a decision adverse to CMS. The ALJ may not require CMS or a MAC to enter a case as a party or draw any adverse inferences if CMS or a MAC decides not to enter as a party. [42 C.F.R. § 405.1012.] CMS or a MAC also will be allowed to participate in an ALJ hearing, including oral hearing, at the request of an ALJ, CMS, or a MAC. [42 C.F.R. § 405.1010.]

Amount-in-controversy requirement. To be entitled to a hearing before an ALJ, the party must meet the amount-in-controversy requirements. Claims may be aggregated to meet the amount in controversy if they involve common issues of law and fact and delivery of